THE ENDURING VISION

THE ENDURING VISION

A History of the American People

Sixth Edition

Volume II: Since 1865

Dolphin Edition

Paul S. Boyer
University of Wisconsin

Clifford E. Clark, Jr.
Carleton College

Joseph F. Kett
University of Virginia

Neal Salisbury
Smith College

Harvard Sitkoff
University of New Hampshire

Nancy Woloch
Barnard College

Houghton Mifflin Company

Boston   New York

Publisher: Suzanne Jeans
Senior Sponsoring Editor: Ann West
Senior Marketing Manager: Katherine Bates
Senior Development Editor: Jeffrey Greene
Senior Project Editor: Bob Greiner
Senior Art and Design Manager: Jill Haber
Cover Design Director: Anthony L. Saizon
Senior Photo Editor: Jennifer Meyer Dare
Senior Composition Buyer: Chuck Dutton
New Title Project Manager: Patricia O'Neill
Editorial Assistant: Evangeline Bermas
Marketing Associate: Lauren Bussard
Editorial Production Assistant: Laura Collins

Cover art: Mary Helmreich, San Francisco Tiburon Ferry, 2006. © 2006 Mary Helmreich.

Printed in the U.S.A.

Library of Congress Catalog Number: 2007937003

ISBN-10: 0-547-05218-9
ISBN-13: 978-0-547-05218-2

1 2 3 4 5 6 7 8 9 – VHO – 11 10 09 08 07

Contents

17

THE TRANSFORMATION OF THE TRANS-MISSISSIPPI WEST, 1860–1900 516

18

THE RISE OF INDUSTRIAL AMERICA, 1865–1900 547

19

IMMIGRATION, URBANIZATION, AND EVERYDAY LIFE, 1860–1900
581

24

**THE GREAT
DEPRESSION AND THE
NEW DEAL,
1929–1939
749**

26

The Cold War Abroad and at Home, 1945–1952
824

27

America at Midcentury, 1952–1960
852

29

**A TIME OF
UPHEAVAL,
1968–1974
917**

30

CONSERVATIVE RESURGENCE, ECONOMIC WOES, FOREIGN CHALLENGES, 1974–1989 943

31

BEYOND THE COLD WAR: CHARTING A NEW COURSE, 1988–2000 974

Preface

Much has changed in America and the world since we began planning *The Enduring Vision* more than two decades ago. Some of these developments have been welcome and positive, others deeply unsettling. This new Dolphin Edition, which is based on the sixth edition of *The Enduring Vision,* fully documents all these changes, as well as the continuities that offer reassurance for the future.

Although the United States of today differs in many ways from the nation of even a few decades ago, the will to live up to the values that give meaning to America—among them individual freedom, social justice, tolerance for diversity, and equality of opportunity—remains a guiding force in our life as a people. Our desire to convey the strength of this enduring vision in a world of change continues to guide our efforts in writing this book.

Since its inception, *The Enduring Vision* has been one of the most widely used American history textbooks. This edition builds on the underlying strategy that has guided us from the beginning. We want our history to be not only comprehensive and illuminating, but also lively, readable, and true to the lived experience of earlier generations of Americans. Within a clear political and chronological framework, we integrate the best recent scholarship in all areas of American history. Our interest in social and cultural history, which shapes our own teaching and scholarship, has suffused *The Enduring Vision* from the outset, and it remains central. We integrate the historical experience of women, African-Americans, Hispanic Americans, Asian Americans, and American Indians—in short, of men and women of all regions, ethnic groups, and social classes who make up the American mosaic.

We created this Dolphin Edition to provide instructors and students with an edition of *The Enduring Vision* that incorporates all of the narrative of the parent text, but in a format that is more concise.

New Interpretations, Expanded Coverage In each new edition of *The Enduring Vision* we carefully assess the coverage, interpretations, and analytic framework to incorporate the latest scholarship and emerging themes. In recent years, American historians have emphasized how deeply our history is embedded within a larger global context. In this edition we have underscored the wider context of American history throughout the narrative. From the origins of agriculture two millennia ago to the impact of globalization today, we have emphasized how the social, economic, and political developments central to our historical experience emerge with fresh new clarity when viewed within a broader world framework. The global theme is also the focus of an innovative new feature, "Beyond America: Global Interactions" (see "Special Features," on the following page).

As in earlier editions, coverage of environmental history, the land, and the West is fully integrated into the narrative, and is treated analytically, not simply "tacked on" to a traditional account. We also incorporate the best of the new political history, stressing the social, cultural, and economic issues at stake in political decisions and debates.

This edition of *The Enduring Vision* continues to emphasize science and technology. From the hunting implements of the Paleo-Indians to the inventions and manufacturing innovations of the industrial age and today's breakthroughs in information processing and genetic engineering, the applications of science and technology are central throughout. We have included new Technology and Culture boxed features (see "Revisions and Innovations in Each Chapter," below).

We again offer extensive coverage of medicine and disease, from the epidemics brought by European explorers and settlers to today's AIDS crisis, bioethics debates, and controversies over health-care financing. We also give careful attention to religious history, from the spiritual values of pre-Columbian communities to the political activism of contemporary conservative Christian groups.

Special Features We are especially proud and excited to introduce a new feature, "Beyond America—Global Interactions," which highlights this edition's intensified global emphasis. The illustrated essays explore the wider context of key developments in American history. The essays examine such topics as "The American Revolution as an International War," "Slavery as a Global Institution," and "The Challenge of Globalization," underscoring how America's history takes on vivid new interest, and can be viewed in strikingly new ways, when seen in its global context. These new essays make clear that just as America has influenced the world, so has the world influenced America.

Revisions and Innovations in Each Chapter A chapter-by-chapter glimpse of some of the changes in this edition highlights its new content and up-to-the-minute scholarship.

Chapter 1 launches the Beyond America feature with a comparative essay on the origins and spread of agriculture, enabling students to view the development of farming America in a global context. The chapter also explicitly links some additional pre-contact cultures with Native American peoples important in later periods of American history.

Chapter 2 incorporates further detail on Spanish colonization in the Caribbean and on Anglo-Indian relations in early Virginia, including a clarification of the roles of John Smith and Pocahontas. The material in the former "Mediterranean Crossroads" section has been distributed among other sections. In Chapter 3, the discussion of the Chesapeake colonies now precedes that of New England.

Chapter 4 offers an expanded definition of mercantilism and additional details on England's Navigation Acts. This chapter also draws a sharper contrast between the experiences of Europeans and Africans who arrived in the colonies in the first half of the eighteenth century. Chapter 5 includes a revised treatment of the Albany Congress and Plan of Union and of the Paxton Boys. This chapter also offers an expanded discussion of military maneuvering and fighting between the battles of Lexington and Concord and the Declaration of Independence.

The Beyond America essay in Chapter 6 presents a fresh perspective on the American Revolution as an international war, and deepens the explanation for Britain's defeat in North America. The chapter offers new material on ordinary soldiers' experiences in the Continental Army, white women's political activities during the Revolution, and the Articles of Confederation.

Chapter 7 considers more fully the implementation of the new national government, the emergence of political parties, Spanish relations with Native Americans in Texas and New Mexico, and Federalist policy toward Native Americans.

Chapter 8 extends the account of Lewis and Clark's negotiations with the Indians. Chapter 9 expands and restructures the discussion of equality and inequality in the early Republic and blacks' efforts to secure education. Chapter 10 offers expanded coverage of the Shakers.

Judicious cuts in Chapter 11 have resulted in an even more readable treatment of technology, culture, and everyday life in pre-Civil War America. An illuminating Beyond America essay in Chapter 12 examines slavery as a global phenomenon while noting how American slavery differed from that found elsewhere.

Chapter 16 includes a new Technology and Culture feature on the sewing machine, a key advance in domestic technology.

Chapter 17 includes a new table on legislation relating to Indians, new material on the Mormons, and a Beyond America feature placing American cowboys in a global context. Chapter 18 adds a new Technology and Culture essay on electricity, a discussion of the South's economy in world perspective, and expanded coverage of black workers in the South and the labor activist Mary Harris ("Mother") Jones.

Chapter 19 includes new material on African-Americans, baseball, and the painter Mary Cassatt. A unique new map illustrates both the Asian and European sources of immigration to the Western Hemisphere in the late nineteenth century. Chapter 20 expands coverage of Clara Barton, founder of the army nursing corps, and Ida B. Wells, the African-American crusader against lynching. A new table lists and explains Gilded Age currency legislation.

Chapter 21's Beyond America essay offers a comparative overview of the reform spirit that gripped many Western countries in the early twentieth century, while a new "Racism and Progressivism" section underscores the pervasiveness of racism in this era, from lynch mobs to the White House. Chapter 22 offers new material on American overseas missionaries, the Mexican leader Pancho Villa, local vigilante movements during World War I, and the growth of the NAACP.

Chapter 23 expands coverage of the 1929 Gastonia textile strike, Hollywood sex scandals, and Herbert Hoover's conservationist policies, and discusses the composer Ruth Crawford Seeger and the African-American filmmaker Oscar Micheaux. The chapter also expands coverage of movies and the National Youth Administration, and offers a concise assessment of New Deal agricultural policies.

The five chapters covering the four decades from 1933 to 1974 offers a new Beyond America essay on the intellectual migration from fascist regimes in Europe in the 1930s.

In addition, Chapter 25 includes more information on the causes and consequences of World War II and the impact of the war on American minorities and on U.S. society in general. Chapter 26 includes a greater emphasis on the Cold War as a global phenomenon and on the early stirrings of postwar conservatism.

Chapter 27 gives greater attention to the shift in the Cold War from Europe to what was then called the Third World, and discusses in more depth the consequences of the rise in TV ownership and viewing. Chapter 28 offers additional background on the American war in Vietnam, environmental issues, and the significance of the 1964 Goldwater campaign in the emergence of postwar conservatism. This chapter also explores more fully the civil rights struggles of African Americans, especially the roles of CORE and SNCC, as well as the activism of American Indians, Hispanic-Americans, and Asian Americans.

Chapter 29 analyzes more fully the conservative resurgence of the 1970s as a reaction to the radicalism of the 1960s and the counterculture. This chapter also gives extensive attention to the rise of the Sunbelt, the Tet offensive as a turning point in the Vietnam War, and the importance of foreign affairs and energy issues in the Nixon administration.

The concluding three chapters, 30 to 32, incorporate new findings from recent scholarship. Chapter 30 expands coverage of popular culture; explores electronic-age privacy issues; and deepens the discussion of deindustrialization, labor activism, the Iran-Iraq War, violence associated with Islamic fundamentalism, and Soviet leader Mikhail Gorbachev's reasons for seeking better relations with the United States.

Chapter 31, extensively revised, now includes both terms of the Clinton Administration and an expanded discussion of the stock market boom, the influence of religious conservatives in the decade's culture wars, and bursts of domestic terrorism. This chapter also examines in more detail President George H. W. Bush's decision not to invade Iraq during the Persian Gulf War and updates the long-term effects of the Welfare Reform Act of 1996. A Beyond America essay weighs the cultural and economic impact of globalization.

Chapter 32 continues the story of American history to the 2006 elections. This chapter describes the Bush administration's response to the September 11, 2001, terrorist attacks, including the invasion of Iraq; new prisoner-detention policies; and domestic surveillance programs. The chapter also explores recent economic developments, social and demographic trends, and the ongoing debate over immigration policy. A new Technology and Culture essay examines the timely issue of global warming.

Paul S. Boyer
Clifford E. Clark, Jr.
Joseph F. Kett
Neal Salisbury
Harvard Sitkoff
Nancy Woloch

About the Authors

PAUL S. BOYER, Merle Curti Professor of History emeritus at the University of Wisconsin, Madison, earned his Ph.D. from Harvard University. An editor of *Notable American Women, 1607–1950* (1971), he also coauthored *Salem Possessed: The Social Origins of Witchcraft* (1974), for which, with Stephen Nissenbaum, he received the John H. Dunning Prize of the American Historical Association. His other works include *Urban Masses and Moral Order in America, 1820–1920* (1978), *By the Bomb's Early Light: American Thought and Culture at the Dawn of the Atomic Age* (1985), *When Time Shall Be No More: Prophecy Belief in Modern American Culture* (1992), and *Promises to Keep: The United States since World War II,* 3rd ed. (2003). He is also editor-in-chief of the *Oxford Companion to United States History* (2001). His articles and essays have appeared in the *American Quarterly, New Republic,* and other journals. He has been a visiting professor at the University of California, Los Angeles, Northwestern University, and the College of William and Mary.

CLIFFORD E. CLARK, JR., M.A. and A.D. Hulings Professor of American Studies and professor of history at Carleton College, earned his Ph.D. from Harvard University. He has served as both the chair of the History Department and director of the American Studies program at Carleton. Clark is the author of *Henry Ward Beecher: Spokesman for a Middle-Class America* (1978), *The American Family Home, 1800–1960* (1986), *The Intellectual and Cultural History of Anglo-America since 1789* in the *General History of the Americas,* and, with Carol Zellie, *Northfield: The History and Architecture of a Community* (1997). He also has edited and contributed to *Minnesota in a Century of Change: The State and Its People since 1900* (1989). A past member of the Council of the American Studies Association, Clark is active in the fields of material culture studies and historic preservation, and he serves on the Northfield, Minnesota, Historical Preservation Commission.

JOSEPH F. KETT, Commonwealth Professor of History at the University of Virginia, received his Ph.D. from Harvard University. His works include *The Formation of the American Medical Profession: The Role of Institutions, 1780–1860* (1968), *Rites of Passage: Adolescence in America, 1790–Present* (1977), *The Pursuit of Knowledge under Difficulties: From Self-Improvement to Adult Education in America, 1750–1990* (1994), and *The New Dictionary of Cultural Literacy* (2002), of which he is coauthor. A former History Department chair at Virginia, he also has participated on the Panel on Youth of the President's Science Advisory Committee, has served on the Board of Editors of the *History of Education Quarterly,* and is a past member of the Council of the American Studies Association.

NEAL SALISBURY, professor of history at Smith College, received his Ph.D. from the University of California, Los Angeles. He is the author of *Manitou and Providence:*

Indians, Europeans, and the Making of New England, 1500–1643 (1982), editor of *The Sovereignty and Goodness of God*, by Mary Rowlandson (1997), and coeditor, with Philip J. Deloria, of *The Companion to American Indian History* (2002). With R. David Edmunds and Frederick E. Hoxie, he has written *The People: A History of Native America* (2007), also published by Houghton Mifflin. He has contributed numerous articles to journals and edited collections, and coedits a book series, Cambridge Studies in North American Indian History. Formerly chair of the History Department at Smith, he has served as president of the American Society for Ethnohistory and is currently a member of the Council of the Omohundro Institute of Early American History and Culture.

HARVARD SITKOFF, professor of history at the University of New Hampshire, earned his Ph.D. from Columbia University. He is the author of *A New Deal for Blacks* (1978), *The Struggle for Black Equality, 1954–1992* (1992), and *Postwar America: A Student Companion* (2000); coauthor of the National Park Service's *Racial Desegregation in Public Education in the United States* (2000) and *The World War II Homefront* (2003); and editor of *Fifty Years Later: The New Deal Reevaluated* (1984), *A History of Our Time*, 6th ed. (2002), and *Perspectives on Modern America: Making Sense of the Twentieth Century* (2001). His articles have appeared in the *American Quarterly, Journal of American History,* and *Journal of Southern History,* among others. A frequent lecturer at universities abroad, he has been awarded the Fulbright Commission's John Adams Professorship of American Civilization in the Netherlands and the Mary Ball Washington Professorship of American History in Ireland.

NANCY WOLOCH received her Ph.D. from Indiana University. She is the author of *Women and the American Experience* (1984, 1994, 1996, 2000, 2002, 2006), editor of *Early American Women: A Documentary History, 1600–1900* (1992, 1997, 2002), and coauthor, with Walter LaFeber and Richard Polenberg, of *The American Century: A History of the United States since the 1890s* (1986, 1992, 1998). She is also the author of *Muller v. Oregon: A Brief History with Documents* (1996). She teaches American history and American Studies at Barnard College, Columbia University.

16

The Crises of Reconstruction, 1865–1877

RECONSTRUCTION POLITICS, 1865–1868

At the end of the Civil War, President Johnson might have exiled, imprisoned, or executed Confederate leaders and imposed martial law indefinitely. Demobilized Confederate soldiers might have continued armed resistance to federal occupation forces. Freed slaves might have taken revenge on former owners and the rest of the white community. But none of these drastic possibilities occurred. Instead, intense *political* conflict dominated the immediate postwar years. In national politics, unparalleled disputes produced new constitutional amendments, a presidential impeachment, and some of the most ambitious domestic legislation ever enacted by Congress, the Reconstruction Acts of 1867–1868. The major outcome of Reconstruction politics was the enfranchisement of black men, a development that few—black or white—had expected when Lee surrendered.

In 1865, only a small group of politicians supported black suffrage. All were Radical Republicans, a minority faction that had emerged during the war. Led by Senator **Charles Sumner** of Massachusetts and Congressman **Thaddeus Stevens** of Pennsylvania, the Radicals had clamored for the abolition of slavery and a demanding reconstruction policy. Any plan to restore the Union, Stevens contended, must "revolutionize Southern institutions, habits, and manners." But the Radicals, outnumbered in Congress by other Republicans and opposed by the Democratic minority, faced long odds. Still, they managed to win broad Republican support for parts of their Reconstruction program, including black male enfranchisement. Just as civil war had led to emancipation, a goal once supported by only a minority of Americans, so Reconstruction policy became bound to black suffrage, a momentous change that originally had only narrow political backing.

The Devastated South   *After the Civil War, parts of the devastated Confederacy resembled a wasteland. Homes, crops, and railroads had been destroyed; farming and business had come to a standstill; and uprooted southerners wandered about. Here, ruins of homes in Baton Rouge, Louisiana.*

Lincoln's Plan   Conflict over Reconstruction began even before the war ended. In December 1863, President Lincoln issued the Proclamation of Amnesty and Reconstruction, which enabled southern states to rejoin the Union if at least 10 percent of those who had cast ballots in the election of 1860 would take an oath of allegiance to the Union and accept emancipation. This minority could then create a loyal state government. Lincoln's plan excluded some southerners from taking the oath: Confederate government officials, army and naval officers, as well as those military or civil officers who had resigned from Congress or from U.S. commissions in 1861. All such persons would have to apply for presidential pardons. Also excluded, of course, were blacks, who had not been voters in 1860. Lincoln hoped to undermine the Confederacy by establishing pro-Union governments within it; to win the allegiance of southern Unionists (those who had opposed secession), especially former Whigs; and to build a southern Republican party.

Radical Republicans in Congress, however, envisioned a slower readmission process that would bar even more ex-Confederates from political life. The Wade-Davis bill, passed by Congress in July 1864, provided that a military governor would rule each former Confederate state and that after at least half the eligible voters took an oath of allegiance to the Union, delegates could be elected to a state convention that would re-

CHRONOLOGY, 1865–1877

1863 • President Abraham Lincoln issues Proclamation of Amnesty and Reconstruction.

1864 • Wade-Davis bill passed by Congress and pocket-vetoed by Lincoln.

1865 • Freedmen's Bureau established.
    Civil War ends.
    Lincoln assassinated.
    Andrew Johnson becomes president.
    Johnson issues Proclamation of Amnesty and Reconstruction.
    Ex-Confederate states hold constitutional conventions (May–December).
    Black conventions begin in the ex-Confederate states.
    Thirteenth Amendment added to the Constitution.
    Presidential Reconstruction completed.

1866 • Congress enacts the Civil Rights Act of 1866 and the Supplementary Freedmen's Bureau Act over Johnson's vetoes.
    Ku Klux Klan founded in Tennessee.
    Tennessee readmitted to the Union.
    Race riots in southern cities.
    Republicans win congressional elections.

1867 • Reconstruction Act of 1867.
    William Seward negotiates the purchase of Alaska.
    Constitutional conventions meet in the ex-Confederate states.
    Howard University founded.

1868 • President Johnson is impeached, tried, and acquitted.
    Omnibus Act.
    Fourteenth Amendment added to the Constitution.
    Ulysses S. Grant elected president.

1869 • Transcontinental railroad completed.

1870 • Congress readmits the four remaining southern states to the Union.
    Fifteenth Amendment added to the Constitution.
    Enforcement Act of 1870.

1871 • Second Enforcement Act.
    Ku Klux Klan Act.

1872 • Liberal Republican party formed.
    Amnesty Act.
    Alabama claims settled.
    Grant reelected president.

1873 • Panic of 1873 begins (September–October), setting off a five-year depression.

1874 • Democrats gain control of the House of Representatives.

1875 • Civil Rights Act of 1875.
    Specie Resumption Act.

1876 • Disputed presidential election: Rutherford B. Hayes versus Samuel J. Tilden.

1877 • Electoral commission decides election in favor of Hayes.
    The last Republican-controlled governments overthrown in Florida, Louisiana, and South Carolina.

1879 • "Exodus" movement spreads through several southern states.

peal secession and abolish slavery. To qualify as a voter or delegate, a southerner would have to take a second, "ironclad" oath, swearing that he had never voluntarily supported the Confederacy. Like the 10 percent plan, the congressional plan did not provide for black suffrage, a measure then supported by only some Radicals. Unlike Lincoln's plan, however, the Wade-Davis scheme would have delayed the readmission process almost indefinitely.

Claiming that he did not want to bind himself to any single restoration policy, Lincoln pocket-vetoed the Wade-Davis bill (that is, he failed to sign the bill within ten days of the adjournment of Congress). The bill's sponsors, Senator Benjamin Wade of Ohio and Congressman Henry Winter Davis of Maryland, blasted Lincoln's act as an outrage. By the war's end, the president and Congress had reached an impasse. Arkansas, Louisiana, Tennessee, and parts of Virginia under Union army control moved toward readmission under variants of Lincoln's plan. But Congress refused to seat their delegates, as it had a right to do. Lincoln, meanwhile, hinted that a more rigorous Reconstruction policy might be in store. What Lincoln's ultimate policy would have been remains unknown. But after his assassination, on April 14, 1865, Radical Republicans turned with hope toward his successor, **Andrew Johnson** of Tennessee, in whom they felt they had an ally.

Presidential Reconstruction Under Johnson

The only southern senator to remain in Congress when his state seceded, Andrew Johnson had served as military governor of Tennessee from 1862 to 1864. He had taken a strong anti-Confederate stand, declaring that "treason is a crime and must be made odious." Above all, Johnson had long sought the destruction of the planter aristocracy. A self-educated man of humble North Carolina origins, Johnson had moved to Greenville, Tennessee, in 1826 and became a tailor. His wife, Eliza McCardle, had taught him how to write. He had entered politics in the 1830s as a spokesman for non-slave-owning whites and rose rapidly from local official to congressman to governor to senator. Once the owner of eight slaves, Johnson reversed his position on slavery during the war. When emancipation became Union policy, he supported it. But Johnson neither adopted abolitionist ideals nor challenged racist sentiments. He hoped mainly that the fall of slavery would injure southern aristocrats. Andrew Johnson, in short, had his own political agenda, which, as Republicans would soon learn, did not coincide with theirs. Moreover, he was a lifelong Democrat who had been added to the Republican, or National Union, ticket in 1864 to broaden its appeal and who had become president by accident.

In May 1865, with Congress out of session, Johnson shocked Republicans by announcing in two proclamations his own program to bring back into the Union the seven southern states still without reconstruction governments—Alabama, Florida, Georgia, Mississippi, North Carolina, South Carolina, and Texas. Almost all southerners who took an oath of allegiance would receive a pardon and amnesty, and all their property except slaves would be restored. Oath takers could elect delegates to state conventions, which would provide for regular elections. Each state convention, Johnson later added, would have to proclaim the illegality of secession, repudiate state debts incurred when the state belonged to the Confederacy, and ratify the Thirteenth Amendment, which abolished slavery. (Proposed by an enthusiastic wartime Congress early in 1865, the amendment would be ratified in December of that year.) As under Lincoln's plan, Confederate civil and military officers would still be disqualified, as would well-off ex-Confederates—those with taxable property worth $20,000 or more. This purge of the plantation aristocracy, Johnson said, would benefit "humble men, the peasantry and yeomen of the South, who have been decoyed . . . into rebellion." Poorer whites would now be in control.

Presidential Reconstruction took effect in the summer of 1865, but with unforeseen consequences. Southerners disqualified on the basis of wealth or high Confederate position applied for pardons in droves, and Johnson handed out pardons liberally—some thirteen thousand of them. He also dropped plans for the punishment of treason. By the end of 1865, all seven states had created new civil governments that in effect restored the status quo from before the war. Confederate army officers and large planters assumed state offices. Former Confederate congressmen, state officials, and generals were elected to Congress. Georgia sent Alexander Stephens, the former Confederate vice president, back to Washington as a senator. Some states refused to ratify the Thirteenth Amendment or to repudiate their Confederate debts.

Most infuriating to Radical Republicans, all seven states took steps to ensure a landless, dependent black labor force: they passed **"black codes"** to replace the slave codes, state laws that had regulated slavery. Because Johnson's plan assured the ratification of the Thirteenth Amendment, all states guaranteed the freedmen some basic rights—to marry, own property, make contracts, and testify in court against other blacks—but the codes harshly restricted freedmen's behavior. Some established racial segregation in public places; most prohibited racial intermarriage, jury service by blacks, and court testimony by blacks against whites. All codes included provisions that effectively barred former slaves from leaving the plantations. South Carolina required special licenses for blacks who wished to enter nonagricultural employment. Mississippi prohibited blacks from buying and selling farmland. Most states required annual contracts between landowners and black agricultural workers and provided that blacks without lawful employment would be arrested as vagrants and their labor auctioned off to employers who would pay their fines.

The black codes left freedmen no longer slaves but not really liberated either. Although "free" to sign labor contracts, for instance, those who failed to sign them would be considered in violation of the law and swept back into involuntary servitude. In practice, many clauses in the codes never took effect: the Union army and the Freedmen's Bureau (a federal agency that assisted former slaves) swiftly suspended the enforcement of racially discriminatory provisions of the new laws. But the black codes revealed white southern intentions. They showed what "home rule" would have been like without federal interference.

Many northerners denounced what they saw as southern defiance. "What can be hatched from such an egg but another rebellion?" asked a Boston newspaper. Republicans in Congress agreed. When Congress convened in December 1865, it refused to seat the delegates of the ex-Confederate states. Establishing the Joint (House-Senate) Committee on Reconstruction, Republicans prepared to dismantle the black codes and lock ex-Confederates out of power.

Congress Versus Johnson Southern blacks' status now became the major issue in Congress. Radical Republicans like Congressman Thaddeus Stevens—who hoped to impose black suffrage on the former Confederacy and delay the readmission of the southern states into the Union—were still a minority in Congress. Conservative Republicans, who tended to favor the Johnson plan, formed a minority too, as did the Democrats, who also supported the president. Moderate Republicans, the largest congressional bloc, agreed with the Radicals that Johnson's plan was too feeble, but they wanted to avoid a dispute with the president. As none of the four congressional blocs could claim the two-thirds majority required to overturn a presidential veto, Johnson's program would prevail unless the moderates and the Radicals joined forces. Ineptly, Johnson alienated a majority of moderates and pushed them into the Radicals' arms.

Two proposals to invalidate the black codes, drafted by a moderate Republican, Senator Lyman Trumbull of Illinois, won wide Republican support. Congress first voted to continue the Freedmen's Bureau, established in 1865, whose term was ending. This federal agency, headed by former Union general O. O. Howard and staffed mainly by army officers, provided relief, rations, and medical care. It also built schools for the freed blacks, put them to work on abandoned or confiscated lands, and tried to protect their rights as laborers. Congress extended the bureau's life for three years and gave it new power: it could run special military courts to settle labor disputes and could invalidate labor contracts forced on freedmen by the black codes. In February 1866, Johnson vetoed the Freedmen's Bureau bill. The Constitution, he declared, did not sanction military trials of civilians in peacetime, nor did it support a system to care for "indigent persons."

In March 1866, Congress passed a second measure proposed by Trumbull, a bill that made blacks U.S. citizens with the same civil rights as other citizens and authorized federal intervention in the states to ensure black rights in court. Johnson vetoed the civil rights bill also. He argued that it would "operate in favor of the colored and against the white race." In April, Congress overrode his veto; the **Civil Rights Act of 1866** was the first major law ever passed over a presidential veto. In July, Congress enacted the Supplementary Freedmen's Bureau Act over Johnson's veto as well. Johnson's vetoes puzzled many Republicans because the new laws did not undercut presidential Reconstruction. The president insisted, however, that both bills were illegitimate because southerners had been shut out of the Congress that passed them. His stance won support in the South and from northern Democrats. But the president had alienated the moderate Republicans, who began to work with the Radicals against him. Johnson had lost "every friend he has," one moderate declared.

Some historians view Andrew Johnson as a political incompetent who, at this crucial turning point, bungled both his readmission scheme and his political future. Others contend that he was merely trying to forge a coalition of the center, made up of Democrats and non-Radical Republicans. In either case, Johnson underestimated the possibility of Republican unity. Once united, the Republicans took their next step: the passage of a constitutional amendment to prevent the Supreme Court from invalidating the new Civil Rights Act and block Democrats in Congress from repealing it.

The Fourteenth Amendment, 1866   In April 1866, Congress adopted the **Fourteenth Amendment,** which had been proposed by the Joint Committee on Reconstruction. To protect blacks' rights, the amendment declared in its first clause that all persons born or naturalized in the United States were citizens of the nation and citizens of their states and that no state could abridge their rights without due process of law or deny them equal protection of the law. This section nullified the *Dred Scott* decision of 1857, which had declared that blacks were not citizens. Second, the amendment guaranteed that if a state denied suffrage to any of its male citizens, its representation in Congress would be proportionally reduced. This clause did not guarantee black suffrage, but it threatened to deprive southern states of some legislators if black men were denied the vote. This was the first time that the word *male* was written into the Constitution. To the dismay of women's rights advocates, woman suffrage seemed a yet more distant prospect. Third, the amendment disqualified from state and national office *all* prewar officeholders—civil and military, state and federal—who had supported the Confederacy, unless Congress removed their disqualifications by a two-thirds vote. In so providing, Congress intended to invalidate Johnson's wholesale distribution of amnesties and pardons. Finally, the amendment repudiated the Confederate debt and maintained the validity of the federal debt.

The most ambitious step that Congress had yet taken, the Fourteenth Amendment revealed Republican legislators' growing receptivity to Radical demands, including black male enfranchisement. The Fourteenth Amendment was the first national effort to limit state control of civil and political rights, and its passage created a firestorm. Abolitionists decried the second clause as a "swindle" because it did not explicitly ensure black suffrage. Southerners and northern Democrats condemned the third clause as vengeful. Southern legislatures, except for Tennessee's, refused to ratify the amendment, and President Johnson denounced it. His defiance solidified the new alliance between moderate and Radical Republicans, and turned the congressional elections of 1866 into a referendum on the Fourteenth Amendment.

Over the summer, Johnson set off on a whistle-stop train tour from Washington to St. Louis and Chicago and back. But this innovative campaign tactic—the "swing around the circle," as Johnson called it—failed. Humorless and defensive, the president made fresh enemies and doomed his hope of creating a new National Union party that would sink the Fourteenth Amendment. Moderate and Radical Republicans defended the amendment, condemned the president, and branded the Democratic Party "a common sewer . . . into which is emptied every element of treason, North and South."

Republicans carried the congressional elections of 1866 in a landslide, winning almost two-thirds of the House and almost four-fifths of the Senate. They had secured a mandate to overcome southern resistance to the Fourteenth Amendment and to enact their own Reconstruction program, even if the president vetoed every part of it.

Congressional Reconstruction, 1866–1867
The congressional debate over reconstructing the South began in December 1866 and lasted three months. Radical Republican leaders called for black suffrage, federal support for public schools, confiscation of Confederate estates, and an extended period of military occupation in the South. Moderate Republicans, who once would have found such a plan too extreme, now accepted parts of it. In February 1867, after complex legislative maneuvers and many late-night sessions, Congress passed the **Reconstruction Act of 1867.** Johnson vetoed the law, and on March 2 Congress passed it over his veto. Later that year and in 1868, Congress passed three further Reconstruction acts, all enacted over presidential vetoes, to refine and enforce the first.

The Reconstruction Act of 1867 invalidated the state governments formed under the Lincoln and Johnson plans. Only Tennessee, which had ratified the Fourteenth Amendment and had been readmitted to the Union, escaped further reconstruction. The new law divided the other ten former Confederate states into five temporary military districts, each run by a Union general. Voters—all black men, plus those white men who had not been disqualified by the Fourteenth Amendment—could elect delegates to a state convention that would write a new state constitution granting black suffrage. When eligible voters ratified the new constitution, elections could be held for state officers. Once Congress approved the state constitution, once the state legislature ratified the Fourteenth Amendment, and once the amendment became part of the federal Constitution, Congress would readmit the state into the Union—and Reconstruction, in a constitutional sense, would be complete.

The Reconstruction Act of 1867 was far more radical than the Johnson program because it enfranchised blacks and disfranchised many ex-Confederates. It fulfilled a central goal of the Radical Republicans: to delay the readmission of former Confederate states until Republican governments could be established and thereby prevent an immediate rebel resurgence. But the new law was not as harsh toward ex-Confederates as it might have been. It provided for only temporary military rule, did not prosecute Confederate leaders for treason or permanently bar them from politics, and made no provision for confiscation or redistribution of property.

During the congressional debates, Radical Republican congressman Thaddeus Stevens had argued for the confiscation of large Confederate estates to "humble the proud traitors" and to provide for the former slaves. He had proposed subdividing such confiscated property into forty-acre tracts to be distributed among the freedmen and selling the rest, some 90 percent of it, to pay off war debts. Stevens wanted to crush the planter aristocracy and create a new class of self-sufficient black yeoman farmers. His land-reform bill won the support of other Radicals but never made progress, for most Republicans held property rights sacred. Tampering with such rights in the South, they feared, would jeopardize those rights in the North. Moreover, Stevens's proposal would alienate southern ex-Whigs from the Republican cause, antagonize other white southerners, and thereby endanger the rest of Reconstruction. Thus land reform never came about. The "radical" Reconstruction acts were a compromise.

Congressional Reconstruction took effect in the spring of 1867, but it could not be enforced without military power. Johnson, as Commander in Chief, impeded its implementation by replacing military officers sympathetic to the Radical cause with conservative ones. Republicans seethed. More suspicious than ever of the president, congressional moderates and Radicals once again joined forces to block Johnson from obstructing Reconstruction.

The Impeachment Crisis, 1867–1868   In March 1867, Republicans in Congress passed two laws to limit presidential power. The **Tenure of Office Act** prohibited the president from removing civil officers without Senate consent. Cabinet members, the law stated, were to hold office "during the term of the president by whom they may have been appointed" and could be fired only with the Senate's approval. The goal was to bar Johnson from dismissing Secretary of War Henry Stanton, a Radical ally needed to enforce the Reconstruction acts. The other law, a rider to an army appropriations bill, barred the president from issuing military orders except through the commanding general, Ulysses S. Grant, who could not be removed without the Senate's consent.

The Radicals' enmity toward Johnson, however, would not die until he was out of office. They began to seek grounds on which to impeach him. The House Judiciary

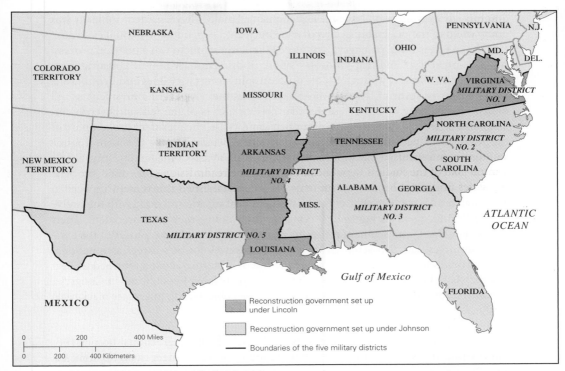

MAP 16.1 **The Reconstruction of the South**

The Reconstruction Act of 1867 divided the former Confederate states, except Tennessee, into five military districts and set forth the steps by which new state governments could be created.

Committee, aided by private detectives, could at first uncover no valid charges against Johnson. But Johnson again rescued his foes by providing the charges they needed.

In August 1867, with Congress out of session, Johnson suspended Secretary of War Stanton and replaced him with General Grant. In early 1868, the reconvened Senate refused to approve Stanton's suspension, and Grant, sensing the Republican mood, vacated the office. Johnson then removed Stanton and replaced him with an aged general, Lorenzo Thomas. Johnson's defiance forced Republican moderates, who had at first resisted impeachment, into yet another alliance with the Radicals: the president had "thrown down the gauntlet," a moderate charged. The House approved eleven charges of impeachment, nine of them based on violation of the Tenure of Office Act. The other charges accused Johnson of being "unmindful of the high duties of office," seeking to disgrace Congress, and not enforcing the Reconstruction acts.

Johnson's trial in the Senate, which began in March 1868, riveted public attention for eleven weeks. Seven congressmen, including leading Radical Republicans, served as prosecutors or "managers." Johnson's lawyers maintained that he was merely seeking a court test by violating the Tenure of Office Act, which he thought was unconstitutional. They also contended, somewhat inconsistently, that the law did not protect Secretary

Stanton, an appointee of Lincoln, not Johnson. Finally, they asserted, Johnson was guilty of no crime indictable in a regular court.

The congressional "managers" countered that impeachment was a political process, not a criminal trial, and that Johnson's "abuse of discretionary power" constituted an impeachable offense. Although Senate opinion split along party lines and Republicans held a majority, some of them wavered, fearful that the removal of a president would destroy the balance of power among the three branches of the federal government. They also distrusted Radical Republican Benjamin Wade, the president pro tempore of the Senate, who, because there was no vice president, would become president if Johnson were thrown out.

Intense pressure weighed on the wavering Republicans. Late in May 1868, the Senate voted against Johnson 35 to 19, one vote short of the two-thirds majority needed for conviction. Seven Republicans had risked political suicide and sided with the twelve Senate Democrats in voting against removal. In so doing, they set a precedent. Their vote discouraged impeachment on political grounds for decades to come. But the anti-Johnson forces had also achieved their goal: Andrew Johnson's career as a national leader would soon end. After serving out the rest of his term, Johnson returned to Tennessee, where he was reelected to the Senate five years later. Republicans in Congress, meanwhile, pursued their last major Reconstruction objective: to guarantee black male suffrage.

The Fifteenth Amendment and the Question of Woman Suffrage, 1869–1870

Black suffrage was the linchpin of congressional Reconstruction. Only with the support of black voters could Republicans secure control of the ex-Confederate states. The Reconstruction Act of 1867 had forced every southern state legislature to enfranchise black men as a prerequisite for readmission to the Union, but much of the North rejected black suffrage at home. Congressional Republicans therefore had two aims. The **Fifteenth Amendment,** drawn up by Republicans and proposed by Congress in 1869, sought to protect black suffrage in the South against future repeal by Congress or the states, and to enfranchise northern and border-state blacks, who would presumably vote Republican. The amendment prohibited the denial of suffrage by the states to any citizen on account of "race, color, or previous condition of servitude."

Democrats argued that the proposed amendment violated states' rights by denying each state the power to determine who would vote. But Democrats did not control enough states to defeat the amendment, and it was ratified in 1870. Four votes came from those ex-Confederate states—Mississippi, Virginia, Georgia, and Texas—that had delayed the Reconstruction process and were therefore forced to approve the Fifteenth Amendment, as well as the Fourteenth, in order to rejoin the Union. Some southerners contended that the new amendment's omissions made it acceptable, for it had, as a Richmond newspaper pointed out, "loopholes through which a coach and four horses can be driven." What were these loopholes? The Fifteenth Amendment neither guaranteed black officeholding nor prohibited voting restrictions such as property requirements and literacy tests. Such restrictions might be used to deny blacks the vote, and indeed, ultimately they were so used.

The debate over black suffrage drew new participants into the political fray. Since the end of the war, a small group of abolitionists, men and women, had sought to revive the cause of women's rights. In 1866, when Congress debated the Fourteenth Amendment, women's rights advocates tried to join forces with their old abolitionist allies to promote both black suffrage and woman suffrage. Most Radical Republicans, however, did not want to be saddled with the woman-suffrage plank; they feared it would impede their primary goal, black enfranchisement.

This defection provoked disputes among women's rights advocates. Some argued that black suffrage would pave the way for the women's vote and that black men deserved priority. "If the elective franchise is not extended to the Negro, he is dead," explained Frederick Douglass, a longtime women's rights supporter. "Woman has a thousand ways by which she can attach herself to the ruling power of the land that we have not." But women's rights leaders Elizabeth Cady Stanton and **Susan B. Anthony** disagreed. In their view, the Fourteenth Amendment had disabled women by including the word *male,* and the Fifteenth Amendment compounded the injury by failing to prohibit the denial of suffrage on account of sex. Instead, Stanton contended, the Fifteenth Amendment established an "aristocracy of sex" and increased women's disadvantages.

The battle over black suffrage and the Fifteenth Amendment split women's rights advocates into two rival suffrage associations, both formed in 1869. The Boston-based American Woman Suffrage Association, endorsed by reformers such as Julia Ward Howe and Lucy Stone, retained an alliance with male abolitionists and campaigned for woman suffrage in the states. The New York–based and more radical National Woman Suffrage Association, led by Stanton and Anthony, condemned its leaders' one-time male allies and promoted a federal woman suffrage amendment.

For the rest of the 1870s, the rival woman suffrage associations vied for constituents. In 1869 and 1870, independent of the suffrage movement, two territories, Wyoming and Utah, enfranchised women. But lacking support, suffragists failed to sway legislators elsewhere. In 1872, Susan B. Anthony mobilized about seventy women to vote nationwide and, as a result, was indicted, convicted, and fined. One of the women who tried to vote in 1872, Missouri suffragist Virginia Minor, brought suit with her husband against the registrar who had excluded her. The Minors based their case on the Fourteenth Amendment, which, they claimed, enfranchised women. In *Minor v. Happersett* (1875), however, the Supreme Court declared that a state could constitutionally deny women the vote. Divided and rebuffed, woman-suffrage advocates braced for a long struggle.

By the time the Fifteenth Amendment was ratified in 1870, Congress could look back on five years of momentous achievement. Since the start of 1865, three constitutional amendments had broadened the scope of American democracy by passing three constitutional amendments. The Thirteenth Amendment abolished slavery, the Fourteenth expanded civil rights, and the Fifteenth prohibited the denial of suffrage on the basis of race. Congress had also readmitted the former Confederate states into the Union. But after 1868 congressional momentum slowed, and in 1869, when Ulysses S. Grant became president, enmity between Congress and the chief executive ceased. The theater of action now shifted to the South, where tumultuous change was under way.

Stanton and Anthony, c. 1870 *Women's rights advocates Susan B. Anthony and Elizabeth Cady Stanton began to promote woman suffrage in 1866 when the issue of black suffrage arose, and subsequently assailed the proposed Fifteenth Amendment for excluding women. By the end of the 1860s, activists had formed two competing suffragist organizations.*

RECONSTRUCTION GOVERNMENTS

During the unstable years of presidential Reconstruction, 1865–1867, the southern states had to create new governments, revive the war-torn economy, and face the impact of emancipation. Social and economic crises abounded. War costs had cut into southern wealth, cities and factories lay in rubble, plantation-labor systems disintegrated, and racial tensions flared. Beginning in 1865, freedmen organized black conventions, political meetings at which they protested ill treatment and demanded equal rights. These meetings occurred in a climate of violence. Race riots erupted in major southern cities, such as Memphis in May 1866 and in New Orleans two months later. Even when Congress imposed military rule, ex-Confederates did not feel defeated. "Having reached bottom, there is hope now that we may rise again," a South Carolina planter wrote in his diary.

Congressional Reconstruction, supervised by federal troops, took effect in the spring of 1867. The Johnson regimes were dismantled, state constitutional conventions met, and voters elected new state governments, which Republicans dominated. In 1868, a majority of the former Confederate states rejoined the Union, and two years later, the last four states—Virginia, Mississippi, Georgia, and Texas—followed.

Readmission to the Union did not end the process of Reconstruction, for Republicans still held power in the South. But Republican rule was very brief, lasting less than a decade in all southern states, far less in most of them, and on average under five years. Opposition from southern Democrats, the landowning elite, thousands of vigilantes, and, indeed, most white voters proved insurmountable. Still, the governments formed under congressional Reconstruction were unique, because black men, including ex-slaves, participated in them. In no other society where slaves had been liberated—neither Haiti, where slaves had revolted in the 1790s, nor the British Caribbean islands, where Parliament had ended slavery in 1833—had freedmen gained democratic political rights.

A New Electorate   The Reconstruction laws of 1867–1868 transformed the southern electorate by temporarily disfranchising 10 to 15 percent of potential white voters and by enfranchising more than seven hundred thousand freedmen. Outnumbering white voters in the South by one hundred thousand, blacks held voting majorities in five states.

The new electorate provided a base for the Republican Party, which had never existed in the South. To scornful Democrats, southern Republicans comprised three types of scoundrels: northern "carpetbaggers," who had allegedly come south seeking wealth and power (with so few possessions that they could be stuffed into traveling bags made of carpet material); southern "scalawags," predominantly poor and ignorant whites, who sought to profit from Republican rule; and hordes of uneducated freedmen, who were ready prey for Republican manipulators. Although the "carpetbag" and "scalawag" labels were derogatory and the stereotypes that they conveyed inaccurate, they remain in use as a form of shorthand. Crossing class and racial lines, the hastily established Republican Party was in fact a loose coalition of diverse factions with often contradictory goals.

To northerners who moved south after the Civil War, the former Confederacy was an undeveloped region, ripe with possibility. The carpetbaggers' ranks included many former Union soldiers who hoped to buy land, open factories, build railroads, or simply enjoy the warmer climate. Albion Tourgee, a young lawyer who had served with the New York and Ohio volunteers, for example, relocated in North Carolina after the war to improve his health; there he worked as a journalist, politician, and Republican judge. Perhaps no more than twenty thousand northern migrants like Tourgee—including veterans, missionaries, teachers, and Freedmen's Bureau agents—headed south immediately after the war, and many returned north by 1867. But those who remained held almost one out of three state offices and wielded disproportionate political power.

Scalawags, white southerners who supported the Republicans, included some entrepreneurs who applauded party policies such as the national banking system and high protective tariffs as well as some prosperous planters, former Whigs who had opposed secession. Their numbers included a few prominent politicians, among them James Orr of South Carolina and Mississippi's governor James Alcorn, who became Republicans in order to retain influence and limit Republican radicalism. Most scalawags, however, were small farmers from the mountain regions of North Carolina, Georgia, Alabama, and Arkansas. Former Unionists who had owned no slaves and felt no loyalty toward the landowning elite, they sought to improve their economic position. Unlike carpetbaggers, they were not committed to black rights or black suffrage; most came from regions with small black populations and cared little whether blacks voted or not. Scalawags held the most political offices during Reconstruction, but they proved the least stable element of the southern Republican coalition: eventually, many drifted back to the Democratic fold.

Freedmen, the backbone of southern Republicanism, provided eight out of ten Republican votes. Republican rule lasted longest in states with the largest black populations—South Carolina, Mississippi, Alabama, and Louisiana. Introduced to politics in the black conventions of 1865–1867, the freedmen sought land, education, civil

Republicans in the South Carolina Legislature, c. 1868 *Only in South Carolina did blacks comprise a majority in the legislature and dominate the legislative process during Reconstruction. This photographic collage of "Radical" legislators, black and white, suggests the extent of black representation. In 1874, blacks won the majority of seats in South Carolina's state senate as well.*

RADICAL. MEMBERS
OF THE S°. C^. LEGISLATURE.

rights, and political equality, and remained loyal Republicans. As an elderly freedman announced at a Georgia political convention in 1867, "We know our friends." Although Reconstruction governments depended on African-American votes, freedmen held at most one in five political offices. Blacks served in all southern legislatures but constituted a majority only in the legislature of South Carolina, whose population was more than 60 percent black. In the House of Representatives, a mere 6 percent of southern members were black, and almost half of these came from South Carolina. No blacks became governor, and only two served in the U.S. Senate, Hiram Revels and Blanche K. Bruce, both of Mississippi. (Still, the same number of African-Americans served in the Senate during Reconstruction as throughout the entire twentieth century.)

Black officeholders on the state level formed a political elite. They often differed from black voters in background, education, wealth, and complexion. A disproportionate number were literate blacks who had been free before the Civil War. In the South Carolina legislature, for instance, most black members, unlike their constituents, came from large towns and cities; many had spent time in the North; and some were well-off property owners or even former slave owners. Color differences were evident, too: 43 percent of South Carolina's black state legislators were mulattos (mixed race), compared to only 7 percent of the state's black population.

Black officials and black voters often had different priorities. Most freedmen cared mainly about their economic future, especially about acquiring land, whereas black officeholders cared most about attaining equal rights. Still, both groups shared high expectations and prized enfranchisement. "We'd walk fifteen miles in wartime to find out about the battle," a Georgia freedman declared. "We can walk fifteen miles and more to find how to vote."

Republican Rule   Large numbers of blacks participated in American government for the first time in the state constitutional conventions of 1867–1868. The South Carolina convention had a black majority, and in Louisiana half the delegates were freedmen. The conventions forged democratic changes in their state constitutions. Delegates abolished property qualifications for officeholding, made many appointive offices elective, and redistricted state legislatures more equitably. All states established universal manhood suffrage, and Louisiana and South Carolina opened public schools to both races. These provisions integrated the New Orleans public schools as well as the University of South Carolina, from which whites withdrew.

But no state instituted land reform. When proposals for land confiscation and redistribution arose at the state conventions, they fell to defeat, as they had in Congress. Hoping to attract northern investment to the reconstructed South, southern Republicans hesitated to threaten property rights or to adopt land-reform measures that northern Republicans had rejected. South Carolina did set up a commission to buy land and make it available to freedmen, and several states changed their tax structures to force uncultivated land onto the market, but in no case was ex-Confederate land confiscated.

Once civil power shifted from the federal army to the new state governments, Republican administrations began ambitious programs of public works. They built roads, bridges, and public buildings; approved railroad bonds; and funded institutions to care for orphans, the insane, and the disabled. Republican regimes also expanded state bureaucracies, raised salaries for government employees, and formed state militia, in which blacks were often heavily represented. Finally, they created public-school systems, almost nonexistent in the South until then.

Because rebuilding the devastated South and expanding state government cost millions, taxes skyrocketed. State legislatures increased poll taxes or "head" taxes (levies on individuals); enacted luxury, sales, and occupation taxes; and imposed new property taxes. Before the war southern states had taxed property in slaves but had barely taxed landed property. Now state governments assessed even small farmers' holdings, and propertied planters paid what they considered an excessive burden. Although northern tax rates still exceeded southern rates, southern landowners resented the new levies. In their view, Reconstruction punished the propertied, already beset by labor problems and falling land values, in order to finance the vast expenditures of Republican legislators.

To Reconstruction's foes, Republican rule was wasteful and corrupt, the "most stupendous system of organized robbery in history." A state like Mississippi, which had an honest government, provided little basis for such charges. But critics could justifiably point to Louisiana, where the governor pocketed thousands of dollars of state funds and corruption permeated all government transactions (as indeed it had before the war). Or they could cite South Carolina, where bribery ran rampant. Besides government officials who took bribes, the main postwar profiteers were the railroad promoters who doled them out. Not all were Republicans. Nor did the Republican regimes in the South hold a monopoly on corruption. After the war, bribery pervaded government transactions North and South, and far more money changed hands in the North. But critics assailed Republican rule for additional reasons.

Counterattacks Ex-Confederates chafed at black enfranchisement and spoke with dread about the "horror of Negro domination." As soon as congressional Reconstruction took effect, former Confederates campaigned to undermine it. Democratic newspapers assailed delegates to North Carolina's constitutional convention as an "Ethiopian minstrelsy . . . baboons, monkeys, mules . . . and other jackasses," and demeaned Louisiana's constitution as "the work of ignorant Negroes cooperating with a gang of white adventurers."

Democrats delayed mobilization until southern states were readmitted to the Union. Then they swung into action, calling themselves Conservatives in order to attract former Whigs. At first, they sought to win the votes of blacks; but when that effort failed, they tried other tactics. In 1868–1869, Georgia Democrats challenged the eligibility of black legislators and expelled them from office. In response, the federal government reestablished military rule in Georgia, but determined Democrats still undercut Republican power. In every southern state, they contested elections, backed dissident Republican factions, elected some Democratic legislators, and lured scalawags away from the Republican Party.

Vigilante efforts to reduce black votes bolstered the Democrats' campaigns to win white ones. Antagonism toward free blacks, long a motif in southern life, had resurged after the war. In 1865, Freedmen's Bureau agents itemized outrages against blacks, including shooting, murder, rape, arson, roasting, and "severe and inhuman beating." Vigilante groups sprang up spontaneously in all parts of the former Confederacy under names like moderators, regulators, and, in Louisiana, Knights of the White Camelia. One group rose to dominance. In the spring of 1866, when the Johnson governments were still in power, six young Confederate war veterans in Tennessee formed a social club, the **Ku Klux Klan,** distinguished by elaborate rituals, hooded costumes, and secret passwords. By the election of 1868, when black men could first vote, Klan dens had spread to all the southern states. Klansmen embarked on night raids to intimidate black voters. No longer a social club, the Ku Klux Klan was now a widespread terrorist movement and a violent arm of the Democratic Party.

The Klan sought to suppress black voting, reestablish white supremacy, and topple the Reconstruction governments. Its members attacked Freedmen's Bureau officials, white Republicans, black militia units, economically successful blacks, and black voters. Concentrated in areas where the black and white populations were most evenly balanced and racial tensions greatest, Klan dens adapted their tactics and timing to local conditions. In Mississippi the Klan targeted black schools; in Alabama it concentrated on Republican officeholders. In Arkansas terror reigned in 1868; in Georgia and Florida Klan strength surged in 1870. Some Democrats denounced Klan members as "cut-throats and riff-raff." But prominent ex-Confederates were also known to be active Klansmen, among them General Nathan Bedford Forrest, the leader of the 1864 Fort Pillow massacre, in which Confederate troops who captured a Union garrison in Tennessee murdered black soldiers after they had surrendered. Vigilantism united southern whites of different social classes and drew on the energy of many Confederate veterans. In areas where the Klan was inactive, other vigilante groups took its place.

Republican legislatures passed laws to outlaw vigilantism, but the state militia could not enforce them. State officials turned to the federal government for help. In response, between May 1870 and February 1871, Congress passed three **Enforcement Acts,** each progressively more stringent. The First Enforcement Act protected black voters, but witnesses to violations were afraid to testify against vigilantes, and local juries refused to convict them. The Second Enforcement Act provided for federal supervision of southern elections, and the Third Enforcement Act, or Ku Klux Klan Act, strengthened punishments for those who prevented blacks from voting. It also empowered the president to use federal troops to enforce the law and to suspend the writ of *habeas corpus* in areas that he declared in insurrection. (The writ of *habeas corpus* is a court order requiring that the detainer of a prisoner bring that person to court and show cause for his or her detention.) The Ku Klux Klan Act generated thousands of arrests; most terrorists, however, escaped conviction.

By 1872, the federal government had effectively suppressed the Klan, but vigilantism had served its purpose. Only a large military presence in the South could have protected black rights, and the government in Washington never provided it. Instead, federal power in the former Confederacy diminished. President Grant steadily reduced troop levels in the South; Congress allowed the Freedmen's Bureau to die in 1869; and the Enforcement acts became dead letters. White southerners, a Georgia politician told congressional investigators in 1871, could not discard "a feeling of bitterness, a feeling that the Negro is a sort of instinctual enemy of ours." The battle over Reconstruction was in essence a battle over the implications of emancipation, and it had begun as soon as the war ended.

THE IMPACT OF EMANCIPATION

"The master he says we are all free," a South Carolina slave declared in 1865. "But it don't mean we is white. And it don't mean we is equal." Emancipated slaves faced daunting handicaps. They had no property, tools, or capital and usually possessed meager skills. Only a minority had been trained as artisans, and more than 95 percent were illiterate. Still, the exhilaration of freedom was overwhelming, as slaves realized, "Now I am for myself" and "All that I make is my own." At emancipation, they gained the right to their own labor and a new sense of autonomy. Under Reconstruction the freed blacks struggled to cast off white control and shed the vestiges of slavery.

Confronting Freedom

For the former slaves, liberty meant they could move where they pleased. Some moved out of the slave quarters and set up dwellings elsewhere on their plantations; others left their plantations entirely. Landowners found that one freed slave after another vanished, with house servants and artisans leading the way. "I have never in my life met with such ingratitude," one South Carolina mistress exclaimed when a former slave ran off. Field workers, who had less contact with whites, were more likely to stay behind or more reluctant to leave. Still, flight remained tempting. "The moment they see an opportunity to improve themselves, they will move on," diarist Mary Chesnut observed.

Emancipation stirred waves of migration within the former Confederacy. Some freed slaves left the Upper South for the Deep South and the Southwest—Florida, Mississippi, Arkansas, and Texas—where planters desperately needed labor and paid higher wages. Even more left the countryside for towns and cities, traditional havens of independence for blacks. Urban black populations sometimes doubled or tripled after emancipation. Overall during the 1860s, the urban black population rose by 75 percent, and the number of blacks in small rural towns grew as well. Many migrants eventually returned to their old locales, but they tended to settle on neighboring plantations rather than with their former owners. Freedom was the major goal. "I's wants to be a free man, cum when I please, and nobody say nuffin to me, nor order me roun'," an Alabama freedman told a northern journalist.

Freed blacks' yearnings to find lost family members prompted much movement. "They had a passion, not so much for wandering as for getting together," a Freedmen's Bureau official commented. Parents sought children who had been sold; husbands and wives who had been separated by sale, or who lived on different plantations, reunited; and families reclaimed youngsters from masters' homes. The Freedmen's Bureau helped former slaves get information about missing relatives and travel to find them. Bureau agents also tried to resolve conflicts that arose when spouses who had been separated under slavery married other people.

Reunification efforts often failed. Some fugitive slaves had died during the war or were untraceable. Other exslaves had formed new relationships and could not revive old ones. "I am married," one husband wrote to a former wife (probably in a dictated letter), "and my wife [and I] have two children, and if you and I meet it would make a very dissatisfied family." But there were success stories, too. "I's hunted an' hunted till I track you up here," one freedman told his wife, whom he found in a refugee camp twenty years after their separation by sale.

Once reunited, freed blacks quickly legalized unions formed under slavery, sometimes in mass ceremonies of up to seventy couples. Legal marriage affected family life. Men asserted themselves as household heads; wives of able-bodied men often withdrew from the labor force to care for homes and families. "When I married my wife, I married her to wait on me and she has got all she can do right here for me and the children," a Tennessee freedman explained.

Black women's desire to secure the privileges of domestic life caused planters severe labor shortages. Before the war at least half of field workers had been women; in 1866, a southern journal claimed, men performed almost all the field labor. Still, by the end of Reconstruction, many black women had returned to agricultural work as part of sharecropper families. Others took paid work in cities, as laundresses, cooks, and domestic servants. (White women often sought employment as well, for the war had incapacitated many white breadwinners, reduced the supply of future husbands, and left families destitute or in diminished circumstances.) However, former slaves continued to view stable, independent domestic life, especially the right to bring up their own children, as a major blessing of freedom. In 1870, eight out of ten black families in the cotton-producing South were two-parent families, about the same proportion as among whites.

African-American Institutions   The freed blacks' desire for independence also led to the postwar growth of black churches. In the late 1860s, some freedmen congregated at churches operated by northern missionaries; others withdrew from white-run churches and formed their own. The African Methodist Episcopal church, founded by Philadelphia blacks in the 1790s, gained thousands of new southern members. Negro Baptist churches sprouted every-where, often growing out o f plantation "praise meetings," religious gatherings organized by slaves.

The black churches offered a fervent, participatory experience. They also provided relief, raised funds for schools, and supported Republican policies. From the outset black ministers assumed leading political roles, first in the black conventions of 1865–1866 and later in the Reconstruction governments. After southern Democrats excluded most freedmen from political life at Reconstruction's end, ministers remained the main pillars of authority in black communities.

Black schools played a crucial role for freedmen as well; exslaves eagerly sought literacy for themselves and even more for their children. At emancipation, blacks organized their own schools, which the Freedmen's Bureau soon supervised. Northern philanthropic societies paid the wages of instructors, about half of them women. In 1869, the bureau reported more than four thousand black schools in the former Confederacy. Within three years, each southern state had a public-school system, at least in principle, generally with separate schools for blacks and whites. Advanced schools for blacks opened as well, to train tradespeople, teachers, and ministers. The Freedmen's Bureau and northern organizations like the American Missionary Association helped found Howard, Atlanta, and Fisk universities (all started in 1866–1867) and Hampton Institute (1868).

Despite these advances, black education remained limited. Few rural blacks could reach the freedmen's schools located in towns. Underfunded black public schools, similarly inaccessible to most rural black children, held classes only for very short seasons and were sometimes the targets of vigilante attacks. At the end of Reconstruction, more than 80 percent of the black population was still illiterate. Still, the proportion of youngsters who could not read and write had declined and would continue to fall.

School segregation and other forms of racial separation were taken for granted. Some black codes of 1865–1866 had segregated public-transit conveyances and public accommodations. Even after the invalidation of the codes, the custom of segregation continued on streetcars, steamboats, and trains as well as in churches, theaters, inns, and restaurants. On railroads, for example, whites could ride in the "ladies' car" or first-class car, whereas blacks had to stay in smoking cars or boxcars with benches. In 1870, Senator Charles Sumner of Massachusetts began promoting a bill to desegregate schools, transportation facilities, juries, and public accommodations. After Sumner's death in 1874, Congress honored him by enacting a new law, the **Civil Rights Act of 1875,** which encompassed many of his proposals, except for the controversial school-integration provision. But in 1883, in the *Civil Rights Cases,* the Supreme Court invalidated the law; the Fourteenth Amendment did not prohibit discrimination by individuals, the Court ruled, only that perpetrated by the state.

White southerners rejected the prospect of racial integration, which they insisted would lead to racial mixing. "If we have social equality, we shall have intermarriage," one white southerner contended, "and if we have intermarriage, we shall degenerate." Urban blacks sometimes challenged segregation practices, and black legislators promoted bills to desegregate public transit. Some black officeholders decried all forms of racial separatism. "The sooner we as a people forget our sable complexion," said a Mobile official, "the better it will be for us as a race." But most freed blacks were less interested in "social equality," in the sense of interracial mingling, than in black liberty and community. The newly formed postwar elite—teachers, ministers, and politicians—served black constituencies and therefore had a vested interest in separate black institutions. Rural blacks, too, widely preferred all-black institutions. They had little desire to mix with whites. On the contrary, they sought freedom from white control. Above all else, they wanted to secure personal independence by acquiring land.

Land, Labor, and Sharecropping   "The sole ambition of the freedman," a New Englander wrote from South Carolina in 1865, "appears to be to become the owner of a little piece of land, there to erect a humble home, and to dwell in peace and security, at his own free will and pleasure." Indeed, to freed blacks everywhere, "forty acres and a mule" (a phrase that originated in 1864 when Union general William T. Sherman set aside land on the South Carolina Sea Islands for black settlement) promised emancipation from plantation labor, from white domination, and from cotton, the "slave crop." Just as garden plots had provided a measure of autonomy under slavery, so did landownership signify economic independence afterward. "We want to be placed on land until we are able to buy it and make it our own," a black minister had told General Sherman in Georgia during the war.

But freedmen's visions of landownership failed to materialize, for, as we have seen, neither Congress nor the southern states imposed large-scale land reform. Some freedmen did obtain land with the help of the Union army or the Freedmen's Bureau, and black soldiers sometimes pooled resources to buy land, as on the Sea Islands of South Carolina and Georgia. The federal government also sought to provide exslaves with land. In 1866, Congress passed the Southern Homestead Act, which set aside 44 million acres of public land in five southern states for freedmen and loyal whites. This acreage contained poor soil, and few former slaves had the resources to survive even until their first harvest. About four thousand blacks resettled on homesteads under the law, but most were unable to establish farms. (White southern homesteaders fared little better.) By the end of Reconstruction, only a small minority of former slaves in each state owned working farms. In Georgia in 1876, for instance, blacks controlled a mere 1.3 percent of total acreage. Without large-scale land reform, the obstacles to black landownership remained overwhelming.

What were these obstacles? First, most freedmen lacked the capital to buy land and the equipment needed to work it. Furthermore, white southerners on the whole opposed selling land to blacks. Most important, planters sought to preserve a black labor force. Freedmen, they insisted, would work only under coercion, and not at all if the possibility of landownership arose. As soon as the war ended, the white South took steps to make sure that black labor would remain available on plantations.

During presidential Reconstruction, southern state legislatures tried to curb black mobility and to preserve a captive labor force through the black codes. Under labor contracts in effect in 1865–1866, freedmen received wages, housing, food, and clothing in exchange for field work. With cash scarce, wages usually took the form of a very small share of the crop, often one-eighth or less, divided among the entire plantation work force. Freedmen's Bureau agents promoted the new labor system; they urged freedmen to sign labor contracts and tried to ensure adequate wages. Imbued with the northern free-labor ideology, which held that wage workers could rise to the status of self-supporting tradesmen and property owners, bureau officials endorsed black wage labor as an interim arrangement that would lead to economic independence. "You must begin at the bottom of the ladder and climb up," Freedmen's Bureau head O. O. Howard exhorted a group of Louisiana freedmen in 1865.

But the freedmen disliked the new wage system, especially the use of gang labor, which resembled the work pattern under slavery. Planters had complaints, too. In some regions the black labor force had shrunk to half its prewar size or less, due to the migration of freedmen and to black women's withdrawal from fieldwork. Once united in defense of slavery, planters now competed for black workers. But the freedmen, whom planters often scorned as lazy or inefficient, did not intend to work as long or as hard as they had labored under slavery. One planter claimed that workers accomplished only "two-fifths of what they did under the old system." As productivity fell, so did land values. To top off the planters' woes, cotton prices plummeted, for during the war northern and foreign buyers had found new sources of cotton in Egypt and India, and the world supply had vastly increased. Finally, the harvests of 1866 and 1867 were extremely poor. By then, an agricultural impasse had been reached: landowners lacked labor, and freedmen lacked land. But free blacks, unlike slaves, had the right to enter into contracts—or to refuse to do so—and thereby gained some leverage.

Planters and freedmen began experimenting with new labor schemes, including the division of plantations into small tenancies. **Sharecropping,** the most widespread arrangement, evolved as a compromise. Under the sharecropping system, landowners subdivided large plantations into farms of thirty to fifty acres, which they rented to freedmen under annual leases for a share of the crop, usually half. Freedmen preferred sharecropping to wage labor because it represented a step toward independence. Heads of households could use the labor of family members. Moreover, a half-share of the crop far exceeded the fraction that freedmen had received as wages under the black codes. Planters often spoke of sharecropping as a concession, but they benefited, too. They retained power over tenants, because annual leases did not have to be renewed; they could expel undesirable tenants at the end of the year. Planters also shared the risk of planting with tenants: if a crop failed, both suffered the loss. Most important, planters retained control of their land and in some cases extended their holdings. The most productive land, therefore, remained in the hands of a small group of owners, as before the war. Sharecropping forced planters to relinquish daily control over the labor of freedmen but helped to preserve the planter elite.

Sharecropping arrangements varied widely. On sugar and rice plantations, the wage system continued; strong markets for sugar and rice meant that planters of those crops could pay their workers in cash—cash that cotton planters lacked. Some freedmen remained independent renters. Some landowners leased areas to white tenants, who then subcontracted with black labor. But by the end of the 1860s, sharecropping prevailed in the cotton South, and the new system continued to expand. A severe depression in 1873 drove many black renters into sharecropping. By then, thousands of independent white farmers had become sharecroppers as well. Stung by wartime losses and by the dismal postwar economy, they sank into debt and lost their land to creditors. Many backcountry residents, no longer able to get by on subsistence farming, shifted to cash crops like cotton and suffered the same fate. At the end of Reconstruction, one-third of the white farmers in Mississippi, for instance, were sharecroppers.

By 1880, 80 percent of the land in the cotton-producing states had been subdivided into tenancies, most of it farmed by sharecroppers, white and black. Indeed, white sharecroppers now outnumbered black ones, although a higher proportion of southern blacks, about 75 percent, were involved in the system. Changes in marketing and finance, meanwhile, made the sharecroppers' lot increasingly precarious.

Toward a Crop-Lien Economy Before the Civil War, planters had depended on factors, or middlemen, who sold them supplies, extended credit, and marketed their crops through urban merchants. These long-distance credit arrangements were backed by the high value and liquidity of slave property. When slavery ended, the factorage system collapsed. The postwar South, with hundreds of thousands of tenants and sharecroppers, needed a far more localized network of credit.

Into the gap stepped the rural merchants (often themselves planters), who advanced supplies to tenants and sharecroppers on credit and sold their crops to wholesalers or textile manufacturers. Because renters had no property to use as collateral, the merchants secured their loans with a lien, or claim, on each farmer's next crop. Exorbitant interest rates of 50 percent or more quickly forced many tenants and sharecroppers into a cycle of indebtedness. Owing part of the crop to a landowner for rent, a sharecropper also owed a rural merchant a large sum (perhaps amounting to the rest of his crop, or more) for supplies. Illiterate tenants who could not keep track of their financial arrangements often fell prey to unscrupulous merchants. "A man that didn't know how to count would always lose," an Arkansas freedman later explained. Once a tenant's debts or alleged debts exceeded the value of his crop, he was tied to the land, to cotton, and to sharecropping.

By the end of Reconstruction, sharecropping and crop liens had transformed southern agriculture. They bound the region to staple production and prevented crop

Sharecroppers during Reconstruction
By the end of the 1870s, about three out of four African-Americans in the cotton-producing states had become sharecroppers. Here, sharecroppers pick cotton in Aiken, South Carolina.

diversification. Despite plunging cotton prices, creditors—landowners and merchants—insisted that tenants raise only easily marketable cash crops. Short of capital, planters could no longer invest in new equipment or improve their land by such techniques as crop rotation and contour plowing. Soil depletion, land erosion, and agricultural backwardness soon locked much of the South into a cycle of poverty.

Trapped in perpetual debt, tenant farmers became the chief victims of the new agricultural order. Raising cotton for distant markets, for prices over which they had no control, remained the only survival route open to poor farmers, regardless of race. But low income from cotton locked them into sharecropping and crop liens, from which escape was difficult. African-American tenants, who attained neither landownership nor economic independence, saw their political rights dwindle, too. As one southern regime after another returned to Democratic control, freedmen could no longer look to the state governments for protection. Nor could they turn to the federal government, for northern politicians were preoccupied with their own problems.

NEW CONCERNS IN THE NORTH, 1868–1876

The nomination of Ulysses S. Grant for president in 1868 launched an era of crises in national politics. Grant's two terms in office featured political scandals, a party revolt, a massive depression, and a steady retreat from Reconstruction policies. By the mid-1870s, northern voters cared more about the economic climate, unemployment, labor unrest, and currency problems than about the "southern question." Responsive to the shift in popular mood, Republicans became eager to end sectional conflict and turned their backs on the freedmen of the South.

Grantism   Republicans had good reason to bypass party leaders and nominate the popular Grant to succeed Andrew Johnson. A war hero, Grant was endorsed by Union veterans, widely admired in the North, and unscathed by the bitter feuds of Reconstruction politics. To oppose Grant in 1868, the Democrats nominated New York governor Horatio Seymour, arch-critic of the Lincoln administration during the war and now a foe of Reconstruction. Grant ran on his personal popularity more than on issues. Although he carried all but eight states, the popular vote was very close; in the South, newly enfranchised freedmen provided Grant's margin of victory.

A strong leader in war, Grant proved a passive president. Although he lacked Johnson's instinct for disaster, he had little political skill. Many of his cabinet appointees were mediocre if not unscrupulous; scandals plagued his administration. In 1869, financier Jay Gould and his partner Jim Fisk tried to corner the gold market with the help of Grant's brother-in-law, a New York speculator. When gold prices tumbled, Gould salvaged his own fortune, but investors were ruined, and Grant's reputation suffered. Then before the president's first term ended, his vice president, Schuyler Colfax, was found to be linked to the Crédit Mobilier, a fraudulent construction company created by the directors of the Union Pacific Railroad to skim off the railroad's profits. Discredited, Colfax was dropped from the Grant ticket in 1872.

More trouble lay ahead. Grant's private secretary, Orville Babcock, was unmasked in 1875 after taking money from the "whiskey ring," a group of distillers who bribed federal agents to avoid paying millions of dollars in whiskey taxes. In 1876, voters learned that Grant's secretary of war, William E. Belknap, had taken bribes to sell lucrative Indian trading posts in Oklahoma. Impeached and disgraced, Belknap resigned.

Although uninvolved in the scandals, Grant loyally defended his subordinates. To his critics, "Grantism" came to stand for fraud, bribery, and political corruption—evils that spread far beyond Washington. In Pennsylvania, for example, the Standard Oil Company and the Pennsylvania Railroad controlled the legislature. Urban politics also provided rich opportunities for graft and swindles. The New York City press revealed in 1872 that Democratic boss William M. Tweed, the leader of Tammany Hall, led a ring that had looted the city treasury and collected at least $30 million in kickbacks and payoffs. When Mark Twain and coauthor Charles Dudley Warner published their satiric novel *The Gilded Age* (1873), readers recognized the book's speculators, self-promoters, and opportunists as familiar types in public life. (The term "Gilded Age" was subsequently used to refer to the decades from the 1870s to the 1890s.)

Grant had some success in foreign policy. In 1872, his competent secretary of state, Hamilton Fish, engineered the settlement of the *Alabama* claims with Britain. To compensate for damage done by British-built ships sold to the Confederacy during the war, an international tribunal awarded the United States $15.5 million. But the Grant administration faltered when it tried to add nonadjacent territory to the United States, as the Johnson administration had done. In 1867, Johnson's secretary of state, William H. Seward, had negotiated a treaty in which the United States bought Alaska from Russia at the bargain price of $7.2 million. Although the press mocked "Seward's Ice Box," the purchase kindled expansionists' hopes. In 1870, Grant decided to annex the eastern half of the Caribbean island of Santo Domingo. Today called the Dominican Republic, the territory had been passed back and forth since the late eighteenth century among France, Spain, and Haiti. Annexation, Grant believed, would promote Caribbean trade and provide a haven for persecuted southern blacks. American speculators anticipated windfalls from land sales, commerce, and mining. But Congress disliked Grant's plan. Senator Charles Sumner denounced it as an imperialist "dance of blood." The Senate rejected the annexation treaty and further diminished Grant's reputation.

As the election of 1872 approached, dissident Republicans expressed fears that "Grantism" at home and abroad would ruin the party. Even Grant's new running mate, Henry Wilson, referred to the president privately as a burden on his fellow Republicans. The dissidents took action. Led by a combination of former Radicals and other Republicans left out of Grant's "Great Barbecue" (a disparaging reference to profiteers who feasted at the public trough), the president's critics formed their own party, the Liberal Republicans.

The Liberals' Revolt

The Liberal Republican revolt marked a turning point in Reconstruction history. By splitting the Republican Party, **Liberal Republicans** undermined support for Republican southern policy. (The label "liberal" at the time referred to those who endorsed economic doctrines such as free trade, the gold standard, and the law of supply and demand.) Liberals attacked the "regular" Republicans on several issues. Denouncing "Grantism" and "spoilsmen" (political hacks who gained party office), they demanded civil-service reform to bring the "best men" into government. Rejecting the usual Republican high-tariff policy, they espoused free trade. Most important, the Liberals condemned "bayonet rule" in the South. Even some Republicans once known for radicalism now claimed that Reconstruction had achieved its goal: blacks had been enfranchised and could manage for themselves from now on. Corruption in government, North and South, Liberals asserted, posed a greater danger than Confederate resurgence. In the South, indeed, corrupt Republican regimes were *kept* in power, Liberals said, because the "best men"—the most capable politicians—were ex-Confederates who had been barred from officeholding.

For president the new party nominated the editor of the *New York Tribune*, Horace Greeley, who had inconsistently supported both a stringent reconstruction policy and leniency toward former rebels. The Democrats endorsed Greeley as well; their campaign slogan explained their support: "Anything to Beat Grant." Horace Greeley proved so diligent a campaigner that he worked himself to death making speeches from the back of a campaign train. He died a few weeks after the election.

Grant, who won 56 percent of the popular vote, carried all the northern states and most of the sixteen southern and border states. But the division among Republicans affected Reconstruction. To deprive the Liberals of a campaign issue, Grant Republicans in Congress, the "regulars," passed the Amnesty Act, which allowed all but a few hundred ex-Confederate officials to hold office. The flood of private amnesty acts that followed convinced white southerners that any ex-Confederate save Jefferson Davis could rise to power. In Grant's second term, Republican desires to discard the "southern question" mounted as a depression of unprecedented scope gripped the nation.

The Panic of 1873   The postwar years brought accelerated industrialization and rapid economic growth; new businesses, factories, and technological advances transformed the nation's economy in the 1870s (see Technology and Culture: The Sewing Machine) Frantic speculation played a role, too. Investors rushed to profit from rising prices, new markets, high tariffs, and seemingly boundless opportunities. Railroads provided the biggest lure. In May 1869, railroad executives drove a golden spike into the ground at Promontory Point, Utah, joining the Union Pacific and Central Pacific lines. The first transcontinental railroad heralded a new era. By 1873, almost four hundred railroad corporations crisscrossed the Northeast, consuming tons of coal and miles of steel rail from the mines and mills of Pennsylvania and neighboring states. Transforming the economy, the railroad boom led entrepreneurs to overspeculate, with drastic results.

Philadelphia banker Jay Cooke, who had helped finance the Union effort with his wartime bond campaign, had taken over a new transcontinental line, the Northern Pacific, in 1869. Northern Pacific securities sold briskly for several years, but in 1873 the line's construction costs outran new investments. In September of that year, his vaults full of bonds he could no longer sell, Cooke failed to meet his obligations, and his bank, the largest in the nation, shut down. A financial panic began; other firms collapsed, as did the stock market. The Panic of 1873 triggered a five-year depression. Banks closed, farm prices plummeted, steel furnaces stood idle, and one out of four railroads failed. Within two years, eighteen thousand businesses went bankrupt, and 3 million employees were out of jobs by 1878. Those still at work suffered repeated wage cuts; labor protests mounted; and industrial violence spread. The depression of the 1870s revealed that conflicts born of industrialization had replaced sectional divisions.

The depression also fed a dispute over currency that had begun in 1865. During the Civil War, Americans had used both national bank notes, yellow in color, which would

The Sewing Machine

"You could scarcely believe . . . that such works were necessary for so small a machine," an observer wrote of the Singer Sewing Machine factory that arose in 1873 in Elizabethport, New Jersey. The massive brick building, which occupied a ten-acre plot near railroad lines and New York harbor, produced every part of the sewing machine except the wooden cabinet—made in South Bend, Indiana. Most parts were cast iron; a vast foundry, the size of a football field, had enough molds laid out on its floor to hold thirty tons of pig iron. The factory also housed the forging shop, rumbling room (to wear off the rough edges of metal pieces), drilling room (to put screw holes in product parts), Japanning room (to give machines a black glossy finish), ornamenting room, assembly room, and adjusting room, where inspectors and seamstresses tested machines. According to John Scott, the lawyer for a Singer executive, the new plant was "believed to be the largest establishment in the world devoted to the production of a single article."

The start of the 1873 factory crowned two decades of explosive growth in the sewing machine industry. In 1856, leading manufacturers set up a patent-sharing pool, the Sewing Machine Combination, as a way to avoid costly lawsuits. The patent pool reflected the complexity of sewing machine technology. The sewing machine did not replicate the movement of the human hand. Instead, inventors developed a process that involved a needle with the eye at the head, two threads, feeding devices, thread tension control, and new types of stitches. The lock-stitch machine, first patented in 1846 by its inventor, Elias Howe, was most effective; it used two spools of thread, one above the material and one below. Subsequent inventions refined this machine, and patents accumulated. Entrepreneur Isaac M. Singer, for instance, received patents in the 1850s for a device that sewed curved as well as straight seams and for a foot treadle (power to run the sewing machine came from the operator until the twentieth century).

Sewing machine production presented challenges. Until the late 1850s, skilled mechanics made each machine by hand; parts were not standardized, labor costs were high, and repairs were difficult. To achieve even a modicum of interchangeable parts required factories with special equipment and heavy investment of capital. By the 1870s, three manufacturers dominated the field: Wheeler and Wilson, Grover and Baker, and I. M. Singer. Each company strove for interchangeability of parts, though to varied degrees, and change was gradual, especially at the Singer company. When the New Jersey factory opened in 1873, Singer had fully adopted the "American" system of manufacturing; all parts were made by special machinery, thereby achieving uniformity though not true interchangeability. The company still relied on "fitters" to file parts so that they fit together. Singer's process remained a fusion of European custom-building and the "American" system until the early 1880s.

Heavy and costly, the earliest sewing machines sold only to factories. Ready-made clothing production had previously depended on seamstresses who worked at home; in the 1850s, sewing machines transformed the industry, first in men's clothing, then in cloaks, hats, and other items. Sewing machines also affected the making of shoes, sails, flags, trunks, valises, harnesses, mattresses, and umbrellas; producers eagerly adapted the machines to suit industrial demands. The impact of machines on garment production, though uneven, was momentous. In the late 1850s, each machine performed the work of six hand-sewers; seamstresses now competed with machine workers of both sexes and faced displacement. Manufacturers, however, gained a competitive edge. In 1860, a New Haven shirt factory that had once paid 2,000 hand-sewers each $3 a week could hire 400 machine workers at $4 each, cut costs, and hike profits, even while paying off the cost of the machines.

But factories were only part of the sewing machine's clientele: a huge home market beckoned. In 1856, Singer introduced the first machine intended solely for home use—its "family" machine—and other manufacturers followed. To appeal to individual purchasers, Edward Clark, a lawyer for the Singer company and later head of it, introduced the "hire-purchase" plan, or installment buying: by paying a percentage of the price, a buyer could "hire" a machine, make monthly payments (with interest), and eventually own it. Poor seamstresses could not afford the machines, but middle-class women flocked to buy them. Mass production of paper patterns, which began in the 1860s, enabled women at home to make up-to-date fashions; attachments and accessories simplified buttonholing, tucking, pleating, and other processes, both at the factory and at home. The zigzag stitch machine, for instance,

patented by inventor Helen Augusta Blanchard in 1873, sealed the edges of seams and made garments sturdier. In the 1870s, the home sewing machine proved a commercial triumph; profits soared. The machine that sold for $64 in 1870 cost only $12 to produce.

To reach the home market, major producers at first used independent agents who worked mainly on commission. Then they established company-owned-and-run centers in the business districts of major cities, such as New York's Union Square. Elegant stores with carpets, chandeliers, marble facades, and plate glass windows greeted customers, who could watch demonstrations by trained personnel. By the 1870s, manufacturers had developed many marketing tactics that included extensive advertising, door-to-door sales, discounts, and trade-in allowances for older models. The first mass-marketed appliance for home use, the sewing machine symbolized a family's middle-class status. Manufacturers promoted the machine as a labor-saving device that provided, in John Scott's words, "whatever saves the busy housewife's time and increases her opportunities for culture."

In the 1870s, the Singer company surged to preeminence. Its executives strove to improve the production process and reduce prices. Between 1874 and 1880, unscathed by the 1873 depression, Singer doubled its annual production of sewing machines to half a million and six years later doubled it again. In 1877, when the last patents in the patent pool of 1856 expired, Singer became an even more competitive marketer. The company reorganized its sales department, imposed a tight managerial scheme, built factories abroad, and found new markets worldwide. Edward Clark, who became Singer's president in 1876, sought to blanket the globe with regional branch offices; three years later, Singer produced three-quarters of the world's sewing machines. At the 1876 Centennial Exhibition in Philadelphia, thirty American firms exhibited sewing machines in "Machinery Hall," but Singer ruled. "Its system of agencies embraces the civilized world," John Scott boasted in 1880. "On every sea are floating the Singer machines."

Questions for Analysis

- Why were sewing machines a challenge to manufacture?

- How did manufacturers promote sales of sewing machines for home use?

- In what ways did the marketing of sewing machines set patterns for the marketing of consumer goods today?

eventually be converted into gold, and greenbacks, a paper currency not "backed" by a particular weight in gold. To stabilize the postwar currency, greenbacks would have to be withdrawn from circulation. This "sound-money" policy, favored by investors, won the backing of Congress. But those who depended on easy credit, both indebted farmers and manufacturers, wanted an expanding currency; that is, more greenbacks. Once the depression began, demands for such "easy money" rose. The issue divided both major parties and was compounded by another one: how to repay the federal debt.

In wartime, the Union government had borrowed what were then astronomical sums, on whatever terms it could get, mainly by selling war bonds—in effect, short-term federal IOUs—to private citizens. Bondholders wanted repayment in coin, gold or silver, even though many had paid for bonds in greenbacks. To pacify bondholders, Senator John Sherman of Ohio and other Republican leaders obtained passage of the Public Credit Act of 1869, which promised repayment in coin. With investors reassured by the Public Credit Act, Sherman guided legislation through Congress that swapped the old short-term bonds for new ones payable over the next generation. In 1872, another bill in effect defined "coin" as "gold coin" by dropping the traditional silver dollar from the official coinage. Through a feat of ingenious compromise, which placated investors and debtors, Sherman preserved the public credit, the currency, and Republican unity. In 1875, he engineered the Specie Resumption Act, which promised to put the nation on the gold standard in 1879, while tossing a few bones to Republican voters who wanted "easy money."

But when Democrats gained control of the House in 1875, with the depression in full force, a verbal storm broke out. Many Democrats and some Republicans demanded restoration of the silver dollar in order to expand the currency and relieve the depression. These "free-silver" advocates secured passage of the Bland-Allison Act of 1878, which partially restored silver coinage by requiring the Treasury to buy $2–4 million worth of silver each month and turn it into coin. In 1876, other expansionists formed the **Greenback Party,** which adopted the debtors' cause and fought to keep greenbacks in circulation, though with little success. As the nation emerged from depression in 1879, the clamor for "easy money" subsided, only to resurge in the 1890s. The controversial "money question" of the 1870s, never resolved, gave politicians and voters another reason to forget about the South.

Reconstruction and the Constitution   The Supreme Court of the 1870s also played a role in weakening northern support for Reconstruction. In wartime, few cases of note had come before the Court. After the war, however, constitutional questions surged into prominence.

First, would the Court support congressional laws to protect freedmen's rights? The decision in *Ex parte* Milligan (1866) suggested not. In *Milligan,* the Court declared that a military commission established by the president or Congress could not try civilians in areas remote from war where the civil courts were functioning. Thus special military courts to enforce the Supplementary Freedmen's Bureau Act were doomed. Second, would the Court sabotage the congressional Reconstruction plan, as Republicans feared? Their qualms were valid, for if the Union was indissoluble, as the North had claimed during the war, then the concept of *restoring* states to the Union would be meaningless. In *Texas v. White* (1869), the Court ruled that although the Union was indissoluble and secession was legally impossible, the process of Reconstruction was still constitutional. It was grounded in Congress's power to ensure each state a republican form of government and to recognize the legitimate government in any state.

The 1869 decision protected the Republicans' Reconstruction plan. But in the 1870s, when cases arose involving the Fourteenth and Fifteenth amendments, the Court backed away from Reconstruction policy. In the **Slaughterhouse cases** of 1873, the Supreme Court began to chip away at the Fourteenth Amendment. The cases involved a business monopoly rather than freedmen's rights, but they provided an opportunity to interpret the amendment narrowly. In 1869, the Louisiana legislature had granted a monopoly over the New Orleans slaughterhouse business to one firm and closed down all other slaughterhouses in the interest of public health. The excluded butchers brought suit. The state had deprived them of their lawful occupation without due process of law, they claimed, and such action violated the Fourteenth Amendment, which guaranteed that no state could "abridge the privileges or immunities" of U.S. citizens. The Supreme Court upheld the Louisiana legislature by issuing a doctrine of "dual citizenship." The Fourteenth Amendment, declared the Court, protected only the rights of *national* citizenship, such as the right of interstate travel or the right to federal protection on the high seas. It did not protect those basic civil rights that fell to citizens by virtue of their *state* citizenship. Therefore, the federal government was not obliged to protect such rights against violation by the states. The *Slaughterhouse* decision came close to nullifying the intent of the Fourteenth Amendment—to secure freedmen's rights against state encroachment.

The Supreme Court again backed away from Reconstruction in two cases in 1876 involving the Enforcement Act of 1870, which had been enacted to protect black suffrage. In *United States v. Reese* and *United States v. Cruikshank,* the Supreme Court undercut the effectiveness of the act. Continuing its retreat from Reconstruction, the Supreme Court in 1883 invalidated both the Civil Rights Act of 1875 and the Ku Klux Klan Act of 1871. These decisions cumulatively dismantled the Reconstruction policies that Republicans had sponsored after the war and confirmed rising northern sentiment that Reconstruction's egalitarian goals could not be enforced.

Republicans in Retreat   The Republicans did not reject Reconstruction suddenly but rather disengaged from it gradually, a process that began with Grant's election to the presidency in 1868. Although not an architect of Reconstruction policy, Grant defended it. But he shared with most Americans a belief in decentralized government and a reluctance to assert federal authority in local and state affairs.

In the 1870s, as the northern military presence shrank in the South, Republican idealism waned in the North. The Liberal Republican revolt of 1872 eroded what remained of radicalism. Although the "regular" Republicans, who backed Grant, continued to defend Reconstruction in the 1872 election, many held ambivalent views. Commercial and industrial interests now dominated both wings of the party, and few Republicans wished to rekindle sectional strife. After the Democrats won control of the House in the 1874 elections, support for Reconstruction became a political liability.

By 1875, the Radical Republicans, so prominent in the 1860s, had vanished from the political scene. Chase, Stevens, and Sumner were dead. Other Radicals had lost office or abandoned their former convictions. "Waving the Bloody Shirt"—defaming Democratic opponents by reviving wartime animosity—now struck many Republicans, including former Radicals, as counterproductive. Party leaders reported that voters were "sick of carpet-bag government" and tiring of both the "southern question" and the "Negro question." It seemed pointless to continue the unpopular and expensive policy of military intervention in the South to prop up Republican regimes that even President Grant found corrupt. Finally, few Republicans shared the egalitarian spirit that had animated Stevens and Sumner. Politics aside, Republican leaders and voters generally agreed with southern Democrats that blacks, although worthy of freedom, were inferior to whites. To insist on black equality would be a thankless, divisive, and politically suicidal undertaking. Moreover, it would quash any hope of reunion between the regions. The Republicans' retreat from Reconstruction set the stage for its demise in 1877.

RECONSTRUCTION ABANDONED, 1876–1877

"We are in a very hot political contest just now," a Mississippi planter wrote to his daughter in 1875, "with a good prospect of turning out the carpetbag thieves by whom we have been robbed for the past six to ten years." Similar contests raged through the South in the 1870s, as the resentment of white majorities grew and Democratic influence surged. By the end of 1872, the Democrats had regained power in Tennessee, Virginia, Georgia, and North Carolina. Within three years, they won control in Texas, Alabama, Arkansas, and Mississippi. As the 1876 elections approached, Republican rule survived in only three states—South Carolina, Florida, and Louisiana. Democratic victories in the state elections of 1876 and political bargaining in Washington in 1877 abruptly ended what little remained of Reconstruction.

"Redeeming" the South   Republican collapse in the South accelerated after 1872. Congressional amnesty enabled ex-Confederate officials to regain office; divisions among the Republicans weakened their party's grip on the southern electorate; and attrition diminished Republican ranks. Some carpetbaggers gave up and returned North; others became Democrats. Scalawags deserted in even larger numbers. Southerners who had joined the Republicans to moderate rampant radicalism tired of northern interference; once "home rule" by Democrats seemed possible, staying Republican meant going down with a sinking ship. Scalawag defections ruined Republican prospects. Unable to win new white votes or retain the old ones, the always-precarious Republican coalition crumbled.

Meanwhile, the Democrats mobilized once-apathetic white voters. The resurrected southern Democratic Party was divided: businessmen who envisioned an industrialized "New South" opposed an agrarian faction called the Bourbons, the old planter elite. But all Democrats shared one goal: to oust Republicans from office. Their tactics varied from state to state. Alabama Democrats won by promising to cut taxes and by getting out the white vote. In Louisiana, the "White League," a vigilante organization formed in 1874, undermined the Republicans' hold. Intimidation also proved effective in Mississippi, where violent incidents—like the 1874 slaughter in Vicksburg of about three hundred blacks by rampaging whites—terrorized black voters. In 1875, the "Mississippi plan" took effect: local Democratic clubs armed their members, who dispersed Republican meetings, patrolled voter-registration places, and marched through black areas. "The Republicans are paralyzed through fear and will not act," the anguished carpetbag governor of Mississippi wrote to his wife. "Why should I fight a hopeless battle?" In 1876, South Carolina's "Rifle Clubs" and "Red Shirts," armed groups that threatened Republicans, continued the scare tactics that had worked so well in Mississippi.

New outbursts of intimidation did not completely squelch black voting, but Democrats deprived Republicans of enough black votes to win state elections. In some counties, they encouraged freedmen to vote Democratic at supervised polls where voters publicly placed a card with a party label in a box. In other instances, employers and landowners impeded black suffrage. Labor contracts included clauses barring attendance at political meetings; planters used the threat of eviction to keep sharecroppers in line. As the Enforcement acts could not be enforced, intimidation and economic pressure succeeded.

"Redemption," the word Democrats used to describe their return to power, introduced sweeping changes. Some states called constitutional conventions to reverse Republican policies. All cut back expenses, wiped out social programs, lowered taxes, and revised their tax systems to relieve landowners of large burdens. State courts limited the rights of tenants and sharecroppers. Most important, the Democrats, or "redeemers," used the law to ensure a stable black labor force. Legislatures restored vagrancy laws, revised crop-lien statutes to make landowners' claims superior to those of merchants, and rewrote criminal law. Local ordinances in heavily black counties often restricted hunting, fishing, gun carrying, and ownership of dogs and thereby curtailed the everyday activities of freedmen who lived off the land. States passed severe laws against trespassing and theft; stealing livestock or wrongly taking part of a crop became grand larceny with a penalty of up to five years at hard labor. By the end of Reconstruction, a large black convict work force had been leased out to private contractors at low rates.

For the freedmen, whose aspirations had been raised by Republican rule, redemption was devastating. The new laws, Tennessee blacks contended at an 1875 convention, would impose "a condition of servitude scarcely less degrading than that endured before the late civil war." In the late 1870s, as the political climate grew more oppressive, an "exodus" movement spread through Mississippi, Tennessee, Texas, and Louisiana. Some African-Americans decided to become homesteaders in Kansas. After a major outbreak of "Kansas fever" in 1879, four thousand **"exodusters"** from Mississippi and

Louisiana joined about ten thousand who had reached Kansas earlier in the decade. But the vast majority of freedmen, devoid of resources, had no migration options or escape route. Mass movement of southern blacks to the North and Midwest would not gain momentum until the twentieth century.

The Election of 1876

By the autumn of 1876, with redemption almost complete, both parties sought to discard the heritage of animosity left by the war and Reconstruction. Republicans nominated Rutherford B. Hayes, three times Ohio's governor, for president. Untainted by the scandals of the Grant years and popular with all factions in his party, Hayes presented himself as a "moderate" on southern policy. He favored "home rule" in the South and a guarantee of civil and political rights for all—two planks that were clearly contradictory. The Democrats nominated Governor Samuel J. Tilden of New York, a millionaire corporate lawyer and political reformer. Known for his assaults on the Tweed Ring that had plundered New York City's treasury, Tilden campaigned against fraud and waste. Both candidates favored sound money, endorsed civil-service reform, and decried corruption, an irony since the 1876 election would be extremely corrupt.

Tilden won the popular vote by a 3 percent margin and seemed destined to capture the 185 electoral votes needed for victory. But the Republicans challenged the pro-Tilden returns from South Carolina, Florida, and Louisiana. If they could deprive the Democrats of these nineteen electoral votes, Hayes would triumph. The Democrats, who needed only one of the disputed electoral votes for victory, challenged (on a technicality) the validity of Oregon's single electoral vote, which the Republicans had won. Twenty electoral votes, therefore, were in contention. But Republicans still controlled the electoral machinery in the three unredeemed southern states, where they threw out enough Democratic ballots to declare Hayes the winner.

The nation now faced an unprecedented dilemma. Each party claimed victory in the contested states, and each accused the other of fraud. In fact, both sets of southern results involved fraud: the Republicans had discarded legitimate Democratic ballots, and the Democrats had illegally prevented freedmen from voting. To resolve the conflict, Congress in January 1877 created a special electoral commission to decide which party would get the contested electoral votes. Made up of senators, representatives, and Supreme Court justices, the commission included seven Democrats, seven Republicans, and one independent, Justice David Davis of Illinois. When Davis resigned to run for the Senate, Congress replaced him with a Republican, and the commission gave Hayes the election by a vote of 8 to 7.

Congress now had to certify the new electoral vote. But since Democrats controlled the House, a new problem loomed. Some Democrats threatened to obstruct debate and delay approval of the electoral vote. Had they done so, the nation would have been without a president on inauguration day, March 4. Room for compromise remained, for many southern Democrats accepted Hayes's election: former scalawags with commercial interests to protect still favored Republican financial policies, and railroad investors hoped that a Republican administration would help them build a southern transcontinental line. Other southerners cared mainly about Democratic state victories and did not mind conceding the presidency as long as the new Republican administration would leave the South alone. Republican leaders, although sure of eventual triumph, were willing to bargain as well, for candidate Hayes desired not merely victory but southern approval.

MAP 16.2 The Disputed Election of 1876

Congress resolved the contested vote of 1876 in favor of Republican Rutherford B. Hayes.

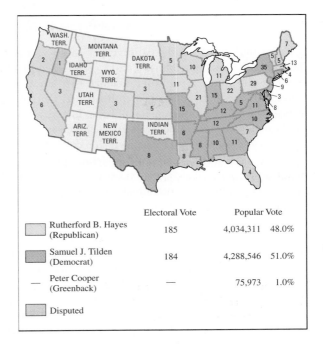

		Electoral Vote	Popular Vote	
	Rutherford B. Hayes (Republican)	185	4,034,311	48.0%
	Samuel J. Tilden (Democrat)	184	4,288,546	51.0%
—	Peter Cooper (Greenback)	—	75,973	1.0%
	Disputed			

A series of informal negotiations ensued, at which politicians exchanged promises. Ohio Republicans and southern Democrats, who met at a Washington hotel, reached an agreement that if Hayes won the election, he would remove federal troops from South Carolina and Louisiana, and Democrats could gain control of those states. In other bargaining sessions, southern politicians asked for federal patronage, federal aid to railroads, and federal support for internal improvements. In return, they promised to drop the filibuster, to accept Hayes as president, and to treat freedmen fairly. With the threatened filibuster broken, Congress ratified Hayes's election. Once in office, Hayes fulfilled some of the promises his Republican colleagues had made. He appointed a former Confederate as postmaster general and ordered federal troops who guarded the South Carolina and Louisiana statehouses back to their barracks. Although federal soldiers remained in the South after 1877, they no longer served a political function. The Democrats, meanwhile, took control of state governments in Louisiana, South Carolina, and Florida. When Republican rule toppled in these states, the era of Reconstruction finally ended, though more with a whimper than with a resounding crash.

But some of the bargains struck in the **Compromise of 1877,** such as Democratic promises to treat southern blacks fairly, were forgotten, as were Hayes's pledges to ensure freedmen's rights. "When you turned us loose, you turned us loose to the sky, to the storm, to the whirlwind, and worst of all . . . to the wrath of our infuriated masters," Frederick Douglass had charged at the Republican convention in 1876. "The question now is, do you mean to make good to us the promises in your Constitution?" The answer provided by the 1876 election and the 1877 compromises was "No."

CONCLUSION

Between 1865 and 1877, the nation experienced a series of crises. In Washington, conflict between President Johnson and Congress led to a stringent Republican plan for restoring the South, a plan that included the radical provision of black male enfranchisement. President Johnson ineptly abetted the triumph of his foes by his defiant stance, which drove moderate Republicans into an alliance against him with Radical Republicans. In the ex-Confederate states, Republicans took over and reorganized state governments. A new electorate, in which recently freed African-Americans were prominent, supported Republican policies. Rebuilding the South cost millions, and state expenditures soared. Objections to taxes, resentment of black suffrage, and fear of "Negro domination" spurred counterattacks on African-Americans by former Confederates.

Emancipation reshaped black communities where former slaves sought new identities as free people. African-Americans reconstituted their families; created black institutions, such as churches and schools; and participated in government for the first time in American history. They also took part in the transformation of southern agriculture. By Reconstruction's end, a new labor system, sharecropping, replaced slavery. Begun as a compromise between freedmen and landowners, sharecropping soon trapped African-Americans and other tenant farmers in a cycle of debt; black political rights waned as well as Republicans lost control of the southern states.

The North, meanwhile, hurtled headlong into an era of industrial growth, labor unrest, and financial crises. The political scandals of the Grant administration and the impact of depression after the Panic of 1873 diverted northern attention from the South. By the mid-1870s, northern politicians were ready to discard the Reconstruction policies that Congress had imposed a decade before. Simultaneously, the southern states returned to Democratic rule, as Republican regimes toppled one by one. Reconstruction's final collapse in 1877 reflected not only a waning of northern resolve but a successful ex-Confederate campaign of violence, intimidation, and protest that had started in the 1860s.

The end of Reconstruction gratified both political parties. Although unable to retain a southern constituency, the Republican Party was no longer burdened by the unpopular "southern question." The Democrats, who had regained power in the former Confederacy, would remain entrenched there for over a century. To be sure, the South was tied to sharecropping and economic backwardness as securely as it had once been tied to slavery. But "home rule" was firmly in place. Reconstruction's end also signified a triumph for nationalism and the spirit of reunion. In the fall of 1877, President Hayes toured the South to champion reconciliation, and similar celebrations continued for decades.

As the nation applauded reunion, Reconstruction's reputation sank. Looking back on the 1860s and 1870s, most late-nineteenth-century Americans dismissed the congressional effort to reconstruct the South as a fiasco—a tragic interlude of "radical rule" or "black reconstruction" fashioned by carpetbaggers, scalawags, and Radical Republicans. With the hindsight of a century, historians continued to regard Reconstruction as a failure, though of a different kind.

No longer viewed as a misguided scheme that collapsed because of radical excess, Reconstruction is now widely seen as a democratic experiment that did not go far enough. Historians cite two main causes. First, Congress did not promote freedmen's independence through land reform; without property of their own, southern blacks lacked the economic power to defend their interests as free citizens. Property ownership, however, does not necessarily ensure political rights, nor does it invariably provide economic security. Considering the depressed state of southern agriculture in the postwar decades, the freedmen's fate as independent farmers would likely have been perilous. Thus the land-reform question, like much else about Reconstruction, remains a subject of debate. A second cause of Reconstruction's collapse is less open to dispute: the federal government neglected to back congressional Reconstruction with military force. Given the choice between protecting blacks' rights at whatever cost and promoting reunion, the government opted for reunion. Reconstruction's failure, therefore, was the federal government's failure to fulfill its own goals and create a biracial democracy in the South. As a result, the nation's adjustment to the consequences of emancipation would continue into the twentieth century.

The Reconstruction era left some significant legacies, including the Fourteenth and Fifteenth amendments. Although neither amendment would be used to protect minority rights for almost a century, they remain monuments to the democratic zeal that swept Congress in the 1860s. The Reconstruction years also hold a significant place in African-American history. The aspirations and achievements of the Reconstruction era left an indelible mark on black citizens. Consigning Reconstruction to history, other Americans turned to their economic futures—to railroads, factories, and mills, and to the exploitation of the country's bountiful natural resources.

17

The Transformation of the Trans–Mississippi West, 1860–1900

CHAPTER OUTLINE

Native Americans and the Trans-Mississippi West • Settling the West • Southwestern Borderlands • Exploiting the Western Landscape • The West of Life and Legend

---

NATIVE AMERICANS AND THE TRANS-MISSISSIPPI WEST

No aspect of the transformation of the West was more visible and dramatic than the destruction of the traditional Indian ways of life. Even before settlers, ranchers, and miners poured onto the Great Plains at midcentury, Indian life in the trans-Mississippi West had changed considerably. In the Southwest, the Spanish had forcibly incorporated pueblo peoples such as the Hopis and Zuñis into their colonial economy. Other tribes, such as the Navajos, had gradually given up migratory life in favor of settled agriculture. To the north, the Cheyenne and the Lakota Sioux, already pushed out of the Great Lakes region by the expansion of the fur trade and later white settlement, had moved onto the grasslands of the Great Plains and had driven their enemies, the Pawnees and the Crows, farther west. These and other nomadic warrior tribes, dispersed in small bands and moving from place to place to follow the bison herds, had developed a resilient culture adapted to the High Plains.

When increasing numbers of whites invaded their territory at midcentury, these Indians protested and resisted. Caught between a stampede of miners and settlers who took their land and the federal government that sought to force them onto reservations, Native Americans fought back. By the 1890s confinement on inferior reservations had become the fate of almost every Indian nation. Undaunted, Native Americans struggled to preserve their customs and rebuild their numbers.

CHRONOLOGY, 1860–1900

1862 • Homestead Act.
     Morrill Anti-Bigamy Act.
     Pacific Railroad Act.

1864 • Nevada admitted to the Union.
     Massacre of Cheyennes at Sand Creek, Colorado.
     George Perkins Marsh, *Man and Nature.*

1867 • Joseph McCoy organizes cattle drives to Abilene, Kansas.
     New Indian policy of smaller reservations adopted.
     Medicine Lodge Treaty.
     Purchase of Alaska.

1868 • Fort Laramie Treaty.

1869 • Board of Indian Commissioners established to reform Indian
     reservation life.
     Wyoming gives women the vote.

1872 • Yellowstone National Park established.

1873 • Panic allows speculators to purchase thousands of acres in the Red River
     valley of North Dakota cheaply.
     Timber Culture Act.
     Biggest strike on Nevada's Comstock Lode.

1874 • Invention of barbed wire.
     Gold discovered in the Black Hills of South Dakota.
     Red River War.

1875 • John Wesley Powell, *The Exploration of the Colorado River.*

1876 • Colorado admitted to the Union, gives women the right to vote in
     school elections.
     Little Bighorn massacre.

1877 • Desert Land Act.

1878 • Timber and Stone Act.
     John Wesley Powell, *Report on the Lands of the Arid Regions of the
     United States.*

1879 • *United States* v. *Reynolds.*

1881 • Helen Hunt Jackson, *A Century of Dishonor.*

1883 • William ("Buffalo Bill") Cody organizes Wild West Show.
     Women's National Indian Rights Association founded.

1884 • Helen Hunt Jackson, *Ramona.*

1886 • Severe drought on the Plains destroys cattle and grain.

1887 • Dawes Severalty Act.
     Edmunds-Tucker Act.

1888 • White Caps raid ranches in northern New Mexico.

1889 • Oklahoma Territory opened for settlement.

1890 • Ghost Dance movement spreads to the Black Hills.
     Massacre of Teton Sioux at Wounded Knee, South Dakota.

1892 • John Muir organizes Sierra Club.

1898 • Curtis Act.

The Plains Indians   The Indians of the Great Plains inhabited three major subregions. The northern Plains, from the Dakotas and Montana southward to Nebraska, were home to several large tribes, most notably the Lakota, as well as Flatheads, Blackfeet, Assiniboins, northern Cheyennes, Arapahos, Crows, Hidatsas, and Mandans. Some of these were allies, but others were bitter enemies frequently at war. In the Central Plains, the so-called Five Civilized Tribes, driven there from the Southeast in the 1830s, pursued an agricultural life in the Indian Territory (present-day Oklahoma). Farther west, the Pawnees of Nebraska maintained the older, more settled tradition characteristic of Plains river valley culture before the introduction of horses, spending at least half the year in villages of earthen lodges along watercourses. On the southern Plains of western Kansas, Colorado, eastern New Mexico, and Texas, the Comanches, Kiowas, Cheyennes, southern Arapahos, and Apaches still maintained a migratory life appropriate to the arid environment.

Considerable diversity flourished among the Plains peoples, and customs varied even within subdivisions of the same tribe. For example, the easternmost branch of the great Sioux Nation, the Dakota Sioux of Minnesota who inhabited the wooded edge of the prairie, led a semisedentary life based on small-scale agriculture, deer and bison hunting, wild-rice harvesting, and maple-sugar production. In contrast, many Plains tribes—not only the Lakota Sioux, but also the Blackfeet, Crows, and Cheyennes—using horses obtained from the Spanish and guns obtained from traders, roamed the High Plains to the west, and followed the bison migrations.

For all the **Plains Indians,** life revolved around extended family ties and tribal cooperation. Within the various Sioux-speaking tribes, for example, children were raised without physical punishment and were taught to treat each adult clan member with the respect accorded to relatives. Families and clans joined forces to hunt and farm, and reached decisions by consensus.

For the various Sioux bands, religious and harvest celebrations provided the cement for village and camp life. Sioux religion was complex. The Lakota Sioux thought of life as a series of circles. Living within the daily cycles of the sun and moon, Lakotas were born into a circle of relatives, which broadened to the band, the tribe, the Sioux Nation, and on to animals and plants. The Lakotas also believed in a hierarchy of spirits whose help could be invoked in ceremonies like the Sun Dance. To gain access to spiritual power, or to fulfill vows made on behalf of their relatives' well-being, young men would "sacrifice" themselves by forgoing food and water, dancing until exhausted, and suffering self-torture. For example, some suspended themselves from poles or cut pieces of their flesh and placed them at the foot of the Sun Dance pole. Painter George Catlin, who recorded Great Plains Indian life before the Civil War, described such a ceremony. "Several of them, seeing me making sketches, beckoned me to look at their faces, which I watched through all this horrid operation, without being able to detect anything but the pleasantest smiles as they looked me in the eye, while I could hear the knife rip through the flesh, and feel enough of it myself, to start involuntary and uncontrollable tears over my cheeks."

On the semiarid High Plains, where rainfall averaged less than twenty inches a year, both the bison and the Native peoples adapted to the environment. The huge bison herds, which at their peak contained an estimated 30 million animals, broke into small groups in the winter and dispersed into river valleys. In the summer, they returned to the High Plains in vast herds to mate and feed on the nutritious short grasses. Like the bison, the Indians dispersed across the landscape to minimize their impact on any one place, wintering in the river valleys and returning to the High Plains in summer. When their herds of horses consumed the grasses near their camps, they moved. Hunting the bison not only supplied the Native peoples with food, clothing, and tipi covers, but also created a valuable trading commodity, buffalo robes. To benefit from this trade, Indians themselves, as the nineteenth century progressed, increased their harvest of animals.

The movement of miners and settlers onto the eastern High Plains in the 1850s eroded the bison's habitat and threatened the Native American way of life. Pioneers who trekked westward occupied the river valley sites, where the buffalo had wintered, and exhausted the grasses. In the 1860s, the whites began systematically to hunt the animals, often with Indian help, to supply the eastern market with carriage robes and industrial belting. **William F. "Buffalo Bill" Cody,** a famous scout and Indian fighter, killed nearly forty-three hundred bison in 1867–1868 to feed construction crews building the Union Pacific Railroad. Army commanders also encouraged the slaughter of buffalo to undermine Indian resistance. The carnage that resulted was almost inconceivable in its scale. Between 1872 and 1875, hunters killed 9 million buffalo, taking only the skin and leaving the carcasses to rot. By the 1880s, the once-thundering herds had been reduced to a few thousand animals, and the Native American way of life dependent on the buffalo had been ruined.

The Assault on Nomadic Indian Life

In the 1850s, Indians who felt pressure from the declining bison herds and deteriorating grasslands faced the onslaught of thousands of pioneers lured by the discovery of gold and silver in the Rocky Mountains. The federal government's response was to reexamine its Indian policies. Abandoning the previous position, which had treated much of the West as a vast Indian reserve, the federal government sought to introduce a system of smaller tribal reservations where the Indians were to be concentrated, by force if necessary. To achieve this goal, the army established outposts along well-traveled trails and stationed troops that could be mobilized at a moment's notice.

Some Native Americans, like the Pueblos of the Southwest (who had adapted to Spanish colonial life), the Crows of Montana, and the Hidatsas of North Dakota, peacefully adjusted to their new life. Others, among them the Navajos of Arizona and New Mexico and the eastern Dakota Sioux, opposed the new policy to no avail. By 1860, eight western reservations had been established.

Significant segments of the remaining tribes on the Great Plains, more than a hundred thousand people, fought against removal for decades. Between 1860 and 1890, the western Sioux, Cheyennes, Arapahos, Kiowas, and Comanches on the Great Plains; the Nez Percés and Bannocks in the northern Rockies; and the Apaches in the Southwest—faced the U.S. army, toughened by its experiences in the Civil War, in a series of final battles for the West.

Misunderstandings, unfulfilled promises, brutality, and butchery marked the conflict. Nowhere was this more evident than in the eroding relationship between the Cheyennes and Arapahos and the settlers near Sand Creek, Colorado, in 1864. During the gold rush six years earlier, more than a hundred thousand people (more than twice the number who went to California in 1849) had stampeded into the area. The Indians, facing starvation because of unfulfilled treaties that had promised food and support, slipped away from the reservations to hunt bison and steal livestock from settlers.

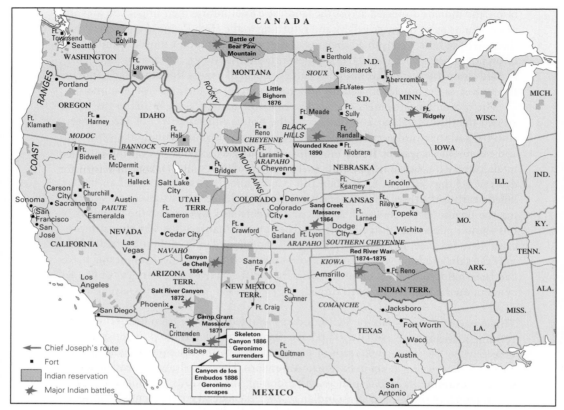

MAP 17.1 **Indian Wars and Reservations in the West**

Although they were never recognized as such in the popular press, the battles between Native Americans and the U.S. army on the Great Plains amounted to a major undeclared war.

In the spring of the year, soldiers from the local militia who had replaced regular army troops fighting in the Civil War, destroyed Cheyenne and Arapaho camps. The Indians retaliated with a flurry of attacks on travelers. The governor, in a panic, authorized Colorado's white citizenry to seek out and kill hostile Indians on sight. He then activated a regiment of troops under Colonel John M. Chivington, a Methodist minister. At dawn on November 29, under orders to "remember the murdered women and children on the Platte [River]," Chivington's troops massacred a peaceful band of Indians, including terrified women and children, camped at Sand Creek, who believed that they would be protected by federal troops.

This massacre and others that followed rekindled public debate over federal Indian policy. In response, in 1867 Congress sent a peace commission to end the fighting, and set aside two large land reserves, one north of Nebraska, the other south of Kansas. There, it was hoped, the tribes would take up farming and convert to Christianity. Behind the federal government's persuasion lay the threat of force. Any Native Americans who refused to "locate in [the] permanent abodes provided for them," warned Commissioner of Indian Affairs Ely S. Parker, himself a Seneca Indian, "would be subject wholly to the control and supervision of military authorities, [and] . . . treated as friendly or hostile as circumstances might justify."

At first the plan appeared to work. Representatives of sixty-eight thousand southern Kiowas, Comanches, Cheyennes, and Arapahos signed the Medicine Lodge Treaty of 1867 and pledged to live on land in present-day Oklahoma. The following year, scattered bands of Sioux, representing nearly fifty-four thousand northern Plains Indians, signed the **Fort Laramie Treaty** and agreed to move to reservations on the so-called Great Sioux Reserve in the western part of what is now South Dakota in return for money and provisions.

But Indian dissatisfaction with the treaties ran deep. As a Sioux chief, Spotted Tail, told the commissioners, "We do not want to live like the white man. . . . The Great Spirit gave us hunting grounds, gave us the buffalo, the elk, the deer, and the antelope. Our fathers have taught us to hunt and live on the Plains, and we are contented." Rejecting the new system, many bands of Indians refused to move to the reservations or to remain on them once there.

In August 1868, war parties of defiant Cheyennes, Arapahos, and Sioux raided settlements in Kansas and Colorado, burning homes and killing whites. In retaliation, army troops attacked Indians, even peaceful ones, who refused confinement. That autumn Lieutenant Colonel George Armstrong Custer's raiding party struck a sleeping Cheyenne village, killing more than a hundred warriors, shooting more than eight hundred horses, and taking fifty-three women and children prisoner. Other hostile Cheyennes and Arapahos were pursued, captured, and returned to the reservations.

In 1869, spurred on by Christian reformers, Congress established a Board of Indian Commissioners drawn from the major Protestant denominations to reform Indian agent abuses on the reservations. But the new and inexperienced church-appointed Indian agents, who distributed government rations and ran the reservations, quickly encountered problems. The pacifist Quaker agent Lawrie Tatum, a big-boned Iowa farmer, for example, failed to persuade the Comanches and Kiowas to stay on their reservations in Oklahoma rather than raid Texas settlements. Other agents were unable to restrain scheming whites who fraudulently purchased reservation lands from the Indians. Frustrated by the manipulation of Indian treaties and irritated by the ineptness of the Indian agents, Congress in 1871 abolished treaty making and replaced treaties with executive orders and acts of Congress. In the 1880s, the federal government ignored the churches' nominations for Indian agents and made its own appointments.

Caught in the sticky web of an ambiguous and deceptive federal policy, and enraged by continuing non-Indian settlement of the Plains, defiant Native Americans struck back in the 1870s. On the southern Plains, Kiowa, Comanche, and Cheyenne raids in the Texas Panhandle in 1874 set off the so-called Red River War. In a fierce winter campaign, regular army troops destroyed Indian supplies and slaughtered a hundred Cheyenne fugitives near the Sappa River in Kansas. With the exile of seventy-four "ringleaders" to reservations in Florida, Native American independence on the southern Plains came to an end. In the Southwest, in present-day Arizona and New Mexico, the Apaches fought an intermittent guerrilla war until their leader, Geronimo, surrendered in 1886.

Custer's Last
Stand, 1876

Of all the acts of Indian resistance against the new reservation policy, none aroused more passion or caused more bloodshed than the battles waged by the western Sioux tribes in the Dakotas, Montana, and Wyoming. The 1868 Treaty of Fort Laramie had set aside the Great Sioux Reserve "in perpetuity." But not all the Sioux bands had fought in the war or signed the treaty.

In 1873, skillfully playing local officials against the federal government, Chief Red Cloud's Oglala band and Chief Spotted Tail's Brulé band won the concession of staying on their traditional lands. To protect their hunting grounds, they raided encroaching non-Indian settlements in Nebraska and Wyoming, intimidated federal agents, and harassed miners, railroad surveyors, and any others who ventured onto their lands.

Non-treaty Sioux found a powerful leader in the Lakota Sioux chief and holy man **Sitting Bull.** Broad-shouldered and powerfully built, Sitting Bull led by example and had considerable fighting experience. "You are fools," he told the reservation Indians, "to make yourselves slaves to a piece of fat bacon, some hard-tack, and a little sugar and coffee."

Pressured by would-be settlers and developers and distressed by the Indian agents' inability to prevent the Sioux from entering and leaving the reservations at will, the federal government took action. In 1874, General William Tecumseh Sherman sent a force under Colonel George Armstrong Custer into the Black Hills of South Dakota, near the western edge of the Great Sioux Reserve. Lean and mustachioed, with shoulder-length reddish-blond hair, the thirty-four-year-old Custer had been a celebrity since his days as an impetuous young Civil War officer.

Custer's mission was to extract concessions from the Sioux. In November 1875, negotiations to buy the Black Hills had broken down because the Indians' asking price was deemed too high. Custer now sought to drive the Indians out of the Black Hills. Indians still outside the reservations after January 31, 1876, the government announced, would be hunted down and taken in by force.

The army mobilized for an assault. In June 1876, leading 600 troops of the Seventh Cavalry, Custer proceeded to the Little Bighorn River area of present-day Montana, a hub of Indian resistance. On the morning of June 25, underestimating the Indian enemy and unwisely dividing his force, Custer, with 209 men, recklessly advanced against a large company of Cheyenne and Sioux warriors led by Chief Sitting Bull, who had encamped along the Little Bighorn. Custer and his outnumbered troops were wiped out.

Americans reeled from this unexpected Indian victory. Newspaper columnists groped to assess the meaning of "Custer's last stand." Some went beyond criticism of Custer's leadership to question the wisdom of current federal policy toward the Indians. Others worried that an outraged public would demand retaliation. Most, however, endorsed the federal government's determination to quash the Native American rebellion. "It is inconsistent with our civilization and with common sense," trumpeted a writer in the *New York Herald*, "to allow the Indian to roam over a country as fine as that around the Black Hills, preventing its development in order that he may shoot game and scalp his neighbors. That can never be. This region must be taken from the Indian."

Defeat at Little Bighorn made the army more determined. In Montana, troops harassed various Sioux bands for more than five years, attacking Indian camps in the

Indian Chiefs   *Early photographs of the Indian leaders Chief Joseph (left) and Sitting Bull (right) captured both their pride and the frustration they felt after years of alternately negotiating and battling with the U.S. army. "I don't want a white man over me," Sitting Bull insisted. "I want to have the white man with me, but not to be my chief. I ask this because I want to do right by my people. . . ."*

dead of winter and destroying all supplies. Even Sitting Bull, who had led his band to Canada to escape the army, surrendered in 1881 for lack of provisions. The slaughter of the buffalo had wiped out his tribe's major food source.

Similar measures were used elsewhere in the West against Chief Joseph and his Nez Percés of Oregon and against the northern Cheyennes, who had been forcibly transported to Oklahoma after the Battle of Little Bighorn. Chief Dull Knife led some 150 survivors, including men, women, and children, north in September 1878 to join the Sioux. But the army chased them down and imprisoned them in Fort Robinson, Nebraska. When the army denied their request to stay nearer to their traditional northern lands, tribal leaders refused to cooperate. The post commander then withheld all food, water, and fuel. On a frigid night in January 1879, a desperate Dull Knife and his followers, in a dramatic escape attempt, shot the guards and broke for freedom. Members of the startled garrison chased the Indians and gunned down half of them in the snow, including women and children as well as Dull Knife himself. The *Atlanta Constitution* condemned the incident as "a dastardly outrage upon humanity and a lasting disgrace to our boasted civilization." Although sporadic Indian resistance continued until the end of the century, these brutal tactics had sapped the Indians' will to resist.

"Saving" the Indians

A growing number of Americans were outraged by the federal government's flagrant violation of its Indian treaties. The Women's National Indian Rights Association, founded in 1883, and other groups took up the cause. **Helen Hunt Jackson,** a Massachusetts writer who had recently moved to Colorado, published *A Century of Dishonor* in 1881 to rally public opinion against the government's record of broken treaty obligations. "It makes little difference . . . where one opens the record of the history of the Indians," she wrote; "every page and every year has its dark stain."

To help Indians abandon hunting and nomadic life, reformers like Jackson advocated the creation of Indian boarding schools, much like those established for emancipated slaves. Richard Henry Pratt, a retired military officer, opened such a school in Carlisle, Pennsylvania, in 1879. Pratt believed that the Indians' customs and languages had halted their progress toward white civilization. His motto therefore became "Kill the Indian and save the man." Modeled after Carlisle, other Indian boarding schools taught farming, carpentry, dress-making, and nursing.

Despite the reformers' best efforts, the attempt to stamp out Indian identity in the boarding schools often backfired. Forming friendships with Indians from many different tribes, boarding school students forged their own sense of Indian identity. As Mitch Walking Elk, a Cheyenne-Arapaho-Hopi student at the Phoenix Indian School, put it, "They put me in the boarding school and they cut off all my hair, gave me an education, but the Apache's still in there."

In addition to their advocacy of boarding schools, well-intentioned humanitarians concluded that the Indians' interests would be best served by breaking up the reservations, ending all recognition of tribal governments, and gradually incorporating individual Native Americans into mainstream society by giving them the rights of citizens. In short, they proposed to eliminate the "Indian problem" by eliminating the Indians as a culturally distinct entity. Inspired by this vision, they supported the **Dawes Severalty Act,** passed in 1887.

The Dawes Act was designed to turn Indians into landowners and farmers. The law emphasized severalty, or the treatment of Indians as individuals rather than as members of tribes, and called for the distribution of 160 acres of reservation land for farming, or 320 acres for grazing, to each head of an Indian family who accepted the law's provisions. The remaining reservation lands (often the richest) were to be sold to speculators and settlers, and the income thus obtained would go toward purchase of farm tools. To prevent unscrupulous people from gaining control of the lands granted to individual Indians, the government would hold the property of each tribal member in trust for twenty-five years. Those Indians who at that point had accepted allotments would also be declared citizens of the United States.

The Dawes Act did not specify a timetable for the breakup of the reservations. Few allotments were made to the Indians until the 1890s. The act proved to be a boon to speculators, who commonly evaded its safeguards and obtained the Indians' best land. By 1934, the act had slashed Indian acreage by 65 percent. Much of what remained in Indian hands was too dry and gravelly for farming. In the twentieth century, ironically, periodic droughts and the fragile, arid High Plains landscape would push many white farmers back off the land.

Although some Native Americans who received land under the Dawes Act prospered enough to expand their holdings and go into large-scale farming or ranching, countless others struggled just to survive. Hunting restrictions on the former reservation lands prevented many Indians from supplementing their limited farm yields. Alcoholism, a continuing problem exacerbated by the prevalence of whiskey as a trade item (and by the boredom that resulted from the disruption of hunting and other traditional pursuits), became more prevalent as Native Americans strove to adapt to the constraints of reservation life.

The Ghost Dance and the End of Indian Resistance on the Great Plains, 1890   Living conditions for the Sioux worsened in the late 1880s. The federal government reduced their meat rations and restricted hunting. When disease killed a third of their cattle, they became desperate. The Sioux, who still numbered almost twenty-five thousand, turned to Wovoka, a new visionary prophet popular among the Great Basin Indians in Nevada. Wovoka foresaw a catastrophic event that would bring the return of dead relatives, the restoration of the bison herds, and the renewal of traditional life. Some versions of his vision included the destruction of European-Americans and their removal from Indian lands. To bring on this new day, the prophet preached a return to traditional ethics, and taught his followers a cycle of ritual songs and dance steps known as the **Ghost Dance.** Wearing sacred Ghost Shirts—cotton or leather vestments decorated to ward off evil—the dancers moved in a circle, accelerating until they reached a trance-like state and experienced visions of the future. Many believed that the Ghost Shirts would protect them from harm.

In the fall of 1890, as the Ghost Dance movement spread among the Sioux in the Dakota Territory, Indian officials and military authorities grew alarmed. The local reservation agent decided that Chief Sitting Bull, whose cabin on the reservation had become a rallying point for the Ghost Dance movement, must be arrested. On a freezing, drizzly December morning, he dispatched a company of Indian policemen from the agency to take Sitting Bull into custody. When two policemen pulled the chief from his cabin, a scuffle ensued, shots rang out, and Sitting Bull was mortally wounded. As bullets whizzed by, Sitting Bull's horse began to perform the tricks it remembered from its days in the Wild West show. Some observers were terrified, convinced that the spirit of the dead chief had entered his horse.

Two weeks later, one of the bloodiest episodes of Indian-white strife on the Plains occurred. On December 29, the Seventh Cavalry was rounding up 340 starving and freezing Sioux at **Wounded Knee,** South Dakota, when someone fired a gun. The soldiers retaliated with cannon fire. Within minutes 300 Indians, including 7 infants, were slaughtered. Three days later, a baby who had miraculously survived was found wrapped in a blanket under the snow. She wore a buckskin cap on which a beadwork American flag had been embroidered. Brigadier General L. W. Colby, who adopted the baby, named her Marguerite, but the Indians called her Lost Bird.

As the frozen corpses at Wounded Knee were dumped into mass graves, a generation of Indian-white conflict on the Great Plains shuddered to a close. Lost Bird, with her poignantly patriotic beadwork cap, highlights the irony of the Plains Indians' response to white expansion. Many Natives did try to adapt to non-Indian ways, and some succeeded fully. Goodbird became a Congregational minister, a prosperous farmer, and a leader of the Hidatsa tribe. He carefully blended his traditional Indian religious beliefs with Christianity. Others did less well economically. Driven onto reservations, many Plains Indians became dependent on governmental support. By 1900, the Plains Indian population had shrunk from nearly a quarter-million to just over a hundred thousand. Nevertheless, the population began to increase slowly after 1900. Against overwhelming odds, the pride, religious traditions, and cultural identities of the Plains Indians survived all efforts at eradication.

Unlike the nomadic western Sioux, the more settled Navajos of the Southwest adjusted more successfully to the reservation system, preserving traditional ways while incorporating elements of the new order in a complex process of cultural adaptation. By 1900, the Navajos had tripled their reservation land, dramatically increased their numbers and their herds, and carved out for themselves a distinct place in Arizona and New Mexico.

These extraordinary changes were forced on the Indian population by the advance of non-Indian settlement. In the name of civilization and progress, non-Indians in the generation after the Civil War pursued a course that involved a mixture of sincere (if misguided) benevolence, coercion wrapped in an aura of legality, and outbursts of naked violence. Many white Americans felt toward the Indians only contempt, hatred, and greed for their land. Others viewed themselves as divinely chosen instruments for uplifting and Christianizing Native peoples. Both groups, however, were blind to the value of Native American life and traditions. And both were unsuccessful in their attempts to shatter proud peoples and their ancient cultures.

SETTLING THE WEST

The successive defeats of the Native Americans opened for settlement a vast territory that reached from the Great Plains to the Sierra Nevada and Cascade Mountains. In the 1840s, when nearly a quarter-million Americans had trudged overland to Oregon and California, they had typically endured a six- to eight-month trip in ox-drawn wagons. After 1870, railroad expansion made the trip faster and considerably easier. In the next three decades, more land was parceled out into farms than in the previous 250 years of American history combined, and agricultural production doubled.

The First Transcontinental Railroad Passed in 1862, the Pacific Railroad Act authorized the construction of a new transcontinental link. The act provided grants of land and other subsidies to the railroads for each mile of track laid, which made them the largest landholders in the West. Over the next half-century, nine major routes, which ran from the South or Midwest to the West, were built. More than any other factor, the expansion of these railroads accelerated the transformation of everyday life west of the Mississippi.

Building the railroad took backbreaking work. Searching for inexpensive labor, the railroads turned to immigrants. The Central Pacific employed Chinese workers to chip and blast rail bed out of solid rock in the Sierra Nevada. The railroad preferred the Chinese laborers because they worked hard for low wages, did not drink, and furnished their own food and tents. Nearly twelve thousand Chinese graded the roadbed while Irish, Mexican-American, and black workers put down the track.

On May 10, 1869, Americans celebrated the completion of the first railroad spanning North America. As the two sets of tracks—the Union Pacific's, stretching westward from Omaha, Nebraska, and the Central Pacific's, reaching eastward from Sacramento,

Immigrants Looking for Homesteads, Kansas Garden City Square & Land Company, 1910 *Railroads often joined forces with land companies to settle foreign immigrants on their holdings. Posed in their Sunday clothes against a background of a productive farm, this picture was meant to suggest the endless acres of land available for those willing to move west.*

California—met at Promontory Point, Utah, beaming officials drove in a final ceremonial golden spike. The nation's vast midsection was now far more accessible than it had ever been.

The railroads quickly proved their usefulness. In the battles against Native Americans, the army shipped horses and men west in the dead of winter to attack the Indians when they were most vulnerable. From the same trains, hunters gained quick access to the bison ranges and increased their harvest of the animals. Once Indian resistance had been broken, the railroads not only expedited the shipment of new settlers and their supplies, but also provided fast access for the shipment of cattle and grain to eastern urban markets. In short, the railroads accelerated the development of the West.

Settlers and
the Railroad

During the decade after the passage of the Pacific Railroad Act, Congress awarded the railroads 170 million acres, worth over half a billion dollars. By 1893, Minnesota and Washington had also deeded to railroad companies a quarter of their state lands; Wisconsin, Iowa, Kansas, North Dakota, and Montana had turned over a fifth of their acreage. As mighty landowners, the railroads had a unique opportunity to shape settlement in the region—and to reap enormous profits.

The railroads set up land sales offices and sent agents to the East Coast and Europe to recruit settlers. While the agents glorified the West as a new Garden of Eden, the land bureaus offered prospective buyers long-term loans and free transportation. Acknowledging that life on the Great Plains could be lonely, the promoters advised young men to bring their wives (because "maidens are scarce") and to emigrate as entire families and with friends.

One unintended consequence of these land promotions was to make land available to single women, or "girl homesteaders" as they were known at the time. In Wyoming, single women made up more than 18 percent of the claimants. Women filed 10 to 20 percent of the claims in Colorado, sometimes as individuals and sometimes to add to family holdings.

In addition to the millions of Americans who migrated from nearby states, the railroads helped bring nearly 2.2 million foreign-born settlers to the trans-Mississippi West between 1870 and 1900. Some agents recruited whole villages of Germans and eastern Europeans to relocate to the North Dakota plains. Irish laborers hired to lay track could be found in every town along the rail lines. By 1905, the Santa Fe Railroad alone had transported sixty thousand Russian Mennonites to the fertile Kansas plains where black pioneers called exodusters had preceded them in the 1870s.

The railroads influenced agriculture as well. To ensure quick repayment of the money owed to them, the railroads urged new immigrants to specialize in cash crops—wheat on the northern Plains, corn in Iowa and Kansas, cotton and tobacco in Texas. Although these crops initially brought in high revenues, many farmers grew dependent on income from a single crop and became vulnerable to fluctuating market forces.

Homesteading on the Great Plains   Liberalized land laws were another powerful magnet pulling settlers westward. The Homestead Act passed in 1862 reflected the Republican Party's belief that free land would enable the poor to achieve economic independence. It offered 160 acres of land to any individual who would pay a ten-dollar registration fee, live on the land for five years, and cultivate and improve it. Although nearly four hundred thousand families claimed land under the provisions of the Homestead Act between 1860 and 1900, the law did not function as Congress had envisioned. Advance agents representing unscrupulous speculators filed false claims for the choicest locations, and railroads acquired huge landholdings. The result was that only one acre in every nine went to the pioneers for whom it was intended.

A second problem resulted from the 160-acre limit specified by the Homestead Act. On the rich soils of Iowa or in the fertile lands in California, Oregon, and Washington, a 160-acre farm was ample, but in the drier areas west of the hundredth meridian, a farmer needed more land. In 1873, to rectify this problem, Congress passed the Timber Culture Act, which gave homesteaders an additional 160 acres if they planted trees on 40 acres. For states with little rainfall, Congress enacted the Desert Land Act in 1877, which made 640 acres available at $1.25 an acre on condition that the owner irrigate part of it within three years. However, this act, along with the Timber and Stone Act of 1878, which permitted the purchase of up to 160 acres of forest land for $2.50 an acre, was abused by grasping speculators, lumber-company representatives, and cattle ranchers seeking to expand their holdings. Yet, even though families did not receive as much land as Congress had intended, federal laws kept alive the dream of the West as a place for new beginnings.

In addition to problems faced by those who chose property in areas that lacked sufficient rainfall to grow crops, almost all settlers faced difficult psychological adjustments to frontier life. The first years of settlement were the most difficult. Toiling to build a house, plow the fields, plant the first crop, and dig a well, the pioneers put in an average of sixty-eight hours of tedious, backbreaking work a week in isolated surroundings. Howard Ruede, a Pennsylvania printer who migrated to Kansas to farm, wrote home in 1877 complaining about the mosquitoes and bedbugs infesting his house, which was cut out of thick grass sod and dug into the ground. He and countless others coping with the severe Plains conditions saw their shining vision of idyllic farm life quickly dim. For blacks who emigrated from the South to Kansas and other parts of the Plains after the Civil War, prejudice compounded the burdens of adjusting to a different life (see Chapter 16).

Many women found adaptation to Plains frontier life especially difficult. At least initially, some were enchanted by the landscape. But far more were struck by the "horrible tribes of Mosquitoes"; the violent weather-drenching summer thunderstorms with hailstones as "big as hen's eggs" and blinding winter blizzards; and the crude sod huts that served as their early homes because of the scarcity of timber. One woman burst into tears upon first seeing her new sod house. The young bride angrily informed her husband that her father had built a better house for his hogs.

The high transience rate on the frontier in these years reflected the difficulty that newcomers faced in adjusting to life on the Great Plains. Nearly half of those who staked homestead claims in Kansas between 1862 and 1890 relinquished their rights to the land and moved on. However, in places like Minnesota and the Pacific Northwest that were populated largely by Germans, Norwegians, and other immigrants with a tradition of family prosperity tied to continuous landownership, the persistence rate (or percentage of people staying for a decade or more) could be considerably higher.

Many who weathered the lean early years eventually came to identify deeply with the land. Within a decade, the typical Plains family that had "stuck it out" had moved into a new wood-framed house and had fixed up the front parlor. Women worked particularly hard on these farms and took pride in their accomplishments. "Just done the chores," wrote one woman to a friend. "I went fence mending and getting out cattle . . . and came in after sundown. I fed my White Leghorns [chickens] and then sat on the step to read over your letter. I forgot my wet feet and shoes full of gravel and giggled joyously."

New Farms, New Markets

Farmers on the Plains took advantage of advances in farm mechanization and the development of improved strains of wheat and corn to boost production dramatically. Efficient steel plows; specially designed wheat planters; and improved grain binders, threshers, and windmills all allowed the typical Great Plains farmer of the late nineteenth century to increase the land's yield tenfold.

Barbed wire, patented in 1874, was another crucial invention that permitted farmers to keep roving livestock out of their crops. But fencing the land touched off violent clashes between farmers and cattle ranchers, who demanded the right to let their herds roam freely until the roundup. Generally the farmers won.

The invention of labor-saving machinery together with increased demand for wheat, milk, and other farm products created the impression that farming was entering a period of unparalleled prosperity. But few fully understood the perils of pursuing agriculture as a livelihood. The cost of the land, horses, machinery, and seed needed to start up a farm could exceed twelve hundred dollars, far more than the annual earnings of the average industrial worker. Faced with substantial mortgage payments, many farmers had to specialize in a crop such as wheat or corn that would fetch high prices. This specialization made them dependent on the railroads for shipping and put them at the mercy of the international grain market's shifting prices.

Far from being an independent producer, the western grain grower was a player in a complex world market economy. Railroad and steamship transport enabled the American farmer to compete in the international market. High demand could bring prosperity, but when world overproduction forced grain prices down, the heavily in-debted grower faced ruin. Confronted with these realities, many Plains farmers quickly abandoned the illusion of frontier independence and easy wealth.

Unpredictable rainfall and weather conditions further exacerbated homesteaders' difficulties west of the hundredth meridian, where rainfall averaged less than twenty inches a year. Farmers compensated through "dry farming"—plowing deeply to stim-ulate the capillary action of the soils and harrowing lightly to raise a covering of dirt that would retain precious moisture after a rainfall. They also built windmills and di-verted creeks for irrigation. But the onset of unusually dry years in the 1870s, together with grasshopper infestations and the major economic depression that struck the United States between 1873 and 1878 (see Chapter 16), made the plight of some mid-westerners desperate.

Building a Society and Achieving Statehood   Despite the hardships, many remote farm settlements blos-somed into thriving communities. Among the first institutions to appear, churches and Sunday schools became humming centers of social activity as well as of worship. Farmers gath-ered for barn raisings and group threshings, and families pooled their energies in quilt-ing and husking bees. Neighbors readily lent a hand to the farmer whose barn had burned or whose family was sick. Cooperation was a practical necessity and a form of insurance in a rugged environment where everyone was vulnerable to instant misfor-tune or even disaster.

When the population increased, local boosters lobbied to turn the territory into a state. Achieving statehood required the residents of the territory to petition Congress to pass an enabling act establishing the territory's boundaries and authorizing an elec-tion to select delegates for a state constitutional convention. Once the state constitution had been drawn up and ratified by popular vote, the territory applied to Congress for admission as a state.

Under these procedures, Kansas entered the Union in 1861, followed by Nevada in 1864 and Nebraska in 1867. Colorado joined in 1876. Not until 1889 did North Dakota, South Dakota, Montana, and Washington gain statehood. Wyoming and Idaho came into the Union the following year. Utah finally entered in 1896. With Oklahoma's admission in 1907 and Arizona's and New Mexico's in 1912, the process of creating permanent political institutions in the trans-Mississippi West was complete.

Although generally socially conservative, the new state governments supported woman suffrage. As territories became states, pioneer women battled for the vote. Seven western states held referenda on this issue between 1870 and 1910. Success came first in the Wyoming Territory, where men outnumbered women 6 to 1. The tiny legis-lature enfranchised women in 1869 in the hope that it would attract women, families, and economic growth. The Utah Territory followed in 1870 and reaffirmed its support

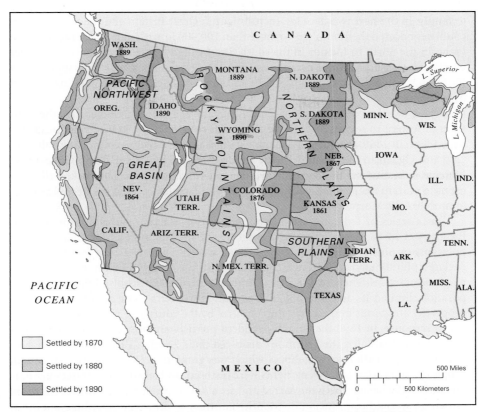

MAP 17.2 The Settlement of the Trans-Mississippi West, 1860–1890
The West was not settled by a movement of peoples gradually creeping westward from the East. Rather, settlers first occupied California and the Midwest and then filled up the nation's vast interior.

for woman suffrage when it became a state. Nebraska in 1867 and Colorado in 1876 permitted women to vote in school elections. Although these successes were significant, by 1910 only four states—Idaho, Wyoming, Utah, and Colorado—had granted women full voting rights. The very newness of their place in the Union may have sensitized legislators in these states to women's important contributions to settlements, and the intense competition among parties may have made them open to experimentation, but by and large, familiar practices persisted.

The Spread of Mormonism   Persecuted in Illinois, members of the Church of Jesus Christ of Latter-day Saints known as Mormons, had moved to the Great Salt Lake Valley in 1847. Led by Brigham Young, their prophet-president, and a Council of Twelve Apostles, they sought to create the independent country of Deseret. Their faith emphasized self-sufficiency and commitment to family. In the next two decades, recruitment in Great Britain and the Scandinavian countries boosted their numbers to more than 100,000 in settlements that ranged from Idaho in the north to Mexico in the south. Increasingly, these Mormon communities conflicted with non-Mormons and with the U.S. government, which disapproved of the church's involvement in politics, its communal business practices, and its support of polygamy.

Trying to balance their territorial claims for the Kingdom of God against the pressures of American secular society, the Mormons sought at first to be economically independent. In 1869, they developed their own railroad branches connecting Salt Lake City and Ogden to the Central Pacific Railroad, and they set up Zion's Cooperative Mercantile Institution to control wholesale and retail activities. They asked all Mormons to abstain from coffee, tea, and alcohol, and established their own People's Party to mobilize the Mormon vote.

But a series of federal acts and court decisions, starting with the Morrill Anti-Bigamy Act in 1862, challenged the authority of their church and their practice of polygamy or plural marriage. In *United States* v. *Reynolds* (1879), the Supreme Court declared plural marriages unlawful and held that freedom of religion did not protect religious practices. Then, in 1887, the **Edmunds-Tucker Act** dissolved the church corporation, limited its assets to $50,000, abolished women's right to vote, and put its properties and funds into receivership (control by the courts).

In response, in 1890 the church president publicly announced the official end of polygamy. A year later, the Mormons dissolved their People's Party. The church supported the application for statehood, which was granted in 1896. Confiscated church properties were returned, voting rights were restored, and jailed polygamists were pardoned, but the balance between sacred and secular had permanently shifted. Mormon settlements would continue in the twentieth century to draw new members and influence economic and social development in western communities.

SOUTHWESTERN BORDERLANDS

The annexation of Texas in 1845 and the Treaty of Guadalupe Hidalgo that had ended the Mexican-American War in 1848 ceded to the United States an immense territory, part of which became Texas, California, Arizona, and New Mexico. At the time, Mexicans had controlled vast expanses of the Southwest. They had built their own churches, maintained large ranching operations, and had traded with the Indians. Although the United States had pledged to protect the liberty and property of Mexicans who remained on American soil, over the next three decades American ranchers and settlers took control of the territorial governments. Like the displacement of the American Indians, much of the Spanish-speaking population was forced off the land. Mexicans who stayed in the region adapted to the new Anglo society with varying degrees of success.

In Texas, the struggle for independence from Mexico had left a legacy of bitterness and misunderstanding. After 1848, Texas cotton planters confiscated Mexican lands and began a racist campaign that labeled Mexicans as nonwhite. Only white people, the Texans asserted, deserved economic and legal rights. Angered by their loss of land and discriminatory treatment, Mexican bandits retaliated by raiding American communities. Tensions peaked in 1859 when Juan Cortina, a Mexican rancher, attacked the Anglo border community of Brownsville, Texas, and freed all the prisoners in jail. Cortina battled the U.S. army for years until the Mexican government, fearing a U.S. invasion, imprisoned him in 1875.

Mexican-Americans in California in the 1850s and 1860s faced similar pressures. A cycle of flood and drought, together with a slumping cattle industry, had ruined many of the large southern California ranches owned by the *californios,* Spanish-speaking descendants of the original Spanish settlers. The collapse of the ranch economy forced many of them to retreat into segregated urban neighborhoods called barrios. Spanish-surnamed citizens made up nearly half the 2,640 residents of Santa Barbara, California, in 1870; because of the influx of new settlers they comprised barely a quarter of the population ten years later. Maintaining a tenacious hold on their traditions, many Spanish-speaking people in Santa Barbara and other towns survived by working as day laborers.

In California, the pattern of racial discrimination, manipulation, and exclusion was similar for Mexicans, Native Americans, and Chinese. At first, the number of new "Anglos" was small. As the number of whites increased, they identified minority racial, cultural, and language differences as marks of inferiority. White state legislators passed laws that made ownership of property difficult for non-Anglos. Relegated to a migratory labor force, non-Anglos were tagged as shiftless and irresponsible. Yet their labor made possible increased prosperity for the farmers, railroads, and households that hired them.

The cultural adaptation of Spanish-speaking Americans to Anglo society initially unfolded more smoothly in Arizona and New Mexico, where Spanish settlement had been sparse and a small class of wealthy Mexican landowners had long dominated a poor, illiterate peasantry. Moreover, since the 1820s, well-to-do Mexicans in Tucson, Arizona, had educated their children in the United States and formed trading partnerships and business alliances with Americans. One of the most successful was Estevan Ochoa, who began a long-distance freight business in 1859 with a U.S. partner and then expanded it into a lucrative merchandising, mining, and sheep-raising operation.

The success of men such as Ochoa, who became mayor of Tucson, helped moderate American settlers' antagonistic attitudes. So, too, did the work of popular writers like Helen Hunt Jackson. By sentimentalizing the gracious colonial Spanish past, Jackson increased public sympathy for Spanish-speaking Americans. Jackson's 1884 romance *Ramona,* a tale of the doomed love of a Hispanicized mixed-blood (Irish-Indian) woman set on a California ranch overwhelmed by the onrushing tide of Anglo civilization, was enormously popular. Jackson's novel also appealed to upper-class Mexican-Americans known as *Nuevomexicanos* who traced their lineage back to the Spanish conquest.

Still, conflicts over property persisted in Arizona and New Mexico. In the 1880s, Mexican-American ranchers organized themselves into a self-protection vigilante group called Las Gorras Blancas (the **White Caps**). In 1888, they tore up railroad tracks and attacked both Anglo newcomers and those upper-class Hispanics who had fenced acreage in northern New Mexico previously considered public grazing land. But this vigilante action did not help, as Anglo-dominated corporate ranchers steadily increased their land holdings. Relations also changed in the urban centers, as discrimination forced Mexican-American businessmen to restrict their business dealings to their own people, and the Spanish-speaking population as a whole became more impoverished. Even in Tucson, where the Mexican-American elite enjoyed considerable economic and political success, 80 percent of the Mexican-Americans in the work force were laborers in 1880, taking jobs as butchers, barbers, cowboys, and railroad workers.

As increasing numbers of Mexican-American men were forced to search for seasonal migrant work, women took responsibility for holding families and communities together. Women managed the households when their husbands were away, and fostered group identification by maintaining traditional customs, kinship ties, and allegiance to the Catholic Church. They served as godmothers for one another's children; tended garden plots; and traded food, soap, and produce with other women. This economy, invisible to those outside the village, stabilized the community in times of drought or persecution by Anglos.

Violence and discrimination against Spanish-speaking citizens of the Southwest escalated in the 1890s, a time of rising racism in the United States. Rioters in Beeville and Laredo, Texas, in 1894 and 1899 attacked and beat up Mexican-Americans. Whites increasingly labeled Mexican-Americans as violent and lazy. For Spanish-speaking citizens, the battle for fair treatment and respect would continue into the twentieth century.

EXPLOITING THE WESTERN LANDSCAPE

The displacement of Mexican-American and Native peoples from their lands opened the way for the exploitation of the natural environment in the trans-Mississippi West. White publicists, developers, and boosters had long promoted the region as a land of boundless opportunity. Between 1860 and 1900, a generation of Americans sought to strike it rich by joining the ranks of miners, ranchers, and farmers intent on making a fortune. Although the mining, ranching, and farming "bonanzas" promised unheard-of wealth, they set in motion a boom-and-bust economy in which many people went bankrupt or barely survived and others were bought out by large-scale enterprises. Of all the groups that surged into the nation's midcontinent in the late nineteenth century, none had to revise their expectations more radically than the speculators and adventurers thirsting for quick fortunes.

The Mining Frontier In the half-century that began with the California gold rush in 1849, a series of mining booms swept from the Southwest northward into Canada and Alaska. Sensational discoveries in California's Sierra Nevada produced more than $81 million worth of gold bullion in 1852. The following year, Henry Comstock, an illiterate prospector, stumbled on the rich **Comstock Lode** along Nevada's Carson River. Later in the same decade, feverishly pursuing rumors of new strikes, prospectors swarmed into the Rocky Mountains and uncovered deep veins of gold and silver near present-day Denver. Over the next five decades, gold was discovered in Idaho, Montana, Wyoming, South Dakota, and, in 1896, in the Canadian Klondike. Although the popular press clearly exaggerated reports of miners scooping up gold by the panful, by 1900 more than a billion dollars' worth of gold had been mined in California alone.

The early discoveries of "placer" gold, panned from streams, attracted a young male population thirsting for wealth and reinforced the myth of mining country as "a poor man's paradise." In contrast to the Great Plains, where ethnic groups recreated their own ethnic enclaves, western mining camps became ethnic melting pots. In the Cali-

Juneau, Alaska, c. 1896 *Like other mining towns, Juneau grew rapidly and haphazardly after Kowee, a local Tlingit man, showed Joe Juneau and Richard Harris the location of gold nuggets in 1880. Between 1881 and 1944 Juneau's mines produced 6.7 million ounces of gold.*

fornia census of 1860, more than thirty-three thousand Irish and thirty-four thousand Chinese had staked out early claims.

Although a few prospectors became fabulously wealthy, the experience of Henry Comstock, who sold out one claim for eleven thousand dollars and another for two mules, was more typical. Because the larger gold and silver deposits lay embedded in veins of quartz deep within the earth, extracting them required huge investments in workers and expensive equipment. Deep shafts had to be blasted into the rock. Once lifted to the surface, the rock had to be crushed, flushed with mercury or cyanide to collect the silver, and smelted into ingots. No sooner had the major discoveries been made, therefore, than large mining companies backed by eastern or British capital bought them out and took them over.

Life in the new mining towns was vibrant but unpredictable. During the heyday of the Comstock Lode in the 1860s and 1870s, Virginia City, Nevada, erupted in an orgy of speculation and building. Started as a shantytown in 1859, it swelled by 1873 into a thriving metropolis of twenty thousand people complete with elaborate mansions, a six-story hotel, an opera house, 131 saloons, 4 banks, and uncounted brothels. Men outnumbered women three to one. Money quickly earned was even more rapidly lost.

The boom-and-bust cycle evident in Virginia City was repeated in towns across the West. Mark Twain captured the thrill of the mining "stampedes" in *Roughing It* (1872). "Every few days," wrote Twain, "news would come of the discovery of a brand-new mining region: immediately the papers would teem with accounts of its richness, and away the surplus population would scamper to take possession. By the time I was fairly inoculated with the disease, 'Esmeralda' had just had a run and 'Humboldt' was beginning to shriek for attention. 'Humboldt! Humboldt!' was the new cry, and straightway Humboldt, the newest of the new, the richest of the rich, the most marvelous of the marvelous discoveries in silver-land, was occupying two columns of the public prints to 'Esmeralda's' one."

One unintended consequence of the gold rush mania was the growth of settlement in Alaska. Small strikes were made there in 1869, two years after the United States had purchased the territory from Russia. More miners arrived in the 1880s after prospector Joe Juneau, for whom the town of Juneau was named, and others developed the Treadwell Mine. But it was the discovery of gold in the Canadian Klondike in 1897 that brought thousands of prospectors into the area and eventually enabled Alaska to establish its own territorial government in 1912.

Word of new ore deposits like the ones in Alaska lured transient populations salivating to get rich. Miners who worked deep within the earth for large corporations typically earned about $2,000 a year at a time when teachers made $450 to $650 and domestic help $250 to $350. But most prospectors at best earned only enough to go elsewhere, perhaps buy some land, and try again. Nevertheless, the production of millions of ounces of gold and silver stimulated the economy, lured new foreign investors, and helped usher the United States into the mainstream of the world economy.

Progress came at a price. The long-term cost to the environment to extract these metals was high. Hydraulic mining, which used water cannons to dislodge minerals, polluted rivers, turned creeks brown, and flushed millions of tons of silt into valleys. The scarred landscape that remained was littered with rock and gravel filled with traces of mercury and cyanide, and nothing would grow on it. Smelters spewed dense smoke containing lead, arsenic, and other carcinogenic chemicals on those who lived nearby and often made them sick. The destruction to the environment is still evident today.

Cowboys and the Cattle Frontier

Like the feverish expansion of the mining frontier during the 1860s and 1870s, open-range cattle ranching boomed in these same decades. In this case, astute businessmen and railroad entrepreneurs, eager to fund their new investments in miles of track, promoted cattle herding as the new route to fame and fortune. The cowboy, once scorned as a ne'er-do-well and drifter, was now glorified as a man of rough-hewn integrity and self-reliant strength.

In 1868, Joseph G. McCoy, a young cattle dealer from Springfield, Illinois, shrewdly combined organizational and promotional skills to turn the cattle industry into a new money-maker. With the forced relocation of the Plains Indians onto reservations and the extension of the railroads into Kansas in the post–Civil War period, McCoy realized that cattle dealers could now amass enormous fortunes by raising steers cheaply in Texas and bringing them north for shipment to eastern urban markets.

McCoy built a new stockyard in Abilene, Kansas. By guaranteeing to transport his steers in railcars to hungry eastern markets, he obtained a five-dollar kickback from the railroads on each cattle car shipped. To make the overland cattle drives from Texas to Abilene easier, McCoy also helped survey and shorten the Chisholm Trail in Kansas. Finally, in a clever feat of showmanship, he organized the first Wild West show, sending four Texas cowboys to St. Louis and Chicago, where they staged roping and riding exhibitions that attracted exuberant crowds. At the end of his first year in business, thirty-five thousand steers were sold in Abilene; the following year the number more than doubled.

The great **cattle drives** of the 1860s and 1870s turned into a bonanza for herd owners. Steers purchased in Texas at nine dollars a head could be sold in Abilene, after deducting four dollars in trail expenses, for twenty-eight dollars. A herd of two thousand head could thus bring a tidy thirty-thousand-dollar profit. But the cattlemen, like the grain growers farther north on the Great Plains, lived at the mercy of high interest rates and an unstable market. During the financial panic of 1873, cattle drovers, unable to get extensions on their loans, fell into bankruptcy by the hundreds.

Little of the money made by the large-scale cattle ranchers found its way into the pockets of the cowboys themselves. The typical cowpunchers who drove herds through the dirt and dust from southern Texas to Abilene earned a mere thirty dollars a month, about the same as common laborers. They also braved the gangs of cattle thieves that operated along the trails. The most notorious of the cattle rustlers, William H. Bonney, better known as Billy the Kid, may have murdered as many as eleven men before he was killed by a sheriff in 1881 at the age of twenty-one. The long hours, low pay, and hazardous work discouraged older ranch hands from applying. Most cowboys were men in their teens and twenties who worked for a year or two and then pursued different livelihoods.

Of the estimated 35,000 to 55,000 men who rode the trails in these years, nearly one-fifth were black or Mexican. Barred by discrimination from many other trades, blacks enjoyed the freedom of life on the trail. Although they were excluded from the position of trail boss, they distinguished themselves as resourceful and shrewd cowpunchers. **Nat Love,** the son of Tennessee slaves, left for Kansas after the Civil War to work for Texas cattle companies. As chief brander, he moved through Texas and Arizona "dancing, drinking, and shooting up the town." By his own account, he was "wild, reckless, free," and "afraid of nothing." On July 4, 1876, when the Black Hills gold rush was in full swing, Love delivered three thousand head of cattle to a point near the hills and rode into Deadwood to celebrate. Local miners and gamblers had raised prize money for roping and shooting contests, and Nat Love won both, as well as a new title, Deadwood Dick.

Close relationships sometimes developed between black and white cowboys. Shortly before Charles Goodnight, a white pioneer trailblazer, died in 1929, he recalled of the black cowboy Bose Ikard, a former slave, that "he was my detective, banker, and everything else in Colorado, New Mexico, and the other wild country I was in. The nearest and only bank was at Denver, and when we carried money I gave it to Bose." Goodnight revealed much about the economic situation of blacks on the Plains, however, when he added that "a thief would never think of robbing him [Ikard]— never think of looking in a Negro's bed for money."

The cattle bonanza, which peaked between 1880 and 1885, produced more than 4.5 million head of cattle for eastern markets. (See Beyond America—Global Interactions: Cattle-Raising in the Americas.) Prices began to sag as early as 1882, however, and many ranchers plunged heavily into debt. When President Grover Cleveland, trying to improve federal observance of Indian treaties, ordered cattlemen to remove their stock from the Cheyenne-Arapaho reservation in 1885, two hundred thousand more cattle were crowded onto already overgrazed ranges. That same year and the following, two of the coldest and snowiest winters on record combined with summer droughts and Texas fever to destroy nearly 90 percent of the cattle in some regions, pushing thousands of ranchers into bankruptcy. The cattle industry lived on, but railroad expansion brought the days of the open range and the great cattle drives to an end. As had the mining frontier, the cattle frontier left behind memories of individual daring, towering fortunes for some, and hard times for many.

Cattle Towns and Prostitutes　　One legacy of the cattle boom was the growth of cities like Abilene, Kansas, which shipped steers to Chicago and eastern markets. Like other cattle towns, Abilene went through an early period of violence that saw cowboys pulling down the walls of the jail as it was being built. But the town quickly established a police force to maintain law and order. City ordinances forbade carrying firearms and regulated saloons, gambling, and prostitution. James B. "Wild Bill" Hickok served as town marshal in 1871, but his tenure was less eventful than legend had it. Dime novelists described him as "a veritable terror to bad men on the border," but during his term as Abilene's lawman, Hickok killed just two men, one of them by mistake. Transient, unruly types certainly gave a distinctive flavor to cattle towns like Abilene, Wichita, and Dodge City, but the overall homicide rates there were not unusually high.

If cattle towns were neither as violent nor as lawless as legend would have it, they did still experience a lively business in prostitution, as did most cities at this time. Given the large numbers of unattached young men and numerous saloons (Abilene, in the 1870s, with a permanent population of 500, had 32 drinking establishments), prostitution thrived. Prostitutes came from all social classes and from as far away as China, Ireland, Germany, and Mexico. Some became prostitutes as an escape from domestic violence or because of economic hardship. Others, like the Chinese, were forced into the trade. But whatever the reasons for entering the business, prostitutes risked venereal disease, physical abuse, and drug and alcohol addiction.

As western towns became more settled, the numbers of women in other occupations increased. Some found work as cooks or laundresses on ranches. Others married merchants, doctors, and businessmen. Although few of the first generation rode the range, their daughters became increasingly involved in the everyday work of the ranch and became proficient riders themselves.

Bonanza Farms　　The enthusiasm that permeated mining and ranching in the 1870s and 1880s also percolated into agriculture. Like the gold rushes and cattle bonanzas, the wheat boom in the Dakota Territory started small but rapidly attracted large capital investments that produced the nation's first agribusinesses.

The boom began during the Panic of 1873, when the failure of numerous banks caused the price of Northern Pacific Railroad bonds to plummet. The railroad responded by exchanging land for its depreciated bonds. Speculators, including the railroad's own president, George W. Cass, jumped at the opportunity and purchased more than three hundred thousand acres in the fertile Red River valley of North Dakota for between fifty cents and a dollar an acre.

Operating singly or in groups, the speculators established factory-like ten-thousand-acre farms, each run by a hired manager, and invested heavily in labor and equipment. On the Cass-Cheney-Dalrymple farm near Fargo, North Dakota, which covered an area six miles long by four miles wide, fifty or sixty plows rumbled across the flat landscape on a typical spring day. The *New York Tribune* reported that Cass, who had invested fifty thousand dollars for land and equipment, paid all his expenses plus the cost of the ten thousand acres with his first harvest alone.

The publicity generated by the tremendous success of a few large investors like Cass and Oliver Dalrymple led to an unprecedented wheat boom in the Red River valley in 1880. Eastern banking syndicates and small farmers alike rushed to buy land. North Dakota's population tripled in the 1880s. Wheat production skyrocketed to almost 29 million bushels by the end of the decade. But the profits so loudly celebrated in the eastern press soon evaporated. By 1890, some Red River valley farmers were destitute.

The wheat boom collapsed for a variety of reasons. Overproduction, high investment costs, too little or too much rain, excessive reliance on one crop, and depressed grain prices on the international market all undercut farmers' earnings. Large-scale farmers who had invested in hopes of getting rich felt lucky just to survive. Oliver Dalrymple lamented in 1889 that "it seems as if the time has come when there is no money in wheat raising."

Large-scale farms proved most successful in California's Central Valley. Using canals and other irrigation systems to water their crops, farmers were growing higher-priced specialty crops and had created new cooperative marketing associations for cherries, apricots, grapes, and oranges by the mid-1880s. Led by the California Citrus Growers' Association, which used the "Sunkist" trademark for their oranges, large-scale agribusinesses in California were shipping a variety of fruits and vegetables in refrigerated train cars to midwestern and eastern markets by 1900.

The Oklahoma Land Rush, 1889   As farmers in the Dakotas and Minnesota were enduring poor harvests and falling prices, hard-pressed would-be homesteaders greedily eyed the Indian Territory, as present-day Oklahoma was then known. The federal government, considering much of this land virtually worthless, had reserved it for the Five Civilized Tribes since the 1830s. Because these tribes (except for some Cherokees) had sided with the Confederacy during the Civil War, Washington had punished them by settling thousands of Indians from other tribes on lands in the western part of the territory. By the 1880s, land-hungry non-Indians argued that the Civilized Tribes' betrayal of the Union justified further confiscation of their land.

In 1889, over the Native Americans' protests, Congress transferred to the federally owned public domain nearly 2 million acres in the central part of the Oklahoma Territory that had not been specifically assigned to any Indian tribe. At noon on April 22, 1889, thousands of men, women, and children in buggies and wagons stampeded into the new lands to stake out homesteads. (Other settlers, the so-called Sooners, had illegally arrived earlier and were already plowing the fields.) Before nightfall tent communities had risen at Oklahoma City and Guthrie near stations on the Santa Fe Railroad. Nine weeks later, six thousand homestead claims had been filed. In the next decade, the Dawes Severalty Act broke up the Indian reservations into individual allotments and opened the surplus to non-Indian settlement. The **Curtis Act** in 1898 dissolved the Indian Territory and abolished tribal governments.

Cattle-Raising in the Americas

Nineteenth-century dime novels and Wild West Shows celebrated cowboys as quintessentially American—independent, self-reliant, tough, and occasionally violent. Driving herds of cattle north from Texas to Kansas, the cowboys, who rode the open range from the end of the Civil War through the mid-1880s, appeared to be the unique product of the American West. From a more global perspective, however, North-American cowboys shared much in common with the Mexican *vaqueros* and Argentinian *gauchos*. Like their counterparts in Latin and South America, they drew on a long tradition of cattle herding that had begun centuries earlier in Africa, England, and Spain.

Spanish conquistadors and English colonists brought to the New World their practice of raising beef cattle on the open range rather than in fixed enclosures. In sixteenth-century Mexico, African slaves often joined mixed-bloods of Spanish and Indian ancestry to brand and tend cattle. On the rich grasslands of Argentina, horsemen first hunted wild cattle that had escaped earlier settlements. Later, after the Indians were driven off the open range, these horsemen, now called *gauchos,* tended cattle on large ranches.

Gauchos and cowboys were colorful characters, usually young men, often from lower-class backgrounds. The English naturalist, Charles Darwin, visiting Argentina in 1833, described them as being "generally tall and handsome, but with a proud and dissolute expression of countenance. They frequently wear their mustaches, and long black hair curling down their backs. With their brightly-colored garments, great spurs clanking about their heels, and knives stuck as daggers (and often so used) at their waists, they look a very different race of men from what might be expected from their name of Gauchos, or simple countrymen." Like cowboys, they busted broncos, taming the wild horses to accept riders, and rounded up strays. They also hunted wild ostriches, whose feathers fetched high prices in Europe. As in North America, some gauchos became bandits, which added to their romantic appeal.

Gauchos and cowboys, like other cattle herders around the world, whether Russian Cossacks, South African Dutch farmers, or Canadian cowhands, were often skilled horsemen. American cowboys drew on both Anglo and Hispanic traditions. Unlike the gauchos in Argentina who used *bolas,* an Indian invention of three balls connected by rawhide thongs, to entangle a steer's feet and immobilize it, American cowboys used the Hispanic *lariat* to rope the necks of their cattle and place them in a corral. Like British herders who used dogs, American cowboys taught their horses to maneuver quickly and sharply to keep the herd in line or to cut out a steer to be branded. Like their counterparts in Canada, they organized rodeos to show off their riding and lassoing skills.

Although horses were universally used to herd cattle throughout the Americas, each open-range cattle-raising region had its own distinctive features. In California, where the open-range cattle boom peaked in the decade after 1848, Hispanic cowhands used rawhide lassos, which they looped around the saddle horn to immobilize steers, and wore the Spanish great-rowel spurs over soft shoes. Since Anglo-Texans adapted British cattle-herding practices that used abrupt turns to cut a steer from the herd, they modified the traditional Spanish saddle by adding a second belt to hold it more securely on the horse, and adopted the pointed-toe, high-heeled riding boot, which would hold the boot, in the stirrup during these tight turns. Cattle-raisers on the Great Plains, while following many Texas cowboy practices, added river irrigation to grow hay fields to help tide their herds over the harsh winters. Canadian cattlemen, in contrast, employed acculturated Indians as cowhands and sometimes followed British practices and used collie dogs as well as horses to help herd cattle.

By the end of the nineteenth century, the cattle booms in both North and South America that depended on open-range grazing practices had passed. By maximizing herd size and fertility, cattle-men had inadvertently destroyed perennial grasses, damaged the landscape, and in some cases caused desertification. Farmers and sheep-raisers competed for grazing land and fenced off access to many ranges. At the same time, the extension of railroad lines made it possible to ship cattle directly from ranches to urban areas, a practice that fundamentally changed the livestock industry. In both North and South America, large-scale ranchers took control of cattle-raising and kept wages low. British investment syndicates, for example, purchased large ranches in Texas and Wyoming where they raised immense herds for eastern urban markets.

Not surprisingly, the idealization and romanticization of the cowboy that occurred after open-range grazing had disappeared in North America produced similar celebrations of gauchos and *vaqueros* in Argentina and Mexico. In all three areas, the reality was different. The colorful cowhands who had stirred the popular imagination as symbols of a freer, more independent way of life had been reduced to seasonal laborers with little chance of advancement.

Questions for Analysis

- What traditions shaped open-range ranching in the Americas?
- What was the popular mythic image of the cowboy, the *vaquero,* and the gaucho?
- What was the environmental impact of open-range grazing?

The Oklahoma land rush demonstrated the continuing power of the frontier myth, which tied "free" land to the ideal of economic opportunity. Despite early obstacles—the 1889 rush occurred too late in the season for most settlers to plant a full crop, and a drought parched the land the following year—Oklahoma farmers remained optimistic about their chances of making it on the last frontier. Most survived because they were fortunate enough to have obtained fertile land in an area where the normal rainfall was thirty inches, ten inches more than in the semiarid regions farther west. Still, within two generations a combination of exploitative farming, poor land management, and sporadic drought would place Oklahoma at the desolate center of what in the 1930s would be called the dust bowl (see Chapter 24).

THE WEST OF LIFE AND LEGEND

In 1893, four years after the last major tract of western Indian land, the Oklahoma Territory, was opened to non-Indian settlement, a young Wisconsin historian, Frederick Jackson Turner, delivered a lecture entitled "The Significance of the Frontier in American History." "[T]he frontier has gone," declared Turner, "and with its going has closed the first period of American history." Although Turner's assertion that the frontier was closed was based on a Census Bureau announcement, it was inaccurate (more western land would be settled in the twentieth century than in the nineteenth). But his linking of economic opportunity with the transformation of the trans-Mississippi West caught the popular imagination and launched a new school of historical inquiry into the effects of the frontier on U.S. history.

Scholars now recognize that many parts of Turner's "frontier thesis," particularly its ethnocentric omission of Native Americans' claims to the land, were inaccurate. Yet his idealized view of the West did reflect ideas popular among his contemporaries in the 1890s. As farmers, miners, ranchers, Indian agents, and prostitutes had pursued their varied activities in the real West, a parallel legendary West had taken deep root in the American imagination. In the nineteenth century, this mythic West was a product of novels, songs, and paintings. In the twentieth century, it would be perpetuated by movies, radio programs, and television shows. The legend merits attention, for its evolution is fascinating and its influence has been far-reaching.

The American Adam and the Dime-Novel Hero　In the early biographies of frontiersmen like Daniel Boone and in the wilderness novels of James Fenimore Cooper, the western hero's personal development sometimes parallels, but more often runs counter to, the interests of society. Mid-nineteenth-century writers, extending the theme of the western wilderness as an alternative to society, presented the frontiersman as a kind of mythic American Adam—simple, virtuous, and innocent—untainted by a corrupt social order. For example, an early biographer of Kit Carson, the Kentucky-born guide who made one of the first recorded crossings of California's Mojave Desert in 1830, depicted him as a perfect antidote to the evils of refined society, an individual of "genuine simplicity, . . . truthfulness . . . [and] bravery." At the end of Mark Twain's *Huckleberry Finn*, Huck rejects the constraints of settled society as represented by Aunt Sally and heads west with the declaration, "I reckon I got to light out for the territory ahead of the rest, because Aunt Sally she's going to adopt me and sivilize me, and I can't stand it. I been there before."

In this version of the legend, the West is a place of adventure, romance, or contemplation where one can escape from society and its pressures.

But even as this conception of the myth was being popularized, another powerful theme had emerged as well. The authors of the dime novels of the 1860s and 1870s offered the image of the western frontiersman as a new masculine ideal, the tough guy who fights for truth and honor. In *Buffalo Bill: King of the Border Men* (1869), a dime novel loosely based on real-life William F. "Buffalo Bill" Cody, Edward Judson (who published under the name Ned Buntline) created an idealized hero who is a powerful moral force as he drives off treacherous Indians and rounds up villainous cattle rustlers.

Cody himself, playing upon the public fascination with cowboys, organized his own **Wild West Show** in 1883. In the show, which toured the East Coast and Europe, cowboys engaged in mock battles with Indians, reinforcing the dime-novel image of the West as an arena of moral encounter where virtue always triumphed.

Revitalizing the Frontier Legend   Eastern writers and artists eagerly embraced both versions of the myth—the West as a place of escape from society and the West as a stage on which the moral conflicts confronting society were played out. Three young members of the eastern establishment, Theodore Roosevelt, Frederic Remington, and Owen Wister, spent much time in the West in the 1880s, and each was intensely affected by the adventure.

Each man found precisely what he was looking for. The frontier that Roosevelt glorified in such books as *The Winning of the West* (four volumes, 1889–1896), and that Remington portrayed in his statues and paintings, was a stark physical and moral environment that stripped away all social artifice and tested each individual's character. Drawing on a popular version of English scientist Charles Darwin's evolutionary theory, which characterized life as a struggle in which only the fittest survived, Roosevelt and Remington exalted the disappearing frontier as the proving ground for a new kind of virile manhood and the last outpost of an honest and true social order.

This version of the frontier myth reached its apogee in **Owen Wister**'s enormously popular novel *The Virginian* (1902), later reincarnated as a 1929 Gary Cooper movie and a 1960s television series. In Wister's tale, the elemental physical and social environment of the Great Plains produces individuals like his unnamed cowboy hero, "the Virginian," an honest, strong, and compassionate man, quick to help the weak and fight the wicked. The Virginian is one of nature's aristocrats—ill-educated and unsophisticated but tough, steady, and deeply moral. The Virginian sums up his own moral code in describing his view of God's justice: "He plays a square game with us." For Wister, as for Roosevelt and Remington, the cowboy was the Christian knight on the Plains, indifferent to material gain as he upheld virtue, pursued justice, and attacked evil.

Needless to say, the western myth was far removed from the reality of the West. Critics delighted in pointing out that not one scene in *The Virginian* showed the hard physical labor of the cattle range. The idealized version of the West also glossed over the darker underside of frontier expansion—the brutalities of Indian warfare, the forced removal of the Indians to reservations, the racist discrimination against Mexican-Americans and blacks, the risks and perils of commercial agriculture and cattle-raising, and the boom-and-bust mentality rooted in the selfish exploitation of natural resources.

Further, the myth obscured the complex links between the settlement of the frontier and the emergence of the United States as a major industrialized nation increasingly tied to a global economy. Eastern and foreign capitalists controlled large-scale mining, cattle, and agricultural operations in the West. The technical know-how of industrial America underlay the marvels of western agricultural productivity. Without the railroad, that quintessential symbol of the new industrial order, the transformation of the West would have been far slower.

Beginning a National Parks Movement
Despite its one-sided and idealized vision, Owen Wister's celebration of the western experience reinforced a growing recognition that many unique features of the western landscape were being threatened by overeager entrepreneurs. One important byproduct of the western legend was a surge of public support for creating national parks and the beginning of an organized conservation movement.

Those who went west in the 1860s and 1870s to map the rugged terrain of the High Plains and the Rocky Mountains were often awed by the natural beauty of the landscape. Major **John Wesley Powell,** the one-armed veteran of the Civil War who charted the Colorado River through the Grand Canyon in 1869, waxed euphoric about its towering rock formations and powerful cataracts. "A beautiful view is presented. The river turns sharply to the east, and seems enclosed by a wall, set with a million brilliant gems. . . . On coming nearer, we find fountains bursting from the rock, high overhead, and the spray in the sunshine forms the gems which bedeck the way."

In his important study, *Report on the Lands of the Arid Regions of the United States* (1878), Powell argued that settlers needed to change their pattern of settlement and readjust their expectations about the use of water in the dry terrain west of the hundredth meridian. Recognizing that incoming farmers had often mistakenly believed that rain would miraculously follow the plow, Powell called for public ownership and governmental control of watersheds, irrigation, and public lands, a request that went largely unheeded.

Around the time Powell was educating Congress about the arid nature of the far West, a group of adventurers led by General Henry D. Washburn visited the hot springs and geysers near the Yellowstone River in northwestern Wyoming and eastern Montana. They were stunned by what they saw. "You can stand in the valley of the Yosemite [the California park land protected by Congress in 1864]," wrote one of the party, "and look up its mile of vertical granite, and distinctly recall its minutest feature; but amid the canyon and falls, the boiling springs and sulphur mountain, and, above all, the mud volcano and the geysers of the Yellowstone, your memory becomes filled and clogged with objects new in experience, wonderful in extent, and possessing unlimited grandeur and beauty." Overwhelmed by the view, the Washburn explorers abandoned their plan to claim the area for the Northern Pacific Railroad and instead petitioned Congress to protect it from settlement, occupancy, and sale. Congress responded in 1872 by creating **Yellowstone National Park** to "provide for the preservation . . . for all time, [of] mineral deposits, natural curiosities, or wonders within said park . . . in their natural condition." In doing so, they excluded the Native Americans who had long considered the area a prime hunting range.

These first steps to conserve a few of the West's unique natural sites reflected the beginning of a changed awareness of the environment. In his influential study *Man and*

Nature in 1864, **George Perkins Marsh,** an architect and politician from Vermont, had attacked the view that nature existed to be tamed and conquered. Cautioning Americans to curb their destructive use of the landscape, he warned the public to change its ways. "Man," he wrote, "is everywhere a disturbing agent. Wherever he plants his foot, the harmonies of nature are turned to discords."

Marsh's plea for conservation found its most eloquent support in the work of **John Muir,** a Scottish immigrant who had grown up in Wisconsin. Temporarily blinded by an accident, Muir left for San Francisco in 1869 and quickly fell in love with the redwood forests. For the next forty years, he tramped the rugged mountains of the West and campaigned for their preservation. A romantic at heart, he struggled to experience the wilderness at its most elemental level. Once trekking high in the Rockies during a summer storm, he climbed the tallest pine he could find and swayed back and forth in the raging wind.

Muir became the late nineteenth century's most articulate publicist for wilderness protection. "Climb the mountains and get their good tidings," he advised city-dwellers. "Nature's peace will flow into you as the sunshine into the trees. The winds will blow their freshness into you, and the storms their energy, while cares will drop off like autumn leaves." Muir's spirited campaign to protect the wilderness contributed strongly to the establishment of Yosemite National Park in 1890. Two years later, the Sierra Club, an organization created to encourage the enjoyment and protection of the wilderness in the mountain regions of the Pacific coast, made Muir its first president.

The precedent established by the creation of Yellowstone National Park remained ambiguous well into the twentieth century. Other parks that preserved the high rugged landforms of the West were often chosen because Congress viewed the sites as worthless for other purposes. Awareness of the need for biological conservation would not emerge until later in the twentieth century (see Chapter 21).

Ironically, despite the crusades of Muir, Powell, and Marsh to educate the public about conservation, the campaign for wilderness preservation reaffirmed the image of the West as a unique region whose magnificent landscape produced tough individuals of superior ability. Overlooking the senseless violence and ruthless exploitation of the land, contemporary writers, historians, and publicists proclaimed that the settlement of the final frontier marked a new stage in the history of civilization, and they kept alive the legend of the western frontier as a seedbed of American virtues.

CONCLUSION

The image of the mythic West has long obscured the transformation of people and landscape that took place there in the second half of the nineteenth century. Precisely because industrialization, urbanization, and immigration were altering the rest of the nation in unsettling ways (see Chapters 18 and 19), many Americans embraced the legend of the West as a visionary, uncomplicated, untainted Eden of social simplicity and moral clarity. The mythic West represented what the entire society had once been like (or so Americans chose to believe), before the advent of cities, factories, and masses of immigrants.

But the reality of westward expansion was more complex than the mythmakers acknowledged. Under the banner of economic opportunity and individual achievement, nineteenth-century Americans used the army to subdue the Indians, undermine their traditional way of life, and drive them onto reservations. They also ruthlessly exploited the region's vast natural resources. In less than three decades, they killed off the enormous buffalo herds, tore up the prairie sod, and littered parts of the landscape with mining debris.

Thus the mythic view of the frontier West as the arena for society building and economic opportunity obscured the dark side of the expansion onto the Great Plains and beyond. Despite the promise of the Homestead Act, which offered 160 acres of free land to those who would settle on it for five years, much of the best land had been given to railroads to encourage their expansion. Speculators had grabbed other prime locations. Homesteaders were often forced to settle on poorer quality tracts in areas where rainfall was marginal. In many places, large business enterprises in mining, ranching, and agribusiness, financed by eastern and European bankers, shoved aside the small entrepreneur and took control of the choicest natural resources.

Nevertheless, the settlement of the vast internal continental land did reinforce the popular image of the United States as a land of unprecedented economic opportunity and as a seedbed for democracy. Although the exclusion of blacks, Indians, and Spanish-speaking Americans belied the voiced commitment to an open society, the founding of new towns, the creation of new territorial and state governments, and the interaction of peoples of different races and ethnicities tested these ideas and, with time, forced their rethinking. The increasing willingness to give women the vote in many of the new western states would spread within the next two decades.

Although the persistence of the mythic view of the West served to hide the more ruthless and destructive features of western expansionism, the experiences gained from settling the interior territories and the utilization of the region's extensive physical resources led to the beginnings of the conservation movement and a reassessment of traditional American views of the environment. By the turn of the century, the thriving farms, ranches, mines, and cities of that region would help make the United States into one of the world's most prosperous nations.

18

The Rise of Industrial America, 1865–1900

THE RISE OF CORPORATE AMERICA

In the early nineteenth century, the corporate form of business organization had been used to raise large amounts of start-up capital for transportation enterprises such as turnpikes and canals. By selling stocks and bonds to raise money, the corporation separated the company's managers, who guided its day-to-day operation, from its owners. After the Civil War, American business leaders pioneered new forms of corporate organization that combined innovative technologies, creative management structures, and limited liability should the enterprise fail. The rise of the giant corporation is a story of risk-taking and innovation as well as of conspiracy and corruption.

The Character of Industrial Change   Six features dominated the world of large-scale manufacturing after the Civil War: first, the exploitation of immense coal deposits as a source of cheap energy; second, the rapid spread of technological innovation in transportation, communication, and factory systems; third, the need for enormous numbers of new workers who could be carefully controlled; fourth, the constant pressure on firms to compete tooth-and-nail by cutting costs and prices, as well as the impulse to eliminate rivals and create monopolies; fifth, the relentless drop in prices (a stark contrast to the inflation of other eras); and finally, the failure of the money supply to keep pace with productivity, a development that drove up interest rates and restricted the availability of credit.

All six factors were closely related. The great coal deposits in Pennsylvania, West Virginia, and Kentucky provided cheap energy to fuel railroad and factory growth. New technologies stimulated productivity and catalyzed breathtaking industrial expansion. Technology also enabled manufacturers to cut costs and hire cheap unskilled or semiskilled labor. Cost cutting enabled firms to undersell one another, destroy weaker competitors, and consolidate themselves into stronger, more efficient, and more ruthless firms. At least until the mid-1890s, cheap energy, cost reduction, new technology, and fierce competition forced down overall price levels.

But almost everyone struggled terribly during the depression years, when the government debated whether it should get involved but did nothing to relieve distress. "The sufferings of the working classes are daily increasing," wrote a Philadelphia worker in 1874. "Famine has broken into the home of many of us, and is at the door of all." Above all, business leaders' unflagging drive to maximize efficiency both created colossal fortunes at the top of the economic ladder and forced millions of wage earners to live near the subsistence level.

Out of the new industrial system poured clouds of haze and soot, as well as the first tantalizing trickle of what would become an avalanche of consumer goods. In turn, mounting demands for consumer goods stimulated heavy industry's production of capital goods—machines to boost farm and factory output even further. Together with the railroads, the corporations that manufactured capital goods, refined petroleum, and made steel became driving forces in the nation's economic growth.

| Railroad Innovations | Competition among the aggressive and innovative capitalists who headed American heavy industry was intense. As the post–Civil War era opened, nowhere was it more intense than among |

the nation's railroads. By 1900, 193,000 miles of railroad track crisscrossed the United States—more than in all of Europe including Russia. These rail lines connected every state in the Union and opened up an immense new internal market. Most important, railroad companies pioneered crucial aspects of large-scale corporate enterprise. These included the creation of national distribution and marketing systems, and the formation of new organizational and management structures.

Railroad entrepreneurs such as Collis P. Huntington of the Central Pacific Railroad, **Jay Gould** of the Union Pacific, and James J. Hill of the Northern Pacific faced enormous financial and organizational problems. To raise the staggering sums necessary for laying track, building engines, and buying out competitors, railroads obtained generous land and loan subsidies from federal, state, and local governments (see Chapter 17). Even so, the larger lines had to borrow heavily by selling stocks and bonds to the public. Bond holders earned a fixed rate of interest; stockholders received dividends only when the company earned a profit. By 1900, the yearly interest repayments required by the combined debt of all U.S. railroads (which stood at an astounding $5.1 billion—nearly five times that of the federal government) cut heavily into their earnings.

In addition to developing ways to raise large amounts of capital, the railroads created new systems for collecting and using information. To coordinate the complex flow of cars across the country, railroads relied heavily on the magnetic telegraph, invented in 1837. To improve efficiency, the railroads set up clearly defined, hierarchical organizational structures and divided their lines into separate geographic units, each with its own superintendent. Elaborate accounting systems documented the cost of every operation for each division, from coal consumption to the repair of engines and cars. Using these reports, railroad officials could set rates and accurately predict profits as early as the 1860s, a time when most businesses had no idea of their total profit until they closed their books at year's end. Railroad management innovations thus became a model for many other businesses seeking a national market.

CHRONOLOGY, 1865–1900

1859 • First oil well drilled in Titusville, Pennsylvania.

1866 • National Labor Union founded.

1869 • Transcontinental railroad completed.
Knights of Labor organized.

1870 • John D. Rockefeller establishes Standard Oil Company.

1873 • Panic of 1873 triggers a depression lasting until 1879.

1876 • Alexander Graham Bell patents the telephone.

1877 • Edison invents phonograph.
Railway workers stage first nationwide strike.

1879 • Henry George, *Progress and Poverty.*
Edison perfects incandescent lamp.

1882 • Standard Oil Trust established.
Edison opens first electric power station in New York City.
Chinese Exclusion Act.

1883 • William Graham Sumner, *What Social Classes Owe to Each Other.*
Lester Frank Ward, *Dynamic Sociology.*

1886 • American Federation of Labor (AFL) formed.
Haymarket riot in Chicago.

1887 • Interstate Commerce Act establishes Interstate Commerce Commission.

1888 • Edward Bellamy, *Looking Backward.*

1889 • Andrew Carnegie, "The Gospel of Wealth."

1890 • Sherman Anti-Trust Act.
United Mine Workers formed.

1892 • Standard Oil of New Jersey and General Electric formed.
Homestead Strike.
Columbian Exposition in Chicago.
Miners strike at Coeur d'Alene, Idaho.

1893 • Panic of 1893 triggers a depression lasting until 1897.

1894 • Pullman Palace Car workers strike.

1901 • J. Pierpont Morgan organizes United States Steel.

Consolidating the Railroad Industry The expansion and consolidation of railroading reflected both the ingenuity and the dishonesty flourishing on the corporate management scene. Although by the 1870s railroads had replaced the patchwork of canal and stagecoach operations that dominated domestic transportation before the Civil War, the industry remained chaotic. Hundreds of small companies used different standards for car couplers, rails, track width, and engine size. Financed by large eastern and British banks, Huntington, Gould, and others devoured these smaller lines to create large, integrated track networks. In the Northeast

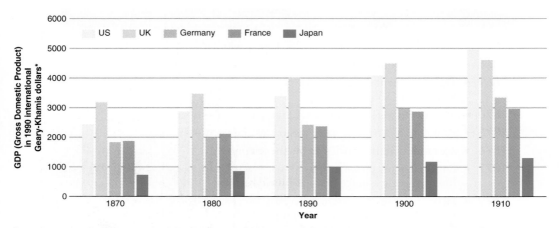

*1990 international Geary-Khamis dollars represent the monetary values of the output of the final goods and services produced in a country in one year converted into 1990 dollars at the exchange rate which would pertain if the goods and services had the same prices in all countries (purchasing power parity). See the statistical definition at the UN site: http://unstats.un.org/unsd/methods/icp/ipc7_htm.htm

Figure 18.1 Late Nineteenth-Century Economic Growth in Global Perspective

four major trunk lines were completed. West of the Mississippi five great lines—the Union Pacific (1869); the Northern Pacific (1883); the Atchison, Topeka, and Santa Fe (1883); the Southern Pacific (1883); and the Great Northern (1893)—controlled most of the track by 1893.

Huntington, Gould, and the other larger-than-life figures who reorganized and expanded the railroad industry in the 1870s and 1880s were often depicted by their contemporaries as villains and robber barons who manipulated stock markets and company policies to line their own pockets. For example, newspaper publisher Joseph Pulitzer called Jay Gould, the short, secretive president of the Union Pacific, "one of the most sinister figures that have ever flitted batlike across the vision of the American people." Recent historians, however, have pointed out that the great industrialists were a diverse group. Although some were ironfisted pirates who engaged in fraudulent practices, others were upstanding businessmen who managed their companies with sophistication and innovation. Indeed, some of their ideas were startling in their originality and inventiveness.

The massive systems created by these entrepreneurs became the largest business enterprises in the world, towering over state and federal governments in the size and scale of their operations. As they consolidated small railroads into a few interlocking systems, these masterminds pioneered the most advanced methods of accounting and large-scale organization. They also standardized all basic equipment and facilities, from engines and cars to automatic couplers, air brakes, signal systems, and outhouses. In 1883, independently of the federal government, the railroads corrected scheduling problems by dividing the country into four time zones. In May 1886 all railroads shifted simultaneously to the new standard 4'8½" gauge track. Finally, cooperative billing arrangements enabled the railroads to ship cars from other roads, including dining and sleeping cars owned by the Pullman Palace Car Company, at uniform rates nationwide.

Abusive Monopoly Power

This Puck cartoon depicts financiers Jay Gould (left) and Cornelius Vanderbilt (right) and suggests that their manipulation of markets and their ownership of railroads, telegraph companies, and newspapers is powerful enough to strangle Uncle Sam.

But the systemization and consolidation of the railroads had its costs. Heavy indebtedness, overextended systems, and crooked business practices forced the railroads to compete recklessly with each other for traffic. They cut rates for large shippers, offered special arrangements for handling bulk goods, showered free passes on politicians, and granted substantial rebates and kickbacks to favored clients. None of these tactics, however, shored up the railroads' precarious financial position. And the continuous push to expand drove some overbuilt lines into bankruptcy.

Caught in the middle of the railroads' tug-of-war and stung by exorbitant rates and secret kickbacks, farmers and small business owners turned to state governments for help. In the 1870s many midwestern state legislatures responded by outlawing rate discrimination. Initially upheld by the Supreme Court, these and other decisions were negated in the 1880s when the Court ruled that states could not regulate interstate commerce. In response in 1887, Congress passed the **Interstate Commerce Act.** A five-member Interstate Commerce Commission (ICC) was established to oversee the practices of interstate railroads. The law banned monopolistic activity like pooling, rebates, and discriminatory short-distance rates.

The railroads challenged the commission's rulings in the federal courts. Of the sixteen cases brought to the Supreme Court before 1905, the justices found in favor of the railroads in all but one, essentially nullifying the ICC's regulatory clout. The Hepburn Act (see Chapter 21), passed in 1906, strengthened the ICC by finally empowering it to set rates.

The railroads' vicious competition weakened in 1893 when a national depression forced a number of roads into the hands of **J. Pierpont Morgan** and other investment bankers. Morgan, a massively built man with piercing eyes and a commanding presence, took over the weakened systems, reorganized their administration, refinanced their debts, and built intersystem alliances. By 1906, thanks to the bankers' centralized management, seven giant networks controlled two-thirds of the nation's rail mileage.

Applying the
Lessons of the
Railroads to Steel

The close connections between railroad expansion, which absorbed millions of tons of steel for tracks, and the growth of corporate organization and management are well illustrated in the career of **Andrew Carnegie.** Born in Scotland, Carnegie immigrated to America in 1848 at the age of twelve. His first job as a bobbin boy in a Pittsburgh textile mill paid only $1.20 a week. Although he worked a sixty-hour week, the aspiring youngster enrolled in a night course to learn bookkeeping. The following year, Carnegie became a Western Union messenger boy. Taking over when the telegraph operators wanted a break, he soon became the city's fastest telegraph operator. Because he had to decode the messages for every major business in Pittsburgh, Carnegie gained an insider's view of their operations.

Carnegie's big break came in 1852 when Tom Scott, superintendent of the Pennsylvania Railroad's western division, hired him as his secretary and personal telegrapher. When Scott became vice president of the Pennsylvania Railroad seven years later, the twenty-four-year-old Carnegie took over as head of the line's western division. A daring innovator, Carnegie, in his six years as division chief, used the complex cost-analysis techniques developed by Scott to more than double the road's mileage and quadruple its traffic. He slashed commuter fares to keep ridership at capacity and developed various cost-cutting techniques. Having invested his earnings in the railroads, by 1868 Carnegie was earning more than $56,000 a year from his investments, a substantial fortune in that era.

In the early 1870s Carnegie decided to build his own steel mill. His connections within the railroad industry, the country's largest purchaser of steel, ensured his success. Starting with his first mill, he introduced a production technology named after its English inventor, Henry Bessemer, which shot a blast of air through an enormous crucible of molten iron to burn off carbon and impurities. Adopting this new technology and combining it with the cost-analysis approach learned from his railroad experience, Carnegie became the first steelmaker to know the actual production cost of each ton of steel.

Carnegie's philosophy was deceptively simple: "Watch the costs, and the profits will take care of themselves." Using rigorous cost accounting and limiting wage increases to his workers, he lowered his production costs and prices below those of his competitors. When these tactics did not drive them out of business, he was not above asking for favors from his railroad-president friends or giving "commissions" to railroad purchasing agents to win business.

Figure 18.2 Iron and Steel Production, 1875–1915

New technologies, improved plant organization, economies of scale, and the vertical integration of production brought a dramatic spurt in iron and steel production. *Source:* Historical Statistics of the United States.

Note: short ton = 2,000 pounds.

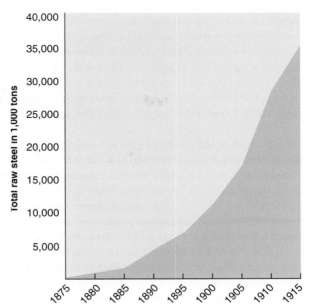

As output climbed, Carnegie discovered the benefits of **vertical integration**—that is, controlling all aspects of manufacturing, from extracting raw materials to selling the finished product. In Carnegie's case, this control embraced every stage from the mining and smelting of ore to the selling of steel rails. Carnegie Steel thus became the classic example of how sophisticated new technology could be combined with innovative management (and brutally low wages) to create a mass-production system that could slash consumer prices.

The management of daily operations by his close associates left Carnegie free to pursue philanthropic activities. While still in his early thirties, Carnegie resolved to donate his money to charitable projects. In his lifetime, he gave more than $300 million to libraries, universities, and international-peace causes.

By 1900, Carnegie Steel, employing twenty thousand people, had become the world's largest industrial corporation. Carnegie's competitors, worried about his domination of the market, decided to buy him out. In 1901, J. Pierpont Morgan, who controlled Federal Steel, asked Charles Schwab, Carnegie Steel's president, to inquire what Carnegie wanted for his share of Carnegie Steel. The next day Carnegie gave Schwab a penciled note asking for nearly half a billion dollars. Morgan's response was simple: "Tell Carnegie I accept his price." Combining Carnegie's companies with Federal Steel, Morgan set up the United States Steel Corporation, the first business capitalized at more than $1 billion. The corporation, made up of two hundred member companies employing 168,000 people, marked a new scale in industrial enterprise.

Throughout his chain of corporate-world triumphs, Carnegie consistently portrayed his success as the result of self-discipline and hard work. The full story was more complex. Carnegie did not mention his uncanny ability to see the larger picture, his cleverness in hiring talented associates who would drive themselves (and the company's factory workers) mercilessly, his ingenuity in transferring organizational systems and cost-accounting methods from railroads to steel, and his callousness in keeping wages as low as possible. To a public unaware of corporate management techniques, however, Carnegie's success reaffirmed the openness of the American economic system. For the new immigrants flooding the nation's shores, Carnegie's career gave credence to the idea that anyone might rise from rags to riches.

The Trust: Creating New Forms of Corporate Organization Between 1870 and 1900, the same fierce competition that had stimulated consolidation in the railroad and steel industries also swept the oil, salt, sugar, tobacco, and meatpacking industries. Like steel, these highly competitive businesses required large capital investments. Entrepreneurs in each industry therefore raced to reduce costs, lower prices, and drive their rivals out of the market. Chicago meatpackers Philip Armour and Gustavus Swift, for example, used every part of the animal. Hides were tanned into leather, bones became fertilizer, and hooves were turned into gelatin. When lowering costs failed to drive out rivals, new organizational methods were pioneered to control competition and preserve market share.

The evolution of the oil industry illustrates the process by which new corporate structures evolved. After Edwin L. Drake drilled the first successful petroleum (or "crude-oil") well in 1859 near Titusville in northwestern Pennsylvania, competitors rushed into the business, sinking wells and erecting small refineries nearby. Petroleum was distilled into oil, which soon replaced animal tallow as the major lubricant, and into kerosene, which became the leading fuel for household and public lighting. By the 1870s the landscape near Pittsburgh and Cleveland, the sites of the first discoveries, was littered with rickety drilling rigs, assorted collection tanks, and ramshackle refineries. Oil spills were a constant problem. "So much oil is produced," reported one Pennsylvania newspaper in 1861, "that it is impossible to care for it, and thousands of barrels are running into the creek; the surface of the river is covered with oil for miles."

In this rush for riches, **John D. Rockefeller,** a young Cleveland merchant, gradually achieved dominance. Although he did not share Andrew Carnegie's outgoing personality, the solemn Rockefeller resembled the opportunistic steelmaker in other respects. Having gotten his start as a bookkeeper, Rockefeller opened his first refinery in 1863. Like Carnegie, Rockefeller had a passion for cost cutting and efficiency. When he became the head of the Standard Oil Company in 1873, he scrutinized every aspect of its operation. In one case, he insisted that a manager find 750 missing barrel stoppers. He realized that in a mass-production enterprise, small changes could save thousands of dollars.

Rockefeller resembled Carnegie, too, in his ability to understand the inner workings of an entire industry and the benefits of vertical integration. The firm that controlled the shipment of oil between the well and the refinery and between the refinery and the retailers, he realized, could dominate the industry. In 1872 he purchased his own tanker cars and obtained not only a 10 percent rebate from the railroads for hauling his oil shipments but also a kickback on his competitors' shipments. When new pipeline technology became available, Rockefeller set up his own massive interregional pipeline network.

Like Carnegie, Rockefeller aggressively forced out his competitors. When local refineries rejected his offers to buy them out, he priced his products below cost and strangled their businesses. When rival firms teamed up against him, Rockefeller set up a pool—an agreement among several companies—that established production quotas and fixed prices. By 1879 Rockefeller had seized control of 90 percent of the country's oil-refining capacity.

Worried about competition, Rockefeller in 1882 decided to eliminate it by establishing a new form of corporate organization, the **Standard Oil Trust.** In place of the "pool" or verbal agreement among companies to control prices and markets, which lacked legal status, the trust created an umbrella corporation that ran them all. To implement his trust, Rockefeller and his associates persuaded the stockholders of forty companies to exchange their stock for trust certificates. Under this arrangement, stockholders retained their share of the trust's profits while enabling the trust to control production. Within three years the Standard Oil Trust had consolidated crude-oil buying throughout its member firms and slashed the number of refineries in half. In this way Rockefeller integrated the petroleum industry both vertically, by controlling every function from production to local retailing, and horizontally, by merging the competing oil companies into one giant system.

Taking a leaf from Rockefeller's book, companies in the copper, sugar, whiskey, lead, and other industries established their own trust arrangements. By limiting the number of competitors, the trusts created an *oligopoly,* the market condition that exists when a small number of sellers can greatly influence prices. But their unscrupulous tactics, semimonopolistic control, and sky-high earnings provoked a public outcry. Both major political parties denounced them in the presidential election of 1888.

Fearful that the trusts would stamp out all competition, Congress, under the leadership of Senator John Sherman of Ohio, passed the **Sherman Anti-Trust Act** in 1890. The Sherman Act outlawed trusts and any other monopolies that fixed prices in restraint of trade and slapped violators with fines of up to five thousand dollars and a year in jail. But the act failed to define clearly either *trust* or *restraint of trade.* The government prosecuted only eighteen antitrust suits between 1890 and 1904. When Standard Oil's structure was challenged in 1892, its lawyers simply reorganized the trust as an enormous holding company. Unlike a trust, which literally owned other businesses, a holding company simply owned a controlling share of the stock of one or more firms. The new board of directors for Standard Oil (New Jersey), the new holding company, made more money than ever.

The Supreme Court further hamstrung congressional antitrust efforts by interpreting the Sherman Act in ways sympathetic to big business. In 1895, for example, the federal government brought suit against the sugar trust in *United States* v. *E. C. Knight Company.* It argued that the Knight firm, which controlled more than 90 percent of all U.S. sugar refining, operated in illegal restraint of trade. Asserting that manufacturing was not interstate commerce and ignoring the company's vast distribution network that enabled it to dominate the market, the Court threw out the suit. Thus vindicated, corporate mergers and consolidations surged ahead at the turn of the century. By 1900, these mammoth firms accounted for nearly two-fifths of the capital invested in the nation's manufacturing sector.

STIMULATING ECONOMIC GROWTH

Although large-scale corporate enterprise significantly increased the volume of manufactured goods in the late nineteenth century, it alone did not account for the colossal growth of the U.S. economy. Other factors proved equally important, including new

Electricity

Of all the technological achievements of the nineteenth century, none seemed more inspiring or mysterious than the ability to generate electricity. Using Alessandro Volta's discovery that chemical reactions in batteries produced a weak electric current, Samuel F. B. Morse had used batteries to power his telegraph in 1837. Alexander Graham Bell followed suit with his telephone in 1876. But higher voltages were needed to run lighting systems and motors. Michael Faraday in England and Joseph Henry in America discovered in 1831 that a rotating magnet surrounded by a conducting wire would produce a continuous flow of electric current. After the Civil War, American inventors used this discovery to develop powerful generators to run incandescent lights (1879), to power motors to run trolley cars (1888), and to drive machines in factories. For many Americans, the ability to harness electricity marked the subjugation of nature and indicated the progress of American civilization.

Nowhere did the knowledge of electricity seem more impressive than its promise to reveal the secrets of the human body. X-rays, discovered in 1895 by the German physicist Wilhelm Roentgen and developed into a practical hospital machine a year later by Thomas Edison, enabled doctors to see inside the body. Physicians discovered that the workings of the nervous system and the brain itself depended on electrical impulses. In short, electrical science, given the breadth of its applications and its power to provide insights into nature, seemed close to being the embodiment of super-

natural power. It was no accident that Edison was known as the "wizard of Menlo Park," where his research laboratory was located.

The spread of electric lighting illustrates how technological advances pushed innovation. Thomas Edison's vision went far beyond the development of a practical light bulb. He conceived of an interrelated system of power plants, transmission lines, and light fixtures, all to be produced by companies that he had established. Edison's system of direct current lighting (DC—which flowed in only one direction in the wires) required that users be located near power plants. But in 1886 George Westinghouse set up a competing company that used the Italian inventor Nikola Tesla's discovery that alternating current (AC—which cycled back and forth within the wires) could send high-voltage electricity efficiently over long distances. Competition between the two systems was finally resolved in 1896 when Edison's successor company, General Electric, agreed to share its patents with the Westinghouse Company. With electric current now standardized as 110 volts AC at 60 Hertz (60 cycles per second), dozens of other inventors developed electric motors, spotlights, electric signs, water pumps, elevators, and household appliances—all drawing power from the same power grid. Only twenty years after the first power station had been built, electrification had started to transform everyday life.

By 1898, when the city of London had sixty-two different utilities that produced thirty-two different voltage levels, American companies had created a unified national electrical system with standardized voltages, and the United States had established itself as a world leader in electrical technology. The remarkable achievements of the American electrical industry resulted from a combination of factors. Skilled inventors such as Edison, Westinghouse, and Frank Sprague, who developed electric motors for trolley and subway cars, were critical. But the efforts might never have made it out of the laboratories without financiers, such as J. P. Morgan and Henry Villard, who funded the enormous investment in electric generators, power plants, and transmission lines. A third factor was the independence of large corporations like General Electric and Westinghouse, which were able to operate nationally and avoid conflicting state regulations. Operating as regional monopolies, these corporations standardized voltage, alternating current, and electrical fixtures nationwide. Finally, the pooling of patents was crucial. The American patent system, by granting inventors property rights in their inventions and by publicly identifying how the discoveries worked, stimulated technological innovation in general.

At first, electricity was very expensive, and the general public could not afford the cost of wiring homes. Still, even confined to the public sphere, the establishment of a national electrical system was one of the greatest technological innovations of the century. Electric streetcars and subways, public lighting systems, and electric elevators transformed urban America, allowing the construction of skyscrapers and the quick transportation of millions of people. The electrification of factories extended the workday into the night and made work safer. In the following decades, electrification made possible the invention of lighting sys-

tems, fans, washing machines, and a host of other devices to ease the drudgery of everyday life.

In the twentieth century, some shortcomings in Americans' love affair with electricity became obvious. In the early years, urban electrification accentuated the differences between city and country life. After World War II, massive power failures showed that the centralization of power distribution systems, first constructed as private monopolies between 1880 and 1932, made them vulnerable to failure when a subsystem problem cascaded throughout the network. The private ownership of power companies, now called utility companies, has enabled them at times to inflate energy prices for their own profit. Most electrical power in the United States today is produced from coal, a nonrenewable resource which also produces acid rain and air pollution. Nevertheless, the creation of a national system of electrical power generation paved the way for remarkable innovations, from lighting to televisions and computers, that remain today closely tied to America's sense of progress and material advancement.

Questions for Analysis

- Why did the early electrical inventions seem to mark the subjugation of nature?

- What technological breakthroughs paved the way for the widespread use of electricity for street lighting and transportation?

- Why did the standardization and consolidation of the electric industry take place more quickly in the United States than in England?

inventions, specialty production, and innovations in advertising and marketing. In fact, the resourcefulness of small enterprises, which combined innovative technology with new methods of advertising and merchandising, enabled many sectors of the economy to grow dramatically by adapting quickly to changing fashions and consumer preferences.

The Triumph of Technology

New inventions not only streamlined the manufacture of traditional products but also stimulated consumer demand by creating entirely new product lines. The development of a safe, practical way to generate electricity, for example, made possible a vast number of electrical motors, household appliances, and lighting systems.

Many of the major inventions that stimulated industrial output and underlay mass production in these years were largely hidden from public view. Few Americans had heard of the improved technologies that facilitated bottle making and glassmaking, canning, flour milling, match production, and petroleum refining. Fewer still knew much about the refrigerated railcars that enabled Gustavus Swift's company to slaughter beef in Chicago and ship it east or about the Bonsack cigarette-making machine that could roll 120,000 cigarettes a day, replacing sixty skilled handworkers.

The inventions that people did see were ones that changed the patterns of everyday life. Inventions like the sewing machine, mass-produced by the Singer Sewing Machine Company beginning in the 1860s (see Chapter 16); the telephone, developed by Alexander Graham Bell in 1876; and the light bulb, perfected by **Thomas A. Edison** in 1879, eased household drudgery and reshaped social interactions. With the advent of the sewing machine, many women were relieved of the tedium of sewing apparel by hand; inexpensive mass-produced clothing thus led to a considerable expansion in personal wardrobes. The spread of telephones—by 1900 the Bell Telephone Company had installed almost eight hundred thousand in the United States—not only transformed communication but also undermined social conventions for polite behavior that had been premised on face-to-face or written exchanges. The light bulb, by further freeing people from dependence on daylight, made it possible to shop after work.

In the eyes of many, Thomas A. Edison epitomized the inventive impulse and the capacity for creating new consumer products. Born in 1847 in Milan, Ohio, Edison, like Andrew Carnegie, had little formal education and got his start in the telegraphic industry. He also was a born salesman and self-promoter. When he modestly said that "genius is one percent inspiration and ninety-nine percent perspiration," he tacitly accepted the popular identification of himself as an inventing "wizard." Edison, moreover, shared Carnegie's vision of a large, interconnected industrial system resting on a foundation of technological innovation (see Technology and Culture: Electricity).

In his early work, Edison concentrated on the telegraph. His experimentation led to his first major invention, a stock-quotation printer, in 1868. The money earned from the patents on this machine enabled Edison to set up his first "invention factory" in Newark, New Jersey, a research facility that he moved to nearby Menlo Park in 1876. Assembling a staff that included university-trained scientists, Edison boastfully predicted "a minor invention every ten days, and a big one every six months."

Buoyed by the success and popularity of his invention in 1877 of a phonograph, or "sound writer" (*phono*: "sound"; *graph*: "writer"), Edison set out to develop a new filament for incandescent light bulbs. Characteristically, he announced his plans for an electricity-generation process before he perfected his inventions and then worked feverishly, testing hundreds of materials before he found a carbon filament that would glow dependably in a vacuum.

Edison realized that practical electrical lighting had to be part of a complete system containing generators, voltage regulators, electric meters, and insulated wiring and that the system needed to be easy to install and repair. It also had to be cheaper and more convenient than kerosene or natural gas lighting, its main competitors. In 1882, having built this system with the support of banker J. Pierpont Morgan, the Edison Illuminating Company opened a power plant in the heart of New York City's financial district, furnishing lighting for eighty-five buildings.

In the following years, Edison and his researchers pumped out invention after invention, including the mimeograph machine, the microphone, the motion-picture camera and film, and the storage battery. By the time of his death in 1931, he had patented 1,093 inventions and amassed an estate worth more than $6 million. Yet Edison's greatest achievement remained his laboratory at Menlo Park. A model for the industrial research labs later established by Kodak, General Electric, and Du Pont, Edison's laboratory demonstrated that the systematic use of science in support of industrial technology paid large dividends. Invention had become big business.

Specialized Production

Along with inventors, manufacturers of custom and specialized products such as machinery, jewelry, furniture, and women's clothes dramatically expanded economic output. Using skilled labor, these companies crafted one-of-a-kind or small batches of articles that ranged in size from large steam engines and machine tools to silverware, furniture, and custom-made dresses. Keenly attuned to innovations in technology and design, they constantly created new products tailored to the needs of individual buyers.

Although they were vastly different in terms of size and number of employees, Philadelphia's Baldwin Locomotive Works and small dressmaking shops were typical of flexible specialization displayed by small batch processors. Both faced sharp fluctuations in the demand for their products as well as the necessity of employing skilled workers to make small numbers of specialized items. Founded before the Civil War, by the 1890s the Baldwin Locomotive Works employed two thousand workers and produced about nine hundred engines a year. Each machine was custom-designed to meet the needs of its purchaser. Construction was systematized through precision plans for every part of an engine, but standardization was not possible since no single engine could meet the needs of every railroad.

Until the turn of the twentieth century, when ready-to-wear clothes came to dominate the market, most women's apparel was custom produced in small shops run by women proprietors. Unlike the tenement sweatshops that produced men's shirts and pants, dressmakers and milliners (a term derived from fancy goods vendors in sixteenth- and seventeenth-century Milan, Italy) paid good wages to highly skilled seamstresses. The small size of the shops together with the skill of the workers enabled them to shift styles quickly to follow the latest fashions.

Thus, alongside of the increasingly rationalized and bureaucratic big businesses like steel and oil in the late nineteenth century, American productivity was also stimulated by small producers who provided a variety of goods that supplemented the bulk-manufactured staples of everyday life.

Advertising and Marketing

As small and large factories alike spewed out an amazing array of new products, business leaders often discovered that their output exceeded what the market could absorb. This was particularly true in two kinds of businesses—those that manufactured devices for individual use such as sewing machines and farm implements, and those that mass-produced consumer goods such as matches, flour, soap, canned foods, and processed meats. Not surprisingly, these industries were trailblazers in developing advertising and marketing techniques. Strategies for whetting consumer demand and for differentiating one product from another represented a critical component of industrial expansion in the post–Civil War era.

The growth of the flour industry illustrates both the spread of mass production and the emergence of new marketing concepts. In the 1870s, the nation's flour mills adopted the most advanced European manufacturing technologies and installed continuous-process machines that graded, cleaned, hulled, ground, and packaged the product in one rapid operation. These companies, however, soon produced more flour than they could sell. To unload this excess, the mills thought up new product lines such as cake flours and breakfast cereals and sold them using easy-to-remember brand names like Quaker Oats.

Through the use of brand names, trademarks, guarantees, slogans, endorsements, and other gimmicks, manufacturers built demand for their products and won enduring consumer loyalty. Americans bought Ivory Soap, first made in 1879 by Procter and Gamble of Cincinnati, because of the absurdly overprecise but impressive pledge that it was "99 and 44/100ths percent pure." James B. "Buck" Duke's American Tobacco Company used trading cards, circulars, box-top premiums, prizes, testimonials, and scientific endorsements to convert Americans to cigarette smoking.

In the 1880s in the photographic field, George Eastman developed a paper-based photographic film as an alternative to the bulky, fragile glass plates then in use. Manufacturing a cheap camera for the masses, the Kodak, Eastman introduced a system whereby customers returned the one-hundred-exposure film and the camera to his Rochester factory. There, for a charge of ten dollars, the film was developed and printed, the camera reloaded, and everything shipped back. In marketing a new technology, Eastman had revolutionized an industry and democratized a visual medium previously confined to a few.

Economic Growth: Costs and Benefits

By 1900, the chaos of early industrial competition, when thousands of companies had struggled to enter a national market, had given way to the most productive economy in the world, supported by a legion of small, specialized companies and dominated by a few enormous ones. An industrial transformation that had originated in railroading and expanded to steel and petroleum had spread to every nook and cranny of American business and raised the United States to a position of world leadership.

For those who fell by the wayside in this era of spectacular economic growth, the cost could be measured in bankrupted companies and shattered dreams. John D. Rockefeller put things with characteristic bluntness when he said he wanted "only the big ones, only those who have already proved they can do a big business" in the Standard Oil Trust. "As for the others, unfortunately they will have to die."

The cost was high, too, for millions of American workers, immigrant and native-born alike. The vast expansion of new products was built on the backs of an army of laborers who were paid subsistence wages and who could be fired on a moment's no- tice when hard times or new technologies made them expendable.

Industrial growth often devastated the environment as well. Rivers fouled by oil or chemical waste, skies filled with clouds of soot, and a landscape littered with reek- ing garbage and toxic materials bore mute witness to the relentless drive for efficiency and profit.

The vast expansion of economic output brought social benefits as well, in the form of labor-saving products, lower prices, and advances in transportation and communi- cations. The benefits and liabilities sometimes seemed inextricably interconnected. The sewing machine, for example, created thousands of new factory jobs, made avail- able a wider variety of clothing, and eased the lives of millions of housewives. At the same time, it encouraged avaricious entrepreneurs to operate sweatshops in which the immigrant poor—often vulnerable young women—toiled long hours for pitifully low wages (see Chapter 21).

Whatever the final balance sheet of social gains and costs, one thing was clear: the United States had muscled its way onto the world stage as an industrial titan. The am- bition and drive of countless inventors, financiers, managerial innovators, and market- ing wizards had combined to lay the groundwork for a new social and economic order in the twentieth century.

THE NEW SOUTH

The South entered the industrial era far more slowly than the Northeast. As late as 1900, total southern cotton-mill output, for example, remained little more than half that of the mills within a thirty-mile radius of Providence, Rhode Island. Moreover, the South's $509 average per capita income was less than half that of northerners.

The reasons for the South's late economic blossoming are not hard to discern. The Civil War's physical devastation, racism, the scarcity of southern towns and cities, lack of capital, illiteracy, northern control of financial markets and patents, and a low rate of technological innovation crippled efforts by southern business leaders to promote industrialization. Economic progress was also impeded by the myth of the Lost Cause, which, through its nostalgic portrayal of pre–Civil War society, perpetuated an image of the South as traditional and unchanging. As a result, southern industrialization inched forward haltingly and was shaped in distinctive ways.

Obstacles to Economic Development Much of the South's difficulty in industrializing arose from its lack of capital and the devastation of the Civil War. So many southern banks failed during the Civil War that by 1865 the South, with more than a quarter of the nation's population, possessed just 2 percent of its banks.

Federal government policies further restricted the expansion of the southern bank- ing system. The Republican-dominated wartime Congress, which had created a na- tional currency and banking structure, required anyone wishing to start a bank to have fifty thousand dollars in capital. Few southerners could meet this standard.

With banks in short supply, country merchants and storekeepers became bankers by default, lending supplies rather than cash to local farmers in return for a lien, or mortgage, on their crops (see Chapter 16). As farmers sank in debt, they increased their production of cotton and tobacco in an effort to stay afloat, and became trapped on the land. As a result, the labor needed for industrial expansion remained in short supply.

The shift from planting corn to specializing in either cotton or tobacco made small southern farmers particularly vulnerable to the fluctuations of commercial agriculture. When the price of cotton tumbled in national and international markets from eleven cents per pound in 1875 to less than five cents in 1894, well under the cost of production, many southern farmers grew desperate.

The South also continued to be the victim of federal policies designed to aid northern industry. High protective tariffs raised the price of machine technology imported from abroad; the demonetization of silver (see Chapter 20) further limited capital availability; and discriminatory railroad freight rates hiked the expense of shipping finished goods and raw materials.

The South's chronic shortage of funds affected the economy in indirect ways as well, by limiting the resources available for education. During Reconstruction northern philanthropists together with the Freedmen's Bureau, the American Missionary Association, and other relief agencies had begun a modest expansion of public schooling for both blacks and whites. But Georgia and many other southern states operated segregated schools and refused to tax property for school support until 1889. As a result, school attendance remained low, severely limiting the number of educated people able to staff technical and managerial positions in business and industry.

Southern states, like those in the North, often contributed the modest funds they had to war veterans' pensions. In this way, southern state governments built a white patronage system for Confederate veterans and helped reinforce southerners' idealization of the old Confederacy—the South's Lost Cause. As late as 1911, veterans' pensions in Georgia ate up 22 percent of the state's entire budget, leaving little for economic or educational development.

The New South Creed and Southern Industrialization   Despite the limited availability of private capital for investment in industrialization, energetic southern newspaper editors such as **Henry W. Grady** of the *Atlanta Constitution* and Henry Watterson of the *Louisville Courier Journal* championed the doctrine that became known as the New South creed. The South's rich coal and timber resources and cheap labor, they proclaimed in their papers, made it a natural site for industrial development.

The movement to industrialize the South gained momentum in the 1880s. To attract northern capital, southern states offered tax exemptions for new businesses, set up industrial and agricultural expositions, and leased prison convicts to serve as cheap labor. Florida, Texas, and other states gave huge tracts of lands to railroads, which expanded dramatically throughout the South and in turn stimulated the birth of new towns and villages. Other states sold forest and mineral rights on nearly 6 million acres of federal lands to speculators, mostly from the North, who significantly expanded the production of iron, sulfur, coal, and lumber.

Following the lead of their northern counterparts, the southern iron and steel industries expanded as well. Birmingham, Alabama, founded in 1871 in the heart of a region blessed with rich deposits of coal, limestone, and iron ore, grew in less than three decades to a bustling city with noisy railroad yards and roaring blast furnaces. By 1900 it was the nation's largest pig-iron shipper. In these same years, Chattanooga, Tennessee, housed nine furnaces, seventeen foundries, and numerous machine shops.

As large-scale recruiters of black workers, the southern iron and steel mills contributed to the migration of blacks to the cities. By 1900, 20 percent of the southern black population was urban. Many urban blacks toiled as domestics or in similar menial capacities, but others entered the industrial work force. Southern industry reflected the patterns of racial segregation in southern life. Tobacco companies used black workers, particularly women, to clean the tobacco leaves while white women, at a different location, ran the machines that made cigarettes. The burgeoning textile mills were lily-white. In the iron and steel industry, blacks, who comprised 60 percent of the unskilled work force by 1900, had practically no chance of advancement. Nevertheless, in a rare reversal of the usual pattern, southern blacks in the iron and steel industry had a higher skill level and on average earned more than did southern white textile workers.

Black miners were also recruited by the West Virginia coal industry that lured them with free transportation, high wages, and company housing. The coal boom at first forced companies to pay similar wages to blacks and whites, and they initially joined biracial labor unions. But, as a result of the depression of 1893, the unions were destroyed, and workers became increasingly confined to separate jobs.

Segregation, both in the coal industry and elsewhere in the South, while restricting black employment in many ways, opened up new opportunities for black barbers, doctors, and businessmen to work with black customers. Still, in many ways, economic opportunities for blacks remained severely limited. In lumbering, which was the South's largest industry, large numbers of blacks worked in the turpentine industry, collecting sap from trees. In good times, wages could be better than those offered to farm laborers, but during economic downturns workers were laid off or confined to work camps by vagrancy laws and armed guards.

The Southern Mill Economy

Unlike the urban-based southern iron and steel industry, the textile mills that mushroomed in the southern countryside in the 1880s often became catalysts for the formation of new towns and villages. (This same pattern had occurred in rural New England in the 1820s.) In those southern districts that underwent the gradual transition from an agricultural to a mill economy, country ways and values suffused the new industrial workplace.

The cotton-mill economy grew largely in the Piedmont, a beautiful highland country of rolling hills and rushing rivers stretching from central Virginia to northern Georgia and Alabama. The Piedmont had long been the South's backcountry, a land of subsistence farming and limited roads. But postwar railroad construction opened the region to outside markets and sparked a period of intense town building and textile-mill expansion. Between 1880 and 1900 track mileage in North Carolina grew dramatically; the number of towns and villages jumped, quickening the pulse of commerce; and the construction of textile mills accelerated. Between 1860 and 1900 cotton-mill capacity shot up 1,400 percent, and by 1920 the South was the nation's leading textile-mill center. Augusta, Georgia, with 2,800 mill workers, became known as the Lowell of the South, named after the mill town in Massachusetts where industrialization had flourished earlier. The expansion of the textile industry nurtured promoters' visions of a new, more prosperous, industrialized South.

Sharecroppers and tenant farmers at first hailed the new cotton mills as a way out of rural poverty. But appearances were deceptive. The chief cotton-mill promoters

Pig Iron Scene, Birmingham, Alabama, by Charles Graham, **1886** *Although Birmingham, Alabama's, extensive foundries turned out inexpensive iron ingots, the northern owners forced factory operators to price their products at the same rate as ingots produced in Pittsburgh.*

were drawn from the same ranks of merchants, lawyers, doctors, and bankers who had profited from the commercialization of southern agriculture (and from the misfortunes of poor black and white tenant farmers and sharecroppers trapped in the new system). R. R. Haynes, a planter and merchant from North Carolina, was typical of the new entrepreneurs. Starting out as a storekeeper, he formed a company in 1884 to finance construction of the Henrietta Mills. By 1913, Haynes owned not only one of the South's largest mills but also banks, railroads, lumber businesses, and general stores.

To run the mills, factory owners commonly hired poor whites from impoverished nearby farms. They promised that textile work would free these farming families from poverty and instill in them the virtues of punctuality and industrial discipline. The reality was different. Cotton-mill entrepreneurs shamelessly exploited their workers, paying just seven to eleven cents an hour, 30 percent to 50 percent less than what comparable mill workers in New England were paid.

The mills dominated most Piedmont textile communities. The mill operator not only built and owned the workers' housing and the company store but also supported the village church, financed the local elementary school, and pried into the morals and behavior of the mill hands. To prevent workers from moving from one mill to another, the mill owner usually paid them just once a month, often in scrip—a certificate redeemable only in goods from the company store. Since few families had enough money to get through a month, they often overspent and fell behind in their payments. The charges were deducted from workers' wages the following month. In this way, the mill drew workers and their families into a cycle of indebtedness very much like that faced by sharecroppers and tenant farmers.

Since farm families shared farm responsibilities together, southern mill superintendents accommodated themselves to local customs and hired whole families, including the children. Mothers commonly brought babies into the mills and kept them in baskets nearby while tending their machines. Little children sometimes learned to operate the machines themselves. Ties among the workers were strong. One employee put it simply: "The mill community was a close bunch of people . . . like one big family. We just loved one another."

To help make ends meet, mill workers kept their own garden patches and raised chickens, cows, and pigs. Southern mill hands thus brought communal farm values, long associated with large farm families and nurtured through cooperative planting and harvesting, into the mills themselves. Although they had to adapt to machine-paced work and received barely enough pay to live on, the working poor in the mill districts, like their prewar counterparts in the North, eased the shift from rural to village-industrial life by embracing a cooperative country ethic.

As northern cotton mills did before the Civil War, southern textile companies exploited the cheap rural labor around them, settling transplanted farm people in paternalistic company-run villages. Using these tactics, the industry underwent a period of steady growth.

The Southern Industrial Lag

Industrialization occurred on a smaller scale and at a slower rate in the South than in the North and also depended far more on outside financing, technology, and expertise. The late-nineteenth-century southern economy remained essentially in a colonial status, subject to domination by northern industries and financial syndicates. U.S. Steel, for example, controlled the foundries in Birmingham, and in 1900 its executives began to price Birmingham steel according to the "Pittsburgh plus" formula based on the price of Pittsburgh steel, plus the freight costs of shipping from Pittsburgh. As a result, southerners paid higher prices for steel than did northerners, despite the cheaper production costs.

An array of factors thus combined to retard industrialization in the South. Banking regulations requiring large reserves, scarce capital, absentee ownership, unfavorable railroad rates, cautious state governments, wartime debts, lack of industrial experience, a segregated labor force, discrimination against blacks, and control by profit-hungry northern enterprises all hampered the region's economic development. Dragged down by a poorly educated white population and by a largely unskilled black population, southern industry languished. While it did grow considerably, not until after the turn of the century did southern industry undergo the restructuring and consolidation that had occurred in northern business enterprise two decades earlier.

As in the North, industrialization brought significant environmental damage, including polluted rivers and streams, decimated forests, grimy coal-mining towns, and soot-infested steel-making cities. Although Henry Grady's vision of a New South may have inspired many southerners to work toward industrialization, economic growth in the South, limited as it was by outside forces, progressed in its own distinctly regional way.

FACTORIES AND THE WORK FORCE

Industrialization proceeded unevenly nationwide, and most late-nineteenth-century Americans still worked in small shops. But as the century unfolded, large factories with armies of workers sprang onto the industrial scene in more and more locales. The pattern of change was evident. Between 1860 and 1900, the number of industrial workers jumped from 885,000 to 3.2 million, and the trend toward large-scale production became unmistakable.

From Workshop to Factory
The transition to a factory economy came not as an earthquake but rather as a series of seismic jolts varying in strength and duration. Whether they occurred quickly or slowly, however, the changes in factory production had a profound impact on artisans and unskilled laborers alike, for they involved a fundamental restructuring of work habits and a new emphasis on workplace discipline. The impact of these changes can be seen by examining the boot and shoe industry. As late as the 1840s, almost every shoe was custom-made by a skilled artisan who worked in a small, independent shop. Shoemakers were aristocrats in the world of labor. Taught in an apprentice system, they took pride in their work and controlled the quality of their products. In some cases they hired and paid their own helpers.

A distinctive working-class culture subdivided along ethnic lines evolved among these shoemakers. Foreign-born English, German, and Irish workers set up ethnic trade organizations and joined affiliated benevolent associations. Bound together by religious and ethnic ties, they observed weddings and funerals according to old-country traditions and relaxed together at the local saloon after work. Living in neighborhood tenements and boardinghouses, they developed a strong community pride and helped one another weather accidents or sicknesses.

As early as the 1850s, even before the widespread use of machinery, changes in the ready-made shoe trade had eroded the status of skilled labor. The manufacturing process was broken down into a sequence of repetitive, easily mastered tasks. Thus instead of crafting a pair of shoes from start to finish, each team member specialized in only one part of the process, such as attaching the heel or polishing the leather.

In the 1880s, shoe factories became larger and more mechanized, and traditional skills largely vanished. Sophisticated sewing and buffing machines allowed shoe companies to replace skilled operatives with lower-paid, less-skilled women and children. By 1890 women made up more than 35 percent of the work force. In many other industries, skilled artisans found their responsibilities and relation to the production process changing. With the exception of some skilled construction crafts such as carpentry and bricklaying, artisans no longer participated in the production process as a whole. Like the laborer whose machine nailed heels on 4,800 shoes a day, even "skilled" workers in the new factories specializing in consumer goods found themselves performing numbingly repetitive tasks.

The Hardships of Industrial Labor
The expansion of the factory system spawned an unprecedented demand for unskilled labor. By the 1880s nearly one-third of the 750,000 workers employed in the railroad and steel industries, for example, were common laborers.

In the construction trades and the garment-making industries, the services of unskilled laborers were procured under the so-called contract system. To avoid the problems of hiring, managing, and firing their own workers, large companies negotiated an agreement with a subcontractor who took responsibility for employee relations. A foreman or boss employed by the subcontractor supervised gangs of unskilled day laborers. These common workers were seasonal help, hired in times of need and laid off in slack periods. The steel industry employed them to shovel ore in the yards and to move ingots inside the mills. The foremen drove the gangs hard; in the Pittsburgh area, the workers called the foremen "pushers."

Notoriously transient, unskilled laborers drifted from city to city and from industry to industry. In the late 1870s unskilled laborers earned $1.30 a day, while bricklayers and blacksmiths earned more than $3. Only unskilled southern mill workers, whose wages averaged a meager eighty-four cents a day, earned less.

Unskilled and skilled workers alike not only worked up to twelve-hour shifts but also faced grave hazards to their health and safety. The alarming incidence of industrial accidents stemmed from a variety of circumstances, including dangerous factory conditions, workers' inexperience, and the rapid pace of the production process. Author Hamlin Garland described the perilous environment of a steel-rail mill at Carnegie's Homestead Steel Works in Pittsburgh. One steelworker recalled that on his first day at the mill, "I looked up and a big train carrying a big vessel with fire was making towards me. I stood numb, afraid to move, until a man came to me and led me out of the mill." Under such conditions the accident rate in the steel mills was extremely high.

In the coal mines and cotton mills, child laborers typically entered the work force at age eight or nine. These youngsters not only faced the same environmental hazards as adults but were especially prone to injury. In the cotton mills, children could be injured by the unprotected pulley belts that powered the machines. They and the adults who toiled in the mills, constantly breathing in cotton dust, fell ill with brown lung, another crippling disease. In the coal industry, children were commonly employed as slate pickers. Sitting at a chute beneath the breakers that crushed the coal, they removed pieces of slate and other impurities. The cloud of coal dust that swirled around them gave them black lung disease—a disorder that leads to emphysema and heart failure.

For adult workers, the railroad industry was one of the most perilous. In 1889, the first year that the Interstate Commerce Commission compiled reliable statistics, almost two thousand rail workers were killed on the job and more than twenty thousand injured.

Disabled workers and widows received minimal financial aid from employers. Until the 1890s, the courts considered employer negligence to be one of the normal risks borne by employees. Railroad and factory owners fought the adoption of state safety and health standards on the grounds that the cost would be excessive. For sickness and accident benefits, workers joined fraternal organizations and ethnic clubs, part of whose monthly dues benefited those in need. But in most cases, the amounts set aside were too low to be of much help. When a worker was killed or maimed in an accident, the family had to rely on relatives or friends for support.

Immigrant Labor   As we shall see in more detail in Chapter 19, factory owners turned to unskilled immigrant workers for the muscle they needed. In Philadelphia, where native-born Americans and recent German immigrants dominated the highly skilled metalworking trades, Irish newcomers remained mired in unskilled horse-carting and construction occupations until the 1890s, when the "new immigrants" from southern and eastern Europe replaced them. Poverty-stricken French

Textile Workers *Young children like this one were often used in the textile mills because their small fingers could tie together broken threads more easily than those of adults.*

Canadians filled the most menial positions in northeastern textile mills. On the West Coast, Chinese immigrants performed the dirtiest and most physically demanding jobs in mining, canning, and railroad construction.

Writing home in the 1890s, eastern European immigrants described the hazardous and draining work in the steel mills. "Wherever the heat is most insupportable, the flames most scorching, the smoke and soot most choking, there we are certain to find compatriots bent and wasted in toil," reported one Hungarian. Yet those immigrants disposed to live frugally in a boardinghouse and to work an eighty-four-hour week could save fifteen dollars a month, far more than they could have earned in their homeland.

Although most immigrants worked hard, few adjusted easily to the fast pace of the factory. Peasants from southern and eastern Europe found it difficult to abandon their seasonal work habits for factory schedules. Factory operations were relentless, dictated by the unvarying speed of the machines. A brochure used by the International Harvester Corporation to teach English to its Polish workers promoted the "proper" values. Lesson 1 read:

I hear the whistle. I must hurry.
I hear the five minute whistle.
It is time to go into the shop.

I take my check from the gate board and hang it
    on the department board.
I change my clothes and get ready to work.
The starting whistle blows.
I eat my lunch.
It is forbidden to eat until then.
The whistle blows at five minutes of starting time.
I get ready to go to work.
I work until the whistle blows to quit.
I leave my place nice and clean.
I put all my clothes in the locker.
I must go home.

As this "lesson" reveals, factory work tied the immigrants to a rigid timetable very different from the pace of farm life.

When immigrant workers resisted the tempo of factory work, drank on the job, or took unexcused absences, employers used a variety of tactics to enforce discipline. Some sponsored temperance societies and Sunday schools to teach punctuality and sobriety. Others cut wages and put workers on the piecework system, paying them only for the items produced. Employers sometimes also provided low-cost housing to gain leverage against work stoppages; if workers went on strike, the boss could simply evict them.

In the case of immigrants from southern Europe whose skin colors were often darker than northern Europeans', employers asserted that the workers were nonwhite and thus did not deserve the same compensation as native-born Americans. Because the concept of "whiteness" in the United States bestowed a sense of privilege and the automatic extension of the rights of citizenship, Irish, Greek, Italian, Jewish, and a host of other immigrants, although of the Caucasian race, were also considered nonwhite. Rather than being a fixed category based on biological differences, the concept of race was thus used to justify the harsh treatment of foreign-born labor.

Women and Work in Industrial America

Women's work experiences, like those of men, were shaped by marital status, social class, and race. Upper-class white married women widely accepted an ideology of "separate spheres" (see Chapter 19) and remained at home, raised children, and looked after the household. The well-to-do hired maids and cooks to ease their burdens.

Working-class married women, in contrast, not only lacked such assistance but also often had to contribute to the financial support of the family. In fact, working for wages at home by sewing, button-making, taking in boarders, or doing laundry had predated industrialization. In the late nineteenth century, unscrupulous urban entrepreneurs exploited this captive work force. Cigar manufacturers would buy or lease a tenement and require their twenty families to live and work there. In the clothing industry, manufacturers hired out finishing tasks to lower-class married women and their children, who labored long hours in crowded apartments.

Young, working-class single women often viewed factory work as an opportunity. In 1870, 13 percent of all women worked outside the home, the majority as cooks, maids, cleaning ladies, and laundresses. But most working women intensely disliked the long hours, low pay, and social stigma of being a "servant." When jobs in industry expanded in the last quarter of the century, growing numbers of single white women abandoned domestic employment for better-paying work in the textile, food-processing, and garment industries. Discrimination barred black working women from following this path. Between 1870 and 1900, the number of women of all races working outside the home nearly tripled. By the turn of the century, women made up 17 percent of the country's labor force.

A variety of factors propelled the rise in the employment of single women. Changes in agriculture prompted many young farmwomen to seek employment in the industrial sector (see Chapter 19), and immigrant parents often sent their daughters to the factories to supplement meager family incomes. Plant managers welcomed young immigrant women as a ready source of inexpensive unskilled labor. But factory owners assumed that many of these women would marry within a short time. They treated them as temporary help and kept their wages low. In 1890, young women operating sewing machines earned as little as four dollars for seventy hours of work while their male counterparts made eight.

Despite their paltry wages, long hours, and often unpleasant working conditions, many young women relished earning their own income and joined the work force in increasing numbers. Although the financial support that these working women contributed to their families was significant, few working women were paid enough to provide homes for themselves. Rather than fostering their independence, industrial work tied them more deeply to a family economy that depended on their earnings.

When the typewriter and the telephone came into general use in the 1890s, office work provided new employment opportunities, and women with high school educations moved into clerical and secretarial jobs earlier filled by men. They were attracted by the clean, safe working conditions and relatively good pay. First-rate typists could earn six to eight dollars a week, which compared favorably with factory wages. Even though women were excluded from managerial positions, office work carried higher prestige and was generally steadier than work in the factory or shop.

Despite the growing number of women workers, the late-nineteenth-century popular press portrayed women's work outside the home as temporary. Few people even considered the possibility that a woman could attain local or even national prominence in the emerging corporate order.

Hard Work and the Gospel of Success Although women were generally excluded from the equation, influential opinion molders in these years preached that any man could achieve success in the new industrial era. In *Ragged Dick* (1867) and scores of later tales, **Horatio Alger,** a Unitarian minister turned dime novelist, recounted the adventures of poor but honest lads who rose through initiative and self-discipline. In his stories shoeshine boys stopped runaway horses and were rewarded by rich benefactors who gave them a start in business. The career of Andrew Carnegie was often offered as proof that the United States remained the land of opportunity and "rags to riches."

Some critics did not accept this belief. In an 1871 essay, Mark Twain chided the public for its naïveté and suggested that business success was more likely to come to those who lied and cheated. In testimony given in 1883 before a Senate committee investigating labor conditions, a New Yorker named Thomas B. McGuire dolefully re-counted how he had been forced out of the horse-cart business by larger, better-financed concerns. Declared McGuire, "I live in a tenement house, three stories up, where the water comes in through the roof, and I cannot better myself. My children will have to go to work before they are able to work. Why? Simply because this present sys-tem . . . is all for the privileged classes, nothing for the man who produces the wealth." Only with starting capital of ten thousand dollars—then a large sum—said McGuire, could the independent entrepreneur hope to compete with the large companies.

What are the facts? Carnegie's rise from abject poverty to colossal wealth was the rare exception, as studies of nearly two hundred of the largest corporations reveal. Ninety-five percent of the industrial leaders came from middle- and upper-class back-grounds. However, even if skilled immigrants and native-born working-class Ameri-cans had little chance to move into management in the largest corporations, they did have a chance to rise to the top in small companies. Although only a few reaped im-mense fortunes, many attained substantial incomes.

The different fates of immigrant workers in San Francisco show the possibilities and perils of moving up within the working class. In the 1860s the Irish-born Donahue brothers grew wealthy from the Union Iron Works they had founded, where six hun-dred men built heavy equipment for the mining industry. In contrast, the nearly fifteen thousand Chinese workers who returned to the city after the Central Pacific's rail line was completed in 1869 were consigned by prejudice to work in cigar, textile, and other light-industry factories. Even successful Chinese entrepreneurs faced discrimination. When a Chinese merchant, Mr. Yung, refused to sell out to the wealthy Charles Crocker, a dry-goods merchant turned railroad entrepreneur who was building a mansion on Nob Hill, Crocker built a thirty-foot-high "spite fence" around Yung's house so that it would be completely sealed from view.

Thus, while some skilled workers became owners of their own companies, the op-portunities for advancement for unskilled immigrant workers were considerably more limited. Some did move to semiskilled or skilled positions. Yet most immigrants, par-ticularly the Irish, Italians, and Chinese, moved far more slowly than the sons of middle- and upper-class Americans who began with greater educational advantages and family financial backing. The upward mobility possible for such unskilled workers was gener-ally mobility within the working class. Immigrants who got ahead in the late nine-teenth century went from rags to respectability, not rags to riches.

One positive economic trend in these years was the rise in real wages, representing gains in actual buying power. Average real wages climbed 31 percent for unskilled workers and 74 percent for skilled workers between 1860 and 1900. Overall gains in purchasing power, however, were often undercut by injuries and unemployment dur-ing slack times or economic slumps. The position of unskilled immigrant laborers was particularly shaky. Even during a prosperous year like 1890, one out of every five nonagricultural workers was unemployed at least one month of the year. During the depressions of the 1870s and 1890s, wage cuts, extended layoffs, and irregular em-ployment pushed those at the bottom of the industrial work force to the brink of starvation.

Thus the overall picture of late-nineteenth-century economic mobility is complex. At the top of the scale, a mere 10 percent of American families owned 73 percent of the nation's wealth in 1890, while less than half of industrial laborers earned more than the five-hundred-dollar poverty line annually. In between the very rich and the very poor, skilled immigrants and small shopkeepers improved their economic position significantly. So although the standard of living for millions of Americans rose, the gap between the poor and the well-off remained a yawning abyss.

LABOR UNIONS AND INDUSTRIAL CONFLICT

Aware that the growth of large corporations gave industrial leaders unprecedented power to control the workplace, labor leaders searched for ways to create broad-based, national organizations that could protect their members. But this drive to create a nationwide labor movement faced many problems. Employers deliberately accentuated ethnic and racial divisions within the work force, including competition between immigrant groups, to hamper unionizing efforts. Skilled craftsworkers, moreover, felt little kinship with low-paid common laborers. Divided into different trades, they often saw little reason to work together. Thus, unionization efforts moved forward slowly and experienced setbacks.

Two groups, the National Labor Union and the Knights of Labor, struggled to build a mass labor movement that would unite skilled and unskilled workers regardless of their specialties. After impressive initial growth, however, both efforts collapsed. Far more effective was the American Federation of Labor (AFL), which represented skilled workers in powerful independent craft unions. The AFL survived and grew, but it represented only a small portion of the total labor force.

With unions weak, labor unrest during economic downturns reached crisis proportions. When pay rates were cut or working conditions became intolerable, laborers walked off the job without union authorization. These actions, called **wildcat strikes,** which were born of desperation, often exploded into violence. The labor crisis of the 1890s, with its strikes and bloodshed, would reshape the legal environment, increase the demand for state regulation, and eventually contribute to a movement for progressive reform.

Organizing
Workers

From the eighteenth century on, skilled workers had organized local trade unions to fight wage reductions and provide benefits for their members in times of illness or accident. In the 1850s some tradesmen had even organized national associations along craft lines. But the effectiveness of these organizations was limited. The challenge that labor leaders faced in the postwar period was how to boost the unions' clout. Some believed that this goal could be achieved by forming one big association that would transcend craft lines and pull in the mass of unskilled workers.

One person inspired by this vision was Philadelphian William H. Sylvis, who in 1863 was elected president of the Iron Molders' International Union, an organization of iron-foundry workers. Strongly built and bearded, Sylvis traveled the country exhorting iron molders to organize. Within a few years, Sylvis had built his union from "a mere pygmy" to a membership of eighty-five hundred.

In 1866, he acted on his dream of a nationwide association that represented all workers and called a convention in Baltimore to form a new organization, the **National Labor Union** (NLU). Reflecting the pre–Civil War idealism, the NLU endorsed the eight-hour-day movement, which insisted that labor deserved eight hours for work,

The Eight-Hour-Day Movement *Striking artisans from more than three hundred companies filled New York streets for weeks in 1872 in a campaign to reduce the workday from ten hours to eight hours. As is evident in this illustration, the eight-hour movement gained additional support from local saloons catering to German immigrants.*

eight hours for sleep, and eight hours for personal affairs. Leaders also called for an end to convict labor, for the establishment of a federal department of labor, and for currency and banking reform. To push wage scales higher, they endorsed immigration restriction, especially of Chinese migrants, whom native-born workers blamed for undercutting prevailing wage levels. The NLU under Sylvis's leadership supported the cause of working women and elected a woman as one of its national officers. It urged black workers to organize as well, though in racially separate unions.

In the winter of 1866–1867, Sylvis's own union became locked in a harrowing strike against the nation's foundry owners. When the strike failed to improve wages, Sylvis turned to national political reform. He invited a number of reformers to the 1868 NLU convention, including woman suffrage advocates Susan B. Anthony and Elizabeth Cady Stanton, who, according to a reporter, made "no mean impression on the bearded delegates." But when Sylvis suddenly died in 1869, the NLU faded quickly. After a brief incarnation in 1872 as the National Labor Reform party, it vanished from the scene.

The dream of a labor movement that combined skilled and unskilled workers lived on in a new organization, the Noble and Holy Order of the **Knights of Labor,** founded in 1869. Led by Uriah H. Stephens, head of the Garment Cutters of Philadelphia, the Knights began as a secret society modeled on the Masonic Order. They welcomed all wage earners or former wage earners; they excluded only bankers, doctors, lawyers, stockbrokers, professional gamblers, and liquor dealers. The Knights demanded equal pay for women, an end to child labor and convict labor, and the cooperative employer-employee ownership of factories, mines, and other businesses. At a time when no federal income tax existed, they called for a progressive tax on all earnings, graduated so that higher-income earners would pay more.

The Knights grew slowly at first. But membership rocketed in the 1880s after Terence V. Powderly replaced Stephens as the organization's head. A young Pennsylvania machinist of Irish-Catholic immigrant origins, Powderly was an unlikely labor leader. He was short and slight, with a blond drooping mustache, elegant attire, and a fastidious, somewhat aloof manner. One journalist expressed surprise at finding such a fashionable man as the leader of "the horny-fisted sons of toil." But Powderly's eloquence, coupled with a series of successes in labor clashes, brought in thousands of new members.

During its growth years in the early 1880s, the Knights of Labor reflected both its idealistic origins and Powderly's collaborative vision. Powderly opposed strikes, which he considered "a relic of barbarism," and organized producer and consumer cooperatives. A teetotaler, he also urged temperance upon the membership. Powderly advocated the admission of blacks into local Knights of Labor assemblies, although he recognized the strength of racism and allowed southern local assemblies to be segregated. Under his leadership the Knights welcomed women members; by 1886 women organizers had recruited thousands of workers, and women made up an estimated 10 percent of the union's membership.

Powderly supported restrictions on immigration and a total ban on Chinese immigration. In the West, fears about competition from low-paid Chinese workers were heightened when California railroad magnate Leland Stanford declared, "[O]pen the door and let everybody come who wants to come . . . until you get enough [immigrants] here to reduce the price of labor to such a point that its cheapness will stop their coming." In 1877, San Francisco workers demonstrating for an eight-hour workday destroyed twenty-five Chinese-run laundries and terrorized the local Chinese population. In 1880 both major party platforms included anti-Chinese immigration plans. Two years later, Congress passed the Chinese Exclusion Act, placing a ten-year moratorium on Chinese immigration. The ban was extended in 1902 and not repealed until 1943.

Although inspired by Powderly's vision of a harmonious and cooperative future, most rank-and-file members of the Knights of Labor strongly disagreed with Powderly's antistrike position. In 1883–1884, local branches of the Knights led a series of spontaneous strikes that gained only reluctant support from the national leadership. In 1885, however, when Jay Gould tried to get rid of the Knights of Labor on his Wabash railroad by firing active union members, Powderly and his executive board instructed all Knights on the Wabash line to walk off the job and those on other lines to refuse to handle Wabash cars. This action crippled the Wabash's operations. To the nation's amazement, Gould met with Powderly and canceled his campaign against the Knights of Labor. "The Wabash victory is with the Knights," declared a St. Louis newspaper; "no such victory has ever before been secured in this or any other country."

With this apparent triumph, membership in the Knights of Labor soared. By 1886, more than seven hundred thousand workers were organized in nearly six thousand locals. Turning to political action that fall, the Knights mounted campaigns in nearly two hundred towns and cities nationwide, electing several mayors and judges (Powderly himself had served as mayor of Scranton since 1878). They secured passage of state laws banning convict labor, and federal laws against the importation of foreign contract labor. Business executives warned that the Knights could cripple the economy and take over the country if they chose.

But the organization's strength soon waned. Workers became disillusioned when a series of unauthorized strikes failed in 1886. By the late 1880s, the Knights of Labor was a shadow of its former self. Nevertheless, the organization had served as a major impetus to the labor movement and had awakened in thousands of workers a sense of group solidarity and potential strength. Powderly, who survived to 1924, always remained proud of his role "in forcing to the forefront the cause of misunderstood and downtrodden humanity."

As the Knights of Labor weakened, another national labor organization, pursuing more immediate and practical goals, was gaining strength. The skilled craft unions had long been uncomfortable with labor organizations like the Knights that welcomed skilled and unskilled alike. They were also concerned that the Knights' broad reform goals would undercut their own commitment to better wages and protecting the interests of their particular crafts. The break came in May 1886 when the craft unions left the Knights of Labor to form the **American Federation of Labor** (AFL).

The AFL replaced the Knights' grand visions with practical tactics aimed at bread-and-butter issues. This philosophy was vigorously pursued by **Samuel Gompers,** the immigrant cigar maker who became head of the AFL in 1886 and led it until his death in 1924. Gompers believed in "trade unionism, pure and simple." For Gompers, higher wages were not simply an end in themselves but were rather the necessary base to enable working-class families to exist decently, with respect and dignity. The stocky, mustachioed labor leader argued that labor, to stand up to the corporations, would have to harness the bargaining power of skilled workers, whom employers could not easily replace, and concentrate on the practical goals of raising wages and reducing hours.

A master tactician, Gompers believed that the trend toward large-scale industrial organization necessitated a comparable degree of organization by labor. He also recognized, however, that the skilled craft unions that made up the AFL retained a strong sense of independence. He knew that he had to persuade craftsworkers from the - various trades to join forces without violating their sense of craft autonomy. Gompers's solution was to organize the AFL as a federation of trade unions, each retaining control of its own members but all linked by an executive council that coordinated strategy during boycotts and strike actions. "We want to make the trade union movement under the AFL as distinct as the billows, yet one as the sea," he told a national convention.

Focusing the federation's efforts on short-term improvements in wages and hours, Gompers at first sidestepped divisive political issues. The new organization's platform did, however, demand an eight-hour workday, employers' liability for workers' injuries, and mine-safety laws. Although women participated in many craft unions, the AFL did little to recruit women workers after 1894 because Gompers and others believed that women workers undercut men's wages. By 1904, under Gompers's careful tutelage, the AFL had grown to more than 1.6 million strong.

Although the unions held up an ideal toward which many might strive, labor organizations before 1900 remained weak. Less than 5 percent of the work force joined union ranks. Split between skilled artisans and common laborers, separated along ethnic and religious lines, and divided over tactics, the unions battled with only occasional effectiveness against the growing power of corporate enterprise. Lacking financial resources, they typically watched from the sidelines when unorganized workers launched wildcat strikes that sometimes turned violent.

Strikes and Labor Violence

Americans had lived with a high level of violence from the nation's beginnings, and the nineteenth century, with its international and civil wars, urban riots, and Indian-white conflict, was no exception. Terrible labor clashes toward the end of the century were part of this continuing pattern, but they nevertheless shocked and dismayed contemporaries. From 1881 to 1905, close to 37,000 strikes erupted, in which nearly 7 million workers participated.

The first major wave of strikes began in 1873 when a Wall Street crash triggered a stock-market panic and a major depression. Six thousand businesses closed the following year, and many more cut wages and laid off workers. Striking Pennsylvania coal miners were fired and evicted from their homes. Tramps roamed the streets in New York and Chicago. The tension turned deadly in 1877 during a wildcat railroad strike. Ignited by a wage reduction on the Baltimore and Ohio Railroad in July, the strike exploded up and down the railroad lines, spreading to New York, Pittsburgh, St. Louis, Kansas City, Chicago, and San Francisco. Rioters in Pittsburgh torched Union Depot and the Pennsylvania Railroad roundhouse. By the time newly installed president Rutherford B. Hayes had called out the troops and quelled the strike two weeks later, nearly one hundred people had died, and two-thirds of the nation's railroads stood idle.

The railroad strike stunned middle-class America. The religious press responded hysterically. "If the club of the policeman, knocking out the brains of the rioter, will answer, then well and good," declared one Congregationalist journal, "[but if not] then bullets and bayonets . . . constitute the one remedy." The same middle-class Americans who worried about Jay Gould and the corporate abuse of power grew terrified of mob violence from the bottom ranks of society.

Employers capitalized on the public hysteria to crack down on labor. Many required their workers to sign "yellow dog" contracts in which they promised not to strike or join a union. Some hired Pinkerton agents, a private police force, to defend their factories and, when necessary, turned to the federal government and the U.S. army to suppress labor unrest.

Although the economy recovered, more strikes and violence followed in the 1880s. On May 1, 1886, 340,000 workers walked off their jobs in support of the campaign for an eight-hour workday. Strikers in Cincinnati virtually shut down the city for nearly a month. Three days later, Chicago police shot and killed four strikers at the McCormick Harvester plant. At a protest rally the next evening in the city's Haymarket Square, someone threw a bomb from a nearby building, killing or fatally wounding seven policemen. In response, the police fired wildly into the crowd and killed four demonstrators.

Public reaction was immediate. Business leaders and middle-class citizens lashed out at labor activists and particularly at the sponsors of the Haymarket meeting, most of whom were associated with a German-language anarchist newspaper that advocated the violent overthrow of capitalism. Eight men were arrested. Although no evidence connected them directly to the bomb throwing, all were convicted of murder, and four were executed. One committed suicide in prison. In Haymarket's aftermath, still more Americans became convinced that the nation was in the grip of a deadly foreign conspiracy, and animosity toward labor unions intensified.

Confrontations between capital and labor became particularly violent in the West. When the Mine Owners' Protective Association cut wages at work sites along Idaho's Coeur d'Alene River in 1892, the miners, who were skilled in the use of dynamite, blew up a mill and captured the guards sent to defend it. Mine owners responded by mustering the Idaho National Guard to round up more than three hundred men and cripple their union.

Back east that same year, armed conflict broke out during the **Homestead Strike** at the Carnegie Steel Company plant in Homestead, Pennsylvania. To destroy the union, managers had cut wages and locked out the workers. When workers fired on the armed men from the Pinkerton Detective Agency who came to protect the plant, a battle broke out. Seven union members and three Pinkertons died. A week later the governor sent eight thousand National Guardsmen to restore order. The union crushed, the mills resumed full operation a month later.

The most systematic use of troops to smash union power came in 1894 during a strike against the Pullman Palace Car Company. In 1880 George Pullman, a manufacturer of elegant dining, parlor, and sleeping cars for the nation's railroads, had constructed a factory and town, called Pullman, ten miles south of Chicago. The carefully planned community provided solid brick houses for the workers, beautiful parks and playgrounds, and even its own sewage-treatment plant. Pullman also closely policed workers' activities, outlawed saloons, and insisted that his properties turn a profit.

When the depression of 1893 hit, Pullman slashed workers' wages without reducing their rents. In reaction thousands of workers joined the newly formed American Railway Union and went on strike. They were led by a fiery young organizer, **Eugene V. Debs,** who vowed "to strip the mask of hypocrisy from the pretended philanthropist and show him to the world as an oppressor of labor." Union members working for the nation's largest railroads refused to switch Pullman cars, paralyzing rail traffic in and out of Chicago, one of the nation's premier rail hubs.

In response, the General Managers' Association, an organization of top railroad executives, set out to break the union. The General Managers imported strikebreakers from among jobless easterners and asked U.S. attorney general Richard Olney, who sat on the board of directors of three major railroad networks, for a federal injunction (court order) against the strikers for allegedly refusing to move railroad cars carrying U.S. mail.

In fact, union members had volunteered to switch mail cars onto any trains that did not carry Pullman cars, and it was the railroads' managers who were delaying the mail by refusing to send their trains without the full complement of cars. Nevertheless, Olney, supported by President Grover Cleveland and citing the Sherman Anti-Trust Act, secured an injunction against the leaders of the American Railway Union for restraint of commerce. When the union refused to order its members back to work, Debs was arrested, and federal troops poured in. During the ensuing riot, workers burned seven hundred freight cars, thirteen people died, and fifty-three were wounded. By July 18 the strike had been crushed.

By playing upon a popular identification of strikers with anarchism and violence, crafty corporate leaders persuaded state and federal officials to cripple organized labor's ability to bargain with business. When the Supreme Court (in the 1895 case *In re Debs*) upheld Debs's prison sentence and legalized the use of injunctions against labor unions, the judicial system gave business a potent new weapon with which to restrain labor organizers.

Yet organizers persisted. In 1897, the feisty Irish-born Mary Harris Jones, known as Mother Jones, persuaded coal miners in Pennsylvania to join the United Mine Workers of America, a union founded seven years earlier. She staged parades of children, invited workers' wives to stockpile food, and dramatized the importance of militant mothers fighting for their families. Her efforts were successful. Wage reductions were restored because no large companies dominated the industry and the owners needed to restore production.

Despite the achievements of the United Mine Workers, whose members had climbed to 300,000 by 1900, the successive attempts by the National Labor Union, Knights of Labor, American Federation of Labor, and American Railway Union to build a national working-class labor movement achieved only limited success. Aggressive employer associations and conservative state and local officials hamstrung their efforts. In sharp contrast to Great Britain and Germany, where state officials often mediated disputes between labor and capital, federal and state officials in the United States increasingly sided with manufacturers. Ineffective in the political arena, blocked by state officials, divided by ethnic differences, harassed by employers, and frustrated by court decisions, American unions failed to expand their base of support. Post–Civil War labor turmoil had sapped the vitality of organized labor and given it a negative public image that it would not shed until the 1930s.

Social Thinkers Probe for Alternatives

Widespread industrial violence was particularly unsettling when examined in the context of working-class poverty. In 1879, after observing three men rummaging through garbage to find food, the poet and journalist Walt Whitman wrote, "If the United States, like the countries of the Old World, are also to grow vast crops of poor, desperate, dissatisfied, nomadic, miserably-waged populations, such as we see looming upon us of late years . . . , then our republican experiment, notwithstanding all its surface-successes, is at heart an unhealthy failure." Whitman's bleak speculation was part of a general public debate over the social meaning of the new industrial order. At stake was a larger issue: should government become the mechanism for helping the poor and regulating big business?

Defenders of capitalism preached the laissez-faire ("hands-off") argument, insisting that government should never attempt to control business. They buttressed their case by citing Scottish economist Adam Smith, who had argued in *The Wealth of Nations* (1776) that self-interest acted as an "invisible hand" in the marketplace, automatically regulating the supply of and demand for goods and services. In "The Gospel of Wealth," an influential essay published in 1889, Andrew Carnegie justified laissez-faire by applying the evolutionary theories of British social scientist Herbert Spencer to human society. "The law of competition," Carnegie argued, "may be sometimes hard for the individual, [but] it is best for the race, because it insures the survival of the fittest in every department."

Tough-minded Yale professor **William Graham Sumner** shared Carnegie's disapproval of government interference. His combative book *What Social Classes Owe to Each Other* (1883) applied the evolutionary theories of British naturalist Charles Darwin to human society. In an early statement of what became known as **Social Darwinism,** Sumner asserted that inexorable natural laws controlled the social order: "A drunkard in the gutter is just where he ought to be. . . . The law of survival of the fittest was not made by man, and it cannot be abrogated by man. We can only, by interfering with it, produce the survival of the unfittest." The state, declared Sumner, owed its citizens nothing but law, order, and basic political rights.

Sumner's argument did not go unchallenged. In *Dynamic Sociology* (1883), Lester Frank Ward, a geologist, argued that contrary to Sumner's claim, the supposed "laws" of nature could be circumvented by human will. Just as scientists had applied their knowledge to breeding superior livestock, government experts could use the power of the state to regulate big business, protect society's weaker members, and prevent the heedless exploitation of natural resources.

Other social theorists offered more utopian solutions to the problems of poverty and social unrest. Henry George, a self-taught San Francisco newspaper editor and economic theorist, proposed to solve the nation's uneven distribution of wealth through what he called the single tax. In *Progress and Poverty* (1879), he noted that speculators reaped huge profits from the rising price of land that they neither developed nor improved. By taxing this "unearned increment," the government could obtain the funds necessary to ameliorate the misery caused by industrialization. The result would bring the benefits of socialism—a state-controlled economic system that distributed resources according to need—without socialism's great disadvantage, the stifling of individual initiative. George's program was so popular that he lectured around the country and only narrowly missed being elected mayor of New York in 1886.

The vision of a harmonious industrialized society was vividly expressed in the utopian novel *Looking Backward* (1888) by Massachusetts newspaper editor Edward Bellamy. Cast as a glimpse into the future, Bellamy's novel tells of Julian West, who falls asleep in 1888 and awakens in the year 2000 to find a nation without poverty or strife. In this future world, West learns, a completely centralized, state-run economy and a new religion of solidarity have combined to create a society in which everyone works for the common welfare. Bellamy's vision of a conflict-free society where all share equally in industrialization's benefits so inspired middle-class Americans fearful of corporate power and working-class violence that nearly five hundred local Bellamyite organizations, called Nationalist clubs, sprang up to try to turn his dream into reality.

Ward, George, and Bellamy did not deny the benefits of the existing industrial order; they simply sought to humanize it. These utopian reformers envisioned a harmonious society whose members all worked together. Marxist socialists advanced a different view. Elaborated by German philosopher and radical agitator Karl Marx (1818–1883) in *Das Kapital* (1867) and other works, **Marxism** rested on the labor theory of value: a proposition (which Adam Smith had also accepted) that the labor required to produce a commodity was the only true measure of that commodity's value. Any profit made by the capitalist employer was "surplus value" appropriated from the exploited workers. As competition among capitalists increased, Marx predicted, wages would decline to starvation levels, and more and more capitalists would be driven out of business. Society would be divided between a shrinking bourgeoisie (capitalists, merchants, and middle-class professionals) and an impoverished proletariat (the workers). The proletariat would then revolt and seize control of the state and of the economy. Although Marx viewed class struggle as the essence of modern history, his eyes were also fixed on the shining vision of the communist millennium that the revolution would eventually usher in—a classless utopia in which the state would "wither away" and all exploitation would cease. To lead the working class in its showdown with capitalism, Marx and his collaborator Friedrich Engels helped found socialist parties in Europe, whose strength grew steadily, beginning in the 1870s.

Despite Marx's keen interest in the United States, Marxism proved to have little appeal in late-nineteenth-century America other than for a tiny group of primarily German-born immigrants. The Marxist-oriented Socialist Labor party (1877) had attracted only about fifteen hundred members by 1890. More alarming to the public at large was the handful of anarchists, again mostly immigrants, who rejected Marxist discipline and preached the destruction of capitalism, the violent overthrow of the state, and the immediate introduction of a stateless utopia. In 1892 Alexander Berkman, a Russian immigrant anarchist, attempted to assassinate Henry Clay Frick, the manager of Andrew Carnegie's Homestead Steel Works. Entering Frick's office with a pistol, Berkman shot him in the neck and then tried to stab him. A carpenter working in Frick's office overpowered the assailant. Rather than igniting a workers' insurrection that would usher in a new social order as he had hoped, Berkman came away with a long prison sentence. His act confirmed the business stereotype of "labor agitators" as lawless and violent.

CONCLUSION

By 1900 industrialization had propelled the United States into the forefront of the world's major powers, lowered the cost of goods through mass production, generated thousands of jobs, and produced a wide range of new consumer products. Using accounting systems first developed by the railroads and sophisticated new technologies, national corporations had pioneered innovative systems for distributing and marketing their goods. In the steel and oil industries, Andrew Carnegie and John D. Rockefeller had vertically integrated their companies, controlling production from the raw materials to the finished product. Through systematic cost-cutting and ruthless underselling of their competitors, they had gained control of most of their industry and lowered prices.

Despite these advantages, most Americans recognized that industrialization's cost was high. The rise of the giant corporations had been achieved through savage competition, exploited workers, shady business practices, polluted factory sites, and the collapse of an economic order built on craft skills. In the South in particular, the devastation of the Civil War and the control of banking and raw materials by northern capitalists encouraged industrialists to adopt a paternalistic, family-oriented approach in the cotton mills and to pay exceedingly low wages.

Outbursts of labor violence and the ominous phenomenon of urban slums and grinding poverty showed starkly that all was not well in industrial America. Although the Knights of Labor and the American Federation of Labor attempted to organize workers nationally, the labor movement could not control spontaneous wildcat strikes and violence. In response, company owners appealed to government authorities to arrest strikers, obtain court injunctions against union actions, and cripple the ability of labor leaders to expand their organizations.

As a result, Americans remained profoundly ambivalent about the new industrial order. Caught between their desire for the higher standard of living that industrialization made possible and their fears of capitalist power and social chaos, Americans of the 1880s and 1890s sought strategies that would preserve the benefits while alleviating the undesirable social byproducts. Efforts to regulate railroads at the state level and such national measures as the Interstate Commerce Act and the Sherman Anti-Trust Act, as well as the fervor with which the ideas of a utopian theorist like Edward Bellamy were embraced, represented early manifestations of this impulse. In the Progressive Era of the early twentieth century, Americans would redouble their efforts to formulate political and social responses to the nation's economic transformation after the Civil War.

19

Immigration, Urbanization, and Everyday Life, 1860–1900

THE NEW AMERICAN CITY

Nowhere were the changes in everyday life more visible than in cities. During the late nineteenth century, American cities grew spectacularly. Not only on the East Coast but also in the South, cities swelled at an astonishing pace. Between 1870 and 1900, New Orleans's population increased by nearly fifty percent, Buffalo's tripled, and Chicago's increased more than fivefold. By the start of the new century, Philadelphia, New York, and Chicago all had more than a million residents, and 40 percent of all Americans lived in cities. (In the census, cities were defined as having more than twenty-five hundred inhabitants.) In 1900, New York's 3.4 million inhabitants almost equaled the nation's entire 1850 urban population.

This spectacular urban growth, fueled by migration from the countryside and the arrival of nearly 11 million immigrants between 1870 and 1900, created a dynamic new environment for economic development. New urban jobs and markets in turn dramatically stimulated national economic expansion. Like the frontier, the city symbolized opportunity for all comers.

The city's unprecedented scale and diversity threatened traditional expectations about community life and social stability. Rural America had been a place of face-to-face personal relations where most people shared the same likes and dislikes. In contrast, the city was a seething caldron where immigrant groups contended with one another and with native-born Americans for jobs, power, and influence. Moreover, the same rapid growth that energized manufacturing and production strained city services, generated terrible housing and sanitation problems, and accentuated class differences.

Backyard Baseball, Boston, 1906, by Lewis Hyne *Often idealized as a rural pastime, baseball at the turn of the century became immensely popular in cities where professional teams turned the sport into entertainment for the masses.*

Native-born city-dwellers complained about the noise, stench, and congestion of this transformed cityscape. They fretted about the newcomers' squalid tenements, fondness for drink, and strange customs. When native-born reformers set about cleaning up the city, they sought not only to improve the physical environment but also to destroy the distinctive customs that made immigrant culture different from their own. The late nineteenth century thus witnessed an intense struggle to control the city and benefit from its economic and cultural potential. The stakes were high, for America was increasingly becoming an urban nation.

Migrants and Immigrants

The growing concentration of industries in urban settings produced demands for thousands of new workers. The promise of good wages and a broad range of jobs (labeled by historians as "pull factors") drew men and women from the countryside and small towns. So great was the migration from rural areas, especially New England, that some farm communities vanished from the map.

Young farmwomen led the exodus to the cities. With the growing mechanization of farming in the late nineteenth century, farming was increasingly male work. Rising sales of factory-produced goods through nationally distributed mail-order catalogs reduced the need for rural women's labor. So young farmwomen flocked to the cities, where they competed for jobs with immigrant, black, and city-born white women.

From 1860 to 1890, the prospect of a better life also attracted nearly 10 million northern European immigrants to East Coast and midwestern cities. Germans made up the largest group, numbering close to 3 million, followed by nearly 2 million Eng-

CHRONOLOGY, 1860–1900

1865 • Vassar College founded.

1869 • Boss William Marcy Tweed gains control of New York's Tammany Hall political machine.
First intercollegiate football game.

1872 • Anthony Comstock founds New York Society for the Suppression of Vice.

1873 • John Wanamaker opens his Philadelphia department store.

1875 • Smith and Wellesley colleges founded.

1876 • National League of baseball organized.

1880 • William Booth's followers establish an American branch of the Salvation Army.

1881 • Josephine Shaw Lowell founds New York Charity Organization Society (COS).

1884 • Mark Twain, *Huckleberry Finn.*

1885 • Stanford University founded.

1889 • Jane Addams and Ellen Gates Starr open Hull House.

1891 • University of Chicago founded.
Basketball invented at Springfield College, Massachusetts.

1892 • Ellis Island Immigration Center opened.
General Federation of Women's Clubs organized.

1895 • Coney Island amusement parks open in Brooklyn, New York.

1899 • Scott Joplin, "Maple Leaf Rag."
Kate Chopin, *The Awakening.*
Thorstein Veblen, *The Theory of the Leisure Class.*

1900 • Theodore Dreiser, *Sister Carrie.*
National Association of Colored Women's Clubs organized.

1910 • Angel Island Immigration Center opens in San Francisco.

lish, Scottish, and Welsh immigrants and almost 1.5 million Irish. Moreover, by 1900 more than eight hundred thousand French-Canadians had migrated south to work in the New England mills, and close to a million Scandinavian newcomers had put down roots in the rich farmlands of Wisconsin and Minnesota. On the West Coast, despite the Chinese Exclusion Act of 1882 (see Chapter 18), more than eighty-one thousand Chinese remained in California and nearby states in 1900.

In the 1890s, these earlier immigrants from northern and western Europe were joined by swelling numbers of **"new immigrants"**—Italians, Slavs, Greeks, and Jews from southern and eastern Europe, Armenians from the Middle East, and, in Hawaii, Japanese from Asia. In the next three decades, these new immigrants, many from peasant backgrounds, would boost America's foreign-born population by more than 18 million.

The overwhelming majority of immigrants settled in cities in the northeastern and north-central states, with the Irish predominating in New England and the Germans in the Midwest. The effect of their numbers was staggering. In 1890, New York City (including Brooklyn, still a legally separate municipality) contained twice as many Irish as Dublin, as many Germans as Hamburg, half as many Italians as Naples, and 2 1/2 times the Jewish population of Warsaw. That same year four out of five people living in New York had been born abroad or were children of foreign-born parents.

Some recent immigrants had been forced out of their home countries by overpopulation, crop failure, famine, religious persecution, violence, or industrial depression. (Historians call these reasons for immigration "push factors," since they drove immigrants out of their homelands.) Emigration from England, for example, spurted during economic downturns in 1873 and 1883. German peasants, squeezed by overpopulation and frustrated by church reorganizations that they opposed, left in large numbers in the 1880s. Others came voluntarily in search of better opportunities. More than one hundred thousand Japanese laborers, for example, were lured to Hawaii in the 1890s to work on sugar plantations by promises of high wages.

Figure 19.1 The Changing Face of U.S. Immigration, 1860–1930

Between 1865 and 1895, the majority of newcomers to America hailed from northern and western Europe. But the early twentieth century witnessed a surge of immigration from southern and eastern Europe.

MAP 19.1 Percent of Foreign-born Whites and Native Whites of Foreign or Mixed Parentage in Total Population, by Counties, 1910 *Source: D. W. Meinig, The Shaping of America—A Geographical Perspective of 500 Years of History. Yale University Press, Volume 3.*

As this map indicates, new immigrants rarely settled in the South.

Legend:

75% and over
50–75%
35–50%
25–35%
15–25%
10–15%
5–10%
Less than 5%

A large number of immigrants were single young men. Birger Osland, an eighteen-year-old Norwegian, explained his reasons for leaving to a friend: "as I now probably have a foundation upon which I can build my own further education, I have come to feel that the most sensible thing I can do is to emigrate to America." Although significant numbers of young men remained in the United States after they had become successful, large numbers, especially Italians and Chinese, returned home as well.

Although single women were less likely to come on their own, Irish women often did so and sent their earnings back home. Most commonly, wives and children waited in the old country until the family breadwinner had secured a job and saved enough money to pay for their passage to America.

Would-be immigrants first had to travel to a port—Hamburg, Germany, was a major embarkation point—where they boarded a crowded steamship. The cramped ocean journey was noted for its poor food, lack of privacy, and rudimentary sanitary facilities. Immigrants arrived tired, fearful, and in some cases sick.

Further complications awaited the travelers when they reached their destination, most often New York City or San Francisco. Customs officials inspected the newcomers for physical handicaps and contagious diseases. After 1892, those with "loathsome" infections such as leprosy, trachoma (a contagious viral disease of the eye), or sexually transmitted diseases were refused admittance and deported. Immigrants who passed the physical examination then had their names recorded. If a customs inspector had difficulty pronouncing a foreign name, he often Anglicized it. One German Jew became flustered when asked for his name and mumbled, "Schon vergessen [already forgotten]," meaning that he could not recall it. The inspector, who did not understand German, wrote "Sean Ferguson" on the man's roster. In this manner, many immigrants ended up with Americanized names.

In 1855, New York State had established a special facility for admitting immigrants at Castle Garden on the tip of Manhattan Island. Later, when the numbers swelled, the federal government took control and built a new station on **Ellis Island** in New York harbor in 1892. Angel Island in San Francisco Bay on the West Coast served a similar purpose after 1910. At the immigrant processing centers, America's newest residents exchanged foreign currency for U.S. dollars, purchased railroad tickets, and arranged lodgings. In other cities immigrants were hounded by tavernkeepers, peddlers, and porters who tried to exploit them. "When you land in America," wrote one Swedish resident to friends back home, "you will find many who will offer their services, but beware of them because there are so many rascals who make it their business to cheat the immigrants."

Those who arrived with sufficient cash, including many German artisans and Scandinavian farmers, commonly traveled west to Chicago, Milwaukee, and the rolling prairies beyond. Most of the Irish, and later the Italians, who hailed largely from poor rural backgrounds, remained in eastern cities like Boston, New York, and Philadelphia. The Irish and Italians who did go west typically made the trip in stages, moving from job to job on the railroad and canal systems.

Adjusting to an Urban Society

For many immigrants the stress of adjusting to a new life was eased by settling among compatriots who had preceded them. (Historians call this tendency to relocate near friends or relatives from one's original town "chain migration.") If a map of New York City's streets and neighborhoods were colored in by nationality, Jacob Riis observed in 1890, it "would show more stripes than on the skin of a zebra, and more colors than any rainbow." The streets of Manhattan between the West Side Irish neighborhoods and the East Side German neighborhoods teemed with Poles, Hungarians, Russians, Italians, and Chinese.

Late-nineteenth-century social commentators often assumed that each nationality clumped together for reasons of national clannishness. But settlement patterns were far more complex. Most immigrants preferred to live near others not merely from their own country but also from their own village or region. On New York's Lower East Side, for example, Italians divided into many different subgroups: Neapolitans and Calabrians at Mulberry Bend, Genoese on Baxter Street, northern Italians west of Broadway, and Tyrolese Italians on Sixty-ninth Street near the Hudson River.

Some immigrant groups adjusted more easily than others. Skilled workers and those familiar with Anglo-American customs had relatively few problems. English-speaking immigrants from the British Isles, particularly those from mill, mining, and manufacturing districts, found comparable work and encountered relatively little discrimination. Ethnic groups that formed a substantial percentage of a city's population also had a major advantage. The Irish, for example, who by the 1880s made up nearly 16 percent of New York's population, 8 percent of Chicago's, and 17 percent of Boston's, facilitated Irish immigrants' entry into the American mainstream by dominating Democratic Party politics and controlling the hierarchy of the Catholic church in all three cities. Because of their success, upwardly mobile Irish became known as "lace curtain" Irish, a reference to their adoption of middle-class ideals.

Ironically, domination of urban institutions by members of larger immigrant groups often made adjustment to American society more difficult for members of smaller groups. Germans and other well-organized and skilled immigrants tended to exclude skilled newcomers from desirable jobs. English and German dominance of the building trades, for example, enabled those nationalities to limit the numbers of Italians hired.

The diversity of immigrants, even those from the same country, was remarkable. Nevertheless, the experience of being labeled a foreigner and of being discriminated against helped create a new common ethnic identity for many groups. Immigrants from the same home country forged a new sense of ethnic distinctiveness as Irish-American, German-American, or Jewish-American that helped them compete for political power and eventually assimilate into mainstream society.

Not all immigrants intended to remain in the United States. Young Chinese and Italian men often worked to save enough money to return home and buy a business. Expecting only a brief stay, they made little effort to learn English or understand American customs. Of the Italians who immigrated to New York before 1914, nearly 50 percent went back to Italy. Although the rate of return migration was greatest among Chinese and Italians, significant numbers of other nationalities eventually returned to their homelands as well.

Various factors thus influenced the ability of immigrants to adapt to urban society in America. Nevertheless, as the number of foreigners in U.S. cities ballooned toward the turn of the century, all immigrant groups faced increasing hostility from white native-born Americans who not only disliked the newcomers' social customs but also worried about their growing influence. Fearing the loss of the privileges and status that were associated with their white skin color, native-born whites often stigmatized immigrants as racially different and inferior. Only gradually, and with much effort, did Irish, Jews, Slavs, and Italians come to be considered "white."

Slums and Ghettos   Every major city had its share of rundown, overcrowded slum neighborhoods. Generally clustered within walking distance of manufacturing districts, slums developed when landlords subdivided long, narrow buildings with few windows, called tenements, and packed in too many residents. The poorer the renters, the worse the slum. Slums became ghettos when laws, prejudice, and community pressure prevented the tenement inhabitants from renting elsewhere. During the 1890s Italians in New York, blacks in Philadelphia and Chicago, Mexican-Americans in Los Angeles, and Chinese in San Francisco increasingly became locked in segregated ghettos.

Life in the slums was particularly difficult for children. Juvenile diseases such as whooping cough (pertussis), measles, and scarlet fever took a fearful toll, and infant mortality was high. In one immigrant ward in Chicago in 1900, 20 percent of infants died in their first year of life.

Since tenements often bordered industrial districts, residents had to put up with the noise, pollution, and foul odors of tanneries, foundries, factories, and packing houses. Because most factories used coal-fired steam engines as their energy source, and because coal was also the preferred fuel for heating apartment houses and businesses, vast quantities of soot and coal dust drifted skyward daily.

Most immigrants stayed in the shabbiest tenements only until they could afford better housing. Blacks, in contrast, were trapped in segregated districts. Driven out of the skilled trades and excluded from most factory work, blacks took menial jobs whose low pay left them little income for housing (see Chapter 18). Racist city-dwellers used high rents, real-estate covenants (agreements not to rent or sell to blacks), and neighborhood pressure to exclude them from areas inhabited by whites. Because the numbers of northern urban blacks in 1890 remained relatively small—for example, they composed only 1.2 percent of Cleveland's population and 1.3 percent of Chicago's—they could not overcome whites' concerted campaigns to shut them out. Instead, wealthy black entrepreneurs established their own churches and charitable organizations in the black neighborhoods where they lived.

Fashionable Avenues and Suburbs   As remains true today, the same cities that harbored slums, filth, suffering, and violence also boasted of neighborhoods of dazzling opulence with the latest lighting and plumbing technologies (see Technology and Culture: Flush Toilets and the Invention of the Nineteenth-Century Bathroom). John D. Rockefeller and Jay Gould lived near Fifth Avenue in New York; other wealthy Americans lived on Commonwealth Avenue in Boston, Euclid Avenue in Cleveland, and Summit Avenue in St. Paul. In the 1870s and 1880s, wealthy city-dwellers began moving to new suburbs. Promoters of the suburban ideal contrasted the rolling lawns and stately houses on the city's periphery with the teeming streets, noisy saloons, and mounds of garbage and horse excrement downtown. Soon, many major cities could boast of their own stylish suburbs: Haverford, Ardmore, and Bryn Mawr outside Philadelphia; Brookline near Boston; and Shaker Heights near Cleveland.

Flush Toilets and the Invention
of the Nineteenth-Century Bathroom

The development of a system of indoor plumbing was typical of the technological breakthroughs that simplified everyday life in the late nineteenth century. In the 1860s, only about 5 percent of American houses had running water. Most Americans used chamber pots or outhouses that emptied into slimy, smelly cesspools. Two decades later, indoor plumbing standards had been established in most major U.S. cities, and wealthier urban Americans used flush toilets connected to municipal sewer systems.

The driving force for change came from outbreaks of cholera, typhoid, and yellow fever, diseases spread by polluted water, that periodically terrorized American cities. Building upon the discovery of germs by Louis Pasteur and Robert Koch, sanitary reformers established stringent metropolitan health laws, created state boards of health, and mandated the licensing of plumbers and the inspection of their work. By the turn of the century, George E. Waring, Jr., a prominent sanitary engineer, could confidently declare that "Plumbing, as we know it, is essentially and almost exclusively an American Institution."

The decision to adopt a water-based system for the removal of human wastes depended on a series of inventions. First, municipal water systems had to be built with reservoirs, pumps, and water towers to provide water to the pipes that supplied buildings. A sewage system of interconnected pipes was also necessary to remove and process wastes. Machines to manufacture lead, cast-iron, and glazed stoneware pipes had to be created,

as did a uniform system of pipe threads and melted lead joints to create a reliable standardized system for connecting them. Finally, a porcelain toilet with a built-in gas trap was needed because the bacteria in feces produce methane or sewer gas. (A trap is a U-shaped joint that uses the water at the low part of the U to prevent gas from seeping back into the bathroom. The gas is then vented through a pipe in the roof.)

Despite its usefulness, the new technology was not rapidly adopted. In 1890, only 24 percent of American dwellings had running water. As late as 1897, over 90 percent of the families in tenements had no baths and had to wash in hallway sinks or courtyard hydrants. By 1920, 80 percent of American houses, particularly those in rural areas, still lacked indoor flush toilets. The reason was simple: indoor plumbing was expensive and depended on the availability of water and sewer systems. Adding indoor plumbing increased the price of a new house by 20 percent.

Advertisers did their best to increase demand. They skillfully used the findings of science to advocate new standards of cleanliness or "hygiene," as it was called, which they associated with upper-class principles of respectability and decorum. Bathing and washing one's hands were touted as symbols of upper-class refinement.

Indoor plumbing not only reinforced higher standards for personal hygiene; it also enmeshed the homeowner in a web of local and state regulations. As sewage and water systems expanded to cover larger constituencies, political control moved from local to state and sometimes national arenas. Once largely independent, the homeowner now had to deal with water and power companies that often functioned regionally.

The adoption of strict sanitation systems and the use of indoor plumbing did achieve their intended result: they dramatically reduced the spread of disease. But the advances had unintended consequences. Indoor plumbing encouraged the phenomenal waste of water. A single faulty toilet could easily leak a hundred gallons of water a day. Not until the

1990s with the development of new low-water-usage toilets, which could save between 18,000 and 26,400 gallons of water a year, would new standards be established to reduce the use of water, an increasingly precious natural resource.

Question for Analysis

- Why does the successful introduction of new technologies often involve a system of inventions rather than a single invention?

Middle-class city-dwellers followed the precedents set by the wealthy. Skilled artisans, shopkeepers, clerks, accountants, and sales personnel moved either to new developments at the city's edge or to outlying suburban communities (although those at the lower fringe of the middle class typically rented apartments in neighborhoods closer to the city center). Lawyers, doctors, small businessmen, and other professionals moved farther out along the main thoroughfares served by the street railway, where they purchased homes on large lots. By the twentieth century, this process would result in suburban sprawl.

In time, a pattern of informal residential segregation by income took shape in the cities and suburbs. Built up for families of a particular income level, certain neighborhoods and suburbs developed remarkably similar standards for lot size and house design. (Two-story houses with front porches, set back thirty feet from the sidewalk, became the norm in many neighborhoods.) Commuters who rode the new street railways out from the city center could identify the social class of the suburban dwellers along the way as readily as a geologist might distinguish different strata on a washed-out riverbank.

By 1900, whirring trolley cars and hissing steam-powered trains had burst the boundaries of the compact midcentury city. As they expanded, cities often annexed contingent suburbs. Within this enlarged city, sharp dissimilarities in building height and neighborhood quality set off business sectors from fashionable residential avenues and differentiated squalid manufacturing districts from parklike suburban subdivisions. Musing about urban America in 1902, James F. Muirhead, a popular Scottish guidebook author, wrote that New York and other U.S. cities reminded him of "a lady in a ball costume, with diamonds in her ears, and her toes out at her boots." To Muirhead, urban America had become a "land of contrasts" in which the spatial separations of various social groups and the increasingly dissimilar living conditions for rich and poor had heightened ethnic, racial, and class divisions. Along with the physical change in American cities, in short, had come a new awareness of class and cultural disparities.

MIDDLE- AND UPPER-CLASS SOCIETY AND CULTURE

Spared the struggle for survival that confronted most Americans after the Civil War, society's middle and upper ranks faced a different challenge: how to rationalize their enjoyment of the products of the emerging consumer society. To justify the position of society's wealthier members, ministers such as Brooklyn preacher Henry Ward Beecher and advice-book writers appealed to **Victorian morality,** a set of social ideas embraced by the privileged classes of England and America during the long reign (1837–1901) of Britain's Queen Victoria.

E. L. Godkin, the editor of *The Nation,* Phillips Brooks, minister to Boston's Trinity Church, and other proponents of Victorian morality argued that the financial success of the middle and upper classes was linked to their superior talent, intelligence, morality, and self-control. They also extended the antebellum ideal of separate spheres by arguing that women were the driving force for moral improvement. While men were expected to engage in self-disciplined, "manly" dedication to the new industrial order, women would provide the gentle, elevating influence that would lead society in its upward march. While Beecher, Godkin, and others defended the superiority of America's middle and upper classes, a network of institutions, from elegant department stores and hotels to elite colleges and universities, reinforced the privileged position of these groups.

Manners and Morals

The Victorian world view, which first emerged in the 1830s and 1840s, rested on a number of assumptions (see Chapter 8). One was that human nature was malleable: people could improve themselves. Hence, Victorian Americans were intensely moralistic and eager to reform practices they considered evil or undesirable. A second assumption was that work had social value: working hard not only developed self-discipline but also helped advance the progress of the nation. Finally, Victorian Americans stressed the importance of good manners and the cultivation of literature and art as marks of a truly civilized society. Although these genteel assumptions were sometimes ignored, they were held up as universal standards.

Before the Civil War, reformers such as Henry Ward Beecher had energized the crusades to abolish slavery and alcoholism by appealing to the ethical standards of Victorian morality. (Both slavery and intemperance threatened feminine virtue and family life.) After the war, Beecher and other preachers became less interested in social reform and more preoccupied with the importance of manners and social protocol. Following their advice, middle- and upper-class families in the 1870s and 1880s increasingly defined their own social standing in terms not only of income but also of behavior. Good manners, especially a knowledge of dining and entertaining etiquette, and good posture became important marks of status.

In her popular advice book *The American Woman's Home* (1869), Catharine Beecher (the sister of Henry Ward Beecher) displayed the typical Victorian self-consciousness about proper manners. The following dinner-table behaviors, she said, should be avoided by those of "good breeding":

> Reaching over another person's plate; standing up to reach distant articles, instead
> of asking to have them passed; . . . using the table-cloth instead of napkins; eating

fast, and in a noisy manner; putting large pieces in the mouth; . . . [and] picking the teeth at the table.

For Beecher and other molders of manners, meals became important rituals that differentiated the social classes. The elaborate china and silver that wealthy families exclusively possessed also provided telltale clues to a family's level of refinement and sophistication.

The Victorian code—with its emphasis on morals, manners, and proper behavior—thus served to heighten the sense of class differences for the post–Civil War generation. Prominent middle- and upper-class Americans made bold claims about their interest in helping others improve themselves. More often than not, however, their self-righteous, intensely moralistic outlook simply widened the gap that income disparities had already opened.

The Cult of Domesticity

Victorian views on morality and culture, coupled with the need to make decisions about a mountain of domestic products, had a subtle but important effect on middle-class expectations about women's role within the home. From the 1840s on, architects, clergymen, and other promoters of the so-called cult of domesticity had idealized the home as "the woman's sphere." They praised the home as a protected retreat where women could express their maternal gifts, including sensitivity toward children and an aptitude for religion. "The home is the wife's province," asserted one writer; "it is her natural field of labor . . . to govern and direct its interior management."

During the 1880s and 1890s, a new obligation was added: to foster an artistic environment that would nurture her family's cultural improvement. For many Victorian Americans of the comfortable classes, houses became statements of cultural aspiration. Excluded from the world of business and commerce, many middle- and upper-class women devoted considerable time and energy to decorating their homes, seeking to make the home, as one advice book suggested, "a place of repose, a refuge from the excitement and distractions of outside . . . , provided with every attainable means of rest and recreation."

Not all middle-class women pursued this domestic ideal. For some, housework and family responsibilities overwhelmed the concern for artistic accomplishment. For others the artistic ideal was not to their taste. Sixteen-year-old Mary Putnam complained privately to a friend that she played the piano because of "an abstract general idea . . . of a father coming home regularly tired at night (from the plow, I believe the usual legend runs), and being solaced by the brilliant yet touching performance of a sweet only daughter upon the piano." She then confessed that she detested the piano. In the 1880s and 1890s, as middle- and upper-class women sought other outlets for their creative energies in settlement-house work, social reform, and women's club activities, the older domestic ideal began to unravel.

Department Stores

Although Victorian social thought justified the privileged status of the well-to-do, many thrifty people who had grown up in the early nineteenth century found it difficult to accept the new preoccupation with accumulation and display. To lure these consumers, merchandisers in the 1880s stressed the high quality and low cost of the objects they sold, encouraging Americans to loosen their purse strings and enjoy prosperity without reservations. This argument particularly appealed to women who, in order to provide for their families, now had to shop for soap, canned foods, and other products formerly made at home.

A key agent in modifying attitudes about consumption was the **department store.** In the final quarter of the nineteenth century, innovative entrepreneurs led by Rowland H. Macy in New York, John Wanamaker in Philadelphia, and Marshall Field in Chicago built giant department stores that transformed the shopping experience for millions of women who became their most important consumers. The stores attracted these new customers by advertising "rock-bottom" prices and engaging in price wars. To avoid keeping their stock too long, they held giant end-of-the-season sales at drastically marked-down prices.

The major department stores tried to make shopping an exciting activity. Rapid turnover of merchandise created a sense of constant novelty. The mammoth stores themselves were imitation palaces, complete with stained-glass skylights, marble stair-cases, sparkling chandeliers, and plush carpets. The large urban department store func-tioned as a workplace for the lower classes and as a kind of social club for comfortably fixed women. For those who could afford it, shopping became an adventure, a form of entertainment, and a way to affirm their place in society.

The Transformation of Higher Education At a time when relatively few Americans had even a high school education, the upper classes dominated U.S. colleges and universities. In 1900, only 4 percent of the nation's eighteen- to twenty-one-year-olds were enrolled in institutions of higher learning.

Wealthy capitalists gained status and a measure of immortality by endowing colleges and universities. Leland Stanford and his wife, Jane Lathrop Stanford, launched Stan-ford University in 1885 with a bequest of $24 million in memory of their dead son; John D. Rockefeller donated $34 million to the University of Chicago in 1891. Industrialists and businessmen dominated the boards of trustees of most educational institutions.

Not only the classroom experience but also social contacts and athletic activities—especially football—prepared affluent young men for later responsibilities in business and the professions. Adapted by American college students in 1869 from English rugby, football was largely an elite sport. But the game, initially played without pads or hel-mets, was marred by violence. In 1905, eighteen students died of playing-field injuries. Many college presidents dismissed football as a dangerous waste of time and money. In 1873, when the University of Michigan challenged Cornell to a game in Ann Arbor, Cornell's president Andrew D. White huffily telegraphed back, "I will not permit thirty men to travel four hundred miles merely to agitate a bag of wind."

But eager alumni and coaches strongly defended the new sport. Some—among them Henry Lee Higginson, the Civil War veteran and Boston banker who gave Har-vard "Soldiers' Field" stadium as a memorial to those who had died in battle—praised football as a character-building sport. Others, including famed Yale coach Walter Camp, insisted that football could function as a surrogate frontier experience in an in-creasingly urbanized society. By 1900, collegiate football had become a popular fall rit-ual, and team captains were campus heroes.

More than 150 new colleges and universities were founded between 1880 and 1900, and enrollments more than doubled. While wealthy capitalists endowed some institu-tions, others, such as the state universities in the South and Midwest, were financed largely

Chemistry Class, Smith College, 1889 *Thanks to their education in science at colleges and universities, increasing numbers of women in the 1890s became physicians. Nevertheless, most medical schools refused to appoint women doctors to their teaching staffs.*

through public funds generated from public land sales under the Morrill Land Grant Act (1862). Many colleges were also founded and funded by religious denominations.

Following the precedent set by Oberlin College in 1836, coeducational private colleges and public universities in the Midwest enrolled increasing numbers of women. In the East, Columbia, Brown, and Harvard universities admitted women to the affiliated but separate institutions of Barnard (1889), Pembroke (1891), and Radcliffe (1894), respectively. Some colleges—Mount Holyoke (1837), Vassar (1865), Wellesley and Smith (1875), and Bryn Mawr (1884)—were founded solely for women. At these institutions, participation in college organizations, athletics, and dramatics enabled female students to learn traditionally "masculine" strategies for gaining power. The generation of women educated at female institutions in the late nineteenth century developed the self-confidence to break with the Victorian ideal of passive womanhood and to compete with men by displaying strength, aggressiveness, and intelligence—popularly considered male attributes. Nationally, the percentage of colleges admitting women jumped from 30 percent to 71 percent between 1880 and 1900. By the turn of the century, women made up more than one-third of the total college-student population.

On the university level, innovative presidents such as Cornell's Andrew D. White and Harvard's Charles W. Eliot sought to change the focus of higher education. New discoveries in science and medicine sparked the reform. In the 1850s, most physicians had attended medical school for only two sixteen-week terms. They typically received their degrees without ever having visited a hospital or examined a patient. The Civil

War exposed the abysmal state of American medical knowledge. Twice as many soldiers died from infections as from wounds. Doctors were so poorly trained and ignorant about sanitation that they often infected soldiers' injuries when they probed wounds with hands wiped on pus-stained aprons. "The ignorance and general incompetency of the average graduate of American medical schools, at the time when he receives the degree which turns him loose upon the community," wrote Eliot in 1870, "is something horrible to contemplate."

In the 1880s and 1890s, leading medical professors, many of whom had studied in France and Germany, began restructuring American medical education. Using the experimental method developed by German scientists, they insisted that all medical students be trained in biology, chemistry, and physics, including working in a laboratory. Although medical school reform improved health care in some areas, it also effectively shut out African-American and poor women who could not afford the tuition. By 1900, graduate medical education had been placed on a firm professional foundation. New educational and professional standards, similarly, were established for architects, engineers, and lawyers.

These changes were part of a larger transformation in higher education, the rise of a new kind of institution, the **research university.** Unlike the best of the mid-nineteenth-century colleges, which focused on teaching Latin and Greek, theology, logic, and mathematics, the new research universities offered courses in a wide variety of subject areas, established professional schools, and encouraged faculty members to pursue basic research. At Cornell University, President Andrew D. White's objective was to create an environment "where any person can find instruction in any study." At Cornell, the University of Wisconsin at Madison, Johns Hopkins, Harvard, and other institutions, this new conception of higher education laid the groundwork for the central role that America's universities would play in the intellectual, cultural, and scientific life of the twentieth century.

WORKING-CLASS POLITICS AND REFORM

The contrast between the affluent world of the college-educated middle and upper classes and the gritty lives of the working class was most graphically on display in the nation's growing urban centers, where immigrant newcomers reshaped political and social institutions to meet their own needs. If fancy department stores and elegant hotels furnished new social spaces for the middle and upper classes, saloons became the poor man's club, and dance halls became single women's home away from home. While the rich and the wellborn looked suspiciously at lower-class recreational activities and sought to force the poor to change their ways, working-class Americans, the immigrant newcomers in particular, fought to preserve their own distinctive way of life. Indeed, the late nineteenth century witnessed an ongoing battle to eradicate social drinking, reform "boss" politics, and curb lower-class recreational activities.

Political Bosses and Machine Politics Earlier in the century the swelling numbers of urban poor had given rise to a new kind of politician, the "boss," who listened to his urban constituents and lobbied to improve their lot. The boss presided over the city's "machine"—an unofficial political organization designed to keep a particular party or faction in office. Whether officially serving as mayor or not, the boss, assisted by local ward or precinct captains, wielded enormous influence in city government. Often a former saloonkeeper or labor leader, the boss knew his constituents well.

For better or worse, the **political machine** was America's unique contribution to municipal government in an era of pell-mell urban growth. Typified by Tammany Hall, the Democratic organization that dominated New York City politics from the 1830s to the 1930s, machines emerged in Baltimore, Philadelphia, Atlanta, San Francisco, and a host of other cities during the Gilded Age.

By the turn of the century, many cities had experienced machine rule. Working through the local ward captains to turn out unusually high numbers of voters (see Chapter 20), the machine rode herd on the tangle of municipal bureaucracies, controlling who was hired for the police and fire departments. It rewarded its friends and punished its enemies through its control of taxes, licenses, and inspections. The machine gave tax breaks to favored contractors in return for large payoffs and slipped them insider information about upcoming street and sewer projects.

At the neighborhood level, the ward boss often acted as a welfare agent, helping the needy and protecting the troubled. To spend three dollars to pay a fine for a juvenile offense meant a lot to the poor, but it was small change to a boss who raked in millions from public-utility contracts and land deals. While the machine helped alleviate some suffering, it entangled urban social services with corrupt politics and often prevented city government from responding to the real problems of the city's neediest inhabitants.

Under New York City's boss **William "Magear" Tweed,** the Tammany Hall machine revealed the slimy depths to which extortion and contract padding could sink. Between 1869 and 1871, Tweed gave $50,000 to the poor and $2,250,000 to schools, orphanages, and hospitals. In these same years, his machine dispensed sixty thousand patronage positions and pumped up the city's debt by $70 million through graft and inflated contracts. The details of the Tweed ring's massive fraud and corruption were brilliantly satirized in *Harper's Weekly* by German immigrant cartoonist Thomas Nast. In one cartoon Nast portrayed Tweed and his cronies as vultures picking at the city's bones. Tweed bellowed in fury. "I don't care a straw for your newspaper articles—my constituents don't know how to read," he told *Harper's,* "but they can't help seeing them damned pictures." Convicted of fraud and extortion, Tweed was sentenced to jail in 1873, served two years, escaped to Spain, was reapprehended and reincarcerated, and died in jail in 1878.

By the turn of the century the bosses were facing well-organized assaults on their power, led by an urban elite whose members sought to restore "good government" (see Chapter 21). In this atmosphere, the bosses increasingly forged alliances with civic organizations and reform leagues. The results, although never entirely satisfactory to any of the parties involved, paved the way for new sewage and transportation systems, expanded parklands, and improved public services—a record of considerable accomplishment, given the magnitude of the problems created by urban growth.

Battling Poverty　　Impatient with political bosses' piecemeal attempts to help the urban poor, middle-class city leaders sought comprehensive solutions for relieving poverty. Jacob Riis and the first generation of reformers believed that the basic cause of urban distress was the immigrants' lack of self-discipline and self-control. Consequently, Riis and his peers focused on moral improvement and exposing squalid tenement housing. Only later would Jane Addams, Florence Kelley, and other settlement-house workers examine the crippling impact of low wages and dangerous working conditions. Although many reformers genuinely sympathized with the suffering of the lower classes, the humanitarians often turned their campaigns to help the destitute into missions to Americanize the immigrants and eliminate customs that they perceived as offensive and self-destructive.

Poverty-relief workers first targeted their efforts at the young, who were thought to be most impressionable. Energized by the religious revivals of the 1830s and 1840s, Protestant reformers started charitable societies to help transient youths and abandoned street children. In 1843, Robert M. Hartley, a former employee of the New York Temperance Society, organized the New York Association for Improving the Condition of the Poor to urge poor families to change their ways.

Hartley's voluntaristic approach was supplemented by the more coercive tactics of Charles Loring Brace, who founded the New York Children's Aid Society in 1853. Brace admired "these little traders of the city . . . battling for a hard living in the snow and mud of the street" but worried that they might join the city's "dangerous classes." Brace established dormitories, reading rooms, and workshops where the boys could learn practical skills; he also swept orphaned children off the streets, shipped them to the country, and placed them with families to work as farm hands.

Where Brace's Children's Aid Society gave adolescents an alternative to living in the slums, the Young Men's Christian Association (YMCA), founded in England in 1841 and exported to America ten years later, provided housing and wholesome recreation for country boys who had migrated to the city. The Young Women's Christian Association (YWCA) similarly provided housing and a day nursery for young women and their children. In the Protestant tradition of moral improvement, both organizations subjected their members to curfews and expelled them for drinking and other forbidden behavior.

By 1900, more than fifteen hundred YMCAs and YWCAs served as havens for nearly a quarter-million young men and women. But YMCA and YWCA leaders reached only a small portion of the young adult population. Some whom they sought to help were put off by the organizations' close supervision and moralistic stance. Others, eager to assert their independence, preferred not to ask for help. Although charity workers made some progress in their efforts to aid youth, the strategy was too narrowly focused to stem the rising tide of urban problems.

New Approaches to Social Reform   The inability of the Children's Aid Society, YMCA, YWCA, and other relief organizations to cope with the explosive growth of the urban poor in the 1870s and 1880s convinced some reformers to search for other ways to fight poverty. One of the earliest and most effective agencies was the **Salvation Army.** A church established along pseudomilitary lines in England in 1865 by Methodist minister "General" William Booth, the Salvation Army sent uniformed volunteers to the United States in 1880 to provide food, shelter, and temporary employment for families. Its members ran soup kitchens and day nurseries and dispatched its "slum brigades" to carry the message of morality to the immigrant poor. The army's strategy was simple. Attract the poor with marching bands and lively preaching; follow up with offers of food, assistance, and employment; and then teach them the solid middle-class virtues of temperance, hard work, and self-discipline.

A similar approach to poor relief was implemented by the New York Charity Organization Society (COS), founded in 1882 by **Josephine Shaw Lowell.** Of a prominent

Boston family, the strong-willed Lowell had been widowed when her husband of a few months was killed during the Civil War, and she wore black for the rest of her life. Trying to make aid to the poor more efficient, Lowell and the COS leaders divided New York City into districts, compiled files on all aid recipients, and sent "friendly visitors," who were trained, salaried women, into the tenements to counsel families on how to improve their lives. Convinced that moral deficiencies lay at the root of poverty and that the "promiscuous charity" of overlapping church welfare agencies undermined the desire to work, the COS tried to foster self-sufficiency in its charges. In 1891, Lowell helped found the Consumers' League of New York, which encouraged women to buy only from manufacturers who paid fair wages and maintained decent working conditions.

Although the COS did serve as a useful coordinator for relief efforts and developed helpful statistics on the extent of poverty, critics justly accused the society of being more interested in controlling the poor than in alleviating their suffering. One of the manuals, for example, stressed the importance of introducing "messy housekeepers" to the "pleasures of a cheery, well-ordered home." Unable to see slum problems from the vantage point of the poor, they failed, for the most part, in their underlying objective: to convert the poor to their own standards of morality and decorum.

The Moral-Purity Campaign

While Josephine Shaw Lowell and other like-minded social disciplinarians worked to eradicate urban poverty, other reformers pushed for tougher measures against sin and immorality. In 1872, **Anthony Comstock,** a pious young dry-goods clerk, founded the New York Society for the Suppression of Vice. The organization demanded that municipal authorities close down gambling and lottery operations and censor obscene publications.

Nothing symbolized the contested terrain between middle- and lower-class culture better than the fight over prostitution. Considered socially degenerate by some and a source of recreation by others, prostitution both exploited women and offered them a steady income and a measure of personal freedom. After the Civil War, the number of brothels—specialized houses controlled by women known as madams where prostitutes plied their trade—expanded rapidly. In the 1880s, saloons, tenements, and cabarets, often controlled by political machines, hired prostitutes of their own. Even though immigrant women do not appear to have made up the majority of big-city prostitutes, reformers often labeled them as the major source of the problem.

In 1892, brothels, along with gambling dens and saloons, became targets for the reform efforts of New York Presbyterian minister Charles Parkhurst. Blaming the "slimy, oozy soil of Tammany Hall" and the New York City police—"the dirtiest, crookedest, and ugliest lot of men ever combined in semi-military array outside of Japan and Turkey"—for the city's rampant evils, he organized the City Vigilance League to clean up the city. Two years later a nonpartisan Committee of Seventy elected a new mayor who pressured city officials to enforce the laws against prostitution, gambling, and Sunday liquor sales.

The purity campaign lasted scarcely three years. The reform coalition quickly fell apart. New York City's population was too large, and its ethnic constituencies too diverse, for middle- and upper-class reformers to curb all the illegal activities flourishing within the sprawling metropolis.

The Social Gospel   In the 1870s and 1880s, a handful of Protestant ministers began to explore several radical alternatives for aiding the poor. Instead of focusing on their alleged moral flaws and character defects, these ministers argued that the rich and the wellborn deserved part of the blame for urban poverty and thus had a responsibility to do something about it.

William S. Rainsford, the Irish-born minister of New York City's Saint George's Episcopal Church, pioneered the development of the so-called institutional church movement. Large downtown churches in once-elite districts that had been overrun by immigrants would provide their new neighbors with social services as well as a place to worship. With the financial help of J. Pierpont Morgan, a warden of his church, Rainsford organized a boys' club, built church recreational facilities for the destitute on the Lower East Side, and established an industrial training program.

Another effort within Protestantism to right contemporary social wrongs was the **Social Gospel** movement launched in the 1870s by Washington Gladden, a Congregational minister in Columbus, Ohio. Gladden insisted that true Christianity commits men and women to fight social injustice wherever it exists. Thus, in response to the wave of violent strikes in 1877, he urged church leaders to mediate the conflict between business and labor. Their attempt to do so was unsuccessful.

If Gladden set the tone for the Social Gospel, Walter Rauschenbusch, a minister at a German Baptist church in New York's notorious "Hell's Kitchen" neighborhood, articulated the movement's central philosophy. Educated in Germany, Rauschenbusch argued that a truly Christian society would unite all churches, reorganize the industrial system, and work for international peace. Rauschenbusch's appeal for Christian unity led to the formation of the Federal Council of Churches in 1908, but his other goals were never achieved. The Social Gospel's attack on what its leaders blasted as the complacent Christian support of the status quo attracted only a handful of Protestants. Nevertheless, their earnest voices blended with a growing chorus of critics bemoaning the nation's urban woes.

The Settlement-House Movement   By the late 1880s, many thoughtful Americans had become convinced that reform pressures applied from the top by the Charity Organization Society and the purity crusaders, however well intentioned, were ineffective. A new approach to social work was needed. Relief workers would have to take up residence in poor neighborhoods, where, in the words of **Jane Addams,** an early advocate of the movement, they could see firsthand "the struggle for existence, which is so much harsher among people near the edge of pauperism." A new institution—the settlement house—was born.

The youngest daughter of a successful Illinois businessman, Jane Addams purchased a dilapidated mansion on Chicago's South Halsted Street in 1889. After overseeing extensive repairs, she and her coworkers opened it as Hull House, the first experiment in the settlement-house approach. Putting the middle-class ideal of true womanhood into action, Addams turned Hull House into an immigrant social center. She and her coworkers invited them to plays; sponsored art projects; held classes in English, civics, cooking, and dressmaking; and encouraged them to preserve their traditional crafts. She set up a kindergarten, a laundry, an employment bureau, and a day nursery for working mothers. Hull House also sponsored recreational and athletic programs and dispensed legal aid and health care.

In the hope of upgrading the filthy and overcrowded housing in its environs, Addams and her coworkers conducted surveys of city housing conditions and pressured politicians to enforce sanitation regulations. For a time, demonstrating her principle of direct engagement with the lives of the poor, Addams even served as garbage inspector for her local ward.

By 1895 at least fifty settlement houses had opened in cities around the nation. Settlement-house leaders trained a generation of young college students, mostly women, many of whom would later serve as state and local government officials. **Florence Kelley,** for example, who had worked at Hull House, became the chief factory inspector for Illinois in 1893. For Kelley as for other young female settlement workers, settlement houses functioned as a supportive sisterhood of reform that taught them how to work effectively with municipal governments. Many settlement-house veterans would later draw on their experience to play an influential role in the regulatory movements of the Progressive Era (see Chapter 21). Through their sympathetic attitudes toward the immigrants and their systematic publication of data about slum conditions, settlement-house workers gave turn-of-the-century Americans renewed hope for urban reform.

But in their attempt to promote class cooperation and social harmony, settlement houses had mixed success. Although many immigrants appreciated the settlement houses' resources and activities, they felt that the reformers were uninterested in increasing their political power. Settlement-house workers did tend to overlook immigrant organizations and their leaders. In 1894, Hull House attracted two thousand visitors per week, but this was only a fraction of the more than seventy thousand people who lived within six blocks of the building. "They're like the rest," complained one immigrant, "a bunch of people planning for us and deciding what is good for us without consulting us or taking us into their confidence."

WORKING-CLASS LEISURE IN THE IMMIGRANT CITY

In colonial America preachers had linked leisure time to "idleness," a dangerous step on the road to sin and wickedness. In the overwhelmingly rural culture of the early nineteenth century, the unremitting routines of farm labor left little time for relaxation. Family picnics, horse races, county fairs, revival meetings, and Fourth of July and Christmas celebrations had provided occasional permissible diversions. But most Americans continued to view leisure activities skeptically. Henry Clay Work's popular song "My Grandfather's Clock" (1876), which praised the ancient timepiece for "wasting no time" and working "ninety years, without slumbering," bore witness to the tenacity of this deep-seated reverence for work and suspicion of leisure.

After the Civil War, as immigration soared, urban populations shot up—and a new class of wealthy entrepreneurs arose—striking new patterns of leisure and amusement emerged, most notably among the urban working class. Although middle-class moralists questioned the wholesomeness of these new forms of recreation, they were little heeded by immigrants in the throbbing cities. After spending long hours in factories, in mills, behind department-store counters, or as domestic servants in the homes of the wealthy, working-class Americans sought relaxation and diversion. Scorning the museums and concert halls favored by the wealthy, they thronged the streets, patronized saloons and dance halls, cheered at boxing matches and baseball games, and organized group picnics and holiday celebrations. As amusement parks, vaudeville theaters, sporting clubs, and racetracks provided further outlets for workers' need for entertainment, leisure became a big business catering to a mass public rather than to a wealthy elite.

For millions of working-class Americans, leisure time took on increasing importance as factory work became routinized and impersonal. Although many recreational activities involved both men and women, others attracted one gender in particular. Saloons offered an intensely male environment where patrons could share good stories, discuss and bet on sporting events, and momentarily put aside pressures of job and family. Young working women preferred to share confidences with friends in informal social clubs, tried out new fashions in street promenading, and found excitement in neighborhood dance halls and amusement parks.

Streets, Saloons, and Boxing Matches   No segment of the population had a greater need for amusement and recreation than the urban working class. Hours of tedious, highly disciplined, and physically exhausting labor left workers tired and thirsting for excitement and escape at the end of the day. A banner carried by the Worcester, Massachusetts, carpenters' union in an 1889 demonstration for the eight-hour workday summed up the importance of workers' leisure hours: "EIGHT HOURS FOR WORK, EIGHT HOURS FOR REST, AND EIGHT HOURS FOR WHAT WE WILL."

City streets provided recreation that anyone could afford. Relaxing after a day's work, shop girls and laborers clustered on busy corners, watching shouting pushcart peddlers and listening to organ grinders and street musicians play familiar melodies. For a penny or a nickel, they could buy bagels, baked potatoes, soda, and other foods and drinks. In the summer, when the heat and humidity in tenement apartments reached unbearable levels, the streets became a hive of neighborhood social life. One immigrant fondly recalled his boyhood on the streets of New York's Lower East Side: "Something was always happening, and our attention was continually being shifted from one excitement to another."

The streets were open to all, but other leisure institutions drew mainly a male clientele. For example, in cities with a strong German immigrant presence like Baltimore, Milwaukee, and Cincinnati, gymnastic clubs (called *Turnverein*) and singing societies (*Gesangverein*) provided both companionship and the opportunity to perpetuate old-world cultural traditions.

For workmen of all ethnic backgrounds, saloons offered companionship, conviviality, and five-cent beer, often with a free lunch thrown in. New York City had an estimated ten thousand saloons by 1900 and Denver nearly five hundred. As neighborhood gathering places, saloons reinforced group identity and became centers for immigrant politics. Saloonkeepers, who often doubled as local ward bosses and turned out the vote in their neighborhoods, performed small services for their patrons, including finding jobs and writing letters for illiterate immigrants. Sports memorabilia and pictures of prominent prizefighters adorned saloon walls. With their rich mahogany bars, etched glass, shiny brass rails, and elegant mirrors, saloons provided patrons with a taste of high-toned luxury. Although working-class women rarely joined their husbands at the saloon, they might send a son or daughter to the corner pub to fetch a "growler"—a large tin pail of beer.

The conventions of saloon culture thus stood in marked contrast to both the socially isolating routines of factory labor and the increasingly private and family-centered social life of the middle class. Nevertheless, it would be a mistake to view the old-time saloon through a haze of sentimental nostalgia. Prostitution and crime flourished in the rougher saloons. Moreover, drunken husbands sometimes beat their wives and children, squandered their limited income, and lost their jobs. The pervasiveness of alcoholism was devastating. Temperance reformers, in their attack on saloons, targeted a widespread social problem.

The Rise of Professional Sports Contrary to the prevailing myth, schoolboy Abner Doubleday did not invent baseball in Cooperstown, New York, in 1839. As an English game called rounders, the pastime had existed in one form or another since the seventeenth century. But if Americans did not create baseball, they unquestionably took a children's game and turned it into a major professional sport. The first organized baseball team, the New York Knickerbockers, was formed in 1845. In the 1860s, the rules were codified, and the sport assumed its modern form. Overhand pitches replaced underhand tosses. Fielders, who now wore gloves, had to catch the ball on the fly to make an out instead of fielding it on one bounce. Games were standardized at nine innings, and bases were spaced ninety feet apart.

In that same decade, promoters organized professional clubs and began to charge admission and compete for players. The Cincinnati Red Stockings, the first team to put its players under contract for the whole season, gained fame in 1869 by touring the country and ending the season with fifty-seven wins and no losses. Team owners organized the National League in 1876, took control from the players by requiring them to sign contracts that barred them from playing for rival organizations, and limited each city to one professional team. Soon the owners were filling baseball parks with crowds of ten to twelve thousand fans and earning enormous profits. By the 1890s, baseball had become big business.

Although baseball attracted a national following from all social levels, the working class particularly took the sport to heart. The most profitable teams were those in major industrial cities with a large working-class population. Workers avidly followed their team's progress. Many saloons reported scores on blackboards and an estimated 50 percent of players worked in saloons in the off season or became saloon owners when they retired from the game.

If baseball helped build solidarity among some ethnic groups, it also fostered discrimination against blacks. Although at least fifty-five blacks played on integrated teams between 1883 and 1898, the refusal of the Chicago White Stockings in 1887 to play a team with George Stovey, a star black pitcher, marked a turning point. That same year, Colored baseball clubs opened in six cities. Increasingly thereafter, blacks were banned from playing on professional teams.

Newspapers thrived on baseball. Joseph Pulitzer introduced the first separate sports page when he bought the *New York World* in 1883, and much of the sporting news in the *World* and other papers was devoted to baseball. Fans who cheered the hometown team provided cities with a shared sports loyalty that reduced ethnic, class, and religious differences, but drinking and gambling continued to plague the game.

Although no organized sport attracted as large a following as baseball, horse racing and boxing contests drew big crowds of spectators and bettors. Louisville's Kentucky

Published by Arthur T. Lumley, New York Illustrated News.

FOR THE HEAVY-WEIGHT CHAMPIONSHIP OF THE WORLD.
John Lawrence Sullivan, the Champion, and James J. Corbett, the Adonis of the Fistic Arena, Who Are to Battle September 7th Next For a Purse and Stakes of $45,000 and the Big Fellow's Title.

World's Heavyweight Boxing Championship, 1892   *In dethroning ring champion John L. Sullivan, "Gentleman Jim" Corbett demonstrated that speed and finesse were more than a match for brute strength.*

Derby became an important social event for the rich, but professional boxing aroused more passionate devotion among laborers. For working-class men, bare-knuckled prizefighting became one of the most popular amusements. Drawing its heroes from the poorer ranks of society, the ring became an arena where lower-class men could assert their individuality and physical prowess.

By far the most popular sports hero of the nineteenth century was heavyweight fighter **John L. Sullivan,** "the Boston Strong Boy." Of Irish immigrant stock, Sullivan began boxing in 1877 at the age of nineteen. His first professional fight came in 1880 when he knocked out John Donaldson, "the Champion of the West," in a Cincinnati beer hall. With his massive physique, handlebar mustache, and arrogant swagger, Sullivan was enormously popular among immigrants. Barnstorming across the country, he vanquished a succession of local strongmen, invariably wearing his trademark green tights with an American flag wrapped around his middle. Cleverly, Sullivan also refused to fight blacks, in deference, he said, to the wishes of his fans. This policy conveniently allowed him to avoid facing the finest boxer of the 1880s, the Australian black, Peter Jackson.

Sullivan loved drink and high living, and by the end of the eighties he was sadly out of shape. But when the editor of the *Police Gazette,* a sensational tabloid, designed a new heavyweight championship belt—allegedly containing two hundred ounces of silver and encrusted with diamonds and pure gold—and awarded it to Sullivan's rival Jake Kilrain, the champion had to defend himself. The two met on a sweltering,

hundred-degree day in New Orleans in July 1889 for the last bare-knuckles championship match. After seventy-five short but grueling rounds, Kilrain's managers threw
in the towel. Newspapers around the nation banner-headlined the story. Contemptu-
ously returning the championship belt to the *Police Gazette* after having had it ap-
praised at $175, Sullivan went on the road to star in a melodrama written specifically
for him. Playing the role of a blacksmith, he (in the words of a recent historian of bare-
knuckles boxing) "pounded an anvil, beat a bully, and mutilated his lines." But his fans
did not care; he was one of them, and they adored him. As one admirer wrote,

> His colors are the Stars and Stripes,
> He also wears the green,
> And he's the grandest slugger that
> The ring has ever seen.

Vaudeville, Amusement Parks, and Dance Halls   In contrast to the male preserve of saloons and prizefights, the world of vaudeville, amusement parks, and neighborhood dance pavilions welcomed all comers regardless of gender. Some of them proved particularly congenial to working-class women.

Vaudeville evolved out of the pre–Civil War blackface minstrel shows in which
white comedians made up as blacks had sung and mocked African-American life.
Vaudeville performances offered a succession of acts, all designed for mass appeal. The
shows typically opened with a trained animal routine or a dance number. These were
followed by a musical interlude featuring sentimental favorites such as "On the Banks
of the Wabash, Far Away" or new hits such as "Meet Me in St. Louis, Louis," a jaunty
spoof of a young wife's frustration with her stick-in-the-mud husband. Comic skits
followed, ridiculing the trials of urban life, satirizing the ineptitude of the police and
municipal officials, poking fun at the babel of accents in the immigrant city, and mining a rich vein of broad ethnic humor and stereotypes. Blackface skits were sometimes
included. After a highbrow operatic aria and acts by ventriloquists, pantomimes, and
magicians, the program ended with a "flash" finale such as flying-trapeze artists swinging against a black background.

By the 1880s, vaudeville was drawing larger crowds than any other form of theater.
Not only did it provide an inexpensive evening of lighthearted entertainment, but in
the comic sketches, immigrant audiences could also laugh at their own experience as
they saw it translated into slapstick and caricature.

The white working class's fascination with vaudeville's blackface acts has been the
subject of considerable recent scrutiny by historians. Some have interpreted it as a way
for the white working class to mock middle-class ideals. By pretending to act like the
popular stereotypes of blacks, white working-class youths could challenge traditional
family structures, the virtue of sexual self-denial, and adult expectations about working hard. In this view popular culture was making fun of the ideals of thrift and propriety being promoted in marketplace and domestic ideology. Other historians have
argued that blackface buffoonery, with its grotesque, demeaning caricatures of
African-Americans, reinforced prejudice against blacks and restricted their escape
from lower-class status. Paradoxically, therefore, the popularity of blackface vaudeville
acts reinforced white racial solidarity and strengthened the expanding wall separating
whites and African-Americans.

Where vaudeville offered psychological escape from the stresses of working-class life by exploiting its comic potential, amusement parks provided physical escape, at least for a day. The prototype of the sprawling urban amusement park was New York's Coney Island, a section of Brooklyn's oceanfront that evolved into a resort for the masses in the 1870s. At Coney Island, young couples went dancing, rode through the dark Tunnel of Love, sped down the dizzying roller coaster in Steeplechase Park, or watched belly dancers in the carnival sideshows. Customers were encouraged to surrender to the spirit of play, forget the demands of the industrial world, and lose themselves in fantasy.

By the end of the nineteenth century, New York City had well over three hundred thousand female wage earners, most of them young, unmarried women working as seamstresses, laundresses, typists, domestic servants, and department-store clerks. For this army of low-paid young working women and their counterparts in other cities, amusement parks exerted a powerful lure. Here they could meet friends, spend time with young men beyond the watchful eyes of their parents, show off their new dresses, and try out the latest dance steps. As a twenty-year-old German immigrant woman who worked as a servant in a wealthy household observed,

> I have heard some of the high people with whom I have been living say that Coney Island is not tony. The trouble is that these high people don't know how to dance. I have to laugh when I see them at their balls and parties. If only I could get out on the floor and show them how—they would be astonished.

For such women, the brightly decorated dance pavilion, the exciting music, and the spell of a warm summer night could seem a magical release from the drudgery of daily life.

Ragtime

Since the days of slavery, black Americans had developed a strong, creative musical culture, and thus it is not surprising that blacks made a major contribution to the popular music of the late nineteenth century in the form of ragtime. Nothing could illustrate more sharply the differences between middle- and working-class culture than the contrasting styles of popular music they favored. The middle class preferred hymns or songs that conveyed a moral lesson. The working class delighted in ragtime, which originated in the 1880s with black musicians in the saloons and brothels of the South and Midwest and was played strictly for entertainment.

Ragtime developed out of the rich tradition of sacred and secular songs through which African-Americans had long eased the burdens of their lives. Like spirituals, ragtime used syncopated rhythms and complex harmonies, but it blended these with marching-band musical structures to create a distinctive style. A favorite of "honky-tonk" piano players, ragtime was introduced to the broader public in the 1890s and became a national sensation.

The reasons for the sudden ragtime craze were complex. Inventive, playful, with catchy syncopations and an infectious rhythm in the bass clef, the music displayed an originality that had an appeal all its own. Part of ragtime's popularity also came from its origin in brothels and its association with blacks, who were widely stereotyped in the 1890s as sexual, sensual, and uninhibited by the rigid Victorian social conventions that restricted whites. The "wild" and complex rhythms of ragtime were widely interpreted to be a freer and more "natural" expression of elemental feelings about love and sex.

Ragtime's great popularity proved a mixed blessing for blacks. It testified to the achievements of brilliant composers like Scott Joplin, helped break down the barriers faced by blacks in the music industry, and contributed to a spreading rebellion against the repressiveness of Victorian standards. But ragtime simply confirmed some whites' stereotype of blacks as primitive and sensual, a bias that underlay the racism of the period and helped justify segregation and discrimination.

CULTURES IN CONFLICT

Even within the elite and middle classes, Victorian morality and genteel cultural standards were never totally accepted. As the century ended, increasing numbers of people questioned these beliefs. Women stood at the center of the era's cultural turbulence. Thwarted by a restrictive code of feminine propriety, middle-class women made their dissatisfactions heard. The rise of women's clubs, the growth of women's colleges, and even the 1890s bicycle fad testified to the emergence of what some began to call the "new woman."

Although Victorian culture was challenged from within the middle class, a widening chasm divided the well-to-do from urban working-class immigrants. In no period of American history have class conflicts—cultural as well as economic—been more open and raw. As middle-class leaders nervously eyed the sometimes disorderly culture of city streets, saloons, boxing clubs, dance halls, and amusement parks, they saw a challenge to their own cultural and social standing. Some middle-class reformers promoted the public school as a way to impose middle-class values on the urban masses. Others battled urban "vice" and "immorality." But ultimately it was the polite mores of the middle class, not urban working-class culture, that proved more vulnerable. By 1900, the Victorian social and moral ethos was crumbling on every front.

The Genteel Tradition and Its Critics

What was this genteel culture that aroused such opposition? In the 1870s and 1880s, a group of upper-class writers and magazine editors, led by Harvard art history professor Charles Eliot Norton and New York editors Richard Watson Gilder of *The Century* magazine and E. L. Godkin of *The Nation,* codified Victorian standards for literature and the arts. They campaigned to improve American taste in interior furnishings, textiles, ceramics, wallpaper, and books. By fashioning rigorous criteria for excellence in writing and design, they hoped to create a coherent national artistic culture.

In the 1880s Norton, Godkin, and Gilder, joined by the editors of other highbrow periodicals such as the *Atlantic Monthly* and *North American Review,* set up new guidelines for serious literature. They lectured the middle class about the value of high culture and the insights to be gained from painting and music. They censored their own publications to remove all sexual allusions, disrespectful treatments of Christianity, and unhappy endings. Expanding their combined circulation to nearly two hundred thousand copies, Godkin and the other editors of "quality" periodicals created an important forum for serious writing. Novelists Henry James, who published virtually all of his work in the *Atlantic,* and William Dean Howells, who served as editor of the same magazine, helped lead this elite literary establishment. James believed that "it is art that makes life. . . . [There is] no substitute whatever for [its] force and beauty. . . ."

This interest in art for art's sake paralleled a broader crusade called the "aesthetic movement," led in England by William Morris, Oscar Wilde, and other art critics, who sought to bring art into every facet of life. In America, Candace Wheeler and other reformers made its influence felt through the work of architects, jewelers, and interior decorators.

Although the magazines initially provided an important forum for new writers, their editors' elitism and desire to control the nation's literary standards soon aroused opposition. Samuel Langhorne Clemens, better known as **Mark Twain,** spoke for many young writers when he declared that he was through with "literature and all that bosh." Attacking aristocratic literary conventions, Twain and other authors who shared his concerns explored new forms of fiction and worked to broaden its appeal to the general public.

These efforts to chart new directions for American literature rested on fundamental changes taking place in the publishing industry. To compete with elite periodicals costing twenty-five to thirty-five cents, new magazines like *Ladies' Home Journal, Cosmopolitan,* and *McClure's* lowered their prices to a dime or fifteen cents and tripled or quadrupled their circulation. Supporting themselves through advertising, these magazines encouraged new trends in fiction while mass-marketing new products. Their editors sought writers who could provide accurate depictions of the "whirlpool of real life" and create a new civic consciousness to heal the class divisions of American society.

Some of these authors have been called regionalists because they captured the distinctive dialect and details of local life in their environs. In *The Country of the Pointed Firs* (1896), for example, Sarah Orne Jewett wrote of the New England village life that she knew in South Berwick, Maine. Others, most notably William Dean Howells, have been called realists because of their focus on the truthful depiction of the commonplace and the everyday, especially in urban areas. Still others have been categorized as naturalists because their novels and stories deny free will and stress the ways in which life's outcomes are determined by economic and psychological forces. Stephen Crane's *Maggie: A Girl of the Streets* (1892), a bleak story of an innocent girl's exploitation and ultimate suicide in an urban slum, is generally considered the first naturalistic American novel. Yet in practice, these categories are imprecise and often overlap. What many of these writers shared was a skepticism about literary conventions and an intense desire to understand the society around them and portray it in words.

The careers of Mark Twain and Theodore Dreiser highlight the changes in the publishing industry and the evolution of new forms of writing. Both authors grew up in the Midwest, outside the East Coast literary establishment. Twain was born near Hannibal, Missouri, in 1835, and Dreiser in Terre Haute, Indiana, in 1871. As young men both worked as newspaper reporters and traveled widely. Both learned from direct and sometimes bitter experience about the greed, speculation, and fraud that figured centrally in Gilded Age life.

Of the two, Twain more incessantly sought a mass-market audience. With his drooping mustache, white hair, and white suits, Twain turned himself into a media personality, lecturing from coast to coast, founding his own publishing house, and using door-to-door salesmen to sell his books. The name Mark Twain became his trademark, identifying him to readers as a literary celebrity much as the labels Coca-Cola and Ivory Soap won instant consumer recognition. Although Dreiser possessed neither

Twain's flamboyant personality nor his instinct for salesmanship, he, too, learned to crank out articles.

Drawing on their own experiences, Twain and Dreiser wrote about the human impact of the wrenching social changes taking place around them: the flow of people to the cities and the relentless scramble for power, wealth, and fame. In *The Adventures of Huckleberry Finn* (1884), Twain tells a story of two runaways, the rebellious Huck and the slave Jim, drifting down the Mississippi in search of freedom. Their physical journey, which contrasts idyllic life on the raft with the tawdry, fraudulent world of small riverfront towns, is a journey of identity that brings with it a deeper understanding of contemporary American society.

Dreiser's *Sister Carrie* (1900) also tells of a journey. In this case, the main character, Carrie Meeber, an innocent girl on her way from her Wisconsin farm home to Chicago, is seduced by a traveling salesman and then moves in with the married proprietor of a fancy saloon. Driven by her desire for expensive department-store clothes and lavish entertainment, Carrie is an opportunist incapable of feeling guilt. She follows her married lover to New York, knowing that he has stolen the receipts from his saloon, abandons him when his money runs out, and pursues her own career in the theater.

Twain and Dreiser broke decisively with the genteel tradition's emphasis on manners and decorum. *Century* magazine readers complained that *Huckleberry Finn* was coarse and "destitute of a single redeeming quality." The publisher of *Sister Carrie* was so repelled by Dreiser's novel that he printed only a thousand copies (to fulfill the legal terms of his contract) and then stored them in a warehouse, refusing to promote them.

Growing numbers of scholars and critics similarly challenged the self-serving certitudes of Victorian mores, including assumptions that moral worth and economic standing were closely linked and that the status quo of the 1870s and 1880s represented a social order decreed by God and nature alike. Whereas Henry George, Lester Ward, and Edward Bellamy elaborated their visions of a cooperative and harmonious society (see Chapter 18), economist Thorstein Veblen in *The Theory of the Leisure Class* (1899) offered a caustic critique of the lifestyles of the new capitalist elite. Raised in a Norwegian farm community in Minnesota, Veblen looked at the captains of industry and their families with a jaundiced eye, documenting their "conspicuous consumption"of expensive purchases and lamenting the widening gap between "those who worked without profit" and "those who profited without working."

Within the new discipline of sociology, Annie MacLean exposed the exploitation of department-store clerks, Walter Wyckoff uncovered the hand-to-mouth existence of unskilled laborers, and W. E. B. Du Bois documented the suffering and hardships faced by blacks in Philadelphia. The publication of these social scientists' writings, coupled with the economic depression and seething labor agitation of the 1890s, made it increasingly difficult for turn-of-the-century middle-class Americans to accept the smug, self-satisfied belief in progress and gentility that had been a hallmark of the Victorian outlook.

Modernism in Architecture and Painting

The challenge to the genteel tradition also found strong support among architects and painters. By the 1890s Chicago architects William Holabird, John Wellborn Root, and others had tired of copying European designs. Breaking with established architects such as Richard Morris Hunt, the designer of French châteaux for New York's Fifth Avenue, these Chicago architects followed the lead of Louis Sullivan, who argued that a building's form should follow its function. In their view, banks should look like the financial institutions they were, not like Greek temples. Striving to evolve functional American design standards, the Chicago architects looked for inspiration to the future—to **modernism**—not to the past.

The Chicago architect **Frank Lloyd Wright** designed "prairie-school" houses that represented a typical modernist break with past styles. Wright scorned the three-story Victorian house with its large attic and basement. His designs, which featured broad, sheltering roofs and horizontal silhouettes, used interconnecting rooms to create a sense of spaciousness.

The call of modernism, with its rejection of Victorian refinement, influenced late-nineteenth-century American painting as well. The watercolors of Winslow Homer, a magazine illustrator during the Civil War, revealed nature as brutally tough and un-sentimental. In Homer's grim, elemental seascapes, lone men struggle against massive waves that constantly threaten to overwhelm them. Thomas Eakins's canvases of swimmers, boxers, and rowers (such as his well-known *Champion Single Sculls,* painted in 1871) similarly captured moments of vigorous physical exertion in everyday life. While Mary Cassatt shared Eakins's interest in everyday life, she often took as her subject the bond between mother and child, as in her painting *The Bath* (c. 1891). After studying at the Pennsylvania Academy of Fine Arts, she moved to Paris in 1874, where she worked closely with French Impressionist painters such as Monet and Degas.

The revolt by architects and painters against Victorian standards was symptomatic of a larger shift in middle-class thought. This shift resulted from fundamental economic changes that had spawned a far more complex social environment than that of the past. As Protestant minister Josiah Strong perceptively observed in 1898, the transition from muscle to mechanical power had "separated, as by an impassable gulf, the simple, homespun, individualistic world of the . . . past, from the complex, closely associated life of the present." The increasingly evident gap between rural or small-town life—a world of quiet parlors and flickering kerosene lamps—and life in the big, glittering, electrified cities of iron and glass made nineteenth-century Americans acutely aware of differences in upbringing and wealth. Given the disparities between rich and poor, between rural and urban, and between native-born Americans and recent immigrants, it is no wonder that pious Victorian platitudes about proper manners and graceful arts seemed out of touch with the new social realities.

Distrusting the idealistic Victorian assumptions about social progress, middle-class journalists, novelists, artists, and politicians nevertheless remained divided over how to replace them. Not until the Progressive Era would social reformers draw on a new expertise in social research and an enlarged conception of the federal government's regulatory power to break sharply with their Victorian predecessors' social outlook.

From Victorian Lady to New Woman
Although middle-class women figured importantly in the revolt against Victorian refinement, their role was complex and ambiguous. Dissatisfaction with the cult of domesticity did not necessarily lead to open rebellion. Many women, although chafing against the constraints of deference and the assumption that they should limit their activities to the home, remained committed to playing a nurturing role within the family. In fact, early advocates of a "widened sphere" for women often fused the traditional Victorian ideal of womanhood with a firm commitment to political action.

The career of temperance leader **Frances Willard** illustrates how the cult of domesticity, with its celebration of special female virtues, could evolve into a broader view of women's social and political responsibilities. Like many of her contemporaries, Willard believed that women were compassionate and nurturing by nature. She was also convinced that drinking encouraged thriftlessness and profoundly threatened family life. Resigning as dean of women and professor of English at Northwestern University in 1874, Willard devoted her energies full-time to the temperance cause. Five years later she was elected president of the newly formed Woman's Christian Temperance Union (WCTU).

Willard took the traditional belief that women had unique moral virtues and transformed it into a rationale for political action. The domestication of politics, she asserted, would protect the family and improve public morality. Choosing as the union's badge a bow of white ribbon, symbolizing the purity of the home, she launched a crusade in 1880 to win the franchise for women so that they could vote to outlaw liquor. Willard soon expanded WCTU activities to include welfare work, prison reform, labor arbitration, and public health. Under her leadership the WCTU, with a membership of nearly 150,000 by 1890, became the nation's first mass organization of women. Through it, women gained experience as lobbyists, organizers, and lecturers, in the process undercutting the assumption of "separate spheres."

An expanding network of women's clubs offered another means by which middle- and upper-class women could hone their skills in civic affairs, public speaking, and intellectual analysis. In the 1870s, many well-to-do women met weekly to study topics of mutual interest. These clubwomen soon became involved in social-welfare projects, public library expansion, and tenement reform. By 1892, the General Federation of Women's Clubs, an umbrella organization established that year, boasted 495 affiliates and a hundred thousand members. Middle-class black women, excluded from many white clubs, formed their own National Association of Colored Women's Clubs in 1900.

While older women eroded the Victorian constraints placed on them by social conventions by joining women's clubs, younger women challenged social conventions by joining the bicycling craze that swept urban America at the turn of the century. The fascination with bicycle riding developed as part of a new interest in health and physical fitness. Middle- and upper-class Americans explored various ways to improve their vigor. Some used health products such as cod liver oil and sarsaparilla for "weak blood." Others played basketball, invented in 1891 by a physical education instructor at Springfield College in Massachusetts to keep students in shape during the winter months. But bicycling, which could be done individually or in groups, quickly became the most popular sport for those who wished to combine exercise with recreation.

Bicycles of various designs had been manufactured since the 1870s, but bicycling did not become a national craze until the invention in the 1880s of the so-called safety bicycle, with smaller wheels, ball-bearing axles, and air-filled tires. By the 1890s, over a million Americans owned bicycles.

Bicycling especially appealed to young women who had chafed under the restrictive Victorian attitudes about female exercise, which held that proper young ladies must never sweat and that the female body must be fully covered at all times. Pedaling along in a shirtwaist or "split" skirt, a woman bicyclist made an implicit feminist statement suggesting that she had broken with genteel conventions and wanted to explore new activities beyond the traditional sphere.

Changing attitudes about femininity and women's proper role also found expression in gradually shifting ideas about marriage. Charlotte Perkins Gilman, a suffrage advocate and speaker for women's rights, asserted that women would make an effective contribution to society only when they won economic independence from men through work outside the home (see Chapter 21). One very tangible indicator of women's changing relationship to men was the substantial rise in the divorce rate between 1880 and 1900. In 1880, one in every twenty-one marriages ended in divorce. By 1900, the rate had climbed to one in twelve. Women who brought suit for divorce increasingly cited their husbands' failure to act responsibly and to respect their autonomy. Accepting such arguments, courts frequently awarded the wife alimony, a monetary settlement payable by the ex-husband to support her and their children.

Women writers generally welcomed the new female commitment to independence and self-sufficiency. In the short stories of Mary Wilkins Freeman, for example, women's expanding role is implicitly compared to the frontier ideal of freedom. Feminist **Kate Chopin** pushed the debate to the extreme by having Edna Pontellier, the married heroine of her controversial 1899 novel *The Awakening*, violate social conventions. First Edna falls in love with another man; then she takes her own life when his ideas about women prove as narrow and traditional as those of her husband.

Despite the efforts of these and other champions of the new woman, attitudes changed slowly. The enlarged conception of women's role in society exerted its greatest influence on college-educated, middle-class women who had leisure time and could reasonably hope for success in journalism, social work, and nursing. For female immigrant factory workers and for shop girls who worked sixty hours a week to try to make ends meet, however, the ideal remained a more distant goal. Although many women were seeking more independence and control over their lives, most still viewed the home as their primary responsibility.

Public Education as an Arena of Class Conflict

While the debate over women's proper role remained largely confined to the middle class, a very different controversy, over the scope and function of public education, engaged Americans of all socioeconomic levels. This debate starkly highlighted the class and cultural divisions in late-nineteenth-century society. From the 1870s on, viewing the public schools as an instrument for indoctrinating and controlling the lower ranks of society, middle-class educators and civic leaders campaigned to expand public schooling and bring it under centralized control. Not surprisingly, the reformers' efforts aroused considerable opposition from ethnic and religious groups whose outlook and interests differed sharply from theirs.

Thanks to the crusade for universal public education started by Horace Mann and other antebellum educational reformers, most states had public school systems by the Civil War, and more than half the nation's children were receiving some formal education. But most attended school for only three or four years, and few went on to high school.

Concerned that many Americans lacked sufficient knowledge to participate wisely in public affairs or function effectively in the labor force, reformers such as William Torrey Harris worked to increase the number of years that children spent in school. First as superintendent of the St. Louis public schools in the 1870s and later as the federal commissioner of education, Harris urged teachers to instill in their students a sense of order,

Interior of an Urban School   *Photographers were careful to picture public elementary schools, such as this one on New York's Lower East Side in 1886, as models of immigrant children's decorum and good behavior.*

decorum, self-discipline, and civic loyalty. Believing that modern industrial society depended on citizens' conforming to the timetables of the factory and the train, he envisioned the schools as models of punctuality and precise scheduling: "The pupil must have his lessons ready at the appointed time, must rise at the tap of the bell, move to the line, return; in short, go through all the evolutions with equal precision."

To achieve these goals and to wrest control of the schools from neighborhood leaders and ward politicians, reform-minded educators like Harris elaborated a philosophy of public education stressing punctuality, centralized administration, compulsory-attendance laws, and a tenure system to insulate teachers from political favoritism and parental pressure. By 1900, thirty-one states required school attendance of all children from eight to fourteen years of age.

The steamroller methods used by Harris and like-minded administrators to systematize public education quickly prompted protests. New York pediatrician Joseph Mayer Rice, who toured thirty-six cities and interviewed twelve hundred teachers in 1892, scornfully criticized an educational establishment that stressed singsong memorization and prisonlike discipline.

Rice's biting attack on public education overlooked the real advances in reading and mathematics made in the previous two decades. Nationally, despite the influx of immigrants, the illiteracy rate in English for individuals ten years and older dropped from 17 percent in 1880 to 13 percent in 1890, largely because of the expansion of urban educational facilities. American high schools were also coeducational, and girls made up the majority of the students by 1900. But Rice was on target in assailing many teachers' rigid emphasis on silence, docility, and unquestioning obedience to the rules. When a Chicago school inspector found a thirteen-year-old boy huddled in the basement of a stockyard building and ordered him back to school, the weeping boy blurted out, "[T]hey hits ye if yer don't learn, and they hits ye if ye whisper, and they hits ye if ye have string in yer pocket, and they hits ye if yer seat squeaks, and they hits ye if ye don't stan' up in time, and they hits ye if yer late, and they hits ye if ye ferget the page."

By the 1880s, several different groups found themselves in opposition to centralized urban public school bureaucracies. Although many working-class families valued education, those who depended on their children's meager wages for survival resisted the attempt to force their sons and daughters to attend school past the elementary grades. Although some immigrant families made great sacrifices to enable their children to get an education, many withdrew their offspring from school as soon as they had learned the rudiments of reading and writing, and sent them to work.

Furthermore, Catholic immigrants objected to the overwhelmingly Protestant orientation of the public schools. Distressed by the use of the King James translation of the Bible and by the schools' failure to observe saints' days, Catholics set up separate parochial school systems. In response, Republican politicians, resentful of Catholic immigrants' overwhelming preference for the Democratic Party, tried unsuccessfully to pass a constitutional amendment cutting off all public aid to church-related schools in 1875. Catholics in turn denounced federal aid to public schools as intended "to suppress Catholic education, gradually extinguish Catholicity in this country, and to form one homogeneous American people after the New England Evangelical type."

At the other end of the social scale, upper-class parents who did not wish to send their children to immigrant-thronged public schools enrolled their daughters in female seminaries such as Chatham Hall in Chatham, Virginia, and their sons in private academies and boarding schools like St. Paul's in Concord, New Hampshire. The proliferation of private and parochial schools, together with the controversies over compulsory education, school funding, and classroom decorum, reveals the extent to which public education had become mired in ethnic and class differences. Unlike Germany and Japan, which created national education systems in the late nineteenth century, the United States, reflecting its social heterogeneity, maintained a system of locally run public and private institutions that allowed each segment of society to retain some influence over the schools attended by its own children. Amid the disputes, school enrollments dramatically expanded. In 1870, fewer than seventy-two thousand students were attending the nation's 1,026 high schools. By 1900 the number of high schools had jumped to more than 5,000 and the number of students to more than half a million.

CONCLUSION

By the 1890s, class conflict was evident in practically every area of city life, from mealtime manners to popular entertainment and recreation. As new immigrants flooded the tenements and spilled out onto neighborhood streets, it became impossible for native-born Americans to ignore their strange religious and social customs. Ethnic differences were compounded by class differences. Often poor and from peasant or working-class backgrounds, the immigrants from southern and eastern Europe took unskilled jobs and worked for subsistence-level wages. The slums and tenements in which they lived had high rates of disease. Middle- and upper-class Americans often responded by moving to fashionable avenues or suburbs and by stigmatizing them as nonwhite and racially inferior.

To distinguish themselves from these newcomers, native-born Americans stressed their commitment to Victorian morality, with its emphasis on manners, decorum, and self-control. Although never fully accepted even among the well-to-do, these Victorian ideals were meant to apply new standards for society. Lavish department stores and artistically designed houses reflected the middle- and upper-class faith that the consumption of material goods indicated good taste.

To raise standards, the prosperous classes expanded the number of high schools and created a new research university system for training educators, lawyers, doctors, and other professionals. As defenders of the new Victorian morality, educated middle- and upper-class women were expected to become the protectors of the home.

In contrast to the upper classes, immigrant newcomers created their own political machines to gain access to work and address the problems of poverty and congestion in the inner city. Although political bosses, at times supported by graft and corruption, handed out jobs and helped many constituents face problems of sickness and misfortune, their efforts were overshadowed by native-born reformers who blamed the immigrants for part of their problems. While Jacob Riis, Jane Addams, and other reformers worked to improve overcrowded housing and dangerous working conditions, Anthony Comstock and less sympathetic reformers attacked immigrant values and cultures in an effort to uplift and Americanize them.

Nowhere was the conflict between the social classes more evident than in the controversy over leisure entertainment. Caught up in the material benefits of a prospering industrial society, middle- and upper-class Americans battled against what they deemed "indecent" lower-class behavior in all its forms, from dancing to ragtime, gambling, and prizefighting to playing baseball on Sunday and visiting bawdy boardwalk sideshows. Even public parks became arenas of class conflict. Whereas the elite favored large, impeccably groomed urban parks that would serve as models of orderliness and propriety, working people fought for parks where they could picnic, play ball, drink beer, and escape the stifling heat of tenement apartments.

Although the well-to-do classes often appeared to have the upper hand in these clashes, significant disagreements about moral standards surfaced early within their own ranks. Critics, among them Charlotte Perkins Gilman, faulted middle-class society for its obsession with polite manners, empty social rituals, and restrictions on the occupations open to women.

By 1900, the contest for power between the elite classes and the largely immigrant working class was heading toward a partial resolution. As Victorian morality eroded, undermined by dissension from within and opposition from without, new standards emerged that blended elements of earlier positions. For example, new rules regulated behavior in the boxing ring and on the baseball field. Still, it was immigrant heroes who captured the popular imagination. The elite vision of sport as a vehicle for instilling self-discipline and self-control was transformed into a new commitment to sports as spectacle and entertainment. Sports had become big business and an important part of the new consumerism.

Similar patterns of compromise and change took place in other arenas. Vaudeville houses, attacked by the affluent for their risqué performances, evolved into the nation's first movie theaters. Ragtime music, with its syncopated rhythms, gave rise to jazz. In short, the dashing, disreputable, and raucous working-class culture of the late-nineteenth-century city can be seen as the seedbed of twentieth-century mass culture. And everywhere popular culture became increasingly dominated by commercial interests that capitalized on the disposable income created by the nation's explosive urban growth.

20

Politics and Expansion in an Industrializing Age, 1877–1900

PARTY POLITICS IN AN ERA OF UPHEAVAL, 1877–1884

Between 1877 and 1894 four presidents squeezed into office by the narrowest of margins; control of the House of Representatives changed hands five times; and seven new western states were admitted into the Union. Competition between political parties was intense. No one party could muster a working majority.

To meet these challenges, Republicans, Democrats, and third-party leaders sought desperately to reshape their political organizations to win over and cement the loyalty of their followers. While the Democrats rebuilt their strength in the South and mounted new challenges, Republicans struggled to maintain the loyalties of the working class, to strengthen their support from business, and to fight off the threat of new third parties. Not until 1896, in the aftermath of a massive depression that hit when the Democrats and a new third party, the Populists, were in office, did the Republicans consolidate their power and build a coalition that would control Congress and the presidency for the next fifteen years.

Contested Political Visions — Between 1876 and 1896, the intense competition between parties produced an incredible turnout of voters. Although most women did not yet have the vote and blacks were increasingly being disenfranchised, more than 80 percent of eligible white males often voted, and in particularly hard-fought state and local elections, the percentage could rise to 95 percent. Voter participation a century later would equal scarcely half that level.

Higher voter turnout resulted in part from the attempts of the major parties to navigate the stormy economy created by postwar industrial and geographic expansion, the influx of millions of immigrants, and the explosive growth of cities (see Chapters 18 and 19). At the same time that voter turnout shot up, however, political parties side-stepped many of the issues created by industrialization, such as taxation of corporations, support for those injured in factory accidents, and poverty relief. Nor was the American labor movement, unlike its counterpart in Europe, able to organize itself effectively as a political force (see Chapter 18). Except for the Interstate Commerce Act of 1887 and the largely symbolic Sherman Anti-Trust Act of 1890, Washington generally ignored the social consequences of industrialization and focused instead on encouraging economic growth.

How can we explain this refusal to address economic concerns and, at the same time, account for the enormous popular support for parties? The answer lies in the political ideology of the period and the two major symbolic and economic issues that preoccupied lawmakers nationally. The first involved the economic issues of the tariff and the money supply. The second issue focused on civil-service reform, aimed at awarding government jobs on the basis of merit rather than political connections.

Political parties in the late nineteenth century energized voters not only by appealing to economic self-interest, as was evident in support for industrialization and pensions for Civil War veterans and their widows, but also by linking their programs to deeply held beliefs about the nature of the family and the proper role of government. In its prewar years, the Republican Party had enhanced economic opportunities for common people by using governmental authority to expand railroads, increase tariff protection for industry, and provide land subsidies to farmers. With encouragement from evangelical ministers, it had also espoused a belief in female moral superiority and a willingness to use government as an instrument to protect family life. Hostility to slavery was based in part on the assumption that slaveholding corroded family values. The Democrats, in contrast, had viewed emancipation as a threat to patriarchal order and racial control.

After the Civil War, these positions hardened into political ideologies. Republicans justified their support for the tariff and defended their commitment to Union widows' pensions as a protection for the family home and female wage earners. Men, in particular, associated loyalty to party with a sense of masculinity. Democrats countered, using metaphors of the seduction and rape of white women by external forces and labeling Republican programs as classic examples of the perils of using excessive government force. High tariffs imperiled the family and threatened economic disaster.

Despite their differences over the tariff and monetary policy, neither Republicans nor Democrats believed that the national government had any right to regulate corporations or to protect the social welfare of workers. Neither party therefore courted the labor union vote (see Chapter 18). Many members of the dominant parties, particularly among the middle and upper classes, embraced the doctrine of **laissez-faire**—the belief that unregulated competition represented the best path to progress. According to this view, the federal government should promote economic development but not regulate the industries that it subsidized.

Rather than looking to Washington, people turned to local or state authorities. On the Great Plains, angry farmers demanded that their state legislatures regulate railroad rates. In the cities, immigrant groups, organized by political bosses, battled for control

CHRONOLOGY, 1877–1902

1878 • Congress requires U.S. Treasury to purchase silver.

1880 • James Garfield elected president.

1881 • Assassination of Garfield; Chester A. Arthur becomes president.

1883 • Pendleton Civil Service Act.

1884 • Grover Cleveland elected president.

1886 • *Wabash v. Illinois.*

1887 • Interstate Commerce Act.

1888 • Benjamin Harrison elected president.

1889 • National Farmers' Alliance formed.

1890 • Sherman Silver Purchase Act.
Sherman Anti-Trust Act.
McKinley Tariff pushes tariffs to all-time high.

1893 • Panic of 1893; depression of 1893–1897 begins.
Repeal of the Sherman Silver Purchase Act.

1894 • Coxey's "army" marches on Washington.
Pullman strike.
Wilson-Gorman Tariff.

1895 • Supreme Court declares federal income tax unconstitutional.

1896 • Free-silver forces capture Democratic Party and nominate William Jennings Bryan.
William McKinley elected president.

1898 • Acquisition of Hawaii.
Spanish-American War.

1898–1902 • Guerrilla uprising in Philippines.

1900 • Currency Act officially places United States on gold standard.

1901 • Platt Amendment retains U.S. role in Cuba.
Regular Army Nursing Corps founded.

1902 • Philippine Government Act.

of municipal governments and local contracts. In response, native-born reformers attempted to oust the political machines and clean up corruption (see Chapter 19).

Moreover, city and state governments vied with each other for control. Cities often could not change their system of government, alter their tax structure, or regulate municipal utilities without state approval. When Chicago wanted to issue permits to street popcorn vendors, for example, the Illinois legislature had to pass a special act.

Party loyalty for both Republicans and Democrats was reinforced by a sense of personal grievance that resulted from the belief, often true, that the other party had engaged in election fraud to steal elections. Although both parties, in both the North and the South, practiced fraud by rigging elections, throwing out opposition votes, and paying for "floaters" who moved from precinct to precinct to vote, each developed a sense of moral outrage at the other's behavior that invigorated party spirit.

By linking economic policy to family values, both parties reinforced the appeal of their platforms and, in the process, encouraged the participation of women in the political process. Although most women could not vote, they played an active role in politics in this period. Frances Willard and her followers in the Woman's Christian Temperance Union (WCTU), for example, helped create a Prohibition and Home Protection Party in the 1880s. A decade later, western women Populists won full suffrage in Colorado, Idaho, and Utah.

Patterns of Party Strength   In the 1870s and 1880s each party had its own ideological appeal and centers of regional strength. The Democrats ruled the South; southern sections of border states like Ohio; midwestern states like Wisconsin; and northern cities with large immigrant populations. In the South, the white Democratic party elite viewed Republicans as villains who had devastated their lands and set up fraudulent carpetbag governments in the defeated Confederacy. The Democrats campaigned for minimal government expenditures, opposed tariff increases, and generally attacked what they considered to be "governmental interference in the economy."

In addition to resisting government support for the economy, Democrats staunchly defended their immigrant followers. On the state and local levels, they fiercely opposed prohibition and other attempts to limit alcohol use and license saloons. They also advocated support for parochial schools and opposed attempts to require immigrant children to attend only those schools that taught in English.

The Republicans, who reigned in rural and small-town New England, Pennsylvania, and the upper Midwest and who drew support from the **Grand Army of the Republic (GAR)**, a social and political lobbying organization of northern Civil War veterans, often "waved the bloody shirt," reminding voters that their party had led the nation during the Civil War. "The Democratic Party," wrote one Republican, "may be described as a common sewer and loathsome receptacle, into which is emptied every element of treason North and South." To solidify their followers, the Republicans ran a series of former Union army generals for president and voted generous veterans' benefits.

State and local party leaders managed campaigns. They chose the candidates, raised money, organized rallies, and—if their candidate won—distributed public jobs to party workers. Bosses like the former saloonkeepers "Big Jim" Pendergast of Kansas City, a Democrat, and George B. Cox of Cincinnati, a Republican, turned out the vote by taking care of constituents, handing out municipal jobs, and financing campaigns with "contributions" extracted from city employees.

Although the struggle to define the legitimate use of governmental authority shaped the general debate between the two major parties on the federal level, family tradition, ethnic ties, religious affiliation, and local issues often determined an individual's vote. Outside the South, ethnicity and religion were the most reliable predictors of party affiliation. Catholics, especially Irish Catholics, and Americans of German ancestry tended to vote Democratic. Old-stock northerners, in contrast, including 75 percent of Methodists and Congregationalists, 65 percent of Baptists, and 60 percent of Presbyterians voted Republican. Among immigrant groups, most British-born Protestants and 80 percent of Swedish and Norwegian Lutherans voted Republican, as did African-Americans, North and South. Although intolerant of racial differences, the Democrats were generally more accepting of religious diversity than were the Republicans.

Political battles often centered on cultural differences, as native-born Protestants tried to force on immigrants their own views on gambling, temperance, and Sabbath observance. No issue on the local level aroused more conflict than prohibition. Irish whiskey drinkers, German beer drinkers, and Italian wine drinkers were equally outraged by antiliquor legislation. State and local prohibition proposals always aroused passionate voter interest.

Regulating the
Money Supply

In the 1870s, politicians confronted a tough problem: how to create a money supply adequate for a growing economy without producing inflation. Americans' almost superstitious reverence for gold and silver added to the difficulty of establishing a coherent monetary policy. The only trustworthy money, many believed, was gold or silver, or certificates exchangeable for these precious metals. Reflecting this notion, all the federally issued currency in circulation in 1860 consisted of gold or silver coins or U.S. Treasury notes redeemable for gold or silver. (Currency from some sixteen hundred state banks was also in circulation, worsening a chaotic monetary situation.)

Opposing groups clashed over the money question. Bankers and creditors, most business leaders, economists, and politicians believed that economic stability required a strictly limited currency supply. Debtors, especially southern and western farmers, favored expanding the money supply to make it easier for them to pay off their debts. The monetary debate focused on a specific question: should the Civil War paper "greenbacks" currently in circulation be retained and even expanded, or phased out, leaving only a currency backed by gold (see Chapter 15)? The hard times associated with the Panic of 1873 sharpened this dispute.

The Greenback party (founded 1877) advocated an expanded money supply, health and safety regulations for the workplace, and other measures to benefit workers and farmers. In the 1878 midterm elections, with the support of labor organizations angered by the government's hostility in the labor unrest of 1877, Greenback candidates won fourteen seats in Congress.

As prosperity returned and the Greenback party faded, the debate became focused on the coinage of silver. In 1873, with little silver being mined, Congress instructed the U.S. mint to stop making silver coins. Silver had been "demonetized." But new discoveries in Nevada (see Chapter 17) vastly increased the silver supply, and debtor groups now demanded that the government resume the coinage of silver.

Enthusiastically backed by the silver-mine owners, silver forces won a partial victory in 1878, when Congress required the treasury to buy up to $4 million worth of silver each month and mint it into silver dollars. But the treasury, dominated by monetary conservatives, sabotaged the law's intent by refusing to circulate the silver dollars that it minted.

Frustrated silver advocates tried a new approach in the **Sherman Silver Purchase Act** of 1890. This measure instructed the treasury to buy, at current market prices, 4.5 million ounces of silver monthly—almost precisely the output of the nation's silver mines. The act further required the government to issue treasury notes, redeemable in gold or silver, equivalent to the cost of these purchases. This law did slightly increase the money supply; but as silver prices fell in 1893 and after, the government paid far less for its monthly purchases and therefore issued fewer treasury notes. The controversy over silver dragged on.

Civil-Service Reform For decades successful candidates in national, state, and local elections had rewarded supporters with jobs ranging from cabinet seats and ambassadorships to lowly municipal posts. To its defenders, this system, originally called rotation in office, seemed a democratic means of filling government positions. But unqualified and incompetent applicants often got jobs simply because of their party loyalty. Once in office, these appointees had to contribute to the reelection campaigns of their political patrons. Because of such abuses, this mode of filling public jobs came to be called the spoils system after the old expression, "To the victor belong the spoils."

For years, a small but influential group of upper-class reformers, including Missouri senator Carl Schurz and editor E. L. Godkin of the *Nation,* had campaigned for a professional civil service based on merit. Well bred, well educated, and wealthy, these reformers favored a civil service staffed by "gentlemen." Whatever their class biases, the reformers had a point. A professional civil service was needed as government grew more complex.

Elected through the compromise that ended Reconstruction (see Chapter 16), Republican president Rutherford B. Hayes cautiously embraced the civil-service cause. In 1877, he launched an investigation of the corruption-riddled New York City customs office and fired two high officials. One, Chester A. Arthur, had played a key role in passing out jobs. Hayes's willingness to confront factions within his own party won praise from civil-service reformers, but critics ridiculed "snivel service" and "Rutherfraud B. Hayes."

When Congressman James A. Garfield won the 1880 Republican presidential nomination, the delegates, to appease the opposing New York faction, chose Chester A. Arthur, the loyalist Hayes had recently fired, as Garfield's running mate. Since Garfield enjoyed excellent health, the choice of the totally unqualified Arthur seemed safe.

The Democrats nominated a career army officer from Pennsylvania, Winfield Scott Hancock, and the Greenbackers gave the nod to Congressman James B. Weaver of Iowa. Garfield's managers stressed his Civil War record and his log-cabin birth. By a razor-thin margin of under forty thousand votes (of 9.2 million cast), Garfield edged out Hancock; Weaver trailed far behind.

Garfield's assassination in 1881, which brought to the White House Vice President Arthur, the very symbol of patronage corruption, gave a powerful emotional thrust to the cause, as civil-service reformers portrayed the fallen president as a spoils-system martyr. In 1883 Congress enacted a civil-service law introduced by Senator George Pendleton of Ohio (Garfield's home state) and drafted by the Civil Service Reform League that had been created two years earlier. The **Pendleton Civil Service Act** set up a commission to prepare competitive examinations and establish standards of merit for a variety of federal jobs; it also forbade political candidates from soliciting contributions from government workers.

Although the Pendleton Act initially covered only about 12 percent of the more than 100,000 federal employees, the number of positions was gradually expanded by subsequent presidents. By the 1890s, the act had opened up new positions for women,

"Where Is the Difference?" 1894   *By equating criminal payoffs to the police to corporate contributions to senators, this cartoon suggests that corruption pervades society and needs to be stopped.*

who now held nearly a third of the jobs as federal clerks in government agencies. The creation of a professional civil service thus helped bring the federal government in step with the modernizing trends transforming society.

As for Chester A. Arthur, the fact that he proved to be a mediocre president pleasantly surprised those who had expected him to be an utter disaster. Arthur supported civil-service reform and proved quite independent. Fed up with the feuding Republicans, in 1882 the voters gave the Democrats a strong majority in the House of Representatives. In 1884, for the first time since 1856, they would put a Democrat in the White House: Grover Cleveland.

POLITICS OF PRIVILEGE, POLITICS OF EXCLUSION, 1884–1892

The stalemate between the two major parties in their battle to establish the standards for economic growth continued under President Cleveland. Although no radical, Cleveland challenged powerful interests by calling for cuts in the tariff and in veterans' pensions. In 1888, business groups and the veterans' lobby rallied to defeat Cleveland and elect Benjamin Harrison of Indiana, a former Civil War general, in one of the most corrupt campaigns in American history. Harrison further alienated voters by passing a high tariff and an expanded pension law that increased the number of pensioners by 43 percent.

Fed up with both the Democrats' and Republicans' fraud and inattention to the needs of rural Americans, farmers mounted protests and began to organize. While the Grange and Farmers' Alliance movements condemned the monopolistic practices of grain and cotton buyers in the post-Reconstruction South, the white majority consolidated their political power by denying the region's black citizens their most basic rights.

A Democrat in the White House: Grover Cleveland, 1885–1889 At a tumultuous Chicago convention in 1884, the Republicans nominated their best-known leader, James G. Blaine. A gifted orator with a keen memory for names and faces, Blaine spoke for the younger, more dynamic wing of the Republican Party eager to shed the taint of corruption, promote economic development, and reinvigorate foreign policy.

But Blaine's name had been stained by the revelation that he, as Speaker of the House, had offered political favors to a railroad company in exchange for stock. For reformers, Blaine epitomized the hated patronage system. To E. L. Godkin, he "wallowed in spoils like a rhinoceros in an African pool."

Sensing Blaine's vulnerability, the Democrats chose a sharply contrasting nominee, Grover Cleveland of New York. In a meteoric rise from reform mayor of Buffalo to governor, Cleveland had fought the bosses and spoilsmen. Short, rotund, and resembling a bulldog, Cleveland was his own man. The shrewdness of the Democrats' choice became apparent when Godkin, Carl Schurz, and other Republican reformers bolted to Cleveland. They were promptly nicknamed **Mugwumps,** an Algonquian term for a renegade chief.

But Cleveland had liabilities, including an illegitimate child he had fathered as a youth. Cleveland admitted the indiscretion, but Republicans still jeered at rallies: "Ma, Ma, where's my pa?" Cleveland also faced opposition from Tammany Hall, the New York City Democratic machine that he had fought as governor. If Tammany's immigrant voters stayed home on election day, Cleveland could lose his own state. But in October a New York City clergyman denounced the Democrats as the party of "Rum, Romanism, and Rebellion." Blaine failed to immediately repudiate the remark. The Cleveland campaign managers widely publicized this triple insult to Catholics, to patriotic Democrats tired of the "bloody shirt," and to drinkers. This blunder and the Mugwumps' defection allowed Cleveland to carry New York State by twelve hundred votes, and with it the election.

Cleveland embraced the belief that government must not meddle in the economy. In Andrew Jackson's day, laissez-faire had been a radical idea endorsed by small entrepreneurs who wanted business conditions favorable to competition; by the 1880s it had become the rallying cry of a corporate elite opposed to any public regulation. Sharing this outlook, Cleveland asserted the power of the presidency mostly through his vetoes and displayed a limited grasp of industrialization's impact. Vetoing a bill that would have provided seeds to drought-stricken farmers in Texas, he warned that people should not expect the government to solve their problems.

One public matter did arouse Cleveland's energies: the tariff, an issue involving a tangle of conflicting economic and political interests. Tariff duties were a major source of revenue in the era before a federal income tax, so the tariff was really a form of taxation. But which imported goods should be subject to duties, and how much? Opinions differed radically.

The producers of such commodities as coal, hides, timber, and wool demanded tariff protection against foreign competition, and industries that had prospered behind tariff walls—iron and steel, textiles, machine tools—wanted protection to continue. Many workers in these industries agreed, convinced that high tariffs meant higher wages. Other manufacturers, however, while seeking protection for their finished products, wanted low tariffs on the raw materials they required. Massachusetts shoe manufacturers, for example, urged high duties on imported shoes but low duties on imported hides. Most farmers, by contrast, hated the protective tariff, charging that it inflated farm-equipment prices and, by impeding trade, made it hard to sell American farm products abroad.

Cleveland's call for lower tariffs arose from a concern over the high tariffs' generation of millions of dollars in surplus federal revenue. This surplus tempted legislators to distribute the money in the form of veterans' pensions or expensive public-works programs in their home districts, commonly called pork-barrel projects. With his horror of paternalistic government, Cleveland viewed the budget surplus as a corrupting influence. In his annual message in 1887, Cleveland argued that lower tariffs not only would cut the federal surplus but would also reduce prices and slow the development of trusts. Although the Democratic campaign of 1888 gave little attention to the issue, Cleveland's talk of lowering the tariff angered many corporate leaders.

Cleveland created another problem when he took on the Grand Army of the Republic. Veterans' disability pensions cost the government millions of dollars annually. No one opposed pensions for the deserving, but by the 1880s fraudulent claims had become a public scandal. Unlike his predecessors, Cleveland investigated these claims and rejected many of them. In 1887 he vetoed a bill that would have pensioned all disabled veterans (even if their disability had nothing to do with military service) and their dependents. The pension list should be an honor roll, he declared, not a refuge for fraud.

Big Business Strikes Back; Benjamin Harrison, 1889–1893
By 1888, some influential interest groups had concluded that Cleveland must go. When Blaine decided not to challenge him, the Republicans turned to Benjamin Harrison of Indiana, the grandson of William Henry Harrison. A corporation lawyer and former senator, Harrison was so aloof that some ridiculed him as the human iceberg. His campaign managers learned to whisk him away after speeches before anyone could talk with him or experience his flabby handshake.

Harrison's managers also developed a new style of electioneering. They brought delegations to Indianapolis and hammered at the tariff issue. Falsely portraying Cleveland as an advocate of "free trade"—the elimination of all tariffs—they warned of the bad effects of such a step. The high protective tariff, they argued, ensured prosperity, decent wages for industrial workers, and a healthy home market for farmers.

The Republicans amassed a $4 million campaign fund from worried business leaders. (Because the Pendleton Civil Service Act had outlawed campaign contributions by government workers, political parties depended more than ever on corporate donors.) This war chest purchased not only posters and buttons but also votes.

Despite such fraud, Cleveland got almost a hundred thousand more votes than Harrison. But Harrison carried the key states of Indiana and New York and won in the Electoral College. The Republicans held the Senate and regained the House. When

Harrison piously observed that Providence had aided the Republican cause, his campaign chairman snorted, "Providence hadn't a damn thing to do with it. . . . [A] number of men . . . approach[ed] the gates of the penitentiary to make him president."

Harrison swiftly rewarded his supporters. He appointed as commissioner of pensions a GAR official who, on taking office, declared "God help the surplus!" The pension rolls soon ballooned from 676,000 to nearly a million. This massive pension system (which was coupled with medical care in a network of veterans' hospitals) became America's first large-scale public-welfare program. In 1890, the triumphant Republicans also enacted the McKinley Tariff, which pushed rates to an all-time high.

Rarely has the federal government been so subservient to entrenched economic interests and so out of touch with the plight of the disadvantaged as during the 1880s. But discontent was rising. The midterm election of 1890, when the Democrats gained sixty-six congressional seats to win control of the House of Representatives, awakened the nation to a tide of political activism engulfing the agrarian South and West. This activism, spawned by chronic problems in rural America, had a long history.

Agrarian Protest and the Rise of the People's Party

As discussed in Chapter 17, Great Plains farming proved far riskier than many had anticipated. Terrible grasshopper infestations consumed nearly half the midwestern wheat crop between 1873 and 1877. Although overall production surged after 1870, the abundant harvests undercut prices. Wheat tumbled from $2.95 a bushel in 1866 to $1.06 in 1880. Countless farmers who had borrowed heavily to finance homesteads and expensive machinery went bankrupt or barely survived. One struggling Minnesota farmer wrote the governor in 1874, "[W]e can see nothing but starvation in the future if relief does not come."

When relief did not come, the farmers responded by setting up cooperative ventures. In 1867, under the leadership of Oliver H. Kelley, a Department of Agriculture clerk, midwestern farmers formed the **Grange**, or "Patrons of Husbandry," as it was officially called. Membership climbed to more than 1.5 million in the early 1870s. Patterned after the Masonic Order, the Grange offered information, emotional support, and fellowship. But the Grange's central concern was farmers' economic plight. An 1874 circular announced the organization's primary purpose: to help farmers "buy less and produce more, in order to make our farms more self-sustaining." Members sought to restore self-sufficiency to the family farm. They negotiated special discounts with farm-machinery dealers and set up "cash-only" cooperative stores and grain-storage elevators to cut out the "middlemen"—the bankers, grain brokers, and merchants who made money at their expense.

Grangers focused their wrath on railroads, which routinely gave discounts to large shippers, bribed state legislators, and charged higher rates for short runs than for long hauls. Stung by these practices, Grangers in Illinois, Wisconsin, Minnesota, and Iowa lobbied state legislatures in 1874 to pass laws fixing maximum rates for freight shipments.

The railroads appealed to the Supreme Court to declare these "Granger laws" unconstitutional. But in *Munn* v. *Illinois* (1877) the Court not only rejected the railroads' appeal but also upheld an Illinois law setting a maximum rate for the storage of grain. The regulation of grain elevators, declared the Court's majority, was legitimate under the federal Constitution's acknowledgment of the right of states to exercise police powers. When the Court in *Wabash* v. *Illinois* (1886) modified this position by prohibit-

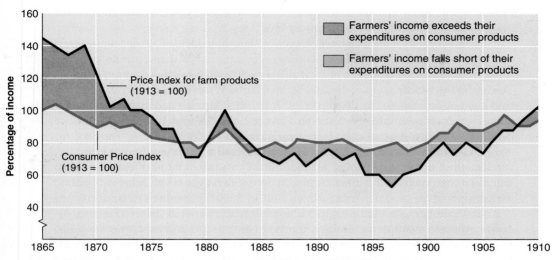

Figure 20.1 Consumer Prices and Farm-Product Prices, 1865–1913

From 1865 to 1895, the prices that farmers received for their crops gradually declined. Even when they increased after 1895, farmers had difficulty in making ends meet. As cycles of drought and debt battered Great Plains wheat growers, a Kansas farmer wrote, "At the age of 52, after a long life of toil, economy, and self-denial, I find myself and family virtually paupers."

ing states from regulating interstate railroad rates, Congress passed the Interstate Commerce Act (1887), reaffirming the federal government's power to investigate and oversee railroad activities and establishing a new agency, the Interstate Commerce Commission (ICC), to do just that. Although the commission failed to curb the railroads' monopolistic practices, it did establish the principle of federal regulation of interstate transportation.

Despite promising beginnings, the Grange movement soon faltered. The railroads, having lost their battle on the national level, lobbied state legislatures and won repeal of most of the rate-regulation laws by 1878. Moreover, the Grange system of cash-only cooperative stores failed because few farmers had sufficient cash. Ultimately, the Grange ideal of complete financial independence proved unrealistic. Under the conditions that prevailed on the Plains, it was impossible to farm without borrowing money.

When the prices of corn, wheat, and cotton briefly revived after 1878, many farmers deserted the Grange. Although the Grange lived on as a social and educational institution, it lost its economic clout because it was ultimately unable to improve its members' financial position. For all its weaknesses, the Grange laid the groundwork for an even more powerful wave of agrarian protest.

While the Grange was centered in the Midwest and the Great Plains, the **Farmers' Alliance** movement first arose in the South and West, where farmers grappled with many of the same problems. In the cotton South, small planters found themselves trapped by the crop-lien system, mortgaging future harvests to cover current expenses.

Mired in debt, many gave up their land and became tenants or sharecroppers. About a third of southern farmers were tenants by 1900.

The Farmers' Alliance movement began in Texas in the late 1870s as poor farmers gathered to discuss their hardships. Soon an organization took shape, promoted by activists who organized hundreds of local alliances. The alliance idea advanced eastward across the Lower South, especially after Texan Charles W. Macune, a self-trained lawyer and a physician, assumed leadership in 1887. By 1889, Macune had merged several regional organizations into the National Farmers' Alliance and Industrial Union, or Southern Alliance. A parallel black organization, the National Colored Farmers' Alliance, had meanwhile emerged in Arkansas and spread to other southern states.

Like the Grange, the Farmers' Alliance initially organized farmers' cooperatives to purchase equipment and market cotton. Many cooperatives failed, however, because farmers lacked the capital to finance them. Still, by 1890 the Southern Alliance claimed 3 million members. An additional 1.2 million joined the National Colored Farmers' Alliance. Alliance members generally comprised not only the poorest farmers but also those most dependent on a single crop and most geographically isolated. As they attended alliance rallies and picnics, read the alliance newspaper, and listened to alliance speakers, hard-hit farm families became increasingly aware of their political potential. An Arkansas member wrote in 1889, "Reform never begins with the leaders, it comes from the people."

Alliance fever soon spread to the Great Plains. In the drought-plagued years of 1880 and 1881, alliances sprang up in Kansas, Nebraska, Iowa, and Minnesota. Membership grew when drought returned, insects destroyed much of the wheat crop, and prices for agricultural produce fell as world production increased. Under these conditions, many settlers returned East. "In God we trusted, in Kansas we busted," some scrawled on their wagons. Western Kansas lost 50 percent of its population between 1888 and 1892. But others hung on, and the Northwestern Alliance grew rapidly. By 1890, the Kansas Alliance claimed 130,000 members, followed closely by alliances in Nebraska, the Dakotas, and Minnesota. What had begun as a desperate attempt to save their farms had now turned into a massive political campaign to change the American political and economic system.

Reformers at first tried to create a biracial movement. Southern Alliance leaders Tom Watson of Georgia and Leonidas Polk of North Carolina urged southern farmers, black and white, to act together. For a time, this message of racial cooperation in the interest of reform offered promise. In Kansas, meanwhile, Jerry Simpson, a rancher who lost his stock in the hard winter of 1886–1887, became a major alliance leader. Mary E. Lease, a Wichita lawyer, burst on the scene in 1890 as a fiery alliance orator.

Other women, veterans of the Granger or prohibition cause, rallied to the new cause, founding the National Women's Alliance (NWA) in 1891. Declared the NWA, "Put 1,000 women lecturers in the field and revolution is here." By no coincidence, a strong feminist strain pervades Ignatius Donnelly's *The Golden Bottle* (1892), a novel portraying the agrarian reformers' social vision.

As the movement swelled, the opposition turned nasty. When Jerry Simpson mentioned the silk stockings of a conservative politician in his district and noted that he had no such finery, a hostile newspaper editor labeled him "Sockless Jerry" Simpson, the nickname he carried to his grave. When Mary Lease advised Kansas to "raise less corn and more hell," another editor sneered: "[Kansas] has started to raise hell, as Mrs.

Lease advised, and [the state] seems to have an overproduction. But that doesn't matter. Kansas never did believe in diversified crops."

All this activity helped shape a new political agenda. In 1889, the Southern and Northwestern Alliances loosely merged and adopted a political litmus test for candidates in the 1890 midterm elections. They focused on increasing government action on behalf of farmers and workers, including tariff reduction, a graduated income tax, public ownership of the railroads, federal funding for irrigation research, a ban on landownership by aliens, and "the free and unlimited coinage of silver."

The 1890 elections revealed the strength of agrarian protest. Southern Democrats who endorsed alliance goals won four governorships and control of eight state legislatures. On the Great Plains, alliance-endorsed candidates secured control of the Nebraska legislature and gained the balance of power in Minnesota and South Dakota. In Kansas, the candidates of the alliance-sponsored People's Party demolished all opposition. Three alliance-backed senators, together with some fifty congressmen (including Watson and Simpson), went to Washington as angry winds from the hinterlands buffeted the political system.

Regional differences, which threatened to divide the movement, were soon overcome by shared economic grievance. Southern Alliance leaders who initially opposed endorsing a third party, fearing that it would weaken the southern Democratic Party, the bastion of white supremacy, eventually adopted the third-party idea, since many Democrats whom they had backed in 1890 had ignored the alliance agenda once in office. In February 1892, alliance leaders organized the People's Party of the United States, generally called the **Populist Party.** At the party convention in Omaha, Nebraska, that August, cheering delegates nominated for president the former Civil War general and Greenback nominee James B. Weaver of Iowa. Courting the South, they chose as Weaver's running mate the Virginian James Field, who had lost a leg fighting for the Confederacy.

The Populist platform restated the alliance goals while adding a call for the direct popular election of senators and other electoral reforms. It also endorsed a **subtreasury plan** devised by alliance leader Charles Macune by which farmers could store their nonperishable commodities in government warehouses, receive low-interest loans using the crops as collateral, and then sell the stored commodities when market prices rose. Ignatius Donnelly's ringing preamble pronounced the nation on "the verge of moral, political, and material ruin" and called for a return of the government "to the hands of 'the plain people' with which class it originated."

African-Americans After Reconstruction

As the Populists geared up for the 1892 campaign, another group of citizens with profound grievances found themselves pushed even farther to the margins of American public life. The end of Reconstruction in 1877 and the restoration of power to the southern white elites, the so-called redeemers (see Chapter 16), was ominous for southern blacks. The redeemer coalition of large landowners, merchants, and "New South" industrialists had little interest in the former slaves except as a docile labor force or as political pawns. However, southern white opinion demanded an end to the hated "Negro rule," and local Democratic Party officials pursued this objective. Suppressing the black vote became a major goal. At first, black disfranchisement was achieved by intimidation, terror, and vote fraud, as blacks were either kept from the

The Knights of Labor
Black delegate Frank J. Farrell introduces Terence V. Powderly, head of the Knights of Labor, at the organization's 1886 convention. The Knights were unusual in accepting both black and female workers.

polls or forced to vote Democratic. Then in 1890 Mississippi amended its state constitution in ways that effectively excluded most black voters, and other southern states soon followed suit.

Because the Fifteenth Amendment (1870) (see Chapter 16) guaranteed all male citizens' right to vote, white southerners used indirect means such as literacy tests (a test of the ability to read), poll taxes (a tax paid to vote), and property requirements (which restricted the right to vote to those who owned property) to disfranchise blacks. The racist intent of these devices was obvious. One stratagem, the so-called grandfather clause, exempted from these electoral requirements anyone with an ancestor who had voted in 1860. Although black disfranchisement proceeded erratically over the South, by the early twentieth century it was essentially complete.

Disfranchisement was only one part of the system of white supremacy laboriously erected in the South. In a parallel development that culminated in the early twentieth century, state after state passed laws imposing strict racial segregation in many realms of life (see Chapter 21).

Black caterers, barbers, bricklayers, carpenters, and other artisans lost their white clientele. Blacks who went to prison—sometimes for minor offenses—faced the convict-lease system, by which cotton planters, railroad builders, coal-mine operators, and other employers "leased" prison gangs and forced them to work under slave-labor conditions.

The convict-lease system not only enforced the racial hierarchy but also played an important economic role as industrialization and agricultural change came to the South. The system brought income to hard-pressed state governments and provided factories, railroads, mines, and large-scale farms with a predictable, controllable, and cheap labor supply. The system also intimidated free laborers. One observer commented, "[O]n account of the convict employment, strikes are of rare occurrence." Recognizing this danger, free miners in Tennessee successfully agitated against the employment of convict labor in their state in the 1890s. Thousands died under the brutal convict-labor system. It survived into the early decades of the twentieth century, ultimately succumbing to humanitarian protest and to economic changes that made it unprofitable.

Lynching became the ultimate enforcer of southern white supremacy. Through the 1880s and 1890s, about a hundred blacks were lynched annually in the United States, mainly in the South. The stated reasons, often the rape of a white woman, frequently arose from rumor and unsubstantiated accusations. The charge of "attempted rape," as the black journalist Ida B. Wells pointed out to a national audience (see Chapter 21), could cover a wide range of behaviors unacceptable to whites, such as questioning authority or talking back.

The lynch mob demonstrated whites' absolute power. In the South, more than 80 percent of the lynchings involved black victims. Lynchings most commonly occurred in the Cotton Belt, and they tended to rise at times of economic distress when cotton prices were falling and job competition between poor whites and poor blacks was most intense. By no coincidence, lynching peaked in 1892 as many poor blacks embraced the Farmers' Alliance movement and rallied to the Populist Party banner. Fifteen black Populists were killed in Georgia alone, it has been estimated, during that year's bitter campaign.

The relationship between southern agrarian protest and white racism was complex. Some Populists, like Georgia's Tom Watson, sought to build an interracial movement. Watson denounced lynching and the convict-lease system. When a black Populist leader pursued by a lynch mob took refuge in his house during the 1892 campaign, Watson summoned two thousand armed white Populists to defend him. But most white Populists clung to racism. Watson complained that most poor whites "would joyously hug the chains of . . . wretchedness rather than do any experimenting on [the race] question."

The white elite, eager to drive a wedge in the protest movement, inflamed lower-class white racism. The agricultural crisis of the period, which included a precipitous decline in cotton prices, had driven poor white tenant farmers in the South to the brink of despair. Those who lost control of their farms felt that they not only faced economic ruin, but also risked loss of their manhood. Conscious of themselves as a racial group, they feared that if they fell further down the economic ladder they would lose the racial privileges that came from their "whiteness" and be treated like blacks, Mexicans, and the foreign born. Hence, they were swayed by conservative Atlanta editor Henry W. Grady when he warned against division among white southerners: the region's only hope, he said, was "the clear and unmistakable domination of the white race."

Even as they warned of the dangers of "Negro rule," the white elite manipulated the urban black vote as a weapon against agrarian radicalism, driving Tom Watson to despair. On balance, the rise of southern agrarian protest deepened racial hatred and ultimately worsened blacks' situation.

While southern blacks suffered racist oppression, the federal government stood aside. A generation of northern politicians paid lip service to egalitarian principles but failed to apply them to blacks.

The Supreme Court similarly abandoned blacks. The Fourteenth Amendment (1868) had granted blacks citizenship and the equal protection of the laws, and the Civil Rights Act of 1875 outlawed racial discrimination on juries, in public places such as hotels and theaters, and on railroads, streetcars, and other such conveyances. But the Supreme Court soon ripped gaping holes in these protective laws.

In the *Civil Rights Cases* (1883), the Court declared the Civil Rights Act of 1875 unconstitutional. The Fourteenth Amendment protected citizens only from governmental infringement of their civil rights, the justices ruled, not from acts by private citizens such as railroad conductors. In **Plessy v. Ferguson (1896),** the justices upheld a Louisiana law requiring segregated railroad cars. Racial segregation was constitutional, the Court held, if equal facilities were made available to each race. (In a prophetic dissent, Associate Justice John Marshall Harlan observed, "Our Constitution is color blind." Segregation, he added, violated the constitutional principle of equality before the law.) With the Supreme Court's blessing, the South segregated its public school system, ignoring the caveat that such separate facilities must be equal. White children studied in nicer buildings, used newer equipment, and were taught by better-paid teachers. Not until 1954 did the Court abandon the "separate but equal" doctrine. Rounding out their dismal record, in 1898 the justices upheld the poll tax and literacy tests by which southern states had disfranchised blacks.

Few northerners protested the South's white-supremacist society. Until the North condemned lynching outright, declared the aged abolitionist Frederick Douglass in 1892, "it will remain equally involved with the South in this common crime." The restoration of sectional harmony, in short, came at a high price: acquiescence by the North in the utter debasement of the South's African-American citizenry. Further, the separatist principle endorsed in *Plessy* had a pervasive impact, affecting blacks nationwide, Mexicans in Texas, Asians in California, and other groups.

Blacks responded to their plight in various ways. The nation's foremost black leader from the 1890s to his death in 1915 was **Booker T. Washington.** Born in slavery in Virginia in 1856, the son of a slave woman and her white master, Washington attended a freedman's school in Hampton, Virginia, and in 1881 organized a black state vocational school in Alabama that eventually became Tuskegee University. Although Washington secretly contributed to lawyers who challenged segregation, he publicly urged accommodation to a racist society. In a widely publicized address in Atlanta in 1895, he insisted that the first task of America's blacks must be to acquire useful skills such as farming and carpentry. Once blacks proved their economic value, he predicted, racism would fade; meanwhile, they must patiently accept their lot. This was a position later challenged by W. E. B. Du Bois (see Chapter 21). Washington lectured widely, and his autobiography, *Up from Slavery* (1901), recounted his rise from poverty thanks to honesty, hard work, and kindly patrons—themes familiar to a generation reared on Horatio Alger's self-help books.

Other blacks responded resourcefully to the racist society. Black churches provided emotional support, as did black fraternal lodges like the Knights of Pythias. Some African-Americans started businesses to serve their community. Two black-owned banks, in Richmond and Washington, D.C., were chartered in 1888. The North Carolina Mutual Insurance Company, organized in 1898 by John Merrick, a prosperous Durham barber, evolved into a major enterprise. Bishop Henry M. Turner of the African Methodist Episcopal church urged blacks to return to Africa and build a great Christian nation. Turner made several trips to Africa in pursuit of his proposal.

African-American protest never wholly died out. Frederick Douglass urged that blacks press for full equality. "Who would be free, themselves must strike the first blow," he proclaimed in 1883. Blacks should meet violence with violence, insisted militant New York black leader T. Thomas Fortune.

Other blacks answered southern racism by leaving the region. In 1879, several thousand moved to Kansas (see Chapter 16). Some ten thousand migrated to Chicago between 1870 and 1890. Blacks who moved north soon found that although white supremacy was not official policy, public opinion sanctioned many forms of de facto discrimination. Northern black laborers, for example, encountered widespread prejudice. The Knights of Labor did welcome blacks and by the mid-1880s had an estimated sixty thousand black members. Its successor, the American Federation of Labor, officially forbade racial discrimination, but in practice many of its member unions excluded blacks.

The rise of the so-called solid South, firmly established on racist foundations, had important political implications. For one thing, it made a mockery of the two-party system in the South. For years, the only meaningful election south of the Potomac was the Democratic primary. Only in the 1960s, in the wake of sweeping social and economic changes, would a genuine two-party system emerge there. The large bloc of southern Democrats elected to Congress each year, accumulating seniority and power, exerted a great and often reactionary influence on public policy. Above all, they mobilized instantly to quash any threat to southern white supremacy. Finally, southern Democrats wielded enormous clout in the national party. No Democratic contender for national office who was unacceptable to them stood a chance.

Above all, the caste system that evolved in the post-Reconstruction South shaped the consciousness of those caught up in it, white and black alike. White novelist Lillian Smith described her girlhood in turn-of-the-century Florida and Georgia: "From the day I was born, I began to learn my lessons. . . . I learned it is possible to be a Christian and a white southerner simultaneously; to be a gentlewoman and an arrogant callous creature at the same moment; to pray at night and ride a Jim Crow car the next morning; . . . to glow when the word democracy was used, and to practice slavery from morning to night."

THE 1890S: POLITICS IN A DEPRESSION DECADE

Discontent with the major parties and their commitment to supporting unrestricted business enterprise, which had smoldered during the 1870s and 1880s, burst into flames in the 1890s. As banks failed and railroads went bankrupt, the nation slid into a grinding depression. The crises of the 1890s laid bare the paralysis of the federal government—dominated by a business elite—when confronted by the new social realities of factories, urban slums, immigrant workers, and desperate farmers. In response, irate farmers, laborers, and their supporters joined a new party, the Populists, to change the system.

1892: Populists Challenge the Status Quo   The Populist Party platform adopted in July 1892 offered a broad vision of national reform. That same month, thirteen people died in a gun battle between strikers and strikebreakers at the Homestead steel plant near Pittsburgh, and President Harrison sent federal troops to Coeur d'Alene, Idaho, where a silver-mine strike had turned violent. Events seemed to justify the Populists' warnings of chaos ahead.

Faced with domestic turmoil and fearful that the powerful European socialist movement would spread to the United States, both major parties acted cautiously. The Republicans renominated Harrison and adopted a platform that ignored escalating unrest. The Democrats turned again to Grover Cleveland, who in four years out of office had made clear his growing conservatism and his opposition to the Populists. Cleveland won by more than 360,000 votes, a decisive margin in this era of close elections. A public reaction against labor violence and the McKinley Tariff hurt Harrison, while Cleveland's support for the gold standard won business support.

Although Populist strength proved spotty, their achievements sparked great hopes for the future. James B. Weaver got just over a million votes—8.5 percent of the total—and the Populists elected five senators, ten congressmen, and three governors. The new party carried Kansas and registered some appeal in the West and in Georgia, Alabama, and Texas, where the alliance movement had taken deep root. But it made no dent in New England, the urban East, or the traditionally Republican farm regions of the Midwest. It even failed to show broad strength in the upper Great Plains. "Beaten! Whipped! Smashed!" moaned Minnesota Populist Ignatius Donnelly in his diary.

Throughout most of the South, racism, ingrained Democratic loyalty, distaste for a ticket headed by a former Union general, widespread intimidation, and voter fraud kept the Populist vote under 25 percent. This failure killed the prospects for interracial agrarian reform in the region. After 1892, as Populism began to revive in the South and Midwest, many southern politicians seeking to appeal to poor whites—including a disillusioned Tom Watson—stayed within the Democratic fold and laced their populism with racism.

Capitalism in Crisis: The Depression of 1893–1897

Cleveland soon confronted a major crisis, an economic collapse in the railroad industry that quickly spread. In the economic boom of the 1880s, railroads had fed the speculative mania by issuing more stock (and enticing investors with higher dividends) than their business prospects warranted. Weakened by agricultural stagnation, railroad growth slowed in the early 1890s. The first hint of trouble flared up in February 1893 when the Philadelphia and Reading Railroad failed.

This bankruptcy came at a time of weakened confidence in the gold standard, the government's pledge to redeem paper money for gold on demand. This diminished confidence had several sources. First, when a leading London investment bank collapsed in 1890, hard-pressed British investors sold millions of dollars' worth of stock in American railroads and other corporations and converted their dollars to gold, draining U.S. gold reserves. Second, Congress's lavish veterans' benefits and pork-barrel appropriations during the Harrison administration drained government resources just as tariff revenues were dropping because of the high McKinley Tariff. Third, the 1890 Sherman Silver Purchase Act further strained the gold reserve. This measure required the government to pay for its monthly silver purchases with treasury certificates redeemable for either silver or gold, and many certificate holders chose to convert them to gold. Finally, the election of Grover Cleveland in 1892 further eroded confidence in the dollar. Although Cleveland endorsed the gold standard, his party harbored many advocates of inflationary policies.

Between January 1892 and March 1893, when Cleveland took office, the gold reserve had fallen sharply to around $100 million, the minimum considered necessary to support the dollar. This decline alarmed those who viewed the gold standard as the only sure evidence of the government's financial stability.

The collapse of a railroad triggered the **Panic of 1893.** Fear fed on itself as alarmed investors converted their stock holdings to gold. Stock prices fell in May and June; gold reserves sank; by the end of the year, seventy-four railroads and more than fifteen thousand commercial institutions, including six hundred banks, had failed. The Panic of 1893 set off four years of hard times.

By 1897, about a third of the nation's railroad mileage had plunged into bankruptcy. Just as the railroad boom had spurred the industrial prosperity of the 1880s, so had the railroad crisis of the early 1890s battered the entire economy as banks and other businesses failed. A full-scale depression gripped the nation.

The crisis took a heavy human toll. Industrial unemployment soared into the 20 to 25 percent range, leaving millions of factory workers with no money to feed their families and heat their homes. Recent immigrants faced disaster. Jobless men tramped the streets and rode freight trains from city to city seeking work.

The unusually harsh winters of 1893 and 1894 made matters worse. In New York City, where the crisis quickly swamped local relief agencies, a minister reported actual starvation. Amid the suffering, a rich New Yorker named Bradley Martin threw a lavish costume ball costing several hundred thousand dollars. Popular outrage over this flaunting of wealth in a prostrate city forced Martin and his family to move abroad.

Rural America, already hard-hit by declining agricultural prices, faced ruin. Farm prices dropped by more than 20 percent between 1890 and 1896. Corn plummeted from fifty cents to twenty-one cents a bushel; wheat, from eighty-four cents to fifty-one cents. Cotton sold for five cents a pound in 1894.

Some desperate Americans turned to protest. In Chicago, workers at the Pullman factory reacted to successive wage cuts by walking off the job in June 1894 (see Chapter 18). In Massillon, Ohio, self-taught monetary expert Jacob Coxey proposed as a solution to unemployment a $500 million public-works program funded with paper money not backed by gold but simply designated "legal tender" (just as it is today). A man of action as well as ideas, Coxey organized a march on Washington to lobby for his scheme. Thousands joined him en route, and several hundred actually reached Washington in late April 1894. Police arrested Coxey and other leaders when they attempted to enter the Capitol grounds, and his "army" broke up. Although some considered Coxey eccentric, his proposal closely resembled programs that the government would adopt during the depression of the 1930s.

As unrest intensified, fear clutched middle-class Americans. A church magazine demanded that troops put "a pitiless stop" to outbreaks of unrest. To some observers, a bloody upheaval seemed imminent.

Business Leaders Respond   In the face of suffering and turmoil, Cleveland refused to intervene. Boom-and-bust economic cycles were inevitable, he insisted, echoing the conventional wisdom of the day; the government could do nothing. Failing to grasp the larger picture, Cleveland focused on a single peripheral issue: defending the gold standard. As the gold reserve dwindled, he blamed the Sherman Silver Purchase Act, and in August 1893 he called on Congress to repeal it. Silver advocates protested, but Congress followed Cleveland's wishes.

Nevertheless, the gold drain continued. In early 1895, with the gold reserve down to $41 million, Cleveland turned to Wall Street. Bankers J. P. Morgan and August Belmont agreed to lend the government $62 million in exchange for U.S. bonds at a special discount. With this loan, the government purchased gold to replenish its reserve.

Meanwhile, Morgan and Belmont resold the bonds for a substantial profit. This complicated deal did help restore confidence in the government's economic stability. The gold drain stopped, and when the treasury offered $100 million in bonds early in 1896, they sold quickly.

Cleveland saved the gold standard, but at a high price. His dealings with Morgan and Belmont, and the bankers' handsome profits on the deal, confirmed radicals' suspicions of an unholy alliance between Washington and Wall Street. Cleveland's readiness to use force against the Pullman strikers and against Jacob Coxey's peaceful marchers deepened such suspicions.

In the ongoing maneuverings of competing interest groups, corporate interests held the whip hand, as a battle over the tariff made clear. Although Cleveland favored tariff reform, the Congress of 1893–1895—despite its Democratic majorities—generally yielded to high-tariff lobbyists. The Wilson-Gorman Tariff of 1894 lowered duties somewhat, but made so many concessions to protectionist interests that Cleveland disgustedly allowed it to become law without his signature.

Hinting at changes ahead, the Wilson-Gorman Tariff imposed a modest income tax of 2 percent on all income over $4,000 (about $40,000 in purchasing power today). But in *Pollock* v. *Farmers' Loan & Trust Co.* (1895), the Supreme Court narrowly held the law unconstitutional, ruling that the federal government could impose such a direct tax on personal property only if it were apportioned according to the population of each state. Whether one looked at the executive, the legislature, or the judiciary, Washington's subordination to financial interests seemed absolute.

Cleveland's policies split the Democratic Party. Farm leaders and silver Democrats condemned his opposition to the Sherman Silver Purchase Act. South Carolina's Ben Tillman, running for the Senate in 1894, proclaimed, "[T]his scoundrel Cleveland . . . is an old bag of beef and I am going to Washington with a pitchfork and prod him in his fat old ribs." This split in the Democratic ranks affected the elections of 1894 and 1896 and reshaped politics as the century ended.

The depression also helped reorient social thought. Middle-class charitable workers, long convinced that individual character flaws caused poverty, now realized—as socialists proclaimed and as the poor well knew—that even sober and hardworking people could succumb to economic forces beyond their control. As the social work profession took form in the early twentieth century, its members spent less time preaching to the poor and more time investigating the social sources of poverty.

Laissez-faire ideology weakened in the 1890s as many depression-worn Americans adopted a broadened view of the government's role in dealing with the social consequences of industrialization. In the early twentieth century, this new view would activate powerful political energies. The depression, in short, not only brought suffering; it also taught lessons.

1894: Protest Grows Louder   Republican gains in the 1894 midterm election revealed the depths of revulsion against Cleveland and the Democrats, who were blamed for the hard times. As 1896 approached, the monetary question became the overriding symbolic issue. Conservatives clung to the gold standard; agrarian radicals rallied to the banner of "free silver." At the 1896 Democratic convention, the nomination went to a young champion of the silver cause, **William Jennings Bryan.** Despite Bryan's eloquence, Republican William McKinley emerged victorious. His triumph laid the groundwork for a major political realignment that would influence American politics for a generation.

With the depression at its worst and President Grover Cleveland deeply unpopular, the midterm election of 1894 spelled Democratic disaster. The Republicans, gaining 5 seats in the Senate and 117 in the House, won both houses of Congress. They also secured control of several key states—including New York, Illinois, and Wisconsin—as immigrant workers, battered by the depression, abandoned their traditional Democratic allegiance.

Populist candidates garnered nearly 1.5 million votes in 1894, an increase of more than 40 percent over their 1892 total. Populism's most impressive gains occurred in the South. Although several western states that had voted Populist in 1892 returned to their traditional Republican allegiance in 1894, the overall results heartened Populist leaders.

The serious economic divisions that split Americans in the mid-1890s focused especially on a symbolic issue: free silver. Cleveland's rigid defense of the gold standard forced his opponents into an equally exaggerated obsession with silver, obscuring the genuine issues that divided rich and poor, creditor and debtor, and farmer and city-dweller. Although agrarian radicals preferred the subtreasury proposal that would have used their stored crops as collateral for loans, the tireless campaign by business leaders for the gold standard led them to counter by emphasizing silver. They were urged on and sometimes financed by western silver-mine owners who stood to profit if silver again became a monetary metal.

Each side had a point. Gold advocates recognized that a nation's paper money must be based on more than a government's ability to run printing presses and that uncontrolled inflation could be catastrophic. The silver advocates knew from experience how tight-money policies depressed prices and devastated farmers. Unfortunately, these underlying realities were rarely expressed clearly. The silverites' most influential propaganda, William H. Harvey's widely distributed *Coin's Financial School* (1894), explained the monetary issue in simplified partisan terms, denounced "the conspiracy of Goldbugs," and insisted that the free coinage of silver would banish debt and end the depression.

Silver Advocates Capture the Democratic Party   At the 1896 Democratic convention in Chicago, western and southern delegates adopted a platform—including a demand for the free and unlimited coinage of silver at the ratio to gold of sixteen to one—that in effect repudiated the Cleveland administration. The front-running candidate was Congressman Richard Bland of Missouri, a silverite. But behind the scenes, the groundwork was being laid for the nomination of a dark horse, William Jennings Bryan, a thirty-six-year-old Nebraska lawyer and politician. During two terms in Congress (1891–1895) he championed western agrarian interests.

Joining Christian imagery with economic analysis, Bryan delivered his major convention speech in the debate over the platform. In an era before electronic amplification, his booming voice easily reached the upper gallery of the cavernous hall. Bryan praised western farmers and scorned advocates of the gold standard. By the time he reached his rousing conclusion—"You shall not press down upon the brow of labor this crown of thorns, you shall not crucify mankind upon a cross of gold"—the wildly cheering delegates had identified their candidate.

Map 20.1 The Election of 1896

Republicans won the election by carrying the urban vote.

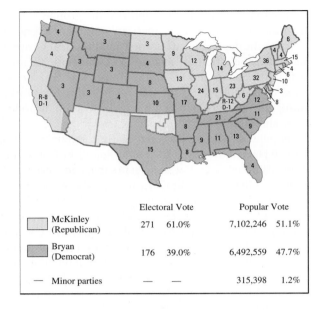

	Electoral Vote		Popular Vote	
McKinley (Republican)	271	61.0%	7,102,246	51.1%
Bryan (Democrat)	176	39.0%	6,492,559	47.7%
— Minor parties	—	—	315,398	1.2%

The silverites' capture of the Democratic Party presented a dilemma to the Populists. They, too, advocated free silver, but only as one reform among many. To back Bryan would be to abandon the broad Populist program. Furthermore, fusion with the Democrats could destroy their influence as a third party. Yet the Populist leaders recognized that a separate Populist ticket would likely siphon votes from Bryan and ensure a Republican victory. Reluctantly, the Populists endorsed Bryan, while preserving a shred of independence (and confusing voters) by naming their own vice-presidential candidate, Tom Watson of Georgia. The Populists were learning the difficulty of organizing an independent political movement in a nation wedded to the two-party system.

The Republicans, meanwhile, had nominated former governor William McKinley, who as an Ohio congressman had given his name to the McKinley Tariff of 1890. The Republican platform embraced the high protective tariff and endorsed the gold standard.

1896: Republicans Triumphant Bryan tried to sustain the momentum of the Chicago convention. Crisscrossing the nation by train, he delivered his free-silver campaign speech to hundreds of audiences in twenty-nine states. One skeptical editor compared him to Nebraska's notoriously shallow Platte River: six inches deep and a mile wide at the mouth.

McKinley's campaign was shrewdly managed by Mark Hanna, a Cleveland industrialist. Dignified and aloof, McKinley could not match Bryan's popular touch. Accordingly, Hanna built the campaign not around the candidate but around posters, pamphlets, and newspaper editorials. These publications warned of the dangers of free silver, caricatured Bryan as a rabid radical, and portrayed McKinley and the gold standard as twin pillars of prosperity.

Women Bryan Supporters   *Although women could not vote in national elections in the 1890s, they actively participated in political campaigns. These women worked to turn out the vote for William Jennings Bryan.*

Drawing on a war chest possibly as large as $7 million, Hanna spent lavishly. J. P. Morgan and John D. Rockefeller together contributed half a million dollars, far more than Bryan's total campaign contributions. Like Benjamin Harrison in 1888, McKinley stayed home in Canton, Ohio, emerging from time to time to read speeches to visiting delegations. Carefully orchestrated by Hanna, McKinley's deceptively bucolic "front-porch" campaign involved elaborate organization. All told, some 750,000 people trekked to Canton that summer.

On election day, McKinley beat Bryan by over six hundred thousand votes. He swept the Northeast and the Midwest and even carried three farm states beyond the Mississippi—Iowa, Minnesota, and North Dakota—as well as California and Oregon. Bryan's strength was limited to the South and the sparsely settled Great Plains and mountain states. The Republicans retained control of Congress.

Why did Bryan lose despite the depression and the protest spirit abroad in the land? Certainly, Republican cash reserves, their influence on the East Coast press, and their scare tactics played a role. But Bryan's candidacy carried its own liabilities. His core constituency, while passionately loyal, was limited. Seduced by free silver and Bryan's oratory, the Democrats had upheld a platform and a candidate with little appeal for factory workers, the urban middle class, or the settled family farmers of the midwestern corn belt. Urban voters, realizing that higher farm prices, a major free-silver goal, also meant higher food prices, went heavily for McKinley. Bryan's weakness in urban America reflected cultural differences as well. To urban Catholics and Jews, this moralistic, teetotaling Nebraskan thundering like a Protestant revival preacher seemed utterly alien.

Finally, although parts of their critique of laissez-faire capitalism were endorsed by Bryan and the Democrats, the Populists' effort to define a humane and democratic alternative relied heavily on visions of a premodern economic order of independent farmers and entrepreneurs. Although appealing, this vision bore little relationship to the new corporate order taking shape in America.

The McKinley administration quickly translated its conservative platform into law. The Dingley Tariff (1897) pushed rates to all-time high levels, and the Currency Act of 1900 officially committed the United States to the gold standard. With returning prosperity, rising farm prices after 1897, and the discovery of gold in Alaska and elsewhere, these measures aroused little protest. Bryan won renomination in 1900, but the fervor of 1896 was missing. The Republican campaign theme of prosperity easily won McKinley a second term.

The elections of 1894 and 1896 produced a Republican majority that, except for Woodrow Wilson's two presidential terms (1913–1921), would dominate national politics until the election of Franklin D. Roosevelt in 1932. Bryan's defeat and the Republicans' emergence as the party of prosperity and the sound dollar killed the Populist Party and drove the Democrats back to their regional base in the South. But although populism collapsed, a new reform movement called progressivism was emerging. Many of the Populists' reform proposals would be enacted into law in the progressive years.

EXPANSIONIST STIRRINGS AND WAR WITH SPAIN, 1878–1901

The same corporate elite that dominated late-nineteenth-century domestic politics influenced U.S. foreign policy as well, contributing to surging expansionist pressures. Not only business leaders but politicians, statesmen, and editorial writers insisted that national greatness required that America match Europe's imperial expansion. Fanned by sensationalistic newspaper coverage of a Cuban struggle for independence and by elite calls for greater American international assertiveness, war between the United States and Spain broke out in 1898.

Roots of Expansionist Sentiment

Ever since the first European settlers colonized North America's Atlantic coast, the newcomers had been an expansionist people. By the 1840s, the push westward had acquired a name: Manifest Destiny. Directed inward after 1865 toward the settlement of the trans-Mississippi West (see Chapter 17), this impulse turned outward in the 1880s as Americans followed the example set by Great Britain, France, Belgium, Italy, Germany, and Japan, which were busily collecting colonies from North Africa to the Pacific islands. National greatness, it appeared, demanded an empire.

Many business leaders believed that continued domestic prosperity required overseas markets. As American industrial capacity expanded, foreign markets offered a safety valve for potentially explosive pressures in the U.S. economy. Secretary of State James Blaine warned in 1890 that U.S. productivity was outrunning "the demands of the home market" and insisted that American business must look abroad.

Advocates of a stronger navy further fueled the expansionist mood. In *The Influence of Sea Power upon History* (1890), **Alfred Thayer Mahan** equated sea power with national greatness and urged a U.S. naval buildup. Since a strong navy required bases abroad, Mahan and other naval advocates supported the movement to acquire foreign territories, especially Pacific islands with good harbors. Military strategy, in this case and others, often masked the desire for access to new markets.

Religious leaders proclaimed America's mission to spread Christianity. This expansionist argument sometimes took on a racist tinge. As Josiah Strong put it in his 1885 work *Our Country*, "God is training the Anglo-Saxon race for its mission"—a mission of Christianizing and civilizing the world's "weaker races."

A group of Republican expansionists, led by Senator Henry Cabot Lodge of Massachusetts, diplomat John Hay, and Theodore Roosevelt of New York, preached imperial greatness and military might. "I should welcome almost any war," declared Roosevelt in 1897; ". . . this country needs one." Advocates of expansionism, like Roosevelt and Lodge, built upon the Social Darwinist rhetoric of the day and argued that war, as a vehicle for natural selection, would test and refurbish American manhood, restore chivalry and honor, and create a new generation of civic-minded Americans. This gendered appeal to renew American masculinity both counterbalanced concerns about women's political activism and helped forge the disparate arguments for expansionism into a simpler, more visceral plea for international engagement that had a broad appeal.

A series of diplomatic skirmishes between 1885 and 1895 revealed the newly assertive American mood and paved the way for the war that Roosevelt desired. In the mid-1880s, quarrels between the United States and Great Britain over fishing rights in the North Atlantic and in the Bering Sea off Alaska reawakened Americans' latent anti-British feelings as well as the old dream of acquiring Canada. A poem published in the *Detroit News* (adapted from an English music-hall song) supplied the nickname that critics would apply to the promoters of expansion—jingoists:

> We do not want to fight,
> But, by jingo, if we do,
> We'll scoop in all the fishing grounds
> And the whole dominion too!

The fishing-rights dispute was resolved in 1898, but by then attention had shifted to Latin America. In 1891, as civil war raged in Chile, U.S. officials seized a Chilean vessel that was attempting to buy guns in San Diego. Soon after, a mob in Valparaiso, Chile, killed two unarmed sailors on shore leave. President Harrison practically called for war. Only when Chile apologized and paid an indemnity was the incident closed.

Another Latin American conflict arose from a boundary dispute between Venezuela and British Guiana in 1895. The disagreement worsened after gold was discovered in the contested territory. When the British rejected a U.S. arbitration offer and condescendingly insisted that America's revered Monroe Doctrine had no standing in international law, a livid Grover Cleveland asked Congress to set up a commission to settle the disputed boundary even without Britain's approval. As patriotic fervor pulsed through the nation, the British in 1897 accepted the commission's findings.

Pacific Expansion   Meanwhile, the U.S. navy focused on the Samoan Islands in the South Pacific, where it sought access to the port of Pago Pago as a refueling station. Britain and Germany had ambitions in Samoa as well, and in March 1889 the United States and Germany narrowly avoided a naval clash when a hurricane wrecked both fleets. Secretary of State Blaine's wife wrote to one of their children, "Your father is now looking up Samoa on the map." Once he found it, negotiations began, and the United States, Great Britain, and Germany established a three-way "protectorate" over the islands.

Attention had by that time shifted to the Hawaiian Islands, which had both strategic and economic significance for the United States. New England trading vessels had visited Hawaii as early as the 1790s, and Yankee missionaries had come in the 1820s. By the 1860s American-owned sugar plantations worked by Chinese and Japanese labor-

Map 20.2 U.S. Territorial Expansion in the Late Nineteenth Century

The major U.S. territorial expansion abroad came in a short burst of activity in the late 1890s, when newspapers and some politicians urged Americans to acquire strategic ports and coaling stations abroad.

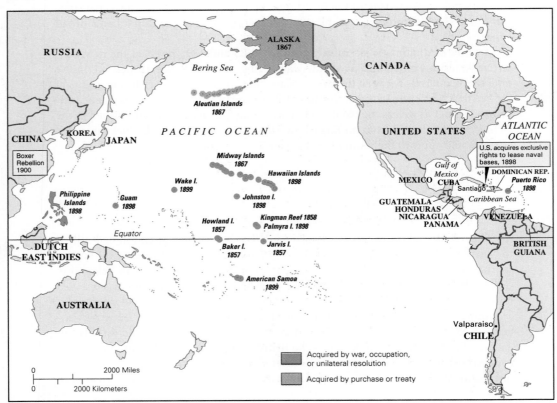

ers dotted the islands. Under an 1887 treaty (negotiated after the planters had forcibly imposed a new constitution on Hawaii's native ruler, Kala-kaua), the United States built a naval base at Pearl Harbor, near Honolulu. American economic dominance and the influx of foreigners angered Hawaiians. In 1891, they welcomed Liliuokalani, a strong-willed woman hostile to Americans, to the Hawaiian throne.

Meanwhile, in 1890, the framers of the McKinley Tariff, pressured by domestic sugar growers, eliminated the duty-free status enjoyed by Hawaiian sugar. In January 1893, facing ruin as Hawaii's wholesale sugar prices plunged 40 percent, the planters deposed Queen Liliuokalani, proclaimed the independent Republic of Hawaii, and re-quested U.S. annexation. The U.S. State Department's representative in Hawaii cabled Washington, "The Hawaiian pear is now fully ripe, and this is the golden hour for the United States to pluck it." But the grab for Hawaii troubled Grover Cleveland, who sent a representative to investigate the situation. This representative's report questioned whether the Hawaiian people actually desired annexation.

Cleveland's scruples infuriated expansionists. When William McKinley succeeded Cleveland in 1897, the acquisition of Hawaii was pushed forward by sugar companies that had similar investments in Cuba. In 1898 Congress proclaimed **Hawaii** an American territory. Sixty-one years later, it joined the Union as the fiftieth state.

Crisis over Cuba   Many of the same expansionists who had argued for the annexation of Hawaii turned their attention in 1898 to the Spanish colony of Cuba, ninety miles off Florida, where in 1895 an anti-Spanish rebellion had broken out. This revolt, organized by the Cuban writer José Martí and other Cuban exiles in New York City, won little support from U.S. business, which had $50 million invested in Cuba and annually imported $100 million worth of sugar and other products from the island. Nor did the rebels initially secure the backing of Washington, which urged Spain to grant Cuba a degree of autonomy.

But the rebels' cause aroused popular sympathy in the United States. This support increased with revelations that the Spanish commander in Cuba, Valeriano Weyler, was herding vast numbers of Cubans into squalid camps. Malnutrition and disease turned these camps into hellholes in which perhaps two hundred thousand Cubans died.

Fueling American anger was the sensationalized reporting of two competing New York City newspapers, William Randolph Hearst's *Journal* and Joseph Pulitzer's *World*. The *Journal*'s color comic strip, "The Yellow Kid," provided a name for Hearst's debased editorial approach: yellow journalism. The Hungarian immigrant Pulitzer normally had higher standards, but in the cutthroat battle for readers, Pulitzer's *World* matched the *Journal*'s sensationalism. Both editors exploited the Cuban crisis. Headlines turned rumor into fact, and feature stories detailed "Butcher" Weyler's atrocities. When a young Cuban woman was jailed for resisting a rape attempt by a Spanish officer, a Hearst reporter helped the woman escape and brought her triumphantly to New York.

In 1897, a new, more liberal Spanish government sought a peaceful resolution of the Cuban crisis. But Hearst and Pulitzer continued to inflame the public. On February 8, 1898, Hearst's *Journal* published a private letter by Spain's minister to the United States that described McKinley as "weak" and "a bidder for the admiration of the crowd." Irritation over this incident turned to outrage when on February 15 an explosion sank the U.S. battleship *Maine* in Havana harbor and killed 266 crewmen. Scholarly opinion about what caused the explosion is still divided, but a careful review of the evidence in 1998 concluded that a mine most likely set off the ammunition explosion that sank the ship. Newspaper headlines at the time blamed the same cause and war spirit flared high.

Despite further Spanish concessions, McKinley sent a war message to Congress on April 11, and legislators enacted a joint resolution recognizing Cuba's independence and authorizing force to expel the Spanish. The Teller Amendment, introduced by Senator Henry M. Teller of Colorado, renounced any U.S. interest in "sovereignty, jurisdiction, or control" in Cuba and pledged that America would leave the island alone once independence was assured.

The Spanish-American War, 1898   The war with Spain involved only a few days of actual combat. The first action came on May 1, 1898, when a U.S. fleet commanded by George Dewey steamed into Manila Bay in the Philippines and destroyed or captured all ten Spanish ships anchored there, at the cost of 1 American and 381 Spanish lives. In mid-August, U.S. troops occupied the capital, Manila.

In Cuba, the fighting centered on the military stronghold of Santiago on the southeastern coast. On May 19, a Spanish battle fleet of seven aging vessels sailed into the Santiago harbor, where five U.S. battleships and two cruisers blockaded them. On July 1, in the war's only significant land action, American troops seized three strongly defended Spanish garrisons on El Caney Hill, Kettleman's Hill, and San Juan Hill overlooking Santiago. Leading the volunteer "Rough Riders" unit in the capture of San Juan Hill was Theodore Roosevelt, who became a war hero. Emphasizing his toughness and sense of honor, Roosevelt would later use his war experience to reaffirm the aptitude of men like himself for political leadership.

On July 3, the Spanish attempted to break through the American blockade to the open sea. The U.S. navy fired and sank their archaic vessels. Spain lost 474 men in this gallant but doomed defense. Americans might have found a cautionary lesson in this sorry end to four hundred years of Spanish rule in the New World, but few had time for somber musings. The *Washington Post* observed, "A new consciousness seems to have come upon us—the consciousness of strength—and with it a new appetite, the yearning to show our strength. . . ." Secretary of State John Hay was more succinct. It had been, he wrote Roosevelt, "a splendid little war."

Many who served in Cuba found the war far from splendid. Ill-trained and poorly equipped, the troops went into summer combat wearing heavy woolen uniforms. The army also lacked adequate medical support. When **Clara Barton,** president of the American Association for Red Cross, visited Santiago, she found wounded soldiers lying in the rain, unable to eat the hardtack rations. Under her leadership, 1,000 trained nurses worked with the medical corps. Despite the efforts of these nurses and doctors, 379 American soldiers died in combat and more than 5,000 succumbed to food poisoning, yellow fever, malaria, and other diseases during and after the war.

Several thousand black troops fought in Cuba. Some, such as the Twenty-fourth Infantry and Tenth Cavalry, were seasoned regular-army "buffalo soldiers" transferred from bases in the West. Others were volunteers from various states. At assembly points in Georgia, and then at the embarkation port of Tampa, Florida, these troops encountered the racism of a Jim Crow society. Tampa restaurants and bars refused them service; Tampa whites disparaged them. On June 6, after weeks of racist treatment, some black troops exploded in riotous rage, storming into restaurants, bars, and other establishments that had barred them. White troops from Georgia restored order. Although white and black troops sailed to Cuba on the same transport ships (actually, hastily converted freighters), the ships themselves were segregated, with black troops often confined to the lowest quarters in the stifling heat, denied permission to mingle on deck with the other units, and in other ways discriminated against.

Despite the racism, African-Americans served with distinction once they reached Cuba. Black troops played key roles in the taking of both San Juan Hill and El Caney Hill. Of the total U.S. troops involved in the latter action, some 15 percent were black.

The Spanish sought an armistice on July 17. In the peace treaty signed that December in Paris, Spain recognized Cuba's independence and, after a U.S. payment of $20 million, ceded the Philippines, Puerto Rico, and the Pacific island of Guam to the United States. Americans now possessed an island empire stretching from the Caribbean to the Pacific.

From 1898 to 1902, the U.S. army governed Cuba under the command of General Leonard Wood. Wood's administration improved public health, education, and sanitation but nevertheless violated the spirit of the 1898 Teller Amendment. The troops eventually withdrew, though under conditions that limited Cuban sovereignty. The 1901 **Platt Amendment,** attached to an army appropriations bill offered by a Connecticut senator at the request of the War Department, authorized American withdrawal only after Cuba agreed not to make any treaty with a foreign power limiting its independence and not to borrow beyond its means. The United States also reserved the right to intervene in Cuba when it saw fit and to maintain a naval base there, an insistence resented by the Cubans. With U.S. troops still occupying the island, the Cuban constitutional convention of 1901 accepted the Platt Amendment, which remained in force until 1934. Under its terms the United States established a naval base at Guantánamo Bay, near Santiago de Cuba, which it still maintains. U.S. investments in Cuba, some $50 million in 1898, soared to half a billion dollars by 1920.

Critics of Empire   The victories of the expansionists in Cuba and the Philippines did not bring universal praise. Some Americans, who had opposed imperialism for more than a decade, were dismayed by the results. Although few in number, the critics, like the Mugwumps who had challenged the spoils system, were influential. Indeed, some of them, like Carl Schurz and E. L. Godkin, were former Mugwumps. Other anti-imperialists included William Jennings Bryan, settlement-house founder Jane Addams, novelist Mark Twain, and Harvard philosopher William James. Steel king Andrew Carnegie gave thousands of dollars to the cause. In 1898, these critics of empire had formed the **Anti-Imperialist League.**

For the United States to rule other peoples, the anti-imperialists believed, was to violate the principles of the Declaration of Independence and the Constitution. As one of them wrote, "Dewey took Manila with the loss of one man—and all our institutions." The military fever that accompanied expansionism also dismayed the anti-imperialists. Some labor leaders feared that imperial expansion would lead to competition from cheap foreign labor and products.

In February 1899, the anti-imperialists failed by one vote to prevent Senate ratification of the peace treaty with Spain. McKinley's overwhelming reelection victory in 1900 and the defeat of expansionist critic William Jennings Bryan eroded the anti-imperialists' cause. Nevertheless, at a time of jingoistic rhetoric and militaristic posturing, they had upheld an older and more traditional vision of America.

The Philippines Quagmire *Anticipating the Vietnam War, the U.S. suppression of the Philippines' independence struggle involved American troops in a long and nasty guerrilla campaign. One of the men in this 1900 photograph scrawled on the back: "27 hours on march, mud and rain, 24 hours without food."*

Guerrilla War in the Philippines, 1898–1902

The worst fears of the anti-imperialists were subsequently borne out by events in the Philippines. When the Spanish-American War ended, President McKinley was faced with the urgent problem of what to do about this group of Pacific islands that had a population of more than 5 million people. At the war's outset, few Americans knew that the Philippines belonged to Spain or even where they were. Without a map, McKinley later confessed, "I could not have told where those darn islands were within two thousand miles."

But the victory over Spain whetted the appetite for expansion. To the U.S. business community, the Philippines offered a steppingstone to the China market. McKinley, reflecting the prevailing mood as always, reasoned that the Filipinos were unready for self-government and would be gobbled up if set adrift in a world of imperial rivalries. McKinley further persuaded himself that American rule would enormously benefit the Filipinos, whom he called "our little brown brothers." A devout Methodist, he explained that America's mission was "to educate the Filipinos, and to uplift and civilize and Christianize them, and by God's grace do the very best we could by them." (In fact, most Filipinos were already Catholic, a legacy of centuries of Spanish rule.) Having prayerfully reached his decision, McKinley instructed the American peace negotiators in Paris to insist on U.S. acquisition of the Philippines.

"Uplifting" the Filipinos required a struggle. In 1896 young **Emilio Aguinaldo** had organized a Filipino independence movement to drive out Spain. In 1898, with arms supplied by George Dewey, Aguinaldo's forces had captured most of Luzon, the Philippines' main island. When the Spanish surrendered, Aguinaldo proclaimed Filipino independence and drafted a democratic constitution. Feeling betrayed when the peace treaty ceded his country to the United States, Aguinaldo ordered his rebel force to attack Manila, the American base of operations. Seventy thousand more U.S. troops were shipped to the Philippines, and by the end of 1899 the initial Filipino resistance had been crushed.

These hostilities became the opening phase of a long guerrilla conflict. Before it ended, over 125,000 American men had served in the Philippines, and 4,000 had been killed. As many as 20,000 Filipino independence fighters died. As in the later Vietnam and Iraq Wars, casualties and suffering ravaged the civilian population as well. Historians estimate that at least 200,000 civilians died in the conflict. Aguinaldo was captured in March 1901, but large-scale guerrilla fighting continued through the summer of 1902.

In 1902, a special Senate committee heard testimony from veterans of the Philippines war about the execution of prisoners, the torture of suspects, and the burning of villages. The humanitarian mood of 1898, when Americans had rushed to save Cuba from the cruel Spaniards, seemed remote indeed. In retrospect, the American troops' ambivalent attitudes about the peoples of the Philippines, while deplorable, are not hard to understand. Despite America's self-image as a beacon of liberty and a savior of the world's peoples, many Americans in the 1880s and 1890s had been deeply troubled by the new immigrants from southern and eastern Europe and had expressed concerns over "backward" and "useless" races. As American nationalism was reformulated in this cauldron of immigration, imperialism, and the "winning of the West," racist attitudes about Native peoples and foreigners intermixed with rhetorical pleas for supervision and stewardship. In the process, as was evident in the treatment of American Indians (see Chapter 17), well-meaning paternalism often degenerated into deadly domination.

The subjugation of the Philippines followed years of expansionism that proclaimed America's debut on the world stage and underscored the global reach of U.S. capitalism. Nevertheless, most Americans remained ambivalent about the acquisition of territory. While anti-imperialist Mark Twain could acidly condemn "the Blessings of Civilization Trust," labor leader Samuel Gompers warned that "an inundation of Mongolians" might steal jobs from white labor. From the debate over the annexation of Hawaii in 1898 to the end of the war against Philippine independence in 1902, white Americans recoiled from making these "barbarian peoples" a part of the United States. Not fit to manage their own affairs, Cuban, Puerto Rican, Hawaiian, and Filipino peoples were placed in a protective status that denied their independence and kept them under U.S. control.

To stabilize relations in the Philippines, Congress passed the Philippine Government Act in 1902, which vested authority in a governor general to be appointed by the president. The act also provided for an elected Filipino assembly and promised eventual self-government. Progress toward this goal inched forward, with intervals of semi-military rule. In 1946, nearly half a century after Admiral Dewey's guns had boomed in Manila Bay, independence finally came to the Philippines.

CONCLUSION

By 1900 immigration, the settlement of the frontier West, and rapid industrial expansion had pushed America to the forefront of the world economy and had sparked a major realignment in American politics. After nearly two decades of hard-fought elections in which political control had seesawed back and forth between the major parties, the Republicans now held power.

It had been difficult to achieve political dominance. The dynamic growth of the American economy together with rapid urbanization and a massive influx of immigrants had initially strained the political process. As the parties struggled to define their vision of the proper role of government in stimulating economic development, they were forced to deal with ethnic, cultural, and racial issues that included prohibition, church schools, and segregation. All this was further complicated by the Democratic Party's attempt to throw off the limits imposed by Reconstruction and gain political control of the South.

On the national level, both parties built a loyal following by linking their positions to deeply held beliefs about the family and the proper role of government. Republicans justified their support for the tariff and soldiers' pensions in terms of patriotic protection of the family. Democrats countered that a high-tariff policy was indicative of precisely the kind of excessive governmental force that would destroy family life. On the local level, both parties secured loyal voters by stressing ethnic and cultural issues. Democrats courted the new immigrants, while Republicans catered to rural and small-town native-born Americans in the Northeast and Midwest.

In the competition for new voters, the needs of rural Americans were often overlooked. Caught between declining prices for grain and cotton, and high railroad and bank rates, farmers struggled to survive. Their precarious position was further strained by years of drought, insect infestation, and overspecialization in one crop. In desperation, farmers turned first to the Grange and Farmers' Alliance movements and then to the Populist Party for help. In the South, after first courting black farmers, members of the Farmers' Alliance and later the Populists joined with Democrats to disfranchise black voters. Using lynching and intimidation, Democrats seized control of southern politics.

In the face of these threats, the Republican Party in 1896 raised huge sums from big business to turn back the Populist challenge and take control of national politics. The fusion of the Populists and Democrats behind William Jennings Bryan and the silver issue created problems of its own. Although he carried the South and almost all the Midwest, the teetotaling Bryan had little appeal for urban workers and the middle class who believed that a monetary policy based on free silver promised only inflation and higher prices. McKinley won by playing down moral reforms such as prohibition and emphasizing patriotism and fiscal responsibility. Republicans won over the urban-industrial core of the nation—the Northeast and much of the Midwest. They would control the House of Representatives for twenty-eight out of the thirty-six years from 1894 to 1930.

McKinley's administration was drawn by events in Cuba and jingoistic advocates within his own party into the Spanish-American War and the subsequent acquisition of Hawaii, Samoa, Guam, the Philippines, and Cuba. Although the Republicans preferred the term "expansionism" to "imperialism," the move to acquire new bases for access to global markets fit the party's probusiness stance. But expansion into the Pacific created its own obstacles when the United States became involved in a guerrilla war with Philippine nationalists. Facing mounting criticism at home, the expansionists adopted the Teller and Platt Amendments, which foreshadowed eventual disengagement from the acquisition of foreign territory.

Notwithstanding these foreign interventions, the fundamental question of late-nineteenth-century American politics persisted: could a government designed for the needs of a small agrarian society serve an industrialized nation of factories and immigrant-crowded cities? The answer was by no means clear. Although issues such as patronage, the tariff, veterans' benefits, and monetary policy had enabled the industrial system to grow dramatically, the needs of farmers, workers, and immigrant Americans had largely been ignored. The Republicans successfully carried the field in 1896, but Populists and other critics who argued that government should play an assertive role in solving social and economic problems would help shape the political environment of the progressive movement.

21

The Progressive Era,
1900–1917

PROGRESSIVES AND THEIR IDEAS

As the twentieth century dawned, local groups across the nation grappled with the problems of the new urban-industrial order. Workers protested unsafe and exhausting jobs. Experts investigated social conditions. Women's clubs embraced reform. Intellectuals challenged the ideological foundations of a business-dominated social order, and journalists publicized municipal corruption and industrialism's human toll. Throughout America, activists worked to make government more democratic, eradicate dangerous conditions in cities and factories, and curb corporate power.

Surveying all these efforts, historians lumped them under a single label: "the progressive movement." In fact, "progressivism" was never a single movement. It is perhaps best understood as a spirit of discontent with the status quo and an exciting sense of new social possibilities. This mood found many outlets and focused on many issues. (See Beyond America—Global Interactions: Progressive Reformers Worldwide Share Ideas and Strategies.)

The Many Faces of Progressivism   Who were the progressives, and what reforms did they pursue? To answer these questions, we must examine the pattern of urban growth in the early twentieth century. Along with immigration, a growing middle class transformed U.S. cities. From the men and women of this class—most of them native-born, white, and Protestant—came many of the progressive movement's leaders and foot soldiers.

From 1900 to 1920, the number of white-collar workers jumped from 5.1 million to 10.5 million—more than double the growth rate of the labor force as a whole. As in-

CHRONOLOGY, 1900–1917

1900 • International Ladies' Garment Workers' Union (ILGWU) founded.
Socialist Party of America organized.
Theodore Dreiser, *Sister Carrie.*
Carrie Chapman Catt becomes president of the National American
Woman Suffrage Association (NAWSA).

1901 • Assassination of McKinley; Theodore Roosevelt becomes president.
J. P. Morgan forms United States Steel Company.

1902 • Jane Addams, *Democracy and Social Ethics.*

1903 • W. E. B. Du Bois, *The Souls of Black Folk.*
Wright brothers' flight.

1904 • Theodore Roosevelt elected president in his own right.
Lincoln Steffens, *The Shame of the Cities.*

1905 • Industrial Workers of the World (IWW) organized.

1906 • Upton Sinclair, *The Jungle.*

1907 • William James, *Pragmatism.*

1908 • William Howard Taft elected president.
Model T Ford introduced.

1909 • Ballinger-Pinchot controversy.
National Association for the Advancement of Colored People (NAACP)
founded.
Herbert Croly, *The Promise of American Life.*
Daniel Burnham, *Plan of Chicago.*

1910 • Insurgents curb power of House Speaker Joseph Cannon.

1911 • Triangle Shirtwaist Company fire.

1912 • Republican Party split; Progressive (Bull Moose) Party founded.
Woodrow Wilson elected president.
International Opium Treaty.

1913 • Sixteenth Amendment (Congress empowered to tax incomes).
Seventeenth Amendment (direct election of U.S. senators).

1914 • American Social Hygiene Association founded.
"Narcotics Act (Harrison Act)"

1915 • D. W. Griffith, *The Birth of a Nation.*

1916 • John Dewey, *Democracy and Education.*
Margaret Sanger opens nation's first birth-control clinic in Brooklyn,
New York.
National Park Service created.
Louis Brandeis appointed to Supreme Court.

1919 • Eighteenth Amendment (national prohibition).

1920 • Nineteenth Amendment (woman suffrage).

The Triangle Fire *The bodies of Triangle Shirtwaist factory workers lie on the sidewalk after they jumped from the burning building.*

dustry grew, so did the ranks of secretaries, civil engineers, and people in advertising. This white-collar class included corporate technicians and desk workers; the owners and managers of local businesses; and professionals such as lawyers, physicians, and teachers. Many new professional groups arose, from the American Association of University Professors (1915) to the American Association of Advertising Agencies (1917). The age of organization had dawned, bringing new professional allegiances and a more standardized, routinized society. For many middle-class Americans, membership in a national professional society provided a sense of identity that might earlier have come from neighborhood, church, or political party. Ambitious, well educated, and valuing social stability, the members of this new middle class were eager to make their influence felt.

For middle-class women, the city offered both opportunities and frustrations. Young unmarried women often became schoolteachers, secretaries, typists, clerks, and telephone operators. The number of women in such white-collar jobs surged from 949,000 in 1900 to 3.4 million in 1920. The ranks of college-educated women, although still small, more than tripled in this twenty-year period.

But for middle-class married women caring for homes and children, city life could mean isolation and frustration. The divorce rate rose from one in twelve marriages in 1900 to one in nine by 1916. As we shall see, many middle-class women joined female white-collar workers and college graduates in leading a revived women's movement. Cultural commentators wrote nervously of the "New Woman."

This urban middle class rallied to the banner of reform. The initial reform impetus came not from political parties but from women's clubs, settlement houses, and private groups with names like the Playground Association of America, the National Child Labor Committee, and the American League for Civic Improvement. In this era of organizations, the reform movement, too, drew strength from organized interest groups.

But the native-born middle class was not the only force behind progressivism. On issues affecting factory workers and slum dwellers, the urban-immigrant political machines—and workers themselves—often took the initiative. Some corporate leaders shaped regulatory measures in ways that served their interests.

What, then, was progressivism? Fundamentally, it was a broad-based response to industrialization and its byproducts: immigration, urban growth, growing corporate power, and widening class divisions. In contrast to populism, progressivism arose in the cities, and it enlisted many more journalists, academics, and social theorists. Finally, most progressives were *reformers*, not radicals. They wished to make the new urban-industrial order more humane, not overturn it entirely.

But which parts of this new order most needed attention, and what remedies were required? Reaching different answers to these key questions, progressive reformers spawned an array of activities that sometimes overlapped, sometimes diverged. Many reformers wanted stricter business regulation, from local transit companies to the almighty trusts. Others focused on protecting workers and the urban poor. Still others tried to reform the structure of government, especially at the municipal level. Some fought for immigration restriction or social-control strategies to regulate city-dwellers' behavior or address threats of urban disorder. All this contributed to the mosaic of progressive reform.

Progressives generally agreed that most social problems could be solved through study and organized effort. They respected science and expert knowledge. Since scientific and technological expertise had produced the new industrial order, such expertise could surely also solve the social problems spawned by industrialism. Progressives marshaled research data, expert opinion, and statistics to support their various causes.

Some historians have portrayed progressivism as an organizational stage that all modernizing societies pass through. This is a useful perspective, provided we remember that it was not an automatic process unfolding independently of human will. Eloquent leaders, gifted journalists, activist workers, and passionate reformers all played a role. Human emotion—whether indignation over child labor, intense moralism, fear of the alien, hatred of corporate power, or raw political ambition—drove the movement forward.

Intellectuals Offer New Social Views   A group of early-twentieth-century thinkers provided progressivism's underlying ideas. As we have seen, some Gilded Age intellectuals had argued that Charles Darwin's theory of evolution justified unrestrained economic competition. In the 1880s and 1890s, sociologist Lester Ward, utopian novelist Edward Bellamy, and leaders of the settlement-house and Social Gospel movements had all attacked this harsh version of Social Darwinism (see Chapters 18 and 19). This attack intensified after 1900.

Economist Thorstein Veblen, a Norwegian-American reared on a Minnesota farm, sharply criticized the new business order. In *The Theory of the Leisure Class* (1899), Veblen satirized the lifestyle of newly rich capitalists. Dissecting their habits the way an anthropologist might study an exotic tribe, he argued that they built showy mansions, threw elaborate parties, and otherwise engaged in "conspicuous consumption" to flaunt their wealth and assert their claims to superiority.

The Harvard philosopher William James argued in *Pragmatism* (1907) that truth emerges not from abstract theorizing but from the experience of coping with life's realities through practical action. Truth is not an absolute; truth happens to ideas as they

Progressive Reformers Worldwide Share Ideas and Strategies

Progressive reform was not an American invention. U.S. progressives drew ideas from Continental Europe, the British Isles, Canada, and even faraway Australia and New Zealand. Sometimes, the exchange flowed in the other direction, as reformers abroad found inspiration in America.

Industrialization and urbanization had transformed other societies as well. The smoky factory cities of Manchester and Birmingham in England; Glasgow in Scotland; Liège in Belgium; and Düsseldorf and Essen in Germany's coal-rich Ruhr Valley all experienced the same social problems as did U.S. industrial cities like Pittsburgh, Chicago, and Cleveland. The grinding poverty of London's East End was as notorious as that of New York's Lower East Side.

The shocked response to these conditions crossed national boundaries as well. Jacob Riis's grim account of life in New York's immigrant wards, *How the Other Half Lives* (1890), echoed the Rev. Andrew Mearns's polemic *The Bitter Cry of Outcast London* (1883). William T. Stead's sensational 1885 exposé of prostitution in London, "The Maiden Tribute of Modern Babylon," helped inspire the American antiprostitution crusade. The sociological studies of poverty in Chicago, Pittsburgh, Philadelphia, and other cities undertaken by American investigators drew inspiration from Charles Booth's massive survey of London poverty. Beginning in 1886, Booth and his collaborators had painstakingly studied conditions in London's slums. Their handwritten data eventually filled 12,000 notebook pages. Booth published detailed maps showing the economic situation street by street,

first in the East End (1887) and eventually in the entire city (1902–1903).

Efforts to solve the problems of the new urban-industrial order crossed national boundaries, giving rise to a transnational reform movement. The breadth and diversity of this movement was showcased at the Paris Exposition of 1900 in a Musée Social (Social Museum) featuring exhibits of many nations' reform innovations.

As early as the 1880s, Germany's conservative Chancellor Otto von Bismarck, trying to keep the socialists from power, instituted a remarkable series of reforms, including a ban on child labor; maximum working hours; and illness, accident, and old-age insurance for workers. Britain's Liberal party, in power in 1906–1914, introduced minimum-wage laws, unemployment insurance, and a health-insurance program on the German model. In France, a coalition of reform parties established a maximum working day, a progressive income tax (one with higher rates for wealthier taxpayers), and a program of medical aid for the elderly poor. Denmark adopted an old-age pension system. Not all the reforms were state sponsored; some relied on voluntary philanthropy. For example, the first settlement house, Toynbee Hall, was started in London in 1884 by the Anglican clergyman Samuel Augustus Barnett and others. While Australia introduced an ambitious program of water-resource planning to promote agricultural development in its vast interior, New Zealand's trailblazing reforms included woman suffrage, arbitration courts to resolve labor disputes, and programs enabling small farmers to lease public lands.

American reformers followed these developments carefully. Jane Addams visited Toynbee Hall repeatedly in the 1880s. In 1900, the muckraking U.S. journalist Henry Demarest Lloyd praised New Zealand as "the political brain of the modern world." American students in German and Swiss universities and the London School of Economics (founded by socialists in 1895) encountered challenges to the laissez-faire doctrine that prevailed back home. The federal government's Bureau of Labor Statistics collected data on European social and labor conditions and labor-related issues, to give government officials and legislators a comparative perspective on issues of concern in America. For the same reason, reform-minded labor historian John R. Commons at the University of Wisconsin plastered his graduate-seminar room with charts showing labor laws around the world. American Social Gospel leaders kept in close touch with like-minded clergy in England and elsewhere. Experiments with publicly owned electric power companies in the Canadian province of Ontario offered a model for municipal reformers who were proposing this innovation in Cleveland and other U.S. cities.

Transatlantic conferences and delegations furthered the exchange of reform strategies. In 1910, ten Americans attended an International Congress on Unemployment in Paris while twenty-eight Americans came to Vienna for an International Housing Congress. The National Civic Federation sent fifteen experts to England and Scotland in 1906 to study new ideas in urban reform. A delegation from the Bureau of Municipal Research spent several months in Frankfurt in 1912 learning about administrative innovations in that city. In 1911, a sociology professor at the City College of

New York offered social workers a package tour including visits to London settlement houses, planned cities elsewhere in England, workers' cooperatives in Belgium, and infant nurseries in Paris.

Reformers committed to causes such as world peace or women's rights often joined forces with kindred spirits abroad. The birth-control advocate Margaret Sanger, pacifist Jane Addams, and woman-suffrage leader Alice Paul all maintained close contact with activists elsewhere who shared their commitments. The introduction of woman suffrage in New Zealand (1893) and Australia (1902) energized the U.S. suffrage movement.

Housing reformers and city planners cultivated international ties as well. The New York State Tenement House Law of 1901, a key reform measure, owed much to the groundbreaking work of English housing reformers. Daniel Burnham's 1909 *Plan of Chicago* (see "Making Cities More Livable") drew inspiration from classical Athens and Rome; Renaissance Florence and Siena; Georges Haussmann's great Paris boulevards of the mid-nineteenth century; and Vienna's Ringstrasse, itself inspired by the Paris model.

Magazines contributed to the global flow of reform ideas. The muckraking journalist Ray Stannard Baker reported on reforms in Germany for *McClure's* magazine in 1900, providing a broader context for the magazine's articles on reform in the United States. Not to be outdone, *Everybody's* magazine sent Charles E. Russell around the world in 1905 to investigate reform initiatives in England, Switzerland, Germany, Australia, New Zealand, and elsewhere.

Reform-minded foreigners also visited the United States to report on the juvenile court system, the playground movement, innovative public schools, and other progressive developments. One English progressive visiting Madison, Wisconsin, in 1911 praised the university's role in promoting reform legislation. "The State has been practically governed by the University . . . ," he wrote. "[E]very question is threshed out in class before it is threshed out by the legislature." The Kansas editor William Allen White, recalling the Progressive Era in his 1946 autobiography, marveled at the movement's transnational character: "We were parts, one of another, . . . the United States and Europe. Something was welding us into one social and economic whole with local political variations, [but] . . . all fighting [for] a common cause."

American progressivism, in short, was simply one manifestation of a larger effort to cope with the social impact of rapid industrialization and urban growth. Through a dense network of publications, conferences, and personal ties, reformers of many nations kept in touch, shared strategies, and drew on a vast storehouse of ideas as they addressed the problems and circumstances of their societies.

Question for Analysis

- What early twentieth-century reforms transcended national boundaries, and how did reformers in different countries share ideas and strategies?

are tested in the real world. James's philosophy of pragmatism deepened the reformers' skepticism toward the older generation's entrenched ideas and strengthened their belief in the necessity of social change.

Herbert Croly shared this faith that new ideas could transform society. The son of reform-minded New York journalists, Croly grew up in a cosmopolitan world where social issues were hotly debated. In *The Promise of American Life* (1909), he called for an activist government of the kind advocated by Alexander Hamilton, the first secretary of the treasury. But rather than serving the interests of the business class, as Hamilton had proposed, Croly argued that this activist government should promote the welfare of all. In 1914, Croly founded the *New Republic* magazine to promote progressive ideas.

The settlement-house leader Jane Addams also played a key role in shaping the ideology of the Progressive Era. In *Democracy and Social Ethics* (1902) and *Twenty Years at Hull House* (1910), Addams rejected the claim that unrestrained competition offered the best path to social progress. Instead, she argued, in a complex industrial society, each individual's well-being depends on the well-being of all. Addams urged middle-class Americans to recognize their common interests with the laboring masses, and to demand better conditions in factories and immigrant slums. Teaching by example, Addams made her Chicago social settlement, Hull House, a center of social activism and legislative-reform initiatives.

With public-school enrollment growing from about 7 million in 1870 to more than 23 million in 1920, the educational reformer John Dewey saw schools as potent engines of social change. Banishing bolted-down chairs and desks from his model school at the University of Chicago, he encouraged pupils to interact with one another. The ideal school, he said in *Democracy and Education* (1916), would be an "embryonic community" where children would learn to live cooperatively as members of a social group.

Oliver Wendell Holmes, Jr., of Harvard Law School focused on changing judicial thinking. In these years, most judges interpreted the law in ways that protected corporate interests and struck down reform legislation. In *The Common Law* (1881), however, Holmes had insisted that law must evolve as society changes. In a phrase much quoted by progressives, he had declared, "The life of the law has not been logic; it has been experience." Appointed to the United States Supreme Court in 1902, Holmes often dissented from the conservative Court majority. As the new social thinking took hold, the courts slowly grew more open to reform legislation.

Novelists, Journalists, and Artists Spotlight Social Problems
While reform-minded intellectuals reoriented American social thought, novelists and journalists roused the reform spirit by chronicling corporate wrongdoing, municipal corruption, slum conditions, and industrial abuses. Advances in printing and photo reproduction ensured a mass audience and sharpened the emotional impact of their message.

In his novel *The Octopus* (1901), Frank Norris of San Francisco portrayed the epic struggle between California railroad barons and the state's wheat growers. Though writing fiction, Norris accurately described the bribery, intimidation, rate manipulation, and other means by which the railroad owners promoted their interests.

Theodore Dreiser's novel *The Financier* (1912) featured a hard-driving business tycoon utterly lacking a social conscience. Dreiser modeled his story on the scandal-ridden career of a railway financier named Charles Yerkes. Like Veblen's *Theory of the Leisure Class,* such works undermined the reputation of the industrial elite and stimulated pressures for tougher regulation of business.

Mass magazines such as *McClure's* and *Collier's* also fanned the flames of reform with articles exposing urban political corruption and corporate wrongdoing. President Theodore Roosevelt criticized the authors as **"muckrakers"** obsessed with dredging up the worst in American life, but the label became a badge of honor. Journalist Lincoln Steffens began the exposé vogue in October 1902 with a *McClure's* article documenting municipal corruption in St. Louis and the reform efforts of a crusading district attorney.

The muckrakers emphasized facts rather than abstractions. To gather material, some worked as factory laborers or lived in slum tenements. In a 1903 series, journalist Maria Van Vorst described her experiences working in a Massachusetts shoe factory where the caustic dyes rotted women's fingernails. The British immigrant John Spargo researched his 1906 book about child labor, *The Bitter Cry of the Children,* by visiting mines in Pennsylvania and West Virginia and attempting to do the work that young boys performed for ten hours a day, picking out slate and other refuse from coal in cramped, dangerous workspaces filled with choking coal dust.

The muckrakers awakened middle-class readers to conditions in industrial America. The circulation of *McClure's* and *Collier's* soared. Some magazine exposés later appeared in book form, including Lincoln Steffens's *The Shame of the Cities* (1904), Ida Tarbell's damning *History of the Standard Oil Company* (1904), and David Graham Phillips's *Treason of the Senate* (1906).

Artists and photographers played a role as well. A group of New York painters dubbed the Ashcan School portrayed the harshness as well as the vitality of slum life.

The Wisconsin-born photographer Lewis Hine captured images of immigrants and factory laborers. For the National Child Labor Committee Hine photographed child workers with stunted bodies and worn expressions. Such images built support for the campaign to outlaw child labor.

STATE AND LOCAL PROGRESSIVISM

Middle-class citizens did more than read about the problems of urban-industrial America. They observed these problems firsthand in their own communities. In fact, the progressive movement began with grass-roots campaigns from New York to San Francisco to end urban political corruption, regulate corporate behavior, and improve conditions in factories and city slums. Eventually, these state and local movements came together in a powerful national surge of reform.

Reforming the Political Process In a series of campaigns beginning in the 1890s, native-born elites and middle-class reformers battled corrupt city governments. These city machines provided services and jobs to immigrants, but often at the price of graft and rigged elections (see Chapter 19). In New York City, Protestant clergy rallied the forces of righteousness against Tammany Hall, the city's entrenched Democratic organization. In Detroit the reform mayor Hazen Pingree (served 1890–1897) brought honesty to city hall, lowered transit fares, adopted a fairer tax structure, and provided public baths and other services. Pingree once slapped a health quarantine on a brothel, holding hostage a well-known business leader until he promised to back Pingree's reforms.

In San Francisco, a courageous newspaper editor led a 1907 crusade against the city's corrupt boss, Abe Ruef. When the original prosecutor was gunned down in court, attorney Hiram Johnson took his place, winning convictions against Ruef and his cronies. Full of reform zeal—one observer called him "a volcano in perpetual eruption"—Johnson rode his newly won fame to the California governorship and the U.S. Senate.

In Toledo, Ohio, a colorful eccentric named Samuel M. ("Golden Rule") Jones led the reform crusade. A self-made businessman converted to the Social Gospel (see Chapter 19), Jones introduced profit sharing in his factory, and as mayor he established playgrounds, free kindergartens, and lodging houses for homeless transients.

The political reformers soon moved beyond simply "throwing the rascals out" to probing the roots of urban misgovernment, including the private monopolies that ran municipal water, gas, electricity, and transit systems. Reformers passed laws regulating the rates these utilities could charge and curbing their political influence. (Some even advocated public ownership of these companies.) This new regulatory structure would remain the rule for a century, until an equally strong deregulatory movement swept the nation in the 1990s.

Reflecting the Progressive Era vogue of expertise and efficiency, some municipal reformers advocated substituting professional administrators and councils chosen in citywide elections for mayors and aldermen elected on a ward-by-ward basis. Disasters sometimes gave a boost to this reform. Dayton, Ohio, adopted a city-manager system after a ruinous flood in 1913. Supposedly above politics, these experts were expected to run the city like an efficient business.

Municipal reform attracted different groups depending on the issue. The native-born middle class, led by clergymen, editors, and other opinion molders, provided the initial impetus and core support. Business interests often pushed for citywide elections and the city-manager system, since these changes reduced immigrants' political clout and increased the influence of the corporate elite. Reforms that promised improved services or better conditions for ordinary city-dwellers won support from immigrants and even from political bosses who realized that explosive urban growth was swamping the old, informal system of meeting constituents' needs.

The electoral-reform movement soon expanded to the state level. By 1910, for example, all states had replaced the old system of voting, which involved preprinted ballots bearing the names of specific candidates, with the secret ballot, which made it harder to rig elections. The direct primary, introduced in Wisconsin in 1903, enabled rank-and-file voters rather than party bosses to select the candidates who would compete in the general election.

Hoping to trim the political power of corporate interests, some western states inaugurated the *initiative, referendum,* and *recall.* By an initiative, voters can instruct the legislature to consider a specific bill. In a referendum, they can actually enact a law or (in a nonbinding referendum) express their views on a proposed measure. By a recall petition, voters can remove a public official from office if they muster enough signatures.

While these reforms aimed to democratize voting, party leaders and interest groups soon learned to manipulate the new electoral machinery. Ironically, the new procedures may have weakened party loyalty and reduced voter interest. Voter-participation rates dropped steeply in these years, while political activity by organized interest groups increased.

Regulating Business, Protecting Workers

The late-nineteenth-century corporate consolidation that produced giants like Carnegie Steel and Standard Oil (see Chapter 18) continued after 1900. The United States Steel Company created by J. P. Morgan in 1901 controlled 80 percent of all U.S. steel production. A year later Morgan combined six competing companies into the International Harvester Company, which dominated the farm-implement business. The General Motors Company, formed in 1908 by William C. Durant with backing from the Du Pont Corporation, brought various independent automobile manufacturers, from the inexpensive Chevrolet to the luxury Cadillac, under one corporate umbrella.

Many workers benefited from this corporate growth. Industrial workers' average annual real wages (defined, that is, in terms of actual purchasing power) rose from $487 in 1900 to $687 by 1915. In railroading and other unionized industries, wages climbed still higher. But even though the cost of living was far lower than today, such wages could barely support a family and provided little cushion for emergencies.

To survive, entire families went to work. Two-thirds of young immigrant women entered the labor force in the early 1900s, working as factory help or domestics or in small establishments like laundries and bakeries. Even children worked. In 1910, the nonfarm labor force probably included at least 1.6 million children aged ten to fifteen employed in factories, mills, tenement sweatshops, and street trades such as shoe shining and newspaper vending. The total may have been higher, since many "women workers" listed in the census were in fact young girls. One investigator found a girl of five working at night in a South Carolina textile mill.

Most laborers faced long hours and great hazards. Despite the eight-hour movement of the 1880s, in 1900 the average worker still toiled 9 1/2 hours a day. Some southern textile mills required workdays of 12 or 13 hours. In one typical year (1907), 4,534 railroad workers and more than 3,000 miners were killed on the job. Few employers accepted responsibility for work-related accidents and illnesses. Vacations and retirement benefits were practically unheard of.

Factory workers accustomed to the rhythms of farm labor faced the discipline of the time clock and the machine. Efficiency experts used time-and-motion studies to increase production and make human labor as predictable as machines. In *Principles of Scientific Management* (1911), Frederick W. Taylor explained how to increase output by standardizing job routines and rewarding the fastest workers. "Efficiency" became a popular catchword, but most workers resented the pressures to speed up.

Many Americans concerned about the social implications of industrialization deplored the expansion of corporate power and the hazards facing the laboring masses. The drive to regulate big business, inherited from the populists, thus became an important component of progressivism. Since corporations had benefited from government policies such as high protective tariffs, reformers reasoned, they should also be subject to government supervision.

Wisconsin under Governor **Robert** ("Fighting Bob") **La Follette** took the lead in regulating railroads, mines, and other businesses. As a Republican congressman, La Follette had feuded with the state's conservative party leadership, and in 1900 he won the governorship as an independent. Challenging long-dominant business interests, La Follette and his administration adopted the direct-primary system, set up a railroad regulatory commission, increased corporate taxes, and limited campaign spending. Reflecting progressivism's faith in experts, La Follette met regularly with reform-minded professors at the University of Wisconsin. He also set up a legislative reference library so lawmakers would not be solely dependent on corporate lobbyists for factual information. La Follette's reforms gained national attention as the "Wisconsin Idea."

If electoral reform and corporate regulation represented the brain of progressivism, the impulse to improve conditions in factories and mills represented its heart. This movement, too, began at the local and state level. By 1907, for example, some thirty states had outlawed child labor. A 1903 Oregon law limited women in industry to a ten-hour workday.

Campaigns for industrial safety and better working conditions won support from political bosses in cities with large immigrant populations, such as New York, Cleveland, and Chicago. New York state senator Robert F. Wagner, a leader of Tammany Hall, headed the investigation of the 1911 Triangle fire. Thanks to his committee's efforts, New York passed fifty-six worker-protection laws, including required fire-safety inspections of factories. By 1914, spurred by the Triangle disaster, twenty-five states had made employers liable for job-related injuries or deaths.

Florence Kelley, a Hull House resident and the daughter of a conservative Republican congressman, helped launch the drive to remedy industrial abuses. In 1893, after investigating conditions in factories and sweatshops, Kelley persuaded the Illinois legislature to outlaw child labor and limit working hours for women. In 1899, she became general secretary of the National Consumers' League, which mobilized consumer pressure for improved factory conditions. Campaigning for a federal child-labor law, Kelley asked, "Why are seals, bears, reindeer, fish, wild game in the national parks, buffalo, [and] migratory birds all found suitable for federal protection, but not children?"

Like many progressive reforms, the crusade for workplace safety relied on expert research. Alice Hamilton, for example, a pioneer in the new field of "industrial hygiene," taught bacteriology at Northwestern University while also working with Jane Addams at Hull House. In 1910, fusing her scientific training and her reformist impulses, she studied lead poisoning among industrial workers. Later, as an investigator for the U.S. Bureau of Labor, Hamilton publicized work-related medical hazards.

Workers themselves, who well understood the hazards of their jobs, provided further pressure for reform. For example, when the granite industry introduced new power drills that created a fine dust that workers inhaled, the *Granite Cutters' Journal* warned of "stone cutters' consumption" and called the new drills "widow makers." Sure enough, investigators soon linked the dust to a deadly respiratory disease, silicosis.

Making Cities More Livable

In the early twentieth century, America became an urban nation. By 1920 the urban population passed the 50 percent mark, and sixty-eight U.S. cities boasted more than a hundred thousand inhabitants. New York City grew by 2.2 million from 1900 to 1920, and Chicago by 1 million.

Political corruption was only one of many problems plaguing urban America. As manufacturing and businesses grew, a tide of immigrants and native-born newcomers engulfed the cities. Overwhelmed by this rapid growth, many cities became sprawling human warehouses. They lacked adequate parks, municipal services, public-health resources, recreational facilities, and other basic civic amenities. As the reform spirit gained momentum, this tangle of urban problems loomed large.

Building on the achievements of Frederick Law Olmsted and others (see Chapter 19), reformers campaigned for parks, boulevards, and street lights and proposed laws against billboards and overhead electrical wires. An influential voice for city planning and beautification was Daniel Burnham, chief architect of the 1893 Chicago world's fair. Burnham led a successful 1906 effort to revive a plan for Washington, D.C., first proposed by Charles L'Enfant in 1791. He also developed plans for Cleveland, San Francisco, and other cities.

Burnham's 1909 *Plan of Chicago* offered a seductive vision of a city both more efficient and more beautiful. He recommended lakefront parks and museums, wide boulevards to improve traffic flow, and a redesign of Chicago's congested major thoroughfare, Michigan Avenue. The focal point of Burnham's dream city was a majestic domed city hall and vast civic plaza. Chicago spent more than $300 million on projects reflecting his ideas. Many Progressive Era urban planners shared Burnham's faith that more beautiful cities and imposing public buildings would produce orderly, law-abiding citizens.

Beyond urban beautification, the municipal reform impulse also included such practical goals as decent housing and better garbage collection and street cleaning. Providing a model for other cities and states, the New York legislature imposed strict health and safety regulations on tenements in 1911.

Public health loomed large as well. With the discovery in the 1880s that germs cause cholera, typhoid fever, and other diseases, municipal hygiene became a high

A Poor Neighborhood in Philadelphia, c. 1915 *Scenes like this in the immigrant wards of America's great cities stirred middle-class reformers to action at the turn of the last century.*

priority. Reformers called for improved water and sewer systems, regulation of food and milk suppliers, school medical examinations and vaccination programs, and campaigns to spread public-health information.

All these efforts bore fruit. From 1900 to 1920, infant mortality (defined as death in the first year of life) dropped from 165 per 1,000 population to around 75, and the tuberculosis death rate fell by nearly half. The municipal health crusades had a social-class dimension. Middle-class reformers set the "sanitary agenda," and the campaigns often targeted immigrants and the poor as the sources of contagion. When Mary Mallon, an Irish-immigrant cook in New York, was found to be a healthy carrier of the typhoid bacillus in 1907, she was confined for years by the city health authorities and demonized in the press as "Typhoid Mary."

Urban reformers also shared the heightened environmental consciousness of these years (see Chapter 17). The battle against air pollution illustrates both the promise and the frustrations of municipal environmentalism. Coal-fueled steam boilers in factories produced massive amounts of soot and smoke. Factory chimneys belching smoke had once inspired pride, but by the early 1900s physicians had linked factory smoke to respiratory problems, and civic reformers were deploring the resulting air pollution.

Like other progressive reforms, the antismoke campaign combined expertise with activism. Civil engineers formed the Smoke Prevention Association in 1906, and researchers at the University of Pittsburgh—one of the nation's smokiest cities with its nearby steel mills—documented the hazards and costs of air pollution. Chicago merchant Marshall Field declared that the "soot tax" he paid to clean his stores was larger than his real-estate taxes. As women's clubs and other civic groups embraced the cause, many cities passed smoke-abatement laws.

Success proved elusive as railroads and corporations fought back in the courts. With coal still providing 70 percent of the nation's energy as late as 1920, cities remained smoky. Not until years later, with the shift to other energy sources, did municipal air pollution significantly diminish.

PROGRESSIVISM AND SOCIAL CONTROL

Progressives' belief that they could improve society through research, legislation, and aroused public opinion sprang from their confidence that they knew what was best for other people. While municipal corruption, unsafe factories, and corporate abuses captured their attention, so, too, did issues of personal behavior, particularly immigrant behavior. The problems they addressed deserved attention, but their moralistic rhetoric and often coercive remedies also betrayed an impulse to impose their own moral standards by force of law.

Moral Control in the Cities
Despite the overcrowded slums, exhausting labor, and other problems, early-twentieth-century cities also offered fun and diversion. Department stores, vaudeville, music halls, and amusement parks (see Chapter 19) continued to flourish. While some vaudeville owners strove for respectability, bawdy routines full of sexual innuendo, including those of the comedienne Mae West, were popular with working-class audiences. New York City's amusement park, Coney Island, drew more patrons than ever. A subway ride from the city, it attracted as many as a million visitors a day by 1914.

For families, amusement parks provided escape from tenements. For female workers, they provided an opportunity to spend time with friends, meet young men, and show off new outfits. With electrification, simply riding the streetcars or taking an evening stroll on well-lit downtown streets became leisure activities in themselves. Orville and Wilbur Wright's successful airplane flight in 1903, and the introduction of Henry Ford's Model T in 1908, transforming the automobile from a toy of the rich to a vehicle for the masses, foretold exciting changes ahead, with cities at the heart of the action.

Jaunty music-hall songs, produced in a district of Manhattan called Tin Pan Alley, added to the vibrancy of city life. The blues, rooted in the chants of southern black sharecroppers, reached a broader public with such songs as W. C. Handy's classic "St. Louis Blues" (1914). Ragtime, another import from the black South (see Chapter 19), enjoyed great popularity in early-twentieth-century urban America. Both the black composer Scott Joplin, with such works as "Maple Leaf Rag" (1899), and the white composer Irving Berlin, with his hit tune "Alexander's Rag-Time Band" (1911), contributed to this vogue.

These years also brought a new medium of mass entertainment—the movies. Initially a part of vaudeville shows, movies soon migrated to five-cent halls called "nickelodeons" in immigrant neighborhoods. At first featuring brief comic sequences like *The Sneeze* or *The Kiss,* the movies began to tell stories with *The Great Train Robbery*

(1903). *A Fool There Was* (1914), with its famous line, "Kiss me, my fool!," made Theda Bara (really Theodosia Goodman of Cincinnati) the first female movie star. The British music-hall performer Charlie Chaplin immigrated to America and appeared in some sixty short two-reel comedies between 1914 and 1917. Like amusement parks, the movies allowed immigrant youth briefly to escape parental supervision. As a New York garment worker recalled, "The one place I was allowed to go by myself was the movies. My parents wouldn't let me go anywhere else."

The diversions that eased city life for the poor struck some middle-class reformers as moral traps no less dangerous than the physical hazards of the factory or the slum. Fearful of immorality and social disorder, reformers campaigned to regulate amusement parks, dance halls, and the movies shown in darkened nickelodeons, which they saw as potential dens of vice. Several states and cities set up film censorship boards, and the Supreme Court upheld such measures in 1915.

Building on the moral-purity crusade of the Woman's Christian Temperance Union (WCTU) and other groups in the 1890s (see Chapter 19), reformers also targeted prostitution, a major urban problem. Male procurers lured young women into the business and then took a share of their income. The paltry wages paid women for factory work or domestic service attracted many to this more-lucrative occupation. One prostitute wrote that she was unwilling "to get up at 6:30 . . . and work in a close stuffy room . . . until dark for $6 or $7 a week" when an afternoon with a man could bring in more.

Adopting the usual progressive approach, investigators gathered statistics on what they called "the social evil." The American Social Hygiene Association (1914), financed by John D. Rockefeller, Jr., sponsored medical research on sexually transmitted diseases, paid for "vice investigations" in various cities, and drafted model municipal statutes against prostitution.

As prostitution came to symbolize the larger moral dangers of cities, a "white slave" hysteria gripped the nation. Novels, films, and magazine articles warned of kidnapped farm girls forced into urban brothels. The Mann Act (1910) made it illegal to transport a woman across a state line "for immoral purposes." Amid much fanfare, reformers shut down the red-light districts of New Orleans, Chicago, and other cities.

Racism, anti-immigrant prejudice, fear of the city, and anxieties about changing sexual mores all fueled the antiprostitution crusade. Authorities employed the new legislation to pry into private sexual behavior. Blackmailers entrapped men into Mann Act violations. In 1913, the African-American boxer Jack Johnson, the heavyweight champion, was convicted under the Mann Act for traveling with a (white) woman across state lines for "immoral purposes." Johnson went abroad to escape imprisonment.

Battling Alcohol and Drugs Temperance had long been part of the American reform agenda, but reformers' objectives changed in the Progressive Era. Most earlier campaigns had urged individuals to give up drink. The powerful **Anti-Saloon League** (ASL), founded in 1895, shifted the emphasis to legislating a ban on the sale of alcoholic beverages. The ASL was a typical Progressive Era organization, run by full-time professionals, with Protestant ministers staffing a network of state committees. The ASL presses in Westerville, Ohio, produced propaganda documenting alcohol's role in many social problems and touting prohibition as the answer.

The Anti-Saloon League encouraged local churches and temperance groups to work for prohibition at the municipal, county, and state levels. As these campaigns built momentum, the ASL moved to its larger goal: national prohibition. Other Progressive Era campaigns followed this strategy of working locally while pursuing national reform as the long-range goal.

This was a heavy-drinking era, and alcohol abuse did indeed contribute to domestic abuse, health problems, and work injuries. But like the antiprostitution crusade, the prohibition campaign became a symbolic battleground pitting native-born citizens against the new immigrants. The ASL, while it raised legitimate issues, also embodied Protestant America's impulse to control the immigrant city.

These years also saw a campaign against drug abuse—and for good reason. Physicians, patent-medicine peddlers, and legitimate drug companies freely prescribed or sold opium (derived from poppies) and its derivatives morphine and heroin. Cocaine, extracted from coca leaves, was widely used as well. Coca-Cola contained cocaine until about 1900.

As reform pressure mounted, the federal government backed a 1912 treaty aimed at the international opium trade. The Narcotics Act of 1914, also known as the Harrison Act, banned the distribution of heroin, morphine, cocaine, and other addictive drugs except by licensed physicians or pharmacists. In this campaign, as in their environmental concerns, the progressives anticipated an issue that remains important today. But this reform, too, had racist undertones. Antidrug crusaders luridly described Chinese "opium dens" (places where this addictive narcotic was smoked) and warned that "drug-crazed Negroes" imperiled white womanhood.

Immigration Restriction and Eugenics

While many of the new city-dwellers came from farms and small towns, immigration remained the main source of urban growth. More than 17 million newcomers arrived from 1900 to 1917 (many passing through New York's immigration center, Ellis Island), and most settled in cities. As in the 1890s (see Chapter 19), the influx came mainly from southern and eastern Europe, but more than two hundred thousand Japanese arrived between 1900 and 1920. An estimated forty thousand Chinese entered in these years, despite the 1882 Chinese Exclusion Act (see Chapter 18), which was not repealed until 1943. Thousands of Mexicans came as well, seeking railroad work. Some immigrants prospered, but many sank into poverty or survived precariously.

The dismay that middle-class Americans felt about urban slum conditions stimulated support not only for protective legislation, but also for immigration restriction. If the immigrant city bred social problems, some concluded, then immigrants should be excluded. Prominent Bostonians formed the Immigration Restriction League in 1894. The American Federation of Labor, fearing job competition, also endorsed restriction.

Like most Progressive Era reformers, advocates of immigration restriction tried to document their case with statistical evidence. In 1911, a congressional commission produced a statistical study allegedly proving the new immigrants' innate degeneracy. Sociologist Edward A. Ross, a prominent progressive, described the recent immigrants as "low-browed, big-faced persons of obviously low mentality."

Led by Massachusetts senator Henry Cabot Lodge, Congress passed literacy-test bills in 1896, 1913, and 1915, only to see them vetoed. These measures would have excluded immigrants over sixteen years old who were unable to read either English or

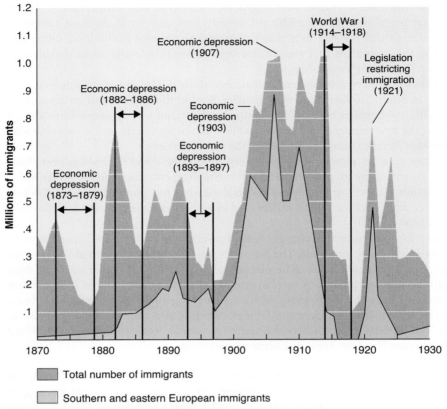

Figure 21.1 Immigration to the United States, 1870–1930

With the end of the depression of the 1890s, immigrants from southern and eastern Europe poured into American cities, spurring an immigration-restriction movement, urban moral-purity campaigns, and efforts to improve the physical and social conditions of immigrant life. *Sources: Statistical History of the United States from Colonial Times to the Present* (Stamford, Conn.: Fairfield Publishers, 1965); and report presented by Senator William P. Dillingham, Senate document 742, 61st Congress, 3rd session, December 5, 1910: Abstracts of Reports to the Immigration Commission.

their native language, thus discriminating against persons lacking formal education. In 1917, one such bill became law over President Woodrow Wilson's veto. Immigrants also faced physical examinations and tests in which legitimate public-health concerns became mixed up with stereotypes of entire ethnic groups as mental or physical defectives.

Anti-immigrant fears helped fuel the eugenics movement. Eugenics is the control of reproduction to alter a plant or animal species, and some U.S. eugenicists believed that human society could be improved by this means. A leading eugenicist, the zoologist Charles B. Davenport, urged immigration restriction to keep America from pollution by "inferior" genetic stock.

In *The Passing of the Great Race* (1916), Madison Grant, a prominent progressive and eugenics advocate, used bogus data to denounce immigrants from southern and eastern Europe, especially Jews. He also viewed African-Americans as inferior. Antici-pating the program of Adolf Hitler in the 1930s (see Chapter 25), Grant called for racial segregation, immigration restriction, and the forced sterilization of the "unfit," including "worthless race types." The vogue of eugenics gave "scientific" respectability to anti-immigrant sentiment, as well as to the racism that pervaded white America in these years. Inspired by eugenics, many states legalized the sterilization of criminals, sex offenders, and persons adjudged mentally deficient. In the 1927 case *Buck* v. *Bell*, the Supreme Court upheld such laws.

Racism and
Progressivism

Progressivism arose at a time of transition in African-American life, and also of intense racism in white America. These reali-ties are crucial to a full understanding of the movement.

In 1900, most of the nation's 10 million blacks lived in the rural South as share-croppers and tenant farmers. As devastating floods and the cotton boll weevil, which spread from Mexico in the 1890s, worsened their lot, many southern blacks left the land. By 1910, over 20 percent of the black population lived in cities, mostly in the South, but many in the North as well. Black men in the cities took jobs in factories, docks, and railroads or became carpenters, plasterers, or bricklayers. Many black women became domestic servants, seamstresses, or workers in laundries and tobacco factories. By 1910, 54 percent of America's black women held jobs.

Across the South, legally enforced racism peaked in the early twentieth century. Local "Jim Crow" laws segregated streetcars, schools, parks, and even cemeteries. The facilities for blacks, including the schools, were invariably inferior. Many southern cities imposed residential segregation by law until the Supreme Court restricted it in 1917. Most labor unions excluded black workers. Disfranchised and trapped in a cycle of poverty, poor education, and discrimination, southern blacks faced bleak prospects.

Fleeing such conditions, two hundred thousand blacks migrated north between 1890 and 1910. Wartime job opportunities drew still more in 1917–1918 (see Chapter 22), and by 1920, 1.4 million African-Americans lived in the North. They found condi-tions only slightly better than in the South. In northern cities, too, racism worsened after 1890 as hard times and immigration heightened social tensions. (Immigrants, competing with blacks for jobs and housing, sometimes exhibited intense racial preju-dice.) Segregation, though not imposed by law, was enforced by custom and sometimes by violence. Blacks lived in run-down "colored districts," attended dilapidated schools, and worked at the lowest-paying jobs.

Their ballots—usually cast for the party of Lincoln—brought little political influ-ence. The only black politicians tolerated by Republican party leaders were those willing to distribute low-level patronage jobs and otherwise keep silent. African-Americans in the segregated army faced hostility from white soldiers and officers, as well as from nearby civilians. Even the movies preached racism. D. W. Griffith's *The Birth of a Na-tion* (1915) disparaged blacks and glorified the Ku Klux Klan.

Smoldering racism sometimes exploded in violence. Antiblack rioters in Atlanta in 1906 murdered twenty-five blacks and burned many black homes. From 1900 to 1920 an average of about seventy-five lynchings occurred yearly. Some lynch mobs used trumped-up charges to justify the murder of blacks whose assertive behavior or eco-nomic aspirations angered whites. Some lynchings involved incredible sadism, with large crowds on hand, victims' bodies mutilated, and graphic photo postcards sold later. Authorities rarely intervened. At a 1916 lynching in Texas, the mayor warned the mob to protect the hanging tree, since it was on city property.

In the face of such hostility, blacks developed strong social institutions and a vigorous culture. Black churches proved a bulwark of support. Working African-American mothers, drawing on strategies dating to slavery days, relied on relatives and neighbors for child care. A handful of black higher-education institutions such as Fisk in Nashville and Howard in Washington, D.C., carried on against heavy odds. John Hope, a classics scholar who became president of Atlanta's Morehouse College in 1906, assembled a distinguished faculty, championed African-American education, and fought racial segregation. His sister Jane (Hope) Lyons was dean of women at Spelman College, another black institution in Atlanta.

The urban black community included several black-owned insurance companies and banks, a small elite of entrepreneurs, teachers, ministers, and sports figures like Jack Johnson. Although major-league baseball excluded blacks, a thriving Negro League attracted many black fans.

In this racist age, progressives compiled a mixed record on racial issues. Lillian Wald, director of New York's Henry Street Settlement, protested racial injustice. Muckraker Ray Stannard Baker documented racism in his 1908 book, *Following the Color Line*. Settlement-house worker Mary White Ovington helped found the National Association for the Advancement of Colored People (see below) and wrote *Half a Man* (1911), about the psychological scars of racism.

But most progressives kept silent as blacks were lynched, disfranchised, and discriminated against. Many saw African-Americans, like immigrants, not as potential allies but as part of the problem. Viewing blacks as inferior and prone to immorality and social disorder, white progressives generally supported or tolerated segregated schools and housing, restrictions on black voting rights, the strict moral oversight of African-American communities, and, at best, paternalistic efforts to "uplift" this supposedly backward and childlike people. Viciously racist southern politicians like Governor James K. Vardaman of Mississippi and Senator Ben Tillman of South Carolina also supported progressive reforms. Southern woman-suffrage leaders argued that granting women the vote would strengthen white supremacy.

At the national level, President Theodore Roosevelt's record on race was marginally better than that of other politicians in this racist age. He appointed a black to head the Charleston customs house despite white opposition, and closed a Mississippi post office rather than yield to demands that he dismiss the black postmistress. In a symbolically important gesture, he dined with Booker T. Washington at the White House. In 1906, however, he approved the dishonorable discharge of an entire regiment of black soldiers, including Congressional Medal of Honor winners, in Brownsville, Texas, because some members of the unit, goaded by racist taunts, had killed a local civilian. The "Brownsville Incident" incensed black Americans. (In 1972, when most of the men were long dead, Congress reversed the dishonorable discharges.)

Under President Woodrow Wilson, racism became rampant in Washington. A Virginia native reared in Georgia, Wilson displayed at best a patronizing attitude toward blacks, praised the racist movie *The Birth of a Nation,* and allowed southerners in his cabinet and in Congress (some of them powerful committee chairmen) to impose rigid segregation on all levels of the government.

BLACKS, WOMEN, AND WORKERS ORGANIZE

The organizational strategy so central to progressivism generally also proved useful for groups facing discrimination or exploitation. African-Americans, middle-class women, and wage workers all organized to address their grievances and improve their situation.

African-American Leaders Organize Against Racism With racism on the rise, Booker T. Washington's accommodationist message (see Chapter 20) seemed increasingly unrealistic, particularly to northern blacks. Washington's self-help theme would appeal to later generations of African-Americans, but in the early twentieth century, many blacks confronting lynching, blatant racism, and rising segregationist pressures tired of his cautious approach. In 1902, William Monroe Trotter, the editor of the *Boston Guardian,* a black newspaper, called Washington's go-slow policies "a fatal blow . . . to the Negro's political rights and liberty."

Another opponent was the black journalist and activist **Ida Wells-Barnett.** Moving to Chicago from Memphis in 1892 after a white mob destroyed her offices, Wells-Barnett mounted a national antilynching campaign, in contrast to Booker T. Washington's public silence on the subject. An eloquent speaker and writer, she toured the United States and Great Britain lecturing against lynching and other racial abuses, and documented the grim record in her 1895 book *A Red Record.*

Booker T. Washington's most potent challenger was **W. E. B. Du Bois** (1868–1963). After earning a Ph.D. in history from Harvard in 1895, Du Bois taught at Wilberforce College in Ohio, the University of Pennsylvania, and then Atlanta University. Openly criticizing Washington in *The Souls of Black Folk* (1903), he rejected Washington's call for patience and his exclusive emphasis on manual skills. Instead, Du Bois demanded full racial equality, including the same educational opportunities open to whites, and called on blacks to resist all forms of racism.

Du Bois's militancy signaled a new era of African-American activism. In 1905, under his leadership, blacks who favored vigorous resistance to racism held a conference at Niagara Falls. For the next few years, participants in the "Niagara Movement" met annually. Meanwhile, a group of white reformers led by newspaper publisher Oswald Garrison Villard, grandson of abolitionist William Lloyd Garrison, had also grown dissatisfied with Washington's cautiousness. In 1909, Villard and his allies joined with Du Bois and other blacks from the Niagara Movement to form the **National Association for the Advancement of Colored People** (NAACP). This new organization called for sustained activism, including legal challenges, to achieve political equality for blacks and full integration into American life. Attracting the urban black middle class, the NAACP by 1914 had six thousand members in fifty branches.

Revival of the Woman-Suffrage Movement As late as 1910, women could vote in only four western states: Wyoming, Utah, Colorado, and Idaho. Woman suffrage failed in six state referenda after 1896. But the active role of women in the progressive reform movement revitalized the suffrage cause. Middle-class women found disfranchisement especially galling when recently arrived immigrant men could vote. A vigorous suffrage movement in Great Britain

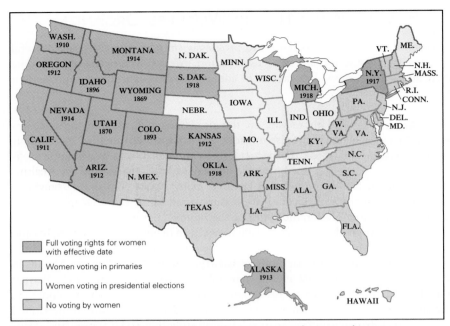

MAP 21.1 **Woman Suffrage Before the Nineteenth Amendment**

Beginning with Wyoming in 1869, woman suffrage made steady gains in western states before 1920. Farther east, key victories came in New York (1917) and Michigan (1918). But much of the East remained an anti-woman-suffrage bastion throughout the period.

reverberated in America as well. Like progressivism itself, this revived campaign in America started at the grass roots. A suffrage campaign in New York State in 1915, though unsuccessful, underscored the new momentum.

So, too, did events in California. Indeed, the California campaign illustrates both the strengths and the limitations of the revived movement. In the 1880s, California's women's clubs focused on cultural and domestic themes. By the early 1900s, they had evolved into a potent statewide organization addressing municipal reforms and public-school issues. This evolution convinced many members that full citizenship meant the right to vote. A state woman-suffrage referendum lost in 1896, but the leaders bounced back to form alliances with labor leaders and male progressives, built on a shared commitment to "good government" and opposition to municipal corruption. But while joining forces with male reformers, the woman-suffrage strategists insisted on the unique role of "organized womanhood" in building a better society. Success came in 1911 when California voters approved woman suffrage.

"Organized womanhood" had its limits. Elite and middle-class women, mainly based in Los Angeles and San Francisco, led the California campaign. Working-class women and farmwomen played little role, while African-American, Mexican-American, and Asian-American women were almost totally excluded.

New leaders translated the momentum in California and other states into a revitalized national movement. When Susan B. Anthony retired from the presidency of the

National American Woman Suffrage Association (NAWSA) in 1900, **Carrie Chapman Catt** of Iowa succeeded her. Under Catt's shrewd direction, NAWSA adopted the so-called Winning Plan: grass-roots organization with tight central coordination.

Suffragists adopted techniques from the new urban consumer culture. They not only lobbied legislators, but also ran newspaper ads; put up posters; waved banners with catchy slogans; organized parades in open cars; arranged photo opportunities for the media; and distributed fans and other items emblazoned with the suffrage message. Gradually, state after state fell into the suffrage column. As in California (and like progressive organizations generally), NAWSA's membership remained largely white, native-born, and middle class. Few black, immigrant, or working-class women joined. Some upper-class women opposed the reform. The leader of the "Antis," the wealthy Josephine Dodge of New York, argued that women already had behind-the-scenes influence, and that to invade the male realm of electoral politics would tarnish their moral and spiritual role.

Not all suffragists accepted Catt's strategy. Alice Paul, who had observed the British suffragists' militant tactics while studying in England, grew impatient with NAWSA's state-by-state approach. In 1913, Paul founded the Congressional Union for Woman Suffrage, renamed the National Woman's Party in 1916, to pressure Congress to enact a woman-suffrage constitutional amendment. Targeting "the party in power"—in this case, the Democrats—Paul and her followers in the 1916 election opposed President Woodrow Wilson and congressional Democrats who had failed to endorse a suffrage amendment. In 1917–1918, with the United States at war, the suffrage cause won key victories in New York and Michigan and advanced toward final success (see Chapter 22).

Enlarging "Woman's Sphere"
As the careers of such women as Florence Kelley, Alice Hamilton, and Ida Wells-Barnett make clear, the suffrage cause did not exhaust women's energies in the Progressive Era. Women's clubs, settlement-house residents, and individual female activists promoted a wide range of reforms. These included the campaigns to bring playgrounds and day nurseries to the slums, abolish child labor, and ban unsafe foods and quack remedies. As Jane Addams observed, the watchful care that women gave their own children could also draw them into broader political activism in an industrial age when hazards came from outside the home as well as inside.

Cultural assumptions about "woman's sphere" weakened as women became active on many fronts. Katherine Bement Davis served as New York City's commissioner of corrections. Emma Goldman crisscrossed the country lecturing on politics, feminism, and modern drama while coediting a radical monthly, *Mother Earth*. A vanguard of pioneering women in higher education included Marion Talbot, first dean of women at the University of Chicago.

In *Women and Economics* (1898) and other works, feminist intellectual Charlotte Perkins Gilman explored the cultural roots of gender roles and linked women's subordinate status to their economic dependence on men. Confining women to the domestic sphere, Gilman argued, was an evolutionary throwback that had become outdated and inefficient. She advocated gender equality in the workplace; the collectivization of cooking, cleaning, and other domestic tasks; and state-run day-care centers. In the utopian novel *Herland* (1915), Gilman wittily critiqued patriarchal assumptions by injecting three naïve young men into an exclusively female society.

Parading for Woman Suffrage *Suffrage leaders built support for the cause by using modern advertising and publicity techniques, including automobiles festooned with flags, bunting, banners, posters, and—in this case—smiling little girls.*

Some Progressive Era reformers challenged federal and state laws banning the distribution of contraceptives and birth-control information. Although countless women, particularly the poor, suffered exhaustion and ill health from frequent pregnancies, artificial contraception was widely denounced as immoral. In 1914, **Margaret Sanger** of New York, a practical nurse and socialist whose mother had died after bearing eleven children, began her crusade for birth control, a term she coined. When her journal *The Woman Rebel* faced prosecution on obscenity charges, Sanger fled to England. Returning in 1916, she opened the nation's first birth-control clinic in Brooklyn; launched a new journal, the *Birth Control Review;* and founded the American Birth Control League, the ancestor of today's Planned Parenthood Federation. Meanwhile, another New Yorker, Mary Ware Dennett, had also emerged as an advocate of birth control and sex education. (Her frank 1919 informational pamphlet for youth, *The Sex Side of Life,* was long banned as obscene.) While Sanger championed direct action to promote the cause, Dennett urged lobbying efforts to change the law. Sanger insisted that only physicians should supply contraceptives; Dennett argued for widespread distribution. These differences, coupled with Sanger's inability to tolerate rivals, soured relations between the two women and their respective organizations.

The birth-control movement stands as one of progressivism's most important legacies. At the time, however, it stirred bitter resistance among conservatives and many religious leaders. Indeed, not until 1965 did the Supreme Court fully legalize the dissemination of contraceptive materials and information.

Workers Organize; Socialism Advances   In this age of organization, labor unions continued to expand. The American Federation of Labor (AFL) grew from 625,000 members in 1900 to 4 million by 1920. This was still only about 20 percent of the industrial work force. With recent immigrants hungry for jobs, union activities could be risky. The boss could always fire an "agitator" and hire a docile newcomer. Judicial hostility also plagued the movement. In the 1908 *Danbury Hatters* case, for example, the Supreme Court forbade unions from organizing boycotts in support of strikes. Such boycotts were a "conspiracy in restraint of trade," said the high court, and thus a violation of the Sherman Anti-Trust Act. The AFL's strength remained in the skilled trades, not in the factories, mills, and sweatshops where most immigrants and women worked.

A few unions did try to reach these laborers. The International Ladies' Garment Workers' Union (ILGWU), founded in 1900 by immigrants working in New York City's needle trades, conducted successful strikes in 1909 and after the 1911 Triangle fire. The 1909 strike began when young Clara Lemlich jumped up as speechmaking droned on at a union meeting and passionately called for a strike. Thousands of women garment workers stayed off the job the next day. Some of the picketers endured police beatings; others lost their jobs. But the strikers did win higher wages and improved working conditions.

Another union that targeted the most exploited workers was the **Industrial Workers of the World** (IWW), nicknamed the Wobblies, founded in Chicago in 1905. The IWW's leader was William "Big Bill" Haywood, a compelling orator. Utah-born Haywood became a miner as a boy and joined the militant Western Federation of Miners in 1896. In 1905 he was acquitted of complicity in the assassination of an antilabor former governor of Idaho. IWW membership peaked at around thirty thousand, mostly western miners, lumbermen, fruit pickers, and itinerant laborers. But it captured the imagination of young cultural rebels in New York City's Greenwich Village, where Haywood often visited.

The IWW led mass strikes of Nevada gold miners; Minnesota iron miners; and timber workers in Louisiana, Texas, and the Northwest. In 1912 it won a bitter textile strike in Massachusetts. This victory owed much to two women: the birth-control reformer Margaret Sanger, and Elizabeth Gurley Flynn, a fiery Irish-American orator who publicized the cause by sending strikers' children to sympathizers in New York City for temporary care. Although the IWW's reputation for violence was much exaggerated, it faced government harassment, especially during World War I, and by 1920 its strength was broken.

Other workers, as well as some middle-class Americans, turned to socialism. All socialists advocated an end to capitalism and public ownership of factories, utilities, railroads, and communications systems, but they differed on how to achieve these goals. The revolutionary ideology of German social theorist Karl Marx won a few converts, but the vision of democratic socialism achieved at the ballot box proved more appealing. In 1900 democratic socialists formed the Socialist Party of America (SPA). Members included Morris Hillquit, a New York City labor organizer; Victor Berger, the leader of Milwaukee's German socialists; and **Eugene V. Debs,** the Indiana labor leader. Debs, a popular orator, was the SPA's presidential candidate five times between 1900 and 1920. Many Greenwich Village cultural rebels embraced socialism as well and supported the radical magazine *The Masses,* founded in 1911.

Socialism's high-water mark came around 1912 when SPA membership stood at 118,000. Debs won more than 900,000 votes for president that year (about 6 percent of the total), and the Socialists elected a congressman (Berger) and hundreds of municipal officials. The Intercollegiate Socialist Society carried the message to college campuses. The party published over three hundred daily and weekly newspapers, many in foreign languages for immigrant members.

NATIONAL PROGRESSIVISM, PHASE I: ROOSEVELT AND TAFT, 1901–1913

By around 1905, local and state reform activities were coalescing into a national movement. Symbolically, in 1906 Wisconsin governor Robert La Follette went to Washington as a U.S. senator. Five years earlier, progressivism had found its first national leader, **Theodore Roosevelt,** nicknamed "TR."

Self-righteous, jingoistic, and fond of speechmaking—but also brilliant, politically savvy, and endlessly interesting—Roosevelt became president in 1901 and at once made the White House a cauldron of activism. Skillfully orchestrating public opinion, the popular young president pursued his goals—labor mediation, consumer protection, conservation, business virtue, and engagement abroad (see Chapter 20)—while embracing and publicizing progressives' ideas and objectives.

Roosevelt's activist approach permanently enlarged the powers of the presidency. TR's handpicked successor, William Howard Taft, proved politically inept, however, and controversy marked his administration. With the Republican Party split, the Democrat Woodrow Wilson, holding a somewhat different vision of progressive reform, won the presidency in 1912.

Roosevelt's Path to the White House On September 6, 1901, in Buffalo, anarchist Leon Czolgosz shot William McKinley. At first recovery seemed likely, and Vice President Theodore Roosevelt proceeded with a hiking trip in New York's Adirondack Mountains. But on September 14, McKinley died. At age forty-two, Theodore Roosevelt became president.

Many politicians shuddered at the thought of the impetuous Roosevelt as president. Republican kingmaker Mark Hanna exclaimed, "My God, that damned cowboy in the White House!" Roosevelt did, indeed, display many traits associated with the West. The son of an aristocratic New York family of Dutch origins, he was sickly as a child. But a bodybuilding program and summers in Wyoming transformed him into a model of physical fitness. When his young wife died in 1884, he stoically carried on. Two years on a Dakota ranch (1884–1886) further toughened him and deepened his enthusiasm for what he termed "the strenuous life."

Although his social peers considered politics unfit for gentlemen, Roosevelt served as a state assemblyman, New York City police commissioner, and a U.S. civil-service commissioner. In 1898, fresh from his Cuban exploits (see Chapter 20), he was elected New York's governor. Two years later, the state's Republican boss, eager to be rid of him, arranged for Roosevelt's nomination as vice president.

As was the case with everything he did, TR found the presidency energizing. "I have been President emphatically . . . ," he boasted; "I believe in a strong executive." He enjoyed public life and loved the limelight. "When Theodore attends a wedding he wants to be the bride," his daughter observed, "and when he attends a funeral he wants to be the corpse." With his toothy grin, machine-gun speech, and amazing energy, he dominated the political landscape. When he refused to shoot a bear cub on a hunting trip, a shrewd toy maker marketed a cuddly new product, the Teddy Bear.

Labor Disputes, Trustbusting, Railroad Regulation The new president's political skills were quickly tested. In May 1902, the United Mine Workers Union (UMW) called a strike to gain not only higher wages and shorter hours but also recognition as a union. The mine owners dug in their heels, and in October, with winter looming, TR acted. Summoning the two sides to the White House and threatening to seize the mines, he forced them to accept an arbitration commission to settle the dispute. The commission granted the miners a 10 percent wage increase and reduced their working day from ten to nine hours.

TR's approach to labor disputes differed from that of his predecessors, who typically sided with management, sometimes using troops as strikebreakers. Though not consistently prolabor, he defended workers' right to organize. When a mine owner insisted that the miners' welfare should be left to those "to whom God in his infinite wisdom has given control of the property interests of the country," Roosevelt derided such "arrogant stupidity."

With his elite background, TR neither feared nor much liked business tycoons. The prospect of spending time with "big-money men," he once wrote a friend, "fills me with frank horror." While he believed that corporations contributed to national greatness, he also embraced the progressive conviction that they must be regulated. A strict moralist, he held corporations, like individuals, to a high standard.

Yet as a political realist, Roosevelt also understood that many Washington politicians abhorred his views—among them Senator Nelson Aldrich of Rhode Island, a wily defender of business interests. Roosevelt's progressive impulses thus remained in tension with his grasp of power realities in capitalist America.

Roosevelt's political skills faced another test in 1901 when J. P. Morgan formed the United States Steel Company, the nation's first billion-dollar business. As public distrust of big corporations deepened, TR dashed to the head of the parade. His 1902 State of the Union message gave high priority to breaking up business monopolies, or "trust-busting." Roosevelt's attorney general soon filed suit against the Northern Securities Company, a giant holding company recently created to control railroading in the Northwest, for violating the Sherman Anti-Trust Act of 1890. On a speaking tour that summer, TR called for a "square deal" for all Americans and denounced special treatment for capitalists. "We don't wish to destroy corporations," he said, "but we do wish to make them . . . serve the public good." In 1904, a divided Supreme Court ordered the Northern Securities Company dissolved.

The Roosevelt administration filed forty-three other antitrust lawsuits. In two key cases decided in 1911, the Supreme Court ordered the breakup of the Standard Oil Company and the reorganization of the American Tobacco Company to make it less monopolistic.

As the 1904 election neared, Roosevelt made peace with J. P. Morgan and other business magnates. When the GOP convention that nominated Roosevelt in Chicago adopted a probusiness platform, $2 million in corporate contributions poured in. The

Democrats, meanwhile, eager to erase the taint of radicalism, embraced the gold standard and nominated a conservative New York judge, Alton B. Parker.

Winning easily, Roosevelt turned to one of his major goals: railroad regulation. He now saw corporate regulation as a more promising strategy than trustbusting. This shift underlay his central role in the passage of the **Hepburn Act** of 1906. This law empowered the Interstate Commerce Commission to set maximum railroad rates and to examine railroads' financial records. It also curtailed the railroads' practice of distributing free passes to ministers and other shapers of public opinion.

The Hepburn Act displayed TR's political talent, as he bargained with Senator Aldrich and other conservatives. In a key compromise, he agreed to delay tariff reform in return for railroad regulation. Although the Hepburn Act did not fully satisfy reformers, it did expand the government's regulatory powers.

Consumer Protection

Of all progressive reforms, the campaign against unsafe food, drugs, and medicine proved especially popular. Upton Sinclair's *The Jungle* (1906) graphically described the foul conditions in some meatpacking plants. Wrote Sinclair in one vivid passage, "[A] man could run his hand over these piles of meat and sweep off handfuls of dried dung of rats. These rats were nuisances, and the packers would put poisoned bread out for them, they would die, and then rats, bread, and meat would go into the hoppers together." (The socialist Sinclair also detailed the exploitation of immigrant workers, but this message proved less potent. "I aimed at the nation's heart, but hit it in the stomach," he later lamented.) Women's organizations and consumer groups rallied public opinion on this issue, and an Agriculture Department chemist, Harvey W. Wiley, helped shape the proposed legislation. Other muckrakers exposed useless or dangerous patent medicines, many laced with cocaine, opium, or alcohol. One tonic "for treatment of the alcohol habit" contained 26.5 percent alcohol. Peddlers of these nostrums freely claimed that they could cure cancer, grow hair, and restore sexual vigor.

Sensing the public mood, Roosevelt supported the **Pure Food and Drug Act** and the Meat Inspection Act, both passed in 1906. The former outlawed the sale of adulterated foods or drugs and required accurate ingredient labels; the latter imposed strict sanitary rules on meatpackers and set up a federal meat-inspection system. The more reputable food-processing, meatpacking, and medicinal companies, eager to regain public confidence, supported these regulatory measures.

Environmentalism Progressive-Style

Environmental concerns loomed large for Theodore Roosevelt. Singling out conservation in his first State of the Union message as America's "most vital internal question," he highlighted an issue that still reverberates.

By 1900 decades of urban-industrial growth and western expansion had taken a heavy toll on the land. In the West, land-use disputes raged as mining and timber interests, farmers, ranchers, sheep growers, and preservationists advanced competing claims.

While business interests and boosters preached exploitation of the West's resources and agricultural groups sought government aid for irrigation projects, organizations such as John Muir's Sierra Club (founded in San Francisco in 1892) battled to preserve wilderness areas. Socially prominent easterners also embraced the wilderness cause. Under an act passed by Congress in 1891, Presidents Harrison and Cleveland had set aside some 35 million acres of public lands as national forests.

In the early twentieth century, amid spreading cities and factories, a wilderness vogue swept America. Popular writers evoked the tang of the campfire and the lure of the primitive. Summer camps, which began in the 1890s, as well as the Boy Scouts (founded in 1910) and Girl Scouts (1912), gave city children a taste of wilderness living.

Between the wilderness enthusiasts and the developers stood government experts like Gifford Pinchot who saw the public domain as a resource to be managed wisely. Appointed by President Roosevelt in 1905 to head the new U.S. Forest Service, Pinchot stressed not preservation but conservation—the planned use of forest lands for public and commercial purposes.

Wilderness advocates viewed Pinchot's Forest Service warily. They welcomed his opposition to mindless exploitation but worried that the multiple-use approach would despoil wilderness areas. As a Sierra Club member wrote, "[T]rees are for human use. But there are . . . uses for the spiritual wealth of us all, as well as for the material wealth of some."

At heart Roosevelt was a preservationist. In 1903, he spent a blissful few days camping in Yosemite National Park with John Muir. He once compared "the destruction of a species" to the loss of "all the works of some great writer." But TR the politician backed the conservationists' call for planned development. He supported the **National Reclamation Act** of 1902, which designated the money from public-land sales for water management in arid western regions, and set up the Reclamation Service to construct dams and irrigation projects.

This measure (also known as the Newlands Act for its sponsor, a Nevada congressman) ranks in importance with the Northwest Ordinance of 1787 for promoting the development of a vast continental region. Reclamation projects increased settlement and productivity between the Rockies and the Pacific. The Roosevelt Dam in Arizona spurred the growth of Phoenix, and a complex of dams and waterways in Idaho's Snake River valley watered thousands of barren acres, stimulating the production of potatoes and other commodities. The law required farmers who benefited from these projects to repay the construction costs, creating a federal fund for further projects. The Newlands Act and other measures of these years helped transform the West from a series of isolated "island settlements" into a thriving, interconnected region.

The competition for scarce water resources in the West sparked bitter political battles. The Los Angeles basin, for example, with 40 percent of California's population in 1900, found itself with only 2 percent of the state's surface water. In 1907, the city derailed a Reclamation Service project intended for the farmers of California's Owens Valley, more than 230 miles to the north, and diverted the precious water to Los Angeles.

Meanwhile, President Roosevelt, embracing Pinchot's multiple-use land-management program, set aside 200 million acres of public land (85 million of them in Alaska) as national forests, mineral reserves, and waterpower sites. But this, too, provoked opposition in the West, and in 1907 Congress revoked the president's authority to create national forests in six timber-rich western states. Before signing the bill, Roosevelt designated 16 million more acres in the six states as national forests. TR also created fifty-three wildlife reserves, sixteen national monuments, and five new national parks. Congress established the National Park Service in 1916 to manage them. The Antiquities Act (1906) protected archaeological sites, especially in the Southwest, some of which later became national parks.

In 1908, Gifford Pinchot organized a White House conservation conference for the nation's governors. There, experts discussed the utilitarian benefits of resource management. John Muir and other wilderness preservationists were not invited. But the struggle between wilderness purists and multiple-use advocates went on. Rallying support through magazine articles, preservationists won key victories. For example, campaigns by private groups, including women's organizations, saved a large grove of California's giant redwoods and a lovely stretch of the Maine coastline from logging.

The Sierra Club lost a major battle to save the Hetch Hetchy Valley in Yosemite National Park when Congress in 1913 approved a dam on the Tuolumne River to provide water and hydroelectric power for San Francisco, 150 miles away. (Other opponents of the dam were less interested in preserving Hetch Hetchy as a pristine wilderness than in developing it for tourism.) While the preservationists lost this battle, the controversy did focus attention on the national-parks movement and publicized the environmentalist cause, as Americans for the first time weighed the aesthetic implications of a major public-works project.

Taft in the White House, 1909–1913   Roosevelt had pledged not to run for a third term, and as the 1908 election approached, the Republican Party's most conservative leaders regained party control. They nominated TR's choice, Secretary of War **William Howard Taft,** for president but selected a conservative vice-presidential nominee and adopted a deeply conservative party platform. The Democrats, meanwhile, nominated William Jennings Bryan for a third time. The Democratic platform called for a lower tariff, denounced the trusts, and embraced the cause of labor.

With Roosevelt's endorsement, Taft coasted to victory. But Bryan bested Alton B. Parker's 1904 vote total by 1.3 million, and progressive Republican state candidates outran the national ticket. Overall, the outcome suggested a lull in the reform movement, not its end.

Republican conservatives welcomed Roosevelt's departure to hunt big game in Africa. Quipped Senator Aldrich, "Let every lion do its duty." But even an ocean away, TR's presence remained vivid. "When I am addressed as 'Mr. President,'" Taft wrote him, "I turn to see whether you are not at my elbow."

Taft, from an old political family in Cincinnati, differed from TR in almost every respect. Whereas TR kept in fighting trim, Taft was obese. Roosevelt had set up a boxing ring in the White House; Taft preferred golf. TR loved speechmaking and battling evildoers; Taft disliked controversy. His happiest days would come later, as chief justice of the United States.

Pledged to support TR's program, Taft backed the Mann-Elkins Act (1910), which beefed up the Interstate Commerce Commission's regulatory authority and extended it to telephone and telegraph companies. The Taft administration actually prosecuted more antitrust cases than had Roosevelt, but without much publicity. To the public, TR remained the mighty trustbuster.

The reform spotlight, meanwhile, shifted from the White House to Congress. During the Roosevelt administration, a small group of reform-minded Republicans, nicknamed the Insurgents, including Senators La Follette and Albert Beveridge of Indiana and Congressman George Norris of Nebraska, had challenged their party's conservative congressional leadership. In 1909, the Insurgents and President Taft fought a bruising battle over the tariff. Taft at first backed the Insurgents' call for a lower tariff. But when high-tariff advocates in Congress pushed through the Payne-Aldrich Tariff raising duties on hundreds of items, Taft infuriated the Insurgents by not only signing the bill but praising it extravagantly.

The Insurgents next set their sights on Speaker of the House Joseph G. Cannon of Illinois, a powerful and reactionary Republican who kept most reform bills from even reaching a vote. In March 1910, the Insurgents joined with the Democrats to trim Cannon's power by removing him from the pivotal Rules Committee. This was a direct slap at Taft, who supported Cannon.

The so-called Ballinger-Pinchot controversy widened the rift. Taft's interior secretary, Richard Ballinger, was a Seattle lawyer who favored unregulated private development of natural resources. In one of several decisions galling to conservationists, Ballinger in 1909 approved the sale of several million acres of public lands in Alaska containing coal deposits to a group of Seattle businessmen. They in turn sold the land to J. P. Morgan and other New York financiers. When a Department of the Interior official protested, he was fired. In true muckraking style, he went public, blasting Ballinger's actions in a *Collier's* magazine article. When Gifford Pinchot of the Forest Service publicly criticized Ballinger, he too got the ax. TR's supporters seethed.

Upon Roosevelt's return to America in June 1910, Pinchot met the boat. Openly breaking with Taft, Roosevelt campaigned for Insurgent candidates in that year's midterm elections. In a speech that alarmed conservatives, he attacked judges who struck down progressive laws and even endorsed the radical idea of reversing judicial rulings by popular vote. Borrowing a term from Herbert Croly's *The Promise of American Life,* TR proposed a "New Nationalism" that would powerfully engage the federal government in reform.

The Democrats captured the House in 1910, and a coalition of Democrats and Insurgent Republicans controlled the Senate. As the reform tide rose, TR sounded more and more like a presidential candidate.

The Four-Way Election of 1912   In February 1912 Roosevelt announced his candidacy for the Republican nomination. But Taft wanted a second term, and a Republican battle loomed. In a series of Republican state primaries and conventions, Roosevelt generally walloped Taft. But Taft controlled the party machinery, and the Republican convention in Chicago disqualified many of Roosevelt's hard-won delegates. Outraged, TR's backers left the convention and formed the **Progressive Party.** What had been a general term for a broad reform movement now became the official name of a political party. Riding an emotional high, the cheering delegates nominated their hero, with California senator Hiram Johnson as his running mate.

"I feel fit as a bull moose," Roosevelt trumpeted, thereby giving his organization its nickname, the Bull Moose Party. The convention platform endorsed nearly every reform cause of the day, including lower tariffs, woman suffrage, business regulation, the abolition of child labor, the eight-hour workday, workers' compensation, the direct primary, and the popular election of senators. The new party attracted a diverse following, united mainly by affection for Roosevelt.

Meanwhile, the reform spirit had also infused the Democratic Party at the local and state levels. In New Jersey in 1910, voters had elected a political novice, **Woodrow Wilson,** as governor. A "Wilson for President" boom soon arose, and when the Democrats assembled in Baltimore in June 1912, Wilson won the nomination, defeating several established party leaders.

MAP 21.2 The Election of 1912

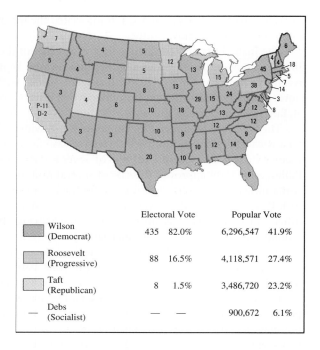

	Electoral Vote		Popular Vote	
Wilson (Democrat)	435	82.0%	6,296,547	41.9%
Roosevelt (Progressive)	88	16.5%	4,118,571	27.4%
Taft (Republican)	8	1.5%	3,486,720	23.2%
Debs (Socialist)	—	—	900,672	6.1%

In the campaign, Taft more or less gave up, happy to have kept his party safe for conservatism. The Socialist Party candidate Eugene Debs proposed an end to capitalism and a socialized economic order. TR preached his New Nationalism. The corporate order was here to stay, he conceded, but big business must be regulated in the public interest, the welfare of workers and consumers safeguarded, and the environment protected.

Woodrow Wilson and William Howard Taft *Having just squared off in the 1912 election campaign, the two politicians share a light moment before Wilson's inauguration on March 4, 1913.*

Wilson, by contrast, called his political vision the "New Freedom." Warning that big corporations were choking off opportunity for ordinary Americans, he nostalgically evoked an era of small government, small businesses, and free competition. "The history of liberty," he said, "is the history of the limitation of governmental power, not the increase of it."

Roosevelt outpolled Taft by 630,000 votes, but the Republican Party's split cost it dearly. Wilson easily won the presidency, and the Democrats took both houses of Congress. More than 900,000 voters opted for Debs and socialism.

The 1912 election linked the Democrats firmly with reform (except on the issue of race)—a link that Franklin D. Roosevelt would strengthen in the 1930s. TR's third-party campaign demonstrated the appeal of reform among grass-roots Republicans while leaving the national party itself in the grip of conservatives.

National Progressivism, Phase II: Woodrow Wilson, 1913–1917

The son and grandson of Presbyterian ministers, Wilson grew up in southern towns in a churchly atmosphere that shaped his oratorical style and moral outlook. Although slow in school (probably because of the learning disorder dyslexia), Wilson graduated from Princeton and earned a Ph.D. in political science from Johns Hopkins University. He taught at Princeton and became its president in 1902. He lost support because of an unwillingness to compromise, and in 1910 left the academic world to enter politics. Three years later he was president of the United States.

Impressive in bearing, with piercing gray eyes, Wilson was an eloquent orator. But the idealism that inspired people could also alienate them. At his best, he excelled at political dealmaking. "He can walk on dead leaves and make no more noise than a tiger," declared one awed politician. But he could also retreat into a fortress of absolute certitude that tolerated no opposition. During his years as president, all these facets of his personality would come into play.

In his first term, Wilson exerted a key leadership role as Congress enacted an array of reform measures. Despite the nostalgia for simpler times he had evoked in the campaign, he proved ready to use government to address the problems of the new corporate order. Under Wilson, the progressive movement gained fresh momentum.

Tariff and Banking Reform   Lowering tariff rates—long a goal of southern and agrarian Democrats—headed Wilson's agenda. Many progressives agreed that high protective tariffs increased corporate profits at the public's expense. Breaking a precedent dating from Thomas Jefferson's presidency, Wilson appeared personally before Congress on April 8, 1913, to read his tariff message. A low-tariff bill quickly passed the House but bogged down in the Senate. Showing his flair for drama, Wilson denounced the tariff lobbyists flooding into Washington. His censure led to a Senate investigation of lobbyists and of senators who profited from high tariffs. Stung by the publicity, the Senate slashed tariff rates even more than the House had done. The Underwood-Simmons Tariff reduced rates an average of 15 percent.

In June 1913 Wilson again addressed Congress, this time to call for banking and currency reform. The nation's banking system clearly needed overhauling. Totally decentralized, it lacked a strong central institution, a "lender of last resort" to help banks survive fiscal crises. The Panic of 1907, when many banks had failed, remained a vivid memory.

No consensus existed on specifics, however. Many reformers wanted a publicly controlled central banking system. But the nation's bankers, whose Senate spokesman was Nelson Aldrich, favored a privately controlled central bank similar to the Bank of England. The large banks of New York City advocated a strong central bank, preferably privately owned, so they could better compete with London banks in international finance. Others, including influential Virginia congressman Carter Glass, opposed any central banking authority, public or private.

No banking expert, Wilson did insist that the monetary system ultimately be publicly controlled. As the bargaining went on, Wilson played a crucial behind-the-scenes role. The result was the **Federal Reserve Act** of December 1913. This compromise measure created twelve regional Federal Reserve banks under mixed public/private control. Each regional bank could issue U.S. dollars, called Federal Reserve notes, to the banks in its district to make loans to corporations and individual borrowers. Overall control of the system was assigned to the heads of the twelve regional banks and a Washington-based Federal Reserve Board, whose members were appointed by the president for fourteen-year terms. (The secretary of the treasury and the comptroller of the currency were made ex officio members.)

The Federal Reserve Act stands as Wilson's greatest legislative achievement. Initially, the Federal Reserve's authority was diffuse, but eventually "the Fed" grew into the strong central monetary institution it remains today, setting interest rates and adopting fiscal policies to prevent financial panics, promote economic growth, and dampen inflationary pressures.

Regulating Business; Aiding Workers and Farmers

In 1914 Wilson and Congress turned to that perennial progressive cause, business regulation. Two key laws resulted: the Federal Trade Commission Act and the Clayton Antitrust Act. Though both sought a common goal, they embodied different approaches.

The first took an administrative approach. This law created a new "watchdog" agency, the **Federal Trade Commission** (FTC), with power to investigate violations of federal regulations, require regular reports from corporations, and issue cease-and-desist orders (subject to judicial review) when it found unfair methods of competition.

The Clayton Antitrust Act, by contrast, took a legal approach. It listed corporate activities that could lead to federal lawsuits. The Sherman Act of 1890, although outlawing business practices in restraint of trade, had been vague about details. The Clayton Act spelled out specific illegal practices, such as selling at a loss to undercut competitors.

Because some of Wilson's appointees to the FTC were conservatives with big-business links, this agency initially proved ineffective. But under the Clayton Act, the Wilson administration filed antitrust suits against nearly a hundred corporations.

Leading a party long identified with workers, Wilson supported the American Federation of Labor and defended workers' right to organize. He also endorsed a Clayton Act clause exempting strikes, boycotts, and picketing from the antitrust laws' prohibition of actions in restraint of trade.

In 1916 (an election year) Wilson and congressional Democrats enacted three important worker-protection laws. The Keating-Owen Act barred from interstate commerce products manufactured by child labor. (This law was declared unconstitutional in 1918, as was a similar law enacted in 1919.) The Adamson Act established an eight-hour day for interstate railway workers. The Workmen's Compensation Act provided accident and injury protection to federal workers. As we have seen, however, Wilson's sympathies for the underdog stopped at the color line.

Other 1916 laws helped farmers. The Federal Farm Loan Act and the Federal Warehouse Act enabled farmers, using land or crops as security, to get low-interest federal loans. The Federal Highway Act, providing matching funds for state highway programs, benefited not only the new automobile industry but also farmers plagued by bad roads.

Progressivism and the Constitution
The probusiness bias of the courts softened a bit in the Progressive Era. Evidence of the changing judicial climate came in *Muller* v. *Oregon* (1908), in which the Supreme Court upheld an Oregon ten-hour law for women laundry workers. Defending the constitutionality of the Oregon law, Boston attorney **Louis Brandeis** offered economic, medical, and sociological evidence documenting how long hours harmed women workers. Rejecting a legal claim long made by business, the high court held that such worker-protection laws did not violate employers' rights under the due-process clause of the Fourteenth Amendment. *Muller* v. *Oregon* marked a breakthrough in making the legal system more responsive to new social realities.

In 1916, Woodrow Wilson nominated Brandeis to the Supreme Court. Disapproving of Brandeis's innovative approach to the law, the conservative American Bar Association protested, as did the *New York Times,* the president of Harvard, and Republican leaders in Congress. Anti-Semites opposed Brandeis because he was a Jew. But Wilson stood by his nominee, and after a fierce battle, the Senate confirmed him.

These years also produced four amendments to the Constitution, the first since 1870. The Sixteenth (ratified in 1913) granted Congress the authority to tax income, thus ending a long legal battle. A Civil War income tax had been phased out in 1872. Congress had authorized an income tax in an 1894 tariff act, but in 1895 the Supreme Court had declared this "communistic" measure unconstitutional. This ruling had spurred the campaign for a constitutional amendment. Exercising its new authority, Congress in 1913 imposed a graduated federal income tax with a maximum rate of 7 percent on incomes over five hundred thousand dollars. Income-tax revenues helped the government pay for the expanded regulatory activities assigned to it by various progressive reform measures.

The Seventeenth Amendment (1913) mandated the direct election of U.S. senators by the voters, rather than their selection by state legislatures as provided by Article I of the Constitution. This reform, earlier advocated by the Populists, sought to make the Senate less subject to corporate influence and more responsive to the popular will.

The Eighteenth Amendment (1919) prohibited the manufacture, sale, or importation of "intoxicating liquors." The Nineteenth (1920) granted women the vote. This remarkable wave of amendments underscored how profoundly the progressive impulse had transformed the political landscape.

1916: Wilson Edges Out Hughes
Wilson easily won renomination in 1916. The Republicans turned to Charles Evans Hughes, a Supreme Court justice and former New York governor. The Progressive Party again courted Theodore Roosevelt, but TR was now obsessed with drawing the United States into the war that had broken out in Europe in 1914 (see Chapter 22). At his urging, the Progressive Party endorsed Hughes and effectively committed political suicide.

With the Republicans now more or less reunited, the election was extremely close. War-related issues loomed large. Wilson won the popular vote, but the Electoral College outcome remained in doubt for several weeks as the California tally seesawed back and forth. Ultimately, Wilson carried the state by fewer than four thousand votes and, with it, the election.

The progressive movement lost momentum as attention turned from reform to war. Final success for the prohibition and woman-suffrage campaigns came later, in 1919–1920, and Congress enacted a few reform measures in the 1920s. But, overall, the movement's zest and drive clearly waned as America went to war in 1917.

CONCLUSION

What we call the progressive movement began as preachers, novelists, journalists, photographers, and painters highlighted appalling conditions in America's cities and factories. Intellectuals offered ideas for reform through the creative use of government.

At the local and state level, reformers like Mayor Hazen Pingree of Detroit and Wisconsin governor Robert M. La Follette, together with a host of reform organizations, worked to combat political corruption, make cities safer and more beautiful, regulate corporations, and improve conditions for workers.

Progressivism had its coercive side. Some reformers concentrated on regulating urban amusements and banning alcohol consumption. Racism and hostility to immigrants comprise a part of the progressive legacy as well.

With the presidencies of Theodore Roosevelt and Woodrow Wilson, progressivism crested as a national movement. Although TR, Wilson, and other national progressive leaders differed in their political ideas, these years saw advances in corporate regulation, environmental conservation, banking reform, and consumer and worker protection. Constitutional amendments granted Congress the power to tax incomes and provided for the direct election of senators, woman suffrage, and national prohibition of alcohol—all aspects of the progressive impulse.

Progressivism's legacy included not only specific laws but also an enlarged view of government's social and economic role. Progressives expanded the meaning of democracy and challenged the cynical view of government as nothing but a tool of the rich and powerful. They did not seek "big government" for its own sake. Rather, they recognized that in an industrial age of great cities and concentrated corporate power, government, too, must grow to serve the public interest and protect society's more vulnerable members.

Unquestionably, this ideal sometimes faltered in practice. Reform laws and regulatory agencies often fell short of their purpose as bureaucratic routine set in. Reforms designed to promote the public good sometimes mainly benefited special interests. Corporations proved adept at manipulating the new regulatory state to their own advantage.

Still, the Progressive Era stands as a time when American politics seriously confronted the social upheavals caused by industrialization. It was also a time when Americans learned to think of government as an arena of possibility where public issues and social problems could be thrashed out. The next great reform movement, the New Deal of the 1930s, would draw on progressivism's legacy.

22

Global Involvements and World War I, 1902–1920

DEFINING AMERICA'S WORLD ROLE, 1902–1914

As we saw in Chapter 20, the annexation of Hawaii, the Spanish-American War, the occupation of the Philippines, and other developments in the 1890s signaled America's growing involvement abroad, especially in Asia and Latin America. These foreign engagements reflected a desire to assert American power in an age of imperial expansion by European nations, to protect and extend U.S. business investments abroad, and to impose American standards of good government beyond the nation's borders. This process of foreign engagement continued under Presidents Theodore Roosevelt, William Howard Taft, and Woodrow Wilson.

America's dealings with Asian and Latin American nations in these years were shaped by both economic and ideological considerations. Certainly U.S. policy makers wanted to expand corporate America's access to foreign markets and raw materials. But they also believed that other societies would benefit by adopting the principles of democracy, individual freedom, and the rule of law. Sometimes the economic motive predominated, sometimes the ideological. Often, both motivations were in play as the United States exerted its power beyond its borders.

The "Open Door": Competing for the China Market
As the campaign to suppress the Philippines insurrection dragged on (see Chapter 20), American policy makers turned their attention farther west, to China. Their aim was not territorial but commercial. Proclaimed Indiana senator Albert J.

Beveridge in 1898, "American factories are making more than the American people can use; American soil is producing more than they can consume. . . . [T]he trade of the world must and shall be ours."

The China market beckoned. Textile producers dreamed of clothing China's millions; investors envisioned railroad construction. As China's 250-year-old Manchu Ch'ing empire grew weaker, U.S. businesspeople watched carefully. In 1896 a consortium of New York capitalists formed a company to promote trade and railroad investment in China.

But other nations were also eyeing the China market. Some pressured the weak Manchu rulers to designate certain regions as "spheres of influence" where they would enjoy exclusive trading and development rights. In 1896, Russia won both the right to build a railway across the Chinese province of Manchuria and a long-term lease on much of the region. In 1897, Germany forcibly secured a ninety-nine-year lease on a Chinese port as well as mining and railroad rights in the adjacent province. The British won concessions as well.

In 1899, U.S. Secretary of State John Hay asked the major European powers to assure American trading rights in China by opening the ports in their spheres of influence to all countries. The nations gave noncommittal answers, but Hay blithely announced that they had accepted the principle of an "Open Door" to American business in China.

Hay's Open Door note showed how commercial considerations were increasingly influencing American foreign policy. It reflected a form of economic expansionism that has been called "informal empire." The U.S. government did not seek Chinese territory, but it did want access to Chinese markets for American businesses.

As Hay pursued this effort, a more urgent threat emerged. For years, antiforeign feeling had simmered in China, fanned by the aged Ch'ing empress, who hated the West's growing influence. In 1899, a fanatical antiforeign secret society known as the Harmonious Righteous Fists (called "Boxers" by Western journalists) killed thousands of foreigners and Chinese Christians. In June 1900, the Boxers occupied Beijing (Peking), the Chinese capital, and besieged the foreign legations. The United States contributed twenty-five hundred soldiers to an international army that marched on Beijing, quashed the **Boxer Rebellion,** and rescued the occupants of the threatened legations.

The Boxers' defeat further weakened China's government. Fearing that the regime's collapse would allow European powers to carve up China, Hay issued a second, more important, series of **Open Door notes** in 1900. He reaffirmed the principle of open trade in China for all nations and announced America's determination to preserve China's territorial and administrative integrity. In general, China remained open to U.S. business interests and Christian missionaries. In the 1930s, when Japanese expansionism menaced China, Hay's policy helped shape the American response.

Along with U.S. economic expansion in China came missionary activity. American Protestant missionaries had come to Hawaii as early as the 1820s, and by the late nineteenth century they had reached China as well. Indeed, by 1900 some five thousand U.S. missionaries were active in China, Africa, India, and elsewhere. As they preached their religious message, the missionaries also spread American influence globally and blazed the way for U.S. economic expansion. As a U.S. diplomat in China wrote in 1895: "Missionaries are the pioneers for American trade and commerce. . . . The missionary, inspired by holy zeal, goes everywhere, and by degrees foreign trade and commerce follow."

CHRONOLOGY, 1902–1920

1899 • First U.S. Open Door note seeking access to China market.
Boxer Rebellion erupts in China.

1900 • Second U.S. Open Door note.

1904 • President Theodore Roosevelt proclaims "Roosevelt Corollary" to Monroe Doctrine.

1905 • Roosevelt mediates the end of the Russo-Japanese War.

1906 • At the request of Roosevelt, San Francisco ends segregation of Asian schoolchildren.
Panama Canal construction begins.

1911 • U.S.-backed revolution in Nicaragua.

1912 • U.S. Marines occupy Nicaragua.

1914 • U.S. troops occupy Veracruz, Mexico.
Panama Canal opens.
World War I begins.
President Wilson proclaims American neutrality.

1915 • U.S. Marines occupy Haiti and the Dominican Republic.
Woman's Peace Party organized.
British liner *Lusitania* sunk by German U-boat.
Wilson permits U.S. bank loans to Allies.

1916 • U.S. punitive expedition invades Mexico, seeking Pancho Villa.
Germany pledges not to attack merchant ships without warning.
Wilson reelected.

1917 • U.S. troops withdraw from Mexico.
Germany resumes unrestricted U-boat warfare; United States declares war.
Selective Service Act sets up national draft.
War Industries Board, Committee on Public Information, and Food Administration created.
Espionage Act passed.
War Risk Insurance Act authorizes payments to servicemen's dependents.
NAACP march in New York City protests upsurge in lynchings.
Bolsheviks seize power in Russia; Russia leaves the war.
New York State passes woman-suffrage referendum.
U.S. government operates the nation's railroads.
Striking miners forcibly expelled from Bisbee, Arizona.

1918 • Wilson outlines Fourteen Points.
Sedition Amendment passed.
Global influenza pandemic takes heavy toll in United States.
National War Labor Board created.

American forces see action at Château-Thierry,
Belleau Wood, St. Mihiel, and Meuse-Argonne campaign.
Republicans win control of both houses of Congress (November 5).
Armistice signed (November 11).

1919 • Eighteenth Amendment added to the Constitution (prohibition).
Peace treaty, including League of Nations covenant, signed at Versailles.
Supreme Court upholds silencing of war critics in *Schenck* v. *United States.*
Upsurge of lynchings; racial violence in Chicago.
Wilson suffers paralyzing stroke.
Versailles treaty, with League covenant, rejected by Senate.

1920 • "Red raids" organized by Justice Department.
Nineteenth Amendment added to the Constitution (woman suffrage).
Warren G. Harding elected president.

The Panama Canal: Hardball Diplomacy Traders had long dreamed of a canal across the forty-mile-wide ribbon of land joining North and South America to eliminate the hazardous voyage around South America. In 1879 a French company secured permission from Colombia to build a canal across Panama, then part of Colombia. But mismanagement and yellow fever doomed the project, and ten years and $400 million later, it went bankrupt. Seeking to recoup its losses, the French company offered its assets, including the concession from Colombia, to the United States for $109 million.

America was in an expansionist mood. In 1902, after the French lowered their price to $40 million, Congress authorized President Theodore Roosevelt to accept the offer. The following year, Secretary of State Hay signed an agreement with a Colombian diplomat granting the United States a ninety-nine-year lease on the proposed canal for a down payment of $10 million and an annual fee of $250,000. But the Colombian senate, seeking a better deal, rejected the agreement. An outraged Roosevelt privately denounced the Colombians as "greedy little anthropoids."

Determined to have his canal, Roosevelt found a willing collaborator in Philippe Bunau-Varilla, an official of the bankrupt French company. Dismayed that his company might lose its $40 million, Bunau-Varilla organized a "revolution" in Panama from a New York hotel room. While his wife stitched a flag, he wrote a declaration of independence and a constitution for the new nation. When the "revolution" occurred as scheduled on November 3, 1903, a U.S. warship hovered offshore. Proclaiming Panama's independence, Bunau-Varilla appointed himself its first ambassador to the United States. John Hay quickly recognized the newly hatched nation and signed a treaty with Bunau-Varilla granting the United States a ten-mile-wide strip of land across Panama "in perpetuity" (that is, forever) on the terms earlier rejected by Colombia. Theodore Roosevelt later summed up the episode: "I took the Canal Zone, and let Congress debate, and while the debate goes on, the canal does also."

The U.S. canal builders' first challenge was the yellow fever that had haunted the French. Leading this effort was Dr. Walter Reed of the Army Medical Corps. Earlier, in a research project in Cuba, Reed and his team had used themselves and army volunteers as experimental subjects to prove that female mosquitoes that bred in stagnant water spread the yellow fever virus. In Panama, Reed organized a large-scale drainage project that eradicated the disease-bearing mosquito—a remarkable public-health achievement. Construction began in 1906, and in 1914 the first ship sailed through the **Panama Canal.** In 1921, implicitly conceding the dubious methods used to acquire the Canal Zone, the U.S. Senate voted a payment of $25 million to Colombia. But the ill feeling generated by Theodore Roosevelt's actions, combined with other instances of U.S. interventionism, would long shadow U.S.–Latin American relations.

Roosevelt and Taft Assert U.S. Power in Latin America and Asia

While the Panama Canal remains this era's best-known foreign-policy achievement, other U.S. actions underscored Washington's growing determination to assert U.S. power and protect U.S. business interests in Latin America and Asia. Two crises early in Theodore Roosevelt's presidency followed European intervention in Latin America. In 1902, German, British, and Italian warships blockaded and bombarded the ports of Venezuela, which had defaulted on its debts to European investors. The standoff ended when all sides agreed to Roosevelt's proposal of arbitration.

The second crisis flared in 1904 when several European nations threatened to invade the Dominican Republic, a Caribbean island nation that had also defaulted on its debts. Roosevelt reacted swiftly. If any nation intervened, he believed, it should be the United States. While denying any territorial ambitions in Latin America, Roosevelt in December 1904 declared that "chronic wrongdoing" by any Latin American nation would justify U.S. intervention.

This pronouncement has been called "the Roosevelt Corollary" to the 1823 Monroe Doctrine, which had warned European powers against meddling in Latin America. Now Roosevelt asserted that in cases of "wrongdoing" (a word he left undefined), the United States had the right to intervene. Suiting actions to words, the Roosevelt administration took over the Dominican Republic's customs service for two years and managed its foreign debt. Roosevelt summed up his foreign-policy approach in a 1901 speech quoting what he said was an old African proverb, "Speak softly and carry a big stick."

The foreign policy of the Taft administration (1909–1913) focused on advancing American commercial interests, a policy some called "dollar diplomacy." A U.S.-backed revolution in Nicaragua in 1911 brought to power Adolfo Díaz, an officer of an American-owned mine. Washington feared growing British influence in Nicaragua's affairs, and also worried that a foreign power might build a canal across Nicaragua to rival the Panama Canal. In exchange for control of Nicaragua's national bank, customs service, and railroad, American bankers lent Díaz's government $1.5 million. When a revolt against Díaz broke out in 1912, Taft sent in the marines to protect the bankers' investment. Except for one brief interval, they remained until 1933.

In Asia, too, both Roosevelt and Taft sought to project U.S. power and advance American business interests. In 1900, exploiting the turmoil caused by the Boxer uprising, Russian troops occupied Manchuria, and Russia promoted its commercial interests by building railroads. This alarmed the Japanese, who also had designs on

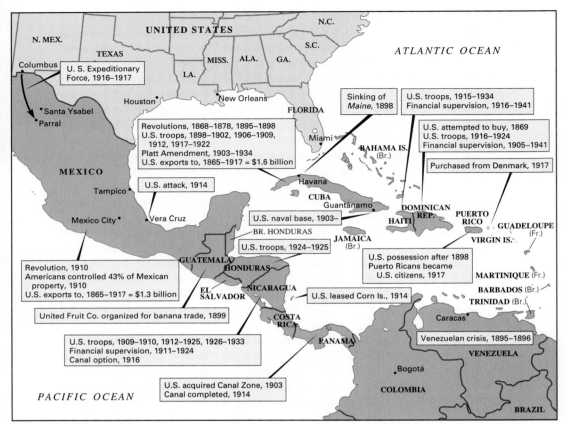

MAP 22.1 U.S. Hegemony in the Caribbean and Latin America, 1900–1941

Through many interventions, territorial acquisitions, and robust economic expansion, the United States became the predominant power in Latin America in the early twentieth century. Acting on Theodore Roosevelt's assertion of a U.S. right to combat "wrongdoing" in Latin America and the Caribbean, the United States dispatched troops to the region, where they met nationalist opposition.

Manchuria and nearby Korea. In February 1904 a surprise Japanese attack destroyed Russian ships anchored at Port Arthur, Manchuria. Japan completely dominated in the Russo-Japanese War that followed. For the first time, an Asian power had checked European imperialist expansion.

Roosevelt, while pleased to see Russian expansionism challenged, believed that a Japanese victory would disrupt the Asian balance of power and threaten America's position in the Philippines. Accordingly, he invited Japan and Russia to a peace conference at Portsmouth, New Hampshire. In September 1905 the two rivals signed a peace treaty. Russia recognized Japan's rule in Korea and made other territorial concessions. After this outcome, curbing Japanese expansionism—peacefully, if possible—became America's major objective in Asia. For his role in ending the war, Roosevelt received the Nobel Peace Prize.

In 1906, U.S.-Japanese relations soured when the San Francisco school board, reflecting West Coast hostility to Asian immigrants, assigned all Asian children to segregated schools. Japan angrily protested this insult. Summoning the school board to Washington, Roosevelt persuaded them to reverse this discriminatory policy. In return, in 1908 the administration negotiated a "gentlemen's agreement" with Japan by which Tokyo pledged to halt Japanese emigration to America. Racist attitudes continued to poison U.S.-Japanese relations, however. In 1913, California prohibited Japanese aliens from owning land.

While Californians warned of the "yellow peril," Japanese journalists, eyeing America's military strength and involvement in Asia, spoke of a "white peril." In 1907 Roosevelt ordered sixteen gleaming U.S. battleships on a "training operation" to Japan. Although officially treated as friendly, this "Great White Fleet" underscored America's growing naval might.

Under President Taft, U.S. foreign policy in Asia continued to focus on dollar diplomacy, which in this case meant promoting U.S. commercial interests in China—the same goal Secretary of State John Hay had sought with his Open Door notes. A plan for a U.S.-financed railroad in Manchuria did not work out, however. Not only did U.S. bankers find the project too risky, but Russia and Japan signed a treaty carving up Manchuria for commercial purposes, freezing out the Americans.

Wilson and Latin America

Taking office in 1913 as the first Democratic president in sixteen years, Woodrow Wilson criticized his Republican predecessors' expansionist policies. The United States, he pledged, would "never again seek one additional foot of territory by conquest." But he, too, soon intervened in Latin America. In 1915, after upheavals in Haiti and the Dominican Republic (two nations sharing the Caribbean island of Santo Domingo), Wilson sent in U.S. marines, who brutally suppressed Haitian resistance to U.S. rule. A Haitian constitution favorable to U.S. commercial interests was overwhelmingly ratified in a 1918 vote supervised by the marines. The marines occupied the Dominican Republic until 1924 and Haiti until 1934.

The most serious crisis Wilson faced in Latin America was the Mexican Revolution. Mexico had won independence from Spain in 1820, but the nation remained divided between a landowning elite and an impoverished peasantry. In 1911, rebels led by the democratic reformer Francisco Madero had ended the thirty-year rule of President Porfirio Díaz, who had defended the interests of the wealthy elite. Early in 1913, just as Wilson took office, Mexican troops loyal to General Victoriano Huerta, a full-blooded Indian, overthrew and murdered Madero.

Amid the chaos, Wilson tried to promote good government, protect U.S. investments, and safeguard U.S. citizens living in Mexico or along its border. Forty thousand Americans had settled in Mexico under Díaz's regime, and U.S. investors had poured some $2 billion into Mexican oil wells and other ventures. Reversing the long-standing U.S. policy of recognizing all governments, Wilson refused to recognize Huerta's regime, which he called "a government of butchers." Authorizing arms sales to General Venustiano Carranza, Huerta's rival, Wilson also ordered the port of Veracruz blockaded to prevent a shipment of German arms from reaching Huerta. Announced Wilson, "I am going to teach the South American republics to elect good men." In April 1914 seven thousand U.S. troops occupied Veracruz and engaged Huerta's forces.

Woodrow Wilson, Schoolteacher *This 1914 political cartoon captures the patronizing tone of Wilson's approach to Latin America, which planted the seeds of long-term resentments.*

Sixty-five Americans and approximately five hundred Mexicans were killed or wounded. Bowing to U.S. might, Huerta abdicated; Carranza took power; and the U.S. troops withdrew.

But the turmoil continued. In January 1916, a bandit chieftain in northern Mexico, Pancho Villa, murdered sixteen U.S. mining engineers. Soon after, Villa's gang burned the town of Columbus, New Mexico, and killed nineteen inhabitants. Enraged Americans demanded action. Wilson dispatched a punitive expedition under General **John J. Pershing.** When Pancho Villa not only eluded Pershing but brazenly staged another cross-border raid into Texas, Wilson ordered 150,000 National Guardsmen to the Mexican border—a massive response that stirred anti-American feelings among Mexico's poor, for whom Villa was a folk hero. (Villa ended his raids in 1920 in exchange for a large grant of land from the Mexican government, but he was assassinated in 1923.)

Although soon overshadowed by World War I, these involvements in Asia and Latin America illuminate the U.S. foreign-policy goal, which was, essentially, to achieve a global order that would welcome both American political values and American business. President Wilson summed up this view in a 1916 speech to the "World's Salesmanship Congress" meeting in Detroit: "[C]arry liberty and justice and the principles of humanity wherever you go. . . . [G]o out and sell goods that will make the world more comfortable and more happy, and convert them to the principles of America." Wilson's vision of an American-based world order shaped his response to a crisis unfolding in Europe.

These early-twentieth-century foreign involvements also illustrate the underlying world view of the old-stock, upper-class men who directed U.S. foreign policy. Convinced of their ethnic, gender, and social superiority, they confidently promoted America's global economic and political interests while viewing with patronizing condescension the "backward" societies they sought to manipulate.

WAR IN EUROPE, 1914–1917

When war engulfed Europe in 1914, most Americans wished only to remain aloof. For nearly three years, the United States officially stayed neutral. But by April 1917 cultural ties to England and France, economic considerations, visions of a world remade in America's image, and German violations of Wilson's definition of neutral rights all combined to draw the United States into the maelstrom.

The Coming of War With Europe at peace through much of the nineteenth century, some concluded that war was a thing of the past. However, a series of ominous developments, including a complex web of alliances, suggested otherwise. Germany, Austria-Hungary, and Italy signed a mutual-defense treaty in 1882, forming the Triple Alliance. In 1904 and 1907, Great Britain signed treaties with France and Russia, creating what came to be called the Triple Entente.

Beyond the treaties, imperial ambitions and nationalistic passions stirred. The once-powerful Ottoman Empire, centered in Turkey, weakened in the 1870s, leaving in its wake such newly independent nations as Romania, Bulgaria, and Serbia.

Serbian patriots dreamed of expanding their boundaries to include Serbs living in Bosnia-Herzegovina, Serbia's neighbor to the west. Russia, home to millions of Slavs, the same ethnic group as the Serbs, supported these ambitions. Meanwhile, the Austro-Hungarian Empire, with its capital in Vienna, also saw opportunities for expansion as Ottoman power faded. In 1908, Austria-Hungary annexed (took over) Bosnia-Herzegovina, alarming Russia and Serbia.

Germany, ruled by Kaiser Wilhelm II, also displayed expansionist impulses. Germany had achieved national unification only in 1871, and many Germans believed that their nation had lagged in the race for empire. Expansion, modernization, and military power became the goal in Berlin.

Such was the context when Archduke Franz Ferdinand of Austria made a state visit to Bosnia in June 1914. As he and his wife rode in an open car through Sarajevo, the Bosnian capital, a young Bosnian Serb gunned them down. In response, Austria declared war on Serbia. Russia, aligned with Serbia by a secret treaty, mobilized for war. Germany declared war on Russia and France. Great Britain, linked by treaty to France, declared war on Germany. An assassin's bullets had plunged Europe into war.

Thus began what contemporaries called the Great War, which we know as World War I. On one side were Great Britain, Russia, and France, called the Allies. On the other side were the Central Powers: Germany and Austria-Hungary. Italy, initially neutral despite its alliance with the Central Powers, joined the Allies in 1915.

The Perils of Neutrality Proclaiming U.S. neutrality, President Wilson urged the nation to be neutral "in thought as well as in action." Most Americans fervently agreed. A popular song summed up the mood: "I Didn't Raise My Boy to Be a Soldier." Fifteen hundred women marched down New York's Fifth Avenue protesting the war. Carrie Chapman Catt and other feminists joined Jane Addams in forming the Woman's Peace Party.

Neutrality proved difficult, however. Wilson privately dreaded a victory by militaristic Germany. Strong economic interests bound the United States and Britain. Many Americans, including Wilson himself, had ancestral ties to England. Well-to-do Americans routinely traveled to England. Schoolbooks stressed the English origins of American institutions. The English language itself—the language of Shakespeare, Dickens, and the King James Bible—deepened the bond. British propaganda subtly stressed the British-American link.

Many German-Americans, by contrast, sympathized with Germany's cause. Irish-Americans speculated that a German victory might free Ireland from British rule. Some Scandinavian immigrants identified more with Germany than with England. But these cultural and ethnic cross-currents did not at first override Wilson's commitment to neutrality. For most Americans, staying out of the conflict became the chief goal.

Neutral in 1914, America went to war in 1917. What caused this turnabout? Fundamentally, Wilson's vision of a world order in America's image conflicted with his neutrality. An international system based on democracy and capitalism would be impossible, he believed, in a world dominated by imperial Germany. Even an Allied victory would not ensure a transformed world order, Wilson gradually became convinced, without a U.S. role in the postwar settlement. To shape the peace, America would have to fight the war.

These underlying ideas influenced Wilson's handling of the immediate issue that dragged the United States into the conflict: neutral nations' rights on the high seas. When the war began, Britain intercepted U.S. merchant ships bound for Germany, insisting that their cargo might aid Germany's war effort. Wilson's protests intensified in late 1914 and early 1915 when Britain declared the North Sea a war zone; planted it with explosive mines; and blockaded all German ports, choking off Germany's imports, including food. Britain was determined to exploit its naval advantage, even if it meant alienating America.

But Germany, not England, ultimately pushed the United States into war. If Britannia ruled the waves, Germany controlled the ocean depths with its torpedo-equipped submarines, or U-boats. In February 1915 Berlin proclaimed the waters around Great Britain a war zone and warned off all ships. Wilson quickly responded: Germany would be held to "strict accountability" for any loss of U.S. ships or lives.

On May 1, 1915, in a small ad in U.S. newspapers, the German embassy cautioned Americans against travel on British or French vessels. Six days later, a U-boat sank the British liner *Lusitania* off the Irish coast, with the loss of 1,198 lives, including 128 Americans. (The *Lusitania*, historians later discovered, had carried munitions destined for England, a secret traffic in weapons known to British officials.)

In three stern notes to Germany, Wilson demanded that Berlin stop unrestricted submarine warfare and pay reparations for the U.S. deaths in the *Lusitania* sinking. Addressing the American public, however, he insisted that the United States could persuade the belligerents to recognize the principle of neutral rights without going to war. "There is such a thing as a man being too proud to fight," he said.

The *Lusitania* disaster exposed deep divisions in U.S. public opinion. Many Americans, now ready for war, ridiculed Wilson's "too proud to fight" speech. Theodore

Roosevelt denounced the president's "abject cowardice." The National Security League, a lobby of bankers and industrialists, promoted a U.S. arms buildup and universal military training and organized "preparedness" parades in major cities. By late 1915 Wilson himself called for a military buildup.

Other citizens, however, deplored the drift toward war. Some progressives warned that war fever was eroding support for reforms. Jane Addams lamented that the international movements to reduce infant mortality and improve care for the aged had been "scattered to the winds by the war." Late in 1915, automaker Henry Ford chartered a vessel to take a group of pacifists to Scandinavia to persuade the belligerents to accept neutral mediation and end the war by Christmas.

Divisions surfaced even within the Wilson administration. Secretary of State William Jennings Bryan, believing that Wilson's *Lusitania* notes were too hostile, resigned in June 1915. His successor, Robert Lansing, proved weak, and Wilson himself played the key role in shaping U.S. policy.

Some neutrality advocates concluded that incidents like the *Lusitania* crisis were inevitable if Americans persisted in sailing on belligerent ships. Early in 1916, Congress considered a bill to ban such travel, but President Wilson successfully opposed it, insisting that the principle of neutral rights must be upheld.

For a time, Wilson's approach seemed to work. Germany ordered U-boats to spare passenger ships, and offered compensation for the Americans lost in the *Lusitania* sinking. In March 1916, however, a German submarine sank a French passenger ship, the *Sussex*, in the English Channel, injuring several Americans. Wilson threatened to break diplomatic relations—a step toward war. In response, Berlin pledged not to attack merchant vessels without warning, provided that Great Britain, too, observed "the rules of international law." Ignoring this qualification, Wilson announced Germany's acceptance of American demands and the crisis eased.

Meanwhile, U.S. banks' support for the Allies eroded the principle of neutrality. Early in the war, Secretary of State Bryan had rejected banker J. P. Morgan's request to extend loans to France. Such loans, said Bryan, would violate "the true spirit of neutrality." But economic considerations, combined with outrage over the *Lusitania* sinking, undermined this policy. In August 1915, Treasury Secretary William G. McAdoo warned Wilson that Allied purchases of American munitions and farm products were essential "[t]o maintain our prosperity." Only substantial loans to England, agreed Secretary of State Lansing, could prevent serious financial problems in the United States, including "unrest . . . among the laboring classes." The neutrality principle must not "stand in the way of our national interests," warned Lansing.

Swayed by such arguments and personally sympathetic to the Allies, Wilson permitted Morgan's bank to lend $500 million to the British and French governments. By April 1917, U.S. banks had lent $2.3 billion to the Allies, in contrast to $27 million to Germany.

While Americans concentrated on neutral rights, the land war settled into a grim stalemate. A September 1914 German drive into France bogged down along the Marne River. The two sides then dug in, constructing trenches across France from the English Channel to the Swiss border. For more than three years, this line scarcely changed. Occasional offensives took a terrible toll. A German attack in February 1916 began with the capture of two forts near the town of Verdun and ended that June with the French recapture of the same two forts, now nothing but rubble, at a horrendous cost in human life. Trench warfare was a nightmare of mud, lice, rats, artillery bursts, poison gas, and random death.

British propaganda focused on the atrocities committed by "the Huns" (a derogatory term for Germans). After the war, much of this propaganda was exposed as false. Seized documents revealing German espionage in U.S. war plants, however, further discredited the German cause.

The war dominated the 1916 presidential election. Wilson faced Republican Charles Evans Hughes, a former New York governor (and future chief justice of the U.S. Supreme Court). The Democrats' campaign theme emerged when a convention speaker, praising Wilson's foreign policy, aroused wild applause as he ended each episode with the refrain "We didn't go to war."

Hughes criticized Wilson's lack of aggressiveness while rebuking him for policies that risked war. Theodore Roosevelt, still much admired, campaigned more for war than for the Republican ticket. The only difference between Wilson and the bearded Hughes, he jeered, was a shave. While Hughes did well among Irish-Americans and German-Americans who considered Wilson too pro-British, Wilson held the Democratic base and won support from women voters in western states that had adopted woman suffrage. Wilson's victory, although close, revealed the strength of the popular longing for peace as late as November 1916.

The United States Enters the War   In January 1917, facing stalemate on the ground, Germany resumed unrestricted submarine warfare. Germany's military leaders believed that even if the United States declared war as a result, full-scale U-boat warfare could bring victory before American troops reached the front.

Events now rushed forward. Wilson broke diplomatic relations on February 3. During February and March, U-boats sank five American ships. A coded telegram from the German foreign secretary, Arthur Zimmermann, to Germany's ambassador to Mexico promised that if Mexico would declare war on the United States, Germany would help restore Mexico's "lost territories" of Texas, Arizona, and New Mexico. Intercepted and decoded by the British, the "Zimmermann telegram" further inflamed the war spirit in America.

Events in distant Russia also helped create favorable conditions for America's entry into the war. In March 1917 Russian peasants, industrial workers, intellectuals inspired by Western liberal values, and revolutionaries who embraced the communist ideology of Karl Marx all joined in an uprising that overthrew the repressive government of Tsar Nicholas II. A provisional government under the liberal Alexander Kerensky briefly seemed to promise a democratic Russia, making it easier for President Wilson to portray the war as a battle for democracy. Many Americans, little understanding conditions in Russia, shared Wilson's hope that a liberal democratic state on the American model would eventually emerge.

On April 2, Wilson appeared before a joint session of Congress and called for a declaration of war. Applause rang out as Wilson described his vision of America's role in creating a postwar international order to make the world "safe for democracy." As the speech ended, Republican senator Henry Cabot Lodge of Massachusetts, one of Wilson's staunchest political foes, rushed forward to shake his hand.

After a short but bitter debate, the Senate voted 82 to 6 for war. The House agreed, 373 to 50. Three key factors—German attacks on American shipping, U.S. economic investment in the Allied cause, and American cultural links to the Allies, especially England—had propelled the United States into the war.

MOBILIZING AT HOME, FIGHTING IN FRANCE, 1917–1918

America's entry into World War I underscored a deepening international involvement that had been underway for several decades. Yet compared to its effects on Europe, the war only grazed the United States. Russia, ill-prepared for war and geographically isolated from its allies, suffered heavily. France, Great Britain, and Germany fought for more than four years; the United States, for nineteen months. Their armies suffered casualties of 70 percent or more; the U.S. casualty rate was 8 percent. The fighting left parts of France and Belgium brutally scarred; North America was physically untouched. Nevertheless, the war profoundly affected America. It changed not only those who participated in it directly, but also the home front and the nation's government and economy.

Raising, Training, and Testing an Army

April 1917 found America's military woefully unprepared. The regular army consisted of 120,000 men, few with combat experience, plus 80,000 National Guard members. An aging officer corps dozed away the years until retirement. Ammunition reserves were paltry. The War Department was a jungle of jealous bureaucrats, one of whom hoarded thousands of typewriters as the war approached.

While army chief-of-staff Peyton C. March brought order to the military bureaucracy, Wilson's secretary of war, Newton D. Baker, concentrated on raising an army. Formerly the reform mayor of Cleveland, Baker lacked administrative talent but was a public-relations genius. The **Selective Service Act** of May 1917 required all men between twenty-one and thirty (later expanded to eighteen through forty-five) to register with local draft boards. Mindful of the Civil War draft riots, Baker planned the draft-registration day, June 5, 1917, as a "festive and patriotic occasion."

By the war's end in November 1918, more than 24 million men had registered, of whom nearly 3 million were drafted. Volunteers and National Guardsmen swelled the total to 4.3 million. Recruits got their first taste of army life in home-front training camps. Along with military discipline and combat instruction, the camps built morale through shows, games, and recreation provided by volunteer organizations. The American Library Association contributed books. YMCA volunteers staffed base clubs and offered classes in literacy, French slang, and Bible study. In Plattsburgh, New York, local women opened a "Hostess House" to provide a touch of domesticity for homesick recruits. The idea soon spread to other communities near military camps.

The War Department monitored the off-duty behavior of young men cut off from family and community. The **Commission on Training Camp Activities** presented films, lectures, and posters on the dangers of alcohol and prostitution. Any soldier disabled by venereal (that is, sexually transmitted) disease, one poster warned, "is a Traitor!" Trainees were confined to camp until nearby towns closed brothels and saloons. The army's antiliquor, antiprostitution policies strengthened the moral-reform campaigns of the Progressive Era (see Chapter 21).

Beginning in December 1917, all recruits also underwent intelligence testing. Psychologists eager to demonstrate the usefulness of their new field claimed that tests measuring recruits' "intelligence quotient" (IQ) could help in assigning their duties and showing who had officer potential. Intelligence testing, declared the president of the American Psychological Association, would "help win the war."

When the psychologists announced that a high percentage of recruits were "morons," editorial writers reacted with alarm. In fact, the tests mostly revealed that many recruits lacked formal education and cultural sophistication. One question asked whether *mauve* was a drink, a color, a fabric, or a food. Another asked in which city a particular make of automobile was built. The testing also reinforced racial and ethnic stereotypes: native-born recruits of northern European origins scored highest; African-Americans and recent immigrants lowest.

In short, the World War I training camps not only turned civilians into soldiers, but also reinforced the prewar moral-control reforms, and signaled changes ahead, including a vogue for standardized testing.

Some twelve thousand Native Americans served in the **American Expeditionary Force** (AEF). While some reformers eager to preserve Indian culture argued for all-Indian units, military officials integrated Native Americans into the general army. Some observers predicted that the wartime experience would hasten the assimilation of Indians into mainstream American life, considered by many a desirable goal at the time.

In April 1917 the African-American leader W. E. B. Du Bois urged African-Americans to "close ranks" and support the war. Some blacks resisted the draft, especially in the South (see "Wartime Intolerance and Dissent"), but most followed Du Bois's advice. More than 260,000 blacks volunteered or were drafted, and 50,000 went to France. Racism pervaded the military, as it did American society. The navy assigned blacks only to menial positions, and the marines excluded them altogether.

Blacks in training camps endured crude racial abuse. One racist senator from Mississippi warned that the sight of "arrogant, strutting" black soldiers would trigger race riots. Tensions exploded in Houston in August 1917 when some black soldiers, endlessly goaded by local whites, seized weapons from the armory and killed seventeen white civilians. After a hasty trial with no appeal process, thirteen black soldiers were hanged and forty-one imprisoned for life. Not since the 1906 Brownsville Incident (see Chapter 21) had black confidence in military justice been so shaken.

Organizing the
Economy for War

The war years of 1917–1918 helped shape modern America. The war's administrative innovations sped up longer-term processes of social reorganization. The war furthered many key developments of the 1920s and beyond—including the spread of mass production; the collaboration between government, business, and labor; and the growth of new professional and managerial elites.

The war led to unprecedented government oversight of the economy and the regulation of corporations, something Populists and progressives had long urged. In 1916, Congress had created an advisory body, the Council of National Defense, to oversee the government's preparedness program. After war was declared, this council set up the **War Industries Board** (WIB) to coordinate military purchasing; ensure production efficiency; and provide weapons, equipment, and supplies to the military. Wilson reorganized the WIB in March 1918 and put Bernard Baruch in charge. A South Carolinian of German-Jewish origin, Baruch had made a fortune on Wall Street. Under Baruch, the WIB controlled the industrial sector. It allocated raw materials, established production priorities, and induced competing companies to standardize and coordinate their products and processes to save scarce commodities. The standardization of bicycle manufacturing, for example, saved tons of steel.

Acting under legislation passed in August 1917, Wilson set up two more new agencies, the Fuel Administration and the Food Administration. The Fuel Administration controlled coal output, regulated fuel prices and consumption, and introduced daylight-saving time—an idea first proposed by Benjamin Franklin. The Food Administration, headed by Herbert Hoover, oversaw the production and allocation of wheat, meat, and sugar to ensure supplies for the army as well as for the desperately food-short Allies. Born in poverty in Iowa, Hoover had prospered as a mining engineer in Asia. He was organizing food relief in Belgium when Wilson brought him back to Washington.

These regulatory agencies relied on voluntary cooperation reinforced by government propaganda. Food Administration posters and magazine ads urged Americans to conserve food. Housewives signed pledges to observe "Meatless Monday" and "Wheatless Wednesday." Slogans such as "Serve Beans by All Means" promoted substitutes for scarce commodities.

Harriot Stanton Blatch, daughter of woman's-rights pioneer Elizabeth Cady Stanton, headed the Food Administration's Speakers' Bureau, which spread the administration's conservation message. Blatch also organized the Woman's Land Army, which recruited women to replace male farm workers.

These agencies were the tip of the regulatory iceberg. Nearly five thousand government boards supervised home-front activities. These included the National War Labor Board, which resolved labor-management disputes that jeopardized production, and the Railroad Administration, headed by Treasury Secretary William McAdoo. When a railroad tie-up during the winter of 1917–1918 threatened the flow of supplies to Europe, the Railroad Administration stepped in and soon transformed the thousands of miles of track operated by competing companies into an efficient national rail system.

American business, much criticized by progressive reformers, utilized the war emergency to improve its image. Corporate executives ran regulatory agencies. Factory owners distributed prowar propaganda to workers. Trade associations coordinated war production.

The war sped up the ongoing process of corporate consolidation and economic integration. In place of trustbusting, the government now encouraged cooperation among businesses. As corporate mergers jumped sharply, one magazine observed, "The war has accelerated . . . a tendency that was already irresistible. . . . Instead of punishing companies for acting in concert, the government is now in some cases forcing them to unite."

Overall, the war was good for business. Despite added taxes imposed by Congress, profits soared. After-tax profits in the copper industry, for example, jumped from 12 percent in 1913 to 24 percent in 1917.

The old laissez-faire suspicion of government, already weakened, eroded further in 1917–1918. The wartime regulatory agencies disappeared quickly after the war, but their influence lingered. In the 1930s, when the nation faced a different crisis, the government activism of World War I would be remembered (see Chapter 24).

With the American Expeditionary Force in France When the United States entered the conflict, Allied prospects looked bleak. German U-boat attacks were taking a horrendous toll on Allied shipping. French troops mutinied after a failed French assault on the Marne. A British offensive along the French-Belgian border in November 1917 gained four miles at a cost of more than four hundred thousand killed and wounded. That same month, the Italian army suffered a disastrous defeat at Caporetto near the Austrian border.

Russia, ill-prepared for war, had suffered serious setbacks, contributing to the revolutionary upheaval. The communist faction of the revolution, the Bolsheviks (Russian for "majority"), gained strength when its top leaders, including Vladimir Lenin and Leon Trotsky, returned from exile abroad. On November 6, 1917 (October 24 by the Russian calendar), a Bolshevik coup overthrew Alexander Kerensky's provisional government and effectively removed Russia from the war. Early in 1918, the Bolsheviks signed an armistice with Germany, the Treaty of Brest-Litovsk, freeing thousands of German troops on the Russian front for fighting in France.

An important advance in military technology came in November 1917 when the British mobilized three hundred tanks along a six-mile section of the front near Cambrai, France, shattering the German defenses. Still the stalemate continued, punctuated by periodic battles.

Initially, U.S. aid to the Allies consisted of munitions and convoys to protect Allied ships crossing the dangerous Atlantic. The first U.S. troops reached France in October 1917. Eventually about 2 million American soldiers served in France as members of the AEF under General John J. Pershing. Ironically, Pershing was of German origin; his family name had been Pfoersching. A West Point graduate and commander of the 1916 expedition against Pancho Villa in Mexico, Pershing was an iron-willed officer with a ramrod bearing, steely eyes, and trim mustache. The death of his wife and three of their children in a fire in 1915 had further hardened him.

Most men of the AEF at first found the war a great adventure. Plucked from towns and farms, they sailed for Europe on crowded freighters; a lucky few traveled on captured German passenger liners. Once in France, railroad freight cars marked "HOMMES 40, CHEVAUX 8" (forty men, eight horses) took them to the front. Then began the routine of marching, training—and waiting.

The African-Americans with the AEF in France worked mainly as mess-boys (mealtime aides), laborers, and stevedores (ship-cargo handlers). Although discriminatory, the latter assignments vitally aided the war effort. Sometimes working twenty-four hours nonstop, black stevedores efficiently unloaded supply ships. Some whites of the AEF pressed the French to treat African-Americans as inferiors, but most ignored this advice and related to blacks without prejudice. This eye-opening experience would remain with black veterans after the war. Except for two segregated divisions, African-Americans did not engage in combat. Only in death was the AEF integrated: graves in military cemeteries were not segregated by race.

For the troops at the front, aerial dogfights between German and Allied reconnaissance planes offered spectacular sideshows. Germany's legendary "Red Baron," Manfred von Richthofen, shot down eighty British and French planes before his luck ran out in April 1918. In 1916, a group of American volunteers had joined the French air corps as the Lafayette Escadrille. Secretary of War Baker, grasping the importance of air power, pushed for plane construction. The program lagged, however—a rare U.S. war-production failure.

France offered other diversions as well, and the U.S. military warned recruits of the danger of venereal disease. One poster declared, "A German bullet is cleaner than a whore." When the French premier, Georges Clemenceau, offered to provide prostitutes for the American troops (as was the French practice), Secretary of War Baker exclaimed, "For God's sake, don't show this to the President, or he'll stop the war."

The YMCA, Red Cross, and Salvation Army, including many young American women volunteers, provided a touch of home. Some 16,500 U.S. women served directly in the AEF as nurses, telephone operators, canteen workers, and secretaries.

To underscore America's distinctive role in the war and to ensure a strong U.S. voice at the peace table, President Wilson insisted that the United States be called an "Associate Power" of the Allies. The Allied generals, facing desperate circumstances, wanted to absorb the Americans into existing units. But for both military and political reasons, Pershing and his superiors in Washington insisted that the AEF be "distinct and separate." Pershing, favoring aggressive combat, abhorred the defensive mentality ingrained by three years of trench warfare.

In March 1918, however, when Germany launched a major offensive along the Somme, the Allies created a unified command under Marshal Ferdinand Foch, chief of the French general staff. Some Americans participated in the fighting around Amiens and Armentières that stemmed the German advance.

The Germans' spring 1918 offensive resumed in May along the Aisne River, where they broke through to the Marne and faced a nearly open route to Paris, fifty miles away. On June 4, as the French government prepared for evacuation, American forces arrived in strength. Parts of three U.S. divisions and a marine brigade helped stop the Germans at the town of Château-Thierry and nearby Belleau Wood. (An AEF division at full strength consisted of twenty-seven thousand men and one thousand officers, plus twelve thousand support troops.)

These two German offensives had punched deep holes (or salients) in the Allied line. A German drive aimed at the cathedral city of Rheims between these two salients was stopped with the help of some eighty-five thousand American troops. This was the war's turning point. At enormous cost, the German offensive had been defeated. Contributing to this defeat was the fact that many German soldiers, already weakened by battle fatigue and poor diet, fell victim to influenza, an infectious disease that would soon emerge as a deadly worldwide epidemic (see "Public-Health Crisis: The 1918 Influenza Pandemic").

Turning the Tide   The final Allied offensive began on July 18, 1918. Some 270,000 U.S. soldiers joined the Allied drive to push the Germans back from the Marne. Rain pelted down as the Americans moved into position. One wrote in his diary, "Trucks, artillery, infantry columns, cavalry, wagons, caissons, mud, MUD, utter confusion." Another 100,000 AEF troops joined a parallel British offensive to expel the Germans from the area north of the Somme.

Pershing's first fully independent command came in September, when Foch authorized an AEF campaign to close a German salient around the town of St. Mihiel on the Meuse River, 150 miles east of Paris. Eager to test his offensive strategy, Pershing assembled nearly five hundred thousand American and one hundred thousand French soldiers. Shelling of German positions began at 1:00 A.M. on September 11. Recorded an American in his diary, "[I]n one instant the entire front . . . was a sheet of flame, while the heavy artillery made the earth quake." Within four days, the salient was

MAP 22.2 The United States on the Western Front, 1918
American troops first saw action in the campaign to throw back Germany's spring 1918 offensive in the Somme and Aisne-Marne sectors. The next heavy American engagement came that autumn as part of the Allies' Meuse-Argonne offensive, which ended the war.

closed. Although some German units had already withdrawn, St. Mihiel still cost seven thousand U.S. casualties.

The war's last battle began on September 26 as some 1.2 million Americans joined the struggle to drive the Germans from the Meuse River and the Argonne Forest north of Verdun. The stench of poison gas (first used by the Germans in 1915) hung in the air, and rats scurried in the mud, gorging on human remains. Americans now endured the filth, vermin, and dysentery familiar to veterans of the trenches. Frontline troops would never forget the terror of combat. As shells streaked overhead at night, one recalled, "We simply lay and trembled from sheer nervous tension." Some welcomed injuries as a ticket out of the battle zone. Others collapsed emotionally and were hospitalized for "shell shock."

The all-black Ninety-second Division saw combat in the Meuse-Argonne campaign. (The Germans showered them with leaflets describing U.S. racism and urging them to defect, but none did.) Four black infantry regiments served under French command. One entire regiment received the French Croix de Guerre, and several hundred black soldiers won French decorations for bravery.

**African-Americans
at the Front**
*Black troops of the
369th Infantry Regi-
ment in the trenches
near Maffrecourt,
France, in 1918.
Most African-
American soldiers
were assigned to
noncombat duty,
such as unloading
supplies and
equipment.*

The AEF was assigned to cut the Sedan-Mezières Railroad, a major German supply route. In the way lay three long, heavily fortified German trenches, called Stellungen. "We are not men anymore, just savage beasts," wrote a young American. Death came in many forms, and without ceremony. Bodies, packs, rifles, photos of loved ones, and letters from home sank indiscriminately into the all-consuming mud. Influenza killed thousands of AEF troops at the front and in training camps back home. One day as General Pershing rode in his staff car, he buried his head in his hands and moaned his dead wife's name: "Frankie, Frankie, my God, sometimes I don't know how I can go on."

Religious and ethical principles faded as men struggled to survive. "Love of thy neighbor is forgotten," recalled one, with "all the falsities of a sheltered civilization." The war's brutality would shape the literature of the 1920s as writers such as Ernest Hemingway stripped away the illusions obscuring the reality of mass slaughter.

But the AEF at last overran the dreaded German trenches, and the survivors slogged northward. In early November the Sedan-Mezières Railroad was cut. The AEF had fulfilled its assignment, at a cost of 26,277 dead.

PROMOTING THE WAR AND SUPPRESSING DISSENT

In their own way, the war's domestic effects were as important as its battles. Spurred by government propaganda, patriotic fervor gripped America. The war fever, in turn, encouraged intellectual conformity and intolerance of dissent. Fueling the repressive spirit, government authorities and private vigilante groups hounded socialists, pacifists, and other dissidents, trampling citizens' constitutional rights.

Advertising the War To President Wilson, selling the war at home was crucial to success in France. "It is not an army we must shape and train for war, it is a nation," he declared. The administration drew on the new professions of advertising and public relations to pursue this goal. Treasury Secretary McAdoo orchestrated a series of government bond drives, called Liberty Loans, that financed about two-thirds of the $35.5 billion (including loans to the Allies) that the war cost the United States.

Posters exhorted citizens to "Fight or Buy Bonds." Liberty Loan parades featured flags, banners, and marching bands. Charlie Chaplin, Mary Pickford, and other movie stars promoted the cause. Schoolchildren purchased "thrift stamps" convertible into war bonds. Patriotic war songs reached a large public through phonograph recordings. Beneath the ballyhoo ran a note of coercion. Only "a friend of Germany," McAdoo warned, would refuse to buy bonds.

The balance of the government's war costs came from taxes. Using the power granted it by the Sixteenth Amendment, Congress imposed wartime income taxes that reached 70 percent at the top levels. War-profits taxes, excise taxes on liquor and luxuries, and increased estate taxes also helped finance the war.

Journalist George Creel headed the key wartime propaganda agency, the **Committee on Public Information** (CPI). While claiming merely to combat rumors with facts, the Creel committee in reality publicized the government's version of events and discredited all who questioned that version. One CPI division distributed posters drawn by leading illustrators. Another wrote propaganda releases that appeared in the press as "news" with no indication of their source. Popular magazines published CPI ads warning of spies, saboteurs, and anyone who "spreads pessimistic stories" or "cries for peace." Theaters screened CPI films bearing such titles as *The Kaiser: The Beast of Berlin.*

The CPI poured foreign-language pamphlets into immigrant neighborhoods and supplied prowar editorials to the foreign-language press. At a CPI media event at Mount Vernon on July 4, 1918, an Irish-born tenor sang "The Battle Hymn of the Republic" while immigrants from thirty-three nations filed reverently past George Washington's tomb. CPI posters in factories attacked the socialists' charge that this was a capitalists' war. Samuel Gompers of the American Federation of Labor headed a prowar "Alliance for Labor and Democracy" funded by the CPI. Seventy-five thousand CPI volunteers, called "Four-Minute Men," gave prowar pep talks to movie audiences and other gatherings. Teachers, writers, editors, and religious leaders overwhelmingly supported the war. These custodians of culture saw the conflict as a struggle to defend threatened values. Historians wrote essays contrasting German brutality with the Allies' lofty ideals. In *The Marne* (1918), expatriate American writer Edith Wharton expressed her love for France. The war poems of Alan Seeger, who volunteered to fight for France and died in action in 1916, enjoyed great popularity. Seeger portrayed the conflict as a noble crusade. An artillery barrage was for him "the magnificent orchestra of war."

Progressive reformers who had applauded Wilson's domestic program now cheered his war. Herbert Croly, Walter Lippmann, and other intellectuals associated with the *New Republic* magazine zealously backed the war. In gratitude, administration officials regularly briefed the editors on the government's policies.

The educator John Dewey endorsed the war and condemned its opponents in a series of *New Republic* essays. Socially engaged intellectuals must accept reality and shape it toward positive social goals, he wrote, not stand aside in self-righteous isolation. The war, he went on, presented exciting "social possibilities." The government's wartime activism could be channeled to reform purposes when peace returned, Dewey argued. Internationally, America's participation in the war would transform an imperialistic struggle into a global democratic crusade.

Wartime Intolerance and Dissent Responding to the propaganda, some Americans became almost hysterical in their strident patriotism and their hostility to radicals and dissenters. Isolated sabotage by German sympathizers, including an attack on a New Jersey munitions dump, fanned the flames. Persons suspected of pro-German sympathies were forced to kiss the flag or recite the Pledge of Allegiance. An Ohio woman accused of disloyalty was wrapped in a flag, marched to a bank, and compelled to buy a war bond. In Collinsville, Illinois, a mob lynched a German-American coal miner, Robert Prager, in April 1918. When a jury freed the mob leaders, a jury member shouted, "Nobody can say we aren't loyal now." The *Washington Post* condemned the lynching but saw it as evidence of "a healthful and wholesome awakening in the interior of the country."

Only when the German press made propaganda use of Prager's murder did President Wilson condemn it. "[N]o man who loves America . . . can justify mob action while the courts of justice are open," he declared in July 1918. But strident calls for patriotic "vigilance" against radicals and war critics created the climate that led to such actions. In a June 1917 speech urging home-front vigilance, Wilson declared ominously: "Woe be to the man or group of men that seeks to stand in our way." An Albany, New York, newspaper, advising direct action against war opponents, added: "You do not require any official authority to do this. . . . [T]he only badge you need is your patriotic fervor."

An Iowa politician charged that "90 percent of all the men and women who teach the German language are traitors." German books vanished from libraries, towns with German names changed them, and on some restaurant menus "liberty sandwich" and "liberty cabbage" replaced "hamburger" and "sauerkraut." The Boston Symphony Orchestra dismissed its German-born conductor for accepting a medal from Kaiser Wilhelm. The Philadelphia Orchestra banned all German music except for Bach, Beethoven, Mozart, and Brahms. A popular evangelist, Billy Sunday, proclaimed, "If you turn hell upside down you will find 'Made in Germany' stamped on the bottom." The zealots also targeted war critics and radicals. A Cincinnati mob horsewhipped a pacifist minister. Theodore Roosevelt branded antiwar Senator Robert La Follette "an unhung traitor." Columbia University fired two antiwar professors. The International Workers of the World faced fierce criticism for its opposition to the war. In Bisbee, Arizona, in July 1917, two thousand well-organized armed vigilantes calling themselves the Citizens Protective League forced twelve hundred striking copper miners, some of whom belonged to the IWW, onto a freight train that dumped them in the New Mexico desert without food, water, or shelter. Declared Theodore Roosevelt: "[N]o human being in his senses doubts that the men deported from Bisbee were bent on destruction and murder."

Despite the persecution, many Americans persisted in opposing the war. Some were immigrants with ancestral ties to Germany. Others were religious pacifists, including Quakers, Mennonites, and Jehovah's Witnesses. Congresswoman Jeannette Rankin of Montana, a pacifist and the first woman elected to Congress, voted against the declaration of war. "I want to stand by my country," she declared, "but I cannot vote for war."

Of some sixty-five thousand men who registered as conscientious objectors (COs), twenty-one thousand were drafted. Assigned to noncombat duty on military bases, such as cleaning latrines, these COs often experienced harsh treatment. Those who rejected this alternative were sent to military prisons. Woodrow Wilson heaped scorn on the pacifists. "[M]y heart is with them, but my mind has contempt for them," he declared in November 1917; "I want peace, but I know how to get it, and they do not."

Socialist leaders such as Eugene Debs and Victor Berger denounced the war as a capitalist struggle for markets, with the soldiers as cannon fodder. The U.S. declaration of war, they insisted, mainly reflected Wall Street's desire to protect its loans to England and France. But other socialists supported the war, dividing the party.

The war split the women's movement as well. While some leaders joined Jane Addams in opposition, others endorsed the war while keeping their own goals in view. In *Mobilizing Woman-Power* (1918), Harriot Stanton Blatch argued that women who wished to help shape the peace must support the war. Anna Howard Shaw, a former president of the National American Woman Suffrage Association (NAWSA), chaired the Woman's Committee of the Council of National Defense, a largely symbolic post.

Carrie Chapman Catt, Shaw's successor as president of NAWSA, had helped start the Woman's Peace Party in 1915. But she supported U.S. entry into the war in 1917, sharing to some extent Wilson's vision of a more liberal postwar world order. Catt continued to focus mainly on woman suffrage, however, insisting that this was NAWSA's "number one war job." For this, some superpatriots accused her of disloyalty.

Draft resistance extended beyond the ranks of conscientious objectors. An estimated 2.4 to 3.6 million young men failed to register, and of those who did, about 12 percent either did not appear when drafted or deserted from training camp. The rural South saw high levels of draft resistance. The urban elites who ran the draft boards were more inclined to defer young men of their own class than poor farmers, white or black, fueling class resentment. In June 1918, a truck carrying U.S. soldiers pursuing draft evaders in rural Georgia crashed when a bridge collapsed, killing three soldiers and injuring others. Investigators found that the bridge supports had been deliberately sabotaged.

Blacks had added reasons to oppose the draft. Of southern blacks who registered, one-third were drafted, in contrast to only one-quarter of whites. White draft boards justified this by arguing that low-income black families could more easily spare a male breadwinner. As an Alabama board observed: "[I]t is . . . common knowledge that it requires more for a white man and his wife to live than it does a negro man and his wife, due to their respective stations in life." But the dynamics of race worked in complex ways: some southern whites, fearful of arming black men even for military service, favored drafting only whites.

The war's most incisive critic was Randolph Bourne, a young journalist. Although Bourne admired John Dewey, he rejected Dewey's prowar argument in several penetrating essays. He dismissed Dewey's contention that reformers could direct the war to their own purposes. "If the war is too strong for you to prevent," he asked, "how is it going to be weak enough for you to . . . mould to your liberal purposes?"

Eventually, many prowar intellectuals came to agree. By 1919, Dewey conceded that the war, far from promoting reform, had encouraged reaction and intolerance. Bourne did not live to see his vindication, however. He died of influenza in 1918, at the age of thirty-two.

Suppressing Dissent by Law Wartime intolerance also surfaced in federal laws and official actions. The **Espionage Act** of June 1917 set fines and prison sentences for a variety of loosely defined antiwar activities. The **Sedition Amendment** (May 1918) imposed stiff penalties on anyone convicted of using "disloyal, profane . . . or abusive language" about the government, the Constitution, the flag, or the military.

Wilson's attorney general, Thomas W. Gregory, used these laws to stamp out dissent. Opponents of the war, proclaimed Gregory, should expect no mercy "from an outraged people and an avenging government." Under the federal legislation and similar state laws, some fifteen hundred pacifists, socialists, IWW leaders, and other war critics were arrested. One socialist, Rose Pastor Stokes, received a ten-year prison sentence (later commuted) for telling an audience, "I am for the people, and the government is for the profiteers." Kate Richards O'Hare, a midwestern socialist organizer, spent over a year in jail for declaring, "The women of the United States are nothing more than brood sows, to raise children to get into the army and be made into fertilizer." Eugene Debs was imprisoned for three years (1918–1921) for a speech discussing the economic causes of the war.

Under the Espionage Act, Postmaster General Albert S. Burleson, a reactionary superpatriot, suppressed socialist periodicals, including *The Masses,* published by radicals in New York City's Greenwich Village. Burleson "didn't know socialism from rheumatism," according to socialist Norman Thomas, but he pursued his repressive crusade. In January 1919 Congressman-elect Victor Berger was convicted under the Espionage Act for publishing antiwar articles in his socialist newspaper, the *Milwaukee Leader.* (The Supreme Court reversed Berger's conviction in 1921.) Upton Sinclair protested to President Wilson that no one of Burleson's "childish ignorance" should wield such power; but Wilson did little to restrain Burleson's excesses.

A patriotic group called the American Protective League and local "Councils of Defense" claiming vague governmental authority further enforced ideological conformity. Local and state volunteer organizations like the Connecticut Home Guard assisted the vigilance effort. A group called "Boy Spies of America" recruited young patriots. The 1917 Bolshevik takeover in Russia sharpened the attacks on domestic radicals. As communists, the Bolsheviks believed in a one-party state and anticipated the violent overthrow of the capitalist system. Some Americans feared that the United States could fall to communism as well.

In three 1919 decisions, the U.S. Supreme Court upheld the Espionage Act convictions of war critics. In *Schenck* v. *United States,* Justice Oliver Wendell Holmes, Jr., writing for a unanimous court, justified such repression in cases where a person's exercise of the First Amendment right of free speech posed a "clear and present danger" to the nation. When the war ended, Wilson vetoed a bill ending the Espionage Act, and it remained in force.

The early wartime mood of idealism had degenerated into persecution of all who failed to meet the zealots' notions of "100 percent Americanism." This climate of conformity and suspicion would linger long after the war's end.

ECONOMIC AND SOCIAL TRENDS IN WARTIME AMERICA

While the war affected the lives of millions of Americans—including industrial workers, farmers, women, and blacks—another of the war's byproducts, a deadly influenza pandemic, took a grievous toll. Some Progressive Era reforms advanced in 1917–1918, but overall the war and its aftermath weakened the reform movement.

Boom Times in Industry and Agriculture

World War I benefited the U.S. economy. From 1914 to 1918, factory output grew by more than one-third. Even with several million men in the military, the civilian work force expanded by 1.3 million between 1916 and 1918, thanks largely to new jobs in war-related industries such as shipbuilding, munitions, steel, and textiles. Prices rose, but so did wages. Even unskilled workers enjoyed wartime wage increases averaging nearly 20 percent. Samuel Gompers urged workers not to strike during the war. Some IWW workers and maverick AFL locals went on strike anyway, but with the economy booming, most workers observed the no-strike request.

The war's social impact took many forms. Job seekers pouring into industrial centers strained housing, schools, and municipal services. The consumption of cigarettes, which soldiers and workers could carry in their shirt pockets with greater ease than pipes or cigars, more than tripled from 1914 to 1918. Reflecting wartime prosperity, automobile production jumped from 460,000 in 1914 to 1.8 million in 1917, then dipped briefly in 1918 as steel went for military production.

Farmers profited, too. With European farm production disrupted, U.S. agricultural prices more than doubled between 1913 and 1918, and farmers' real income rose significantly. Cotton prices soared from twelve cents a pound in 1913 to twenty-nine cents a pound by 1918, and corn prices surged as well.

This agricultural boom proved a mixed blessing. Farmers who borrowed heavily to expand production faced a credit squeeze when farm prices fell after the war. In the 1920s and 1930s, hard-pressed farmers would look back to the war years as a golden age of prosperity.

Blacks Migrate Northward

The war sped the exodus of southern blacks. An estimated half-million African-Americans moved north during the war, and most settled in cities. Each day, fresh arrivals crowded the railroad stations of Philadelphia, New York, Detroit, and Pittsburgh. Chicago's black population grew from 44,000 in 1910 to 110,000 in 1920, Cleveland's from 8,000 to 34,000.

With European immigration disrupted by the war, booming industries hired more black workers. Some companies sent labor agents south to recruit black workers. African-American newspapers like the *Chicago Defender* spread the word, as did letters and word-of-mouth reports. One southern black, newly settled near Chicago, wrote home, "Nothing here but money, and it is not hard to get." A Pittsburgh newcomer presented a more balanced picture: "They give you big money for what you do, but they charge you big things for what you get." As economic opportunity beckoned, impoverished southern blacks welcomed the prospect of earning three dollars a day or more in a region where racism seemed less intense. By 1920, 1.5 million African-Americans were working in northern factories and other urban-based jobs.

This vast population movement had social, political, and cultural ramifications. New city churches and storefront missions met the spiritual and social needs of deeply religious migrants from the South. The National Association for the Advancement of Colored People (NAACP) grew from 9,000 members before the war to nearly 100,000 by the early 1920s. Tireless NAACP organizers built a sturdy network of local branches throughout the nation. NAACP leaders pointed to African-American support for the war to buttress their demand for racial equality. The struggle against racism faced setbacks in the reactionary 1920s, but the heightened race consciousness and activism of the war years helped create the groundwork for the civil-rights movement that lay ahead. The concentration of blacks in New York City also prepared the way for the Harlem Renaissance, a cultural flowering of the 1920s (see Chapter 23).

Still, these African-American newcomers in northern cities faced severe challenges. White workers resented the labor competition, and white homeowners lashed out as jammed black neighborhoods spilled over into surrounding areas. A bloody outbreak erupted on July 2, 1917, in East St. Louis, Illinois, home to thousands of recently arrived southern blacks. In a coordinated attack, a white mob torched black homes and shot the residents as they fled. At least thirty-nine blacks died, including a two-year-old who was shot and then thrown into a burning house.

A few weeks later, a silent march down New York's Fifth Avenue organized by the NAACP protested racist violence. One banner echoed Wilson's phrase justifying U.S. involvement in the war: "Mr. President, Why Not Make AMERICA Safe for Democracy?"

Women in Wartime   From one perspective, World War I seems a uniquely male experience. Male politicians led their nations into war. Male officers ordered other men into battle. Yet war touches all of society, not just half of it. The war affected women differently, but it affected them profoundly.

Feminist leaders like Carrie Chapman Catt hoped that the war would lead to full equality and greater opportunity for women. For a time, these goals seemed attainable. In addition to the women in the AEF and in wartime volunteer agencies, about 1 million women worked in industry. Thousands more held other jobs, from streetcar conductors to bricklayers. "Out of . . . repression into opportunity is the meaning of the war to thousands of women," wrote Florence Thorne of the American Federation of Labor in 1917.

As the woman-suffrage movement gained momentum, a key victory came in November 1917 when New York voters amended the state constitution to permit women to vote. In Washington, Alice Paul and members of her National Woman's Party (see Chapter 21) picketed the White House and posted banners criticizing President Wilson for opposing woman suffrage at home while championing democracy abroad. Several protesters were jailed and, when they went on a hunger strike, force-fed. Under growing pressure from all wings of the suffrage movement, Wilson declared that women's war service had earned them the right to vote. In 1919, barraged by prosuffrage petitions, the House and Senate overwhelmingly passed the **Nineteenth Amendment** granting women the vote. Ratification followed in 1920.

Beyond this victory, however, the war did little to better women's status permanently.

Relatively few women actually entered the work force for the first time in 1917–1918; most simply moved to better-paying jobs. Despite protests and War Labor Board rulings, even in these jobs most earned less than the men they replaced. As for the women in the AEF, the War Department refused their requests for military rank and benefits.

At the war's end, many women lost their jobs to returning veterans. The New York labor federation advised, "The same patriotism which induced women to enter industry during the war should induce them to vacate their positions after the war." Male streetcar workers in Cleveland went on strike to force women conductors off the job. In 1920, the percentage of U.S. women in the paid labor force was actually slightly lower than it had been in 1910.

Public-Health Crisis: The 1918 Influenza Pandemic   Amid battlefield casualties and home-front social changes, the nation in 1918 also coped with a global outbreak of influenza, a highly contagious viral infection. The **influenza pandemic,** spread by a particularly deadly strain of the virus, killed as many as 30 million people worldwide. Despite medical and public-health advances, doctors had few weapons against the flu in 1918.

Moving northward from its origins in southern Africa, the deadly flu spread from the war zone in France to U.S. military camps, striking Fort Riley, Kansas, in March and quickly advancing to other bases and the urban population. In September, an army health official visiting Camp Devens in Massachusetts wrote, "I saw hundreds of young stalwart men in uniform coming into . . . the hospital. . . . The faces wore a bluish cast, a cough brought up blood-stained sputum. In the morning, the dead bodies are stacked about the morgue like cordwood."

The flu hit the cities hard. In Philadelphia on September 19, 1918, the day after a massive Liberty Loan rally, doctors reported 635 new influenza cases. Many cities forbade all public gatherings. The worst came in October, when the flu killed 195,000 Americans. The total U.S. death toll was about 550,000, over six times the total of AEF battle deaths in France. More than 50,000 died in Canada.

In 1998 researchers with the U.S. Armed Forces Institute of Pathology recovered samples of the 1918 flu virus from the frozen corpse of a female victim buried in the Alaska tundra. Using this sample and tissue preserved from two U.S. soldiers who had died of influenza, scientists in 2004 announced that they had synthesized the 1918 virus for research purposes.

In 1997, a new avian (bird) virus similar to the 1918 flu virus killed six persons in Hong Kong. By 2005, the virus had spread to poultry in Asia, Turkey, and eastern Europe, and more than sixty people had died after direct contact with infected birds. Though the risk appeared low, public-health agencies worldwide took measures to prevent another global pandemic like that of 1918.

The War and Progressivism   As one weighs the war's effects on Progressive Era reform movements, a mixed picture emerges. As we have seen, the war strengthened the coercive, moral-control aspect of progressivism, including the drive for the prohibition of alcohol. Exploiting anti-German sentiment, prohibitionists pointed out that the nation's biggest breweries bore such German names as Pabst, Schlitz, and Anheuser-Busch. Beer, they hinted, was part of a

German plot to undermine American fitness. With food conservation a high priority, they stressed the wastefulness of using grain to make liquor. When the **Eighteenth Amendment** establishing national prohibition passed Congress in December 1917, it was widely seen as a war measure. Ratified in 1919, it went into effect on January 1, 1920.

Similarly, the war strengthened the Progressive Era antiprostitution campaign. The War Department closed red-light districts near military bases, including New Orleans's famed Storyville. (As Storyville's jazz musicians moved north, jazz reached a national audience.) Congress appropriated $4 million to combat venereal disease among soldiers and war workers. In San Antonio, a major military hub, an antiprostitution leader reflected the war mood when he declared, "We propose to fight vice . . . with the cold steel of the law, and to drive in the steel from the point to the hilt until the law's supremacy is acknowledged."

In the wartime climate of "vigilance," the antiprostitution drive expanded to a broader policing of morals. Female lecturers hired by the Commission on Training Camp Activities urged women to uphold standards of sexual morality. "Do Your Bit to Keep Him Fit" one pamphlet advised women. Urban "protective bureaus" set up with government authority monitored women's behavior. In Massachusetts, female social workers hid in the Boston Common after dark to apprehend young women dating soldiers from nearby bases.

All this moral-reform activity convinced some that traditional codes of sexual behavior, weakening before the war, had been restored. One antiprostitution crusader exulted, "Young men of today . . . are nearer perfection in conduct, morals, and ideals than any similar generation . . . in the history of the world. Their minds have been raised to ideals that would never have been attained save by the heroism of . . . the World War."

Along with woman suffrage, other reforms advanced as well. The **War Labor Board** (WLB), spurred by progressives interested in the cause of labor, encouraged workers to join unions and guaranteed unions' right to bargain with management. The WLB also pressured factory owners to introduce the eight-hour workday, end child labor, and open their plants to safety and sanitation inspectors. The Railroad Administration also recognized railway workers' right to unionize. Under these favorable conditions, union membership rose from 2.7 million in 1916 to more than 5 million by 1920.

Another wartime agency, the United States Housing Corporation, built housing projects for workers, including some that encompassed schools, playgrounds, and recreational centers. Several state legislatures, concluding that worker-protection laws would help the war effort, passed wage-and-hour laws and other measures benefiting factory laborers.

The **Bureau of War Risk Insurance** (BWRI), created in October 1917 to aid soldiers' families, established a precedent of government help for families at risk. As Julia Lathrop, head of the Federal Children's Bureau, observed, "The least a democratic nation can do, which sends men into war, is to . . . [care for] the families." By the war's end, the BWRI was sending regular checks to 2.1 million families.

Overall, however, at least in the short run, the war weakened the progressive social-justice impulse. While the war brought increased regulation of the economy—a key progressive goal—business interests often dominated the regulatory agencies, and they were quickly dismantled after the war.

The government's repression of radicals and antiwar dissenters fractured the fragile coalition of left-leaning progressives, women's groups, trade unionists, and some socialists that had provided the momentum for prewar worker-protection laws, and ushered in a decade of reaction. The 1918 midterm election signaled the shift: the Democrats lost both houses of Congress to a deeply conservative Republican Party.

Nevertheless, taking a longer view, reform energies, after diminishing in the 1920s, would reemerge in the depression decade of the 1930s. And as Franklin D. Roosevelt's New Deal took shape (see Chapter 24), the memory of such World War I agencies as the War Labor Board, the United States Housing Corporation, and the Bureau of War Risk Insurance provided ideas and inspiration.

JOYOUS ARMISTICE, BITTER AFTERMATH, 1918–1920

In November 1918, the war finally ended. The peace conference that followed stands as a high point of America's growing internationalist involvement, but it also triggered a sharp domestic reaction against that involvement. Woodrow Wilson dominated the peace conference but failed in his most cherished objective—American membership in the League of Nations. At home, as racism and intolerance worsened, the electorate repudiated Wilsonianism and in 1920 sent a conservative Republican to the White House.

Wilson's Fourteen Points; The Armistice From the moment the United States entered the war, President Wilson planned to put his personal stamp on the peace. He and his reform-minded supporters believed that U.S. involvement could transform a sordid struggle for power and empire into a crusade for a democratic world order. Wilson recruited a group of advisers called The Inquiry to translate his vision into specific war aims. The need for a statement of U.S. war objectives grew urgent after the Bolsheviks, having seized power in Russia, published many of the self-serving secret treaties signed by European powers prior to 1914.

In a speech to Congress in January 1918, Wilson summed up U.S. war aims in fourteen points. Eight of these spelled out Wilson's belief that the subject peoples of the Austro-Hungarian and Ottoman empires should have the right of self-determination—that is, the freedom to choose their own political futures. A ninth point insisted that colonial disputes take into account the interests of the colonized peoples. The remaining five points offered Wilson's larger postwar vision: a world of free navigation, free trade, reduced armaments, openly negotiated treaties, and "a general association of nations" to resolve conflicts peacefully. The **Fourteen Points** helped solidify American support for the war, especially among liberals. They seemed proof that the United States had entered the war not for selfish reasons but out of noble motives.

In early October 1918, reeling from the Allies' advances, Germany proposed an armistice based on Wilson's Fourteen Points. The British and French hesitated, but when Wilson threatened to negotiate a separate peace, they agreed. Meanwhile, in Berlin, Kaiser Wilhelm II had abdicated and a German republic had been proclaimed.

In the early morning of November 11, 1918, the Allied commander Marshal Foch and his German counterparts signed an armistice ending hostilities at 11:00 A.M. Rockets burst over the front that night, not in anger but in relief and celebration. Back home, cheering throngs (some wearing protective masks against the influenza epidemic) filled the streets. "Everything for which America has fought has been accomplished," Wilson proclaimed.

Troop transports soon ferried the soldiers home. One returnee, artillery captain Harry Truman of Missouri, described his feelings in a letter to his fiancée, Bess Wallace:

> I've never seen anything that looks so good as the Liberty Lady in New York Harbor. . . . [T]he men . . . have been in so many hard places that it takes something real to give them a thrill, but when the band . . . played "Home Sweet Home" there were not many dry eyes. The hardest of hard-boiled cookies even had to blow his nose a time or two.

The Versailles Peace Conference, 1919 Eager to play a central role in the peace conference, Wilson decided to lead the U.S. delegation himself. This was probably a mistake. The strain of long bargaining sessions soon took its toll on his frail nerves. Wilson compounded his mistake by naming only one Republican to the delegation, an elderly diplomat with little influence in the party. Selecting some prominent Republicans might have spared Wilson future grief. The Democrats' loss of Congress in the 1918 midterm election was a further ill omen.

Nevertheless, spirits soared on December 4, 1918, as the *George Washington*, a converted German liner, left New York, bearing Wilson to Europe—the first president to cross the Atlantic while in office. Ships' whistles blared as Wilson waved to the crowd on shore. The giddy mood continued when Wilson reached France. In Paris, shouts of "Voodrow Veelson" rang out as he rode up the Champs-Élysées, the city's ceremonial boulevard. When he visited England, children at the dock in Dover spread flowers in his path. In Italy, a local official compared him to Jesus Christ.

The euphoria faded once the peace conference began at the palace of Versailles near Paris, where the treaty ending the Revolutionary War had been signed 136 years before. Joining Wilson were the other Allied heads of state: Italy's Vittorio Orlando; the aged and cynical Georges Clemenceau of France; and England's David Lloyd George, of whom Wilson said, "He is slippery as an eel, and I never know when to count on him." Japan participated as well.

The European statesmen at the **Versailles Peace Conference** were determined to avenge their nations' horrendous wartime losses, which they blamed directly on German aggression. Their goals bore little relation to Wilson's liberal vision. As Clemenceau remarked, "God gave us the Ten Commandments and we broke them. Mr. Wilson has given us the Fourteen Points. We shall see."

Differences surfaced quickly. Italy demanded a port on the eastern Adriatic Sea. Japan insisted on keeping the trading rights it had seized from Germany in the Chinese province of Shandong (Shantung). Clemenceau was obsessed with revenge. At one point, an appalled Wilson threatened to leave the conference.

Reflecting this toxic climate, the peace treaty signed by a sullen German delegation in June 1919 was harshly punitive. Though its industrial infrastructure remained intact, Germany was disarmed, stripped of its colonies, forced to admit sole blame for the war, and saddled with reparation payments of $56 billion. France regained the provinces of Alsace and Lorraine lost to Germany in 1871 and took control for fifteen years of Germany's coal-rich Saar Basin. The treaty demilitarized Germany's western border and transferred a slice of eastern Germany to Poland. All told, the treaty cost Germany one-tenth of its population and one-eighth of its territory. The treaty granted Japan's Shandong claims and gave Italy a slice of Austria that contained two hundred thousand German-speaking inhabitants. These harsh terms, bitterly resented in Germany, planted the seeds of an even more devastating future war.

Some treaty provisions did reflect Wilson's themes of democracy and self-determination. Germany's former colonies went to the various Allies under a "mandate" or trusteeship system that in theory would lead to eventual independence. The treaty also recognized the independence of Poland and the Baltic states of Estonia, Latvia, and Lithuania (territories seized by Germany in its 1918 peace treaty with Bolshevik Russia). Separate treaties provided for the independence of Czechoslovakia and Yugoslavia, new nations carved from the Austro-Hungarian and Ottoman empires.

Palestine, a part of Turkey's collapsed Ottoman Empire, went to Great Britain under a mandate arrangement. In 1917, after gaining military control of Palestine, the British had issued the Balfour Declaration supporting a Jewish "national home" in the region while also acknowledging the rights of the non-Jewish Palestinians.

But the treaty makers ignored the aspirations of colonized peoples in Asia and Africa. For example, Ho Chi Minh, a young Vietnamese nationalist who would later become head of his nation, tried unsuccessfully at Versailles to secure Vietnamese independence from France.

Nor did the peacemakers come to terms with revolutionary Russia. Indeed, in August 1918 a fourteen-nation Allied army, including some seven thousand U.S. troops, had landed at various Russian ports, ostensibly to secure them from German attack and to protect Allied war equipment. In fact, the aim was to overthrow the new Bolshevik regime, whose communist ideology stirred deep fear in the capitals of Europe and America. Wilson, having welcomed the liberal Russian revolution of March 1917, viewed the Bolshevik coup and Russia's withdrawal from the war as a betrayal of the Allies and of his hopes for a democratic Russia. The Versailles treaty reflected this hostility. Its territorial settlements in eastern Europe were designed to weaken Russia. Wilson and the other Allied leaders agreed to support a Russian military leader waging a last-ditch struggle against the Bolsheviks. Not until 1933 would the United States recognize the Soviet Union.

The Fight over the League of Nations Dismayed by the treaty's vindictive features, Wilson focused on his one shining achievement at Versailles—the creation of a new international organization, the **League of Nations.** The agreement or "covenant" to establish the League, written into the treaty, embodied Wilson's vision of a new world order of peace and justice.

But Wilson's League faced major hurdles. A warning sign had come in February 1919 when thirty-nine Republican senators and senators-elect, including Henry Cabot Lodge, signed a letter rejecting the League in its present form. Wilson had retorted defiantly, "You cannot dissect the Covenant from the treaty without destroying the whole vital structure."

When Wilson sent the treaty to the Senate for ratification in July 1919, Lodge bottled it up in the Foreign Relations Committee. Convinced that he could rally popular opinion to his cause, Wilson left Washington on September 3 for a speaking tour. Covering more than nine thousand miles by train, Wilson defended the League in thirty-seven speeches in twenty-two days. Crowds were large and friendly. People wept as Wilson described his visits to American war cemeteries in France and cheered his vision of a new world order.

But the trip exhausted Wilson, and on September 25 he collapsed in Colorado. His train sped back to Washington, where Wilson suffered a stroke on October 2 that for a time left him near death. He spent the rest of his term mostly in bed or in a wheelchair, a reclusive invalid, his mind clouded, his fragile emotions betraying him into vindictive actions and tearful outbursts. He broke with close advisers, refused to see the British ambassador, and dismissed Secretary of State Lansing, accusing him of disloyalty. In January 1920, his physician advised him to resign, but Wilson refused.

Wilson's first wife, Ellen, had died in 1914. His strong-willed second wife, Edith Galt, played a crucial role behind the scenes during this crisis. She hid Wilson's condition from the public, controlled his access to information, and decided who could see him. Cabinet members, diplomats, and congressional leaders were barred from the White House. When one leader seeking a meeting urged Mrs. Wilson to consider "the welfare of the country," she snapped, "I am not thinking of the country now, I am thinking of my husband." Since the Twenty-fifth Amendment, dealing with issues of presidential disability, was not adopted until 1967, the impasse continued.

The League drama unfolded against this grim backdrop. On September 10, 1919, the Foreign Relations Committee at last sent the treaty to the Senate, but with a series of amendments. The Senate split into three groups. First were Democrats who supported the League covenant without changes. Second were Republican "Irreconcilables," led by Hiram Johnson of California, Wisconsin's Robert La Follette, and Idaho's William Borah, who opposed the League absolutely. Progressive on domestic issues, but also intensely nationalistic, they feared that League membership would dangerously restrict U.S. freedom of action and entangle America with foreign powers they viewed as corrupt and reactionary. Finally, a group of Republican "Reservationists," led by Lodge, demanded amendments as a condition of their support. The Reservationists especially objected to Article 10 of the covenant, which pledged each member nation to preserve the political independence and territorial integrity of all other members. This provision, the Reservationists believed, limited America's sovereignty and infringed on Congress's constitutional power to declare war.

Had Wilson accepted compromise, the Senate would probably have ratified the Versailles treaty, including the League covenant. But Wilson's illness aggravated his tendency toward rigidity. Isolated in the White House, he instructed Senate Democrats to vote against the treaty, which now included Lodge's reservations. Although international-law specialists argued that these reservations would not significantly weaken U.S. participation in the League, Wilson rejected them as "a knife thrust at the heart of the treaty."

Despite Wilson's speaking tour, the public did not rally behind the League. The reactionary mood that Wilson's own administration had helped create was not conducive to bold gestures of political idealism. As the editor of *The Nation* magazine observed, "If [Wilson] loses his great fight for humanity, it will be because he was deliberately silent when freedom of speech and the right of conscience were struck down in America."

On November 19, 1919, pro-League Democrats obeying Wilson's instructions and anti-League Irreconcilables joined forces to defeat the version of the Versailles treaty that included Lodge's reservations. A second vote in March 1920 produced the same result. The United States would not join the League. A president elected amid high hopes in 1912, cheered when he called for war in 1917, and adulated in Europe in 1918 lay embittered and impotent. What might have been Wilson's crowning achievement had turned to ashes.

Racism and Red Scare, 1919–1920

The wartime spirit of "100 percent Americanism" left a bitter aftertaste. The years 1919–1920 saw new racial violence and antiradical hysteria. Seventy-six blacks were lynched in 1919, the worst toll in fifteen years. The victims included ten veterans, several still in uniform. In Omaha, Nebraska, a mob of 5,000 or more, inflamed by sensational newspaper stories, seized a black prisoner, Will Brown, from the county courthouse, in the process burning the building and assaulting the mayor. The mob hanged Brown from a lamppost, shot him multiple times, dragged his body through the streets, and burned it. Fourteen-year-old Henry Fonda, a future film actor, witnessed the lynching from his father's print shop. "It was the most horrendous sight I'd ever seen," he later recalled.

The worst violence exploded in Chicago, where simmering racial tension erupted on a hot afternoon in July 1919. When a black youth swimming at a Lake Michigan beach drowned after whites had pelted him with stones, black neighborhoods erupted in fury. A thirteen-day reign of terror followed as white and black marauders engaged in random attacks and arson. Black gangs stabbed an Italian peddler; white gangs pulled blacks from streetcars and shot or whipped them. Before an uneasy calm returned, the outbreak left fifteen whites and twenty-three blacks dead, over five hundred injured, and more than a thousand families, mostly black, homeless.

Wartime antiradicalism crested in a postwar Red Scare. (Communists were called "reds" because of the red flag favored by revolutionary organizations.) For some, the 1917 triumph of bolshevism in Russia offered a grim foretaste of what might happen in America. A rash of strikes in 1919 deepened such fears. When the IWW and other unions called a general strike in Seattle early that year, the mayor accused the strikers of seeking to "duplicate the anarchy of Russia" and called for federal troops to maintain order. Anxiety crackled again in April, when various public officials received packages containing bombs. One severely injured a senator's maid; another damaged the home of Attorney General A. Mitchell Palmer. When 350,000 steelworkers went on strike in September, mill owners ran newspaper ads describing the walkout as a plot by "Red agitators."

Antiradical paranoia also infected politics. In November 1919, the House of Representatives refused to seat Milwaukee socialist Victor Berger because of his indictment under the Espionage Act. Milwaukee voters promptly reelected him, but the House stood firm. The New York legislature expelled several socialist members. The Justice Department set up an antiradical division under young J. Edgar Hoover, future head of the Federal Bureau of Investigation, who ordered the arrest of hundreds of suspected communists and radicals. In December 1919, the government deported 249 Russian-born aliens, including Emma Goldman, a prominent radical and leader of the birth-control movement.

On January 2, 1920, in a Justice Department dragnet, federal marshals and local police raided the homes of suspected radicals and the headquarters of radical organizations in thirty-two cities. Without search warrants or arrest warrants, they arrested more than 4,000 persons (some 550 were eventually deported) and seized papers and records. In Lynn, Massachusetts, police arrested a group of people who were meeting to plan a cooperative bakery. In Boston, police paraded arrested persons through the streets in handcuffs and chains and then confined them in crowded and unsanitary cells without formal charges or the right to post bail.

Attorney General Palmer, ambitious for higher office, coordinated these "Red raids." A Quaker and one-time reform-minded congressman, Palmer had succumbed to the anticommunist hysteria. He later described the menace he believed the nation faced in 1919:

> The blaze of revolution was sweeping over every American institution of law and order . . . eating its way into the homes of the American workman, its sharp tongues of revolutionary heat . . . licking at the altars of the churches, leaping into the belfry of the school bell, crawling into the sacred corners of American homes, . . . burning up the foundations of society.

The Red Scare soon subsided. When a bomb exploded in New York City's financial district in September 1920, killing thirty-eight people, most Americans saw the deed as the work of an isolated fanatic, not evidence of approaching revolution.

The Election of 1920   In this unsettled climate, the election of 1920 approached. Wilson, out of touch with political reality, considered seeking a third term, but was persuaded otherwise. Few heeded his call to make the election a "solemn referendum" on the League. "The bitterness toward Wilson is everywhere . . . ," wrote a Democratic campaign worker; "he hasn't a friend."

Treasury Secretary McAdoo and Attorney General Palmer harbored presidential hopes. But when the Democrats convened in San Francisco, the delegates nominated James M. Cox, the mildly progressive governor of Ohio. As Cox's running mate they

"Convict No. 9653 for President" *Although socialist Eugene V. Debs was in prison in 1920 for his antiwar speeches in 1917–19, he still received over 900,000 votes for president.*

chose the young assistant secretary of the navy, Franklin D. Roosevelt, who possessed a potent political name.

The confident Republicans, meeting in Chicago, nominated Senator **Warren G. Harding** of Ohio, an amiable politician of little distinction. As one GOP leader observed, "There ain't any first raters this year. . . . We got a lot of second raters, and Harding is the best of the second raters." For vice president, they chose Massachusetts governor Calvin Coolidge, who had won attention in 1919 with his denunciation of a Boston policemen's strike.

Harding's vacuous campaign speeches reminded one critic of "an army of pompous phrases moving over the landscape in search of an idea." But his reassuring promise of a return to "normalcy" resonated with many voters, and he won by a landslide—16 million votes against 9 million for Cox. Nearly a million citizens defiantly voted for socialist Eugene Debs, who remained behind bars in an Atlanta penitentiary for his earlier antiwar speeches.

The election dashed all hope for American entry into the League of Nations. During the campaign, Harding vaguely endorsed some form of "international organization," but once elected he bluntly declared the League question "dead." Senator Lodge, who had praised Wilson's idealistic war message so highly, now expressed grim satisfaction that the voters had ripped "Wilsonism" up by the roots. The sense of high purpose that Wilson had evoked so eloquently in April 1917 seemed remote indeed as Americans turned to a new president and a new era.

Conclusion

The early twentieth century saw intensifying U.S. involvement abroad. Focused initially on Latin America and Asia, this new globalism arose from a desire to promote U.S. business interests internationally; export American values to other societies; and extend the power of a newly confident, industrialized United States as a counterweight to the expansive ambitions of Great Britain, Germany, and other imperial nations.

After 1914 this new internationalism focused on the European war. The nation's 1917 decision to enter the war on the Allied side reflected a combination of cultural ties, economic interests, concern for neutral rights, and President Wilson's vision of a transformed world order that would emerge from the struggle.

By a conservative estimate, World War I cost 10 million dead and 20 million wounded. Included in this toll were 112,000 deaths in the American military—49,000 in battle and 63,000 from diseases, mostly influenza. The conflict brought advances in the technology of slaughter, from U-boat torpedoes and primitive aerial bombs to tanks, poison gas, and deadlier machine guns.

The war also had far-reaching social, political, and economic effects. It advanced some reforms, notably woman suffrage and the campaigns against prostitution and alcohol. As a war measure, the government expanded its regulatory power over corporations and took steps to ensure workers' well-being and right to organize. Wartime regulatory agencies and social programs offered models that would prove influential in the future.

But the war undermined other aspects of progressivism—its openness to new ideas, its larger commitment to social justice, and its humanitarian concern for the underdog. As government propaganda encouraged ideological conformity and fear of radicalism, the reform impulse withered. The climate of reaction intensified in 1919–1920, as the nation repudiated Wilsonian idealism.

The war at least temporarily improved the economic prospects of many workers, farmers, blacks, and women, and enhanced the standing of the corporate executives, psychologists, public-relations specialists, and other professionals who contributed their expertise to the cause. Internationally, despite the wrangles that kept America out of the League of Nations, the conflict propelled the United States to the center of world politics and left the nation's businesses and financial institutions poised for global expansion.

Some of these changes endured; others proved fleeting. Cumulatively, however, their effect was profound. The nation that celebrated the armistice in November 1918 was very different from the one that Woodrow Wilson had solemnly taken into battle only nineteen months earlier.

23

The 1920s: Coping with Change, 1920–1929

A NEW ECONOMIC ORDER

Fueled by new consumer products and new methods of producing and selling goods, the economy surged in the 1920s. Not everyone benefited, and farmers in particular suffered chronic economic woes. Still, the overall picture appeared rosy. As we shall see, these economic changes influenced the decade's political, social, and cultural climate, as Americans struggled to cope with a rapidly changing society.

Booming Business, Ailing Agriculture A recession struck in 1920 after the government canceled wartime defense contracts and returning veterans reentered the job market. Recovery came in 1922, however, and for the next few years the nonfarm economy hummed. Unemployment fell to as low as 3 percent, prices held steady, and the gross national product (GNP) grew by 43 percent from 1922 to 1929.

With the growth of cities, new consumer goods, including home electrical products, fed the prosperity. Many factories already ran on electricity, but now many urban households joined the grid as well. By the mid-1920s, with more than 60 percent of the nation's homes electrified, new appliances, from refrigerators and vacuum cleaners to fans and razors, filled the stores. The manufacture of such appliances, as well as of hydroelectric generating plants and equipment, provided a massive economic stimulus.

The automobile helped fuel the boom. Introduced before the war (see Chapter 21), the automobile came into its own in the 1920s. By 1930, some 60 percent of U.S. families owned cars. The Ford Motor Company led the market until mid-decade, when General Motors (GM) spurted ahead by touting greater comfort and a range of colors (Ford's Model T came only in black). GM's lowest-priced car, named for French auto-

CHRONOLOGY, 1920–1929

1920–1921 • Postwar recession.

1920 • Warren G. Harding elected president.
Radio station KDKA, Pittsburgh, broadcasts election returns.
Sinclair Lewis, *Main Street.*

1921 • Economic boom begins; agriculture remains depressed.
Sheppard-Towner Act.
Shuffle Along, all-black musical review.

1921–1922 • Washington Naval Arms Conference.

1922 • Supreme Court declares child-labor law unconstitutional.
Fordney-McCumber Tariff restores high rates.
Herbert Hoover, *American Individualism.*

1923 • Harding dies; Calvin Coolidge becomes president.

1924 • Teapot Dome scandals investigated.
National Origins Act (immigration restriction).
Calvin Coolidge elected president.

1925 • Scopes Trial.
Ku Klux Klan scandal in Indiana.
Alain Locke, *The New Negro.*
DuBose Heyward, *Porgy.*
F. Scott Fitzgerald, *The Great Gatsby.*

1926 • Book-of-the-Month Club founded.
National Broadcasting Company founded.
Langston Hughes, *The Weary Blues.*

1927 • *The Jazz Singer,* first sound movie.
Coolidge vetoes the McNary-Haugen farm bill.
Henry Ford introduces the Model A.
Ford apologizes for anti-Semitic publications.
Execution of Sacco and Vanzetti.
Charles A. Lindbergh's transatlantic flight.
Marcus Garvey deported.
Mississippi River flood.

1928 • Herbert Hoover elected president.

1929 • Federal Farm Board created.
Sheppard-Towner program terminated.
Textile strike in Gastonia, North Carolina.
Ernest Hemingway, *A Farewell to Arms.*
Claude McKay, *Home to Harlem.*

motive designer Louis Chevrolet, proved especially popular. Meeting the challenge, in 1927 **Henry Ford** introduced the stylish Model A in various colors. By the end of the decade, the automobile industry accounted for about 9 percent of all wages in manufacturing and had stimulated such industries as rubber, gasoline and motor oil, advertising, and highway construction.

The stock market at first reflected the prevailing prosperity, and then far outran it, as a speculative frenzy gripped Wall Street. By 1929, stock prices had reached stratospheric levels, creating conditions for a horrendous collapse (see Chapter 24).

The business boom had a global impact. To supply overseas markets, Ford, GM, and other corporations built production facilities abroad. Other U.S. firms acquired foreign factories or sources of raw materials. U.S. meatpackers built plants in Argentina; Anaconda Copper acquired Chile's biggest copper mine; the mammoth United Fruit Company established plants across Latin America. U.S. private investment abroad also increased as American investment firms loaned European nations money to repay war debts and modernize their economies. But the era of economic globalization still lay far in the future. Economic nationalism prevailed in the 1920s, as the industrialized nations, including the United States, erected high tariff barriers. The Fordney-McCumber Tariff (1922) and the Smoot-Hawley Tariff (1930) pushed U.S. import duties to all-time highs, benefiting domestic manufacturers but stifling foreign trade. The percentage of the GNP represented by exports actually fell between 1913 and 1929. Manufactured goods increasingly replaced agricultural commodities in U.S. exports, however, rising to 61 percent of the total by 1930.

While prosperity lifted overall wage rates, workers benefited unequally, reflecting regional variations and discriminatory practices by employers. The variation between North and South loomed largest. In 1928, unskilled laborers in New England earned an average of forty-seven cents an hour, in contrast to twenty-eight cents in the South. Textile corporations moved south in search of lower wage rates, devastating New England mill towns. Women workers, blacks, Mexican-Americans, and recent immigrants clustered at the bottom of the wage scale. African-Americans, including many recent migrants from the rural South, faced special difficulties. "Last hired and first fired," they generally held the most menial jobs.

For farmers, wartime prosperity gave way to hard times. Grain prices plummeted when government purchases for the army dwindled, European agriculture revived, and America's high tariffs depressed agricultural exports. Ironically, when tractors and other new machinery increased farm production, the resulting surpluses further weakened prices. Farmers who had bought land and equipment on credit during the war now felt the squeeze as payments came due.

New Modes of Producing, Managing, and Selling

The 1920s saw striking increases in productivity. New assembly-line techniques boosted the per capita output of industrial workers by some 40 percent. At the Ford plants near Detroit, workers stood in place and performed repetitive tasks as chains conveyed the partly assembled vehicles past them.

Assembly-line work influenced employees' behavior. Managers discouraged individual initiative. Even talking or laughter could distract workers from their task. Ford employees learned to speak without moving their lips and adopted an expressionless mask that some called "Fordization of the face." As work became more routine, job satisfaction diminished. Assembly-line labor did not foster the pride that came from farming or mastering a craft. Nor did it offer much prospect of advancement. In Muncie, Indiana, factories employing over four thousand workers announced only ten openings for foremen in 1924 and 1925.

Still, the new mass-production methods had a global impact. *Fordism* became a synonym worldwide for American industrial might and assembly-line methods. In Russia, which purchased twenty-five thousand Ford tractors in the 1920s, people "ascribed a magical quality to the name of Ford," a visitor reported.

Business consolidation, spurred by the war, continued. By the late 1920s, over a thousand companies a year vanished through merger. Corporate giants dominated the major industries: Ford, GM, and Chrysler in automobiles; General Electric and Westinghouse in electricity; and so forth. Samuel Insull, longtime president of Chicago's Commonwealth Edison Company, presided over a multi-billion-dollar empire of local and regional power companies and electric railroads. By 1930, one hundred corporations controlled nearly half the nation's business. Without actually merging, companies that made the same product often cooperated through trade associations on such matters as pricing, product specifications, and division of markets.

As U.S. capitalism matured, management structures evolved. Giant corporations set up separate divisions for product development, market research, economic forecasting, employee relations, and so on, each run by a professional manager.

The modernization of business affected wage policies. Rejecting the old view that employers should pay the lowest wages possible, business leaders now concluded that higher wages would improve productivity and increase consumer buying power. Henry Ford had led the way in 1914 by paying his workers five dollars a day, well above the average for factory workers. Other companies soon followed suit.

New systems for distributing goods emerged as well. Automobiles reached consumers through dealer networks. By 1926, nearly ten thousand Ford dealerships dotted the nation. The A&P grocery chain boasted 17,500 stores by 1928. Chain stores accounted for about a quarter of all retail sales by 1930. Department stores grew more inviting, with remodeled interiors and attractive display windows. Air conditioning, an early-twentieth-century invention, made department stores (as well as movie theaters and restaurants) welcome havens on summer days.

Advertising and credit sales further strengthened the new consumer economy. In 1929, corporations spent nearly $2 billion on radio, billboard, newspaper, and magazine ads, and advertising companies employed some six hundred thousand people. Chicago advertising baron Albert Lasker owned the Chicago Cubs baseball team and his own golf course. As they still do, 1920s' advertisers used celebrity endorsements, promises of social success, and threats of social embarrassment. Beneath a picture of a sad young woman, a Listerine mouthwash ad proclaimed: "She was a beautiful girl and talented too. . . . Yet in the one pursuit that stands foremost in the mind of every girl and woman—marriage—she was a failure." Her problem was "halitosis," or bad breath. The remedy, of course, was Listerine, and lots of it.

Advertisers offered a seductive vision of the new era of abundance. Portraying a fantasy world of elegance, grace, and pleasure, ads aroused desires that the new consumer-oriented capitalist system happily fulfilled. One critic in 1925 described the "dream world" created by advertising:

[S]miling faces, shining teeth, schoolgirl complexions, cornless feet, perfect fitting [underwear], distinguished collars, wrinkleless pants, odorless breath, regularized bowels, . . . charging motors, punctureless tires, perfect busts, shimmering shanks, self-washing dishes, backs behind which the moon was meant to rise.

The ballyhoo of advertising also stirred a skeptical reaction. *Your Money's Worth* (1927), by Stuart Chase and F. J. Schlink, cast a critical eye on advertisers' claims. One observer called the book "the *Uncle Tom's Cabin* of the consumer movement." The *Consumers' Research Bulletin,* launched by Chase and Schlink in 1929, tested products and reported the results to consumers.

Americans of the 1920s increasingly bought major purchases on credit. In earlier days, credit had typically involved pawnbrokers, personal loans, or informal arrangements between buyers and sellers. Now retailers routinely offered credit plans for big-ticket items such as automobiles, furniture, and refrigerators. By 1929 credit purchases accounted for 75 percent of automobile sales.

What some have called "the cult of business" saturated 1920s' U.S. culture. "America stands for one idea: Business . . . ," proclaimed the *Independent* magazine in 1921; "Thru business, . . . the human race is finally to be redeemed." Presidents Harding and Coolidge praised business values and hobnobbed with corporate leaders. Magazines profiled business tycoons. A 1923 opinion poll ranked Henry Ford as a leading presidential prospect. In *The Man Nobody Knows* (1925), ad man Bruce Barton described Jesus Christ as a managerial genius who "picked up twelve men from the bottom ranks of business and forged them into an organization that conquered the world."

Women in the New Economic Era Although the ranks of women employed outside the home increased in the 1920s, their share as a proportion of the total female population hardly changed, hovering at about 24 percent. Male workers dominated the auto plants and other assembly-line factories.

Women who did enter the workplace faced wage discrimination. In 1929, for example, a male trimmer in the meatpacking industry received fifty-two cents an hour; a female trimmer, thirty-seven cents. The weakening of the union movement (see next section) hit women workers hard. By 1929, the proportion of women workers belonging to unions fell to a minuscule 3 percent.

Most women workers, especially recent immigrants and members of minority groups, held low-paying, unskilled positions. By 1930, however, some 2 million women were working in corporate offices as secretaries, typists, or filing clerks, although rarely at higher ranks. Indeed, office-space arrangements often segregated male managers and female clerks.

As for higher education, nearly fifty thousand women received college degrees in 1930, almost triple the 1920 figure. Of those who entered the workplace, most took clerical jobs or entered such traditional "women's professions" as nursing, librarianship, and school teaching. With medical schools imposing a 5 percent quota on female admissions, the number of women physicians actually declined from 1910 to 1930. A handful of women, however, following the lead of Progressive Era feminist trailblazers, pursued postgraduate education to become faculty members in colleges and universities.

While marginalized in the workplace, women were courted as consumers. In the decade's advertising, glamorous women smiled behind the steering wheel, swooned over new appliances, and smoked cigarettes in romantic settings. (One ad man promoted cigarettes for women as "torches of freedom.") In the advertisers' dream world, housework became an exciting challenge. As one ad put it, "Men are judged . . . according to their power to delegate work. Similarly the wise woman delegates to electricity all that electricity can do."

Struggling Labor Unions in a Business Age

Organized labor faced tough sledding in the 1920s. Union membership fell from 5 million in 1920 to 3.4 million in 1929. Several factors underlay this decline. For one thing, despite inequities and regional variations, overall wage rates rose in the decade, reducing the incentive to join a union. Further, the union movement's strength lay in older industries like printing, railroading, mining, and construction. These unions were ill suited to the new mass-production factories.

Management hostility further weakened organized labor. Henry Ford hired thugs to intimidate union organizers. In 1929, anti-union violence flared in North Carolina, where textile workers faced low wages, long hours, and appalling work conditions. In Marion, deputy sheriffs shot and killed six striking workers. In Gastonia, the communist-led National Textile Workers Union organized the strike. The mill's absentee owners refused to negotiate and evicted strikers from their company-owned homes. When armed thugs in league with the owners raided an encampment of strikers, the police chief was shot, possibly by one of his own deputies. Sixteen union leaders were indicted for murder, but released after a mistrial was declared. Later, a sniper shot and killed strike leader and balladeer Ella May Wiggins en route to a union rally. In the end, these strikes failed, and the textile industry remained nonunion.

Gastonia, North Carolina, 1929 *Two women textile workers confront an armed guard in a bitter strike that took several lives.*

As the wartime antiradical mood continued, opponents of labor unions often smeared them with the "communist" label, whether accurate or not. The anti-union campaign took subtler forms as well. Manufacturers' associations renamed the non-union shop the "open shop" and dubbed it the "American Plan" of labor relations. Some corporations provided cafeterias and recreational facilities for employees or sold them company stock at bargain prices. Corporate publicists praised "welfare capitalism" (the term for this anti-union strategy) as evidence of employers' benevolent concern for their workers.

Black membership in labor unions stood at only about eighty-two thousand by 1929, mostly miners, dockworkers, and railroad porters. The American Federation of Labor officially prohibited racial discrimination, but most AFL unions in fact barred African-Americans. Corporations often hired jobless blacks as strikebreakers, increasing organized labor's hostility toward them.

THE HARDING AND COOLIDGE ADMINISTRATIONS

With Republicans in control of Congress and the White House, politics reflected the decade's business orientation. Unsettled by rapid social change, many voters turned to conservative candidates who seemed to represent stability and traditional values. In this climate, former progressives, would-be reformers, and exploited groups had few political options.

Standpat Politics in a Decade of Change While the white South and the immigrant cities remained heavily Democratic, the Republican Party continued to attract northern farmers, businesspeople, native-born white-collar workers and professionals, and some skilled blue-collar workers. The GOP also benefited from the antiradical mood that had produced the early postwar Red Scare (see Chapter 22) and fed the decade's anti-union sentiment. Exploiting such fears, the Republican-led New York legislature set up a committee to investigate "seditious activities," expelled five socialist members, and required loyalty oaths of public-school teachers.

With Republican progressives having bolted to Theodore Roosevelt in 1912, GOP conservatives controlled the 1920 convention and nominated Senator **Warren G. Harding** of Marion, Ohio, for president. As a young newspaper editor, Harding had married the local banker's daughter, Florence Kling, who helped manage his election to the Senate in 1915. A genial backslapper, he enjoyed good liquor, a good poker game, and at least one long-term extramarital relationship. In the election, Harding swamped his Democratic opponent James M. Cox. After the stresses of war and Wilson's lofty moralizing, voters welcomed Harding's blandness and soothing oratory.

Harding made some notable cabinet selections: Henry C. Wallace, the editor of an Iowa farm periodical, as secretary of agriculture; **Charles Evans Hughes,** former New York governor and 1916 presidential candidate, secretary of state; and **Andrew Mellon,** a Pittsburgh financier, treasury secretary. **Herbert Hoover,** the wartime food czar, became secretary of commerce.

Harding also made some disastrous appointments: his political manager, Harry Daugherty, as attorney general; a Senate pal, Albert Fall of New Mexico, as secretary of the interior; a wartime draft dodger, Charles Forbes, as Veterans' Bureau head. Such men set the low ethical tone of Harding's presidency. By 1922, Washington rumor hinted at corruption in high places. "I have no trouble with my enemies . . . ," Harding told an associate; "[b]ut . . . my goddamn friends . . . keep me walking the floor nights." In July 1923, vacationing in the West, Harding suffered a heart attack; on August 2 he died in a San Francisco hotel.

A 1924 Senate investigation exposed the full scope of the scandals. Charles Forbes, convicted of stealing Veterans' Bureau funds, evaded prison by fleeing abroad. The bureau's general counsel committed suicide, as did an aide to Attorney General Daugherty accused of influence peddling. Daugherty himself narrowly escaped conviction in two criminal trials. Interior Secretary Fall went to jail for leasing government oil reserves, one in Teapot Dome, Wyoming, to two oilmen in return for a $400,000 bribe. Like "Watergate" in the 1970s, **"Teapot Dome"** became a shorthand label for a tangle of scandals.

With Harding's death, Vice President **Calvin Coolidge,** on a family visit in Vermont, took the presidential oath by lantern light from his father, a local magistrate. After graduating from Amherst College in Massachusetts, Coolidge had entered politics. Elected Massachusetts governor in 1918, he secured the Republican vice-presidential nomination in 1920.

Coolidge's image as "Silent Cal," a prim Yankee embodiment of old-fashioned virtues, was carefully crafted. The advertising executive Bruce Barton, an early master of political image-making, guided Coolidge's bid for national office in 1919–1920. Having persuaded the Boston publisher Houghton Mifflin to issue a book of Coolidge's speeches, Barton sent autographed copies to key GOP convention delegates. Barton planted pro-Coolidge articles in popular periodicals; organized "spontaneous" letter-writing campaigns to magazines urging more attention to Coolidge; and in general marketed his candidate as one would a soap or an automobile. The very name *Calvin Coolidge,* he wrote in a 1919 *Collier's* article building brand recognition, "seems cut from granite; one could almost strike sparks with such a name, like a flint." Targeting newly enfranchised women, Barton composed a "Message to Women" published under Coolidge's name in the March 1920 *Woman's Home Companion.*

Once Coolidge became president, Barton wrote speeches for him, arranged more book deals, and set up interviews with friendly reporters. Coolidge good-naturedly cooperated with Barton's image-making, donning cowboy hats and Indian war bonnets for photographers and reinforcing his "Silent Cal" reputation. When a journalist asked for a parting message to the people of California at the close of a presidential visit, Coolidge responded "Good-bye."

Long before Franklin D. Roosevelt's "fireside chats" of the 1930s (see Chapter 24), Barton understood the political potential of radio. He advised Coolidge to speak conversationally in his radio addresses, avoiding the spread-eagle oratory of earlier times. Wrote an admirer of Barton: "No man is his equal in [analyzing] the middle-class mind and directing an appeal to it."

Republican Policy Making in a Probusiness Era | While Coolidge raised the ethical tone of the White House, the probusiness policies, symbolized by high tariffs, continued. Prodded by Treasury Secretary Mellon, Congress lowered income-tax rates for the wealthy from their high wartime levels. Promoting what would later be called the "trickle-down theory" of prosperity, Mellon preached that tax cuts for the rich encouraged business investment and thus benefited everyone. In the same probusiness spirit, the Supreme Court under Chief Justice William Howard Taft (appointed by Harding in 1921) overturned a federal ban on child labor passed in 1919.

While promoting corporate interests, Coolidge opposed government assistance for other groups. This position faced a test in 1927 when torrential spring rains caused severe flooding on the Mississippi River. Soil erosion resulting from poor farming practices worsened the flood conditions, as did ill-considered engineering projects aimed at draining the river's natural floodplain for development purposes. One official described the river as "writh[ing] like an imprisoned snake" within its artificial confines. From Cairo, Illinois, to the Gulf of Mexico, water poured over towns and farms, flooding twenty-seven thousand square miles. Hundreds died, and the toll of the homeless, including many African-Americans, reached several hundred thousand. Disease spread in makeshift refugee camps. In an eerie preview of Hurricane Katrina in 2005, floodwaters swept over New Orleans's low-lying black neighborhoods.

Despite the flood's toll, Coolidge rejected calls for aid to the victims. The government had no duty to protect citizens "against the hazards of the elements," he declared. Coolidge did, however, sign the Flood Control Act of 1928 funding a ten-year program of levee construction along the Mississippi.

Another test of Coolidge's views came when hard-pressed farmers rallied behind the **McNary-Haugen Bill,** a price-support plan under which the government would annually purchase the surplus of six basic farm commodities—cotton, corn, rice, hogs, tobacco, and wheat—at their average price in 1909–1914 (when farm prices were high). The government would then sell these surpluses abroad at market prices and recover the difference, if any, through a tax on domestic sales of these commodities. Coolidge twice vetoed the McNary-Haugen bill, in 1927 and 1928, warning of "the tyranny of bureaucratic regulation and control." The government ought not favor a single interest group, he argued, even though corporations had long benefited from high tariffs and other measures. These vetoes led many angry farmers to vote Democratic in 1928. In the 1930s, New Deal planners would draw upon the McNary-Haugen approach in shaping farm policy (see Chapter 24).

Independent Internationalism   Although U.S. officials participated informally in some League of Nations activities, the United States refused to join the League or its International Court of Justice (the World Court) in the Netherlands. Despite isolationist tendencies, however, the Republican administrations of the 1920s pursued global policies they saw as serving America's national interest—an approach historians have called independent internationalism.

President Harding's most notable achievement was the **Washington Naval Arms Conference.** After the war ended, the United States, Great Britain, and Japan edged toward a dangerous (and costly) naval-arms race. In 1921, Secretary of State Hughes called for a conference in Washington to address the problem. He startled the delegates by outlining a specific ratio of warships among the world's naval powers. He even proposed scrapping some vessels, which he mentioned by name. Great Britain and Japan, together with Italy and France, accepted Hughes's plan, and agreed to halt all battleship construction for ten years. The United States and Japan also pledged to respect each other's territorial holdings in the Pacific. Although this treaty ultimately failed to prevent war, it did represent an early arms-control effort.

Another U.S. peace initiative was mainly symbolic. In 1928, the United States and France, eventually joined by sixty other nations, signed the Kellogg-Briand Pact renouncing aggression and calling for the outlawing of war. Lacking enforcement mechanisms, this high-sounding document accomplished little.

The Republican administrations of these years used diplomacy to promote U.S. economic interests. For example, they vigorously sought repayment of $22 billion in Allied war debts and German reparation payments. A study commission in 1924 sharply reduced these claims, but high U.S. tariffs and Europe's economic problems, including runaway inflation in Germany, made repayment of even the reduced claims unrealistic. When Adolf Hitler rose to power in Germany in 1933 (see Chapter 25), he repudiated all reparations payments.

With U.S. foreign investments expanding, the Harding and Coolidge administrations promoted American business interests abroad. For example, they opposed Mexico's efforts to regain control of oilfields earlier granted to U.S. companies. Efforts to negotiate the issue collapsed in 1928 when Mexico's president was assassinated. Complicating U.S.-Mexican relations was Washington's fear that Mexico, gripped by revolutionary upheaval, might go communist. These fears deepened in 1924 when Mexico recognized the Soviet Union, nine years before the United States took the same step.

Progressive Stirrings, Democratic Party Divisions The reform spirit survived feebly in the legislative branch. Congress staved off Andrew Mellon's proposals for even deeper tax cuts for the rich. Senator George Norris of Nebraska prevented the Coolidge administration from selling a federal hydroelectric facility at Muscle Shoals, Alabama, to Henry Ford at bargain prices. And in 1927 Congress created the Federal Radio Commission, extending the regulatory principle to this new industry.

In the 1922 midterm election, an alliance of labor and farm groups helped defeat some conservative Republicans. In 1924, this alliance revived the Progressive Party and nominated Senator Robert La Follette for president. The Socialist Party and the American Federation of Labor endorsed La Follette.

The 1924 Democratic convention in New York City split evenly between urban and rural wings. By one vote, the delegates defeated a resolution condemning the **Ku Klux Klan** (see below). While the party's rural, Protestant, southern wing favored former Treasury Secretary William G. McAdoo, the big-city delegates rallied behind New York's Catholic governor **Alfred E. Smith,** of Irish, German, and Italian immigrant origins. The Democratic split mirrored deep divisions in the nation. After 102 ballots, the exhausted delegates nominated an obscure New York corporation lawyer, John W. Davis.

Calvin Coolidge, aided by his media adviser Bruce Barton, easily won the Republican nomination. The GOP platform praised the high protective tariff and urged tax cuts and reduced government spending. With the economy humming, Coolidge polled nearly 16 million votes, about twice Davis's total. La Follette's 4.8 million votes cut into the Democratic total, contributing to the Coolidge landslide.

Women and Politics in the 1920s: A Dream Deferred Suffragists' hope that votes for women would transform politics survived briefly after the war. Polling places shifted from saloons to schools and churches. The 1920 major-party platforms endorsed several measures proposed by the League of Women Voters. The Women's Joint Congressional Committee, a coalition of activist groups, lobbied for child-labor laws, protection of women workers, and federal support for education. It also backed the **Sheppard-Towner Act** (1921), which funded rural prenatal and baby-care centers staffed by public-health nurses.

Overall, however, the Nineteenth Amendment, though a historic achievement, had little short-term political effect. As former suffrage advocates scattered across the political spectrum, the women's movement lost focus. The League of Women Voters, drawing middle-class and professional women, abandoned feminist activism and instead conducted nonpartisan studies of civic issues. Alice Paul's National Woman's Party proposed a constitutional amendment guaranteeing women equal rights, but other reformers argued that such an amendment could jeopardize gender-based laws protecting women workers. Politically active African-American women battled racial discrimination rather than addressing feminist issues; Hispanic women in the Southwest put their energies into labor-union organizing.

The reactionary political climate intensified this retreat from feminism. Patriotic groups accused Jane Addams and other women's-rights leaders of communist sympathies. Younger women, bombarded by ads that defined liberation in terms of consumption, rejected the prewar feminists' civic idealism. One in 1927 criticized the prewar "fighting feminists" for their lack of "feminine charm" and their "constant clamor about equal rights."

The few reforms women's groups did achieve proved short-lived. The Supreme Court in 1922–1923 struck down child-labor and women's-protective laws. A 1924 constitutional amendment banning child labor passed Congress, but few states ratified it. The Sheppard-Towner Act, denounced by the American Medical Association as a threat to physicians' monopoly of health care, expired in 1929.

MASS SOCIETY, MASS CULTURE

As a conservative reaction dominated U.S. politics, major transformations were reshaping society. Assembly lines, new consumer products, advertising, the spread of mass entertainment, and innovations in corporate organization all signaled profound changes in American life. Some citizens found these changes exciting; others recoiled in fear and apprehension.

Cities, Cars, Consumer Goods

In the 1920 census, for the first time, the urban population (defined as persons living in communities of twenty-five hundred or more) surpassed the rural. The United States had become an urban nation.

Urbanization affected different groups of Americans in different ways. African-Americans, for example, migrated cityward in massive numbers, especially after the 1927 Mississippi River floods. By 1930, more than 40 percent of the nation's 12 million blacks lived in cities, 2 million of them in Chicago, Detroit, New York, and other urban centers of the North and West. The first black congressman since Reconstruction, Oscar De Priest of Chicago, won election in 1928.

For many women, city life meant eased housework thanks to laborsaving appliances: gas stoves, electric irons, refrigerators, washing machines, and vacuum cleaners. Store-bought clothes replaced hand-sewn apparel. Home baking and canning declined as commercial bakeries arose and supermarkets offered canned fruit and vegetables.

For social impact, however, nothing matched the automobile. In *Middletown* (1929), a study of Muncie, Indiana, Robert and Helen Lynd reported one resident's comment: "Why . . . do you need to study what's changing this country? I can tell you . . . in just four letters: A-U-T-O."

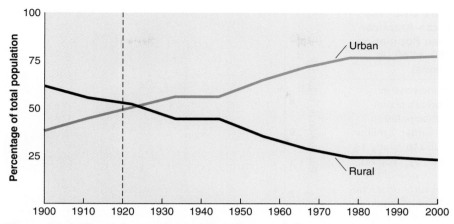

Figure 23.1 The Urban and Rural Population of the United States, 1900–2000

The urbanization of America in the twentieth century had profound political, economic, and social consequences. *Source:* Census Bureau, *Historical Statistics of the United States,* updated by relevant Statistical Abstracts of the United States.

The A-U-T-O's social impact was decidedly mixed, including traffic jams, parking problems, and highway fatalities (more than twenty-six thousand in 1924). In some ways, the automobile brought families together. Family vacations, rare a generation earlier, became more common. Tourist cabins and roadside restaurants served vacationing families. But the automobile also eroded family cohesion and parental authority. Young people could borrow the car to go to the movies, attend a distant dance, or simply park in a secluded lovers' lane.

Middle- and upper-class women welcomed the automobile. They could now drive to work, attend meetings, visit friends, and gain a sense of personal empowerment. Stereotypes of feminine delicacy faded as women mastered this new technology. As the editor of an automotive magazine wrote in 1927, "[E]very time a woman learns to drive, . . . it is a threat to yesterday's order of things."

For farm families, the automobile offered easier access to neighbors and to the city, lessening rural isolation. The automobile's country cousin, the tractor, proved instantly popular, with nearly a million in use in America by 1930, increasing productivity and reducing the physical demands of farm labor. Yet increased productivity did not always mean increased profits. And as farmers bought automobiles, tractors, and other mechanized equipment on credit, the rural debt crisis worsened.

Ads celebrated the freedom the automobile offered, in contrast to the fixed routes and schedules of trains and streetcars. Yet the automobile and other forms of motor transport in many ways further standardized American life. One-room schoolhouses stood empty as buses carried children to consolidated schools. Neighborhood grocery stores declined as people drove to supermarkets served by trucks bringing commercial foods from distant facilities. With the automobile came the first suburban shopping center (in Kansas City), and the first fast-food chain (A & W Root Beer).

Figure 23.2 The African-American Urban Population, 1880–1960 (in millions)

The increase in America's urban black population from under 1 million in 1880 to nearly 14 million by 1960 represents one of the great rural-urban migrations of modern history. *Source: Historical Statistics of the United States, Colonial Times to 1970* (Washington, D.C.: Bureau of the Census, 1975), vol. I, p. 12.

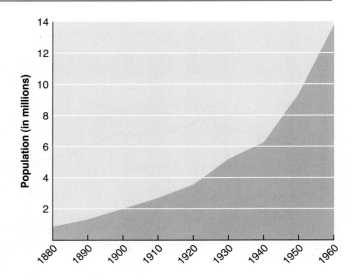

Even at $300 or $400, and despite a thriving used-car market, the automobile remained too expensive for many. The "automobile suburbs" that sprang up beyond the streetcar lines attracted mainly the well-to-do, widening class divisions in American society.

Soaring Energy Consumption and a Threatened Environment

Electrification and the spread of motorized vehicles placed heavy demands on the nation's natural resources and the environment. As electrical use soared, generating plants consumed growing quantities of coal. In 1929, with 20 million cars on the road, U.S. refineries used over a billion barrels of petroleum to meet the demand for gasoline and lubricating oil.

Rising gasoline consumption underlay Washington's efforts to ensure U.S. access to Mexican oil; played a role in the Teapot Dome scandal; and triggered fevered activity in the oilfields of Texas and Oklahoma as Texaco, Gulf, and many now-forgotten companies struggled for dominance. The natural gas found with petroleum seemed so abundant that it was simply burned off. In short, heavy fossil-fuel consumption, though small by later standards, already characterized America in the 1920s.

The wilderness that had inspired nineteenth-century artists and writers became more accessible as cars, improved roads, and tourist facilities gave vacationers easier access to the national parks and once-pristine regions. This development, too, had mixed effects. On one hand, it created a broader constituency for environmental protection and wilderness preservation. On the other, it subjected the nation's parks and wilderness areas to heavy pressures as visitors expected good highways, service stations, restaurants, and hotels.

Three Young Hispanic Women of Tucson, Arizona *In this posed photograph featuring an open touring car, these confident and fashionably dressed young women make their social aspirations clear.*

These contradictions worried Secretary of Commerce Herbert Hoover. He believed that urban dwellers benefited from returning to nature, but he recognized the strains that tourism placed on parks and wilderness areas. Hoover called a National Conference on Outdoor Recreation to consider ways to balance the preservationist ethic and the vacation-minded leisure culture of the 1920s.

The Sierra Club and other groups worked to protect wilderness and wildlife. In 1923, the Izaak Walton League, devoted to recreational fishing, persuaded Congress to halt a private-development scheme to drain a vast stretch of wetlands on the upper Mississippi. Instead, Congress declared this beautiful waterway a wildlife preserve. Aldo Leopold of the U.S. Forest Service warned of technology run amok. For too long, Leopold wrote in 1925, "a stump was our symbol of progress." However, few Americans in the expansive 1920s worried about the environmental issues that would occupy future generations.

Mass-Produced Entertainment Growing prosperity and routinized work stimulated interest in leisure activities in the 1920s. In their free hours, Americans sought the fulfillment many found missing in the workplace.

Mass-circulation magazines provided diversion. By 1922, ten U.S. magazines boasted circulation of more than 2.5 million. The venerable *Saturday Evening Post,* with its Norman Rockwell covers and fiction featuring small-town life, specialized in nostalgia. *Reader's Digest,* founded in 1921 by DeWitt and Lila Wallace, offered condensed versions of articles first published elsewhere. A journalistic equivalent of the Model T, the *Digest* offered standardized fare for mass consumption.

Book publishers broadened their market by selling through department stores or directly to the public via the Book-of-the-Month Club, launched in 1926. While critics accused such mass-market ventures of debasing literary taste, they did help sustain a common national culture in an increasingly diverse society.

In an age of standardized consumer goods, radio and the movies offered standardized cultural fare. The radio era began on November 2, 1920, when Pittsburgh station KDKA reported Warren Harding's election. In 1922, New York's WEAF began a regular news program, and a Newark station broadcast the World Series (the New York Giants beat the Yankees). In 1922, five hundred new stations began operations, as radio fever gripped America.

In 1926 three corporations—General Electric, Westinghouse, and the Radio Corporation of America—formed the first radio network, the National Broadcasting Company (NBC). The Columbia Broadcasting System (CBS) followed in 1927. Testing popular taste through market research, the networks soon ruled broadcasting. Americans everywhere laughed at the same jokes, heard the same news, and absorbed the same commercials.

WEAF broadcast the first sponsored program in 1922. Some public-policy commentators advocated preserving radio as a public educational and cultural medium, free of advertising, but commercial sponsorship soon won out. The first network comedy show, *Amos 'n' Andy* (1928), enriched its sponsor, Pepsodent toothpaste. White actors played the black characters on the program, which softened the realities of a racist society with stereotyped caricatures of African-American life.

Featuring stars like Valentino, the movies reached all social classes as they expanded from the nickelodeons of the immigrant wards into elegant uptown pleasure palaces with names like Majestic, Ritz, and Orpheum. In 1922, facing protests about sexually suggestive movies, and after a lurid sex scandal involving film star Roscoe "Fatty" Arbuckle, the movie industry named Will Hays, a member of President Harding's cabinet and former head of the Republican National Committee, to police movie morals. While enforcing a code of standards, Hays also served a public-relations role, promoting Hollywood films.

Despite charges that the movies undermined morality, they often reinforced traditional values. Charlie Chaplin, who had played anarchic, anti-authority figures in his prewar comedies, now softened his character in such feature-length films as *The Gold Rush* (1925). "America's sweetheart," Mary Pickford, with her golden curls and look of frail vulnerability, played innocent girls in need of protection, reinforcing traditional gender stereotypes at a time when many young women were challenging them. (Pickford sometimes played plucky young women facing danger courageously, and in real life was a shrewd businesswoman who became enormously wealthy.) *The Ten Commandments* (1923), directed by Cecil B. De Mille (the son of an Episcopal clergyman), warned of the consequences of breaking moral taboos.

Technical innovations kept moviegoers coming. Al Jolson's *The Jazz Singer* (1927) introduced sound. Walt Disney's cartoon *Steamboat Willie* (1928) not only marked the debut of Mickey Mouse but also showed the potential of animation. With technical advances came greater standardization. By 1930, with weekly attendance approaching 80 million, the corporate giants Metro-Goldwyn-Mayer, Warner Brothers, and Columbia, relying on formulaic plots and typecast stars, produced most films. As U.S. business expanded abroad, Hollywood, too, sought overseas markets for its product.

Like advertising, the movies created a dream world only loosely tethered to reality. One ad promised "all the adventure, . . . romance, . . . [and] excitement you lack in your daily life." These mass-produced fantasies shaped behavior and values, especially of the young. Hollywood, observed novelist John Dos Passos, offered a "great bargain sale of five-and-ten-cent lusts and dreams." The movies also stimulated consumption with alluring images of the good life. Along with department stores, mass magazines, and advertising, they opened new vistas of consumer abundance.

This spread of mass culture was a byproduct of urbanization. Even when advertisers, radio programmers, filmmakers, and magazine editors nostalgically evoked rural or small-town life, they did so from big-city offices and studios.

For all its influence, the new mass culture penetrated society unevenly. It had less impact in rural America, and met resistance among evangelical Christians suspicious of worldly amusements. Mexican-Americans preserved traditional festivals and leisure activities despite the "Americanization" efforts of non-Hispanic priests and well-intentioned outsiders. Working-class African-Americans flocked to concerts by performers outside the mass-culture mainstream like blues singers Bessie Smith and Gertrude "Ma" Rainey. Black-oriented "race records" catered to this specialized market.

Local radio stations broadcast not only network shows, but also farm reports, local news, religious programs, community announcements, and ethnic or regional music. Similarly, along with the downtown movie palaces, neighborhood theaters provided opportunities for socializing and for exuberant responses to the film. The *Chicago Defender,* the voice of the city's black middle class, deplored the raucousness of movie theaters in poor black neighborhoods, where "during a death scene . . . you are likely to hear the orchestra jazzing away." In short, despite the new mass culture, America still had room for diversity in the 1920s.

Celebrity Culture   Professional sports and media-promoted spectacles provided diversion as well. In 1921, Atlantic City promoters launched a bathing-beauty contest they grandly called the Miss America Pageant. Celebrities dominated professional sports: Babe Ruth of the New York Yankees, who hit sixty home runs in 1927; Ty Cobb, the Detroit Tigers' manager, whose earlier record of 4,191 hits still inspired awe; prizefighters Jack Dempsey and Gene Tunney, whose two heavyweight fights drew thousands of fans and massive radio audiences. Ruth was a coarse, heavy-drinking womanizer; Cobb, an exceedingly foul-tempered if not borderline psychotic racist. Yet the alchemy of publicity transformed them into heroes with contrived nicknames: "the Sultan of Swat" (Ruth) and "the Georgia Peach" (Cobb).

This celebrity culture illuminates the stresses facing ordinary Americans in these years of social change. For young women uncertain about society's shifting expectations, the beauty pageants offered one ideal to which they could aspire. For men grappling with unsettling developments from feminism to Fordism, the exploits of sports heroes like Dempsey or Ruth could help restore damaged self-esteem.

Celebrity worship reached a crescendo in the response to **Charles Lindbergh,** a daredevil stunt pilot who flew solo across the Atlantic in his small single-engine plane, *The Spirit of St. Louis,* on May 20–21, 1927. A Minnesotan of Swedish ancestry, Lindbergh had entered a $25,000 prize competition offered by a New York hotel for the first nonstop New York to Paris flight. His success gripped the public's imagination. In New York, thousands turned out for a ticker-tape parade. Radio, newspapers, magazines, and movie newsreels offered saturation coverage.

An instant celebrity, Lindbergh became a kind of blank screen onto which people projected their hopes, fears, and ideologies. President Coolidge praised the flight as a triumph of American business and corporate technology. Many editorial writers, by contrast, saw Lindbergh as proof that despite standardization and mechanization, the individual still counted. Others praised this native-born midwesterner of Scandinavian roots as more authentically American than the recent immigrants crowding the cities.

Overall, the new mass media had mixed social effects. Certainly, they promoted cultural standardization and uniformity of thought. But mass magazines, radio, and movies also helped forge a national culture and introduced new viewpoints and ways of behaving. Implicitly they conveyed a potent message: a person's immediate surroundings need not limit his or her horizons. If the larger world they opened for ordinary Americans was often superficial or tawdry, it could also be exciting and liberating.

CULTURAL FERMENT AND CREATIVITY

American life in the 1920s involved more than politics, assembly lines, and celebrity worship. Young people savored the postwar moment when familiar pieties and traditional ways came under challenge. As writers, artists, and musicians contributed to the modernist spirit of cultural innovation, African-Americans created a cultural flowering known as the Harlem Renaissance.

The Jazz Age and the Postwar Crisis of Values The war and its disillusioned aftermath sharpened the cultural restlessness already evident before the war. The year 1918, wrote Randolph Bourne, marked "a sudden . . . stop at the end of an intellectual era." Poet Ezra Pound hammered the same point in 1920. America had gone to war, he wrote, to save "a botched civilization; . . . an old bitch gone in the teeth."

The postwar cultural ferment, summed up in the phrase "the Jazz Age," took many forms. Some young people—especially affluent college students—boisterously assailed conventional notions of proper behavior. Seizing the freedom offered by the automobile, they threw parties, drank bootleg liquor, flocked to jazz clubs, and danced the Charleston. Asked her favorite activity, a California college student replied, "I adore dancing; who doesn't?" Unaware of the risks, and urged by advertisers, many young women, especially college students and urban workers, defied prevailing taboos and took up cigarettes. For some, smoking became a feminist issue. As one woman college student put it, "[W]hy [should] men . . . be permitted to smoke while girls are expelled for doing it?"

Young people also discussed sex more freely than their elders had. Sigmund Freud, the Viennese physician who explored the sexual aspects of human psychology, enjoyed a popular vogue in a postwar climate that encouraged challenges to old taboos.

Despite much talk about sex and charges of rampant immorality, however, the 1920s' "sexual revolution" is hard to pin down. Premarital intercourse remained exceptional and widely disapproved. What *can* be documented are changing courtship patterns. "Courting" had once been a formal prelude to marriage. The 1920s brought the more casual practice of "dating," through which young people gained social confidence and a degree of sexual experience without necessarily contemplating marriage. Wrote novelist F. Scott Fitzgerald, "None of the Victorian mothers had any idea how casually their daughters were accustomed to be kissed." A Methodist bishop denounced new dances that brought "the bodies of men and women in unusual relation to each other."

The 1920s saw greater erotic freedom, but within bounds, as most young people drew a clear line between permissible and taboo behavior.

For women, these postwar changes in some ways proved liberating. Female sexuality was more openly acknowledged. Skirt lengths crept up; makeup became more acceptable; and the elaborate armor of petticoats and corsets fell away. The awesome matronly bosom mysteriously deflated as a more boyish figure became the fashion ideal.

The most enduring twenties stereotype is the flapper, the sophisticated, pleasure-mad young woman. The term originated with a magazine illustration of a fashionable young woman whose rubber rain boots were open and flapping. Although a journalistic creation, the flapper image played a significant cultural role. In the nineteenth century, the idealized woman on her moral pedestal had symbolized an elaborate complex of cultural ideals. The flapper, with her bobbed hair, defiant cigarette, lipstick, and short skirt, similarly epitomized youthful rejection of entrenched stereotypes.

But this image also objectified young women as decorative sexual objects. Many young women, while rejecting older taboos, now molded their appearance according to standards dictated by fashion magazines like *Vogue* and *Vanity Fair*. Advertisers and movies encouraged women to pursue a "glamorous" lifestyle by purchasing new fashions, cosmetics, silk stockings, and other consumer accessories. Further, the double standard, which held women to a stricter code of conduct, remained in force. Young men could boast of sexual exploits, but young women reputed to be "fast" risked damaged reputations. In some ways, in short, 1920s' popular culture worked against full gender equality nearly as effectively as had the older Victorian stereotypes.

Around 1922, according to F. Scott Fitzgerald, adults embraced the rebelliousness of the young. As middle-aged Americans "discovered that young liquor will take the place of young blood," he wrote, "the orgy began." But such sweeping cultural generalizations can mislead. During the years of Fitzgerald's alleged national orgy, the divorce rate remained constant, and many Americans adhered to traditional standards, rejecting alcohol and wild parties. Most farmers, industrial workers, blacks, Hispanics, and recent immigrants found economic survival more pressing than the latest fads and fashions.

The entire Jazz Age was partially a media and literary creation. Fitzgerald's romanticized novel about affluent postwar youth, *This Side of Paradise* (1920), spawned many imitators. With his movie-idol good looks, Fitzgerald not only wrote about the Jazz Age but lived it. But if the Jazz Age stereotype obscured the complexity of the 1920s, it did capture a part of the postwar scene, especially the brassy new mass culture and the hedonism and materialism of the well-to-do as they basked in the era's prosperity.

Alienated Writers Like Fitzgerald, many young writers found the cultural turbulence of the 1920s energizing. Rejecting the moralistic pieties of the old order, they also disliked the business pieties of the new. In *Main Street* (1920), the novelist Sinclair Lewis satirized the smugness and cultural barrenness of Gopher Prairie, a fictional midwestern town based on his native Sauk Centre, Minnesota. In *Babbitt* (1922), Lewis skewered a mythic larger city, Zenith, and the title character George F. Babbitt, a real-estate agent trapped in middle-class conformity.

H. L. Mencken, a journalist, editor, and critic, in 1924 launched the iconoclastic *American Mercury* magazine, an instant success with the decade's alienated intellectuals and young people. Mencken championed writers like Lewis and Theodore Dreiser while ridiculing politicians, small-town America, Protestant fundamentalism, and the middle-class "Booboisie." His essays on Harding, Coolidge, and Bryan remain classics of political satire. Asked why he stayed in America, Mencken replied, "Why do people visit zoos?"

For the novelist Ernest Hemingway, seriously wounded in 1918 while serving as a Red Cross volunteer in northern Italy, World War I was a watershed experience. In 1926, now an expatriate in Paris, Hemingway published *The Sun Also Rises,* portraying a group of American and English young people, variously damaged by the war, as they drift around Spain. His *A Farewell to Arms* (1929), loosely based on his own experiences, depicts the war's futility and politicians' empty rhetoric. In one passage, the narrator says,

> I was always embarrassed by the words sacred, glorious, and sacrifice and the expression in vain. We . . . had read them, on proclamations that were slapped up . . . over other proclamations, now for a long time, and I had seen nothing sacred, and the things that were glorious had no glory and the sacrifices were like the stockyards at Chicago if nothing was done with the meat except to bury it.

Although writers like Lewis and Hemingway deplored the inflated rhetoric of the war and the vulgarity of postwar culture, they remained American at heart, striving to create a more authentic national culture. Even F. Scott Fitzgerald, himself caught up in Jazz Age excesses, was fundamentally a moralist. Fitzgerald's masterpiece, *The Great Gatsby* (1925), portrayed not only the party-filled lives of the decade's moneyed class, but also their decadence, selfishness, and heedless disregard for the less fortunate.

Architects, Painters, and Musicians Confront Modern America   A burst of architectural activity transformed the urban skyline in the 1920s. By 1930, America's cities boasted 377 buildings over seventy stories tall. The skyscraper, proclaimed one writer, "epitomizes . . . American civilization." The cultural critic Lewis Mumford, by contrast, in magazine essays and his 1924 book *Sticks and Bones,* deplored the modern city with its skyscrapers and automobile-clogged streets. Mumford preferred smaller communities and regional cultures to the congested cities and mass culture of 1920s' America.

The decade's leading painters took America as their subject—either the real nation around them or an imagined one. While Thomas Hart Benton evoked a past of cowboys, pioneers, and riverboat gamblers, Edward Hopper portrayed faded towns and lonely cities of the present. Hopper's painting *Sunday* (1926), picturing a man slumped on the curb of an empty street of abandoned stores, conveyed both the bleakness and potential beauty of urban America.

The painter and photographer Charles Sheeler found inspiration in factories, including Henry Ford's plant near Detroit. The Italian immigrant Joseph Stella captured New York's excitement and energy in such paintings as *The Bridge* (1926), an abstract representation of the Brooklyn Bridge. Wisconsin's Georgia O'Keeffe, who moved to New York City in 1918, evoked the allure of the metropolis in her paintings of the later 1920s.

The creative ferment of the 1920s inspired composers as well. Ruth Crawford Seeger arranged American folksongs for the poet Carl Sandburg's *American Songbag* (1927). Carl Ruggles set a Walt Whitman poem to music in 1923. And Frederick Converse's ambitious 1927 tone poem about the automobile, "Flivver Ten Million," featured such episodes as "May Night by the Roadside" and "The Collision."

Of all the musical innovations, jazz best captured the modernist spirit. The Original Dixieland Jass Band—white musicians imitating the black jazz bands of New Orleans—had debuted in New York City in 1917, launching a vogue that spread by live performances, radio, and phonograph records. The white bandleader Paul Whiteman offered watered-down "jazz" versions of standard tunes, and white composers embraced jazz as well. Aaron Copland's *Music for Theatre* (1925) and George Gershwin's *Rhapsody in Blue* (1924) and *An American in Paris* (1928) revealed strong jazz influences.

Meanwhile, black musicians preserved authentic jazz and explored its potential. The 1920s recordings of trumpeter Louis Armstrong and his "Hot Five" and "Hot Seven" groups decisively influenced the future of jazz. While the composer and bandleader Duke Ellington performed to sellout audiences at Harlem's Cotton Club, Fletcher Henderson's band, featuring singer Ethel Waters and saxophonist Coleman Hawkins, held forth at New York's Roseland Ballroom and recorded for the Black Swan and Columbia labels. Meanwhile, the piano's jazz potential was demonstrated by Fats Waller, Ferdinand "Jelly Roll" Morton, and Earl Hines, who joined Louis Armstrong's band in 1927. Although much of 1920s' popular culture faded quickly, jazz endured.

The Harlem Renaissance

Jazz was only one of many black contributions to 1920s' American culture. The social changes of these years energized African-American cultural life, especially in New York City's Harlem. An elite white suburb before World War I, Harlem attracted many African-Americans during and after the war, and by 1930 most of New York's 327,000 blacks lived within its boundaries. This concentration, plus the proximity of Broadway theaters, record companies, book publishers, and the NAACP's national headquarters, all contributed to the Harlem Renaissance.

This cultural flowering took varied forms. The Mississippi-born black composer William Grant Still, moving to Harlem in 1922, produced many works, including *Afro American Symphony* (1931). The painter Aaron Douglas and the sculptor Augusta Savage worked in the visual arts. In 1921 Savage, a Florida native, arrived in Harlem, where she opened a studio and later an art school. The 1921 Broadway hit *Shuffle Along* launched a series of popular all-black musicals. Oscar Micheaux made films featuring black actors and black story lines. The multitalented Paul Robeson gave vocal concerts; made films; and appeared on Broadway in Eugene O'Neill's *The Emperor Jones* and other plays.

Among a host of writers, poet Langston Hughes drew upon southern black oral traditions in *The Weary Blues* (1926), and the Jamaican-born poet and novelist Claude McKay evoked Harlem's vibrant, sometimes sinister nightlife in *Home to Harlem* (1928). In *Cane* (1923), Jean Toomer used poetry, drama, and fictional vignettes to convey the world of the rural black South. Nella Larsen, from the Danish West Indies, told of a mulatto woman's struggle with her mixed ethnicity in the 1928 novel *Quicksand*. In *The New Negro* (1925), Alain Locke, a philosophy professor at Howard University, assembled essays, poems, short stories, and reproductions of artworks to convey Harlem's rich cultural life.

Jazz Pioneer Ferdinand (Jelly Roll) Morton *Born to Creole parents in New Orleans in 1890, Morton came to Chicago, where in 1926 his group, Jelly Roll Morton and His Red Hot Peppers, made some of the earliest jazz recordings for the Victor phonograph company.*

The white cultural establishment took notice. Book publishers and magazine editors courted black writers. Broadway producers mounted black shows. Whites crowded Harlem's jazz clubs. The 1929 Hollywood film *Hallelujah*, featuring an all-black cast, romanticized plantation life and dramatized the city's dangers. DuBose Heyward's 1925 novel *Porgy* (adapted for the stage by Heyward and his wife Dorothy) offered a sympathetic picture of Charleston's African-American community. George Gershwin's musical version, *Porgy and Bess*, premiered in 1935.

The Harlem Renaissance reached beyond America's borders. Jazz won a following in Europe. Langston Hughes and Claude McKay were admired in Africa, Latin America, and Europe. The dancer and singer Josephine Baker, after debuting in Harlem, moved to Paris in 1925, where her highly erotic performances created a sensation.

Along with white support came misunderstanding and attempts at control. Rebellious young whites romanticized Harlem nightlife, ignoring the community's overcrowding, poverty, and social problems. Some whites idealized the spiritual or "primitive" qualities of black culture. When Langston Hughes's poems confronted the gritty realities of black life in America, his wealthy white patron angrily withdrew her support. Wrote Hughes: "Concerning Negroes, she felt that they were America's great link with the primitive. . . . But unfortunately I did not feel the rhythms of the primitive surging through me. . . . I was not Africa. I was Chicago and Kansas City and Broadway and Harlem."

The hard times of the 1930s ended the Harlem Renaissance. Nevertheless, this burst of creativity stands as a memorable achievement. Future black writers, artists, musicians, and performers would owe a great debt to their predecessors of the 1920s.

A SOCIETY IN CONFLICT

The social changes of the 1920s produced a backlash, as a series of divisive episodes and social movements highlighted the era's tensions. While Congress restricted immigration, highly publicized court cases in Massachusetts and Tennessee underscored the nation's social and cultural divisions. Millions of whites embraced the racist bigotry and moralistic rhetoric of a revived Ku Klux Klan, and many newly urbanized African-Americans rallied to Marcus Garvey, a magnetic black leader with a riveting message of racial pride. Prohibition stirred further controversy in this conflict-ridden decade.

Immigration Restriction

Fed by wartime efforts to enforce patriotism, the old impulse to remake America into a nation of like-minded, culturally homogeneous people revived in the 1920s.

The **National Origins Act** of 1924, a revision of the immigration law, restricted annual immigration from any foreign country to 2 percent of the number of persons of that "national origin" in the United States in 1890. Since the great influx of southern and eastern Europeans had come after 1890, the intent of this provision was clear: to reduce the immigration of these nationalities. As Calvin Coolidge observed on signing the law, "America must be kept American."

In 1929, Congress changed the base year for determining "national origins" to 1920, but even under this formula, Poland's annual quota stood at a mere 6,524; Italy's at 5,802; and Hungary's, 869. This quota system, which survived to 1965, represented a strong counterattack by native-born Protestant America against the immigrant cities. Total immigration fell from 1.2 million in 1914 to 280,000 in 1929. The law excluded Asians and South Asians entirely.

Court rulings underscored the nativist message. In *Ozawa v. United States* (1922), the U.S. Supreme Court rejected a citizenship request by a Japanese-born student at the University of California. In 1923, the Supreme Court upheld a California law limiting the right of Japanese immigrants to own or lease farmland. That same year, the Supreme Court rejected an immigration application by a man from India who claimed that he was "Caucasian" and thus eligible for entry under the Nationality Act of 1790, which had limited naturalized citizenship to "free white persons." The 1790 law, the court ruled, referred only to "the type of man whom [the authors of the law] knew as white . . . [those] from the British Isles and northwestern Europe."

Needed Workers/ Unwelcome Aliens: Hispanic Newcomers

With all its restrictive provisions, the 1924 law placed no limits on immigration from the Western Hemisphere. Accordingly, immigration from Latin America (as well as from French Canada) soared. Poverty and political turmoil propelled thousands of Mexicans northward. By 1930, at least 2 million Mexican-born people lived in the United States, mostly in the Southwest. California's Mexican-American population surged from 90,000 to nearly 360,000 in the decade.

Many of these immigrants worked in low-paid migratory jobs in the region's large-scale agribusinesses. Mexican labor sustained California's citrus industry. Cooperatives such as the Southern California Fruit Growers Exchange (which marketed its fruit under the brand name "Sunkist") hired itinerant workers on a seasonal basis, provided substandard housing in isolated settlements the workers called *colonias,* and fought the migrants' attempts to form labor unions.

Not all Mexican immigrants were migratory workers; many settled into U.S. communities. Mexican-Americans in the Midwest worked not only in agriculture but also in the automobile, steel, and railroad industries. While still emotionally linked to "México Lindo" (Beautiful Mexico), they formed local support networks and cultural institutions. The Mexican-American community was divided, however, between recent arrivals and earlier immigrants who had become U.S. citizens. The strongest Mexican-American organization in the 1920s, the League of United Latin-American Citizens, ignored the migrant laborers of the Southwest.

Though deeply religious, Mexican-Americans found little support from the U.S. Catholic Church. Earlier, European Catholic immigrants had attended ethnic parishes and worshiped in their own languages, but church policy had changed by the 1920s. In parishes with non-Hispanic priests, Spanish-speaking Mexican newcomers encountered pressure to abandon their language and traditions.

In the larger society, Mexican immigrants faced ambivalent attitudes. Their labor was needed, but their presence disturbed nativists eager to preserve a "white" and Protestant nation. Would-be immigrants confronted strict literacy and means tests, and in 1929 Congress made illegal entry a criminal offense. The flow northward continued, however, as an estimated one hundred thousand Mexican newcomers arrived annually, legally and clandestinely, to fill the U.S. labor market's pressing demands.

Nativism, Antiradicalism, and the Sacco-Vanzetti Case The immigration-restriction movement reflected deep strains of ethnic, racial, and religious prejudice in 1920s' America. Anti-Semitic propaganda filled the *Dearborn Independent,* a weekly newspaper owned by Henry Ford. Distributed through Ford dealerships and mailed free to schools and libraries, the *Dearborn Independent* at its peak reached 600,000 readers. The anti-Semitic articles were reprinted in a series of pamphlets entitled *The International Jew.* Sued for defamation by a California Jewish attorney, Ford in 1927 issued an evasive apology (drafted by a prominent Jewish leader in New York) blaming subordinates.

Nativist, antiradical prejudices emerged starkly in the **Sacco-Vanzetti Case,** a Massachusetts murder case that began in April 1920, when robbers shot and killed the paymaster and guard of a shoe factory in South Braintree, Massachusetts, and stole two cash boxes. In 1921, a jury found two Italian immigrants, Nicola Sacco and Bartolomeo Vanzetti, guilty of the crime. After many appeals and a review by a commission of notable citizens, they were electrocuted on August 23, 1927.

These bare facts hardly convey the passions the case aroused. Sacco and Vanzetti were anarchists, and the prosecution harped on their radicalism. The judge barely concealed his hostility to the pair, whom he privately called "those anarchist bastards." While many conservatives supported the death sentence, liberals and socialists rallied to their cause. As the two went to the chair, John Dos Passos wrote a bitter poem that ended:

All right you have won you will kill the brave men our friends tonight . . . all right we are two nations.

Later research on Boston's anarchist community and ballistics tests on Sacco's gun pointed to their guilt. But the prejudices that tainted the trial remain indisputable, as does the case's symbolic importance in exposing the deep fault lines in 1920s' American society.

Fundamentalism and the Scopes Trial   Meanwhile, an equally celebrated case in Tennessee highlighted another front in the cultural wars of the 1920s: the growing prestige of science. While scientists were "individually powerless," wrote the Harvard philosopher Alfred North Whitehead in *Science and the Modern World* (1925), they were "ultimately the rulers of the world." While many Americans welcomed the advance of science, some religious believers found it threatening. Their fears had deepened as scholars had subjected the Bible to critical scrutiny, psychologists and sociologists had studied supernatural belief systems as human social constructs and expressions of emotional needs, and biologists had embraced Charles Darwin's naturalistic explanation for the variety of life forms on Earth advanced in *Origin of Species* (1859).

While liberal Protestants had generally accepted the findings of science, evangelical believers had resisted. This gave rise to a movement called **Fundamentalism,** after *The Fundamentals,* a series of essays published in 1909–1914. Fundamentalists insisted on the Bible's literal truth, including the Genesis account of Creation.

In the early 1920s, fundamentalists targeted Darwin's theory of evolution as a threat to their faith. Many states considered legislation to bar public schools from teaching evolution, and several southern states enacted such laws. Texas governor Miriam "Ma" Ferguson personally censored textbooks that discussed evolution. "I am a Christian mother," she declared, "and I am not going to let that kind of rot go into Texas textbooks." The former Democratic presidential candidate and secretary of state William Jennings Bryan, still widely admired in the American heartland, endorsed the antievolution cause.

When Tennessee's legislature barred the teaching of evolution in the state's public schools in 1925, the American Civil Liberties Union (ACLU) offered to defend any teacher willing to challenge this law. A high-school teacher in Dayton, Tennessee, John T. Scopes, encouraged by local businessmen eager to promote their town, accepted the offer. Scopes summarized Darwin's theory to a science class and was arrested. Famed criminal lawyer Clarence Darrow headed the defense, while Bryan assisted the prosecution. Journalists poured into Dayton; a Chicago radio station broadcast the proceedings live; and the **Scopes Trial** became a media sensation.

Cross-examined by Darrow, Bryan embraced the fundamentalist view of the Bible and dismissed evolutionary theory. Although the jury found Scopes guilty (in a decision later reversed on a technicality), the trial exposed Fundamentalism to ridicule. When Bryan died of a heart attack soon after, H. L. Mencken wrote a column mercilessly deriding him and his fundamentalist admirers.

The Scopes Trial exposed broader tensions in a rapidly changing society. In his testimony, Bryan shrewdly appealed to citizens fearful of cultural forces outside their control, centered in distant cities. Let parents and local communities decide what children are taught, he pled, evoking memories of his earlier populist campaigns defending the common folk against the rich and powerful. Despite the setback in Dayton, Fundamentalism remained alive and well. Mainstream Protestant denominations grew more liberal, but many local congregations, radio preachers, Bible schools, and new conservative denominations upheld the traditional faith. So, too, did the flamboyant evangelist Billy Sunday, who remained popular in the 1920s. Southern and western states continued to pass antievolution laws, and textbook publishers deleted or modified their treatment of evolution to appease local school boards.

In Los Angeles, Aimee Semple McPherson, anticipating later TV evangelists, filled her cavernous Angelus Temple and reached thousands more by radio. The charismatic McPherson entranced audiences with theatrical sermons. She once used a gigantic electric scoreboard to illustrate the triumph of good over evil. Her followers, mainly transplanted midwesterners, embraced her fundamentalist theology while enjoying her mass-entertainment techniques. At her death in 1944, her International Church of the Foursquare Gospel had more than six hundred branches in the United States and abroad.

The Ku Klux Klan

The tensions gnawing at American society of the 1920s also emerged in a resurrected Ku Klux Klan (KKK). The original Klan of the post–Civil War South had faded by the 1870s (see Chapter 16), but in 1915 hooded men who had gathered at Stone Mountain, Georgia, revived it. D. W. Griffith's glorification of the Klan in his 1915 movie *The Birth of a Nation* provided further inspiration.

The movement remained obscure until 1920, when two Atlanta entrepreneurs organized a national membership drive to exploit the appeal of the Klan's ritual and its nativist, white-supremacist ideology. Their wildly successful scheme involved a ten-

The Ku Klux Klan in Washington, D.C. *In a brazen display of power, the Ku Klux Klan organized a march in the nation's capital in 1926. By this time, the Klan was already in decline.*

dollar membership fee divided among the salesman (called the Kleagle), the local sales manager (King Kleagle), the district sales manager (Grand Goblin), the state leader (Grand Dragon), and the national leader (Imperial Wizard)—with a rake-off to themselves. The sale of Klan robes, masks, horse blankets, and the bottled Chattahoochee River water used in initiation rites added to the take.

Under the umbrella term "100 percent Americanism," the Klan demonized not only African-Americans but also Catholics, Jews, and aliens. Some Klan groups targeted whites suspected of sexual immorality or prohibition-law violations. Membership estimates for the KKK and its women's auxiliary in the early 1920s range as high as 5 million. From its southern base, the Klan spread through the Midwest and across the country from Long Island to the West Coast. The white working class and lower middle class in cities with native-born Protestant majorities proved especially receptive. In 1922 Imperial Wizard Hiram Wesley Evans admitted the Klan's image as a haven of "hicks" and "rubes" and urged college graduates to support the great cause.

Although corrupt at the top and basically a money-making scam, the Klan was not a haven for criminals or fanatics. Observers commented on members' ordinariness. (Evans, a Texas dentist, called himself "the most average man in America.") The Klan's promise to restore the nation's lost purity—racial, ethnic, religious, and moral— appealed to many economically marginal old-stock Protestants disoriented by social change. For some small businessmen threatened by the new corporate order, the Klan's litany of menace offered a vocabulary for articulating economic anxieties. Some citizens upset by changing sexual mores welcomed the Klan's defense of "the purity of white womanhood." Klan membership, in short, gave a sense of empowerment to people who felt adrift in a new social order of great corporations; a raucous mass culture; changing behavior; and immigrant-filled cities. The rituals, parades, and cross burnings added drama and a sense of camaraderie to lonely, unfulfilling lives.

But if individual Klan members seemed more needy than sinister, the Klan's menace as a mass movement was real. Some KKK groups employed threats, beatings, and lynching in their quest to purify America. In several states, the Klan won political power. Oklahoma's Klan-controlled legislature impeached and removed an anti-Klan governor. In Oregon, the Klan elected a governor and pushed through legislation requiring all children to attend public school, an attempt to destroy the state's Catholic schools.

The Klan collapsed with shocking suddenness. In March 1925, Indiana's Grand Dragon, David Stephenson, brutally raped his young secretary. When she swallowed poison, Stephenson panicked and refused to call a physician. The woman died several weeks later, and Stephenson went to prison, where he revealed sordid details of political corruption in Indiana. Its moral pretensions in shreds, the KKK faded. It did not disappear, however, and when African-Americans demanded equal rights in the 1950s, the Klan again reared its head.

The Garvey Movement

Among African-Americans who had fled southern rural poverty and racism only to experience discrimination and racism in the urban North, the decade's social strains produced a different kind of mass movement, led by the spellbinding **Marcus Garvey** and his Universal Negro Improvement Association (UNIA). Born in Jamaica in 1887, the son of a stonemason, Garvey founded UNIA in 1914 and two years later moved to Harlem, which became the movement's headquarters. In a white-dominated society, Garvey glorified all things black. Urging black economic solidarity and relying on capitalist enterprise as the lever of racial advance, he founded UNIA grocery stores and other businesses. He summoned blacks to return to "Motherland Africa" and established the Black Star Steamship Line to help them get there.

An estimated eighty thousand blacks joined UNIA, and thousands more felt the lure of Garvey's oratory, the excitement of UNIA parades and uniforms, and the appeal of the vision of economic self-sufficiency and a glorious future in Africa. Garvey's popularity unsettled black church leaders and the NAACP's middle-class leaders, who saw the African-American future in America, not in Africa, and advocated racial integration rather than separation. W. E. B. Du Bois was among Garvey's sharpest critics.

The movement also highlighted social tensions in Harlem, where two streams of the African diaspora, one from the Caribbean, the other from the American South, converged in the 1920s. The resulting economic and political rivalry shaped attitudes toward the UNIA, since Garvey was Jamaican, and Caribbean immigrants figured prominently in UNIA's leadership.

In 1923, a federal court convicted Garvey of fraud in the management of his Black Star Steamship Line. In 1927, after two years' imprisonment, he was deported to Jamaica, and the UNIA collapsed. But this first mass movement in black America had revealed both the social aspirations and the activist potential of African-Americans in the urban North. "In a world where black is despised," commented an African-American newspaper after Garvey's fall, "he taught his followers that black is beautiful."

The NAACP, meanwhile, remained active even in a reactionary decade with racism rampant. In some 300 branches nationwide, members kept the civil-rights cause alive and patiently laid the groundwork for legal challenges to segregation.

Prohibition: Cultures in Conflict   A bitter controversy over alcohol further exposed the fissures in American society. As noted in Chapter 21, the Progressive Era **prohibition** campaign was both a legitimate effort to address social problems associated with alcohol abuse and a weapon in the struggle of native-born Americans to control the immigrant cities. These tensions persisted in the 1920s.

When the Eighteenth Amendment took effect in 1920, prohibitionists rejoiced. Billy Sunday proclaimed,

> The reign of tears is over. The slums will soon be only a memory. We will turn our prisons into factories and our jails into storehouses and corncribs. Men will walk upright now. Women will smile and children will laugh.

Sunday's dream seemed attainable as saloons closed, liquor advertising vanished, and arrests for drunkenness declined. In 1921, alcohol consumption stood at about one-third the prewar level. Yet prohibition gradually lost support, and in 1933 it ended.

What went wrong? Essentially, prohibition's failure illustrates the difficulty in an open society of enforcing a widely opposed law. The Volstead Act, the 1919 prohibition law, was underfunded and weakly enforced, especially in antiprohibition areas. New York, for example, repealed its prohibition-enforcement law as early as 1923. Would-be drinkers grew bolder as enforcement faltered. For rebellious youths, alcohol's illegality increased its appeal. Challenging the prohibition law, declared one college student, represented "the natural reaction of youth to rules and regulations."

Rum-runners smuggled liquor from Canada and the West Indies, and every city harbored speakeasies where customers could buy drinks. People concocted home brew, shady entrepreneurs sold flavored industrial-grade alcohol, and sacramental wine sales soared. By 1929, alcohol consumption reached about 70 percent of prewar levels.

Organized crime helped circumvent the law. Chicago, where rival gangs battled to control the liquor business, witnessed 550 gangland killings in the 1920s. Speakeasies controlled by Chicago gangster Al Capone generated annual profits of $60 million. Although not typical, Chicago's crime wave underscored prohibition's failure. A reform designed to improve the nation's morality was turning citizens into lawbreakers and mobsters into celebrities.

Thus prohibition, too, became a battleground in the decade's cultural wars. The "drys"—usually native-born Protestants—praised it. The "wets"—liberals, Jazz Age rebels, big-city immigrants—condemned it as moralistic meddling. One college student newspaper suggested a campus distillery as the senior class gift, "with the proceeds going to the college."

Prohibition influenced the 1928 presidential campaign. While Democratic candidate Al Smith advocated repeal of the Eighteenth Amendment, Republican Herbert Hoover praised it as "a great social and economic experiment, noble in motive and far-reaching in purpose." Once elected, Hoover characteristically appointed a study commission. In a confusing 1931 report, the commission admitted prohibition's failure, but urged its retention. A journalist parodied the findings:

Prohibition is an awful flop.
  We like it.
It can't stop what it's meant to stop.
  We like it.
It's left a trail of graft and slime,
It's filled our land with vice and crime,
It don't prohibit worth a dime,
  Nevertheless we're for it.

When the Eighteenth Amendment was finally repealed in 1933, prohibition seemed little more than a relic of another age.

HOOVER AT THE HELM

Herbert Hoover, elected president in 1928, appeared well fitted to sustain the nation's prosperity. No standpat conservative like Harding and Coolidge, his social and political philosophy reflected his engineering background. In some ways, he seemed the ideal president for the new technological age.

The Election of 1928

A Hollywood casting agent could not have chosen two individuals who better personified America's divisions than the 1928 presidential candidates. New York governor Al Smith easily won the Democratic nomination. The party's urban-immigrant wing had gained strength since the deadlocked 1924 convention. A Catholic and a wet, Smith exuded the flavor of immigrant New York. Originally a machine politician and basically conservative, he had impressed reformers by backing social-welfare measures. His inner circle

Map 23.1 The Election of 1928

Although Hoover won every state but Massachusetts and six Deep South states, Smith's 1928 vote in the Midwestern farm belt and the nation's largest cities showed significant gains over 1924.

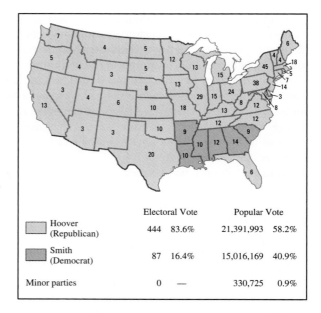

		Electoral Vote		Popular Vote	
Hoover (Republican)		444	83.6%	21,391,993	58.2%
Smith (Democrat)		87	16.4%	15,016,169	40.9%
Minor parties		0	—	330,725	0.9%

included several reform-minded women, notably Frances Perkins, the head of the state industrial board, and Belle Moskowitz, a key adviser.

Herbert Hoover won the Republican nomination after Calvin Coolidge chose not to run. Some conservative party leaders mistrusted the brilliant but aloof Hoover, who had never held elective office and had spent much of his adult life abroad. Born in Iowa and orphaned at an early age, Hoover had put himself through Stanford University and made a fortune as a mining engineer in China and Australia. His service as wartime food administrator had won him a place as secretary of commerce in the Harding and Coolidge cabinets.

Hoover disdained conventional campaigning. Instead, he issued "tons of reports on dull subjects" (in H. L. Mencken's jaundiced view) and read radio speeches in a droning monotone that obscured the originality of some of his ideas. Smith, by contrast, campaigned spiritedly across the nation. This may actually have hurt him, however, because his big-city wisecracking and New York accent put off many voters.

How Smith's Catholicism affected his candidacy remains debatable. Hoover urged tolerance, and Smith denied any conflict between his faith and the duties of the presidency, but anti-Catholic prejudice played a role. Rumors circulated that Smith would follow the Vatican's orders if he won. (A post-election joke had Smith sending the pope a one-word telegram, "Unpack.") But Smith's religion attracted Catholic voters, and in any event the decisive issue was probably not popery but prosperity. Republican orators pointed to the booming economy and warned of "soup kitchens instead of busy factories" if Smith won. In his nomination-acceptance speech, Hoover grandly predicted "the final triumph over poverty."

Hoover won in a landslide, grabbing 58 percent of the vote and even making deep inroads in the Democratic "solid South." Socialist Norman Thomas received only

Presidential Voting by Selected Ethnic Groups in Chicago, 1924, 1928, and 1932

	Percent Democratic		
	1924	1928	1932
Blacks	10	23	21
Czechoslovaks	40	73	83
Germans	14	58	69
Italians	31	63	64
Jews	19	60	77
Lithuanians	48	77	84
Poles	35	71	80
Swedes	15	34	51
Yugoslavs	20	54	67

Source: John M. Allswang, *A House for All Peoples: Ethnic Politics in Chicago, 1890–1936* (Lexington: University Press of Kentucky, 1971).

267,000 votes. However, the outcome also hinted at an emerging political realignment. Smith did well in the rural Midwest, where hard-pressed farmers, angered by Coolidge's insensitivity to their plight, abandoned their normal Republican allegiance. In northern cities, Catholic and Jewish wards voted heavily Democratic. Smith carried the nation's twelve largest cities, all of which had gone Republican in 1924. Should prosperity falter, these portents suggested, the Republican Party faced trouble.

Herbert Hoover's Social Thought   Americans looked hopefully to their new president, whom admirers dubbed "the Great Engineer." Although a self-made man himself, he did not uncritically praise big business. His Quakerism, humanitarian activities, engineering experience, and Republican loyalties combined to produce a unique social outlook, summed up in his 1922 book *American Individualism.*

Like Theodore Roosevelt (whom he had supported in 1912), Hoover opposed cut-throat capitalist competition. Rational economic development, he insisted, demanded corporate cooperation in marketing, wage policy, raw-material allocation, and product standardization. The economy, in short, should operate like an efficient machine. Believing that businesses must behave ethically, Hoover welcomed the growth of welfare capitalism. But above all, he advocated voluntarism. The smoothly functioning, socially responsible economic order he envisioned must arise from the voluntary action of capitalist leaders, not government coercion or labor-management power struggles.

Putting into practice his philosophy of corporate cooperation, Hoover as secretary of commerce had convened more than 250 conferences where business leaders discussed such issues as job creation and labor-management relations. He urged higher wages to increase consumer purchasing power, and in 1923 he persuaded the steel industry to adopt an eight-hour workday as an efficiency measure. During the 1927 Mississippi River floods, as President Coolidge remained in Washington, Hoover had rushed to the stricken area to mobilize private relief efforts.

A conservationist and environmentalist, Hoover as secretary of commerce had pushed for flood control, planned use of water resources, and protection of rivers and lakes. Pollution, he warned in 1924, "is destroying . . . our fisheries . . . [and] beaches and endangering our harbors." In 1922, he negotiated a compact among Western states for a division of Colorado River water. This agreement, implemented in 1929, opened the way for a dam on the Colorado to provide hydroelectric power and water for irrigation, and control spring flooding from the Rocky Mountain snowmelt. Construction began on Hoover Dam in 1930. (In an act of petty politics, Democrats changed the name to Boulder Dam in 1933, but Congress restored the original name in 1947.)

Hoover's ideology had limitations. He showed more enthusiasm for cooperation among capitalists than among consumers or workers. His belief that capitalists would behave ethically and voluntarily embrace enlightened labor policies overestimated the role of altruism in business decision making. And his opposition to government economic intervention brought him grief when such intervention became urgently necessary.

Hoover's presidency began promisingly. He set up a Council on Recent Social Trends and other commissions to gather data to guide policy makers. Responding to the farm problem, he persuaded Congress to create a Federal Farm Board to promote cooperative marketing. This, he hoped, would raise farm prices while preserving the voluntarist principle. But while Hoover applied his social philosophy to the business of government, a crisis was approaching that would overwhelm and ultimately destroy his presidency.

CONCLUSION

Reacting against Woodrow Wilson's exalted wartime idealism, America pursued a nationalistic foreign policy in the 1920s. But the myth of U.S. isolationism is belied by expanding foreign investment and corporate expansion in Europe and Latin America.

At home, the twenties brought new consumer products, new modes of mass production, new marketing and advertising strategies, and new entertainment media. As the economy exuded a glow of prosperity, Americans grappled with massive technological and social changes. Like jet-lagged world travelers, people struggled to adapt to the new order. Skyscrapers, radio, the automobile, the movies, and electrical appliances—all familiar today—were exciting novelties in 1920s America.

While the Harding and Coolidge administrations celebrated the new corporate, consumerist culture and pursued probusiness policies, society seethed in ferment. Ironically, the same stresses that sparked angry social conflict also stimulated cultural creativity. The young people adapting to Jazz Age fashions and behavior standards; the Mexican immigrants seeking a better life in the United States; the native-born advocates of immigration restriction, prohibition, and Fundamentalism; the whites who joined the Klan; the blacks who rallied to Marcus Garvey; the artists and writers of the Harlem Renaissance; the young musicians, painters, and novelists who revitalized American culture were all, in their different ways, responding to the promise and uncertainties of modernity.

24

The Great Depression and the New Deal, 1929–1939

CRASH AND DEPRESSION, 1929–1932

The prosperity of the 1920s came to a jolting end in October 1929 with the collapse of the stock market. The Wall Street crash, and the economic problems that underlay it, launched a depression that hit every household. President Hoover struggled with the crisis, but his commitment to private initiative and his horror of government coercion limited his effectiveness. In November 1932 voters turned to the Democratic Party and its new leader, Franklin Roosevelt. This key election set the stage for a vast expansion in the federal government's role in addressing social and economic issues.

Black Thursday and the Onset of the Depression   Stock prices had risen steadily through much of the 1920s, but 1928–1929 brought a frenzied upsurge as speculators plunged into the market. In 1925 the market value of all stocks had stood at about $27 billion; by October 1929, it hit $87 billion. With stockbrokers lending buyers up to 75 percent of a stock's cost, credit or "margin" buying spread. The income-tax cuts promoted by Treasury Secretary Andrew Mellon had increased the flow of money into the market. Upbeat statements also fed the speculative boom. In March 1929, former president Calvin Coolidge declared stocks "cheap at current prices." "Investment trusts," akin to today's mutual funds, but totally unregulated, lured novices into the market. The construction industry declined sharply in 1928–1929, signaling a glut in the housing market and a decline in business expansion.

In 1928, and again in September 1929, the Federal Reserve Board tried to dampen speculation by raising the interest rate on Federal Reserve notes. Early in 1929, the Fed warned member banks to tighten their lending policies. But with speculators paying up to 20 percent interest to buy more stock, lending institutions continued to loan money freely—an act akin to dumping gasoline on a raging fire.

The collapse came on October 24, 1929—"Black Thursday." As prices fell, some stocks found no buyers at all: they had become worthless. On Tuesday, October 29, a record 16 million stocks changed hands. In the ensuing weeks, feeble upswings alternated with further plunges.

President Hoover, in the first of many optimistic statements, pronounced the economy "sound and prosperous." Indeed, a weak upswing early in 1930 suggested that the worst might be over. Instead, the economy went into a long tailspin, producing a full-scale depression.

What were the underlying causes of this depression? Many economists focus on structural problems that made 1920s' prosperity so unstable. The agricultural sector remained depressed throughout the decade. In the industrial sector, wage increases did not keep pace with factory output, and this reduced consumer purchasing power. At the same time, assembly-line methods encouraged overproduction. By summer 1929, not only housing, but also the automobile, textile, tire, and other durable-goods industries were seriously overextended. Further, important sectors of industry—including railroads, steel, textiles, and mining—lagged technologically in the 1930s and could not attract the investment needed to stimulate recovery.

Some economists, called monetarists, also focus on the Federal Reserve System's tight-money policies in the early 1930s. This policy, they argue, strangled any hope of economic recovery by reducing the amount of money available to businesses for investment and growth.

All analysts link the U.S. depression to a global economic crisis. European economies, struggling with war-debt payments and a severe trade imbalance with the United States, collapsed in 1931, dealing a heavy blow to U.S. exports.

The worsening depression devastated the U.S. economy. From 1929 to 1932, the gross national product dropped from $104 billion to $59 billion. Farm prices, already low, fell by nearly 60 percent. By early 1933 more than fifty-five hundred banks had closed, and unemployment stood at 25 percent, or nearly 13 million workers. In some cities the jobless rate surged far higher. In Toledo in 1932, for example, it stood at 80 percent. Many who still had jobs faced cuts in pay and hours.

Hoover's Response Historically, Americans had viewed depressions as acts of nature: little could be done other than ride out the storm. President Hoover, with his activist impulses, disagreed. Drawing upon his experience as U.S. food administrator in World War I and as secretary of commerce, Hoover initially responded boldly. But his belief in localism and in private initiative limited his options.

Hoover urged business leaders to maintain wages and employment. Viewing unemployment as a local issue, he advised city and state officials to create public-works projects. In October 1930, he set up an Emergency Committee for Employment to coordinate voluntary relief efforts. In 1931, he persuaded the nation's largest banks to set up a private lending agency to help hard-pressed smaller banks make business loans.

Despite these initiatives, public opinion turned against Hoover as the crisis worsened. In the 1930 midterm election, the Republicans lost the House of Representatives and gave up eight Senate seats. In 1931, dreading a budget deficit, Hoover called for a tax increase, further angering hard-pressed Americans. That same year, despite their

CHRONOLOGY, 1929–1939

1929 • Stock market crash; onset of depression.

1932 • Reconstruction Finance Corporation.
Veterans' bonus march.
Franklin D. Roosevelt elected president.

1933 • Repeal of Eighteenth Amendment.
Civilian Conservation Corps (CCC).
Federal Emergency Relief Act (FERA).
Tennessee Valley Authority (TVA).
Agricultural Adjustment Administration (AAA).
National Recovery Administration (NRA).
Public Works Administration (PWA).

1934 • Securities and Exchange Commission (SEC).
Taylor Grazing Act.
Indian Reorganization Act.

1934–1936 • Strikes by Mexican-American agricultural workers in the West.

1935 • Supreme Court declares NIRA unconstitutional.
Works Progress Administration (WPA).
Resettlement Administration.
National Labor Relations Act (Wagner Act).
Social Security Act.
NAACP campaign for federal antilynching law.
Huey Long assassinated.
Revenue Act raises taxes on corporations and the wealthy.
Supreme Court reverses conviction of the "Scottsboro Boys."
Harlem riot.

1935–1939 • Era of the Popular Front.

1936 • Supreme Court declares AAA unconstitutional.
Roosevelt wins landslide reelection victory.
Autoworkers' sit-down strike against General Motors begins (December).

1937 • Roosevelt's "court-packing" plan defeated.
Farm Security Administration.
GM, U.S. Steel, and Chrysler sign union contracts.

1937–1938 • The "Roosevelt recession."

1938 • Fair Labor Standards Act.
Republicans gain heavily in midterm elections.
Congress of Industrial Organizations (CIO) formed.
Carnegie Hall concert by Benny Goodman Orchestra.

1939 • Hatch Act.
Marian Anderson concert at Lincoln Memorial.
John Steinbeck, *The Grapes of Wrath.*
1940 • Ernest Hemingway, *For Whom the Bell Tolls.*

pledges, U.S. Steel, General Motors, and other big corporations slashed wages. The crisis quickly swamped private charities and local welfare agencies. Philadelphia, with more than three hundred thousand jobless by 1932, cut weekly relief payments to $4.23 per family and then stopped them entirely.

In 1932, a presidential election year, Hoover swallowed his principles and took a bold step. In January, at Hoover's recommendation, Congress set up a new agency, the **Reconstruction Finance Corporation** (RFC), to make loans to banks and other lending institutions. By July, the RFC had pumped $1.2 billion into the economy. Congress also authorized the RFC to grant $2 billion to state and local governments for job-creating public-works programs, and allocated $750 million for loans to struggling businesses.

Hoover supported these measures reluctantly, warning that they could open the door to "socialism and collectivism." Blaming global forces for the depression, he argued that only international measures would help. His call for a moratorium on war-debt and reparations payments by European nations made sense, but seemed irrelevant to the plight of ordinary Americans.

As Hoover endlessly urged self-help and local initiative and saw recovery "just around the corner," his unpopularity deepened. When he appointed a new press secretary disliked by journalists, one reporter called it the first instance of a rat boarding a sinking ship. An administration launched so hopefully in 1929 was ending in bitterness and failure.

Mounting
Discontent
and Protest

An ominous mood spread as hordes of the jobless waited in breadlines, slept on park benches, trudged the streets, and rode freight trains seeking work. Americans reared on the ethic of hard work and self-reliance experienced chronic unemployment as a shattering emotional blow. The families of the jobless suffered as well.

Newspapers humanized the crisis. The *New York Times* described "Hoover Valley"—a section of Central Park where jobless men lived in boxes and packing crates. In winter they wrapped themselves in layers of newspapers they called Hoover blankets. The suicide rate soared. In Youngstown, Ohio, a jobless father of ten whose family faced eviction jumped to his death from a bridge. Violence threatened in some cities when landlords evicted people unable to pay their rent.

Hard times battered the nation's farms. Many underwent mortgage foreclosures or forced sales because of tax delinquency, with Iowa and the Dakotas especially hard hit. At some forced farm auctions, neighbors bought the foreclosed farm for a trivial sum, and returned it to the evicted family.

In 1931, midwestern farmers organized a boycott movement called the Farmers' Holiday Association to force prices up by withholding grain and livestock from the market. Dairy farmers angered by low prices dumped milk in Iowa and Wisconsin.

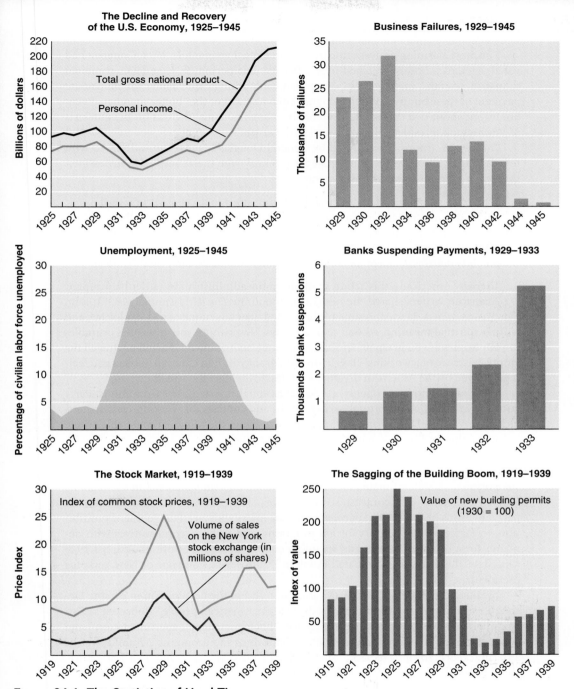

FIGURE 24.1 The Statistics of Hard Times

Figures on the gross national product, personal income, unemployment, the stock market, and business failures all show the Depression's shattering impact, with gradual and uneven improvement as the 1930s wore on. *Sources:* C. D. Bremmer, *American Bank Failures* (New York: Columbia University Press, 1935), 42; Thomas C. Cochran, *The Great Depression and World War II: 1929–1945* (Glenview, Ill. : Scott, Foresman, 1968); *Historical Statistics of the United States, Colonial Times to 1970* (Washington, D.C.: U.S. Government Printing Office, 1975).

The most alarming protest came from World War I veterans. In 1924, Congress had voted veterans a bonus stretched over a twenty-year period. In June 1932, some ten thousand veterans, many jobless, descended on Washington to lobby for immediate payment of these bonuses. When Congress refused, most of the "bonus marchers" went home, but about two thousand stayed on, building makeshift shelters on the outskirts of Washington. President Hoover called in the army.

On July 28, troops commanded by General Douglas MacArthur and armed with tear gas, tanks, and machine guns drove the veterans from their camp and burned their shelters. A journalist described the scene:

[The veterans and their families] wandered from street to street or sat in ragged groups, the men exhausted, the women with wet handkerchiefs laid over their smarting eyes, the children waking from sleep to cough and whimper from the tear gas in their lungs. . . . Their shanties and tents had been burned, their personal property destroyed, except for the few belongings they could carry on their backs.

To many Americans, this action symbolized the administration's utter bankruptcy. American writers shared the despairing mood. In *The 42nd Parallel* (1930), John Dos Passos drew a dark panorama of the United States as money-mad, exploitive, and lacking spiritual meaning. As one character says, "Everything you've wanted crumbles in your fingers as you grasp it." In *Young Lonigan* (1932), James T. Farrell portrayed the empty existence of a working-class Irish-immigrant youth in Chicago. Jobless and feeling betrayed by the American dream, he aimlessly wanders the streets.

Some radical novelists openly attacked the capitalist system. The Communist Party encouraged such fiction through writers' clubs and contests for working-class writers. Jack Conroy's *The Disinherited* (1933) dealt with life in the Missouri coal fields, where his own father and brother had died in a mine disaster.

The Election of 1932

Gloom pervaded the 1932 Republican convention that renominated Hoover. The Democrats who gathered in Chicago, by contrast, scented victory. Their platform, crafted to erase the party divisions of the 1920s, appealed to urban voters with a call for repeal of prohibition, to farmers with support for aid programs, and to fiscal conservatives with demands for a balanced budget and spending cuts. Rejecting Al Smith, the party's 1928 candidate, the delegates nominated Franklin D. Roosevelt, governor of New York, for president.

Breaking precedent, FDR flew to Chicago to accept the nomination in person. Despite a rousing speech pledging "a new deal for the American people," Roosevelt's campaign offered few specifics. He called for "bold persistent experimentation" and compassion for "the forgotten man at the bottom of the economic pyramid," yet he also attacked Hoover's "reckless" spending and insisted that "only as a last resort" should Washington play a larger depression-fighting role.

But Roosevelt exuded confidence, and above all he was not Hoover. On November 8, FDR and his running mate, Texas congressman John Nance Garner, received nearly 23 million votes, compared with fewer than 16 million for Hoover. Roosevelt carried every state but Pennsylvania, Connecticut, Vermont, New Hampshire, and Maine. Both houses of Congress went heavily Democratic. How would Roosevelt use this impressive mandate? The nation waited.

THE NEW DEAL TAKES SHAPE, 1933–1935

The Roosevelt years began in a whirl of activity. An array of emergency measures proposed by Roosevelt and passed by Congress reflected three basic goals: industrial recovery through business-government cooperation and pump-priming federal spending; agricultural recovery through crop reduction; and short-term emergency relief distributed through state and local agencies when possible, but directly by the federal government if necessary. Taken together, these programs conveyed the sense of an activist government addressing urgent national problems. Hovering over the bustle loomed a confident Franklin Roosevelt, cigarette holder jauntily tilted upward, a symbol of hope. By 1935, however, the New Deal faced problems, and opposition was building.

Roosevelt and His Circle   FDR's inaugural address dedicated his administration to helping a people in crisis. "The only thing we have to fear," he intoned, "is fear itself." In an outpouring of support, half a million letters deluged the White House.

Roosevelt seemed an unlikely popular hero. Like his distant cousin Theodore, FDR was of the social elite, with merchants and landowners among his Dutch-immigrant ancestors. He attended Harvard College and Columbia Law School. But as a state senator and governor of New York, he had backed the Democratic Party's urban-immigrant wing. When the depression hit, he had introduced innovative measures in New York, including unemployment insurance and a public-works program. Intent on promoting recovery while preserving capitalism and democracy, Roosevelt encouraged competing proposals, compromised (or papered over) differences, and then backed the measures he sensed could be sold to Congress and the public.

Roosevelt brought to Washington a circle of advisers nicknamed the brain trust. It included Columbia University professor Rexford G. Tugwell and lawyer Adolph A. Berle. Shaped by the progressive reform tradition, Tugwell and Berle advocated federal economic planning and corporate regulation. But no single ideology or set of advisers controlled the New Deal, for FDR sought a broad range of opinions.

Eleanor Roosevelt played a key role. A niece of Theodore Roosevelt, she had been active in settlement-house work and in Florence Kelley's National Consumers' League. Through her, FDR met reformers, social workers, and advocates of minority rights. Recalled Rexford Tugwell: "No one who ever saw Eleanor Roosevelt sit down facing her husband, and holding his eyes firmly, say to him 'Franklin, I think you should . . . ,' or 'Franklin, surely you will not . . .' will ever forget the experience." Mrs. Roosevelt traveled ceaselessly and served as an astute observer for her wheelchair-bound husband. (A Washington newspaper once headlined "MRS. ROOSEVELT SPENDS NIGHT AT WHITE HOUSE.") In 1935, she began a newspaper column, "My Day."

Roosevelt's cabinet reflected the New Deal's diversity. Postmaster General James Farley, FDR's top political adviser, distributed patronage jobs, managed his campaigns, and dealt with state and local Democratic leaders. Secretary of Labor **Frances Perkins,** the first woman cabinet member, had served as industrial commissioner of New York. Interior Secretary **Harold Ickes** had organized liberal Republicans for Roosevelt in 1932. Secretary of Agriculture Henry A. Wallace of Iowa held the same post his father had occupied in the 1920s. Treasury Secretary Henry Morgenthau, Jr., FDR's neighbor and political ally, though a fiscal conservative, tolerated the spending necessary to finance New Deal anti-depression programs.

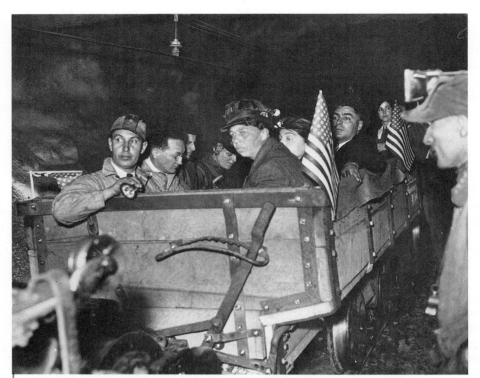

Eleanor Roosevelt Visits a West Virginia Coal Mine, 1933 *A New Yorker cartoon of 1933 portrayed one coal miner exclaiming to another: "Oh migosh, here comes Mrs. Roosevelt." But reality soon caught up with humor, as the First Lady immersed herself in the plight of the poor and the exploited.*

A host of newcomers poured into Washington in 1933—former progressives, liberal-minded professors, bright young lawyers. They drafted bills, staffed government agencies, and debated recovery strategies. From this pressure-cooker environment emerged the laws, programs, and agencies gathered under a catch-all label: the New Deal.

The Hundred Days Between March and June 1933, a period labeled the "Hundred Days," Congress enacted more than a dozen key measures. Rooted in the experience of the Progressive Era, World War I, and the Hoover presidency, these measures expanded Washington's involvement in the nation's economic life.

FDR first addressed the banking crisis. As borrowers defaulted, depositors withdrew savings, and homeowners missed mortgage payments, thousands of banks had failed, undermining confidence in the entire system. On March 5 Roosevelt ordered all banks to close for four days. At the end of this so-called bank holiday, he proposed an Emergency Banking Act. This law and a later one permitted healthy banks to reopen, set up procedures for managing failed banks, increased government oversight of banking, and required banks to separate their savings deposits from their investment funds. Congress also created the Federal Deposit Insurance Corporation (FDIC) to insure bank deposits up to five thousand dollars. In the first of a series of radio talks dubbed "fireside chats," the president assured Americans that they could again trust their banks.

Other measures of the Hundred Days addressed the urgent problem of relief for Americans struggling to survive. Two new agencies assisted those who were losing their homes. The Home Owners Loan Corporation (HOLC) helped city-dwellers refinance their mortgages. The Farm Credit Administration provided loans to rural Americans.

Another early relief program, the **Civilian Conservation Corps** (CCC), employed jobless youths in such government projects as reforestation, park maintenance, and erosion control. The CCC thus combined work relief with environmental programs. By 1935 half a million young men were earning thirty-five dollars a month in CCC camps—a godsend to desperate families.

The principal relief measure of the Hundred Days, the **Federal Emergency Relief Act,** appropriated $500 million for state and local relief agencies that had exhausted their funds. To head this program, FDR chose **Harry Hopkins,** the relief administrator in New York State, who soon emerged as a powerful New Deal figure.

While supplying immediate relief, the early New Deal also faced the longer-term challenge of promoting agricultural and industrial recovery. In tackling the chronic problem of low farm prices, New Dealers held different opinions. Some favored the approach of the 1920s McNary-Haugen bill (see Chapter 23), by which the government would buy agricultural surpluses and sell them abroad. Others, however, advocated reduced production as a way to raise farm income, and this approach won the day.

As a first step to cutting production, the government paid southern cotton planters to plow under much of their crop and midwestern farmers to slaughter some 6 million piglets and pregnant sows. Destroying crops and killing pigs amid widespread hunger proved a public-relations nightmare. Pursuing the same goal more systematically, Congress passed the Agricultural Adjustment Act in May 1933. This law gave payments, called subsidies, to producers of the major agricultural commodities—including hogs, wheat, corn, cotton, and dairy products—in return for cutting production. A tax on grain mills and other food processors (a tax ultimately passed on to consumers) financed these subsidies. A new agency, the **Agricultural Adjustment Administration** (AAA), supervised the program.

The other key recovery measure of the Hundred Days, the National Industrial Recovery Act, appropriated $3.3 billion for large-scale public-works projects to provide jobs and stimulate the economy. The **Public Works Administration** (PWA), headed by Interior Secretary Harold Ickes, ran this program.

This law also created the **National Recovery Administration** (NRA). The NRA brought together business leaders to draft codes of "fair competition" for their industries. These codes set production limits, prescribed wages and working conditions, and forbade price cutting and unfair competitive practices. The aim was to promote recovery by breaking the cycle of wage cuts, falling prices, and layoffs. This approach revived the trade associations that Washington had encouraged during World War I (see Chapter 22). Indeed, the NRA's head, Hugh Johnson, had served with the War Industries Board of 1917–1918. The NRA also echoed the theme of business-government cooperation that Herbert Hoover had promoted as secretary of commerce in the 1920s.

The NRA depended on voluntary support by business and the public. The flamboyant Johnson used parades, billboards, magazine ads, and celebrity events to persuade people to buy only from companies that subscribed to an NRA code and that displayed the NRA symbol, a blue eagle, and its slogan, "We Do Our Part."

While the NRA's purpose was economic recovery, some New Dealers saw its reform potential as well. Under pressure from Labor Secretary Frances Perkins, the NRA's textile-industry code banned child labor. And thanks to Senator Robert Wagner of New York, Section 7a of the National Industrial Recovery Act affirmed workers' right to organize unions.

The Reconstruction Finance Corporation, dating from the Hoover years, remained active in the New Deal era. Under its chairman Jesse Jones, a Houston banker, the RFC lent large sums to banks, insurance companies, and even new business ventures, making it a potent financial resource for corporate America. The early New Deal thus had a strong probusiness tone. In his speeches of 1933–1935, FDR always included business in the "all-American team" working for recovery.

A few measures adopted during the Hundred Days, however, took a tougher approach to business. The stock-market crash had produced an antibusiness reaction. A Senate investigation of Wall Street revealed that none of the twenty partners of the Morgan Bank had paid any income tax in 1931 or 1932. People jeered when the head of the New York Stock Exchange told a Senate committee considering regulatory measures, "You gentlemen are making a big mistake. The Exchange is a perfect institution."

Reflecting the public mood, Congress in 1933 passed the Federal Securities Act requiring corporations to inform the government fully on all stock offerings. This law also made executives personally liable for any misrepresentation of securities their companies issued. (In 1934 Congress curbed the purchase of stock on credit—a practice that had contributed to the crash—and created the Securities and Exchange Commission [SEC] to enforce the new regulations.)

The most innovative program of the Hundred Days was the **Tennessee Valley Authority** (TVA). This program had its origins in a World War I hydroelectric station on the Tennessee River in Alabama built by the War Department to power a nearby munitions plant. In the 1920s, Senator George Norris of Nebraska had urged the use of this facility to supply electricity to nearby farmers.

Expanding Norris's idea, TVA advanced the economic and social development of the entire Tennessee River valley, a region mired in poverty. A European visitor in the 1930s described the region's farms: "[K]itchens with ovens burning wood . . . ; no icebox . . . ; dim, smoking, smelly oil lamps . . . ; clothes [washed] by hand in antiquated tubs . . . ; the water . . . brought into the house by women and children, from wells invariably situated at inconvenient and tiring distances."

Such conditions stunted children's lives. Wrote a Tennessee school administrator of the pupils in her district, "Due to insufficient clothing and food, many are unable to attend school. . . . It is not uncommon for a child to have but one dress or one shirt. They have to stay at home the day the mother launders them."

While creating construction jobs, TVA dams brought electricity to the region, provided recreational facilities, and reduced flooding and soil erosion. Under director David Lilienthal, TVA proved one of the New Deal's most popular and enduring achievements.

The mind-boggling burst of laws and the "alphabet-soup" of new agencies during the Hundred Days symbolized both the dynamism and the confusion of the New Deal. How these new programs and agencies would work in practice remained to be seen.

Problems and Controversies Plague the Early New Deal

As the depression persisted, several early New Deal programs, including the NRA and the AAA, faced difficulties. The NRA's problems related partly to the personality of the hard-driving, hard-drinking Hugh Johnson, who left in 1934. But the trouble went deeper. As the unity spirit of the Hundred Days faded, corporate America chafed under NRA regulation. Code violations increased. Small businesses complained that the codes favored big corporations. The agency itself, meanwhile, became bogged down in drafting trivial codes. The shoulder-pad industry, for example, had its own code. Corporate trade associations used the codes to stifle competition and fix prices.

In May 1935, the Supreme Court unanimously ruled the NRA unconstitutional. The Court cited two reasons: first, the law gave the president regulatory powers that constitutionally belonged to Congress; second, the NRA regulated commerce within states, violating the constitutional provision limiting federal regulation to interstate commerce. Few mourned. As a recovery measure, the NRA had failed.

The AAA fared better, but it too proved controversial. Farm prices did rise as production fell, and from 1933 to 1937 overall farm income increased by 50 percent. But the AAA did not help farm laborers or migrant workers; indeed, its crop-reduction payments actually hurt southern tenants and sharecroppers, who faced eviction as cotton planters removed acreage from production. One Georgia sharecropper wrote Harry Hopkins, "I have Bin farming all my life But the man I live with Has Turned me loose. . . . I can't get a Job."

Some victims of this process resisted. In 1934 the interracial Southern Tenant Farmers' Union, led by the Socialist Party, emerged in Arkansas. Declared one black sharecropper at the organizing meeting, "The same chain that holds my people holds

MAP 24.1 The Dust Bowl

From the Dakotas southward to the Mexican border, farmers in the Great Plains suffered from a lack of rainfall and severe soil erosion in the 1930s, worsening the hardships of the Great Depression.

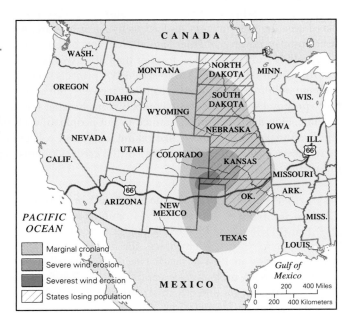

your people too. . . . [We should] get together and stay together." The landowners struck back, harassing union organizers.

While some New Dealers focused on raising total agricultural income, others took a more class-based approach and urged attention to the poorest farmers. Their cause was strengthened as a parching drought centered in the Oklahoma panhandle region turned much of the Great Plains into a dust bowl. The rains failed in 1930, devastating wheat and livestock on the southern plains. In 1934, dust clouds spread across the nation, darkening the skies over Boston, Washington, D.C., and Savannah. As a particularly dense dust cloud passed over Washington, one legislator commented: "There goes Oklahoma." On "Black Sunday," April 14, 1935, racing winds created dunes fifty feet high. Through 1939, each summer brought a new scourge of dust.

Even night brought no relief. Recalled a Kansas woman, "A trip for water to rinse the grit from our lips, and then back to bed with washcloths over our noses. We try to lie still, because every turn stirs the dust on the blankets." Folk singer Woody Guthrie recalled the most vivid memory of his 1930s' boyhood in Oklahoma and Texas in a song called "The Great Dust Storm."

Battered by debt, drought, and dust, many families gave up. Nearly 3.5 million people left the Great Plains in the 1930s. Some migrated to nearby cities, further swamping relief rolls. Others packed their meager belongings into old cars and headed west. Though coming from various states, they all bore a derisive nickname, Okies. The plight of dust-bowl migrants further complicated New Deal agricultural planning.

Policy differences also plagued the New Deal relief program. As unemployment continued, Harry Hopkins convinced FDR to support direct federal relief programs, rather than channeling funds through state and local agencies. Late in 1933, FDR named Hopkins to head a temporary agency, the Civil Works Administration (CWA). Through the winter the CWA funded short-term work projects for the jobless, but when warm weather returned, FDR abolished it. Like his conservative critics, FDR feared creating a permanent underclass living on welfare. As local relief agencies ran out of money, however, further federal programs became inevitable.

Hopkins and Harold Ickes, head of the Public Works Administration, competed to control federal relief policy. Large-scale PWA projects such as bridges, dams, and government buildings did promote economic recovery, but as the cautious Ickes examined every proposal with a fine-tooth comb, billions in relief funds remained stalled in the pipeline. Hopkins, by contrast, wanted to put people to work and get money circulating. Even make-work projects like raking leaves and collecting litter, he argued, furthered these goals. Given the urgency of the crisis, Hopkins's approach proved more influential.

1934–1935: Challenges from Right and Left

Despite the New Deal's brave beginnings, the depression persisted. In 1934 national income rose about 25 percent above 1933 levels, but remained far below that of 1929. Millions had been jobless for three or four years. The rising frustration found expression in 1934 in nearly two thousand strikes, some of them communist-led. With the NRA under attack, conflict flaring over farm policy, and relief spending growing, criticism mounted. Conservatives attacked the New Deal as socialistic. In 1934 several business leaders, joined by an embittered Al Smith, formed the anti–New

Deal American Liberty League. Anti-Roosevelt jokes circulated among the rich, many of whom denounced him as a traitor to his class.

But the New Deal remained popular, reflecting both its promise and FDR's political skills. Assisted by speechwriters and publicists, Roosevelt commanded the political stage. Pursuing his "national unity" theme, he exhorted Americans to join the battle for economic recovery just as they had united in 1917 against a foreign foe. Although Republican newspaper publishers remained hostile, FDR enjoyed good relations with the working press, and journalists responded with favorable stories.

Unlike Hoover, Roosevelt loved public appearances and took naturally to radio. Frances Perkins described his radio talks: "His head would nod and his hands would move in simple, natural, comfortable gestures. His face would smile and light up as though he were actually sitting . . . with [his listeners]." The nickname of these radio talks, "fireside chats," underscored their informal nature. Roosevelt's mastery of radio would provide a model for politicians of the television era.

The 1934 midterm election ratified the New Deal's popularity. Reversing the usual pattern, the Democrats increased their congressional majorities. As for FDR, Kansas journalist William Allen White observed, "He's been all but crowned by the people." As the returns rolled in, Harry Hopkins exulted to a group of New Deal associates, "Boys, this is our hour!"

Despite this outcome, the political scene was highly unstable in 1934–1935. While conservatives criticized the New Deal for going too far, critics on the left attacked it for not going far enough. Socialists and communists ridiculed Roosevelt's efforts to include big business in his "all-American team." Clifford Odets's 1935 play *Waiting for Lefty* portrayed noble workers battling evil bosses.

Pushing the New Deal's experimental spirit still further, demagogues peddled more radical nostrums. The Detroit Catholic priest and radio spellbinder Charles Coughlin attacked FDR as a "great betrayer and liar," made anti-Semitic allusions, and called for nationalization of the banks. For a time, Coughlin's movement, the National Union of Social Justice, drawn mainly from the lower middle class, seemed a potent force.

Meanwhile, California physician Francis Townsend proposed that the government pay two hundred dollars a month to all retired citizens, requiring them to spend it within thirty days. This plan, Townsend insisted, would help the elderly, stimulate the economy, and create jobs by encouraging retirement. The scheme would have bankrupted the nation, but many older citizens rallied to Townsend's banner.

FDR's wiliest rival was Huey Long of Louisiana. A country lawyer elected governor in 1928, Long built highways, schools, and public housing while fostering a climate of graft and political corruption. He roared into Washington as a senator in 1933, preaching his "Share Our Wealth" program: a 100 percent tax on all incomes over $1 million and appropriation of all fortunes over $5 million. With this money, Long promised, every family could enjoy a comfortable income, a house, a car, old-age benefits, and free college education. "Every man a king," Long proclaimed. By 1935 he boasted 7.5 million supporters. The title of his 1935 book, *My First Days in the White House,* made clear his ultimate goal. An assassin's bullet killed Long that September, but his organization survived.

Battling back, Roosevelt regained the political high ground in 1935 with a series of bold initiatives. The result was a fresh surge of legislation that rivaled that of the Hundred Days.

THE NEW DEAL CHANGES COURSE, 1935–1936

As the 1936 election neared, Roosevelt shelved the unity theme and championed the poor and the working class. His 1935 State of the Union address outlined six initiatives: expanded public-works programs, assistance to the rural poor, support for organized labor, benefits for retired workers and other at-risk groups, tougher business regulation, and heavier taxes on the well-to-do. These priorities translated into a bundle of reform measures some called "the Second New Deal." FDR's landslide victory in 1936 solidified a new Democratic coalition. The New Deal also addressed environmental issues and launched public-works and power projects in the West that stimulated the region's economic development.

Expanding Federal Relief   With unemployment still high, Congress passed the $5 billion Emergency Relief Appropriation Act in April 1935. Roosevelt swiftly set up the **Works Progress Administration** (WPA), with Harry Hopkins in charge, to funnel assistance directly to the jobless. Roosevelt insisted that the WPA provide work, not handouts. Over its eight-year life, the WPA employed more than 8 million Americans and constructed or improved vast numbers of bridges, roads, schools, post offices, and other public facilities.

The WPA also assisted writers, performers, and artists. The Federal Writers' Project (FWP) employed some ten thousand jobless writers nationwide to produce state and city guides and histories of ethnic and immigrant groups. In the South, research teams recorded the oral-history reminiscences of former slaves. Responding to the rise of totalitarian regimes abroad (see Chapter 25), the FWP encouraged cultural nationalism while recognizing regional and ethnic differences. Sterling Brown, the FWP's "Negro Affairs editor," pushed for the inclusion of African-American history and voices in FWP publications.

Under the WPA's Federal Music Project, unemployed musicians gave free concerts, often featuring American composers. By 1938, more than 30 million Americans had attended these events. Artists working for the Federal Arts Project designed posters, offered courses, and painted murals on public buildings.

The Federal Theatre Project (FTP) employed actors. One FTP project, the Living Newspaper, which dramatized current social issues, was criticized as New Deal propaganda. Nervous WPA officials canceled one FTP-funded production, Marc Blitzstein's radical musical *The Cradle Will Rock* (1937), before the opening-night performance. The cast and audience defiantly walked to another theater, and the show went on. Touring FTP drama companies gave many citizens their first taste of theater.

Another 1935 agency, the National Youth Administration (NYA), provided job training for unemployed youth and part-time work to enable college students to remain in school. Eleanor Roosevelt, viewing young people as the hope of the future, took particular pride in the NYA.

Harold Ickes's Public Works Administration, after a slow start, eventually completed some thirty-four thousand major construction projects, employing thousands of workers. Among the PWA's undertakings were New York City's Triborough Bridge and Lincoln Tunnel, and the awesome Grand Coulee Dam on the Columbia River.

All this relief spending generated large federal budget deficits, cresting at $4.4 billion in 1936. According to British economist John Maynard Keynes, governments should deliberately use deficit spending during depressions to fund public-works programs, thereby increasing purchasing power and stimulating recovery. The New Deal approach, however, was not Keynesian. Because every dollar spent on relief programs was withdrawn from the economy through taxation or government borrowing, the stimulus effect was nil. FDR saw deficits as an unwelcome necessity, not a positive good.

Aiding Migrants, Supporting Unions, Regulating Business, Taxing the Wealthy   The New Deal's second phase more frankly targeted the needs of workers, the poor, and the disadvantaged. Social-justice advocates like Frances Perkins and Eleanor Roosevelt helped shape this program, but so did hard-headed politics. Looking to 1936, FDR's political advisers feared that the followers of Coughlin, Townsend, and Long could siphon off enough votes to cost him the election. This worry underlay FDR's 1935 political agenda.

The Second New Deal's agricultural policy addressed the plight of sharecroppers (a plight the AAA had helped create) and other poor farmers. The Resettlement Administration (1935), directed by Rexford Tugwell, made loans to help tenant farmers buy their own farms and to enable displaced sharecroppers, tenants, and dust-bowl migrants to move to more productive areas.

The Resettlement Administration also funded two brilliant documentary films directed by Pare Lorenz. *The Plow That Broke the Plains* (1936) explained the farming practices that led to the dust bowl. *The River* (1938) dealt with the devastating effects of flooding in the Mississippi River valley, and the promise of TVA and other New Deal flood-control projects. Lorenz's films today rank among the outstanding cultural productions of the 1930s.

The Rural Electrification Administration, also started in 1935, made low-interest loans to utility companies and farmers' cooperatives to extend electricity to the 90 percent of rural America that still lacked it. By 1941, 40 percent of U.S. farms enjoyed electric power.

The agricultural-recovery program suffered a setback in January 1936 when the Supreme Court declared the Agricultural Adjustment Act unconstitutional. The processing tax that funded the AAA's subsidies, the Court held, was an illegal use of the government's tax power. To replace the AAA, Congress passed a soil-conservation act that paid farmers to plant grasses and legumes instead of soil-depleting crops such as wheat and cotton (which also happened to be the major surplus commodities).

Organized labor won a key victory in 1935, again thanks to Senator Robert Wagner. During the New Deal's national-unity phase, FDR had criticized Wagner's campaign for a prolabor law as "special interest" legislation. But in 1935, when the Supreme Court outlawed the NIRA, including Section 7a protecting union members' rights, as unconstitutional, FDR called for a labor law that would survive court scrutiny. The **National Labor Relations Act** of July 1935 (the Wagner Act) guaranteed collective-bargaining rights, permitted closed shops (in which all employees must join a union), and outlawed such management tactics as blacklisting union organizers. The law created the National Labor Relations Board (NLRB) to enforce the law and supervise shop elections. A wave of unionization soon followed (see below).

The Second New Deal's more class-conscious thrust shaped other 1935 measures as well. The Banking Act strengthened the Federal Reserve Board's control over the nation's financial system. The Public Utilities Holding Company Act, targeting the sprawling public-utility empires of the 1920s such as that of Samuel Insull (see Chapter 23), restricted gas and electric companies to one geographic region.

In 1935, too, Roosevelt called for steeper taxes on the rich to combat the "unjust concentration of wealth and economic power." Congress responded with a revenue act, also called the Wealth Tax Act, that raised taxes on corporations and on the well-to-do. This law had many loopholes and was not quite the "soak the rich" measure some believed, but it did express the Second New Deal's more radical spirit.

The Social Security Act of 1935; End of the Second New Deal
The **Social Security Act** of 1935 stands out among New Deal laws for its long-range significance. Drafted by a committee chaired by Frances Perkins, this measure drew upon Progressive Era ideas and the social-welfare programs of England and Germany. It established a mixed federal-state system of workers' pensions; unemployment insurance; survivors' benefits for victims of industrial accidents; and aid for disabled persons and dependent mothers with children.

Taxes paid partly by employers and partly by workers (in the form of sums withheld from their paychecks) funded the pension and survivors' benefit features. This cut in take-home pay helped bring on a recession in 1937. But it made sense politically because workers would fight any effort to end a pension plan they had contributed to. As FDR put it, "With those taxes in there, no damned politician can ever scrap my social security program."

The initial Social Security Act paid low benefits and bypassed farmers, domestic workers, and the self-employed. But it established the principle of federal responsibility for social welfare and laid the foundation for a vastly expanded welfare system in the future.

By September 1935, when Congress adjourned, the Second New Deal was complete. Without embracing the panaceas of Coughlin, Townsend, or Long, FDR had addressed the grievances they had exploited. Although conservatives called this phase of the New Deal "antibusiness," FDR insisted that he had saved capitalism by addressing the social problems it spawned. During much of the post–Civil War era the business class had dominated government, marginalizing other groups. Business remained influential in the 1930s, but as the New Deal evolved, it acted as a broker for all organized interest groups, including labor, not just corporate America. And in 1935, with an election looming, New Deal strategists reached farther still, to address the situation of sharecroppers and migrant workers, the disabled, the elderly, and others whose plight had rarely concerned politicians of the past.

In the process, the New Deal enlarged the role of the federal government in American life, as well as the power of the presidency. Building on earlier precedents set by Theodore Roosevelt, FDR so dominated 1930s' politics that Americans began to expect presidents to offer "programs," address national issues, and shape the public debate. This decisively altered the power balance between the White House and Congress. The New Deal's importance thus lies not only in specific laws, but also in the way it redefined the scope of the presidency and, more broadly, the social role of the state.

The 1936 Roosevelt Landslide and the New Democratic Coalition

With the Second New Deal in place, FDR confidently faced the 1936 campaign. "There's one issue . . . ," he told an aide; "it's myself, and people must be either for me or against me."

The Republican candidate, Kansas governor Alfred Landon, a fiscal conservative who nevertheless believed that government must address social issues, proved an inept campaigner. ("Wherever I have gone in this country, I have found Americans," he revealed in one speech.) FDR, by contrast, responded zestfully when Republicans lambasted his alleged dictatorial ambitions or charged that the social security law would require all workers to wear metal dog tags. The forces of "selfishness and greed . . . are united in their hatred for me," he declared at a tumultuous election-eve rally in New York City, "and I welcome their hatred."

In the greatest landslide since 1820, FDR carried every state but Maine and Vermont. Landon even lost Kansas. Pennsylvania went Democratic for the first time since 1856. The Democrats increased their already top-heavy majorities in Congress. Roosevelt buried his minor-party opponents as well. Socialist Norman Thomas received under 200,000 votes, the Communist Party's presidential candidate only about 80,000. The Union Party, a coalition of Coughlinites, Townsendites, and Huey Long supporters, seemingly so formidable in 1935, polled under 900,000 votes.

The 1936 election signaled the emergence of a new Democratic coalition. Since Reconstruction, the Democrats had counted on three bases of support: the white South, parts of the West, and urban white ethnic voters. FDR retained these centers of strength. He rarely challenged state or local party leaders who produced the votes, whether they supported the New Deal or not. In Virginia he even withdrew support from a pro–New Deal governor who clashed with the state's conservative but powerful Democratic senators. When the Democratic boss of Jersey City, Frank Hague, faced mail-tampering charges, FDR told Jim Farley, "Tell Frank to knock it off . . . , but keep this thing quiet because we need Hague's support if we want New Jersey."

Building on Al Smith's urban breakthrough in 1928, FDR carried the nation's twelve largest cities in 1936. Aided by New Deal relief programs, many city-dwellers idolized Roosevelt. When he visited New York, Boston, or other cities, cheering crowds lined the route. FDR also turned to the newer urban-immigrant groups, including Catholics and Jews, in filling New Deal positions.

Expanding the Democratic base, FDR also reached out to farmers, union members, northern blacks, and women. Midwestern farmers, long rock-ribbed Republicans, liked the New Deal's agricultural program and voted accordingly. In Iowa, a GOP bastion in the 1920s, FDR won decisively in 1936. Union members, too, joined the Roosevelt bandwagon in 1936, and the unions pumped money into Roosevelt's campaign chest (though far less than business gave the Republicans). Despite his early criticism of the Wagner bill, FDR's reputation as a "friend of labor" proved unassailable.

Although most southern blacks remained disfranchised, northern blacks could vote, and as late as 1932, two-thirds of them went for Hoover, leading one African-American editor to insist: "[T]urn Lincoln's picture to the wall. That debt has been paid in full." The New Deal caused a historic shift. In 1934, Chicago's black voters replaced Republican congressman Oscar DePriest with a Democrat. In 1936, 76 percent of black voters supported FDR.

In economic terms, this shift made sense. Owing mainly to workplace racism, blacks' jobless rates in the 1930s outran those of the work force as a whole. Thus, New Deal relief programs greatly aided blacks. On racial-justice issues, however, the New Deal's record was mixed at best. Some NRA codes included racially discriminatory clauses, causing black activists to deride the agency as "Negroes Ruined Again." TVA and other New Deal agencies tolerated racial bias. Lynchings increased in the 1930s as some whites translated economic worries into racial violence, but Roosevelt kept aloof from an NAACP campaign to make lynching a federal crime. An antilynching bill passed the House of Representatives in 1935, but southern Democratic senators killed it with a filibuster. To protect his legislative program and retain southern white voters, FDR did little. "[T]he Roosevelt administration [has] nothing for [blacks]," the NAACP concluded bitterly.

In limited ways, FDR did address racial issues. He cautiously tried to rid New Deal agencies of blatant racism. He appointed more than a hundred blacks to policy-level and judicial positions, including Eleanor Roosevelt's friend Mary McLeod Bethune as director of minority affairs in the National Youth Administration. Bethune, a Florida educator and founder of the National Council of Negro Women (1936), led the so-called black cabinet that linked the administration and black organizations. The "Roosevelt Supreme Court" that took shape after 1936 issued antidiscrimination rulings in cases involving housing, voting rights, wage inequity, and jury selection.

The New Deal also supported racial justice in symbolic ways. In 1938, when the participants in a welfare conference in Birmingham, Alabama, were segregated in compliance with local statutes, Mrs. Roosevelt pointedly placed her chair halfway between the white and black delegates. In 1939, when the Daughters of the American Revolution barred black contralto Marian Anderson from performing in Washington's Constitution Hall, Mrs. Roosevelt resigned from the organization, and Harold Ickes arranged an Easter concert by Anderson at the Lincoln Memorial. Even symbolic gestures outraged many southern whites. When a black minister delivered the invocation at the 1936 Democratic convention, a South Carolina senator noisily stalked out.

Molly Dewson, head of the Democratic Party's women's division and a friend of the Roosevelts, led the party's effort to court women voters. In the 1936 campaign Dewson mobilized fifteen thousand women to distribute flyers describing New Deal programs. "[W]e did not make the old-fashioned plea that our nominee was charming," she recalled; ". . . we appealed to [women's] intelligence."

Unlike earlier feminists, Dewson did not promote a specifically feminist agenda. The New Deal's recovery and social-welfare programs, she argued, served the interests of both sexes. She did, however, successfully push for more women in policy-level positions. FDR appointed the first woman cabinet member, the first woman ambassador, and a number of female federal judges. Through Dewson's efforts, the 1936 Democratic platform committee reflected a fifty-fifty gender balance.

Symbolic gestures and the appointment of a few blacks and women, while noteworthy, ought not be overemphasized. Racism and sexism pervaded U.S. society in the 1930s, and Roosevelt, grappling with the depression, did relatively little to change things. That challenge would await a later time.

The Environment and the West

Environmental issues loomed large in the 1930s, reflecting FDR's priorities. While still in the New York Senate, he had sought to regulate logging that threatened wildlife. As presi-

Power to the People *The New Deal's massive hydroelectric power projects were celebrated in this 1937 "Living Newspaper" production by the WPA's Federal Theatre Project.*

dent, he strongly supported the Civilian Conservation Corps' program of planting trees, thinning forests, and building hiking trails.

Soil conservation emerged as a major priority. The 1930s' dust storms resulted not only from drought, but from years of overgrazing and poor farming practices. For decades, Great Plains' wheat farmers had used powerful tractors, combines, and heavy-duty plows called "sodbusters" to uproot the native prairie grasses that anchored the soil. When the rains failed, as they periodically do in this drought-prone region, little remained to hold the baked earth in place, and parching winds whipped up devastating dust storms. By the 1930s, 9 million acres of farmland had been lost to erosion in the Great Plains, the South, and elsewhere.

In response, the Department of Agriculture's Soil Conservation Service set up projects to show the value of contour plowing, crop rotation, and soil-strengthening grasses. The Taylor Grazing Act of 1934 restricted the grazing on public lands that had contributed to the problem. The TVA helped control the floods that worsened erosion in the Tennessee valley.

New Deal planners also promoted the national-park movement. Olympic National Park in Washington, Virginia's Shenandoah National Park, and Kings Canyon National Park in California all date from the 1930s. The administration also created some 160 new national wildlife refuges. Roosevelt even closed a Utah artillery range that threatened a nesting site of the endangered trumpeter swan.

The wilderness-preservation movement gained momentum in the 1930s, supported by such diverse groups as the Wilderness Society (1935), started by environmentalist

Aldo Leopold and others, and the National Wildlife Federation (1936), funded by firearms makers eager to preserve wilderness areas for hunters. Under pressure from such groups, Congress set aside a portion of Kings Canyon National Park as a wilderness area. Building on these beginnings, the United States by 2006 had 680 officially designated national wilderness areas, comprising 105 million acres.

By later standards, the New Deal's environmental record was spotty. The decade's massive hydroelectric projects, while necessary at a time when many rural families still lacked electricity, had ecological consequences little noted at the time. The Grand Coulee Dam, for example, destroyed salmon spawning on much of the Columbia River's tributary system. Other New Deal dams disrupted fragile ecosystems and adversely affected local residents, particularly Native American communities, who depended on these ecosystems for their livelihood.

Viewed in context, however, the New Deal's environmental record remains impressive. While coping with a grave economic crisis, the Roosevelt administration focused a level of attention on environmental issues that had not been seen since the Progressive Era, and would not be seen again for a generation.

The New Deal had a big impact on the West, especially because the federal government owned a third or more of the land in eleven western states, with the figure rising far higher in some states. New Deal agencies and laws such as the AAA, the Soil Conservation Service, the Taylor Grazing Act, and the Farm Security Administration (see below) set new rules for western agriculture from the grain and cattle of the Great Plains to the Pacific coast citrus groves and truck farms dependent on migrant labor.

Some of the largest PWA and WPA projects were built in the West, including thousands of public buildings (246 in Washington State alone), from courthouses and post offices to tourist facilities such as beautiful Timberline Lodge on Oregon's Mount Hood. The highways linking the West to the rest of America, such as the Lincoln Highway from Philadelphia to San Francisco and Route 66 from Chicago to Los Angeles, were upgraded in the 1930s with federal assistance.

Above all, the PWA in the West built dams—not only Grand Coulee, but also Shasta on the Sacramento River, Bonneville on the Columbia, Glen Canyon on the Colorado, and others. The PWA completed Hoover Dam on the Colorado, authorized by Congress in 1928 (see Chapter 23), well ahead of schedule. Despite their ecological downside, these great undertakings—among the largest engineering projects in human history—supplied electric power to vast regions while also contributing to flood control, irrigation, and soil conservation. (Las Vegas owed its post–World War II emergence as a gambling and entertainment mecca to power from nearby Hoover Dam.)

A New Deal initiative especially important for the West was Harold Ickes's National Planning Board of 1934, later renamed the National Resources Planning Board. This agency, which extended Herbert Hoover's promotion of cooperative, multistate planning of western water resources (see Chapter 23), facilitated state and regional management of water, soil, timber, and minerals.

THE NEW DEAL'S END STAGE, 1937–1939

Buoyed by his 1936 victory, Roosevelt launched an abortive attack on the Supreme Court. After this bruising fight, FDR confronted both a stubborn recession and newly energized conservative opposition. A few final measures in 1937–1938 brought the New Deal to a close.

FDR and the
Supreme Court

In 1937, four of the Supreme Court's nine elderly justices were archconservatives who abhorred the New Deal. Joined by others of more moderate views, these conservatives had struck down the NRA, the AAA, and progressive state laws. Roosevelt feared that key measures of the Second New Deal, including the Social Security Act and the Wagner Act, would meet a similar fate. Indeed, some corporate lawyers were so sure that the Social Security Act would be found unconstitutional that they advised their clients to ignore it.

In February 1937, FDR proposed a bill that would have allowed him to appoint an additional Supreme Court member for each justice over age seventy, up to a total of six. Roosevelt blandly insisted that this would ease aging justices' heavy workload, but his political motivation was obvious.

FDR hoped that his popularity would assure support for his Court plan, but the press and public reacted with sharp hostility. The Supreme Court's size (unspecified in the Constitution) had fluctuated in the early Republic, but the membership of nine, dating to 1869, had become almost sacrosanct. Warning of a power grab by FDR, conservatives blasted the "court-packing" scheme and the devious way FDR had presented it. Even many Democrats disapproved. When the Senate voted down the scheme in July, FDR quietly dropped it.

But was this a defeat? One conservative justice retired in May 1937; others announced retirement plans. In April and May the Court upheld several New Deal measures, including the Wagner Act, as well as a state minimum-wage law. This outcome may have been Roosevelt's objective all along. His challenge to the Court, plus his 1936 victory, sent powerful political signals that the justices heeded. From 1937 to 1939 FDR appointed four new Supreme Court justices, creating a judicial legacy that would long outlive him.

The Roosevelt
Recession

After showing signs of recovery, the economy dipped ominously in August 1937. Industrial production slumped. Soaring unemployment again dominated the headlines. This "Roosevelt recession" resulted in part from federal policies that reduced consumer income. Social-security payroll taxes withdrew some $2 billion from circulation. The Federal Reserve Board had raised interest rates to forestall inflation, further contracting the money supply. FDR, meanwhile, concerned about mounting deficits, had seized on the signs of recovery to cut back the New Deal relief programs.

Echoing Hoover, FDR assured his cabinet, "Everything will work out . . . if we just sit tight." Meanwhile, however, John Maynard Keynes's advocacy of deficit spending as the key to recovery had persuaded some New Dealers. Aware that political rather than economic arguments carried more weight with FDR, they warned him of a political backlash if breadlines and soup kitchens returned. Convinced, FDR in April 1938 authorized new spending on work-relief projects by the WPA, PWA, and other New Deal agencies. By late 1938, unemployment had declined and industrial output increased. As late as 1939, however, more than 17 percent of the labor force remained jobless.

A Camera's-Eye View of Depression-Era America *This 1937 image by Dorothea Lange, a photographer with the Farm Security Administration, pictures migrants from the Texas dust bowl gathered at a roadside camp near Calipatria in southern California.*

Final Measures; Growing Opposition

Preoccupied by the Supreme Court fight, the recession, and menacing events abroad (see Chapter 25), FDR offered few domestic initiatives after 1936. Congress, however, enacted several significant measures.

In 1937, Congress created the **Farm Security Administration** (FSA), replacing Rexford Tugwell's underfunded Resettlement Administration. The FSA made low-interest loans to help tenant farmers and sharecroppers buy their own farms. These loans, totaling more than $1 billion through 1941, did help some rural folk become more self-sufficient. Ironically, however, the FSA often rejected the poorest farmers' loan applications, considering them a bad credit risk.

The FSA operated camps offering shelter and medical services to migrant farm workers living in wretched conditions. FSA nurses and home economists provided health, hygiene, and housekeeping advice to poor farm families. The FSA also commissioned gifted photographers to record the lives of migrant workers, tenant farmers, and uprooted dust-bowl families. These FSA photographs, published in various periodicals, helped shape a realistic documentary style that pervaded 1930s' popular culture, including Hollywood movies and Henry Luce's photo magazine *Life*, launched in 1936. Today they comprise a haunting album of depression-era images.

Other measures set precedents for the future. The 1937 Housing Act appropriated $500 million for urban slum clearance and public housing—projects that would loom large in the 1950s. The **Fair Labor Standards Act** of 1938 banned child labor and set a national minimum wage (initially forty cents an hour) and a maximum workweek of forty hours. This measure reflected not only humanitarianism but also some northern legislators' desire to undermine the competitive edge of the South, with its low wages. Despite many loopholes, the law helped exploited workers, and underscored the government's role in regulating abuses by employers.

In a final stab at raising farm income, the Agricultural Adjustment Act of 1938 created a mechanism by which the government, in years of big harvests and low prices, would make loans to farmers and warehouse their surplus crops. When prices rose, farmers could repay their loans and sell their commodities. This complicated system set the framework of federal farm price support for decades.

Overall, New Deal farm policy produced mixed results. Large-scale growers benefited from subsidy payments, but the cumbersome price-support mechanisms involved problems that would worsen with time. The FSA provided short-term help to some tenants, sharecroppers, and small farmers (though often not the neediest), but did little to slow the long-term decline of family farms and the rise of agribusinesses. In reality, many small farmers themselves aspired to become large-scale commercial operators. Most did not succeed, however, and gradually left the land.

The New Deal's slower pace after 1935 also reflected the rise of an anti–New Deal congressional coalition of Republicans and conservative southern Democrats. In 1937, this coalition rejected FDR's proposal to reorganize the executive branch. The plan made administrative sense, but critics again warned darkly of a White House power grab.

The conservative coalition also slashed relief appropriations; cut corporate taxes in 1938; and in 1939 killed the WPA's Federal Theatre Project for its alleged radicalism. Under Texas congressman Martin Dies, the House Un-American Activities Committee (created in 1937) investigated New Deal agencies for communist infiltration. The 1939 Hatch Act, barring federal employees from electoral campaigning, reflected conservatives' suspicions that FDR was using WPA staff for campaign purposes.

Although FDR campaigned actively in the 1938 midterm elections, the Republicans gained heavily in the House and Senate and won a net of thirteen governorships. In the Democratic primaries Roosevelt tried to defeat several anti–New Deal Democratic senators, but most bested their primary challengers and went on to win in November. Focusing on foreign affairs in his January 1939 State of the Union message, FDR proposed no new domestic measures and merely noted the need to "preserve our reforms." The New Deal was over.

SOCIAL CHANGE AND SOCIAL ACTION IN THE 1930s

American life in the 1930s involved more than politics. The depression affected most Americans, including the jobless and their families; working women; and all age groups. For industrial workers, African-Americans, a growing Hispanic community, and Native Americans, the crisis brought hard times, but the activist climate of the era also encouraged organized resistance to exploitation and brought new legislative initiatives.

The Depression's Psychological and Social Impact

The depression caused untold human suffering and marked all who lived through it. Despite the New Deal, unemployment never fell below about 14 percent in the 1930s, and for much of the decade it was considerably higher. A quarter of all farm families had to accept public or private assistance during the 1930s. Even the employed often had to take jobs below their level of training: college alumni pumped gas; business-school graduates sold furniture; a retired navy captain became an usher in a movie theater.

Psychologists described "unemployment shock": jobless persons who walked the streets seeking work and then lay awake at night worrying. When shoe soles wore out, cardboard or folded newspapers had to serve. Tacks pierced worn shoe heels, cutting the skin. "You pass . . . shoe-shops where a tack might be bent down," one young man observed bitterly, "but you can't pull off a shoe and ask to have that done—for nothing."

Advertisements for mouthwashes, deodorants, and correspondence courses exploited feelings of shame and failure. Women's magazines described low-cost meals and other budget-trimming strategies. Habits of scrimping and saving acquired in the 1930s often survived into more affluent times. As Caroline Bird wrote in *The Invisible Scar* (1966), a social history of the 1930s, the depression for many boiled down to "a dull misery in the bones."

New York senator Robert Wagner called the working woman in the depression "the first orphan in the storm." Indeed, for the 25 percent of U.S. women employed in 1930, the depression brought difficult times. The female jobless rate exceeded 20 percent for much of the decade. Women desperate to continue working often took lower-paying jobs. Laid-off factory workers became waitresses. Young women new to the job market took temporary or part-time work. Jobless men competed with women even for such traditional "women's work" as library work and school teaching.

Married women workers endured harsh criticism. Although most worked because of economic necessity, they were accused of stealing jobs from men. Even Secretary of Labor Frances Perkins urged married women to stay out of the labor market so more men could work. Many cities refused to employ married women as teachers and even fired women teachers who married.

Women workers also faced wage discrimination. In 1939, women teachers earned on average nearly 20 percent less than male teachers with comparable experience. Some NRA codes authorized lower pay for women workers. Many women workers were not covered by the minimum-wage clause of the Fair Labor Standards Act, including the more than 2 million who worked for wages in private households.

The late 1930s' unionization drive (see below) had mixed effects on women workers. Those employed in some mass-production industries benefited, but the most heavily female sectors of the labor force—textiles, sales, and clerical and service work—resisted unionization. Male managers and even male union leaders opposed a 1937 campaign to unionize mostly female clerical workers.

Despite the criticism, the percentage of married women holding wage-earning jobs increased from under 12 percent in 1930 to nearly 16 percent in 1940. The depression may actually have hastened the long-term movement of women into the workplace as married women took jobs out of necessity. When her husband gave up trying to find work in 1932, one working wife explained, "[At] twenty-eight, with two little girls, . . . I took a job as a salesclerk . . . , and worked through the Depression."

As this story suggests, the depression profoundly affected family life. The birthrate fell in the early thirties as married couples postponed a family or limited its size. Birth control became easier as condoms and diaphragms became more accessible. A declining birthrate plus reduced immigration held population growth in the 1930s to a scant 7 percent, in contrast to an average of 20 percent per decade from 1900 to 1930.

Making ends meet and holding one's family together posed major challenges. Parents patched clothes, stretched food resources, and sought public assistance when necessary. In homes with a tradition of strong male authority, the husband's loss of a job could prove a devastating psychological blow. "I would rather turn on the gas and put an end to the whole family than let my wife support me," one man told a social investigator. Desertions increased, and the divorce rate, after a dip in the early and mid-1930s, edged upward, hitting a then all-time high by 1940.

The depression spared neither old nor young. Bank failures wiped out the savings of many older Americans. By 1935, a million citizens over sixty-five were on relief. As for young people, one observer compared them to runners waiting for a starting gun that never sounded. High-school enrollment increased as many youths, lacking job prospects, simply stayed in school. The marriage rate declined as young people facing bleak prospects postponed this step. Commented Eleanor Roosevelt in 1934, "I have moments of real terror when I think we might be losing this generation. We have got to bring these young people into the active life of the community and make them feel that they are necessary."

Children found vacation plans canceled, birthdays with few presents, and mealtimes tense with anxious discussions. Maria Tighe of Long Island, who was seven years old in 1929, recalled sneaking to 6 A.M. mass so her friends would not see her ugly shoes, provided by the welfare bureau. Depression-era children wrote sad letters to Eleanor Roosevelt. A Michigan high-school senior described her shame at not having a graduation dress. "I give all I earn for food for the family," she explained. A thirteen-year-old Arkansas girl wrote, "I have to stay out of school because I have no books or clothes to ware."

Depression-era families also rediscovered traditional skills. They baked bread, canned fruit and vegetables, painted their own houses, and repaired their own cars. Many would later recall the 1930s as a time of simple, inexpensive pleasures and neighborly sharing of scant resources.

For the neediest—among them blacks, Hispanics, and southern sharecroppers—the depression imposed added misery on poverty-blighted lives. In his novel *Native Son* (1940), Richard Wright vividly portrayed the desperate conditions in Chicago's black slums. Yet hope survived. Emotional resilience, ingrained patterns of mutual aid, and survival skills honed through years of oppression helped poor families cope. In New York's Harlem a charismatic black religious leader calling himself Father Divine institutionalized this cooperative spirit by organizing kitchens that distributed thousands of free meals daily.

Industrial Workers Unionize   Between 1900 and 1930, the ranks of factory workers had soared from 3.7 million to 7.7 million. Yet most of these workers remained unorganized. Major industries such as steel, au-

FIGURE **24.2 The Growth of Labor Union Membership, 1933–1946**

The CIO's industrial unions grew rapidly with passage of the pro-union National Labor Relations Act in 1935. Union membership increased still more as war plants hired workers in the early 1940s. *Source: Historical Statistics of the United States, Colonial Times to 1970 (1975), 176–177.*

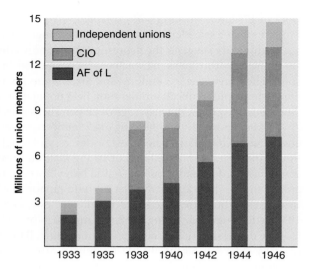

tomobiles, and textiles had resisted workers' attempts to unionize. The conservative mood of the 1920s had further weakened the labor movement.

But hard times and a favorable government climate bred a new labor militancy in the 1930s. Only through collective action, workers realized, could they pressure management to provide better wages and working conditions. The Wagner Act's guarantee of workers' right to organize energized some American Federation of Labor leaders. In November 1935, John L. Lewis of the United Mine Workers and Sidney Hillman of the Amalgamated Clothing Workers, frustrated by the AFL's slowness in organizing factory workers, started the Committee for Industrial Organization (CIO) within the AFL. Young CIO activists preached unionization in Pittsburgh steel mills, Detroit auto plants, Akron rubber factories, and southern textile mills. Unlike the craft-based and racially exclusive AFL unions, CIO unions welcomed all workers in a particular industry, regardless of race, gender, or degree of skill.

In 1936 a CIO-sponsored organizing committee geared up for a strike to unionize the steel industry. (In fact, John L. Lewis had already secretly worked out a settlement with the head of U.S. Steel.) In March 1937, U.S. Steel recognized the union, raised wages, and introduced a forty-hour workweek. Other big steel companies followed suit, and soon four hundred thousand steelworkers had signed union cards.

Other CIO organizers targeted General Motors, an anti-union stronghold. Their leader was a redheaded young autoworker and labor activist, Walter Reuther. Reuther's father, of German-immigrant stock, was a committed socialist, and when the depression hit, young Reuther rediscovered his radical roots. On December 30, 1936, employees at GM's two body plants in Flint, Michigan, stopped work and peacefully occupied the factories. This "sit-down" strategy (adopted so GM could not hire strikebreakers to keep the plants operating) paralyzed GM's production.

Although women workers did not participate in the plant occupation (to avoid gossip that might discredit the strike), they picketed on the outside. A Women's Auxiliary led by strikers' families provided meals, set up a speakers' bureau, and organized marches supporting the strike.

GM sent spies to union meetings, called in police to harass the strikers, and threatened to fire them. A showdown with the police led to the formation of the Women's Emergency Brigade, whose members remained on twenty-four-hour alert for picket duty or to surround the plants in case of further police raids.

GM asked President Roosevelt and the governor of Michigan to send troops to expel the strikers, as Herbert Hoover had done with the bonus marchers in 1932. Both officials declined, however. Although FDR disapproved of the sit-down tactic, he refused to intervene.

On February 11, 1937, GM signed a contract recognizing the United Automobile Workers (UAW). Bearded workers who had vowed not to shave until victory was won streamed out of the plants. As Chrysler fell into line also, the UAW soon boasted more than four hundred thousand members. Unionization of the electrical and rubber industries moved forward as well.

In 1938 the Committee for Industrial Organization broke with the AFL to become the **Congress of Industrial Organizations,** a 2-million-member association of industrial unions including the autoworkers. In response to the CIO challenge, the AFL began to adapt to the changed nature of the labor force. Overall, union membership in the United States shot from under 3 million in 1933 to over 8 million in 1941.

Some big corporations fought on. Henry Ford hated unions, and his tough lieutenant Harry Bennett organized a squad of union-busting thugs to fight the UAW. In 1937 Bennett's men viciously beat Walter Reuther and other UAW officials outside Ford's plant near Detroit. Not until 1941, faced with a wildcat (unauthorized) strike after Bennett fired several union sympathizers, did Ford yield to the union's pressure.

The Republic Steel Company, headed by a union hater named Tom Girdler, dug in as well. Even after the major steelmakers signed with the CIO, Republic and a group of smaller companies known collectively as "Little Steel" resisted. In May 1937 workers in twenty-seven Little Steel plants, including Republic's factory in South Chicago, walked off the job. Anticipating the strike, Girdler had assembled an arsenal of riot guns and tear gas. On May 30, Memorial Day, a group of strikers approached over 250 police guarding the factory. When someone threw a large stick at the police, they responded with gunfire that left four strikers dead and scores wounded. An investigative committee found that the police killings had been "clearly avoidable." In 1941, under growing pressure, the Little Steel companies, including Republic, finally accepted the CIO union.

Another holdout was the textile industry, with over six hundred thousand workers, mostly in the South and 40 percent female. Most textile workers earned little and had no recourse against autocratic bosses. The AFL's textile-workers union had made little headway in the 1920s owing to mill owners' hostility and the AFL's policy of admitting only skilled workers. In 1934, the CIO launched a new drive. Some four hundred thousand textile workers went on strike, but the mill owners fought back. Southern governors mobilized the National Guard to fight the strike. Several strikers were killed and thousands arrested. The strike failed, and most textile workers still did not belong to a union as the decade ended.

Indeed, despite the wave of unionization, more than three-quarters of the nonfarm labor force remained unorganized in 1940, including department-store and clerical workers and low-paid manual laborers, domestic workers, and restaurant and laundry employees—categories that included many women, blacks, and recent immigrants. Nevertheless, the unionization of key sectors of America's industrial work force ranks as one of the decade's memorable developments.

Why did powerful corporations yield to unionization after years of resistance? Certainly workers' militancy and the tactical skill of union organizers were crucial. But a changed government climate contributed as well. Historically, corporations had called on the government to help break strikes. Although this still happened in the 1930s, as in the textile-industry strike, in general the Roosevelt administration and key state officials refused to intervene on the side of management. A series of New Deal labor laws made clear that Washington would no longer automatically back management in labor disputes. Once corporate managers realized this, unionization often followed.

Organized labor's successes in the later 1930s concealed some complex tensions. A hard core of activists, some of them communists or socialists, led the unionizing drive. But most rank-and-file workers had no desire to overthrow the capitalist system. Indeed, many held back from striking, fearful for their jobs. But once the CIO's militant minority showed that picket lines and sit-down strikes could win union contracts and tangible gains, workers signed up by the thousands. As they did, the radical organizers lost influence, and the unions became more conservative.

Even Walter Reuther, despite his socialist roots, turned increasingly conservative. After World War II, in a different political climate, Reuther purged from the CIO some of the same radicals and leftists who had led the organizational battles of the 1930s.

Black and Hispanic Americans Resist Racism and Exploitation

The depression also stirred activism within the African-American and Hispanic communities. Although black migration northward slowed in the 1930s, four hundred thousand southern blacks moved to northern cities in the decade. By 1940, nearly one-quarter of the nation's 12 million blacks lived in the urban North.

Rural or urban, life was hard. Black tenant farmers and sharecroppers often faced eviction. Among black industrial workers, the depression-era jobless rate far outran the rate for whites, largely because of racism and discriminatory hiring. Although black workers in some industries benefited from the CIO's nondiscriminatory policy, workplace racism remained a fact of life.

Over one hundred blacks died by lynching in the 1930s, and other miscarriages of justice continued, especially in the South. In 1931 an all-white jury in Scottsboro, Alabama, sentenced eight black youths to death on highly suspect charges of rape. In 1935, after heavy publicity and an aggressive defense, the Supreme Court ordered a new trial for the "Scottsboro Boys" because they had been denied legal counsel and blacks had been excluded from the jury. Five of the group were again convicted, however, and served long prison terms.

But rising activism signaled changes ahead. The NAACP battled in courts and legislatures against lynching, segregation, and the denial of voting rights. Under the banner "Don't Shop Where You Can't Work," black protesters picketed and boycotted businesses that refused to hire blacks, particularly in black neighborhoods. In March 1935, hostility toward discriminatory white-owned businesses in Harlem, intensified

Young Mexican Cotton Picker in the 1930s
Whether in agricultural labor or urban barrios, Mexican-Americans endured harsh conditions during the depression.

by anger over racism and joblessness, ignited a riot that caused an estimated $200 million in damage and left three blacks dead.

The Communist Party publicized lynchings and racial discrimination, and supplied lawyers for the "Scottsboro Boys," as part of a depression-era recruitment effort in the black community. But despite a few notable recruits (including the novelist Richard Wright), few blacks joined the party.

Other minority groups also faced discrimination. California continued to restrict landownership by Japanese-Americans. In 1934, Congress set an annual limit of fifty on immigration from the Philippines, still a U.S. possession—lower than that for any other nation. Congress also offered free travel "home" for Filipinos long settled in the United States.

The more than 2 million Hispanic Americans faced trying times as well. Some were citizens with ancestral roots in the Southwest, but most were recent arrivals from Mexico or Caribbean islands such as Jamaica, Cuba, and Puerto Rico (a U.S. holding whose residents were and are American citizens). While the Caribbean immigrants settled in East Coast cities, most Mexican newcomers worked as migratory agricultural laborers in the Southwest and elsewhere, or in midwestern steel or meatpacking plants.

As the depression deepened, Mexican-born residents endured rising hostility. The western trek of thousands of "Okies" fleeing the dust bowl worsened the job crisis for Hispanic farm workers. By 1937 more than half of Arizona's cotton workers were out-of-staters who had supplanted Mexican-born laborers. With their patterns of migratory work disrupted, Mexican-Americans poured into the barrios (Hispanic neighborhoods) of southwestern cities. Lacking work, half a million Mexicans returned to their native land in the 1930s. While many did so voluntarily, others were repatriated by immigration officials and local authorities. Los Angeles welfare officials announced free one-way transportation to Mexico. The savings in relief payments, they calculated, would more than offset the cost of sending *repatriados* to Mexico. Though the plan was "voluntary," those who remained were denied relief payments or jobs with New Deal work programs. Under federal and local pressure, an estimated seventy thousand Mexicans left Los Angeles in 1931 alone.

Mexican-American farm workers who remained endured appalling conditions and near-starvation wages. A wave of protests and strikes (some led by Communist Party organizers) swept California. A labor organization called the Confederación de Uniones de Campesinos y Obreros Mexicanos (Confederation of Unions of Mexican Workers and Farm Laborers) emerged from a 1933 strike of grape workers in El Monte, California. More strikes erupted in 1935–1936 from the celery fields and citrus groves around Los Angeles to the lettuce fields of the Salinas Valley.

Organizations like the California Fruit Growers Exchange (which marketed its citrus under the brand name Sunkist) fought the unions, sometimes with violence. In October 1933, bullets ripped into a cotton pickers' union hall in Pixley, California, killing two men and wounding others. Resisting intimidation, the strikers won a 20 percent pay increase. Striking cotton pickers and other Mexican-American farm workers gained hard-fought victories as well. These strikes awakened at least some Americans to the plight of one of the nation's most exploited groups.

A New Deal for Native Americans

The 1930s also focused attention on the nation's 330,000 Native Americans, most of whom endured poverty, scant education, poor health care, and bleak prospects. The 1887 Dawes Act (see Chapter 17) had dissolved the tribes as legal entities, allocated some tribal lands to individual Indians, and offered the rest for sale. By the 1930s, whites held about two-thirds of the land that Indians had possessed in 1887, including much of the most valuable acreage. Indians had gained voting rights in 1924, but this did little to improve their lot.

In the 1920s a reform movement arose to reverse the Dawes Act approach. John Collier, who had lived among New Mexico's Pueblo Indians, founded the American Indian Defense Association in 1923 to preserve what he saw as the spiritual harmony of traditional Indian life. The National Council of American Indians, headed by Gertrude Bonnin, a Yankton Dakota Sioux, while not sharing all of Collier's goals, also pressed for reform.

Appointed commissioner of Indian affairs in 1933, Collier gathered funds from various New Deal agencies to construct schools, hospitals, and irrigation systems on reservations, and to preserve sites of cultural importance. The Civilian Conservation Corps employed twelve thousand Indian youths to work on projects on Indian lands.

Pursuing his vision of renewed tribal life, Collier drafted a bill to halt the sale of tribal land and restore the remaining unallocated lands to tribal control. Collier's bill also gave broad powers to tribal councils and required Indian schools to teach Native American history and handicrafts. Some Indian leaders criticized it as a plan to transform reservations into living museums and to treat Native Americans as an exotic people cut off from modern life. Indians who were thriving as individual property owners or entrepreneurs rejected the bill's tribalist assumptions. The bill did, indeed, reflect the idealism of well-meaning outsiders rather than the views of the nation's diverse Native American groups.

The **Indian Reorganization Act** of 1934, a compromise measure, halted the sale of tribal lands and enabled tribes to regain title to unallocated lands. But Congress scaled back Collier's proposals for tribal self-government and dropped his calls for renewal of traditional tribal culture.

A majority of tribes approved the law (a requirement for it to go into effect), but opinion differed. Of 258 tribes that voted, 181 favored the measure, while 77 did not. America's largest tribal group, the 40,000-strong Navajo, voted no, largely because the law, to promote soil conservation, restricted grazing rights.

Indian policy clearly remained contentious. But the law did recognize Indian interests and the value of cultural diversity. The restoration of tribes as legal entities laid the groundwork for later tribal business ventures as well as tribal lawsuits seeking to enforce long-violated treaty rights (see Chapter 30).

THE AMERICAN CULTURAL SCENE IN THE 1930S

Hard times and the New Deal shaped American cultural life in the 1930s. Radio and the movies offered mostly escapist fare, though some films addressed depression-era realities. The response of novelists, artists, playwrights, and photographers changed over time. When the depression first struck, as we have seen, their view of capitalist America tended to be highly critical. As the decade went on, however, a more positive view of America emerged, reflecting both optimism about the New Deal and apprehension about events abroad.

Avenues of Escape: Radio and the Movies

The standardization of mass culture continued in the 1930s. Each evening, Americans turned to their radios for network news, musical programs, and comedy shows. Radio humor flourished as hard times battered the real world. Comedians like Jack Benny and the husband-and-wife team George Burns and Gracie Allen attracted millions.

So, too, did the fifteen-minute afternoon domestic dramas known as soap operas (for the soap companies that sponsored them). Despite their assembly-line quality, these daily dollops of romance and melodrama won a devoted audience, consisting mostly of housewives. Identifying with the ordeals of the radio heroines, female listeners gained at least temporary escape from their own difficulties. As one put it, "I can get through the day better when I hear they have sorrows, too."

The movies, with their affordable ten or twenty-five cent admission, remained extremely popular. In 1939, 65 percent of Americans went to the movies at least once a week. Motion pictures, declared one Hollywood executive, had become "as necessary as any other daily commodity."

Films of the early 1930s like *Street Scene* (1931) and *I Am a Fugitive from a Chain Gang* (1932) captured the grimness of the early depression. The popular Marx Brothers movies reflected the confusion and uncertainty of the Hoover years, when the economy and the social order itself seemed on the verge of collapse. In zanily anarchic comedies like *Animal Crackers* (1930) and *Duck Soup* (1933), these vaudeville troupers of German-Jewish immigrant origins ridiculed authority and satirized the established order.

After Roosevelt took office, Warner Brothers studio (with close ties to the administration) made several topical films that presented the New Deal as the answer to the nation's problems. These included *Wild Boys of the Road* (1933), about unemployed youth; *Massacre* (1934), on the mistreatment of Indians; and *Black Fury* (1935), dealing with striking coal miners.

The gangster movies of the early thirties, inspired by real-life criminals like Al Capone and John Dillinger, served up a different style of film realism. Films like *Little Caesar* (1930) and *The Public Enemy* (1931) offered gritty images of depression America: menacing streets; forbidding industrial sites; gunfights between rival gangs. When civic groups protested the glorification of crime, Hollywood simply made the police and "G-men" (FBI agents) the heroes, while retaining the violence. The movie gangsters played by Edward G. Robinson and James Cagney, variants of the Horatio Alger hero battling adversity, appealed to depression-era moviegoers facing equally heavy odds.

Above all, Hollywood offered escape—the chance briefly to forget the depression. The publicist who claimed that the movies "literally laughed the big bad wolf of the depression out of the public mind" exaggerated, but cinema's escapist function in the 1930s is clear. Musicals such as *Gold Diggers of 1933* (with its theme song, "We're in the Money") offered dancing, music, and cheerful plots involving the triumph of pluck over all obstacles. In Frank Capra's *Mr. Deeds Goes to Town* (1936) and *Mr. Smith Goes to Washington* (1939), virtuous heroes representing "the people" triumph over entrenched interests. When color movies arrived in the late 1930s, they seemed an omen of better times ahead.

African-Americans appeared in 1930s' movies, if at all, only as stereotypes: the scatterbrained maid played by Butterfly McQueen in *Gone with the Wind* (1939); the indulgent house servant played by tap dancer Bill Robinson and patronized by child star Shirley Temple in *The Little Colonel* (1935). Under the denigrating screen name Stepin Fetchit, black actor Lincoln Perry played the slow-witted buffoon in many movies.

In representing women, Hollywood offered mixed messages. While some 1930s' movie heroines found fulfillment in marriage and domesticity, other films chipped away at the stereotype. Joan Bennett played a strong-willed professional in *The Wedding Present* (1936). Katharine Hepburn portrayed autonomous, independent-minded women in such films as *Spitfire* (1934) and *A Woman Rebels* (1936). Mae West, brassy, openly sexual, and fiercely independent, mocked conventional stereotypes in *I'm No Angel* (1933) and other 1930s' hits.

The Later 1930s: Opposing Fascism; Reaffirming Traditional Values   As the 1930s ended, many Americans viewed the nation more favorably. It had survived the depression. The social fabric remained whole; revolution had not come. As other societies collapsed into dictatorships, American democracy endured. Writers, composers, and other cultural creators reflected the changed mood, as despair gave way to a more upbeat and patriotic outlook.

International developments and a domestic political movement known as the **Popular Front** influenced this shift. In the early 1930s, the U.S. Communist Party attacked Roosevelt and the New Deal. But in 1935 Russian dictator Joseph Stalin, fearing attack by Nazi Germany, called for a worldwide alliance, or Popular Front, against Adolf

Hitler and his Italian fascist ally, Benito Mussolini. (Fascism is a form of government involving one-party rule, extreme nationalism, hostility to minority groups, and the forcible suppression of dissent.) Parroting the new Soviet line, U.S. communists now praised FDR and summoned writers and intellectuals to the antifascist cause. Many noncommunists, alarmed by developments in Europe, responded to the call.

The Popular Front's high-water mark came during the Spanish Civil War of 1936–1939. In July 1936 Spanish fascist general Francisco Franco began a military revolt against Spain's legally elected government, a coalition of left-wing parties. With aid from Hitler and Mussolini, Franco won backing from Spanish monarchists, landowners, industrialists, and the Catholic Church.

In America, the anti-Franco Spanish Loyalists (that is, those loyal to the elected government) won support from writers, artists, and intellectuals who backed the Popular Front. The novelist Ernest Hemingway, who visited Spain in 1936–1937, was among the writers who backed the Loyalists. In contrast to his antiwar novels of the 1920s (see Chapter 23), Hemingway's *For Whom the Bell Tolls* (1940) told of a young American volunteer who dies while fighting with the Loyalists. "The Spanish Civil War offered something which you could believe in wholly and completely," Hemingway later wrote, "and in which you felt an absolute brotherhood with the others who were engaged in it."

The Popular Front collapsed in August 1939 when the Soviet Union and Nazi Germany signed a nonaggression pact. Overnight, enthusiasm for joining with communists under the "antifascism" banner faded. But while it lasted, the Popular Front helped shape U.S. culture and alerted Americans to threatening events abroad.

The New Deal's programs for writers, artists, and musicians, as well as its turn leftward in 1935–1936, also contributed to the cultural shift of the later 1930s. The cynical tone of the 1920s and early 1930s now gave way to a more upbeat view. In John Steinbeck's best-selling novel *The Grapes of Wrath* (1939), an uprooted dust-bowl family, the Joads, make their difficult way from Oklahoma to California along Route 66. Steinbeck stressed the strength and endurance of ordinary Americans as well as their cooperation and mutual support. As Ma Joad tells her son Tom, "They ain't gonna wipe us out. Why, we're the people—we go on." Made into a movie by John Ford, and starring Henry Fonda, *The Grapes of Wrath* stands as a memorable cultural document of the later 1930s.

In 1936 journalist James Agee and photographer Walker Evans spent several weeks with Alabama sharecropper families while researching a magazine article. From this experience came Agee's masterpiece, *Let Us Now Praise Famous Men* (1941). Enhanced by Evans's powerful photographs, Agee's intensely personal work evoked the endurance and decency of Americans living on society's margins.

The new cultural mood also reached the stage. Thornton Wilder's play *Our Town* (1938) portrayed a New England town in which everyday events become, in memory, infinitely precious. William Saroyan's *The Time of Your Life* (1939) celebrated the foibles and virtues of a colorful collection of American "types" gathered in a San Francisco waterfront bar.

Composers, too, caught the spirit of cultural nationalism. In such works as *Billy the Kid* (1938), Aaron Copland drew upon American legends and folk melodies. George Gershwin's 1935 musical *Porgy and Bess,* based on the 1920s' novel and play by DuBose and Dorothy Heyward (see Chapter 23), brought this portrayal of black street life in Charleston, South Carolina, to a new and larger audience.

Jazz surged in popularity thanks to swing, a danceable style originated by the pianist Fletcher Henderson and popularized by the big bands of Count Basie, Benny Goodman, Duke Ellington, and others. The Basie band started at Kansas City's Reno Club, where, as Basie later recalled, "We played from nine o'clock in the evening to five or six the next morning. . . . [T]he boys in the band got eighteen dollars a week and I got twenty one." Moving to New York in 1936, Basie helped launch the swing era.

Benny Goodman, of a Chicago immigrant family, had played the clarinet as a boy at Jane Addams's Hull House. Challenging the color line in jazz, Goodman included black musicians like pianist Teddy Wilson and vibraphonist Lionel Hampton in his orchestra. A turning point in the acceptance of jazz came in 1938, when Goodman's band performed at New York's Carnegie Hall, a citadel of high culture.

The later 1930s also saw a heightened interest in regional literature, painting, and folk art. Zora Neale Hurston's novel *Their Eyes Were Watching God* (1937), exploring a black woman's search for fulfillment, was set in rural Florida. In *Absalom, Absalom!* (1936) William Faulkner continued the saga of his mythic Yoknapatawpha County in Mississippi. Painters Thomas Hart Benton of Missouri (a descendant of the nineteenth-century senator of the same name), John Steuart Curry of Kansas, and Grant Wood of Iowa struck strongly regional notes in their work.

Galleries displayed folk paintings, Amish quilts, and New England weather vanes. A 1938 show at New York's Museum of Modern Art introduced Horace Pippin, a black Philadelphia laborer partially disabled in World War I. In such paintings as *John Brown Going to His Hanging,* Pippin revealed a genuine, if untutored, talent. In 1939 the same museum featured seventy-nine-year-old Anna "Grandma" Moses of Hoosick Falls, New York, whose memory paintings of her farm girlhood enjoyed great popularity.

The surge of cultural nationalism heightened interest in the nation's past. Americans flocked to historical re-creations such as Henry Ford's Greenfield Village near Detroit and Colonial Williamsburg in Virginia, restored by John D. Rockefeller, Jr. Texans restored the Alamo in San Antonio, the "Cradle of Texas Liberty." Historical novels like Margaret Mitchell's Civil War epic *Gone with the Wind* (1936) became best sellers. These restorations and fictions often distorted history. Slavery was downplayed or sentimentalized at Colonial Williamsburg and in Mitchell's novel. "Texas Liberty" resonated differently for the state's Hispanic, African-American, and Indian peoples than it did for the patriotic organizations that turned the Alamo into a tourist shrine.

Streamlining and a World's Fair: Corporate America's Utopian Vision

A design style called streamlining also shaped the visual culture of the late 1930s. This style originated in the 1920s when industrial designers, inspired by the airplane, introduced smoothly flowing curves into the design of commercial products. Streamlining appealed to consumers—a vital business consideration during the depression. When Sears Roebuck streamlined its Coldspot refrigerators, sales surged. As products ranging from house trailers to pencil sharpeners and cigarette lighters emerged in sleek new forms, streamlining helped corporate America rebuild its image and present itself as the benevolent shaper of a better future.

Under the theme "The World of Tomorrow," the 1939 New York World's Fair represented the high point of the streamlining vogue and of corporate America's public-relations blitz. The fair's futuristic theme was symbolized by the Trylon and Perisphere: a seven-hundred-foot tapered tower and a globe that seemed to float on a pool of water. Inside the Perisphere, visitors found "Democracity," a revolving diorama portraying an idealized city of the future.

The hit of the fair was Futurama, the General Motors exhibit. Visitors entered a darkened circular auditorium where, amid piped-in music and a resonant recorded narration, a vision of America in the distant year 1960 slowly unfolded. A multilane highway network complete with cloverleaf exits and stacked interchanges dominated the imagined landscape. A brilliant public-relations investment by GM, Futurama built support for the interstate highway system that would soon become a reality. Forget the depression and even the bitter Flint strike of 1937, GM's exhibit seemed to whisper; behold the exciting future we are preparing for you.

Also featuring such wonders as television and automatic dishwashers, the World's Fair did, indeed, offer a glimpse of "The World of Tomorrow" as a harmonious technological utopia made possible by the nation's great corporations. A visit to the fair, a business magazine editorialized, "should convince [any doubters] that American business has been the vehicle which carried the discoveries of science and the benefits of machine production to . . . American consumers." The fair epitomized corporate America's version of the patriotism and hopefulness that pervaded U.S. culture as the 1930s ended.

But the hopefulness was tinged with fear. The nation had survived the depression, yet danger loomed beyond the seas. The anxiety triggered by the menacing world situation surfaced on October 31, 1938, when CBS radio aired an adaptation of H. G. Wells's science-fiction story *War of the Worlds* directed by Orson Welles. In realistic detail, the broadcast reported the landing of a spaceship in New Jersey, the emergence of aliens with ray guns, and their advance toward New York City. The show sparked a panic. Some terrified listeners jumped in their cars and sped off into the night. Others prayed. A few attempted suicide. Beneath the terror lay a more well-founded fear: of approaching war. For a decade, as America had battled the depression, the international situation had steadily worsened. By October 1938 another European war loomed on the horizon.

The panic triggered by Orson Welles's Halloween prank quickly faded, but the anxieties aroused by the all-too-real dangers abroad only escalated. By the time the New York World's Fair offered its vision of "The World of Tomorrow," the actual world of 1939 had become very scary indeed.

CONCLUSION

The 1929 stock-market crash and the ensuing Great Depression exposed major weaknesses in the U.S. and world economies. These ranged from chronically low farm prices and uneven income distribution to trade barriers, a glut of consumer goods, and a constricted money supply. As the crisis deepened, President Hoover struggled to respond. In 1932, with Hoover's reputation in tatters, Franklin D. Roosevelt and his promised "New Deal" brought a surge of hope.

Initially focusing on immediate economic relief and recovery, Roosevelt welcomed big business in his depression-fighting coalition. By 1935, however, the New Deal adopted a more class-based approach. FDR now addressed the plight of the poor, including sharecroppers and migrants; pursued tougher business regulation and higher taxes for the wealthy; and championed such fundamental reforms as the Social Security Act, centerpiece of the welfare state, and the Wagner Act, guaranteeing workers' right to unionize. FDR's smashing reelection victory in 1936 solidified the Democratic coalition he had forged, including the white South, farmers, urban ethnics, union members, and African-Americans. By 1938, facing rising conservative opposition and menaces abroad, the New Deal's reformist energies faded.

The depression and the New Deal affected different groups in different ways. For Tennessee valley residents and citizens across the West, public-works projects brought hydroelectric power and economic growth. Amid widespread joblessness, women were told to stay home so men could find work. Many resisted, however, and the female labor force expanded. For industrial workers, the decade's spirit of militance and favorable legislation brought a wave of strikes and unionization campaigns.

While African-Americans benefited from New Deal relief programs, the Roosevelt administration failed to address lynching and racial discrimination. Exploited Mexican-born farm laborers, facing deportation threats, organized strikes demanding better wages and working conditions. For Native Americans, New Deal legislation restored tribes' legal status, laying the groundwork for future enterprises and treaty claims.

American culture in the 1930s reflected the decade's economic and social realities. While the movies and radio offered diversion, writers, painters, and other cultural creators initially expressed despair and cynicism over capitalism's failure. But as New Deal programs assisted writers and artists, and as foreign threats loomed in the later 1930s, the cultural climate grew more patriotic and affirmative.

The New Deal has its downside. Some programs failed, and recovery proved elusive. Only in 1943, as war plants boomed, was full employment finally achieved. On racial issues, symbolic gestures substituted for genuine engagement. But the New Deal's achievements remain noteworthy, reflecting an unprecedented level of engagement with social and economic issues. The New Dealers radically reshaped the nature of the presidency, the nation's political agenda, and citizens' understanding of the role of government.

Looming over the decade is the larger-than-life image of Franklin D. Roosevelt. Neither saint nor superman, FDR could be devious, superficial, and cavalier about details. But for most Americans of the 1930s—and most historians since—his strengths outweighed his liabilities. His experimental approach served a suffering nation well. He once compared himself to a football quarterback, deciding which play to call after seeing how the last one worked out.

Above all, Roosevelt's optimism inspired a demoralized people. "We Americans of today . . . ," he told an audience of young people in 1939, "are characters in the living book of democracy. But we are also its author. It falls upon us now to say whether the chapters . . . to come will tell a story of retreat or a story of continued advance."

25

Americans and a World in Crisis, 1933–1945

THE UNITED STATES IN A MENACING WORLD, 1933–1939

Apart from improving relations with Latin America, the early administration of President Franklin D. Roosevelt (FDR) remained largely aloof from the crises in the world. Americans reacted ambivalently as Italy, Germany, and Japan grew more aggressive. Millions of Americans, determined not to stumble into war again, supported neutrality. Only a minority wanted the United States to help embattled democracies abroad. All the while, the world slid toward the precipice.

Nationalism and the Good Neighbor   During the Great Depression, Roosevelt put U.S. economic interests above all else. He showed little interest in free trade or international economic cooperation.

He did, however, adopt an internationalist approach in Latin America, where bitterness over decades of "Yankee imperialism" ran high. He declared a **"Good Neighbor" policy,** renouncing any nation's right to intervene in the affairs of another. To support this policy, FDR withdrew the last U.S. troops from Haiti and the Dominican Republic, and terminated the Platt Amendment, which had given the United States its right to intervene in Cuba since 1901. The key tests of the Good Neighbor policy came in Cuba and Mexico. In Cuba, an economic crisis in 1933 brought to power a leftist regime that the United States opposed. Instead of sending in the marines, as earlier administrations might have done, the United States provided indirect aid to a conservative revolt led by Fulgencio Batista in 1934 that overthrew the radical government. American economic assistance would then allow Batista to retain power until his overthrow by Fidel Castro in 1959.

In Mexico, a reform government came to power in 1936 and promptly nationalized several oil companies owned by U.S. and British corporations. While insisting on fair compensation, the United States refrained from military intervention and conceded Mexico's right to nationalize the companies. Subsequently, Mexico and the oil companies reached a compromise compensation agreement.

The Good Neighbor policy did not end U.S. interference in Latin American affairs. But it did substitute economic leverage for heavy-handed intervention and military occupation. The better relations fostered by FDR would help the United States pursue hemispheric solidarity in World War II, and later in the Cold War.

The Rise of Aggressive States in Europe and Asia

As early as 1922, economic and social unrest in Italy enabled **Benito Mussolini** to seize power. Dictator until 1943, Mussolini suppressed dissent and liberty, imposed one-party rule, strictly controlled business and labor, invaded Ethiopia in October 1935, and began to persecute Jews in 1938.

The rise of **Adolf Hitler** in Germany proved more menacing. Hitler's National Socialist (Nazi) Party had gained broad support as a result of the depression and German resentment of the harsh Versailles treaty, and Hitler became Germany's chancellor in January 1933. Crushing opponents and rivals, Hitler imposed a brutal dictatorship on Germany and began a program to purify it of Jews—whom he considered an "inferior race" responsible for Germany's defeat in World War I.

Violating the Versailles treaty, Hitler began rearming Germany in 1935. A year later, German troops reoccupied the Rhineland, a region between the Rhine River and France specifically demilitarized by the Versailles treaty. In 1938, as German tanks rolled into Vienna, Hitler proclaimed an *Anschluss* (union) between Austria and Germany. London, Paris, and Washington murmured their disapproval but took no action. An emboldened Hitler then claimed Germany's right to the Sudetenland, a part of neighboring Czechoslovakia containing 3 million ethnic Germans. British prime minister Neville Chamberlain and his French counterpart, insisting that their countries could not endure another war like that of 1914–1918, yielded to Hitler's demands in return for his assurance that Germany had no further territorial ambitions—a policy dubbed **appeasement**—at a conference in Munich in September 1938.

In Japan, meanwhile, militarists gained control of the government and launched a fateful course of expansion. In 1931, Japan sent troops into the northern Chinese province of Manchuria, and within two years took control of the province. In July 1937, it initiated a full-scale war against China itself, and soon controlled key parts of that nation. Weak protests by Washington did little to deter Japan's plans for further aggression.

The American Mood: No More War

The feeble American response reflected the people's belief that the decision to go to war in 1917 had been a mistake. This conviction was rooted in the nation's isolationist tradition—its wish to avoid military and political entanglements in Old World quarrels—as well as in its desire to have the government focus on economic matters, not foreign affairs, in the midst of the Great Depression. Popular books stressing American disillusionment with World War I's failure to make the world safe for democracy strengthened isolationist sentiment. So did a 1934–1936 Senate investigation

CHRONOLOGY, 1933–1945

1931–1932 • Japan invades Manchuria and creates a puppet government.

1933 • Adolf Hitler becomes chancellor of Germany and assumes dictatorial powers.

1934–1936 • Nye Committee investigations.

1935–1937 • Neutrality Acts.

1937 • Japan invades China.

1938 • Germany annexes Austria; Munich Pact gives Sudetenland to Germany. *Kristallnacht,* night of Nazi terror against German and Austrian Jews.

1939 • Nazi-Soviet Pact.
Germany invades Poland; World War II begins.

1940 • Germany conquers the Netherlands, Belgium, France, Denmark, Norway, and Luxembourg.
Germany, Italy, and Japan sign the Tripartite Pact.
Selective Service Act.
Franklin Roosevelt elected to an unprecedented third term.

1941 • Lend-Lease Act.
Roosevelt establishes the Fair Employment Practices Commission (FEPC).
Germany invades the Soviet Union.
Japan attacks Pearl Harbor; the United States enters World War II.
War Powers Act.

1942 • Battles of Coral Sea and Midway halt Japanese offensive.
Internment of Japanese-Americans.
Revenue Act expands graduated income-tax system.
Allies invade North Africa (Operation TORCH).
First successful atomic chain reaction.
CORE founded.

1943 • Soviet victory in Battle of Stalingrad.
Coal miners strike; Smith-Connally War Labor Disputes Act.
Detroit and Los Angeles race riots.
Allied invasion of Italy.
Roosevelt, Churchill, and Stalin meet in Tehran.

1944 • Allied invasion of France (Operation Overlord).
U.S. forces invade the Philippines.
Roosevelt wins fourth term.
Battle of the Bulge.

1945 • Yalta Conference.
Battles of Iwo Jima and Okinawa.
Roosevelt dies; Harry S Truman becomes president.
Germany surrenders.
Truman, Churchill, and Stalin meet in Potsdam.

United States drops atomic bombs on Hiroshima and Nagasaki; Japan surrenders.

headed by Republican Gerald P. Nye of North Dakota, which concluded that banking and munitions interests, whom it called "merchants of death," had tricked the United States into war to protect their loans and weapon sales to England and France.

By the mid-1930s an overwhelming majority of Americans thought that the "mistake" of intervention should not be repeated. Congress responded by passing a series of Neutrality Acts in 1935–1937. To prevent a repetition of 1917, these measures outlawed arms sales and loans to nations at war and barred Americans from traveling on the ships of belligerent powers. The high point of antiwar sentiment came in 1938 when Indiana congressman Louis Ludlow proposed a constitutional amendment requiring a national referendum on any U.S. declaration of war except in cases of direct attack. Only a direct appeal from FDR steeled Congress to reject the Ludlow Amendment by the narrowest of margins.

With the public firmly isolationist and some American companies, like IBM, with large financial investments in German industry, confrontation with fascism came solely in sports. At the 1936 Olympics in Berlin, African-American track star Jesse Owens made a mockery of Nazi theories of racial superiority by winning four gold medals and breaking or tying three world records. In 1938, in a boxing match laden with symbolism, the black American Joe Louis knocked out German fighter Max Schmeling in the first round of their world heavyweight championship fight. Although Americans cheered Lewis, they still opposed any policies that might involve them in war.

The Gathering Storm: 1938–1939   The reduced tension that followed the Munich Pact proved tragically brief. Five and a half months later, on March 15, 1939, Nazi troops occupied what remained of Czechoslovakia, violating the Munich accords. Five months after that, Hitler reached an agreement with Soviet leader **Joseph Stalin** in the German-Soviet Nonaggression Pact that their nations would not fight one another and that they would divide Poland after Germany invaded it. No longer worried about a Soviet reaction, Hitler took aim on Poland despite claims by Britain and France that they would come to an invaded Poland's assistance.

Although isolationist sentiment remained strong in the United States, opinion began to shift rapidly. After the fall of Czechoslovakia, Roosevelt called for actions "short of war" to demonstrate America's will to check fascism, and he asked Hitler and Mussolini to pledge not to invade thirty-one listed nations. A jeering Hitler ridiculed FDR's message to the Reichstag (legislative assembly), while Mussolini mocked Roosevelt's physical disability, joking that the president's paralysis must have reached his brain.

Roosevelt, however, did more than send messages. In October 1938 he asked Congress for a $300 million military appropriation; in November he instructed the Army Air Corps to plan for an annual production of twenty thousand planes; and in January 1939 he submitted a $1.3 billion defense budget. Hitler and Mussolini, the now-aroused president proclaimed, were "two madmen" who "respect force and force alone."

America and the Jewish Refugees   Hitler and the Nazis had used the power of the state and their own paramilitary organizations to assault German Jews, confiscate their property, and force them to emigrate. The Nuremberg Laws of 1935 stripped Jews of the rights of German citizenship, and increased restrictions on Jews in all spheres of German educational, social, and economic life. This campaign of hatred reached a violent crescendo on November 9–10, 1938, when the Nazis unleashed *Kristallnacht* (Night of the Broken Glass), a frenzy of arson, destruction, and looting against Jews throughout Germany.

No longer could anyone mistake the perilous situation of German Jews or misunderstand Hitler's evil intent. Some 300,000 Jews left Germany by 1939, and about 200,000 emigrated from Austria (see Beyond America—Global Interactions: Refugees from Fascism: The Intellectual Migration to the United States). But given the magnitude of the Great Depression and America's own anti-Semitism, Roosevelt did little other than deplore Hitler's persecution of the Jews, and Congress consistently rejected efforts to liberalize the immigration law or abolish its discriminatory quotas (see Chapter 23). When asked by pollsters in 1938 whether the immigration law should be changed to admit "a larger number of Jewish refugees from Germany," 75 percent said no.

The consequences of such attitudes became clear in June 1939 when the *St. Louis*, a vessel jammed with nine hundred Jewish refugees, asked permission to put its passengers ashore at Fort Lauderdale, Florida. Immigration officials refused the request, and a Coast Guard cutter stood by "to prevent possible attempts by refugees to jump off and swim ashore." The *St. Louis* turned slowly away from the lights of America and

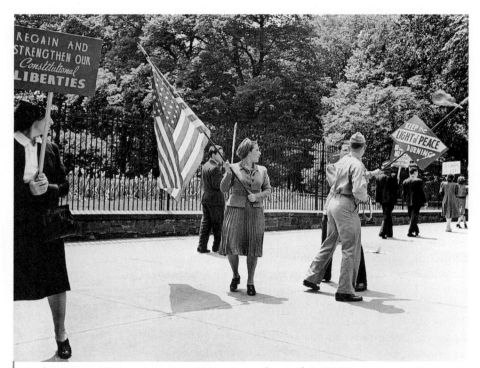

Isolationism Versus Interventionism   *In front of the White House in 1941, an American soldier grabs a sign from an isolationist picketing against the United States entering the war in Europe. A diverse group, isolationists ran the gamut from pacifists who opposed all wars, to progressives who feared the growth of business and centralized power that a war would bring, to ultra-rightists who sympathized with fascism and/or shared Hitler's anti-Semitism.*

sailed back to Germany, where more than 700 of its passengers died at the hands of the Nazis.

INTO THE STORM, 1939–1941

After a decade of crises—worldwide depression and regional conflicts—war erupted in Europe in 1939. Following the lightning German victories in western Europe in the spring of 1940, President Roosevelt's policy of neutrality to keep America out of war gave way to a policy of economic intervention. He knew that extending increasing amounts of aid to those resisting aggression by the so-called Rome-Berlin-Tokyo Axis, as well as his toughening conduct toward Germany and Japan, could, as he said, "push" the U.S. into the crisis of worldwide war. Japan's attack on the U.S. fleet at Pearl Harbor would provide the push.

The European War   Hitler began the war in Europe by demanding that Poland return the city of Danzig (Gdansk), taken from Germany after World War I. When Poland refused, Nazi troops poured into Poland on September 1, 1939. Two days later, Britain and France, honoring commitments to Poland, declared war on Germany. Although FDR invoked the Neutrality Acts, he would not ask Americans to be impartial in thought and deed (as had President Wilson in 1914).

Tailoring his actions to the public mood, which favored both preventing a Nazi victory and staying out of war, FDR persuaded Congress in November to amend the Neutrality Acts to allow the belligerents to purchase weapons from the United States if they paid cash and carried the arms away in their own ships. But "cash-and-carry" did not stop the Nazis. In the spring of 1940, Hitler's armies taught the world the meaning of *Blitzkrieg* (lightning war) as they quickly overwhelmed Denmark, Norway, Belgium, Holland, Luxembourg, and France and pinned the British army against the sea at Dunkirk. Narrowly escaping disaster, the British used every possible craft to evacuate their army and some French troops across the English Channel. By then, however, Hitler virtually controlled western Europe, and on June 22 he dictated France's surrender in the same railway car in which Germany surrendered in 1918.

Hitler now took aim at Great Britain. Round-the-clock aerial assaults by the *Luftwaffe* (air force) killed or wounded thousands of civilians, destroyed the city of Coventry, and reduced parts of London to rubble. Britain's new prime minister, **Winston Churchill,** who replaced Chamberlain in May 1940, pleaded for more U.S. aid. Most Americans, shocked at the use of German air power against British civilians, favored such aid. But a large and vocal minority opposed it as wasteful of materials needed for U.S. defenses or as a ruse to lure Americans into a war not vital to their interests.

From Isolation to Intervention   In the United States in 1940, news of the "battle of Britain" competed with speculation about whether FDR would break with tradition and run for an unprecedented third term. Not until the eve of the Democrats' July convention did he reveal that, given the world crisis, he would consent to being drafted by his party. The Axis threat clinched his renomination and forced conservative Democrats to accept the very liberal Henry Wallace, FDR's former secretary of agriculture, as his running mate. Republicans bowed to the

Refugees from Fascism: The Intellectual Migration to the United States

In line with Adolf Hitler's obsessive and virulent anti-Semitism, the Nazi government undertook a systematic campaign to deprive German Jews of their legal rights. In 1933, they were dismissed from government service, and from the universities, where, although less than 1 percent of the German population, they constituted 12 percent of the professors. In 1935, the Nuremberg laws deprived Jews of the rights of citizenship, prohibited intermarriage with non-Jews, and excluded them from hospitals, theaters, museums, and athletic fields. In November 1938, Nazi gangs murdered scores of Jews, destroyed 267 synagogues, and vandalized thousands of Jewish businesses throughout Germany. In this pogrom known as the Night of the Broken Glass (Kristallnacht), for the many Jewish shop windows smashed by the brown shirts, the Nazis sent between twenty and thirty thousand Jews to concentration camps and ordered the rest to wear yellow Stars of David. Meanwhile, Hitler also stepped up his persecution of non-Jewish intellectuals, like Thomas Mann, who opposed his murderous regime.

Some Jews in central Europe (particularly Austria, Germany, and Hungary) saw the handwriting on the wall and sought to escape. Although most lacked the means to emigrate—being forbidden to bring their property out of the country with them—or found their way blocked by countries who refused to accept refugees, Nazi anti-Semitism and political repression led perhaps a half million immigrants, between 1933 and 1941, to seek safe haven in western Europe, Switzerland, or the United States—whose rigid numerical quotas on immigration blocked entry to most.

However, as the news of Nazi persecutions made its way out of Germany, various groups organized to find refuge for the many prominent artists, scholars, and scientists who were Jews or opponents of fascism. The British Academic Assistance Council and the American Emergency Committee in Aid of Displaced Foreign Scholars worked to obtain university positions in the United States for émigré scholars. To take a stand for academic freedom and add eminence to their faculty the presidents of some American colleges formed the Emergency Committee in Aid of German Displaced Scholars. The New School for Social Research, in New York, hired German émigrés to train American graduate students in its new University in Exile. Similarly, the Institute for Advanced Study at Princeton, North Carolina's Black Mountain College, and scores of other academic, artistic, and scientific institutions opened their doors to thousands of exiles.

Although the Nazis had sought to destroy what they sneered at as Jewish science and culture, they, as one refugee scholar wrote, "spread it all over the world. Only Germany would be the loser." The United States, given the extraordinary number and talents of the refugees it accepted, would be the big winner.

Because the Second World War was in no small part a struggle of opposing scientists, the intellectual migration weakened the Axis and strengthened the Allies. The most decisive impact of the émigré scientists came in the field of nuclear physics.

Fearing the possibility that Hitler might develop atomic weapons, two refugee physicists, Leo Szilard (from Hungary) and Enrico Fermi (from Italy) convinced fellow refugee Albert Einstein to sign a letter to President Roosevelt warning about recent German discoveries in uranium fission. The result would eventually be the Manhattan Project, an Anglo-American effort to produce atomic bombs. In it, scores of émigré scientists brought their different skills and intellectual traits to bear on the single objective of beating the Germans in building a super-bomb. The refugee scientists—Hans Bethe, James Franck, Edward Teller, Eugene Wigner, among others—succeeded, and changed the world.

Mainly due to the efforts of the American Psychoanalytic Association and the Menninger Clinic in Topeka, Kansas, a lion's share of Europe's psychoanalytic teachers, therapists, and thinkers, among whom Jews predominated, also came to the United States in the 1930s and had a huge impact. Bruno Bettelheim, Erich Fromm, and other psychologists influenced by Sigmund Freud changed America's approach to mental illness, stressing the value of therapy. They influenced Americans to have greater tolerance for adolescent rebellious behavior, and convinced parents to pay attention to the psychological needs of the young. They also shaped attitudes toward crime and criminals—from punishment to rehabilitation; made public relations and sales experts more savvy about what motivates buyers; and popularized the notion that everyone has a right to self-fulfillment and happiness.

Significant changes similarly came in the social sciences and humanities. The leading lights among Austrian intellectuals, known as the Vienna Circle, advanced the school of logical positivism in American philosophy. Joseph Schumpeter and Ludwig von Mises changed the teaching of economics in the United States, much as Hannah Arendt, Theodor Adorno, and Herbert Marcuse influenced political thought. Virtually en masse, the many political and social scientists at the Institute for Social Research in Frankfurt escaped to the United States with the assistance of sympathetic Columbia University faculty. They would go on to make fundamental changes in sociology, emphasizing both a quantitative approach to studying social issues and a psychological approach to social phenomena, especially prejudice and discrimination.

Some of the brightest stars in the new American firmament were émigré artists. From Germany's Bauhaus school of design, furniture-maker Marcel Breuer and architects Walter Gropius and Ludwig Mies van der Rohe became the giants of postwar American design. Great musicians—the conductors Otto Klemperer, Erich Leinsdorf, Pierre Monteux, George Szell, and Bruno Walter; the composers Paul Hindemith, Darius Milhaud, and Arnold Schoenberg; and the pianists Artur Rubinstein, Rudolf Serkin, and Vladimir Horowitz, among many others—added luster to the concert stage and, as master teachers, influenced an entire generation of American musicians.

No other immigrant group in history had ever brought such gifts as these émigré artists and scholars brought to the United States in the 1930s. They found in the United States the freedom of thought and freedom from fear that enabled them to pursue their talents and ideas. Despite the financial difficulties of the Great Depression, private American generosity provided the funds for many of the positions in colleges, laboratories, and music schools that enabled the refugees to earn a living. And most of the Americans they worked with welcomed them, and judged them on their abilities rather than their religion or place of birth. The government, moreover, displayed unprecedented trust in these foreign-born, hiring scores of them for positions of responsibility in the atomic bomb project and other war work.

In return, most of these refugees quickly learned English, sought and obtained American citizenship, and left an indelible mark on American life. Summing up her account of these "illustrious immigrants," Laura Fermi, the wife of atomic scientist Enrico Fermi, who had fled Italy's anti-Semitism and fascism with her husband in 1938, wrote: "In making room for countless Europeans

and saving many whose lives were threatened, America proved once more a land of opportunity and a haven to which the persecuted of the world might continue to look with confidence." In return, the United States would be more than repaid in full "in a currency compounded of prestige, knowledge, and a general enrichment of culture."

Questions for Analysis

- What were the major contributions to American life made by the refugees in the Intellectual Migration?

- What steps did Americans take to welcome émigré scholars and artists and facilitate their profound impact on American life and thought?

public mood by nominating Wendell Willkie of Indiana, an all-out internationalist who championed greater aid to Britain.

FDR adroitly played the role of the crisis leader too busy to engage in politics. He appointed Republicans Henry Stimson and Frank Knox as secretaries of war and the navy. He signed the Selective Service and Training Act, the first peacetime draft in U.S. history, and approved an enormous increase in spending for rearmament. With Willkie's support, FDR engineered a "destroyers-for-bases" swap with England, sending fifty vintage ships to Britain in exchange for leases on British naval and air bases in the Western Hemisphere. Although FDR pictured the agreement as a way to keep the country out of war, it infuriated isolationists.

In the 1930s the isolationist camp had included prominent figures from both major parties and both the Right and Left. But in 1940 the arch-conservative America First Committee was isolationism's dominant voice. Largely financed by Henry Ford, the committee featured pacifist Charles Lindbergh as its most popular speaker. It insisted that "Fortress America" could stand alone. But a majority of Americans supported Roosevelt's effort to assist Great Britain while staying out of war. Reassured by the president's promise never to "send an American boy to fight in a foreign war," 55 percent of the voters chose to give Roosevelt a third term.

Calling on the United States to be the "great arsenal of democracy," Roosevelt proposed a **"lend-lease"** program to supply war materiel to cash-strapped Britain. While Roosevelt likened the plan to loaning a garden hose to a neighbor whose house was on fire, isolationist senator Robert Taft compared it to chewing gum: after a neighbor uses it, "you don't want it back." A large majority of Americans supported lend-lease, however, and Congress approved the bill in March 1941, abolishing the "cash" provision of the Neutrality Acts and allowing the president to lend or lease supplies to any nation deemed "vital to the defense of the United States." Shipments to England began at once, and after Hitler invaded the USSR in June, U.S. war supplies flowed to the Soviet Union. To defeat Hitler, FDR confided, "I would hold hands with the Devil."

Moving toward war with Germany, Roosevelt in April 1941 authorized the U.S. navy to help the British track U-boats. In mid-summer he ordered the navy to begin convoying British ships carrying lend-lease supplies, with orders to destroy enemy vessels if necessary to protect the shipments. U.S. forces also occupied Greenland and Iceland to keep those strategic Danish islands out of Nazi hands.

In August, Roosevelt met with Churchill aboard a warship off the coast of Newfoundland to map strategy. They issued a document, the **Atlantic Charter,** that condemned international aggression, affirmed the right of national self-determination, and endorsed the principles of free trade, disarmament, and collective security. The Charter envisioned a postwar world in which the peoples of "all the lands may live out their lives in freedom from fear and want."

After a U-boat torpedoed and sank the *Reuben James,* killing 115 American sailors, Roosevelt persuaded Congress in November to permit the arming of merchant ships and their entry into belligerent ports in war zones. Virtually nothing remained of the Neutrality Acts. Unprepared for a major war, America was already fighting a limited one, and full-scale war seemed imminent.

Pearl Harbor and the Coming of War   Hitler's triumphs in western Europe encouraged Japan to expand farther into Asia. Seeing Germany as its primary danger, the Roosevelt administration tried to apply just enough pressure to frighten off the Japanese without provoking Tokyo to war before the United States had built the "two-ocean navy" authorized by Congress in 1940. "It is terribly important for the control of the Atlantic for us to keep peace in the Pacific," Roosevelt told Harold Ickes in mid-1941. "I simply have not got enough navy to go around—and every episode in the Pacific means fewer ships in the Atlantic."

Both Japan and the United States hoped to avoid war, but neither would compromise. Japan's desire to create a Greater East Asia Co-Prosperity Sphere (an empire embracing much of China, Southeast Asia, and the western Pacific) matched America's insistence on the Open Door in China and the status quo in the rest of Asia. Japan saw the U.S. stand as a ploy to block its rise to world power; and the United States viewed Japan's talk of legitimate national aspirations as a smoke screen to hide aggression.

The two nations became locked in a deadly dance. In 1940, believing that economic coercion would force the Japanese out of China, the United States ended a long-standing trade treaty with Japan and banned the sale of aviation fuel and scrap metal to it. Tokyo responded by occupying northern Indochina, a French colony, and signing the Tripartite Pact with Germany and Italy in September, creating a military alliance, the Berlin-Rome-Tokyo Axis, that required each government to help the others in the event of a U.S. attack.

With the French and Dutch defeated by Germany, and Britain with its back to the wall, Japan gambled on a war for hegemony in the western Pacific. It chose to conquer

Remember Pearl Harbor   *At Minneapolis's Northern Pump Co., nightshift workers heralded the new year, 1942, with a demonstration of national unity and determination. Rather than resorting to drafting workers or compelling them to work in certain areas, the government relied primarily on what FDR called "voluntary cooperation" to fill the labor shortages in war-related jobs.*

new lands to obtain the resources it needed rather than retreat from China to gain a resumption of trade with the United States. Fatefully, Japan overran the rest of Indochina in July 1941. In turn, expecting that firmness would more likely deter Japan than provoke her to war, FDR froze all Japanese assets in the United States, imposed a new fuel embargo, and clamped a total ban on trade with Japan. But as Japan's fuel meters dropped toward empty, the expansionist General Hideki Tojo replaced a more conciliatory prime minister in October. Tojo set the first week in December as a deadline for a preemptive attack if the United States did not yield.

By late November U.S. intelligence's deciphering of Japan's top diplomatic code alerted the Roosevelt administration that war was imminent. Negotiators made no concessions, however, during the eleventh-hour talks under way in Washington. "I have washed my hands of it," Secretary of State Hull told Secretary of War Stimson on November 27, "and it is now in the hands of you and Knox—the Army and the Navy." War warnings went out to all commanders in the Pacific, advising that negotiations were deadlocked and that a Japanese attack was expected. But where? U.S. officials assumed that the Japanese offensive would continue southward, striking Malaya or the Philippines. The Japanese banked on a knockout punch; they believed that a surprise raid on

Pearl Harbor would destroy America's Pacific fleet and compel a Roosevelt preoccupied with Germany to seek accommodation with Japan.

On Sunday morning, December 7, 1941, Japanese dive-bombers and torpedo planes attacked the U.S. fleet at anchor in Pearl Harbor on the Hawaiian island of Oahu. Pounding the harbor and nearby airfields, the Japanese sank or crippled nearly a score of warships, destroyed or damaged some 350 aircraft, killed more than 2,400 Americans, and wounded another 1,200. American forces suffered their most devastating loss in history, and simultaneous attacks by Japan on the Philippines, Malaya, and Hong Kong opened the way for Japan's advance on Australia.

Critics later charged that Roosevelt knew the attack on Pearl Harbor was coming and deliberately left the fleet exposed in order to bring the United States into the war against Germany. There is no conclusive evidence to support this accusation. Roosevelt and his advisers knew that war was close but did not expect an assault on Pearl Harbor. Neither did the U.S. military officials at Pearl Harbor, who took precautions only against possible sabotage by the Japanese in Hawaii. Due to their own prejudices, Americans underestimated the resourcefulness, skill, and daring of the Japanese. They simply did not believe that Japan would attack an American stronghold five thousand miles from its home islands. At the same time, Japanese leaders erred in counting on a paralyzing blow to compel the soft, weak-willed Americans, unready for a two-ocean war, to compromise rather than fight. That miscalculation assured an aroused and united nation determined to avenge the attack.

On December 8 Congress declared war against Japan. (The only dissenter was Montana's Jeannette Rankin, who had also cast a nay vote against U.S. entry into World War I.) Three days later, honoring Germany's treaty obligation to Japan, Hitler declared war on the "half Judaized and the other half Negrified" American people; Mussolini followed suit. Congress immediately reciprocated without a dissenting vote. Confidently, Roosevelt cabled Churchill, "Today all of us are in the same boat with you and the people of the Empire, and it is a ship which will not and can not be sunk." Nevertheless, the United States faced a global war that it was not ready to fight.

After Pearl Harbor, U-boats wreaked havoc in the North Atlantic and prowled the Caribbean. Every twenty-four hours, five more Allied vessels went to the bottom. German submarines even bottled up the Chesapeake Bay for nearly six weeks. By the end of 1942, U-boat "wolf packs" had sunk more than a thousand Allied ships, offsetting the pace of American ship production. The United States was losing the Battle of the Atlantic.

The war news from Europe and Africa was, as Roosevelt admitted, "all bad." Hitler had painted the swastika across an enormous swath of territory, from the outskirts of Moscow and Leningrad—a thousand miles deep into Russia—to the Pyrenees on the Spanish-French border, and from northern Norway to the Libyan desert. In North Africa the German Afrika Korps swept toward Cairo and the Suez Canal, the British oil lifeline. It seemed as if the Mediterranean would become an Axis sea and that Hitler would be in India to greet Tojo marching across Asia before the United States was ready to fight.

Japan followed its attack on Pearl Harbor by seizing Guam, Wake Island, Singapore, Burma, and the Dutch East Indies. Having pushed the U.S. garrison on the Philippines first onto the Bataan peninsula and then onto the tiny island of Corregidor, Japan took more than eleven thousand American soldiers prisoner early in May 1942. Japan's Rising Sun flag blazed over hundreds of islands in the Pacific and over the entire eastern perimeter of the Asian mainland from the border of Siberia to the border of India.

AMERICA MOBILIZES FOR WAR

In December 1941, American armed forces numbered just 1.6 million, and war production accounted for only 15 percent of U.S. industrial output. Pearl Harbor changed everything. Congress passed a War Powers Act granting the president unprecedented authority over all aspects of the war. Volunteers and draftees swelled the armed forces; by war's end more than 15 million men and nearly 350,000 women would serve. More would work in defense industries. Mobilization required unprecedented coordination of the American government, economy, and military. In 1942 those responsible for managing America's growing war machine moved into the world's largest building, the newly constructed Pentagon. Like the Pentagon, which was intended to house civilian agencies after the war, American attitudes, behavior, and institutions would also be significantly altered by far-reaching wartime domestic changes.

Organizing
for Victory

To direct the military engine, Roosevelt formed the Joint Chiefs of Staff, made up of representatives of the army, navy, and army air force. (Only a minor "corps" within the army as late as June 1941, the air force would grow more dramatically than any other branch of the service, achieve virtual autonomy, and play a vital role in combat strategy.) The changing nature of modern warfare also led to the creation of the Office of Strategic Services (OSS), forerunner of the Central Intelligence Agency, to conduct the espionage required for strategic planning.

To organize the conversion of American industry to war production, Roosevelt established a host of new government agencies. The **War Production Board** (WPB) allocated materials, limited the production of civilian goods, and distributed contracts among manufacturers. The War Manpower Commission (WMC) supervised the mobilization of men and women for the military, agriculture, and industry, while the National War Labor Board (NWLB) mediated disputes between management and labor. Finally, the **Office of Price Administration** (OPA) rationed scarce products and imposed price and rent controls to check inflation. "The Americans can't build planes," a Nazi commander had jeered, "only electric iceboxes and razor blades." But soon after February 1942, when the last civilian car came off an assembly line, the United States achieved a miracle of war production. Automakers retooled to produce planes and tanks; a merry-go-round factory switched to fashioning gun mounts; a pinball-machine maker converted to armor-piercing shells. By late 1942 a third of the economy was committed to war production, equaling the military output of Germany, Italy, and Japan combined. Whole new industries appeared virtually overnight. With almost all of the nation's crude-rubber supply now in Japanese-controlled territory, the government built some fifty new synthetic-rubber plants. By the end of the war, the United States, once the world's largest importer of crude rubber, had become the world's largest exporter of synthetic rubber.

America also became the world's greatest weapons manufacturer, producing twice as much war material than all its Axis enemies by 1944. "To American production," Stalin would toast FDR and Churchill, "without which the war would have been lost." Indeed, the three hundred thousand military aircraft, 2.6 million machine guns, 6 million tons of bombs, and more than five thousand cargo ships and eighty-six thousand warships assembled by Americans did essentially win the war for the United States and its allies. Henry J. Kaiser, who had supervised the construction of Boulder Dam, introduced prefabrication to cut the time needed to produce a Liberty-class merchant ship from six months in 1941 to less than two weeks in 1943, and then just ten days. In 1945 Kaiser, dubbed "Sir Launchalot," and other shipbuilders were completing a cargo ship a day.

Such breakneck production had its costs. The size and powers of the government swelled as defense spending zoomed from 9 percent of the GNP in 1940 to 46 percent in 1945 and the budget soared from $9 billion to $98 billion. The number of federal civilian employees mushroomed from 1.1 million to 3.8 million. The executive branch, directing the war effort, grew the most; and an alliance formed between the defense industry and the military. (A generation later, Americans would call these concentrations of power the "imperial presidency" and the "military-industrial complex.") Because the government sought the greatest volume of war production in the shortest possible time, it encouraged corporate profits. "If you are going to try to go to war in a capitalist country," Secretary of War Stimson pointed out, "you have to let business make money out of the process or business won't work."

"Dr. New Deal," in FDR's words, gave way to "Dr. Win the War." To encourage business to convert to war production and expand its capacity, the government guaranteed profits, provided generous tax write-offs and subsidies, and suspended antitrust prosecutions. America's ten biggest corporations got a third of the war contracts, and two-thirds of all war-production spending went to the hundred largest firms, greatly accelerating trends toward economic concentration.

The War Economy   The United States spent more than $320 billion ($250 million a day) to defeat the Axis—ten times more than the cost of World War I in real dollars and nearly twice the amount that had been spent by the government since its founding. This massive expenditure ended the depression and stimulated an industrial boom that brought prosperity to most American workers. It doubled U.S. industrial output and the per capita GNP, created 17 million new jobs, increased corporate after-tax profits by 70 percent, and raised the real wages or purchasing power of industrial workers by 50 percent.

The government poured nearly $40 billion into the West, more than any other region, and four times as much as it had in the preceding decade, making the West an economic powerhouse. California alone secured more than 10 percent of all federal funds, and by 1945 nearly half the personal income in the state came from expenditures by the federal government.

A newly prospering South also contributed to the emergence of a dynamic Sunbelt. In an arc stretching from the Southeast to the Southwest, the billions spent by Uncle Sam meant millions of jobs in the textile, oil and natural gas, chemical, and aluminum industries, as well as in the shipyards of Norfolk, Mobile, and New Orleans, and the aircraft plants in Dallas–Fort Worth and Marietta, Georgia. The South's industrial capacity increased by 40 percent, and per capita income tripled. Boom times enabled hundreds of thousands of sharecroppers and farm tenants to leave the land for better-paying industrial jobs. While the South's farm population decreased by 20 percent in the 1940s, its urban population grew 36 percent.

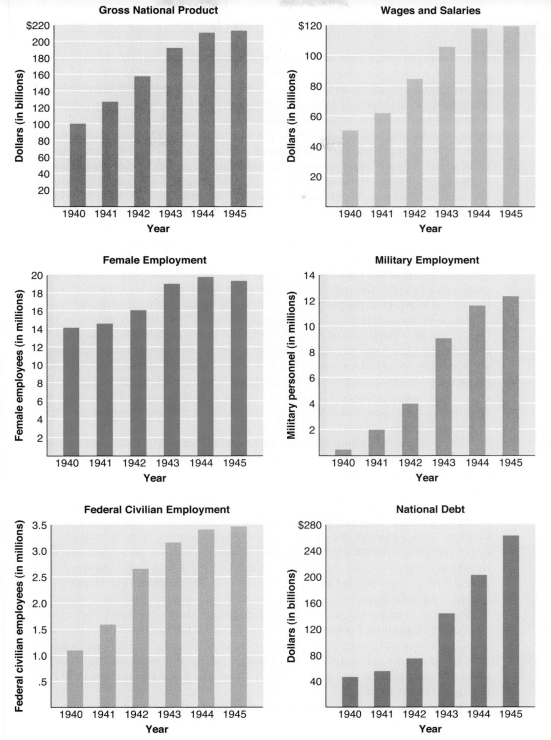

FIGURE 25.1 U.S. Wartime Production

Between 1941 and 1945, the economy grew at a remarkable pace.

Full employment, longer workweeks, larger paychecks, and the increased hiring of minorities, women, the elderly, and teenagers brought a middle-class standard of living to millions of families. In California, the demand for workers in the shipyards and aircraft factories opened opportunities for thousands of Chinese-Americans previously confined to menial jobs within their own communities. In San Diego, 40 percent of retirees returned to work. Deafening factories hired the hearing-impaired, and aircraft plants employed dwarfs as inspectors because of their ability to crawl inside small spaces. The war years produced the only significant shift toward greater equality in the distribution of income in the twentieth century. The earnings of the bottom fifth of all workers rose 68 percent, and those of the middle class doubled. The richest 5 percent, conversely, saw their share of total disposable income drop from 23 to 17 percent.

Large-scale commercial farmers prospered as a result of higher consumer prices and increased productivity thanks to improved fertilizers and more mechanization. As the consolidation of small farms into fewer large ones proceeded, corporations dominated commercial farming. Organized agriculture (later called agribusiness) took its seat in the council of power, alongside big government, big business, and organized labor.

Labor-union membership leaped from 9 million in 1940 to 14.8 million in 1945 (35 percent of nonagricultural employment). This growth resulted from the huge increase in the work force and the NWLB's "maintenance-of-membership" rule, which automatically enrolled new workers in unions and required workers to retain their union membership through the life of a contract. In return, unions agreed not to strike and to limit wage increases to 15 percent. In lieu of higher pay, they negotiated unprecedented fringe benefits for their members, including paid vacation time, health insurance, and pension plans.

Only a minority of unionists broke the no-strike pledge. Most occurred in "wildcat strikes," not authorized by union officials and of brief duration, which swept the country from 1943 to 1945. All told, however, strikes amounted to less than one-tenth of 1 percent of wartime working hours, barely affecting war production. In the most glaring exception, John L. Lewis, the iron-willed head of the United Mine Workers (UMW), led more than half a million coal-field workers out of the pits three times in 1943. Although the miners won wage concessions, their victory cost the union movement dearly. Many states passed laws to limit union power, and, over Roosevelt's veto, Congress passed the Smith-Connally War Labor Disputes Act of 1943, which empowered the president to take over any facility where strikes interrupted war production.

Far more than strikes, inflation threatened the wartime economy. Throughout 1942 prices climbed by 2 percent a month as a result of the combination of increased spending power and a scarcity of consumer goods. At the end of the year, Congress gave the president authority to control wages, prices, and rents, and as the OPA clamped down, inflation slowed dramatically. Consumer prices rose just 8 percent during the last two years of war.

The OPA also instituted rationing to combat inflation and conserve scarce materials. Under the slogan "Use it up, wear it out, make it do or do without," the OPA rationed gasoline, coffee, sugar, butter, cheese, and meat. Americans endured "meatless Tuesdays" and cuffless trousers, ate sherbet instead of ice cream, and put up with imitation chocolate that tasted like soap and imitation soap that did not lather. American men and women planted 20 million victory gardens, served as air-raid wardens, and organized collection drives to recycle cooking grease and used paper and tires, while their children, known as "Uncle Sam's Scrappers" and "Tin-Can Colonels," scoured their neighborhoods for scrap metal and other valuable trash.

Buying war bonds further curtailed inflation by decreasing consumer purchasing power, while giving civilians a sense of involvement in the distant war. The sale of bonds—"bullets in the bellies of Hitler's hordes!" claimed the Treasury Department—to schoolchildren, small investors, and corporations raised almost half the money needed to finance the war. Roosevelt sought to raise the rest by drastically increasing taxes. Congress refused the president much of what he sought. Still, the Revenue Act of 1942 raised the top income-tax rate from 60 percent to 94 percent and imposed income taxes on middle- and lower-income Americans for the first time, quadrupling the number of people who paid taxes. Beginning in 1943, the payroll-deduction system automatically withheld income taxes from wages and salaries. By 1945 the federal government was taking in nearly twenty times the tax revenue that it had in 1940.

"A Wizard War"   Winston Churchill labeled the conflict "a wizard war" in tribute to the importance of wartime scientific and technological developments. Mathematicians went to work deciphering enemy codes, psychologists devised propaganda, and, as never before, the major combatants mobilized scientists into virtual armies of invention. Their labors brought forth both miracles in healing and advances in the technology of killing. They became as indispensable to national defense as military officers, both as creators of new weapons technologies and as advisers on their use and their consequences for national security. In 1941, Roosevelt formed a committee to organize scientists for a weapons race against the Axis, and created the Office of Scientific Research and Development (OSRD) for the development of new ordnance and military medicine. OSRD spent more than $1 billion to generate radar and sonar devices, rocket weapons, and bomb fuses. It advanced the development of jet aircraft and high-altitude bombsights, and its employment of scientists to devise methods for utilizing new weapons resulted in a brand-new field called operational analysis. The need to improve military radar spurred the development of the laser, while research in quantum physics to build atomic bombs later became the basis for transistors and semiconductors. The need to supply rapidly advancing troops with unspoiled food resulted in the instant mashed potatoes on sale today.

The quest for greater accuracy in ordinance, moreover, required the kind of rapid, detailed calculations that only computing machines could supply. So a half-dozen teams of scientists went to work in 1942 to develop what would become the earliest computers. By mid-1944 navy personnel in the basement of Harvard's physics laboratory were operating IBM's Automatic Sequence Controlled Calculator, known as Mark I—a cumbersome device 51 feet long and 8 feet high that weighed five tons, used 530 miles of wire, and contained 760,000 parts. ENIAC (electronic numerical integrator and computer), developed to improve artillery accuracy for the army, reduced the time required to multiply two tenth-place numbers from Mark I's three seconds to less than three-thousandths of a second.

Nothing saved the lives of more wounded servicemen than blood plasma and improvements in blood-transfusion and blood-banking techniques. Military needs led to advances in heart and lung surgery, and to the use of synthetic antimalarial drugs to substitute for scarce quinine and toxoid vaccine to prevent tetanus. So-called miracle drugs, antibiotics to combat infections, a rarity on the eve of war, would be copiously produced. The military, which had only enough penicillin for about a hundred patients at the Battle of Midway in June 1942, had enough for all major casualties by D-Day in June 1944, and far more than it could use by V-J Day in August 1945, allowing the beginning of the sale of penicillin for civilian use.

Insecticides initially seemed as much a miracle. The use of DDT cleared many islands of malaria-carrying mosquitoes, like those at Guadalcanal that had caused five times as many casualties as combat in 1942. DDT also stopped an incipient typhus epidemic in Naples in January 1944. Along with innovations like the Mobile Auxiliary Surgical Hospital (MASH), science helped save tens of thousands of lives, halving the World War I death rate of wounded soldiers who reached medical installations. It improved the health of the nation as well. Life expectancy rose by three years during the war, and infant mortality fell by more than a third.

No scientific endeavor had a higher priority than the **Manhattan Project** to develop the atomic bomb. In August 1939 physicist Albert Einstein, a Jewish refugee, warned Roosevelt that German scientists were seeking to construct a weapon of extraordinary destructiveness, based on the discovery of nuclear fission—the splitting of the uranium atom and the release of nuclear energy. The president promptly established an advisory committee and in late 1941 launched an Anglo-American secret program—the Soviets were excluded—to produce atomic bombs. In 1942 the participating physicists, both Americans and Europeans, achieved a controlled atomic chain reaction under the University of Chicago football stadium, the first step toward developing the bomb. In 1943–1944 the Manhattan Engineer District—the code name for the atomic project—stockpiled uranium-235 at Oak Ridge, Tennessee, and plutonium at Hanford, Washington. In 1945, engineers and scientists headquartered on an isolated mesa in Los Alamos, New Mexico, assembled two bombs utilizing fissionable materials. By then the Manhattan Project employed more than 120,000 people and had spent nearly $2 billion.

Just before dawn on July 16, 1945, a blinding fireball with "the brightness of several suns at midday" rose over the Alamogordo, New Mexico, desert at a test site named Trinity. A huge, billowing mushroom cloud soon towered 40,000 feet above the ground. With a force of twenty thousand tons of TNT, the blast shattered windows more than 120 miles away. "A few people laughed, a few people cried," recalled J. Robert Oppenheimer, the Manhattan Project's scientific director. "Most people were silent. I remembered the line from the Hindu scripture, the Bhagavad-Gita: 'Now I am become Death, the destroyer of worlds.'" The atomic age had dawned.

Propaganda and Politics   People as well as science and machinery had to be mobilized for the global conflict. To sustain a spirit of unity and fan the fires of patriotism, the Roosevelt administration managed public opinion. The Office of Censorship examined letters going overseas and worked with publishers and broadcasters to suppress information that might hinder the war effort. A year passed before casualty and damage figures from Pearl Harbor were disclosed. Fearful of demoralizing the public, the government banned the publication of photographs of American war dead until 1943. Then, concerned that the public had become overconfident, the media were prompted to display pictures of American servicemen killed by the enemy and to emphasize accounts of Japan's atrocities against American prisoners.

To shape public opinion and sell the faraway war to the American people, Roosevelt created the Office of War Information (OWI) in June 1942. The OWI employed more than four thousand artists, writers, and advertising specialists to explain the war and counter enemy propaganda. The OWI depicted the war as a mortal struggle between good and evil and harped on the necessity of totally destroying, not merely defeating, the enemy.

Hollywood answered the OWI directive—"Will this help win the war?"—by highlighting the heroism and unity of the American forces, while inciting hatred of the enemy. Films about the war portrayed the Japanese, in particular, as treacherous and cruel, as beasts in the jungle, as "slant-eyed rats." Jukeboxes blared songs like "We're Gonna Have to Slap the Dirty Little Jap." U.S. propaganda also presented the war as a struggle to preserve the "American way of life," usually depicted in images of small-town, middle-class, white Americans enjoying a bountiful consumer society.

While the Roosevelt administration concentrated on the war, Republican critics seized the initiative in domestic politics. Full employment and higher wages undercut the appeal of the New Deal, and resentment over wartime shortages and dismay over Axis victories further weakened the Democrats. With voter turnout low because many soldiers and defense workers were far from the hometowns where they had registered and were thus unable to vote, the Republicans gained forty-four seats in the House and nine in the Senate in 1942.

Politics shifted to the Right. The conservative coalition of Republicans and southern Democrats abolished some New Deal agencies, such as the WPA and CCC, drastically curtailed others, and rebuffed the adoption of new liberal programs. But the dynamics of the war enormously expanded governmental power, especially the power of the executive branch. As never before, the federal government managed the economy, molded public opinion, funded scientific research, and influenced people's daily lives.

THE BATTLEFRONT, 1942–1944

Following the Japanese attack on Pearl Harbor, the outlook for the Allies appeared critical. Then America's industrial might and Soviet manpower turned the tides of war, and diplomacy followed in its wake. Allied unity dwindled as Germany and Japan weakened, and the United States, Soviet Union, and Great Britain each sought wartime strategies and postwar arrangements best suited to its own interests.

Liberating Europe   British and American officials agreed to concentrate on defeating Germany first and then smashing Japan. But they differed on where to attack. While German U-boats sank Allied ships at an appalling rate in early 1942, Hitler's forces advanced toward the Suez Canal in Egypt and penetrated deeper into the Soviet Union. Roosevelt sought to placate Stalin, who demanded a second front in western Europe to relieve the pressure on the Soviet Union, which faced the full fury of two hundred German divisions. But Churchill, fearing a repeat of the World War I slaughter in the trenches of France and wanting American assistance in maintaining British control of the vital Suez Canal, persuaded FDR to postpone the "second front" in Europe and invade North Africa instead. In Operation TORCH, begun in November 1942, American forces landed in Morocco and Algeria, and pressing eastward trapped the German and Italian armies being driven westward by the British, forcing some 260,000 German and Italian troops to surrender, despite Hitler's orders to fight to the death.

The Soviet Union proved to be the graveyard of the Wehrmacht (German army). In the main turning point of the European war, the Russians defeated the Germans in the protracted Battle of Stalingrad (August 1942–January 1943. As the Russian snow turned red with blood (costing each side more battle deaths in half a year than the United States suffered in the entire war), and its hills strewn with human bones became "white fields," Soviet forces defended Moscow, saved Stalingrad, and relieved besieged Leningrad.

Stalin pleaded again for a second front; Churchill objected again; and again Roosevelt gave in to Churchill, agreeing to invade Sicily. In summer 1943, after a month of fighting, the Allies seized Sicily and landed in southern Italy. Italian military officials deposed Mussolini and surrendered to the Allies in early September. But as Allied forces moved up the Italian peninsula, German troops poured into Italy. Facing elite

"Full Victory—Nothing Else!" *Commander-in-Chief of the Allied Expeditionary Force General Dwight D. ("Ike") Eisenhower gives the order of the day to U.S. paratroopers in England on the eve of D-Day.*

MAP 25.1 World War II in Europe and Africa

The momentous German defeats at Stalingrad and in Tunisia early in 1943 marked the turning point in the war against the Axis. By 1945 Allied conquest of Hitler's "thousand-year" Reich was imminent.

Nazi divisions in strong defensive positions, the Allies spent eight months inching their way 150 miles to Rome. They were still battling through the mud and snow of northern Italy when the war in Europe ended in 1945.

In 1943–1944 the Allies turned the tide in the Atlantic and instituted round-the-clock bombardment of Germany. American science and industry developed sophisticated radar and sonar systems and better torpedoes and depth charges, and produced ever-increasing quantities of destroyers and aircraft. Britain's Royal Air Force by night and the U.S. army air force by day rained thousands of tons of bombs on German cities. In raids on Hamburg in July 1943 Allied planes dropped incendiary bombs mixed with high explosives, killing at least 35,000 people and leveling the city, much as they had earlier done to Cologne and would do to Dresden in February 1945, where an estimated sixty thousand people died and another thirty-seven thousand were injured.

Meanwhile, in July 1943 German and Soviet divisions fought the largest tank battle in history near the city of Kursk in the Ukraine, and the victorious Red Army began an offensive that rid the Soviet Union of Germans by mid-1944. It then plunged into Poland and established a puppet government, took control of Romania and Bulgaria, and assisted communist guerrillas led by Josip Broz Tito in liberating Yugoslavia.

As the Soviets swept across eastern Europe, Allied forces finally opened the long-delayed second front. Early on the morning of June 6, 1944—D-Day—nearly two hundred thousand American, British, and Canadian troops, accompanied by six hundred warships and more than ten thousand planes, stormed a sixty-mile stretch of the Normandy coast in the largest amphibious invasion in history. Led by General Eisenhower, now Supreme Commander of the Allied Expeditionary Force in Western Europe, **Operation OVERLORD** gradually pushed inland, securing the Low Countries, liberating Paris, and approaching the border of Germany. There, in the face of supply problems and stiffened German resistance, the Allied offensive ground to a halt. In mid-December, as the Allies prepared for a full-scale assault on Germany, Hitler threw his last reserves against Americans in the forest of Ardennes. The **Battle of the Bulge**—named for the eighty-mile-long and fifty-mile-wide "bulge" that the German troops drove inside the American lines—raged for nearly a month, and ended with American forces on the banks of the Rhine, the German army depleted, and the end of the European war in sight.

War in the Pacific   The day after the Philippines fell to Japan in mid-May 1942, the U.S. and Japanese fleets clashed in the Coral Sea off northeastern Australia in the first battle in history fought entirely by planes from aircraft carriers. Each lost a carrier, but the battle stymied the Japanese advance on Australia.

Less than a month later, a Japanese armada headed toward Midway Island, a crucial American outpost between Hawaii and Japan. The U.S. Signal Corps, however, had broken the Japanese naval code. Knowing the plans and locations of Japan's ships, the U.S. carriers and planes won a decisive victory, sinking four Japanese carriers and destroying hundreds of planes. Suddenly on the defensive, the stunned Japanese could now only try to hold what they had already won.

On the offensive, U.S. marines waded ashore at Guadalcanal in the Solomon Islands in August 1942. Facing fierce resistance as well as tropical diseases like malaria, the Americans needed six months to take the island, a bitter preview of the battles to come. As the British moved from India to retake Burma, the United States began a two-pronged advance toward Japan in 1943. The army, under General Douglas MacArthur, advanced north on the islands between Australia and the Philippines, and the navy and marines, under Admiral Chester Nimitz, "island-hopped" across the central Pacific to seize strategic bases and put Tokyo in range of American bombers. In fall 1944 the navy annihilated what remained of the Japanese fleet at the battles of the Philippine Sea and Leyte Gulf, giving the United States control of Japan's air and shipping lanes and leaving the Japanese home islands open to invasion.

MAP 25.2 World War II in the Pacific

American ships and planes stemmed the Japanese offensive at the Battles of the Coral Sea and Midway Island. Thereafter, the Japanese were on the defensive against American amphibious assaults and air strikes.

Legend:
- Japanese Empire, 1936
- Japanese-controlled areas, Aug. 1942
- Allied Powers
- Soviet Union and its allies (entered Pacific war Aug. 1945)
- Allied advances
- Major battles
- Atomic bombs

Map labels:
SOVIET UNION
MONGOLIA
MANCHUKUO (MANCHURIA)
Aug. 1945
CHINA
Chungking
Nanking
TIBET
INDIA (Br.)
BURMA (Br.)
THAILAND
FRENCH INDOCHINA (Vichy)
MALAYA
Singapore
Sumatra
Borneo
Java
Celebes
NETHERLANDS EAST INDIES
South China Sea
Hong Kong
Formosa (Taiwan)
KOREA
JAPAN
Tokyo
Sakhalin I.
Kamchatka
KURILE IS.
Bering Sea
ALASKA (U.S.)
ALEUTIAN IS.
Kiska I.
Attu I.
May 1943
PACIFIC OCEAN
INDIAN OCEAN
AUSTRALIA
New Guinea
NEW HEBRIDES (Fr. - Br.)
FIJI IS. (Br.)
New Caledonia (Fr.)
SOLOMON IS.
Rabaul
Lae
Guadalcanal Aug. 7, 1942 - Feb. 9, 1943
Coral Sea May 7 - 8, 1942
Apr. 1942
Aug. 1942
ELLICE IS. (Br.)
GILBERT IS. (Br.)
Tarawa Nov. 20, 1943
Nov. 1943
MARSHALL IS.
Eniwetok Feb. 17, 1944
Japanese Mandate
CAROLINE IS.
MARIANA IS.
Guam July 21 - Aug. 10, 1944 □ (U.S.)
Wake I. (U.S.)
Midway Is. (U.S.) Midway June 3 - 6, 1942
HAWAIIAN IS. (U.S.)
Pearl Harbor Dec. 7, 1941
Nov. 1943
PHILIPPINE IS.
Leyte Gulf Oct. 23 - 26, 1944
Apr. 1945
Iwo Jima Feb. 19 - Mar. 16, 1945
Okinawa Apr. 1 - June 21, 1945
Hiroshima Aug. 6, 1945
Nagasaki Aug. 9, 1945

Scale:
1000 Miles
1000 Kilometers

The Grand Alliance President Roosevelt had two main goals for the war: the total defeat of the Axis at the least possible cost in American lives, and the establishment of a world order strong enough to preserve peace, open trade, and ensure national self-determination in the postwar era. Aware that only a common enemy fused the Grand Alliance together, Roosevelt tried to promote harmony by concentrating on military victory and postponing divisive postwar matters.

Churchill and Stalin had other goals. Britain wanted neither the United States nor the Soviet Union to reshape and dominate the postwar world; it especially sought to retain its imperial possessions. As Churchill said, he had "not become the King's First Minister to preside over the liquidation of the British Empire." The Soviet Union wanted a permanently weakened Germany and a sphere of influence (a region whose governments can be counted on to do a great power's bidding) in eastern Europe. To hold together this fragile alliance, FDR relied on personal diplomacy to mediate conflicts.

The first president to travel by plane while in office, Roosevelt arrived in Casablanca, Morocco's main port, in January 1943 to confer with Churchill. They resolved to attack Italy before invading France and proclaimed that the war would continue until the "unconditional surrender" of the Axis. By so doing, they sought to reduce Soviet mistrust of the West, which had deepened because of the postponement of the second front. Ten months later, in Cairo, Roosevelt met with Churchill and Jiang Jieshi (Chiang Kai-shek), the anticommunist head of the Chinese government. To keep China in the war, FDR promised the return of Manchuria and Taiwan to China and a "free and independent Korea." From Cairo, FDR and Churchill continued on to Tehran, Iran's capital, to meet with Stalin. Here they set the invasion of France for June 1944, and agreed to divide Germany into zones of occupation and to impose reparations on the Reich. Most importantly to Roosevelt, Stalin pledged to enter the war against Japan after Hitler's defeat.

Roosevelt then turned his attention to domestic politics. Increasing conservative sentiment in the nation led him to drop the liberal Henry A. Wallace from the ticket and accept Harry S Truman as his vice-presidential candidate. A moderate senator from Missouri, now dubbed "the new Missouri Compromise," Truman restored a semblance of unity to the Democrats for the 1944 campaign. To compete, the Republicans nominated moderate and noncontroversial New York governor Thomas E. Dewey. The campaign focused more on personalities than on issues, and the still-popular FDR defeated his dull GOP opponent, but with the narrowest margin since 1916—winning 53 percent of the popular vote. A weary Roosevelt, secretly suffering from hypertension and heart disease, now directed his waning energies toward defeating the Axis and constructing an international peacekeeping system.

WAR AND AMERICAN SOCIETY

The crisis of war altered the most basic patterns of American life, powerfully affecting those on the home front as well as those who served in the armed forces. Few families were untouched: more than 15 million Americans went to the war, an equal number were on the move, and unprecedented numbers of women went to work outside the home. As well, the war opened some doors of opportunity for African-Americans and other minorities, although many remained closed. It heightened minority aspirations and widened cracks in the wall of white racist attitudes and policy, while maintaining much of America's racial caste system, thereby tilling the ground for future crises.

The GIs' War

Most Americans in the armed forces griped about regimentation and were more interested in dry socks than in ideology. They knew little of the big strategies, and cared less. They fought because they were told to and wanted to stay alive. Reluctant recruits rather than heroic warriors, most had few aims beyond returning to a safe, familiar United States.

But the GIs' war dragged on for almost four years, transforming them in the process. Millions who had never been far from home traveled to unfamiliar cities and remote lands, shedding their parochialism. Sharing tents and foxholes with Americans of different religions, ethnicities, and classes, their military service acted as a "melting pot" experience that freed them from some prewar prejudices.

In countless ways, the war modified how GIs saw themselves and others. Besides serving with people they had never previously encountered, over a million married overseas, broadening personal horizons and sowing the seeds of a more tolerant and diverse national culture that placed far less emphasis on divisions of class, national origin, region, and religion. At the same time many GIs became evermore distrustful of foreigners and outsiders, and returned home obsessed with the flag as a symbol of patriotism.

Physical misery, chronic exhaustion, and, especially, intense combat took a heavy toll, leaving lasting psychological as well as physical wounds. Both American and Japanese troops saw the other in racist images, as animals to be exterminated, and brutality became as much the rule as the exception in "a war without mercy." Both sides machine-gunned hostile flyers in parachutes; both tortured and killed prisoners in cold blood; both mutilated enemy dead for souvenirs. In the fight against Germany, cruelties and atrocities also occurred, although on a lesser scale. A battalion of the Second Armored Division calling itself "Roosevelt's Butchers" boasted that it shot all the German soldiers it captured. Some U.S. pilots laughed at the lifeboats they strafed and the bodies they exploded out of trucks. Some became cynical about human life; others, haunted by nightmares about the war, would long languish in veterans' hospitals.

The Home Front

Nothing transformed the social topography more than the vast internal migration of an already mobile people. About 15 million men moved because of military service, often accompanied by family members. Many other Americans moved to secure new economic opportunities, especially in the Pacific coast states. Nearly a quarter of a million found jobs in the shipyards of the Bay area and at least as many in the aircraft industry that arose in the orange groves of southern California. More than one hundred thousand worked in the Puget Sound shipyards of Washington State and half as many in the nearby Boeing airplane plants. Others flocked to the world's largest magnesium plant in Henderson, Nevada, to the huge Geneva Steel Works near Provo, Utah, and to the Rocky Mountain Arsenal and Remington Rand arms plant outside Denver.

At least 6 million people left farms to work in urban areas, including several million southern blacks and whites. They doubled Albuquerque's population and increased

San Diego's some 90 percent. This mass uprooting of people from familiar settings made Americans both more cosmopolitan and lonelier. Some who moved far from their hometowns left behind their traditional values. Housing shortages left millions living in converted garages and trailer camps, even in cars. Some workers in Seattle lived in chicken coops. The swarms of migrants to Mobile, Alabama, attracted by a new aluminum plant, two massive shipyards, an air base, and an army supply depot, transformed a sleepy fishing village into a symbol of urban disorder.

Overcrowding, and wartime separations, strained family and community life. High rates of divorce, mental illness, family violence, and juvenile delinquency reflected the disruptions caused in part by the lack of privacy, the sense of impermanence, the absence of familiar settings, and the competition for scarce facilities. Few boom communities had the resources to supply their swollen populations with transportation, recreation, and social services. Urban blight and conflicts between newcomers and old-timers accelerated.

While military culture fostered a sexist mentality, emphasizing the differences between "femininity" and "masculinity," millions of American women donned pants, put their hair in bandannas, and went to work in defense plants. Reversing a decade of efforts to exclude women from the labor force, the federal government urged women into war production in 1942. Songs like "We're the Janes Who Make the Planes" encouraged women to take up war work. Propaganda called upon them to take jobs and "release able-bodied men for fighting." More than 6 million women entered the labor force during the war, increasing the number of employed women to 19 million. Less than a quarter of the labor force in 1940, women constituted well over a third of all workers in 1945.

Before the war most female wage earners had been young and single. By contrast, 75 percent of the new women workers were married, 60 percent were over thirty-five, and more than 33 percent had children under the age of fourteen. They tended blast furnaces, operated cranes, greased locomotives, drove taxis, welded hulls, loaded shells, and worked in coke plants and rolling mills. On the Pacific coast, more than one-third of all workers in aircraft and shipbuilding were women. **"Rosie the Riveter,"** holding a pneumatic gun in arms bulging with muscles, became the symbol of the woman war worker; she was, in the words of a popular song, "making history working for victory."

Yet traditional attitudes and gender discrimination existed throughout the war. Women earned only about 65 percent of what men earned for the same work, and were often denied equal seniority rights. Labor unions often stipulated that women had to give up their jobs to men on their return from military service, and government propaganda portrayed women's war work as a temporary response to an emergency. "A woman is a substitute," claimed a War Department brochure, "like plastic instead of metal." As a result, the public attitude about women's employment changed little in World War II. In 1945, only 18 percent of the respondents in a poll approved of married women working.

Traditional notions of a woman's place and the stigma attached to working mothers also shaped government resistance to establishing child-care centers for women employed in defense. "A mother's primary duty is to her home and children," the Labor Department's Children's Bureau stated. "This duty is one she cannot lay aside, no matter what the emergency." New York mayor Fiorello LaGuardia proclaimed that the worst mother was better than the best nursery. Funds for federal child-care centers covered fewer than 10 percent of defense workers' children, and the young suffered. Terms like "eight-hour orphans" and "latch-key children" described unsupervised children forced to take care of themselves. Fueling the fears of those who believed that the employment of women outside the home would cause the family to disintegrate, juvenile delinquency increased fivefold and the divorce rate zoomed from 16 per 100 marriages in 1940 to 27 per 100 in 1944.

The impact of war on women and the family proved multifaceted and even contradictory. As the divorce rate soared, so did marriage rates and birthrates. Although some women remained content to roll bandages for the Red Cross, more than three hundred thousand joined the armed forces and, for the first time in American history, were given regular military status and served in positions other than that of nurse. As members of the Women's Army Corps (WACs) and the Navy's Women Appointed for Volunteer Emergency Service (WAVES), they replaced men in such noncombat jobs as mechanics and radio operators, and served as mapmakers and ferry pilots. About a thousand women became civilian pilots with the WASPs (Women's Airforce Service Pilots). When they left the service, moreover, women had the same rights and privileges as male veterans.

Despite lingering notions of separate spheres, female workers gained unprecedented employment opportunities and public recognition. Although some eagerly gave up their jobs at the end of the war, others did not relish losing the income, independence, and self-esteem they had gained in contributing to the war effort. As Inez Sauer, who went to work for Boeing in Seattle, recalled,

> My mother warned me when I took the job that I would never be the same. She said, "You will never want to go back to being a housewife." She was right, it definitely did. At Boeing I found a freedom and an independence I had never known. After the war I could never go back to playing bridge again, being a clubwoman and listening to a lot of inanities when I knew there were things you could use your mind for. The war changed my life completely.

Overall, women gained a new sense of their potential. The war proved their capabilities and widened their world. Recalled one war wife whose returning husband did not like her independence, "He had left a shrinking violet and come home to a very strong oak tree." Wartime experiences markedly affected a generation of women and the sons and daughters they later raised.

Some of these women were among the 350,000 teachers who took better-paying war work or joined the armed services, leaving schools badly understaffed. Students, too, abandoned school in record numbers. High school enrollments sank as the full-time employment of teenagers rose from 900,000 in 1940 to 3 million in 1944.

The loss of students to war production and the armed services forced colleges to admit large numbers of women and to contract themselves out to the armed forces. Nearly a million servicemen took college classes in science, engineering, and foreign languages. The military presence was all-pervasive. Harvard University awarded four military-training certificates for every academic degree it conferred. The chancellor of one branch of the University of California announced that his school was "no longer an academic tent with military sideshows. It is a military tent with academic sideshows." Higher education became more dependent on the federal government, and most universities sought increased federal contracts and subsidies, despite their having to submit to greater government interference and regulation. The universities in the West received some $100 billion from the Office of Scientific Research and Development, more money than had been spent on scientific research by all the western universities since their founding.

The war profoundly affected American culture. Spending on books and theater entertainment doubled. More than 60 million people (in a population of 135 million) attended movies weekly, and the film industry reached its zenith in 1945–1946. But as the war dragged on, people tired of patriotic war films, and Hollywood reemphasized romance and nostalgia with such stars as Katharine Hepburn and Judy Garland.

Similarly, popular music early in the war featured patriotic themes. "Goodbye, Mama, I'm Off to Yokohama" became the first hit of 1942. As the war continued, themes of lost love and loneliness dominated lyrics. Numbers like "They're Either Too Young or Too Old" expressed the laments of women separated from the men they loved. So, too, did the dozens of "dream songs" in which love denied by the real world could be achieved only in a dream. By 1945 bitterness rather than melancholy pervaded the lyrics of best-selling records, and songs like "Saturday Night Is the Loneliest Night of the Week" revealed impatience for the war's end.

In bookstores, nonfiction ruled the roost and every newsmagazine increased its circulation. The Government Printing Office published Armed Services Editions, paperback reprints of classics and new releases; and the nearly 350 million copies distributed free to soldiers sped up the American acceptance of quality paperbacks, which were introduced in 1939 by the Pocket Book Company. Wendell Willkie's *One World* (1943) became the fastest-selling title in publishing history to that time, with 1 million copies snapped up in two months. A euphoric vision of a world without military alliances and spheres of influence, this brief volume expressed hope that an international organization would extend peace and democracy through the postwar world. Most startlingly, Willkie attacked "our imperialisms at home." Unless the United States ended its own racism, he concluded, nonwhites around the globe would rebuff its claim to world leadership. "If we want to talk about freedom, we must mean freedom for everyone inside our frontiers."

An avid interest in wartime news also spurred the major radio networks to increase their news programs from 4 percent to nearly 30 percent of broadcasting time, and enticed Americans to listen to the radio an average of 4½ hours a day. Daytime radio serials, like those featuring Dick Tracy tracking down Axis spies, reached the height of their popularity, as did juvenile comic books in which a platoon of new superheroes, including Captain America and Captain Marvel, saw action on the battlefield. Even Bugs Bunny donned a uniform to combat America's foes.

Racism and New Opportunities

Recognizing that the government needed the loyalty and labor of a united people, black leaders entered World War II determined to secure equal rights. In 1942 civil-rights spokesmen insisted that African-American support of the war hinged on America's commitment to racial justice. They demanded a *"Double V"* campaign to gain victory over racial discrimination at home as well as over the Axis abroad.

Membership in the NAACP multiplied nearly ten times, reaching half a million in 1945. The association pressed for legislation outlawing the poll tax and lynching, decried discrimination in defense industries and the armed services, and sought to end black disfranchisement. The campaign for voting rights gained momentum when the Supreme Court, in *Smith* v. *Allwright* (1944), ruled the Texas all-white primary unconstitutional. The decision eliminated a bar that had existed in eight southern states, although these states promptly resorted to other devices to minimize voting by blacks.

A new civil-rights organization, the Congress of Racial Equality (CORE), was founded in 1942. Employing the same forms of nonviolent direct action that Mohandas Gandhi used in his campaign for India's independence, CORE sought to desegregate public facilities in northern cities.

Also proposing nonviolent direct action, **A. Philip Randolph,** president of the Brotherhood of Sleeping Car Porters, in 1941 called for a "thundering march" of one hundred thousand blacks on Washington "to wake up and shock white America as it has never been shocked before." He warned Roosevelt that if the president did not end discrimination in the armed services and the defense industry, angry African-Americans would besiege Washington. FDR agreed to compromise.

In June 1941 Roosevelt issued Executive Order 8802, the first presidential directive on race since Reconstruction. It prohibited discriminatory employment practices by federal agencies and all unions and companies engaged in war-related work, and established the Fair Employment Practices Commission (FEPC) to monitor compliance. Although the FEPC lacked effective enforcement powers, booming war production and a labor supply depleted by military service resulted in the employment of some 2 million African-Americans in industry and two hundred thousand in the federal civil service. Between 1942 and 1945 the proportion of blacks in war-production work rose from 3 to 9 percent. Black membership in labor unions doubled to 1.25 million, and the number of skilled and semiskilled black workers tripled. Formerly mired in low-paying domestic and farm jobs, some three hundred thousand black women found work in factories and the civil service. "Hitler was the one that got us out of the white folks' kitchen," recalled one black woman who went to work for Boeing in Seattle, a city whose black population rose from four thousand to forty thousand during the war. Overall, the average wage for African-Americans increased from $457 to $1,976 a year, compared with a gain from $1,064 to $2,600 for whites.

About 1 million African-Americans served in the armed forces. Wartime needs forced the military to end policies of excluding blacks from the marines and coast guard, restricting them to jobs as mess boys in the navy, and confining them to noncombatant units in the army. From just five in 1940—three of them chaplains—the number of black officers grew to over seven thousand in 1945. The all-black 761st Tank Battalion gained distinction fighting in Germany, and the 99th Pursuit Squadron won eighty Distinguished Flying Crosses for its combat against the *Luftwaffe* in Europe. In 1944 both the army and navy began token integration in some training facilities, ships, and battlefield platoons.

The great majority of blacks, however, served throughout the war in segregated service units commanded by white officers. This indignity, made worse by the failure of military authorities to protect black servicemen off the post and by the use of white military police to keep blacks "in their place," sparked rioting on army bases. At least fifty black soldiers died in racial conflicts during the war. "I used to sing gospel songs until I joined the Army," recalled blues-guitar great B. B. King, "then I sang the blues."

Violence within the military mirrored growing racial tensions on the home front. As blacks protested against discrimination, many whites resisted all efforts by blacks to improve their economic and social status. Numerous clashes occurred. Scores of cities reported pitched battles between blacks and whites. Race riots erupted in 1943 in Harlem, Mobile, and Beaumont, Texas. The bloodiest melee exploded in Detroit that year when white mobs assaulted blacks caught riding on trolleys or sitting in movie theaters and blacks smashed and looted white-owned stores and shops. After thirty hours of racial beatings, shootings, and burning, twenty-five African-Americans and nine whites lay dead, more than seven hundred had been injured, and over $2 million of property had been destroyed. The fear of continued violence led to a greater emphasis on racial tolerance by liberal whites and to a reduction in the militancy of African-American leaders.

Yet the war brought significant changes that would eventually result in a successful drive for black civil rights. The migration of over seven hundred thousand blacks from the South turned a southern problem into a national concern. It created a new attitude of independence in African-Americans freed from the stifling constraints of caste. Despite the continuation of racial prejudice and discrimination, most who left the rural South found a more abundant and hopeful life than the one they had left behind. As the growing numbers of blacks in northern cities began to vote, moreover, African-Americans could hold a balance of power in close elections. This prompted politicians in both major parties to extend greater recognition to blacks and to pay more attention to civil-rights issues.

African-American expectations of greater government concern for their rights also resulted from the new prominence of the United States as a major power in a predominantly nonwhite world. As Japanese propaganda appeals to the peoples of Asia and Latin America emphasized lynchings and race riots in the United States, Americans had to confront the peril that white racism posed to their national security. In addition, the horrors of Nazi racism discredited America's own white-supremacist attitudes and practices. A former governor of Alabama complained, Nazism has "wrecked the theories of the master race with which we were so contented so long." And Roosevelt proclaimed, "There never has been, there isn't now, and there never will be, any race of people on earth fit to serve as masters over their fellow men." A pluralist vision of American society now became part of official rhetoric, and of the liberal-left agenda. The contradiction between American ideals of freedom and equality and the actual state of African-Americans became manifest. Swedish economist Gunnar Myrdal, in his massive study of race problems, *An American Dilemma* (1944), concluded that "not since Reconstruction had there been more reason to anticipate fundamental changes in American race relations. . . . [T]here is bound to be a redefinition of the Negro's status as a result of this War." Returning black veterans, and African-Americans who had served the nation on the home front, expected to soon gain all the rights enjoyed by whites.

War and Diversity   Wartime winds of change also brought new opportunities and difficulties to other minorities. More than twenty-five thousand Native Americans served in the armed forces, including 400 Navajo "code talkers" who confounded the Japanese by using their complex native language to relay messages between U.S. command centers. "Were it not for the Navajos, the Marines would never have taken Iwo Jima," one Signal Corps officer declared.

Another fifty thousand Indians left the reservation to work in defense industries, mainly on the West Coast. The Rosebud Reservation in South Dakota lost more than a quarter of its population to migration during the war. It was the first time most had lived in a non-Indian world, and the average income of Native American households tripled during the war. Such economic improvement encouraged many Indians to remain outside the reservation and to try to assimilate into mainstream life. But anti-Indian discrimination, particularly in smaller towns near reservations such as Gallup, New Mexico, and Billings, Montana, forced many Native Americans back to their reservations, which had suffered severely from budget cuts during the war. Prodded by those who coveted Indian lands, lawmakers demanded that Indians be taken off the backs of the taxpayers and "freed from the reservations" to fend for themselves. To mobilize against the campaign to end all reservations and trust protections, Native Americans organized the National Congress of American Indians in 1944.

To relieve labor shortages in agriculture, caused by conscription and the movement of rural workers to city factories, the U.S. government negotiated an agreement with Mexico in July 1942 to import *braceros,* or temporary workers. Classified as foreign laborers rather than as immigrants, an estimated two hundred thousand *braceros,* half of them in California, received short-term contracts promising adequate wages, medical care, and decent living conditions. But farm owners frequently violated the terms of these contracts and also encouraged an influx of illegal migrants from Mexico desperate for employment. Unable to complain about their working conditions without risking arrest and deportation, hundreds of thousands of Mexicans were exploited by agribusinesses in Arizona, California, and Texas. At the same time, tens of thousands of Chicanos left agricultural work for jobs in factories, shipbuilding yards, and steel mills. By 1943 about half a million Chicanos were living in Los Angeles County, 10 percent of the total population. In New Mexico nearly 20 percent of Mexican-American farm laborers escaped from rural poverty to urban jobs. Even as their occupational status and material conditions improved, most Mexican-Americans remained in communities called *colonias,* segregated from the larger society and frequently harassed by the police.

Much of the hostility toward Mexican-Americans focused on young gang members who wore "zoot suits"—a fashion that originated in Harlem and emphasized long, broad-shouldered jackets and pleated trousers tightly pegged at the ankles. Known as pachucos, zoot-suited Mexican-Americans aroused the ire of servicemen stationed or on leave in Los Angeles who saw them as delinquents and draft dodgers. After a luridly publicized trial arising from a Mexican-American gang fight at a swimming hole called Sleepy Lagoon, and newspaper headlines of a Chicano "crime wave," bands of sailors from nearby bases and soldiers on leave in Los Angeles rampaged through the city in early June 1943, stripping pachucos, cutting their long hair, and beating them. Military authorities looked the other way. City police intervened only to arrest Mexican-Americans. *Time* magazine described the violence as "the ugliest brand of mob action since the coolie race riots of the 1870s"; yet Los Angeles officials praised the servicemen's actions, and the city council made the wearing of a zoot suit a misdemeanor. Nothing was done about the substandard housing, disease, and racism Hispanics had to endure.

Unlike African-Americans, however, more than 350,000 Mexican-Americans served in the armed forces without segregation, and in all combat units. They volunteered in much higher numbers than warranted by their percentage of the population and earned a disproportionate number of citations for distinguished service as well as seventeen Medals of Honor. Air corps hero Jose Holguin from Los Angeles won the Distinguished Flying Cross, the Air Medal, and the Silver Star. Returning Mexican-American GIs joined established antidiscrimination groups, like the League of United Latin American Citizens (LULAC), and organized their own associations, like the American GI Forum, to press for equal rights.

Thousands of gay men and lesbians who served in the armed forces also found new wartime opportunities. Although the military officially barred those they defined as "sexual perverts," the urgency of building a massive armed forces led to just four to five thousand men out of 18 million examined for induction to be excluded because of homosexuality. For the vast majority of gays not excluded, being emancipated from traditional expectations and the close scrutiny of family and neighbors, and living in overwhelmingly all-male or all-female environments, brought freedom to meet like-minded gay men and women. Like other minorities, many gays saw the war as a chance to prove their worth under fire. Yet some suspected of being gay were dishonorably discharged, sent to psychiatric hospitals, or imprisoned in so-called queer stockades. In 1945, gay veterans established the Veteran's Benevolent Association, the first organization in the United States to combat discrimination against homosexuals.

The Internment of Japanese-Americans

Far more than any other minority in the United States, Japanese-Americans suffered grievously during the war. The internment of about thirty-seven thousand first-generation Japanese immigrants (Issei) and nearly seventy-five thousand native-born Japanese-American citizens of the United States (Nisei) in "relocation centers" guarded by military police was a tragic reminder of the fragility of civil liberties in wartime.

The **internment of Japanese-Americans** reflected forty years of anti-Japanese sentiment on the West Coast, rooted in racial prejudice and economic rivalry. Nativist politicians and farmers who wanted Japanese-American land had long decried the "yellow peril." Following the attack on Pearl Harbor, they whipped up the rage of white Californians, aided by a government report falsely blaming Japanese-Americans in Hawaii for aiding the Japanese naval force. Patriotic associations and many newspapers clamored for evacuating the Japanese-Americans, as did the army general in charge of the Western Defense Command, who proclaimed, "It makes no difference whether he is an American citizen or not. . . . I don't want any of them."

In February 1942, President Roosevelt gave in to the pressure and issued Executive Order 9066, authorizing the removal from military areas of anyone deemed a threat. Although not a single Japanese-American was apprehended for espionage or sedition and neither the FBI nor military intelligence uncovered any evidence of disloyal behavior by Japanese-Americans, the military ordered the eviction of all first-generation Japanese immigrants (Issei) and native-born Japanese-American citizens of the United States (Nisei) from the West Coast. Only Hawaii was excepted. Despite the far larger number of Hawaiians of Japanese ancestry, as well as of Japanese living in Hawaii, no internment policy was implemented there, and no sabotage occurred.

Forced to sell all they owned at whatever prices they could obtain, Japanese-Americans lost an estimated $2 billion in property and possessions. Tagged with numbers rather than names, they were herded into barbed-wire-encircled detention camps in the most desolate parts of the West and Great Plains—places, wrote one historian, "where nobody had lived before and no one has lived since." Few other Americans protested the incarceration. Stating that it would not question government claims of military necessity during time of war, the Supreme Court upheld the constitutionality of the evacuation in the *Korematsu* case (1944). By then the hysteria had subsided, and the government had begun a program of gradual release, allowing some Nisei to attend college or take factory jobs (but not on the West Coast); about eighteen thousand served in the military. The 442nd Regimental Combat Team, entirely Japanese-American, became the most decorated unit in the military.

In 1982 a special government commission concluded in its report, *Personal Justice Denied,* that internment "was not justified by military necessity." It blamed the Roosevelt administration's action on "race prejudice, war hysteria, and a failure of political leadership" and apologized to Japanese-Americans for "a grave injustice." In 1988 Congress voted to pay twenty thousand dollars in compensation to each of the nearly sixty-two thousand surviving internees; and in 1998 President Bill Clinton further apologized for the injustice by giving the nation's highest civilian honor, the Presidential Medal of Freedom, to Fred Korematsu, who had protested the evacuation decree all the way to the Supreme Court.

TRIUMPH AND TRAGEDY, 1945

Spring and summer 1945 brought stunning changes and new crises. In Europe a new balance of power emerged after the collapse of the Third Reich. In Asia continued Japanese reluctance to surrender led to the use of atomic bombs. And in the United States a new president, Harry Truman, presided over both the end of World War II and the beginning of the Cold War and the nuclear age.

The Yalta Conference By the time Roosevelt, Churchill, and Stalin met in the Soviet city of Yalta in February 1945, the military situation favored the Soviet Union. The Red Army had overrun Poland, Romania, and Bulgaria; driven the Nazis out of Yugoslavia; penetrated Austria, Hungary, and Czechoslovakia; and was massed just fifty miles from Berlin. American forces, in contrast, were still recovering from the Battle of the Bulge and facing stiff resistance on the route to Japan. The Joint Chiefs of Staff, contemplating the awesome cost in American casualties of an invasion of Japan, insisted that Stalin's help was worth almost any price. And Stalin was in a position to make demands. The Soviet Union had suffered most in the war against Germany, it already dominated eastern Europe, and, knowing that the United States did not want to fight a prolonged war against Japan, Stalin had the luxury of deciding whether and when to enter the Pacific war.

The **Yalta accords** reflected these realities. Stalin again vowed to declare war on Japan "two or three months" after Germany's surrender, and in return Churchill and Roosevelt reneged on their arrangement with Jiang Jieshi and promised the Soviet Union concessions in Manchuria and the territories it had lost in the Russo-Japanese War (1904). The Big Three delegated a final settlement of the German reparations issue to a postwar commission, and left vague the matter of partitioning Germany and its eventual reunification. The conference also vaguely called for interim governments in eastern Europe "broadly representative of all democratic elements" and for eventual freely elected permanent governments. On the matter dearest to FDR's heart, the negotiators accepted a plan for a new international organization and agreed to a founding conference of the new United Nations in San Francisco in April 1945.

Stalin proved adamant about the nature of the postwar Polish government. Twice in the twentieth century German troops had used Poland as a springboard for invading Russia. Stalin would not expose his land again, and after the Red Army had captured Warsaw in January 1945 he installed a procommunist regime and brutally

Yalta Conference, 1945   *The palaces where Roosevelt, Churchill, Stalin, and their advisers gathered were still standing, but the rest of Yalta had been reduced to ruin during the German occupation.*

subdued the anticommunist Poles. Conservative critics would later charge that FDR "gave away" eastern Europe. Actually, the Soviet Union gained little it did not already control, and short of going to war against the Soviet Union while still battling Germany and Japan, FDR could only hope that Stalin would keep his word.

Victory in Europe   As the Soviets prepared for their assault on Berlin, American troops crossed the Rhine at Remagen in March 1945 and encircled the Ruhr Valley, Germany's industrial heartland. Churchill now proposed a rapid thrust to Berlin. But Eisenhower, with Roosevelt's backing, overruled Churchill. They saw no point in risking high casualties to rush to an area of Germany that had already been designated as the Soviet occupation zone. So Eisenhower advanced methodically along a broad front until the Americans met the Russians at the Elbe River on April 25. By then the Red Army had taken Vienna and reached the suburbs of Berlin. On April 30, as Soviet troops approached his headquarters, Hitler committed suicide. Berlin fell to the Soviets on May 2, and on May 8 a new German government surrendered unconditionally.

Jubilant Americans celebrated Victory in Europe (V-E) Day less than a month after they had mourned the death of their president. On April 12 an exhausted President Roosevelt had abruptly clutched his head, moaned that he had a "terrific headache," and fell unconscious. A cerebral hemorrhage ended his life. As the nation grieved, Roosevelt's unprepared successor assumed the burden of ending the war and dealing with the Soviet Union.

"I don't know whether you fellows ever had a load of hay or a bull fall on you," Harry S Truman told reporters on his first full day in office, "but last night the moon, the stars, and all the planets fell on me." An unpretentious politician awed by his new responsibilities, Truman struggled to continue FDR's policies. But Roosevelt had made no effort to familiarize his vice president with world affairs. Perhaps sensing his own inadequacies, Truman adopted a tough pose toward adversaries. In office less than two weeks, he lashed out at Soviet ambassador V. M. Molotov that the United States was tired of waiting for the Russians to allow free elections in Poland, and he threatened to cut off lend-lease aid if the Soviet Union did not cooperate. The Truman administration then reduced U.S. economic assistance to the Soviets and stalled on their request for a $1 billion reconstruction loan. Simultaneously, Stalin strengthened his grip on eastern Europe, ignoring the promises he had made at Yalta.

The United States neither conceded the Soviet sphere of influence in eastern Europe nor tried to end it. Although Truman still sought Stalin's cooperation in establishing the United Nations and in defeating Japan, Soviet-American relations deteriorated. By June 1945, when the Allied countries succeeded in framing the United Nations Charter, hopes for a new international order had dimmed, and the United Nations emerged as a diplomatic battleground. Truman, Churchill, and Stalin met at Potsdam, Germany, from July 16 to August 2 to complete the postwar arrangements begun at Yalta. But the Allied leaders could barely agree to demilitarize Germany and to punish Nazi war criminals. All the major divisive issues were postponed and left to the Council of Foreign Ministers to resolve later. Given the diplomatic impasse, only military power remained to determine the contours of the postwar world.

The Holocaust

When news of the **Holocaust**—the term later given to the Nazis' extermination of European Jewry—first leaked out in early 1942, many Americans discounted the reports. Not until November did the State Department admit knowledge of the massacres. A month later the American broadcaster Edward R. Murrow, listened to nationwide, reported on the systematic killing of millions of Jews: "It is a picture of mass murder and moral depravity unequalled in the history of the world. It is a horror beyond what imagination can grasp. . . . There are no longer 'concentration camps'—we must speak now only of 'extermination camps.'" Most Americans considered the annihilation of Europe's 6 million Jews beyond belief. There were no photographs to prove it, and, some argued, the atrocities attributed to the Germans in World War I had turned out to be false. So few took issue with the military's view that the way to liberate those enslaved by Hitler was by speedily winning the war. Pleas by American Jews for the Allies to bomb the death camps and the railroad tracks leading to them fell on deaf ears. In fall 1944 U.S. planes flying over Auschwitz in southern Poland bombed nearby factories but left the gas chambers and crematoria intact, in order, American officials explained, not to divert air power from more vital raids elsewhere. "How could it be," historian David Wyman has asked, "that Government officials knew that a place existed where 2,000 helpless human beings could be killed in less than an hour, knew that this occurred over and over again, and yet did not feel driven to search for some way to wipe such a scourge from the earth?"

How much could have been done remains uncertain. Still, the U.S. government never seriously considered rescue schemes or searched for a way to curtail the Nazis' "final solution" to the "Jewish question." Its feeble response was due to its overwhelming focus on winning the war as quickly as possible, congressional and public fears of an influx of destitute Jews into the United States, Britain's wish to placate the Arabs by keeping Jewish settlers out of Palestine, and the fear of some Jewish-American leaders that pressing the issue would increase anti-Semitism at home. The War Refugee Board managed to save the lives of just two hundred thousand Jews and twenty thousand non-Jews. Six million other Jews, about 75 percent of the European Jewish population, were gassed, shot, and incinerated, as were several million gypsies, communists, homosexuals, Polish Catholics, and others deemed unfit to live in the Third Reich.

"The things I saw beggar description," wrote General Eisenhower after visiting the first death camp liberated by the U.S. army. He sent immediately for a delegation of congressional leaders and newspaper editors to make sure Americans would never forget the gas chambers and human ovens. Only after viewing the photographs and newsreels of corpses stacked like cordwood, boxcars heaped with the bones of dead prisoners, bulldozers shoving emaciated bodies into hastily dug ditches, and liberated, barely alive living skeletons lying in their own filth, their vacant, sunken eyes staring through barbed wire, did most Americans see that the Holocaust was no myth.

The Atomic Bombs   Meanwhile, the war with Japan ground on. Early in 1945 an assault force of marines invaded Iwo Jima, 700 miles from Japan. In places termed the "Meat Grinder" and "Bloody Gorge," the marines savagely battled thousands of Japanese soldiers hidden in tunnels and behind concrete bunkers and pillboxes. Securing the five-square-mile island would cost the marines nearly twenty-seven thousand casualties, and one-third of all the marines killed in the Pacific. In June American troops waded ashore on Okinawa, 350 miles from Japan and a key staging area for the planned U.S. invasion of the Japanese home islands. Death and destruction engulfed Okinawa as waves of Americans attacked nearly impregnable Japanese defenses head-on, repeating the bloody strategy of World War I. After eighty-three days of fighting on land and sea, twelve thousand Americans lay dead and three times as many wounded, a 35 percent casualty rate, higher than at Normandy.

The appalling rate of loss on Iwo Jima and Okinawa weighed on the minds of American strategists as they thought about an invasion of the Japanese home islands. The Japanese Cabinet showed no willingness to give up the war despite Japan's being blockaded and bombed daily (on March 9–10 a fleet of B-29s dropped napalm-and-magnesium bombs on Tokyo, burning sixteen square miles of the city to the ground and killing some eighty-four thousand). Its military leaders insisted on fighting to the bitter end; surrender was unthinkable. Japan possessed an army of over 2 million, plus up to 4 million reservists and five thousand kamikaze aircraft, and the U.S. Joint Chiefs estimated that American casualties in invasions of Kyushu and Honshu (the main island of Japan) might exceed 1 million.

The successful detonation of history's first nuclear explosion at Alamogordo in mid-July gave Truman an alternative. On July 25, while meeting with Stalin and Churchill in Potsdam, Truman ordered the use of an atomic bomb if Japan did not surrender before August 3. The next day, in the **Potsdam Declaration,** he warned Japan to surrender unconditionally or face "prompt and utter destruction." Japan refused, and on August 6 a B-29 bomber named *Enola Gay* took off from the Marianas island of Tinian and dropped a uranium bomb on Hiroshima. It plunged the city into what Japanese novelist Masuji Ibuse termed "a hell of unspeakable torments." The 300,000 degree centigrade fireball incinerated houses and vaporized people. More than sixty thousand died immediately from the blast, and another seventy-five thousand died from burns and radiation poisoning by late 1945. On August 8 Stalin declared war on Japan, and U.S. planes dropped leaflets on Japan warning that another bomb would be dropped if it did not surrender. Japan refused. Its military leaders preferred death to surrender. The next day, at high noon, the *Bock's Car* flattened Nagasaki with a plutonium bomb, killing over thirty-five thousand, and injuring more than sixty thousand. On August 14, Japan accepted the American terms of surrender, which implicitly permitted the emperor to retain his throne but subordinated him to the U.S. commander of the occupation forces. General MacArthur received Japan's surrender on the battleship *Missouri* on September 2, 1945. The war was over.

While Americans at the time overwhelmingly backed the atomic bombings of Japan as the necessary way to end the war quickly and with the least cost in lives, many critics later contended that Japan would have soon surrendered without the horrendous bombing. Some believed that racist American attitudes toward the Japanese motivated the decision to drop the bombs. As war correspondent Ernie Pyle wrote, "The Japanese are looked upon as something inhuman and squirmy—like some people feel about cockroaches or mice." While racial hatred undoubtedly stirred exterminationist sentiment, those involved in the Manhattan Project had regarded Germany as the target; and, considering the ferocity of the Allied bombings of Hamburg and Dresden, there is little reason to assume that the Allies would not have dropped atomic bombs on Germany had they been available. By 1945 the Allies as well as the Axis had abandoned restraints on attacking civilians.

Other critics maintain that demonstrating the bomb's terrible destructiveness on an uninhabited island would have moved Japan to surrender. We will never know for sure. American scientists rejected a demonstration bombing because the United States had an atomic arsenal of only two bombs, and they did not know whether the mechanism for detonating them in the air would work. A large number of those critical of Truman's decision believe that the president, aware of worsening relations between the United States and the USSR, ordered the atomic attack primarily to end the Pacific war before Stalin could enter it and share in the postwar occupation of Japan. At the same time, its use might also intimidate Stalin into making concessions in eastern Europe. Referring to the Soviets, President Truman noted just before the atomic test at Alamogordo, "If it explodes, as I think it will, I'll certainly have a hammer on those boys." Truman's new secretary of state, James Byrnes, thought that the bomb would "make Russia more manageable" and would "put us in a position to dictate our own terms at the end of the war."

Although the president and his advisers believed that the atomic bombs would strengthen their hand against the Soviets, the foremost reason for Truman's decision was to shorten the war and save American lives. As throughout the war, American leaders in August 1945 relied on production and technology to win the war with the minimum loss of American life. Every new weapon was put to use; the concept of "total war" easily accommodated the bombing of civilians; and the atomic bomb was one more item in an arsenal that had already wreaked enormous destruction on the Axis. The rules of war that had once stayed the use of weapons of mass destruction against enemy civilians no longer prevailed. No responsible official counseled that the United States should sacrifice American servicemen to lessen death and destruction in Japan, or not use a weapon developed with 2 billion taxpayer dollars. To the vast majority of Americans, the atomic bomb was, in Churchill's words, "a miracle of deliverance" that saved Allied lives. So E. B. Sledge and his comrades in the First Marine Division, slated to take part in the first wave of the invasion of Japan's home islands, breathed "an indescribable sense of relief." Hearing the news of the atomic bombs and Japan's surrender, Sledge wrote, they sat in stunned silence:

> We remembered our dead. So many dead. So many maimed. So many bright futures consigned to the ashes of the past. So many dreams lost in the madness that engulfed us. Except for a few widely scattered shouts of joy, the survivors of the abyss sat hollow-eyed and silent, trying to comprehend a world without war.

The atomic bombs ended the deadliest war in history. A truly global conflict, involving over half the world's peoples, with armies ranging over continents and navies fighting on every ocean, the war affected women, men, and children as victims of civilian bombing campaigns, as war workers, as slave laborers, and comfort women. Neither side gave much quarter in seeking to destroy the other's will and resources. Some 50 million died—more than half of them noncombatants. The Soviet Union lost roughly 20 million people, China 15 million, Poland 6 million, Germany 4 million, and Japan 2 million. Much of Asia and Europe was rubble. Some four hundred thousand American servicemen had also perished, and, although physically unscathed, the United States had changed profoundly—for better and worse.

CONCLUSION

Most Americans, and their government, initially responded to the war clouds over Asia and Europe by intensifying their post–World War I isolationism. As one senator proclaimed, prior to the vote that defeated Roosevelt's effort to have the United States join the World Court, "To hell with Europe and the rest of those nations!" Not till the Japanese attack on the American fleet at Pearl Harbor, more than two years after the war in Europe had begun, did the United States enter the fray, and even then it waited until Hitler and Mussolini declared war on it before joining the armed struggle engulfing the world. Once engaged, the Americans rapidly went on a war footing. Mobilization transformed the scope and authority of the federal government, vastly expanding presidential powers. It ended the unemployment of the depression and made American industry more productive than it had ever been, and most Americans more prosperous than they had ever been. It tilted the national economic balance toward the South Atlantic, Gulf, and Pacific coasts. It accelerated trends toward bigness in business, agriculture, and labor. It involved the military in the economy and education as never before.

To achieve an unconditional victory, with the least possible cost in American lives, Roosevelt concentrated on defeating Germany first, yet delaying a second front in Europe until Soviet forces had routed the German army in eastern Europe. Meanwhile, half a world away, a two-pronged American offensive, across the central Pacific and north from Australia, brought Japan to the brink of defeat. On the home front, the war catalyzed vital changes in racial and social relations, sometimes intensifying prejudices against minorities and women, but also broadening educational and employment opportunities that widened public spheres and heightened expectations. Fighting and winning the greatest war in history, moreover, restored American faith in capitalism and democratic institutions. It was a vital coming-of-age experience for an entire generation that did much to give postwar American society a confident "can-do" spirit for the "American Century" that they knew lay ahead.

The awesome development and use of an atomic bomb bolstered that spirit and enabled the United States to defeat Japan promptly, to try to force the Soviets to be more manageable, and to avoid an invasion of the Japanese home islands that might have cost tens, possibly hundreds, of thousands of American casualties. The mass destruction of the war and total defeat of the Axis, however, brought new crises to cloud the bright dawn of peace. The world's two superpowers—the United States and USSR—soon squared off in a Cold War that would see the United States play a role in global affairs that would have seemed inconceivable to most Americans just five years before.

26

The Cold War Abroad and at Home, 1945–1952

THE POSTWAR POLITICAL SETTING, 1945–1946

The Cold War profoundly changed the United States for better and for worse. It spurred more than a quarter of a century of economic growth and prosperity, the longest such period in American history. It propelled research in medicine and science that, for the most part, made lives longer and better. And it contributed to a vast expansion of higher education that enabled many Americans to become middle class.

Demobilization and Reconversion
When the war ended, GIs and civilians alike wanted those who had served overseas "home alive in '45." Troops demanding transport ships barraged Congress with threats of "no boats, no votes." On a single day in December 1945, sixty thousand postcards arrived at the White House with the message "Bring the Boys Home by Christmas." Truman bowed to popular demand, and by 1948 American military strength had dropped from 12 million to just 1.5 million.

Returning veterans faced readjustment problems intensified by a soaring divorce rate and a drastic housing shortage. Others feared the return of mass unemployment and economic depression as war plants closed, and memories revived of the hard times immediately after World War I (see Chapter 22). Defense spending dropped from $76 billion in 1945 to under $20 billion in 1946, and more than a million defense jobs vanished.

By the end of the decade more women were working outside the home than during World War II. Most took jobs in traditional women's fields, especially office work and sales, to pay for family needs. Although the postwar economy created new openings for women in the labor market, many public figures urged women to seek fulfillment at

CHRONOLOGY, 1945–1952

1944 • Servicemen's Readjustment Act (GI Bill).

1945 • Postwar strike wave begins.

1946 • Employment Act.
George Kennan's "long telegram."
Winston Churchill's "iron curtain" speech.
Coal miners' strike.
Inflation soars to more than 18 percent.
Republicans win control of Congress.

1947 • Truman Doctrine.
Federal Employee Loyalty Program.
Jackie Robinson breaks major league baseball's color line.
Taft-Hartley Act.
National Security Act.
President's Committee on Civil Rights issues *To Secure These Rights*.
HUAC holds hearings on Hollywood.

1948 • Communist coup in Czechoslovakia.
State of Israel founded.
Berlin airlift.
Congress approves Marshall Plan to aid Europe.
Truman orders an end to segregation in the armed forces.
Communist leaders put on trial under the Smith Act.
Truman elected president.

1949 • North Atlantic Treaty Organization (NATO) established.
East and West Germany founded as separate nations.
Communist victory in China; People's Republic of China established.
Soviet Union detonates an atomic bomb.

1950 • Soviet spy ring at Los Alamos uncovered.
Joseph McCarthy launches anticommunist crusade.
Korean War begins.
McCarran Internal Security Act.
Truman accepts NSC-68.
China enters the Korean War.

1951 • Julius and Ethel Rosenberg convicted of espionage.

1952 • First hydrogen bomb exploded.
Dwight D. Eisenhower elected president.
Republicans win control of Congress.

home. Popular culture romanticized married bliss and demonized career women as a threat to social stability.

The GI Bill of Rights The Servicemen's Readjustment Act of 1944, commonly called the GI Bill of Rights or **GI Bill,** was designed to forestall the expected recession by easing veterans back into the work force, and to reward the "soldier boys" and reduce their fears of female competition. The GI Bill gave veterans priority for many jobs, occupational guidance, and, if need be, fifty-two weeks of unemployment benefits. It also established veterans' hospitals and provided low-interest loans to returning GIs who were starting businesses or buying homes or farms. Almost four million veterans bought homes with government loans, fueling a baby boom, suburbanization, and a record demand for new goods and services.

Most vitally, the government promised to pay up to four years of further education or job training for veterans. Not all Americans approved. Some opposed it as opening the door to socialism or to demands by minorities to special entitlements. Many university administrators, fearing that "riffraff" would sully their bastions of privilege,

Veterans Go to College   *So many World War II veterans wanted to use their GI benefits for higher education that colleges were overwhelmed; many had to turn away students. In 1946, registration of new students was done at temporary desks set up in Wildermuth Field House at Indiana University.*

FIGURE 26.1 Gross National Product, 1929–1990

Following World War II, the United States achieved the highest living standard in world history. Between 1950 and 1970, the real GNP, which factors out inflation and reveals the actual amount of goods and services produced, steadily increased. However, in 1972, 1974–1975, 1980, and 1982 the real GNP declined. *Source: Economic Report of the President, 1991.* Note: Data shown in 1982 dollars.

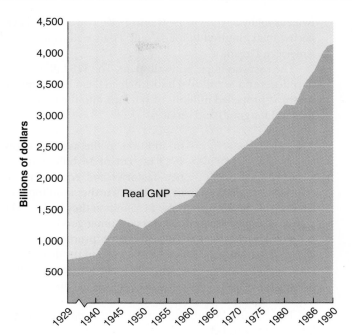

echoed the complaint of the University of Chicago president that their hallowed halls of learning would become "educational hobo jungles."

In 1946, flush with stipends of sixty-five dollars a month—ninety dollars for those with dependents—and up to five hundred dollars a year for tuition and books, 1.5 million veterans were attending college, spurring a huge increase in higher education and the creation of many new state and community colleges. California State University established additional campuses in Fullerton, Hayward, Long Beach, Los Angeles, Northridge, Sacramento, and San Bernardino. Various "normal schools" for the training of teachers were upgraded into full-fledged colleges to create the State University of New York in 1948. Veterans made up over half of all college students in 1947. Often married and the fathers of young children, they were less interested in knowledge ("what good will it do me?") than in a degree and a higher-paying job. To accommodate them, colleges converted old military barracks and Quonset huts into so-called Veterans' Village housing units and featured accelerated programs and more vocational or career-oriented courses.

To make room for the millions of GIs pursuing higher education after the war, many colleges limited the percentage of women admitted or barred students from out of state. The percentage of female college graduates dropped from 40 percent in 1949 to 25 percent in 1950. By then most women students were the working wives of the 8 million veterans who took advantage of the GI Bill to go college.

The GI Bill democratized higher education. By 1956 nearly 10 million veterans had used the GI Bill to enroll in colleges, universities, and vocational training programs (most the first in their families to do so). No longer a citadel of privilege, universities awarded twice as many degrees in 1950 as in 1940. Two decades later, these educated veterans expected their children to follow suit. Higher education became an accepted part of the American Dream.

The cost was huge, but well spent. The $15 billion that veterans received sent them to colleges and technical schools, helped them buy homes, and financed their new businesses. It propelled millions of veterans into the middle class, heightening the postwar demand for goods and services.

The Economic Boom Begins

In addition to the assistance given returning servicemen, a 1945 tax cut of $6 billion spurred corporate investment in new factories and equipment and helped produce an economic boom that began in late 1946. Further kindling postwar growth and prosperity, Americans spent much of the $135 billion they had saved from wartime work and service pay to satisfy their desire for consumer goods formerly beyond their means or not produced during the war. Advertisements promising "a Ford in your future" and an "all-electric kitchen of the future" also increased the desire to consume, and sales of homes, cars, and appliances skyrocketed. Scores of new products—televisions, high-fidelity phonographs, filter cigarettes, automatic transmissions, freezers, and air conditioners—became hallmarks of the middle-class lifestyle.

The Bretton Woods Agreement (1944) among the Allies had set the stage for the United States to become economic leader of the noncommunist world. It created the International Monetary Fund (IMF) to stabilize exchange rates by valuing ("pegging") other currencies in relation to the U.S. dollar; established the International Bank for Reconstruction and Development (World Bank) to help rebuild war-battered Asia and Europe; and laid the groundwork for the 1947 General Agreement on Tariffs and Trade (GATT) to break up closed trading blocs and expand international trade. Since the United States largely controlled and funded these powerful economic institutions, they gave the United States an especially favorable position in international trade and finance.

With many nations in ruins, American firms could import raw materials cheaply; with little competition from other industrial countries, they could increase exports to record levels. U.S. economic dominance also resulted from the 35 percent increase in the productivity of American workers in the decade following the war. Wartime advances in science and technology, which led to revolutionary developments in such industries as electronics and plastics, further bolstered visions of limitless growth and the dawn of "the American century."

Truman's Domestic Program

Americans' hunger for the fruits of affluence left them with little appetite for extending the New Deal. Truman agreed. "I don't want any experiments," he confided. "The American people have been through a lot of experiments and they want a rest." His only major domestic accomplishment in the Seventy-ninth Congress was the **Employment Act of 1946.** It committed the federal government to ensuring economic growth and established the Council of Economic Advisers to confer with the president and formulate policies for maintaining employment, production, and purchasing power. Congress, however, gutted both the goal of full employment and the enhanced executive powers to achieve that objective.

Congressional eagerness to dismantle wartime controls worsened the nation's chief economic problem: inflation. Consumer demand outran the supply of goods, intensifying the pressure on prices. The Office of Price Administration (OPA) sought to hold the line by enforcing price controls, but food producers, manufacturers, and retailers opposed continuing wartime controls. While some consumers favored the OPA, others deplored it as an irksome relic of wartime regulations. In June 1946, Truman vetoed a bill that would have extended the OPA's life, but deprived it of power, effectively ending all price controls. Within a week food costs rose 16 percent and the price of beef doubled. "PRICES SOAR, BUYERS SORE, STEERS JUMP OVER THE MOON," headlined the *New York Daily News*.

Congress then passed, and Truman signed, a second bill extending price controls in weakened form. Protesting any price controls, however, farmers and meat producers threatened to withhold food from the market. Knowing that "meatless voters are opposition voters," Truman lifted controls on food prices just before the 1946 midterm elections. When Democrats fared poorly anyway, Truman ended all price controls. By then the consumer price index had jumped nearly 25 percent since the end of the war.

Sharp price rises and shrinking paychecks shorn of overtime goaded organized labor to demand higher wages. More than 4.5 million workers went on strike in 1946. When a United Mine Workers walkout paralyzed the economy for forty days, Truman ordered the army to seize the mines. A week later, after Truman had pressured owners to grant most of the union's demands, the miners returned to work, only to walk out again six months later. Meanwhile, on the heels of the first mine workers settlement, railway engineers and trainmen announced that they would shut down the nation's railroad system for the first time in history. "If you think I'm going to sit here and let you tie up this whole country," Truman shouted at the heads of the two unions, "you're crazy as hell." In May he asked Congress for authority to draft workers who struck vital industries. Before he could finish his speech, the unions gave in. Still, Truman's threat alienated labor leaders.

By the fall of 1946, Truman had angered most major interest groups. Less than a third of the Americans polled approved of his performance. "To err is Truman," some gibed. Summing up the public discontent, Republicans asked, "Had enough?" In the 1946 elections, they captured twenty-five governorships and, for the first time since 1928, won control of both houses of Congress.

The public mood reflected more than just economic discontent. Under the surface laughter at stores advertising atomic sales or bartenders mixing atomic cocktails ran a new, deep current of fear, symbolized by the rash of "flying saucer" sightings that had begun after the war. An NBC radio program depicted a nuclear attack on Chicago in which most people died instantly. "Those few who escaped the blast, but not the gamma rays, died slowly after they had left the ruined city," intoned the narrator. "No attempt at identification of the bodies or burial ever took place. Chicago was simply closed." There was much talk of urban dispersal—resettling people in small communities in the country's vast open spaces—and of how to protect oneself in a nuclear attack. Schoolchildren wore dog tags in order to be identified after an atomic attack, and practiced crawling under their desks and putting their hands over their heads— "Duck and Cover"—to protect themselves from the bomb. The end of World War II had brought an uneasy peace.

ANTICOMMUNISM AND CONTAINMENT, 1946–1952

By late 1946 the simmering antagonisms between Moscow and Washington had come to a boil. With the Nazis defeated, the "shotgun wedding" between the United States and the USSR dissolved into a struggle to fill the power vacuums left by the defeat of Germany and Japan, the exhaustion of Western Europe, and the crumbling of colonial empires in Asia and Africa. Misperception and misunderstanding mounted as the two powers sought greater security, each feeding the other's fears. The Cold War resulted.

Polarization and Cold War The destiny of Eastern Europe, especially Poland, stood at the heart of the strife between the United States and the USSR. Wanting to end the Soviet Union's vulnerability to invasions from the West, Stalin insisted on a demilitarized Germany and a buffer zone of nations friendly to Russia along its western flank. He considered a Soviet sphere of influence in Eastern Europe essential to Russian security, a just reward for bearing the brunt of the war against Germany, and no different than the American spheres of influence in Western Europe, Japan, and Latin America. Stalin also believed that Roosevelt and Churchill had implicitly accepted a Soviet zone in Eastern Europe at the Yalta Conference (see Chapter 25).

With the Red Army occupying half of Europe at war's end, Stalin installed pro-Soviet puppet governments in Bulgaria, Hungary, and Romania, and supported the establishment of communist regimes in nominally independent Albania and Yugoslavia. Ignoring the Yalta Declaration of Liberated Europe, Stalin barred free elections in Poland and brutally suppressed Polish democratic parties. Poland, he said, was "not only a question of honor for Russia, but one of life and death."

Stalin's insistence on dominance in Eastern Europe collided with Truman's unwillingness to concede Soviet supremacy beyond Russia's borders. What Stalin saw as critical to Russian security, Truman viewed as a violation of national self-determination, a betrayal of democracy, and a cover for communist aggression. Truman and his advisers believed that the appeasement of dictators only fed their appetites for expansion. They thought that traditional balance-of-power politics and spheres of influence had precipitated both world wars, and that only a new world order based on the self-determination of all nations working in good faith within the United Nations could guarantee peace.

Truman also thought that accepting the "enforced sovietization" of Eastern Europe would betray American war aims and condemn nations rescued from Hitler's tyranny to another totalitarian dictatorship. He worried, too, that a Soviet stranglehold on Eastern Europe would hurt American businesses dependent on exports and on access to raw materials. In addition, Truman understood that the Democratic Party would invite political disaster if he reneged on the Yalta agreements. The Democrats counted on winning most of the votes of the 6 million Polish-Americans and millions of other Americans of Eastern European origin, who remained keenly interested in the fates of their homelands. He resolved not to appear "soft on communism."

Combativeness fit the temperament of the feisty Truman. Eager to demonstrate his command, the president matched Stalin's intransigence on controlling Poland with his own demands for Polish free elections. Encouraged by America's monopoly of atomic weapons and its position as the world's economic superpower, the new president hoped that the United States could control the terms of the postwar settlement. His foreign policy sought, in the words of a November 1945 State Department document, to "establish the kind of world we want to live in."

The Iron Curtain Descends
As Truman's assertiveness deepened Stalin's mistrust of the West, the Soviet Union tightened its grip on Eastern Europe, stepped up its confiscation of materials and factories from occupied territories, and forced its satellite nations (countries under Soviet control) to close their doors to American trade and influence. In a February 1946 speech that the White House considered a "declaration of World War III," Stalin asserted that there could be no lasting peace with capitalism and vowed to overcome the American lead in weaponry no matter what the cost.

Two weeks later, **George F. Kennan,** an American diplomat in Moscow, wired a long telegram to the State Department. A leading student of Russian affairs, Kennan described Soviet expansionism as moving "inexorably along a prescribed path, like a toy automobile wound up and headed in a given direction, stopping only when it meets some unanswerable force." Therefore, U.S. policy must be the "long-term, patient but firm and vigilant containment of Russian expansive tendencies," with the expectation that the Soviet state would eventually mellow or break up. Truman, who had already insisted that the time had come "to stop babying the Soviets" and "to get tough with Russia," accepted Kennan's advice. **Containment**—a policy uniting military, economic, and diplomatic strategies to "contain" any further Soviet communist expansion and to enhance America's security and influence abroad—became Washington gospel.

In early March 1946 Truman accompanied Winston Churchill to Westminister College in Missouri. In a speech, the former British prime minister warned of a new threat to Western democracies, this time from Moscow. Stalin, he said, had drawn an iron curtain across the eastern half of Europe. To meet the threat of further Soviet aggression, Churchill called for an alliance of the English-speaking peoples and the maintenance of an Anglo-American monopoly of atomic weapons: "There is nothing the Communists admire so much as strength and nothing for which they have less respect than for military weakness."

Truman agreed. In spring 1946, he threatened to send in American combat troops unless the Soviets withdrew from oil-rich Iran. In June he submitted an atomic-energy control plan to the United Nations requiring the Soviet Union to stop all work on nuclear weapons and to submit to UN inspections before the United States destroyed its own atomic arsenal. As expected, the Soviets rejected the proposal and offered an alternative plan equally unacceptable to the United States. As mutual hostility escalated, the Soviets and Americans rushed to develop their own doomsday weapons. In 1946 Congress established the Atomic Energy Commission (AEC) to develop nuclear energy and nuclear weaponry. The AEC devoted more than 90 percent of its effort to atomic weapon development. By 1950, one AEC adviser reckoned, the United States "had a stockpile capable of somewhat more than reproducing World War II in a single day."

Thus, less than a year after American and Soviet soldiers had jubilantly met at the Elbe River to celebrate Hitler's defeat, the Cold War had begun. It would be waged by economic pressure, nuclear intimidation, propaganda, subversion, and proxy wars (fought by governments and peoples allied to the principals rather than a direct military clash of the principals). Many Americans would view it as an ideological conflict pitting democracy against dictatorship, freedom against totalitarianism, religion against atheism, and capitalism against socialism. It would affect American life as decisively as any military engagement that the nation had fought.

Containing Communism   On February 21, 1947, the British informed the United States that they could no longer afford to assist Greece and Turkey in their struggles against communist-supported insurgents and Soviet pressure for access to the Mediterranean. A stricken Britain asked the United States to bear the costs of thwarting communism in the eastern Mediterranean. The harsh European winter, the most severe in memory, intensified the sense of urgency in Washington. The economies of Western Europe had come to a near-halt. Famine and tuberculosis plagued the Continent. European colonies in Africa and Asia had risen in revolt. Cigarettes and candy bars circulated as currency in Germany, and the communist parties in France and Italy appeared ready to topple democratic coalition governments. Truman decided to meet the challenge.

He first had to mobilize support for a radical departure from the American tradition of avoiding entangling alliances. In a tense White House on February 27, the new secretary of state, former army chief of staff George C. Marshall, presented the case for

American Food for a Hungry Europe   *Grateful English mothers line up for orange juice sent by the United States to assist Europeans devastated by the Second World War.*

aid to Greece and Turkey. Congressional leaders balked, more concerned about inflation at home than civil war in Greece. But Dean Acheson, the newly appointed undersecretary of state, seized the moment. The issue, he said, was not one of assisting the repressive Greek oligarchy and Turkey's military dictatorship, but rather a universal struggle of freedom against tyranny. "Like apples in a barrel infected by the corruption of one rotten one," he warned, the fall of Greece or Turkey would open Asia, Western Europe, and the oil fields of the Middle East to the Red menace. "The Soviet Union [is] playing one of the greatest gambles in history," Acheson declaimed. "We and we alone are in a position to break up this play." Shaken, the congressional leaders agreed to support the administration's request if Truman could "scare hell out of the country."

Truman could and did. On March 12, 1947, addressing a joint session of Congress and a national radio audience, he asked for $400 million in military assistance to Greece and Turkey. Going far beyond the immediate issues in the two countries, the **Truman Doctrine** pictured the matter as part of a global struggle "between alternative ways of life." One way promised "freedom" and "liberty," the other "oppression" and "terror." In a world endangered by evil communism, therefore, the United States must support free peoples everywhere "resisting attempted subjugation by armed minorities or by outside pressures." His rhetorical defense of freedom—using the words "free" or "freedom" twenty-four times in an eighteen-minute speech—worked. Congress appropriated funds that helped the Greek monarchy defeat the rebel movement and helped Turkey stay out of the Soviet orbit.

The Truman Doctrine of active U.S. engagement to contain communism persisted long after the crisis in the Mediterranean. It proclaimed the nation's intention to be a global policeman, everywhere on guard against advances by the Soviet Union and its allies, and it became as comprehensive as the Monroe Doctrine's "Keep Out" sign posted on the Western Hemisphere. Most Americans accepted its notion of America defending freedom against the forces of darkness as the essence of the Cold War, and the doctrine guided American foreign policy for much of the next four decades.

To back up the new international initiative, Congress passed the **National Security Act of 1947,** unifying the armed forces under a single Department of Defense, creating the National Security Council (NSC) to provide foreign-policy information to the White House and advise the president on strategic matters, and establishing the Central Intelligence Agency (CIA) to gather information abroad and engage in covert activities in support of the nation's security. Congress also approved the administration's proposal for massive U.S. assistance for European recovery in 1947. Advocated by the secretary of state, and thus called the **Marshall Plan,** the European Recovery Plan (ERP) was to be another weapon in the arsenal against the spread of communism. With Europe, in Churchill's words, "a rubble heap . . . a breeding ground of pestilence and hate," Truman wanted to end the economic devastation believed to spawn communism. Truman correctly guessed that the Soviet Union and its satellites would refuse to take part in the plan, because of the controls linked to it, and accurately foresaw that Western European economic recovery would expand sales of American goods abroad and promote prosperity in the United States.

Although denounced by the Left as a "Martial Plan" and by isolationist voices on the Right as a "Share-the-American-Wealth Plan," the Marshall Plan more than fulfilled its sponsors' hopes. By 1952, industrial production had risen 200 percent in Western Europe, and the economic and social chaos that communists had exploited had been overcome in the sixteen nations that shared the $17 billion in aid provided by the ERP. Its slogan, "Prosperity Makes You Free," had been vindicated, and, not incidentally, Western Europe had become a major center of American trade and investment.

Confrontation in Germany   The Soviet Union reacted to the Truman Doctrine and the Marshall Plan by tightening its grip on Eastern Europe. Communist takeovers added Hungary and Czechoslovakia to the Soviet bloc in 1947 and 1948, and Stalin set his sights on Germany. The 1945 Potsdam Agreement had divided Germany into four separate zones (administered by France, Great Britain, the Soviet Union, and the United States) and created a joint four-power administration for Germany's capital, Berlin, lying 110 miles within the Soviet-occupied eastern zone. As the Cold War intensified, the Western powers moved toward uniting their zones into an anti-Soviet West German state to help contain communism. Stalin responded in June 1948 by blocking all rail and highway routes through the Soviet zone into Berlin. He calculated that the Western powers would be unable to provision the 2 million Berliners under their control and would either have to abandon plans to create a West German nation or accept a communist Berlin.

Truman resolved neither to abandon Berlin nor to shoot his way into the city and possibly trigger World War III. Instead he ordered a massive airlift to provide Berliners with the food and fuel necessary for survival. American cargo planes landed in West Berlin every three minutes around the clock, bringing a mountain of supplies. To prevent the Soviets from shooting down the U.S. planes, Truman hinted that he would use "the bomb" if necessary and ordered a fleet of B-29s, the only planes capable of delivering atomic bombs, to English bases in July 1948. Tensions rose. The president confided to his diary "we are very close to war." Meanwhile, the **Berlin airlift** continued to provide the blockaded city with a precarious lifeline.

In May 1949 the Soviets ended the blockade. Stalin's gambit had failed. The airlift highlighted American determination and technological prowess, revealed Stalin's readiness to use innocent people as pawns, and dramatically heightened anti-Soviet feeling in the West. U.S. public-opinion polls in late 1948 revealed an overwhelming demand for "firmness and increased 'toughness' in relations with Russia."

Continuing fears of a Soviet attack on Western Europe fostered support for a rearmed West German state and for an Atlantic collective security alliance. In May 1949 the United States, Britain, and France ended their occupation of Germany and approved the creation of the Federal Republic of Germany (West Germany). A month earlier, ten nations of Western Europe had signed the North Atlantic Treaty, establishing a mutual defense pact with the United States and Canada in which "an armed attack against one or more of them . . . shall be considered an attack against them all." For the first time in its history, the United States entered into a peacetime military alliance. In effect, Western Europe now lay under the American "nuclear umbrella," protected from Soviet invasion by the U.S. threat of nuclear retaliation. Senator Robert Taft of Ohio, speaking for a small band of Republican senators, warned that this agreement would provoke the Soviets to respond in kind, stimulate a massive arms race, and open the floodgates of American military aid to Europe. But the Senate overwhelmingly approved the treaty, and in July the United States officially joined the **North Atlantic Treaty Organization (NATO),** marking the formal end of U.S. isolationism.

Truman ranked the Marshall Plan and NATO as his proudest achievements, convinced that if the latter had been in existence in 1914 and 1939, the world would have been spared two disastrous wars. Accordingly, he spurred Congress to authorize $1.3 billion for military assistance to NATO nations, persuaded General Dwight D. Eisenhower to become supreme commander of NATO forces, and authorized the stationing of four American army divisions in Europe as the nucleus of the NATO armed force. As Taft had predicted, the Soviet Union responded in kind. It created the German Democratic Republic (East Germany) in 1949, exploded its own atomic bomb that same year, and, in 1955, set up a rival Eastern bloc military alliance, the Warsaw Pact. The United States and Soviet Union had divided Europe into two armed camps.

The Cold War in Asia　　Moscow-Washington hostility also carved Asia into contending camps. The Russians created a sphere of influence in Manchuria; the Americans denied Moscow a role in postwar Japan; and both partitioned a helpless Korea.

As head of the U.S. occupation forces in Japan, General Douglas MacArthur oversaw that nation's transformation from an empire in ruins into a prosperous democracy. In 1952, the occupation ended, but a military security treaty allowed the U.S. to retain its Japanese bases on the Soviet-Asian perimeter and brought Japan under the American "nuclear umbrella." In further pursuit of containment, the United States helped crush a procommunist insurgency in the Philippines and aided French efforts to reestablish colonial rule in Indochina (Vietnam, Laos, and Cambodia), despite American declarations in favor of national self-determination and against imperialism.

In China, however, U.S. efforts to block communism failed. The Truman administration first tried to mediate the civil war between the Nationalist government of Jiang Jieshi and the communist forces of **Mao Zedong,** hoping to arrange a coalition government that would end the bloody conflict raging since the 1930s. It also sent nearly $3 billion in aid to the Nationalists between 1945 and 1949. But American dollars could not force Jiang's corrupt and unpopular government to reform itself and win the support of the Chinese people. As Mao's well-disciplined and motivated troops marched south, Jiang's soldiers mutinied or surrendered without a fight. Unable to stem revolutionary sentiment or to hold the countryside, where 85 percent of the population lived and where the communists, in Mao's words, "swam like fishes in the peasant sea," Jiang's regime collapsed and withdrew to the island of Taiwan.

Mao's establishment of the communist People's Republic of China (PRC) shocked Americans. The most populous nation in the world, seen by Washington as a counterforce to Asian communism and a market for American exports, had become "Red China." Although the Truman administration insisted that it could have done nothing to alter the outcome and placed the blame for Jiang's defeat on his failure to reform China, most Americans were unconvinced. China's "fall" especially embittered conservatives who believed that America's interests lay in Asia, not Europe. "China asked for a sword," proclaimed one Republican senator, "and we gave her a dull paring knife." The pressure from conservatives influenced the administration's refusal to recognize the PRC, block its admission to the United Nations, and proclaim Jiang's Nationalist regime in Taiwan as the legitimate government of China.

In September 1949, as the "Who lost China" debate raged, the president announced that the Soviet Union had exploded an atomic bomb. The loss of the nuclear monopoly

MAP 26.1 The Postwar Division of Europe, 1945–1989

The wartime dispute between the Soviet Union and the Western Allies over Poland's future hardened after World War II into a Cold War that split Europe into competing American and Russian spheres of influence. Across an "iron curtain," NATO countries faced the Warsaw Pact nations.

shattered illusions of American invincibility. Ordinary Americans sought safety in civil defense. Public schools held air-raid drills. "We took the drills seriously," recalled novelist Annie Dillard; "surely Pittsburgh, which had the nation's steel, coke, and aluminum, would be the enemy's first target." Four million Americans volunteered to be Sky Watchers, looking for Soviet planes. More than a million purchased or constructed their own family bomb shelters. Those who could not afford a bomb shelter were advised by the Federal Civil Defense Administration to "jump in any handy ditch or gutter . . . bury your face in your arms . . . never lose your head."

In January 1950, stung by charges that he was "soft on communism," Truman ordered a crash program to build a fusion-based hydrogen bomb (H-bomb). In November 1952, the United States exploded its first thermonuclear bomb, nicknamed Mike, 500 times more powerful than an atomic bomb. The blast completely vaporized one of the Marshall Islands in the Pacific, carved a mile-long crater in the ocean floor, and

**FIGURE 26.2
National Defense
Spending,
1941–1960**

In 1950, the defense budget was $13 billion, less than a third of the total federal outlay. In 1961, defense spending reached $47 billion, fully half of the federal budget and almost 10 percent of the gross national product. *Source:* From *American Promise, Vol. 2, 4th ed.,* by James A. Henretta et al. Reprinted with permission of Bedford/St. Martin's.

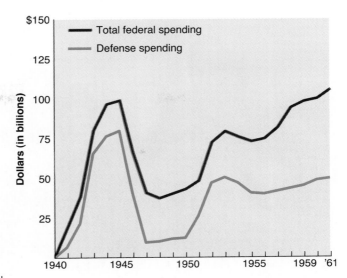

spilled radioactive dust over thousands of square miles. "You would swear the whole world was on fire," a sailor wrote home. Nine months later the Soviets detonated their own H-bomb. The balance of terror escalated.

Truman also called for a top-secret review of defense policy by the National Security Council in early 1950. Completed in April, its secret report, **NSC-68,** emphasized the Soviet Union's military strength and aggressive intentions. To counter the USSR's "design for world domination"—the mortal challenge posed by the Soviet Union "not only to this Republic but to civilization itself"—NSC-68 urged massive increases in America's nuclear arsenal, a large standing army, vigorous covert actions by the CIA, and a quadrupling of the defense budget to wage a global struggle against communism. Truman hesitated to swallow the NSC's expensive medicine. An aide to Secretary of State Acheson recalled, "We were sweating over it, and then, with regard to NSC-68, thank God Korea came along." By the end of 1950 NSC-68 had become official U.S. policy.

The Korean War, 1950–1953

After World War II the United States and Soviet Union temporarily divided Korea, which had been controlled by Japan since the Russo-Japanese War of 1904, at the thirty-eighth parallel. This line then solidified into a *de facto* border between the American-supported Republic of Korea, or South Korea, and the Soviet-backed Democratic People's Republic of Korea in the north, each claiming the sole right to rule all of Korea, and each seeking to undermine the other with economic pressure and military raids.

On June 24, 1950, North Korean troops, aided by Soviet arms and Chinese training, swept across the thirty-eighth parallel to attack South Korea. Truman decided to fight back, viewing the assault not as an intensification of a simmering Korean civil war but rather as a communist test of U.S. will and its containment policy. "Korea is the Greece

A Racially Integrated Unit in the Korean War *The Korean War was the first war in U.S. history in which most soldiers fought in racially integrated units. President Truman had ordered the integration of the armed forces in 1948, despite the oppositon of many military officers, and the successful performance of African-Americans in Korea accelerated acceptance of military integration.*

of the Far East," Truman maintained. "If we are tough enough now, if we stand up to them like we did in Greece . . . they won't take any next steps." Mindful of the failure of appeasement at Munich in 1938, he believed that the communists were doing in Korea exactly what Hitler and the Japanese had done in the 1930s: "Nobody had stood up to them. And that is what led to the Second World War." Having been accused of "selling out" Eastern Europe and "losing" China, Truman needed to prove he could stand up to "the Reds."

Without consulting Congress, Truman ordered air and naval forces to Korea from their bases in Japan on June 27. That same day he asked the United Nations to authorize action to repel the invasion. The Soviet delegate was boycotting the Security Council to protest the UN's unwillingness to seat a representative from Mao's China, and Truman gained approval for a UN "police action" to restore South Korea's border. He appointed General Douglas MacArthur to command the UN effort and ordered American ground troops into what now became the **Korean War.** The Cold War had turned hot.

North Korean forces initially routed the disorganized American and South Korean troops. "All day and night we ran like antelopes," recalled Sergeant Raymond Remp. "We didn't know our officers. They didn't know us. We lost everything we had." Then, in mid-September, with UN forces cornered on the tip of the peninsula around Pusan, struggling to avoid being pushed into the sea, MacArthur's troops landed at Inchon in a brilliant amphibious maneuver. Within two weeks, U.S. and South Korean forces

MAP 26.2 The Korean War, 1950–1953

The experience of fighting an undeclared war for the limited objective of containing communism confused the generation of Americans who had just fought an all-out war for the total defeat of the Axis. General MacArthur spoke for the many who were frustrated by the Korean conflict's mounting costs in blood and dollars: "There is no substitute for victory."

United States and United Nations forces
North Korean forces
Intervention by Chinese forces, Oct. 1950

U.S.S.R.

CHINA

MANCHURIA

Tumen

Chongjin

Hyesahjin
Kanggye

Chosan   Yalu

Angtung
Sinuiju   Unsan   Chosin Res.

Taedong   Hungnam

Farthest U.S. advance, Oct.–Nov. 1950

NORTH KOREA

Sea of Japan

Pyongyang

Nan

Armistice line, July 7, 1953

Kaesong

38th Parallel

Panmunjom
Seoul
Inchon   Han

U.S. landing Sept. 1950

SOUTH KOREA

Farthest Chinese/ North Korean advance, Jan. 1951

Taejon   Naktong   Yongdok

Pohang

Yellow Sea

Taegu

Farthest North Korean advance, Sept. 1950

Pusan

Strait

Korea   TSUSHIMA

0   50   100 Miles
0   50   100 Kilometers

drove the North Koreans back across the thirty-eighth parallel. Basking in victory, MacArthur persuaded Truman to let him go beyond the UN mandate to repel aggression and to cross the border to liberate all of Korea from communism.

As UN troops approached the Yalu River—the boundary between Korea and China—the Chinese warned that they would not "sit back with folded hands and let the Americans come to the border." Dismissing the threat as "hot air," MacArthur deployed his forces in a thin line below the river. On November 25, thirty-three Chinese divisions (about three hundred thousand men) counterattacked, driving stunned marines and soldiers below the thirty-eighth parallel in what *Time* magazine called "the worst military setback the United States has ever suffered." By March 1951, the fighting was deadlocked at roughly the original dividing line between the two Koreas.

"We were eyeball to eyeball," recalled Bev Scott, one of the first black lieutenants to head a racially integrated infantry squad.

> Just 20 meters of no man's land between us. We couldn't move at all in the daytime without getting shot at. . . . It was like World War I. We lived in a maze of bunkers and deep trenches. . . . There were bodies strewn all over the place. Hundreds of bodies frozen in the snow. We could see the arms and legs sticking up. Nobody could get their dead out of there.

Stalemated, Truman reversed course and sought a negotiated peace based on the original objective of restoring the integrity of South Korea. MacArthur rocked the boat, however, calling for an escalation of the war. Chafing at civilian control of the military, the general wanted authority to blockade and bomb Mao's China and to "unleash" Jiang Jieshi's forces to invade the mainland. But Truman, fearing such actions would bring the Soviet Union into the conflict and perhaps trigger a nuclear war, would have none of it. "We are trying to prevent a world war—not start one."

When MacArthur bluntly and repeatedly criticized Truman's limited war—the "appeasement of Communism"—the president fired the general for insubordination on April 10, 1951, replacing him with General Matthew Ridgway. The Joint Chiefs endorsed Truman's decision, but public opinion backed the general. He returned to the United States a genuine folk hero. The very idea of limited war, of containing rather than defeating the enemy, baffled many Americans; and the mounting toll of American casualties in pursuit of a stalemate angered them. It seemed senseless. Despite the warning by General Omar Bradley, chairman of the Joint Chiefs of Staff, that MacArthur's proposals "would involve us in the wrong war at the wrong place in the wrong time and with the wrong enemy," a growing number of Americans listened sympathetically to Republican charges that communist agents controlled American policy.

Truman, meanwhile, found himself bogged down in Korea, unable to win the war or craft a peace. After two more years of fighting, the two sides reached an armistice in July 1953 that left Korea as divided as it had been at the start of the war. The "limited" conflict cost the United States 54,246 lives (about 33,700 of them direct battlefield deaths), another 103,284 wounded, and some $54 billion. The Chinese lost about 900,000 men, and the two Korean armies lost some 800,000. Following the pattern of World War II, massive U.S. "carpet bombing" killed over 2 million civilians, and left North Korea looking like a moonscape.

The Korean War had significant consequences. It accelerated implementation of NSC-68 and the expansion of the containment doctrine into a global commitment. Between 1950 and 1953, defense spending zoomed from $13 billion to $60 billion—from one-third to two-thirds of the entire federal budget—the U.S. army grew from about half a million men to 3.6 million, and the American atomic stockpile mushroomed from 150 to 750 nuclear warheads. The United States acquired new bases around the world, committed itself to rearm West Germany, and joined a mutual-defense pact with Australia and New Zealand. Increased military aid flowed to Jiang Jieshi on Taiwan, and American dollars supported the French army fighting the communist Ho Chi Minh in Indochina. By 1954, the United States was paying three-quarters of French war costs in Vietnam.

Truman's intervention in Korea preserved a precarious balance of power in Asia, and stepped up the administration's commitment to the anticommunist struggle. Containment, originally advanced to justify U.S. aid to Greece and Turkey, had become the ideological foundation for a major war in Korea and, ominously, for a deepening U.S. involvement in Vietnam, intensifying public fears of communist aggression and subversion. Truman's actions enhanced the powers of an already powerful presidency and set the precedent for later undeclared wars. They also helped spark an economic boom, added fuel to a second Red Scare, and fostered Cold War attitudes that lasted long after the war ended.

THE TRUMAN ADMINISTRATION AT HOME, 1945–1952

Since 1929 many Americans had known little but the sufferings and shortages of depression and war. They now wanted to enjoy life. The Cold War both hindered that desire and helped create a postwar affluence that changed dreams into reality. Americans flocked to the suburbs, launched a huge baby boom, and rushed to buy refrigerators and new cars. Sales of TV sets soared from fewer than seven thousand in 1946 to more than 7 million by 1949; by 1953 half of all U.S. homes had at least one television. However, not all Americans shared these good times. Poverty remained a stark fact of life for millions. Minorities experienced the grim reality of racism. Yet a major movement by African-Americans for equality gradually emerged from these Cold War years.

But it did not triumph. Family and career, not public issues, interested most Americans. An increasingly conservative temper trumped liberalism. Some second- and third-generation white Americans, whose recent prosperity had dimmed memories of the Great Depression, and who no longer felt the pull of the New Deal, began to reject liberals at the polls. They worried about high taxes, not unemployment, and they favored a fiscally responsible administration more than one committed to social justice. These former Democratic voters cared more about the growing crime rate and the decline in family authority than about the civil rights of African-Americans. They feared communist subversives, not the loss of civil liberties. Fervently patriotic, they championed a muscular anticommunism, demanding victory, not stalemate, in the Cold War. Although Truman occasionally sought liberal measures, the stirrings of conservative sentiments in places like southern California undercut efforts for progressive change.

The Eightieth Congress, 1947–1948

Many Republicans in the Eightieth Congress interpreted the 1946 elections as a mandate to reverse the New Deal. As "Mr. Republican," Senator Robert A. Taft of Ohio, declared, "We have got to break with the corrupting idea that we can legislate prosperity, legislate equality, legislate opportunity." Congress defeated Democratic bills to raise the minimum wage and to provide federal funds for education and housing.

Truman and the conservatives waged their major battle over the pro-union Wagner Act of 1935 (see Chapter 24). Massive postwar strikes had created a national consensus for curbing union power. In 1947, more than twenty states passed laws to restrict union activities, and Congress passed the **Taft-Hartley Act** (officially the Labor-Management Relations Act), which barred the closed shop—a workplace where only union members could be hired—outlawed secondary boycotts, required union officials to sign loyalty oaths, and permitted the president to call a cooling-off period to delay any strike that might endanger national safety or health. The act weakened organizing drives in the nonunion South and West, hastening the relocation of labor-intensive industries, such as textiles, from the Northeast and Midwest to the Sunbelt. It also helped drive leftists out of CIO leadership positions, weakening organized labor as a force for social justice.

Eager for labor's support in the 1948 presidential election, Truman vetoed the bill. Congress overrode the veto. But Truman had taken a major step in regaining organized labor's support and reforging FDR's New Deal coalition. Truman now played the role of a staunch New Dealer to the hilt, urging Congress to repeal Taft-Hartley; raise the minimum wage, social-security benefits, and price supports for farmers; enact federal aid to education and housing; and adopt a federal health-insurance program. To woo ethnic voters of Eastern European descent, Truman stressed his opposition to the Iron Curtain. To court Jewish-American voters as well as express his deep sympathy toward Holocaust survivors, he overrode the objections of the State Department, which feared alienating the oil-rich Arab world, and extended diplomatic recognition to the new state of Israel immediately after it proclaimed independence on May 14, 1948.

The Politics of Civil Rights and the Election of 1948 As the head of the NAACP noted in 1945, "World War II has immeasurably magnified the Negro's awareness of the disparity between the American profession and practice of democracy." The war heightened African-American expectations for racial equality, and numerous blacks demanded a permanent Fair Employment Practices Commission (FEPC), the outlawing of lynching, and the right to vote. Voter-registration drives raised the percentage of southern blacks registered to vote from 2 percent in 1940 to 12 percent in 1947.

Fearful of the increasing assertiveness of African-Americans to, in the words of Harlem congressman Adam Clayton Powell, Jr., "make the dream of America become flesh and blood, bread and butter, freedom and equality," some southern whites reacted brutally. In 1946, whites killed several black war veterans who had voted that year in rural Georgia, flogged to death an "uppity" black tenant farmer in Mississippi, blow-torched a young black in Louisiana for daring to enter a white woman's house, and blinded a black soldier for failing to sit in the rear of a bus in South Carolina. In Columbia, Tennessee, in 1946 whites rioted against blacks who insisted on their rights. Police arrested seventy blacks and looked the other way as a white mob broke into the jail to murder two black prisoners.

President Truman, responding to the pressure brought by local black protest movements and knowing the political importance of the growing black vote, particularly in northern cities, vowed to act. He understood that white racism damaged U.S. relations with much of the world. The USSR highlighted the mistreatment of African-Americans, both to undercut U.S. appeals to the nonwhites of Africa, Asia, and Latin America, and to counter criticism of its own repression behind the Iron Curtain. Accordingly, Truman established the first **President's Committee on Civil Rights.** Its 1947 report, *To Secure These Rights,* dramatized the inequities of life in Jim Crow America and emphasized all the compelling moral, economic, and international reasons for the government to enact federal legislation outlawing lynching and the poll tax, establishing a permanent FEPC, desegregating the armed forces, and supporting a legal assault on segregation in education, housing, and interstate transportation.

Southern segregationists accused Truman of "stabbing the South in the back" and warned of a boycott of the national Democratic ticket. Truman backtracked. Fearful of

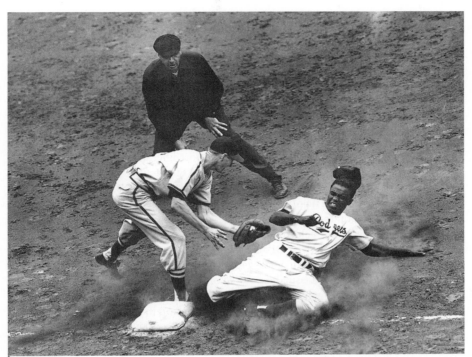

Jackie Robinson, 1947 *Before he became the first African-American to play major-league baseball, Robinson had excelled at track as well as baseball at UCLA and had been an army officer in World War II. Even his brilliant play for the Brooklyn Dodgers did not save him from racial taunts of fans and players or exclusion from restaurants and hotels that catered to his white teammates.*

losing the Solid South, he dropped plans to submit civil-rights bills to Congress and endorsed a weak civil-rights plank for the Democratic platform. But liberals and urban politicians who needed the votes of African-Americans rejected the president's feeble civil-rights plank at the Democratic convention in July 1948 and committed the party to act on Truman's original proposals. Thirty-five delegates from Alabama and Mississippi stalked out, joining other segregationists to form the States' Rights Democratic Party, which nominated Governor Strom Thurmond of South Carolina for the presidency. The "Dixiecrats" hoped to restore their dominance in the Democratic Party, and preserve the segregationist "southern way of life." The Dixiecrats would be an important step toward future Republican conservatism in the South; in 1948, placing their electors on the ballot as the regular Democratic ticket in several states, they posed a major roadblock to Truman's chances of victory.

Truman's 1948 electoral hopes faded further when left-wing Democrats joined with communists to launch a new Progressive Party and nominated Henry A. Wallace for president. The Wallace candidacy threatened Truman's chances in northern states, where many urban Democrats saw Wallace as the true heir of New Deal liberalism. To capitalize on Democratic divisions, Republicans played it safe, nominating the moderate governor of New York, Thomas E. Dewey. Confident of victory, Dewey ran a complacent campaign designed to offend the fewest people. Truman, in contrast, campaigned vigorously, blasting the "no-good, do-nothing" Republican-controlled Eightieth Congress. To shouts of "Give 'em hell, Harry," the president hammered away at the GOP as the party of "privilege, pride, and plunder." Pollsters applauded Truman's spunk but predicted a Dewey victory.

Yet the president won the biggest electoral upset in U.S. history. Ironically, the Progressives and Dixiecrats had helped Truman. Their radicalism had kept moderate Democrats safely in the fold. The Berlin crisis, a coup in Czechoslovakia, and Wallace's failure to repudiate communist support forced most liberals away from the Progressives. Although the support for Thurmond signaled the first cracks in the Solid South, few southern Democrats felt sufficiently threatened by Truman's civil-rights stand to desert the party in 1948. "The only sane and constructive course to follow is to remain in the house of our fathers—even though the roof leaks, and there be bats in the belfry, rats in the pantry, a cockroach in the kitchen and skunks in the parlor," explained a southern officeholder. Moreover, Dixiecrat defections had freed Truman to campaign as a champion of civil rights. In July 1948, responding to a protest campaign led by A. Philip Randolph, Truman issued executive orders barring discrimination in federal employment and ending racial segregation in the armed services. Truman also benefited from Supreme Court decisions declaring segregation in interstate bus transportation unconstitutional (*Morgan* v. *Virginia,* 1946) and outlawing restrictive housing covenants that forbade the sale or rental of property to minorities (*Shelley* v. *Kraemer,* 1948).

The Fair Deal

Despite his narrow victory margin, Truman proposed a **Fair Deal** agenda that included civil rights, national health-care legislation, and federal aid to education. Unlike the New Deal, the Fair Deal was based on the belief in continual economic growth: the constantly expanding economic pie would mean a progressively bigger piece for most Americans (so they would not resent helping those left behind) and for the government (so it would have the revenue to pay for social-welfare programs).

The Eighty-first Congress extended existing programs but rejected new Fair Deal measures. It raised the hourly minimum wage from forty to seventy-five cents; increased social-security benefits and coverage; expanded appropriations for public power, conservation, and slum clearance; and authorized the construction of nearly a million low-income housing units. It also enacted the Displaced Persons Act of 1948, which allowed entry to the United States to 205,000 persons, primarily non-Jews, who had survived the concentration camps, fled the Axis forces, or refused repatriation to the Eastern zone. Another act, in 1950, eliminated the anti-Jewish provisions of the 1948 measure and allowed entry to an additional 200,000 persons. But Congress rejected federal aid to education, national health insurance, civil-rights legislation, and repeal of the Taft-Hartley Act.

Congress's rejection of most Fair Deal proposals stemmed from Truman's own lessening commitment to domestic reform in favor of foreign and military affairs, as well as from the strengthening of the congressional coalition of Republicans and conservative Democrats. The postwar congresses mirrored the public lack of enthusiasm for liberal reform caused by increasing prosperity and by fears of communism.

THE POLITICS OF ANTICOMMUNISM

As the Cold War worsened, some Americans concluded that the roots of the nation's difficulties abroad lay in domestic treason and subversion. How else could the communists have defeated Jiang in China and built an atomic bomb? Millions of fearful Americans enlisted in a crusade that equated dissent with disloyalty and blamed scapegoats for the nation's problems.

Similar intolerance had prevailed in the Red Scare of 1919–1920 (see Chapter 22). Since its establishment in 1938, the House Committee on Un-American Activities (later called the House Un-American Activities Committee, or HUAC) had served as a platform for right-wing denunciations of the New Deal as a communist plot. Only the extreme Right initially took such charges seriously. But after World War II mounting numbers of Democrats and Republicans climbed aboard the anti-Red bandwagon.

The **Second Red Scare** influenced both governmental and personal actions. Millions of Americans were subjected to security investigations and loyalty oaths. Anticommunist extremism destroyed the Left, undermined labor militancy, and discredited liberalism. It spawned a "silent generation" of college students, and ensured anticommunist foreign-policy rigidity.

Loyalty and Security

The Cold War raised legitimate concerns about American security. The Communist Party had claimed eighty thousand members in the United States during the Second World War, and far more sympathizers. Just how many party members or secret communists occupied sensitive government and military positions no one knew. In mid-1945 a raid on the offices of a procommunist magazine revealed that classified documents had been given to the periodical by State Department employees and a naval intelligence officer. Then the Canadian government exposed a major spy network that had passed American atomic secrets to the Soviets during the war. Republicans accused the Democratic administration of being "soft on communism."

A week after his Truman Doctrine speech of March 1947, the president issued Executive Order 9835, establishing the Federal Employee Loyalty Program to root out subversives in the government. The first such peacetime program, it barred members of the Communist Party and anyone guilty of "sympathetic association" with it from federal employment. "Reasonable grounds for belief that the person is disloyal," which was defined to include being homosexual, led to dismissal. Those suspected were allowed neither to face their accusers nor to require investigators to reveal sources. Instead of focusing on potential subversives in high-risk areas, review boards extended the probe to the associations and beliefs of every government worker.

Mere criticism of American foreign policy could result in an accusation of disloyalty. Clouds of suspicion hovered over those who liked foreign films or who favored the unionization of federal workers. "Of course the fact that a person believes in racial equality doesn't prove he's a communist," mused an Interior Department Loyalty Board chairman, "but it certainly makes you look twice, doesn't it?" Some people lost jobs because they associated with radical friends or had once belonged to organizations now declared disloyal.

Of the 4.7 million jobholders and applicants who underwent loyalty checks by 1952, 560 were fired or denied jobs on security grounds, several thousand resigned or withdrew their applications, and countless more were intimidated. Although Loyalty Board probes uncovered no evidence of espionage or subversion, they heightened fears of what Truman called "the enemy within," adding credibility to the Red Scare. "If communists like apple pie and I do," claimed one federal worker, "I see no reason why I should stop eating it. But I would."

The Anticommunist Crusade The very existence of a federal loyalty probe fed mounting anticommunist hysteria. It promoted fears of communist infiltrators and legitimated a witch-hunt for subversives. At Yale, the FBI, with the consent of the college administration, spied on students and faculty, screening candidates for jobs and fellowships. Many universities banned controversial speakers, and popular magazines featured articles like "Reds Are After Your Child." Comics joined the fray: "Beware, commies, spies, traitors, and foreign agents! Captain America, with all loyal, free men behind him, is looking for you, ready to fight until the last one of you is exposed for the yellow scum you are." Truman's Office of Education introduced a "Zeal for Democracy" campaign, providing local school boards with curriculum materials to combat "communist subversion."

By the end of Truman's term, thirty-nine states had created loyalty programs. Few had any procedural safeguards. Schoolteachers, college professors, and state and city employees throughout the nation had to sign loyalty oaths or lose their jobs. No one knows for sure how many were dismissed, denied tenure, or drifted away, leaving behind colleagues too frightened to speak out.

In 1947, the **House Un-American Activities Committee** began hearings to expose communist influence in American life. HUAC's probes blurred distinctions between dissent and disloyalty, between radicalism and subversion. Those called to testify were in a bind. When asked whether they had ever been members of the Communist Party, witnesses could say yes and be forced to reveal the names of others; say no and be vulnerable to charges of perjury; or refuse to answer, pleading the First or Fifth Amendment, and risk being viewed by the public as a communist. To gain publicity for itself and to influence the content of movies, HUAC investigated Hollywood. They saw as proof of communist activity wartime films about the Soviet Union showing Russians smiling, or movies featuring the line "share and share alike, that's democracy." In 1947, HUAC cited for contempt of Congress a group of film directors and screenwriters who, claiming the freedom of speech and assembly guaranteed by the First Amendment, refused to say whether they had been members of the Communist Party. The so-called Hollywood Ten—some of them communists, all of them leftists—were convicted of contempt and sent to prison. The threat of further investigations prompted the movie colony, financially dependent on favorable press and public opinion, to deny work to other "unfriendly witnesses." Soon the studios established a blacklist barring the employment of anyone suspected of having been a communist.

HUAC also frightened the labor movement into expelling communists and avoiding progressive causes. Fearful of appearing "red," or even "pink," most unions focused on securing better pay and benefits for their members.

The 1948 presidential election campaign also fed national anxieties. Truman lambasted Henry Wallace as a Stalinist dupe and accused the Republicans of being "unwittingly the ally of the communists." In turn, the GOP dubbed the Democrats "the party of treason." To blunt such accusations, Truman's Justice Department prosecuted eleven top leaders of the American Communist Party under the Smith Act of 1940, which outlawed any conspiracy advocating the overthrow of the government. The Supreme Court upheld the Smith Act's constitutionality (*Dennis* v. *United States*, 1951), declaring that Congress could curtail freedom of speech if national security required such restriction, and affirmed the conviction and jailing of the communists, despite the absence of any acts of violence or espionage.

Ironically, the Communist Party was fading into obscurity at the very time when politicians magnified its threat. By 1950 its membership had shrunk to fewer than thirty thousand. Yet Truman's attorney general warned that American Reds "are everywhere— in factories, offices, butcher stores, on street corners, in private businesses—and each carries in himself the germ of death for society."

Alger Hiss and
the Rosenbergs

Nothing set off more alarms of a diabolic Red conspiracy in Washington than the matter of **Alger Hiss and Whittaker Chambers.** During the 1948 political campaign, HUAC had conducted a hearing in which Chambers, a *Time* editor and former Soviet agent who had broken with the communists in 1938, identified Hiss as an underground communist in the 1930s.

A rumpled, repentant, former communist and college dropout, Chambers seemed a tortured soul crusading to save the West from the Red peril. The elegant Hiss, in contrast, symbolized the liberal establishment: a Harvard-trained lawyer who had clerked for Supreme Court Justice Oliver Wendell Holmes, he had served FDR in the New Deal and later as a State Department official, presiding over the inaugural meeting of the United Nations. For conservative Republicans, a better villain could not have been invented. Hiss denied any communist affiliation and claimed not to know Chambers. Most liberals believed him. They saw him as a victim of conservatives bent on tarnishing New Deal liberalism. Truman denounced Chambers's allegation as a "red herring" to deflect attention from the failures of the Eightieth Congress.

To those suspicious of the Roosevelt liberal tradition, Chambers's persistence and Hiss's fumbling retreat intensified fears that the Democratic administration teemed with communists. Under relentless questioning by Congressman (and later president) Richard Nixon, Hiss finally admitted that he had known Chambers and had even let Chambers have his car and live in his apartment. But he denied ever having been a communist. Chambers then broadened his accusation, claiming that Hiss had committed espionage in the 1930s by giving him secret State Department documents to be sent to the Soviet Union. To prove his charge, Chambers led federal agents to his farm in Maryland, where, in a hollowed-out pumpkin, he had microfilm copies of confidential government papers that had been copied on a typewriter traced to Hiss. A grand jury indicted Hiss for perjury, or lying under oath. (The statute of limitations for espionage prevented a charge of treason.) In January 1950 Hiss was convicted and given a five-year prison sentence. Republican conservatives were emboldened. Who knew how many other bright young New Dealers had betrayed the country?

Hard on the heels of the Hiss conviction, another spy case shocked Americans. In February 1950, the British arrested Klaus Fuchs, a German-born scientist involved in the Manhattan Project, for passing atomic secrets to the Soviets during the Second World War. Fuchs's confession led to the arrest of his American accomplice and a machinist who had worked at Los Alamos, who then named his brother-in-law and sister,

Julius and Ethel Rosenberg, as co-conspirators in the wartime spy network. The Rosenbergs insisted they were victims of anti-Semitism and were being prosecuted for their leftist beliefs. In March 1951, a jury found them both guilty of conspiring to commit espionage. Declaring their crime "worse than murder," the trial judge sentenced them to die in the electric chair. Offered clemency if they named other spies, neither Rosenberg would confess. On June 19, 1953, they were executed—the first American civilians to lose their lives for espionage.

Both the Rosenbergs and Alger Hiss protested their innocence to their end, and their defenders continued to do so for decades. Soviet secret documents released by the National Security Agency in the 1990s—called the Venona Intercepts—lent weight to Chambers's charges against Hiss and confirmed Julius Rosenberg's guilt. (Ethel's role in her husband's spying remained uncertain.)

McCarthyism

At this point, when few Americans could separate fact from fantasy, the Hiss and Rosenberg cases tarnished liberalism and fueled other loyalty investigations. Only a conspiracy, it seemed, could explain U.S. weakness and Soviet might. Frustrated by their unexpected failure to win the White House in 1948, Republicans eagerly exploited the fearful mood and accused the "Commiecrats" of selling out America.

No individual would inflict so many wounds on the Democrats as Republican senator **Joseph R. McCarthy** of Wisconsin. Falsely claiming to be a wounded war hero, "Tail-Gunner Joe" won a Senate seat in the 1946 Republican landslide, and promptly gained a reputation for lying and heavy drinking. His political future in jeopardy, McCarthy decided to imitate Republicans like Richard Nixon who had gained popularity by accusing Democrats of being "soft on communism." In February 1950 McCarthy told an audience in Wheeling, West Virginia, that the United States found itself in a "position of impotency" because of "the traitorous actions" of high officials in the Truman administration. "I have here in my hands a list of 205," McCarthy boldly claimed as he waved a laundry ticket, "a list of names known to the Secretary of State as being members of the Communist party and who nevertheless are still working and shaping policy." Although McCarthy offered no evidence to support his accusations, the newspapers printed his charges, giving him a national forum. McCarthy soon repeated his accusations, reducing his numbers first to 81, then to 57, and finally to "a lot," and reducing his indictment from "card-carrying communists" to "subversives" to "bad risks." A Senate committee found McCarthy's charges "a fraud and a hoax," but he persisted.

Buoyed by the partisan usefulness of Senator McCarthy's onslaught, Republicans encouraged even more accusations. Even the normally fair-minded Robert Taft, who privately dismissed McCarthy's charges as "nonsense," urged him "to keep talking, and if one case doesn't work, try another." He did, and "McCarthyism" became a synonym for personal attacks on individuals by means of indiscriminate allegations and unsubstantiated charges.

As the Korean War dragged on, McCarthy's efforts to "root out the skunks" escalated. He ridiculed Secretary of State Dean Acheson as the "Red Dean," termed Truman's dismissal of MacArthur "the greatest victory the communists have ever won," and charged George Marshall with having "aided and abetted a communist conspiracy so immense as to dwarf any previous such venture in the history of man."

McCarthyism especially appealed to midwestern Republicans indignant about the Europe-first emphasis of Truman's foreign policy and eager to turn the public's fears into votes for the GOP. For many in the American Legion and the Chambers of Commerce, anticommunism was a weapon of revenge against liberals and internationalists, as well as a means to regain the controlling position that conservative forces had once held. McCarthy also won a devoted following among blue-collar workers who identified with his charge that a person was either a true American who detested "communists and queers" or an "egg sucking phony liberal." Laborers praised his demand that the war against communism be fought with brass knuckles, not kid gloves, while both small and big businessmen sniffed an opportunity to destroy the power of organized labor. McCarthy's flag-waving appeals held a special attraction for traditionally Democratic Catholic ethnics, who sought to gain acceptance as "100 percent Americans" through a show of anticommunist zeal. Countless Americans also shared McCarthy's scorn for the privileged, for the "bright young men who are born with silver spoons in their mouths," for the "striped-pants boys in the State Department." His conspiracy theory, moreover, offered a simple answer to the perplexing questions of the Cold War.

McCarthy's political power rested on the support of the Republican establishment and Democrats fearful of antagonizing him. McCarthy appeared invincible after he helped GOP candidates in the 1950 congressional elections unseat Democrats who had denounced him. "Look out for McCarthy," warned the new majority leader, Democrat Lyndon B. Johnson of Texas; "Joe will go that extra mile to destroy you." Few dared incur McCarthy's wrath.

Over Truman's veto, Congress in 1950 adopted the **McCarran Internal Security Act,** which required organizations deemed communist by the attorney general to register with the Department of Justice. It also authorized the arrest and detention during a national emergency of "any person as to whom there is reason to believe might engage in acts of espionage or sabotage." As part of this effort, a Senate committee sought to root out homosexuals holding government jobs. The linking of disloyalty with homosexuality in turn legitimated the armed forces' effort to dismiss "queers" and the raiding of gay bars by city police. The McCarran-Walter Immigration and Nationality Act of 1952, also adopted over Truman's veto, maintained the quota system that severely restricted immigration from southern and eastern Europe and from Asia, but did end the ban on Japanese immigration and made Issei eligible for naturalized citizenship. In the name of national security, moreover, the law increased the attorney general's authority to exclude or deport "undesirable" aliens, particularly those suspected of homosexuality or supporting communism.

The Election of 1952

In 1952 public apprehension about the loyalty of government employees combined with frustration over the Korean stalemate to sink Democratic hopes to their lowest level since the 1920s. Both business and labor also resented Truman's freeze on wages and prices during the Korean conflict. Revelations of bribery and influence peddling by some of Truman's old political associates gave Republicans ammunition for charging the Democrats with "plunder at home, and blunder abroad."

With Truman too unpopular to run for reelection, dispirited Democrats drafted Governor Adlai Stevenson of Illinois. But Stevenson could not separate himself politically from Truman, and his lofty speeches failed to stir most voters. An intellectual out of touch with the common people, he was jokingly referred to as an "egghead," someone with more brains than hair. Above all, Stevenson could not overcome the widespread sentiment that twenty years of Democratic rule was enough.

Compounding Democratic woes, the GOP nominated the hugely popular war hero Dwight D. Eisenhower. Essentially apolitical, Eisenhower had once insisted that "lifelong professional soldiers should abstain from seeking higher political office." But in 1952 he answered the call of the moderate wing of the Republican Party and accepted the nomination. As a concession to the hard-line anticommunists in the party, "Ike" chose as his running mate Richard Nixon, who had won a seat in the Senate in 1950 by red-baiting his opponent, Helen Gahagan Douglas, as "pink right down to her underwear."

Eisenhower and Nixon proved unbeatable. With a captivating grin and unimpeachable record of public service, Eisenhower projected both personal warmth and the vigorous authority associated with military command. His smile, wrote one commentator, was one "of infinite reassurance." At the same time, Nixon kept public apprehensions at the boiling point. Accusing the Democrats of treason, he charged that the election of "Adlai the appeaser ... who got a Ph.D. from Dean Acheson's College of Cowardly Communist Containment" would bring "more Alger Hisses, more atomic spies."

The GOP ticket stumbled when newspapers revealed the existence of a "slush fund" that California businessmen created to keep Nixon in "financial comfort." But Nixon saved himself with a heart-tugging television defense. Less than two weeks before the election, Eisenhower dramatically pledged to "go to Korea" to end the stalemated war. It worked, and 62.7 percent of those eligible to vote (compared to just 51.5 percent in 1948) turned out in 1952 and gave the Republican ticket 55 percent of the ballots. Ike cracked the Solid South, carrying thirty-nine states (and 442 electoral votes). Enough Republicans rode his coattails to give the GOP narrow control of both houses of Congress.

CONCLUSION

After nearly two decades of depression and war, the end of World War II meant the beginning of a better life and a new era of hope for most Americans. Millions of returning veterans took advantage of the GI Bill to go to college and to receive low-interest loans to start businesses and purchase homes. Although temporarily disadvantaging women in securing employment or a college degree, the GI Bill, in the long run, democratized higher education, helped fuel a baby boom and suburbanization, and played a major role in the postwar economic boom that for the first time provided a middle-class standard of living for a majority of Americans.

At the same time, an assertive United States, eager to protect and expand its influence and power in the world, sought to contain a Soviet Union obsessed with its own security and self-interest. Stalin's aggressive posture toward Eastern Europe and the Persian Gulf was met by an American policy of containment, in whose name the United States aided Greece and Turkey, established the Marshall Plan, airlifted supplies into Berlin for a year, approved the creation of the Federal Republic of Germany (West Germany), established NATO, implemented NSC-68, financed France's war in Vietnam, and went to war in Korea. The resulting stalemate would last for four decades, define American politics and society, transform its economy, and condition the thinking of a generation.

The Cold War obsession with communism, as well as postwar prosperity, weakened the appeal of liberal reform. In a political climate far more conservative than that of the

1930s, New Deal measures remained in place, but Truman's Fair Deal to assist the disadvantaged with new initiatives in education, health insurance, and civil rights failed. Anticommunist hysteria squashed the left and narrowed the range of politically acceptable ideas. Bold proposals to end racism and discrimination—often labeled "communistic" by segregationists—had little chance in Congress; but the need of the United States to appeal to the nonwhites of the world during the Cold War brought racial issues to the fore in American politics and forced President Truman to take executive actions. Most immediately, and of paramount consequence, Truman's actions at home and abroad fed America's fear of communism. The president's responses to the Soviet detonation of an atomic bomb, the fall of China to the communists, and the invasion of South Korea, in addition to his own loyalty probe to root out subversive government workers, spawned anxieties. In an atmosphere of paranoia, caused by witch-hunts for communism in American life and the discovery of a Soviet atomic spy ring, Truman's actions encouraged others to seek scapegoats for American failures abroad and legitimated conservative accusations that equated dissent with disloyalty. The Republicans would ride "McCarthyism" back to the seat of power in Washington; it would be up to President Eisenhower to restore unity and renew hopefulness.

27

America at Midcentury, 1952–1960

THE EISENHOWER PRESIDENCY

Rarely in U.S. history has a president better fit the national mood than did **Dwight David Eisenhower.** Exhausted by a quarter-century of upheaval—the depression, World War II, the Cold War—Americans craved peace and stability. Eisenhower delivered. He gave a nation weary of partisanship a sense of unity; he inspired confidence; and his moderate politics, steering a middle course between Democratic liberalism and traditional Republican conservatism, pleased most Americans. So did his largely hands-off approach to McCarthyism and the desegregation of public schools.

"Dynamic Conservatism"   The most lauded American general of the Second World War, Eisenhower projected the image of a plain but good man. He expressed complicated issues in simple terms, yet governed a complex, urban, technological society. A grandfatherly figure, a hero who had vanquished Hitler, Ike comforted an anxious people.

Born in Denison, Texas, on October 14, 1890, Dwight Eisenhower grew up in Abilene, Kansas, in a poor, strongly religious family. More athletic than studious, he graduated from the U.S. Military Academy at West Point in 1915. A brilliant war planner, respected for his managerial ability and skill at conciliation, Eisenhower's approach to the presidency reflected his wartime leadership style. He concentrated on "the big picture," delegating authority while reconciling contending factions. His restrained view of presidential powers stemmed from his respect for the constitutional balance of power as well as his sense of the dignity of the Oval Office. He rarely intervened publicly in the legislative process. He shunned using his office as a "bully pulpit." He promised his cabinet that he would "stay out of its hair." This low-key style led Democrats to scoff at Eisenhower as a bumbler who preferred golf to government, who "reigned but did not rule."

CHRONOLOGY ,1952–1960

1946 • ENIAC, the first electronic computer, begins operation.

1947 • Levittown, New York, development started.

1948 • Bell Labs develops the transistor.

1950 • *Asosiación Nacional México-Americana* established.

1952 • Dwight D. Eisenhower elected president.

1953 • Korean War truce signed.
Earl Warren appointed chief justice.
Operation Wetback begins.

1954 • Army-McCarthy hearings.
Brown v. *Board of Education of Topeka*.
Fall of Dienbienphu; Geneva Conference.
Father Knows Best begins on TV.

1955 • Salk polio vaccine developed.
AFL-CIO merger.
First postwar U.S.-Soviet summit meeting.
James Dean stars in *Rebel Without a Cause*.
Montgomery bus boycott begins.

1956 • Interstate Highway Act.
Suez crisis.
Soviet intervention in Poland and Hungary.

1957 • Eisenhower Doctrine announced.
Civil Rights Act (first since Reconstruction).
Little Rock school-desegregation crisis.
Soviet Union launches *Sputnik*.
Peak of baby boom (4.3 million births).
Southern Christian Leadership Conference founded.

1958 • National Defense Education Act.
United States and Soviet Union halt atomic tests.
National Aeronautics and Space Administration (NASA) founded.

1959 • Fidel Castro comes to power in Cuba.
Khrushchev and Eisenhower meet at Camp David.

1960 • U-2 incident.
Second Civil Rights Act.
Suburban population almost equals that of central city.

The image of passivity actually masked an active and occasionally ruthless politician. Determined to govern the nation on business principles, Eisenhower staffed his administration with corporate executives. "Eight millionaires and a plumber," jested one journalist about the cabinet. (The "plumber" was union leader Martin Durkin, who headed the Labor Department, and soon resigned.) The president initially worked with the Republican-controlled Congress to reduce the size of government and to slash the federal budget. He promoted the private development of hydroelectric and nuclear power, and persuaded Congress to turn over to coastal states the oil-rich "tidelands" that the Supreme Court had awarded to the federal government.

For the most part, however, the Eisenhower administration followed a centrist course, which the president labeled "dynamic conservatism" and "modern Republicanism." More pragmatic than ideological, he wished to reduce taxes, contain inflation, and govern efficiently without surrendering the fundamentals of the New Deal. When recessions struck in 1953 and 1957, Eisenhower abandoned his balanced budgets and increased spending to restore prosperity. As Milton Eisenhower summed up his brother's views: "We should keep what we have, catch our breath for a while, and improve administration; it does not mean moving backward."

Ike supported extending social-security benefits, raising the minimum wage, adding 4 million more workers to those eligible for unemployment benefits, and providing federally financed public housing for low-income families. He also approved establishing a Department of Health, Education and Welfare; constructing the St. Lawrence Seaway, linking the Great Lakes and the Atlantic Ocean; and building freeways (see Technology and Culture: The Interstate Highway System). With the Republicans crowing "Everything's booming but the guns," Ike won reelection in 1956 by a landslide over Democrat Adlai Stevenson. Despite having suffered a major heart attack in 1955, Eisenhower carried all but seven states.

The Downfall of Joseph McCarthy

Although he despised McCarthy—and called him a "pimple on the path to progress," Eisenhower considered it beneath his dignity to "get into the gutter with that guy." Fearing a direct confrontation with the senator, he first tightened security requirements for government employees, to steal McCarthy's thunder, and then allowed McCarthy to grab plenty of rope in hopes that the demagogue would hang himself. He did. Angry that one of his aides had not received a draft deferment, the senator accused the army in 1954 of harboring communist spies. The army countered that McCarthy had tried to get preferential treatment for the aide who had been drafted.

The resulting nationally televised Senate investigation, begun in April 1954, brought McCarthy down. A national audience witnessed McCarthy's boorish behavior firsthand on television. His dark scowl, raspy voice, endless interruptions ("point of order, Mr. Chairman, point of order"), and disregard for the rights of others repelled many viewers. He behaved like the bad guy in a TV western, observed novelist John Steinbeck: "He had a stubble of a beard, he leered, he sneered, he had a nasty laugh. He bullied and shouted. He looked evil." In June McCarthy slurred the reputation of a young lawyer assisting Joseph Welch, the army counsel. Suddenly the mild-mannered Welch turned his wrath on McCarthy, "Until this moment, Senator, I think I really never gauged your cruelty or your recklessness. . . . Have you no sense of decency?" The gallery burst into applause.

The Interstate Highway System

As a young captain after World War I, Dwight Eisenhower had been given the task of accompanying a convoy of army trucks across the country. The woefully inadequate state of the roads for military transport dismayed him then as much as he would later be impressed by the German autobahns that allowed Hitler to deploy troops around Germany with incredible speed. Not surprisingly, when he became president he sought a transportation system that would facilitate the rapid movement of the military, as well as increase road safety and aid commerce. The arms race with the Soviet Union, moreover, necessitated a network of highways for evacuating cities in case of a nuclear attack—a change, according to the *Bulletin of the Atomic Scientists,* from "Duck and Cover" to "Run Like Hell."

In 1954 Eisenhower set up a high-powered commission to recommend a highway program that would cost as much as a war. He appointed an army general to head it to emphasize the connection between highways, national defense, and the concerns Americans had about their security. The next year, with the entire federal budget at $71 billion, Eisenhower asked Congress for a $40 billion, forty-one-thousand-mile construction project, to be financed by government bonds. Conservative Republicans, fearful of increasing the federal debt, balked. So Ike switched to a financing plan based on new gasoline, tire, bus, and trucking taxes. The federal government would use the taxes to pay 90 percent of the construction costs in any state willing to come up with the other 10 percent.

Millions of suburbanites commuting to central cities loved the idea of new multilane highways. So did motorists dreaming of summer travel; the powerful coalition of automobile manufacturers, oil companies, asphalt firms, and truckers, who stood to benefit financially the most; and the many special interests in virtually every congressional district, including real-estate developers, shopping mall entrepreneurs, engineers, and construction industries. Indeed, the interstate highway bill promised something to almost everybody except the inner-city poor. It sailed through Congress in 1956, winning by voice vote in the House and by an 89 to 1 margin in the Senate.

The largest and most expensive public-works scheme in American history, the interstate highway system was designed and built as a single project for the entire country, unlike the haphazard development of the canal and railroad networks. It required taking more land by eminent domain than had been taken in the entire history of road building in the United States. Expected increases in highway use, speed of travel, and weight of loads necessitated drastic changes in road engineering and materials. Utilizing the technological advances that had produced high-quality concrete and asphalt, diesel-powered roadbed graders, reinforced steel, and safely controlled explosives, construction crews built superhighways with standardized twelve-foot-wide lanes, ten-foot shoulders, and median strips of at least thirty-six feet in rural areas. Terrain in which a dirt trail was difficult to blaze was laced with cloverleaf intersections and some sixteen thousand exits and entrances. More than fifty thousand bridges, tunnels, and overpasses traversed swamps, rivers, and mountains. Road curves were banked for speeds of seventy miles per hour, with grades no greater than 3 percent and minimum sight distances of six hundred feet. The massive amounts of concrete poured, Ike later boasted, could have made "six sidewalks to the moon" or sixty Panama Canals.

The network of four-to-eight-lane roads linking cities and suburbs made it possible to drive from New York to San Francisco without encountering a stoplight. It more than fulfilled the initial hopes of most of its backers, enormously speeding the movement of goods and people across the country, invigorating the tourist industry, providing steady work for construction firms, enriching those who lived near the interstates and sold their lands to developers, and hastening suburban development.

The freeways that helped unify Americans by increasing the accessibility of once-distant regions also helped homogenize the nation with interchangeable shopping malls, motels, and fast-food chains. In 1955, Ray Kroc, who supplied the Multimixers for milk shakes to the original McDonald's drive-in in San Bernardino, California, began to franchise similar family restaurants beside highways, each serving the same standardized foods under the instantly rec-ognizable logo of the golden arches. By century's end, McDonald's would be the world's largest private real-estate enterprise, as well as the largest food provider, serving more than 40 million meals daily in some hundred countries.

Moreover, the expressways boosted the interstate trucking business and hastened the decline of the nation's railroad lines and urban mass-transportation systems. The highways built to speed commuters into the central cities—"white men's roads through black men's bedrooms," said the National Urban League—often bulldozed minority neighborhoods out of existence or served as barriers between black and white neighborhoods. The beltways that lured increasingly more residents and businesses to suburbia eroded city tax bases, which, in turn, accelerated urban decay, triggering the urban crisis that then furthered suburban sprawl. The interstates had locked the United States into an ever-increasing reliance on cars and trucks, drastically increasing air pollution and American dependence on a constant supply of cheap and plentiful gasoline.

Questions for Analysis

- Why did Congress authorize the construction of an interstate highway system?

- Describe some of the unintended consequences of the new highway system.

McCarthy's popularity ratings plummeted. With the GOP no longer needing him to drive the "Commiecrats" from power, and the Democrats eager to be rid of their scourge, the Senate, with Eisenhower applying pressure behind the scenes, voted in December 1954 to censure McCarthy for contemptuous behavior. This powerful rebuke—only the third in the Senate's history—demolished McCarthy as a political force. McCarthyism, Ike gloated, had become "McCarthywasism."

In 1957 McCarthy died from alcoholism. But the fears he exploited lingered. Congress continued to fund the House Un-American Activities Committee's search for suspected radicals. State and local governments continued to require teachers to take loyalty oaths.

McCarthyism also remained a rallying call of conservatives disenchanted with the postwar consensus. Young conservatives like William F. Buckley, Jr. (a recent Yale graduate who founded the *National Review* in 1955), and the Christian Anti-Communist Crusade continued to claim that domestic communism was a major subversive threat. None did so more than the John Birch Society, which denounced Eisenhower as a conscious agent of the communist conspiracy, and equated liberalism with treason. Its grass-roots network of as many as a hundred thousand activists promoted like-minded political candidates, while waging local struggles against taxes, gun control, and sex education in the schools. Although few saw all the dangers lurking in every shadow that the John Birch Society did, Barry Goldwater and Ronald Reagan, among others, used its anticommunist, antigovernment rhetoric to advantage. Stressing victory over communism, rather than its containment, the self-proclaimed "new conservatives" (or radical right, as their opponents called them) criticized the "creeping socialism" of Eisenhower, advocated a return to traditional moral standards, and condemned the liberal rulings of the Supreme Court.

Jim Crow in Court   Led by a new chief justice, **Earl Warren** (1953), the Supreme Court incurred conservatives' wrath for defending the rights of persons accused of subversive beliefs. In *Jencks* v. *United States* (1957) the Court held that the accused had the right to inspect government files used by the prosecution. In *Yates* v. *United States* (1957) the justices overturned the convictions of Communist Party officials under the Smith Act (see Chapter 26), emphasizing the distinction between unlawful concrete acts and the teaching of revolutionary ideology. *Yates* essentially ended further prosecutions of communists, and right-wing opponents of the decision demanded limitations on the Court's powers and plastered "Impeach Earl Warren" posters on highway billboards.

These condemnations paled beside those of segregationists following ***Brown* v. *Board of Education of Topeka*** (May 17, 1954). Following a series of cases brought by the NAACP in the 1930s and 1940s, which did not attack segregation head-on but rather called for greater equality within "separate but equal," the NAACP's Thurgood Marshall combined lawsuits from four states and the District of Columbia, reflecting the growing determination of black Americans to demand their rights, in which black plaintiffs claimed that segregated public education *per se* was unconstitutional. *Brown* built on an earlier federal court ruling that had prohibited the segregation of Mexican-American children in California schools, as well as on decisions in 1950 in which the Supreme Court had significantly narrowed the possibility of separate law school and graduate education being in fact equal education, and thus constitutional. Chief Justice Warren, speaking for a unanimous Court, reversed *Plessy* v. *Ferguson* (see Chapter 20). Largely citing psychological studies, the high court held that separating schoolchildren "solely because of their race generates a feeling of inferiority as to their status in the community that may affect their hearts and minds in a way unlikely ever to be undone," thereby violating the equal protection clause of the Fourteenth Amendment. "In the field of public education," the Court concluded, "the doctrine of 'separate but equal' has no place. Separate educational facilities are inherently unequal." A year later, the Court ordered federal district judges to monitor compliance with *Brown,* vaguely requiring that desegregation proceed "with all deliberate speed"—an oxymoron that implied gradualism—the price Warren paid to gain a unanimous decision.

In the border states, African-American and white students sat side by side for the first time in history. But in the South, where segregation was deeply entrenched in law and custom, politicians vowed resistance, and Eisenhower refused to press them to comply: "I don't believe you can change the hearts of men with laws or decisions." Although not personally a racist, Ike never publicly endorsed the *Brown* decision and privately called his appointment of Earl Warren "the biggest damn fool mistake I ever made."

Public-opinion polls in 1954 indicated that some 80 percent of white southerners opposed the *Brown* decision. Encouraged by the president's silence, white resistance stiffened. White Citizens Councils sprang up, and the Ku Klux Klan revived. Declaring *Brown* "null, void, and of no effect," southern legislatures claimed the right to "interpose" themselves against the federal government and adopted a strategy of "massive resistance" to thwart compliance with the law. They closed down or denied state aid to school systems that desegregated, and enacted pupil-placement laws that permitted school boards to assign black and white children to different schools.

In 1956, more than a hundred members of Congress signed the **Southern Manifesto,** denouncing *Brown* as "a clear abuse of judicial power." White southern politicians competed in their opposition to desegregation. When a gubernatorial candidate in Alabama promised to go to jail to defend segregation, his opponent swore that he would die for it. Segregationists also resorted to violence and economic reprisals against blacks to maintain all-white schools. At the end of 1956, not a single African-American attended school with whites in the Deep South, and few did so in the Upper South.

The Laws of the Land

Southern resistance reached a climax in September 1957. Although the Little Rock school board had accepted a federal court order to desegregate Central High School, Arkansas governor Orval E. Faubus mobilized the state's National Guard to bar nine African-American students from entering the school. After another court order forced Faubus to withdraw the guardsmen, an angry mob of whites blocked the black students' entry.

Although Eisenhower sought to avoid the divisive issue of civil rights, he believed he had to uphold federal law. He worried that the Soviets were "gloating over this incident and using it everywhere to misrepresent our whole nation." The Cold War had made segregation in the United States a national security liability. Understanding that racism at home hampered American efforts to gain the support of nonwhite Third World nations, the president federalized the Arkansas National Guard and, for the first time since Reconstruction, dispatched federal troops to protect blacks' rights. To ensure the safety of the black students, soldiers patrolled Central High for the rest of the year. Rather than accept integration, however, Faubus shut down Little Rock's public high schools for two years. At the end of the decade, fewer than 1 percent of African-American students in the Deep South attended desegregated schools.

Nevertheless, Little Rock strengthened the determination of African-Americans to end Jim Crow. The crisis foreshadowed television's vital role in the demise of Jim Crow.

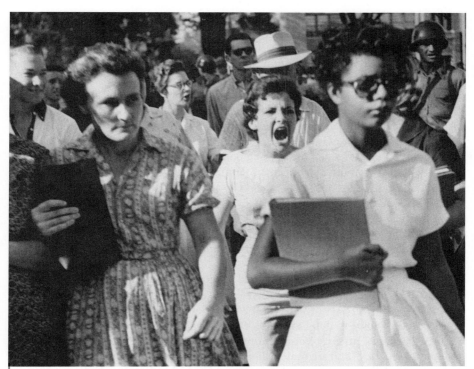

Little Rock, 1957   *Elizabeth Eckford, age fifteen, one of the nine black students to desegregate Central High School, endures abuse on her way to school, September 4, 1957. Such scenes of angry whites jeering, screaming, and threatening African-American students were televised to the nation, showing the human suffering caused by racist hatred in the South. By so doing, television made Americans aware of the stark consequences of racism. Forty years later, the young white woman in this picture shouting insults asked for forgiveness.*

The contrast between the images of howling white racists and those of resolute black students projected on the TV screen immensely aided the civil-rights cause. According to a 1957 public-opinion poll, fully 90 percent of whites outside the South approved the use of federal troops in Little Rock.

Most northern whites also favored legislation to enfranchise southern blacks, and during the 1956 campaign Eisenhower proposed a voting rights bill. The Civil Rights Act of 1957, the first since Reconstruction, established a permanent commission on civil rights with broad investigatory powers, but did little to guarantee the ballot to blacks. The Civil Rights Act of 1960 only slightly strengthened the first measure's enforcement provisions. Neither act empowered federal officials to register African-Americans to vote. Like the *Brown* decision, however, these laws implied a changing view of race relations by the federal government, and that further encouraged blacks to fight for their rights.

THE COLD WAR CONTINUES

Eisenhower continued Truman's containment policy. Stalin's death in 1953 and Eisenhower's resolve to reduce the risk of nuclear war brought a thaw in the Cold War, but the United States and the USSR remained deadlocked. Neither the Cold War nor American determination to check communism ceased. Global fear of a nuclear holocaust mounted in step with both countries' increasingly destructive weapons.

Honoring his campaign pledge, Eisenhower visited South Korea in December 1952, but the fate of thousands of prisoners of war (POWs) who did not want to return to communist rule remained the sticking point preventing a settlement. Then the uncertainty in the communist world after Stalin's death and Eisenhower's veiled threat to use nuclear weapons broke the stalemate. The armistice signed in July 1953 established a panel from neutral nations to oversee the return of POWs and set the boundary between North and South Korea once again at the thirty-eighth parallel. Some Americans claimed that communist aggression had been thwarted and containment vindicated; others condemned the truce as peace without honor.

Ike and Dulles   Eager to ease Cold War tensions, Eisenhower first had to quiet the GOP right-wing's clamor to roll back the Red tide. To do so he chose as his secretary of state, **John Foster Dulles.** A rigid Presbyterian whose humorlessness led some to dub him "Dull, Duller, Dulles," the secretary of state talked of a holy war against "atheistic communism," rejected containment as a "negative, futile and immoral policy," and advocated "liberating" the captive peoples of Eastern Europe and unleashing Jiang Jieshi against communist China. He threatened "instant, massive retaliation" with nuclear weapons in response to Soviet aggression, and insisted on the necessity of "brinksmanship," the art of never backing down in a crisis, even if it meant risking war.

Such saber-rattling pleased the Right, but Eisenhower preferred conciliation. Partly because he feared a nuclear war with the Soviet Union, which had tested its own H-bomb in 1953, Eisenhower refused to translate Dulles's rhetoric into action. Aware of the limits of American power, the United States did nothing to check the Soviet interventions that crushed uprisings in East Germany (1953) and Hungary (1956).

As multimegaton thermonuclear weapons replaced atom bombs in the U.S. and Soviet arsenals, Eisenhower worked to reduce the probability of mutual annihilation. He proposed an "atoms for peace" plan, whereby both superpowers would contribute fissionable materials to a new UN agency for use in industrial projects. In the absence of a positive Soviet response, the government began construction of an electronic air defense system to provide warning of a missile attack.

Work also began on commercial nuclear plants in the mid-1950s, promising electricity "too cheap to meter." However, most money for nuclear research continued to be military-related, like that going to naval captain Hyman Rickover's development of nuclear-powered submarines. Mounting fears over radioactive fallout from atmospheric atomic tests, especially the 1954 U.S. test series in the Pacific that spread strontium 90 over a wide area, heightened world concern about the nuclear-arms race.

In 1955 Eisenhower and Soviet leaders met in Geneva for their first summit conference since World War II. Mutual talk of "peaceful coexistence" led reporters to hail the "spirit of Geneva." The two nations could not agree on a plan for arms control, but

Moscow suspended further atmospheric tests of nuclear weapons in March 1958, and the United States followed suit.

Still, the Cold War continued. Dulles negotiated mutual-defense pacts with any nation that would join the United States in opposing communism. His "pactomania" committed the United States to the defense of forty-three nations. The administration relied primarily on the U.S. nuclear arsenal to deter the Soviets. Tailored to suit fiscally conservative Republicans, the "New Look" defense program promised "more bang for the buck" by emphasizing nuclear weapons over conventional forces. It spurred the Soviets to seek "more rubble for the ruble" by enlarging their nuclear stockpile. In anticipation of nuclear war, Congress built a 112,000-square-foot bunker for itself 700 feet below the grounds of the elegant Greenbrier resort in West Virginia. It featured dormitories, a restaurant, an operating clinic, decontamination showers, and chambers in which the legislators would meet.

As the decade wore on, the focus of the Cold War shifted from Europe to the Third World, the nonwhite developing nations. In 1959, Alaska and Hawaii became, respectively, the forty-ninth and fiftieth states in the Union. The first states not contiguous to the continental forty-eight, they were geographically important because of Hawaii's strategic location in the Pacific Ocean and Alaska's closeness to the Soviet Union and Asia. Both were racially and culturally diverse, moreover, and their diversity was seen as an aid to the United States in its relations with nonwhite nations.

CIA Covert Actions To command the Central Intelligence Agency, Eisenhower chose **Allen Dulles,** a veteran of wartime OSS cloak-and-dagger operations and the brother of the secretary of state. Established in 1947 to conduct foreign intelligence gathering, the CIA became increasingly involved in secret operations to topple regimes friendly to communism. By 1957 half its personnel and 80 percent of its budget were devoted to "covert action"—assassinations, political coups, financially supporting foreign political parties and leaders, and subsidizing foreign newspapers and labor unions that hewed a pro-American line.

To woo influential foreigners away from communism, the CIA also sponsored intellectual conferences and jazz concerts. It bankrolled exhibitions of abstract expressionist paintings to counter Soviet socialist realism art. It purchased the film rights to George Orwell's *Animal Farm* and *1984* to make their messages more overtly anticommunist. It subsidized magazines to publish articles supporting Washington's foreign policy. And it recruited businessmen and college students traveling abroad as "fronts" in clandestine CIA activities.

In 1953, the CIA orchestrated a coup to overthrow the government of Iran. Fearing that the prime minister, who had nationalized oil fields, might open oil-rich Iran to the Soviets, the CIA replaced him with pro-American Shah Reza Pahlavi. The United States thus gained a loyal ally on the Soviet border, and American oil companies prospered when the shah made low-priced oil available to them. But Iranian hatred of America took root—an enmity that would haunt the United States a quarter-century later.

Also in 1953, the CIA intervened in Philippine elections to ensure a pro-American government. The next year, a CIA-trained and -financed band of mercenaries overthrew the leftist elected government in Guatemala, which had nationalized and redistributed tracts of land owned by the United Fruit Company. The new pro-American military dictatorship returned the expropriated lands to United Fruit and trampled political opposition.

The Great Debate, July 24, 1959   *At the opening of the American National Exhibit in Moscow, Vice President Richard Nixon and Soviet premier Nikita Khrushchev engaged in a "kitchen debate," arguing not about the strength of their rockets or bombs but about the relative merits of American and Soviet washing machines and television sets.*

The Vietnam Domino

The most extensive CIA covert operations during the 1950s took place in Indochina. As a result of Mao Zedong's victory in China and the outbreak of war in Korea, the United States viewed Indochina as a key battleground in the Cold War. The Truman administration provided France with large-scale military assistance to fight the Vietminh, a broad-based Vietnamese nationalist coalition led by the communist Ho Chi Minh (see Chapter 26). By 1954 American aid accounted for three-quarters of French expenditures. Nevertheless, France tottered near defeat. In early 1954, the Vietminh besieged twelve thousand French troops in the northern valley of Dienbienphu.

France appealed for U.S. intervention, and some American officials toyed with the idea of a nuclear strike. "You boys must be crazy," the president replied. "We can't use those awful things against Asians for the second time in ten years." With the Korean War just recently ended, Ike also refused to involve the United States in another land war in Asia. In May, the French surrendered at Dienbienphu. An international conference in Geneva arranged a cease-fire and temporarily divided Vietnam at the seventeenth parallel, pending elections in 1956 to choose the government of a unified nation.

Although unwilling to go to war, Eisenhower would not accept a communist takeover of Vietnam. In what became known as the **domino theory**, Eisenhower warned that if Vietnam went communist, then Thailand, Burma, Indonesia, and ultimately all of Asia would fall like dominos. The United States refused to sign the Geneva Peace Accords, and in late 1954 created the Southeast Asia Treaty Organization (SEATO), a military alliance patterned on NATO.

The United States installed Ngo Dinh Diem, a fiercely anticommunist Catholic, as premier and then president of an independent South Vietnam. CIA agents helped Diem train his armed forces and secret police, eliminate political opposition, and block the 1956 election to reunify Vietnam specified by the Geneva agreement. As Eisenhower admitted, "possibly 80 percent of the population would have voted for the communist Ho Chi Minh as their leader." Washington pinned its hopes on Diem, and Vietnam became a test of its ability to defeat communism in Asia with American dollars rather than American lives.

The autocratic Diem's Catholicism alienated the predominantly Buddhist population, and his refusal to institute land reform and to end corruption spurred opposition. In December 1960, Diem's opponents coalesced in the **National Liberation Front** (NLF). Backed by North Vietnam, the insurgency attracted broad support and soon controlled half of South Vietnam. The administration's commitment to "sink or swim with Ngo Dinh Diem" had cost over $1 billion, and Diem was sinking.

Troubles in the Third World

In 1956, Eisenhower faced his greatest challenge in the Middle East, the **Suez crisis.** In 1954, Gamal Abdel Nasser came to power in Egypt, determined to modernize his nation. To woo him, the United States offered to finance a dam at Aswan to harness the Nile River. When Nasser purchased arms from Czechoslovakia and officially recognized the People's Republic of China, Dulles canceled the loan. Nasser then nationalized the British-owned Suez Canal.

Viewing the canal as the lifeline of its empire, Britain planned to take it back by force. The British were supported by France, which feared Arab nationalism in their Algerian colony, and by Israel, which feared the Egyptian arms buildup. The three countries, America's closest allies, attacked Egypt in October 1956 without consulting Eisenhower. Ike fumed that the military action would drive the Arab world and its precious oil to the Russians. When Moscow threatened to intervene, Eisenhower forced his allies to withdraw their troops.

The Suez crisis had major consequences. It swelled antiwestern sentiment in the Third World, and the United States replaced Britain and France as the protector of Western interests in the Middle East. Determined to guarantee the flow of oil to the West, the president announced the **Eisenhower Doctrine** in 1957, proclaiming that the United States would send military aid and, if necessary, troops to any Middle Eastern nation threatened by "Communist aggression." To show he meant it, Eisenhower ordered fourteen thousand marines into Lebanon in July 1958 to quell a threatened Muslim revolt against its prowestern regime.

Such interventions intensified anti-American feelings in the Third World. Shouting "yanqui imperialism," angry crowds in Peru and Venezuela spat at Vice President Nixon and stoned his car in 1958. In 1959, Fidel Castro overturned a dictatorial regime in Cuba. He confiscated without compensation American properties constituting 90 percent of Cuban mining operations, 80 percent of its utilities, and nearly half its sugar operations. In 1960 anti-American riots in Japan forced Eisenhower to cancel a trip there.

An even tougher blow struck on May 1, 1960. Two weeks before a scheduled summit conference with Soviet premier Nikita Khrushchev, the Soviets shot down a U.S. spy plane far inside their border. Khrushchev displayed the captured CIA pilot and the photos he had taken of Soviet missile sites. Eisenhower refused to apologize and the summit to limit nuclear testing collapsed.

The Eisenhower Legacy   Just before leaving office, Eisenhower offered Americans a farewell and warning. The demands of national security, he stated, had produced the "conjunction of an immense military establishment and a large arms industry that is new in the American experience." Swollen defense budgets had yoked American economic well-being to military expenditures. Military contracts had become the staff of life for research scholars, politicians, and the nation's largest corporations. This combination of interests, Eisenhower believed, exerted enormous leverage and threatened the traditional subordination of the military in American life. "We must guard against the acquisition of unwarranted influence . . . by the **military-industrial complex.** The potential for the disastrous rise of misplaced power exists and will persist."

The president concluded that he had avoided war but that lasting peace was not in sight. Most scholars agreed. Eisenhower ended the Korean War, avoided direct intervention in Vietnam, began relaxing tensions with the Soviet Union, and suspended atmospheric nuclear testing. At the same time, he presided over an accelerating nuclear-arms race and a widening Cold War. He encouraged the CIA to intervene in local conflicts around the globe, which, in Vietnam, would soon lead to the most disastrous military conflict in American history.

The moderate Eisenhower pleased neither Left nor Right. His acceptance of New Deal social-welfare measures angered conservative Republicans, while liberal Democrats faulted his passivity toward McCarthyism and racism. Yet Ike had given most Americans what they most wanted—prosperity, reassurance, and a breathing spell in which to relish the comforts of life.

THE AFFLUENT SOCIETY

In 1958, the economist John Kenneth Galbraith published *The Affluent Society,* a study of postwar America whose title reflected the broad-based prosperity that made the 1950s seem the fulfillment of the American Dream. By the end of the decade, about 60 percent of American families owned homes; 75 percent, cars; and 87 percent, at least one TV. Government spending, a huge upsurge in productivity, and steadily increasing consumer demand pushed the gross national product (GNP) up 50 percent.

Three brief recessions and a national debt of almost $290 billion by 1961 evoked concern but did little to stifle economic growth or optimism. The United States had achieved the world's highest living standard ever. By 1960 the average worker's income, adjusted for inflation, was 35 percent higher than in 1945. With just 6 percent of the world's population, the United States produced and consumed nearly half of everything made and sold on Earth.

The New Industrial Society Federal spending constituted a major source of economic growth. It nearly doubled in the 1950s to $180 billion, and the outlays of state and local governments kept pace. Federal expenditures (accounting for 17 percent of the GNP in the mid-1950s, compared to just 1 percent in 1929) built roads and airports, financed home mortgages, supported farm prices, and provided stipends for education. More than half the federal budget—10 percent of the GNP—went to defense spending. Continued superpower rivalry in atomic munitions, missile-delivery systems, and the space race kept the federal government the nation's main financier of scientific and technological research and development (R&D).

For the West, especially, it was as if World War II never ended, as the new Air Force Academy in Colorado Springs signified. Politicians from both parties labored to keep defense spending flowing westward. Liberal and conservative members of Congress from California sought contracts for Lockheed. So did those from Texas for General Dynamics and those from Washington State for Boeing. By the late 1950s California alone received half the space budget and a quarter of all major military contracts. By then, Denver had the largest number of federal employees outside Washington, D.C.; Albuquerque boasted more Ph.D. degrees per capita than any other U.S. city; and over a third of workers in Los Angeles depended on defense industries. Utah, once the Mormon dream of an agricultural utopia, received the nation's highest per capita expenditures on space and defense research. Government spending transformed the mythic West of individualistic cowboys, miners, and farmers into a West of bureaucrats, manufacturers, and scientists dependent on federal funds.

Science became a ward of the state, with government funding and control transforming both the U.S. military and industry. Financed by the Atomic Energy Commission (AEC) and utilizing navy scientists, the Duquesne Light Company began construction in Shippingport, Pennsylvania, of the nation's first nuclear-power plant in 1954. Chemicals surged from the fiftieth-largest industry before the war to the nation's fourth-largest in the 1960s. As chemical fertilizers and pesticides contaminated groundwater supplies, and as the use of plastics for consumer products reduced landfill space, Americans—unaware of the hidden perils—marveled at fruits and vegetables covered with Saran Wrap and delighted in their Dacron suits, Orlon shirts, Acrilan socks, and Teflon-coated pots and pans.

Electronics became the fifth-largest American industry, providing industrial equipment and consumer appliances. Electricity consumption tripled in the 1950s as industry automated and consumers, "to live better electrically," as commercials urged, purchased electric washers and dryers, freezers, blenders, television sets, and stereos. Essential to the expansion of both the chemical and the electronics industries was inexpensive petroleum. With domestic crude-oil production increasing close to 50 percent and petroleum imports rising from 74 million to 371 million barrels between 1945 and 1960, oil replaced coal as the nation's main energy source. Hardly anyone paid attention when a physicist warned in 1953 that "adding 6 billion tons of carbon dioxide to the atmosphere each year is warming up the Earth."

Plentiful, cheap gasoline fed the growth of the automobile and aircraft industries. The nation's third-largest industry in the 1950s, aerospace depended heavily on defense spending and on federally funded research. In Washington State, the manufacturers of jet aircraft, ballistic missiles, and space equipment employed more people than did logging and timbering firms. Seattle, Dallas–Fort Worth, San Diego, and Los Angeles accounted for nearly all of the nation's aircraft production. The automobile industry, still the titan of the American economy, also utilized technological R&D. Where machines had earlier replaced some human workers, automation now controlled the machines. Between 1945 and 1960 the industry halved the number of hours and of workers required to produce a car. Other industries followed, investing $10 billion a year throughout the fifties on laborsaving machinery.

| The Age of Computers | The computer was a major key to the technological revolution. In 1944, International Business Machines (IBM), cooperating with Harvard scientists, had produced the Mark I calculator to |

decipher secret Axis codes. It was a slow, cumbersome device with five hundred miles of wiring. In late 1945, to improve artillery accuracy, the military devised ENIAC, the first electronic computer. Still unwieldly, with eighteen thousand vacuum tubes, ENIAC could perform five thousand calculations per second. Next came the development of operating instructions, or programs, that could be stored inside the computer's memory; the substitution of printed circuits for wired ones; and in 1948, at Bell Labs, the invention of tiny solid-state transistors that ended reliance on radio tubes.

The computer changed the American economy and society as fundamentally as the steam engine in the First Industrial Revolution and the electric motor and internal combustion engine in the Second. Sales of electronic computers to industry rose from twenty in 1954 to more than a thousand in 1957 and more than two thousand in 1960. Major manufacturers used them to monitor production lines, track inventory, and ensure quality control. The government, which used three machines in computing the 1950 census returns, employed several hundred on the 1960 census. They became as indispensable to Pentagon strategists playing war games as to the Internal Revenue Service, as integral to meteorologists as to scientists "flying" rockets on the drawing board. By the mid-1960s more than thirty thousand mainframe computers were used by banks, hospitals, and universities. Further developments led to the first integrated circuits and to what would ultimately become the Internet, fundamentally changing the nature of work as well as its landscape.

The development of the high-technology complex known as Silicon Valley began with the opening of the Stanford Industrial Park in 1951. Seeking to develop its landholdings around Palo Alto and to attract financial aid from business and the military, Stanford University utilized its science and engineering faculties to design and produce products for the Fairchild Semiconductor and Hewlett-Packard companies. This relationship became a model followed by other high-tech firms. Soon apricot and cherry orchards throughout the Santa Clara valley gave way to industrial parks filled with computer firms and pharmaceutical laboratories. Initially a far cry from dirty eastern factories, these campus-like facilities would eventually choke the valley with traffic congestion, housing developments, and smog. Similar developments would follow the military-fueled research complexes along Boston's Route 128, near Austin, Texas, and in North Carolina's Research Triangle.

| The Costs of Bigness | Rapid technological advances accelerated the growth and power of big business. In 1950, twenty-two U.S. firms had assets of more than $1 billion; ten years later more than fifty did. |

By 1960 one-half of 1 percent of all companies earned more than half the total corporate income in the United States. The wealthiest, which could afford huge R&D outlays, became oligopolies, swallowing up weak competitors. Three television networks monopolized the nation's airwaves; three automobile and three aluminum companies produced more than 90 percent of America's cars and aluminum; and a handful of firms controlled the lion's share of assets and sales in steel, petroleum, chemicals, and electrical machinery. Corporations acquired overseas facilities to become "multinational" enterprises, and formed "conglomerates" by merging companies in unrelated industries: International Telephone and Telegraph (ITT) branched out from communications into car rental, home building, motel chains, insurance, and more. Despite talk of "people's capitalism," the oil-rich Rockefeller family alone owned more corporate stock than all the nation's wage earners combined.

Growth and consolidation meant greater bureaucratization. "Executives" replaced "capitalists." Success required conformity not creativity, teamwork not individuality. According to sociologist David Riesman's *The Lonely Crowd* (1950), the new "company people" were "other-directed," eager to follow the cues from their peers and not think innovatively or act independently. In the old nursery rhyme "This Little Pig Went to Market," Riesman noted, each pig went his own way. "Today, however, all little pigs go to market; none stay home; all have roast beef, if any do; and all say 'we-we.'"

Changes in American agriculture paralleled those in industry. Farming grew increasingly scientific and mechanized. Technology cut the work hours necessary to grow crops by half between 1945 and 1960, causing many farm families to migrate to cities. In 1956 alone, one-eleventh of the farm population left the land. Meanwhile, heavily capitalized farm businesses, running "factories in the field," prospered by using more machines, more chemicals, and more migrant laborers.

Until the publication of Rachel Carson's *Silent Spring* in 1962, few Americans understood the extent to which fertilizers, herbicides, and pesticides poisoned the environment. Carson, a former researcher for the Fish and Wildlife Service, dramatized the problems caused by the use of the insecticide DDT and its spread through the food chain. Her depiction of a "silent spring" caused by the death of songbirds from DDT toxicity led many states to ban its use. The federal government followed suit. But the incentives for cultivating more land, and more marginal land, led to further ravages. The Army Corps of Engineers and the Bureau of Reclamation dammed the waters of the West, turning the Columbia and Missouri Rivers into rows of slack-water reservoirs, killing fish and wildlife as well as immersing hundreds of square miles of Indian tribal lands.

Blue-Collar Blues   Consolidation also transformed the labor movement. In 1955, the merger of the AFL and CIO brought 85 percent of union members into a single federation. Although labor leadership promised aggressive unionism, organized labor fell victim to its success at the bargaining table. Higher wages, shorter workweeks, paid vacations, health-care coverage, and automatic wage hikes tied to the cost of living led most workers to view themselves as middle class rather than the proletariat. The 1950s saw far fewer strikes than the 1930s.

A decrease in the number of blue-collar workers further sapped labor militancy. Most of the new jobs in the 1950s were in the service sector and in public employment, which banned collective bargaining by labor unions. Automation cut membership in the once-mighty coal, auto, and steelworkers' unions by more than half; and unions' very success in raising wages led employers to mechanize more aspects of manufacturing. In 1956, for the first time in U.S. history, white-collar workers outnumbered blue-collar workers. Some proclaimed the United States a "postindustrial" society. This notion minimized the fact that more service jobs involved manual labor than intellect. Most office work was as routinized as any factory job. Yet few unions sought to woo white-collar workers. The percentage of the unionized labor force dropped from a high of 36 percent in 1953 to 31 percent in 1960, and kept falling.

Prosperity and the Suburbs

As real income (adjusted for inflation) rose, Americans spent less of their income on necessities and more on powered lawnmowers and air conditioners. They heaped their shopping carts with frozen, dehydrated, and fortified foods. When they lacked cash, they borrowed. In 1950 Diner's Club issued the first credit card; American Express followed in 1958. Installment buying, home mortgages, and auto loans tripled Americans' total private indebtedness in the 1950s. Advertising expenditures also tripled. Appealing to the desire for status and glamour in its effort to convince people to buy what they did not need, business spent more on advertising than the nation did on public schools. "Our ability to consume is endless," gloated the head of the Macy's department store. "The luxuries of today are the necessities of tomorrow."

Responding to the slogan "You auto buy now," Americans purchased 58 million new cars during the 1950s. Manufacturers enticed people to trade in and up by offering flashier models, two-tone color, tail fins, and extra-powerful engines—like Pontiac's 1955 "Sensational Strato-Streak V-8," which could go more than twice as fast as any speed limit. Seat belts remained an unadvertised extra-cost option. The consequences were increases in highway deaths, air pollution, oil consumption, and "autosclerosis"—clogged urban arteries.

Government policy as well as "auto mania" spurred white Americans' exodus to the suburbs. Federal spending on highways skyrocketed from $79 million in 1946 to $2.6 billion in 1960, putting once-remote areas within "commuting distance" for city workers (see Technology and Culture: The Interstate Highway System). The income tax code stimulated home sales by allowing deductions for home-mortgage interest payments and for property taxes. Both the Federal Housing Administration (FHA) and Veterans Administration (VA) offered low-interest loans; and both continued to deny loans to blacks who sought to buy homes in white neighborhoods. New homeowners frequently had to sign a contract pledging never to sell or rent to "members of other than the Caucasian race," despite the Supreme Court's 1948 ruling that state courts could not enforce restrictive covenants (see Chapter 26). In 1960 suburbia was 98 percent white.

Eighty-five percent of the 13 million new homes built in the 1950s were in the suburbs. While social critics lampooned the "ticky-tacky" houses in "disturbia," many families considered them the embodiment of the American Dream. They longed for single-family homes of their own, good schools, a safe environment for the children, fresh air, and friendly neighbors just like themselves.

Park Forest, Illinois, was carefully planned to be a "complete community for middle-income families with children." While wives stayed home to raise the kids and shop at the Plaza, husbands commuted the thirty miles to Chicago on the Illinois Central Rail-

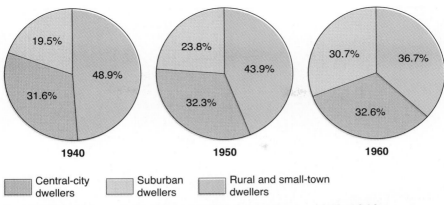

Figure 27.1 Urban, Suburban, and Rural Americans, 1940–1960

In the fifteen years following World War II, more than 40 million Americans migrated to the suburbs, where, as one father put it, "a kid could grow up with grass stains on his pants." Over the same period, fourteen of the fifteen largest U.S. cities lost population. *Source:* Adapted from U.S. Bureau of the Census, *Current Censuses,* 1930–1970 (Washington, D.C.: U.S. Government Printing Office).

road or drove into the city on Western Avenue. On Long Island, some thirty miles from midtown Manhattan, Alfred and William Levitt used the mass-production construction techniques they perfected during the war to construct thousands of standardized 720-square-foot houses as quickly as possible. All looked alike. Deeds to the property required door chimes, not buzzers, prohibited picket fences, mandated regular lawn mowing, and even specified when the wash could be hung to dry in the backyard. All the town streets curved at the same angle. A tree was planted every twenty-eight feet. The Levitts then built a second, larger Levittown in Bucks County, Pennsylvania, and a third in Willingboro, New Jersey.

In the greatest internal migration in its history, some 20 million Americans moved to the suburbs in the 1950s—doubling the numbers and making the suburban population equal to that of the central cities. Contractors built 2 million new homes a year, 85 percent of them in the suburbs. By 1960 over 60 percent of American families owned their homes—the symbol of the affluent society.

Many former servicemen who had first glimpsed the Sunbelt in military camps returned to take up residence, as did others lured by job opportunities, the climate, and the pace of life. California's population went from 9 to 19 million between 1945 and 1964, supplanting New York as the most populous state. Los Angeles epitomized the enormous expansion of the suburbs as well as the rapid growth of the Sunbelt. It boasted the highest per capita ownership of private homes and automobiles of any city, as well as 250 miles of freeways by 1960. Initially designed to lure shoppers downtown, the highway system instead had become the road to a home in the suburbs. Orange County, bordering Los Angeles, doubled its population in the 1940s and then tripled it in the 1950s.

Industry also headed south and west, drawn by low taxes, low energy costs, and anti-union right-to-work laws. Senior citizens, attracted to places like Sun City, Arizona,

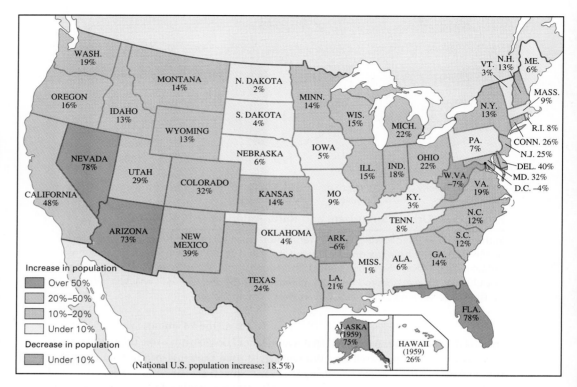

MAP 27.1 Rise of the Sunbelt, 1950–1960

The years after the Second World War saw a continuation of the migration of Americans to the Sunbelt states of the Southwest and the West Coast.

"a complete community geared to older Americans," also brought a more conservative outlook to the Southwest. By 1980 the population of the **Sunbelt,** which stretched from the old Confederacy across Texas to southern California, exceeded that of the North and East. The political power of the Republican Party rose accordingly.

CONSENSUS AND CONSERVATISM

Not everyone embraced the conformity of 1950s consumer culture. Intellectuals found an audience for their attack on "an America of mass housing, mass markets, massive corporations, massive government, mass media, and massive boredom." David Riesman, in *The Lonely Crowd* (1950), described modern Americans as "other-directed" conformists, shaped by the opinions of their peers rather than by their own consciences, and lacking the inner resources to dare be different. Other critics targeted "organization men" incapable of independent thought and "status seekers" pursuing external rewards to compensate for inner insecurities. Some took aim at the consumerist middle class: "all items in a national supermarket—categorized, processed, labeled, priced, and readied for merchandising."

This social criticism oversimplified reality. It ignored ethnic and class diversity. It overlooked the acquisitiveness and conformity of earlier generations—the peer-group pressures in small-town America. It failed to gauge the currents of dissent swirling beneath the surface. It caricatured rather than characterized American society. But the critique rightly spotlighted the elevation of comfort over challenge, and of private pleasures over public affairs. It was, in the main, a time of political passivity and preoccupation with personal gain.

Togetherness and the Baby Boom

In 1954, *McCall's* magazine coined the term *togetherness* to celebrate the "ideal" couple: the man and woman who centered their lives on home and children. Confident in continued economic prosperity and influenced by popular culture, Americans in the 1950s wed at an earlier age than had their parents (one woman in three married by age nineteen), and had more babies sooner. The fertility rate (the number of births per thousand women) was 80 in 1940, and peaked at 123 in 1957, when an American baby was born every seven seconds.

New antibiotics subdued diphtheria and whooping cough, and the Salk and Sabin vaccines ended the dread of polio. The decline in childhood mortality helped raise American life expectancy from 65.9 years in 1945 to 70.9 years in 1970. Coupled with the "baby boom," it led to a 19 percent increase in the U.S. population during the 1950s—a larger jump than in any previous decade. By 1960 children under fourteen constituted one-third of the population.

The immense size of the **baby-boom** generation (the 76 million Americans born between 1946 and 1964) ensured its impact and historical importance. Its needs and expectations at each stage of life would be as contorting as the digestion of a pig by a boa constrictor. First came the bulge in baby carriages; in the 1950s school construction boomed; and in the 1960s college enrollments soared. Then in the 1970s—as the baby boomers had their own families—home construction peaked. The 1980s and 1990s brought a surge in retirement investments, and the twenty-first century a preoccupation with health matters. In the 1950s, the baby boom also made child rearing a huge concern, reinforcing the idea that women's place was in the home. With Americans convinced of the psychological importance of early childhood experiences, motherhood became an increasingly vital, demanding calling.

No one did more to emphasize children's need for the love and care of full-time mothers than **Dr. Benjamin Spock.** Only the Bible outsold his *Common Sense Book of Baby and Child Care* (1946) in the 1950s. Spock urged mothers not to work outside the home, in order to create the atmosphere of warmth and intimacy necessary for their children to mature into well-adjusted adults. Crying babies were to be comforted so that they would not feel rejected. Breast-feeding came back into vogue. Spock's advice also led to less scolding and spanking and to more "democratic" family discussions. In some homes his "permissive" approach produced a "filiarchy" in which kids ruled the roost; in many it unduly burdened mothers.

Domesticity

Popular culture in the 1950s glorified marriage and parenthood, emphasizing a woman's role as a helpmate to her husband and a full-time mother to her children. As Hollywood actress Debbie Reynolds declared in *The Tender Trap* (1955), "A woman isn't a woman until she's been married and had children."

Television mostly pictured women as at-home mothers. Women's magazines featured articles with titles like "Cooking to Me Is Poetry." *Life* lauded Marjorie Sutton for marrying at sixteen, cooking and sewing for the family, raising four children, being a pillar of the PTA and Campfire Girls, and working out on a trampoline "to keep her size 12 figure." *Housekeeping Monthly* published "The Good Wife's Guide" in 1955 to remind women:

- Catering to his comfort will provide you with immense personal satisfaction.
- Don't complain if he's home late for dinner or stays out all night.
- Don't ask him questions about his actions or question his judgement.
- A good wife always knows her place.

Education reinforced these notions. While girls learned typing and cooking, boys were channeled into carpentry and courses leading to professional careers. Guidance counselors cautioned young women not to "miss the boat" of marriage by pursuing higher education. "Men are not interested in college degrees but in the warmth and humanness of the girls they marry," stressed a textbook on the family. More men than women went to college, and only one-third of college women completed a degree. They dropped out, women joked, to get their M.R.S. degree or a Ph.T.—"Putting Hubbie Through." The laughter sometimes hid dissatisfaction: cooking the perfect dinner could still leave a woman starved for fulfillment.

Profound changes, however, were under way. Despite domesticity's holding sway, increasing numbers of women entered the work force. By 1952, 2 million more women worked outside the home than had during the war; and by 1960, twice as many did as in 1940. In 1960 one-third of the labor force was female, and one out of three married women worked outside the home. Of all women workers that year, 60 percent were married, while 40 percent had school-age children. Their median wage, however, was less than half that for men.

Forced back into low-paying, gender-segregated jobs, most women worked to add to the family income, not to fulfill personal aspirations or challenge stereotypes. White women mostly filled clerical positions, while African-Americans held service jobs in private households and restaurants. Some women, as during World War II, developed a heightened sense of expectations and empowerment as a result of employment. Transmitted to their daughters, their experience would lead to a feminist resurgence in the late 1960s.

Religion and Education

"Today in the U.S.," *Time* claimed in 1954, "the Christian faith is back in the center of things." Domestic anxieties and Cold War fears catalyzed a surge of religious activity. Evangelist **Billy Graham,** Roman Catholic Bishop Fulton J. Sheen, and Protestant minister Norman Vincent Peale all had syndicated newspaper columns, best-selling books, and radio and television programs. None was more influential than Graham. Backed to the hilt by the Hearst press and Luce publications, Graham peddled a potent mixture of religious salvation and aggressive anticommunism. In what he pictured as a duel to the death against the atheistic Kremlin, Graham supported McCarthyism and backed GOP demands to "unleash" Jiang's troops against mainland China. He termed communism "a great sinister anti-Christian movement masterminded by Satan" and echoed Billy Sunday's emphasis on the traditional morality of the nineteenth-century American village, lashing out at homosexuals and working wives.

The turn to religion found expression in Hollywood religious extravaganzas, such as *Ben Hur* and *The Ten Commandments,* and in popular songs like "I Believe" and "The Man Upstairs." Sales of Bibles reached an all-time high. Television proclaimed that "the family that prays together stays together." Dial-a-Prayer offered telephone solutions for spiritual problems. Congress added "under God" to the Pledge of Allegiance and required "IN GOD WE TRUST" to be put on all U.S. currency.

"Everybody should have a religious faith," President Eisenhower declared, "and I don't care what it is." Buffalo Bob agreed: kids watching *The Howdy Doody Show* were regularly exhorted to worship "at the church or synagogue of your choice." Church attendance swelled, and the percentage of people who said they belonged to a church or synagogue increased from 49 percent in 1940 to 55 percent in 1950, and to a historic-high 69 percent in 1959. It had become "un-American to be unreligious," noted *The Christian Century.*

While increasing numbers of Americans identified with some denomination, the intensity of religious faith diminished for many. Religious belief was intermixed with patriotism, family togetherness, and Thursday night bingo. Mainstream Protestant churches downplayed sin and evil and emphasized fellowship, offering a sense of belonging in a rapidly changing society. Many Jews spurned the orthodoxy of their parents for the easier-to-follow practices of Reform or Conservative Judaism. Catholicism broadened its appeal as a new pope, John XXIII, charmed the world with ecumenical reforms.

Similarly, education swelled in the 1950s yet seemed less rigorous than in earlier decades. Primary school enrollment rose by 10 million in the 1950s (compared with 1 million in the 1940s). California opened a new school every week throughout the decade and still faced a classroom shortage. The proportion of college-age Americans in higher education climbed from 15 percent in 1940 to more than 40 percent by the early 1960s. "Progressive" educators promoted sociability and self-expression over science, math, and history. The "well-rounded" student became more prized than the highly skilled or intelligent student. Surveys of college students found them conservative, conformist, and careerist, a "silent generation" seeking security and comfort.

While administrators ran universities like businesses, few faculty challenged the economic structure or ideology of the United States, or addressed the problems of minorities and the poor. Historians downplayed past class conflicts, and highlighted the pragmatic ideas and values held by most Americans. Consensus—the widely shared agreement on most matters of importance, especially respect for private property, individualism, and equal opportunity—was frequently depicted as an integral part of America's history and the key to its greatness.

The Culture of the Fifties

American culture reflected the expansive spirit of prosperity as well as Cold War anxieties. With increasing leisure time and fatter paychecks, Americans spent one-seventh of their GNP on entertainment. Yellowstone National Park lured four times as many people through its gates each summer as lived in Wyoming; Glacier National Park attracted more visitors than lived in Montana. Spectator sports boomed; new symphony halls opened; and book sales doubled.

With the opening of a major exhibit of abstract expressionists by the Museum of Modern Art in 1951, New York replaced Paris as the capital of the art world. Like the immense canvases of Jackson Pollock and the cool jazz of trumpeter Miles Davis, introspection and improvisation characterized the major novels of the era. Their personal yearnings sharply contrasted with the political engagement and social realism of literature in the 1930s. Novels like John Updike's *Rabbit Run* (1960) presented characters dissatisfied with jobs and home, longing for a more vital and authentic existence, yet incapable of decisive action.

Southern, African-American, and Jewish-American writers turned out the decade's most vital fiction. William Faulkner continued his dense saga of Yoknapatawpha County, Mississippi, while Eudora Welty evoked southern small-town life in *The Ponder Heart* (1954). The black experience found memorable expression in James Baldwin's *Go Tell It on the Mountain* (1953) and Ralph Ellison's *Invisible Man* (1951). Bernard Malamud's *The Assistant* (1957) explored the Jewish immigrant world of New York's Lower East Side, and Philip Roth's *Goodbye Columbus* (1959) dissected the very different world of upwardly mobile Jews.

The many westerns, musicals, and costume spectacles churned out by Hollywood reflected the diminished interest in political issues. Most films about contemporary life portrayed Americans as one happy white, middle-class family. Minorities and the poor remained invisible, and the independent career women of films of the 1940s were replaced by "dumb blondes" and cute helpmates. But as TV viewing soared, movie attendance dropped 50 percent. A fifth of the nation's theaters became bowling alleys and supermarkets by 1960. Hollywood tried to recoup by developing three-dimensionality and wide-screen processes that accentuated the difference from television's small black-and-white image. No technological wizardry, however—not even Smell-O-Vision and its rival Aroma-Rama—could stem TV's astounding growth.

The Television Culture

No cultural medium ever became as popular and as powerful as quickly, or so reinforced the public mood, as television. Ownership of a TV set soared from one of every eighteen thousand households in 1946 to nine of ten American homes by 1960. By then, more Americans had televisions than had bathrooms.

Business capitalized on the phenomenon. The three main radio networks—ABC, CBS, and NBC—gobbled up virtually every TV station in the country, and, just as in radio, they profited by selling time to advertisers who wanted to reach the largest possible audiences. By the mid-fifties, the three networks each had larger advertising revenues than any other communications medium in the world. By 1959, their advertising income would top $1.5 billion.

Introduced in 1952, *TV Guide* outsold every other periodical and was being published in fifty-three separate regional editions by 1960. The TV dinner, first marketed in 1954, altered the nation's eating habits. When Walt Disney produced a show on Davy Crockett in 1955, stores could not keep up with the massive demand for "King of the Wild Frontier" coonskin caps. Corporations spent fortunes on TV ads, convincing middle-class suburban viewers that the good life was based on endless consumption. "The message of the media," a critic noted, "is the commercial."

Geared to its initial small audiences, TV showcased talent and creativity. Opera performances appeared in prime time, as did sophisticated comedies and political dramas, and documentaries like Edward R. Murrow's *See It Now*. Early situation comedies such as *The Life of Riley* and *The Goldbergs* featured ethnic working-class families. As the price of TV sets came down and program producers felt the chill of McCarthyism, the networks' appetite for a mass audience transformed TV into a cautious celebration of conformity and consumerism. Controversy went off the air. Only a few situation comedies, like Jackie Gleason's *The Honeymooners,* set in Brooklyn, did not feature suburban, consumer-oriented, upper-middle-class families. Most, like *Father Knows Best* and *The Adventures of Ozzie and Harriet,* portrayed perfectly coiffed moms who loved to vacuum in high heels, frisky yet ultimately obedient kids, and all-knowing dads who never lost their tempers.

Decrying TV's mediocrity in 1961, the head of the Federal Communications Commission dared broadcasters to watch their own shows for a day: "I can assure you that you will observe a vast wasteland." A steady parade of soaps, unsophisticated comedies, and violent westerns led others to call TV the "idiot box."

Measuring television's impact is difficult. Depending on the many factors that differentiate individuals, people read the "texts" of TV (or of movies or books) their own way and so receive their own messages or signals from the media. While TV bound some to the status quo, it brought others glimpses of possibilities that raised expectations. It functioned simultaneously as conservator and spur to change. In the main, television reflected existing values and institutions. It stimulated the desire to be included in American society, not to transform it. It spawned mass fads for Barbie dolls and hula hoops, spread the message of consumerism, and made Americans ever more name-brand conscious. It reinforced gender and racial stereotypes. TV rarely showed African-Americans and Latinos—except in servile roles or prison scenes. It extolled male violence in fighting evil; and it portrayed women as either zany madcaps (*My Friend*

Figure 27.2 The Television Revolution, 1950–1994

As televisions became commonplace in the 1950s, TV viewing altered the nature of American culture and politics. *Source:* Statistical Abstracts of the United States.

Motorala TV Family Ad *The television set itself, so grandly advertised and displayed, was a symbol of postwar affluence, and both advertising and programming, which featured largely middle-class, consumption-oriented suburban familes, stimulated the consumer culture. Overall, TV powerfully reinforced the conservative, celebratory values of everyday American life in the 1950s.*

Irma) or self-effacing moms (*The Donna Reed Show*). It virtually ended network radio, returning local stations to a music-based format, especially "Top-40" programs geared to youth. While promoting professional baseball and football into truly national phenomena, TV decreased the audience of motion picture theaters and of general interest magazines such as *Look* and *Life*.

Television also changed the political life of the nation. Politicians could effectively appeal to the voters over the heads of party leaders, and appearance mattered more than content. The millions watching Senator Estes Kefauver grill mobsters about their ties to city governments instantly made him a serious contender for the presidency. The 20 million observing the combative Senator Joseph McCarthy bully and demean witnesses during his crusade against the army doomed his career. The 58 million who witnessed Richard Nixon's appeal for support in the "Checkers" speech saved his place on the GOP ticket. And Eisenhower's pioneering use of brief "spot advertisements" clinched Ike's smashing presidential victories. In 1960, John F. Kennedy's "telegenic" image would play a major role in his winning the presidency.

Television vastly increased the cost of political campaigning while decreasing the content level of political discussion. It helped produce a more national culture, diminishing provincialism and regional differences. Its overwhelming portrayal of a contented citizenry reinforced complacency and hid the reality of "the other America."

THE OTHER AMERICA

"I am an invisible man," declared the African-American narrator of Ralph Ellison's *Invisible Man;* "I am invisible, understand, simply because people refuse to see me." Indeed, few middle-class white Americans perceived the extent of social injustice in the United States. "White flight" from cities to suburbs produced physical separation of the races and classes. New expressways walled off ghettos and rural poverty from middle-class motorists speeding by. Popular culture focused on affluent Americans enjoying the "good life." In the consensus of the Eisenhower era, deprivation had supposedly disappeared. In reality, poverty and racial discrimination were rife and dire, and the struggles for social justice intensified.

Poverty and Urban Blight   Although the percentage of poor families (defined as a family of four with a yearly income of less than three thousand dollars) declined from 34 percent in 1947 to 22 percent in 1960, 35 million Americans remained below the "poverty line." Eight million senior citizens existed on annual incomes below one thousand dollars. A third of the poor lived in depressed rural areas, where 2 million migrant farm workers experienced the most abject poverty. Observing a Texas migratory-labor camp in 1955, a journalist reported that 96 percent of the children had consumed no milk in the previous six months; eight out of ten adults had eaten no meat; and most slept "on the ground, in a cave, under a tree, or in a chicken house." In California's Imperial Valley, the infant death rate among migrant workers was more than seven times the statewide average.

The bulk of the poor huddled in decaying inner-city slums. Displaced southern blacks and Appalachian whites, Native Americans forced off reservations, and newly arrived Hispanics strained cities' inadequate facilities. Nearly two hundred thousand Mexican-Americans were herded into San Antonio's Westside barrio. A local newspaper described them as living like cattle in a stockyard, "with roofed-over corrals for homes and chutes for streets." A visitor to New York City's slums in 1950 found "25 human beings living in a dark and airless coal cellar ten feet below the street level. . . . No animal could live there long, yet here were 17 children, the youngest having been born here two weeks before." The " 'promised land' that Mammy had been singing about in the cotton fields for many years," observed Claude Brown, had become a slum, "a dirty, stinky, uncared-for closet-size section of a great city."

As described by Michael Harrington in *The Other America: Poverty in the United States* (1962), the poor were trapped in a vicious cycle of want and a culture of deprivation. Because they could not afford good housing, a nutritious diet, and doctors, the poor got sick more often and for longer than more affluent Americans. Losing wages and finding it hard to hold steady jobs, they could not pay for the decent housing, good food, or doctors that would keep them from getting and staying sick. The children of the poor started school disadvantaged, quickly fell behind, and, lacking encouragement and expectation of success, dropped out. Living with neither hope nor the necessary skills to enter the mainstream of American life, the poor bequeathed a similar legacy to their children.

The pressing need for low-cost housing went unanswered. In 1955 fewer than 200,000 of the 810,000 public-housing units called for in the Housing Act of 1949 had been built. A decade later only 320,000 had been constructed. "Slum clearance" generally meant "Negro clearance," and "urban renewal" meant "poor removal," as developers razed low-income neighborhoods to put up parking garages and expensive housing. The Los Angeles barrio of Chavez Ravine was bulldozed to construct Dodger Stadium.

At the same time, landlords, realtors, and bankers deliberately excluded nonwhites from decent housing. Half of the housing in New York's Harlem predated 1900. A dozen people might share a tiny apartment with broken windows, faulty plumbing, and gaping holes in the walls. Harlem's rates of illegitimate births, infant deaths, narcotics use, and crime soared above the averages for the city and the nation. "Where flies and maggots breed, where the plumbing is stopped up and not repaired, where rats bite helpless infants," black social psychologist Kenneth Clark observed, "the conditions of life are brutal and inhuman."

Blacks' Struggle for Justice   The collision between the hopes raised by the 1954 *Brown* decision and the indignities of persistent discrimination and segregation sparked a new phase in the civil-rights movement. To sweep away the separate but rarely equal Jim Crow facilities in the South, African-Americans turned to new tactics, organizations, and leaders. They utilized nonviolent direct-action protest to engage large numbers of blacks in their own freedom struggle and to arouse white America's conscience.

In the 1950s racism still touched even the smallest details of daily life. In Montgomery, Alabama, black bus riders had to surrender their seats so that no white rider would stand. Although they were more than three-quarters of all passengers, the African-Americans had to pay their fares at the front of the bus, leave, and reenter through the back door, sit only in the rear, and then give up their seats to any standing white passengers.

On December 1, 1955, **Rosa Parks,** for many years an officer of the Montgomery NAACP and a veteran of civil-rights protests in the 1930s and 1940s, refused to get up so that a white man could sit. "I was not tired physically," she later wrote. "No, the only tired I was, was tired of giving in." Her arrest sparked Jo Ann Robinson of the Women's Political Council, and other blacks who had been engaged in the freedom struggle in Montgomery, to propose a boycott of the buses—the beginning of the mass phase of the civil-rights movement. They founded the Montgomery Improvement Association (MIA) to organize the protest, and elected **Martin Luther King, Jr.,** a twenty-seven-year-old African-American minister, to lead the boycott. "There comes a time when people get tired," declared King, articulating the anger of Montgomery blacks, "tired of being segregated and humiliated; tired of being kicked about by the brutal feet of oppression." The time had come, he continued, to cease being patient "with anything less than freedom and justice." In King, Montgomery blacks found a spokesman who repeatedly stirred their souls and encouraged them to boycott the buses for a year, organize carpools or walk miles to work, brave legal harassment and violence. "My soul has been tired for a long time," an old woman told a minister who had stopped his car to offer her a ride; "now my feet are tired, and my soul is resting." When the city leaders would not budge, the blacks challenged the constitutionality of bus segregation. In November 1956, the U.S. Supreme Court affirmed a lower-court decision outlawing segregation on the buses.

The Montgomery bus boycott demonstrated African-American strength and determination. It shattered the myth that African-Americans approved of segregation and that only outside agitators opposed Jim Crow. It affirmed the possibility of social change and inspired protests elsewhere in the South. It vaulted Dr. King, whose oratory simultaneously inspired black activism and touched white consciences, into the national spotlight. As no one before, King presented the case for black rights in a vocabulary that echoed both the Bible and the freedom values of the Founding Fathers.

King's philosophy of civil disobedience fused the spirit of Christianity with the strategy of achieving racial justice by nonviolent resistance. His emphasis on direct action gave every African-American an opportunity to demonstrate the moral evil of racial discrimination; and his insistence on nonviolence diminished the likelihood of bloodshed. Preaching that blacks must lay their bodies on the line to provoke crises that would force whites to confront their racism, King urged his followers to love their enemies. By so doing, he believed, blacks would convert their oppressors and bring "redemption and reconciliation." In 1957 King and a group of black ministers formed the Southern Christian Leadership Conference (SCLC) "to carry on nonviolent crusades against the evils of second-class citizenship." Yet more than on leaders, the movement's triumphs would depend on the domestic servants who walked instead of riding the buses, the children on the front lines of the battle for school desegregation, and the tens of thousands of ordinary people who marched, rallied, and demonstrated extraordinarily.

Latinos and Latinas   Hispanic Americans initially made less headway in ending discrimination. High unemployment on the Caribbean island and the advent of direct air service to New York in 1945 brought a steady stream of Puerto Ricans, who as U.S. citizens could enter the mainland without restriction. From seventy thousand in 1940 to a quarter of a million in 1950 and then nearly a million in 1960, El Barrio in New York City's East Harlem had a larger Puerto Rican population and more bodegas than San Juan by the late 1960s.

In New York they suffered from inadequate schools and police harassment, and were denied decent jobs and political recognition. More than half lived in inadequate housing. Like countless earlier immigrants, Puerto Ricans gained greater personal freedom in the United States while losing the security of a strong cultural tradition. Family frictions flared in the transition to unaccustomed ways. Parents felt upstaged by children who learned English and obtained jobs that were closed to them. The relationship between husbands and wives changed as women found readier access to jobs than did men. One migrant explained, "Whether I have a husband or not I work . . . and if my husband dare to complain, I throw him out. That is the difference; in Puerto Rico Ishould have to stand for anything a man asks me to do because he pays the rent. Here I belong to myself." Others hoped to earn money in the United States and then return home. Most stayed. Yet however much they tried to embrace American ways, many could not enjoy the promise of the American Dream because of their skin color, culture, and language. Increasingly they turned to organizations like Antonia Pantoja's Puerto Rican Association for Community Affairs (PRACA), which sought to end discrimination against Puerto Ricans and *Nuyoricans*—those born in New York City.

Mexican-Americans suffered the same indignities. Most were underpaid, overcharged, and segregated from mainstream American life. The presence of countless "undocumented aliens" compounded their woes.

After World War II, new irrigation systems added 7.5 million acres to the agricultural lands of the Southwest, stimulating farm owners' desire for cheap Mexican labor. In 1951, to stem the resulting tide of illegal Mexican immigrants, Congress reintroduced

Mexican Wetbacks Being Pulled Back into Mexico by Mexican Police
Following World War II, the U.S goverment continued to use the bracero *program when it needed inexpensive laborers to do the arduous work in the hot agricurtural fields of the Sunbelt, and then deported millions of Mexicans when it no longer needed them, as in this photo taken during "Operation Wetback" in the recession of 1953–1955.*

the ***bracero* program,** a wartime "temporary worker" measure that brought in seasonal farm laborers. The *braceros* were supposed to return to Mexico at the end of their labor contract, but many stayed without authorization, joining a growing number of Latinos who entered the country illegally.

During the 1953–1955 recession, the Eisenhower administration's "Operation Wetback" (*wetback* was a term of derision for illegal Mexican immigrants who supposedly swam across the Rio Grande to enter the United States) deported some 3 million allegedly undocumented entrants. Periodic roundups, however, did not substitute for a sound labor policy or an effective enforcement strategy, and millions of Mexicans continued to cross the poorly guarded two-thousand-mile border. The *bracero* program itself peaked in 1959, admitting 450,000 workers. Neither the *Asociación Nacional México-Americana* (founded in 1950) nor the older League of United Latin American Citizens (LULAC) could stop their exploitation or the widespread violations of the rights of Mexican-American citizens.

The Mexican-American population of Los Angeles County doubled to more than six hundred thousand, and the *colonias* of Denver, El Paso, Phoenix, and San Antonio grew proportionately as large. The most rural of all major ethnic groups in 1940, the percentage of Mexican-Americans living in urban areas rose to 65 percent in 1950 and to 85 percent by 1970. As service in World War II gave Hispanics an increased sense of their own American identity and a claim on the rights supposedly available to all American citizens, urbanization gave them better educational and employment opportunities. Unions like the United Cannery, Agricultural, Packing and Allied Workers of America sought higher wages and better working conditions for their Mexican-American members, and such middle-class organizations as LULAC, the GI Forum, and the Unity League campaigned to end discrimination and segregation, and won important court decisions that declared school segregation of Mexican-Americans unconstitutional (*Mendez,* 1947, and *Delgado,* 1948) and ended their exclusion from Texas jury lists (*Hernandez,* 1954).

The mobilization of Hispanic voters led to the election of the first Mexican-American mayor, in El Paso in 1958. Latinos also took pride in baseball star Roberto Clemente and their growing numbers in the major leagues, in Nobel Prize winners like biologist Severo Ochoa, and in such Hollywood stars as Ricardo Montalban and Anthony Quinn. But the existence of millions of undocumented aliens and the continuation of the *bracero* program stigmatized all people of Spanish descent and depressed their wages. The median income of Hispanics was less than two-thirds that of Anglos. At least a third lived in poverty.

Native Americans Native Americans remained the poorest minority, with a death rate three times the national average. Unemployment rates on reservations during the 1950s reached 70 percent for the Blackfeet of Montana and the Hopi of New Mexico, and a staggering 86 percent for the Choctaw of Mississippi. After World War II Congress veered away from John Collier's efforts to reassert Indian sovereignty and cultural autonomy and had moved toward the goal of assimilation. This meant terminating treaty relationships with tribes, ending the federal trusteeship of Indians. Some favored it as a move toward Indian self-sufficiency; others desired an end to the communal culture of Indians; and still others wanted access to Indian lands and mineral resources. Between 1954 and 1962 Congress passed a dozen termination bills, withdrawing financial support from sixty-one reservations.

First applied to Menominees of Wisconsin and Klamaths of Oregon, who owned valuable timberlands, the termination policy proved disastrous. Further impoverishing the Indians whom it affected, the law transferred more than five hundred thousand acres of Native American lands to non-Indians. To lure Indians off the reservations and into urban areas, and to speed the sale of Indian lands to developers, the government established the Voluntary Relocation Program. It provided Native Americans with moving costs, assistance in finding housing and jobs, and living expenses until they obtained work. "We're like wheat," said one Hopi woman who went to the city. "The wind blows, we bend over. . . . You can't stand up when there's wind."

By the end of the decade about sixty thousand reservation Indians had been relocated to cities. Some became assimilated into middle-class America, marrying whites and losing their tribal identity. Others could not find work and ended up on state welfare rolls living in rundown shantytowns, addicted to alcohol. A third returned to the reservations. Not surprisingly, the National Congress of American Indians vigorously opposed termination, and most tribal politicians advocated Indian sovereignty, treaty rights, federal trusteeship, and the special status of Indians.

SEEDS OF DISQUIET

Late in the 1950s, apprehension ruffled the calm surface of American life. Questions about the nation's values and goals, periodic recessions, rising unemployment, and the growing national debt made Khrushchev's 1959 warning that the Soviet Union would bury the United States economically and his boast that "your grandchildren will live under communism" ring in American ears. Third World anticolonialism, especially in Cuba, diminished Americans' sense of national pride. So did the growing alienation of American youth and a technological breakthrough by the Soviet Union.

Sputnik   On October 4, 1957, the Soviet Union launched the first artificial satellite, *Sputnik* ("Little Traveler"). Weighing 184 pounds and a mere twenty-two inches in diameter, *Sputnik* dashed the American myth of unquestioned technological superiority. When *Sputnik II,* carrying a dog, went into a more distant orbit on November 3, Democrats charged that Eisenhower had allowed a "technological Pearl Harbor."

The Eisenhower administration publicly disparaged the Soviet achievement. Behind the scenes it hurried to have the American Vanguard missile launch a satellite. On December 6, with millions watching on TV, the Vanguard rose six feet in the air and exploded. Newspapers ridiculed America's "Flopnik."

Eisenhower did not laugh. He doubled the funds for missile development to $4.3 billion in 1958 and then raised the amount to $5.3 billion in 1959. He also established the Science Advisory Committee, whose recommendations led to the creation of the National Aeronautics and Space Administration (NASA) in July 1958. By decade's end, the United States had launched several space probes and successfully tested the Atlas intercontinental ballistic missile (ICBM).

Spurred by *Sputnik,* Americans embarked on a crash program to improve American education. The National Defense Education Act (1958) for the first time provided direct federal funding to higher education, especially to improve the teaching of the sciences, mathematics, and foreign languages. Far more funds went to university research to ensure national security. By 1960, nearly a third of scientists and engineers on university faculties worked full-time on government research, primarily defense projects. Some observers dubbed it the "military-industrial-educational complex."

The number of college students skyrocketed from 2.5 million in 1955 to 3.6 million in 1960. That year the U.S. government funneled $1.5 billion to universities, a hundred-fold increase over 1940. Linked directly to the Cold War, this hike in federal aid to education raised unsettling questions.

A Different Beat   Few adults considered the social implications of their affluence on the young, or the consequences of having a teenage generation stay in school instead of working. Few pondered growing up in an age when traditional values like thrift and self-denial had declining relevance, or of maturing when young people had the leisure and money to shape their own subculture. Little attention was paid to the decline in the age of menarche (first menstruation), or the ways that the relatively new institution of the junior high school affected the behavior of youth. Despite talk of family togetherness, busy fathers paid little attention to their children, and mothers sometimes spent more time chauffeuring their young than listening to them. Indeed, much of what adults knew about teenagers (a noun that first appeared in the 1940s and was not commonly used until the 1950s) they learned from the mass media, which focused on the sensational and the superficial.

Accounts of juvenile delinquency abounded, portraying high schools as war zones, city streets as jungles, and teenagers as zip-gun-armed hoodlums. A cover story in *Time* blared "Teenagers on the Rampage." Highly publicized hearings by a Senate subcommittee on juvenile delinquency stoked the fears. Teenage crime, in fact, had barely increased. Male teenagers aroused alarm by sporting leather jackets and slicking their hair in a "ducktail."

As dismaying to parents, young Americans embraced rock-and-roll. In 1951, Alan Freed, the host of a classical music program on Cleveland radio, had observed white teenagers dancing to rhythm-and-blues records by such black performers as Chuck Berry, Bo Diddley, and Little Richard. In 1952, Freed started a new radio program to play "race music," and in 1954 he took the program to New York, creating a national craze for "rock-and-roll," the very term that had been used in blues songs for sexual intercourse.

Just as white musicians in the 1920s and 1930s had adapted black jazz for white audiences, white performers in the 1950s transformed rock-and-roll. In 1954, Bill Haley and the Comets dropped the sexual allusions from Joe Turner's "Shake, Rattle, and Roll," added country-and-western guitar riffs, and had the first major white rock-and-roll hit. When Haley performed "Rock Around the Clock" in *The Blackboard Jungle,* a 1955 film about juvenile delinquency, many parents linked rock-and-roll with disobedience and crime. Red-hunters saw it as a communist plot to corrupt youth. Segregationists claimed it was a ploy "to mix the races." Psychiatrists feared it was "a communicable disease." Some churches condemned it as the "devil's music."

Nothing confirmed their dismay as much as raucous, swaggering **Elvis Presley.** Born in Tupelo, Mississippi, Elvis was a nineteen-year-old truck driver in 1954 when he paid four dollars to record two songs at a Memphis studio. He melded the Pentecostal music of his boyhood with the powerful beat and sexual energy of the rhythm-and-blues music he heard on Memphis's Beale Street, and his songs like "Hound Dog" and "All Shook Up" transformed the cloying pop music that youth found wanting into a proclamation of teenage "separateness." Presley's gyrating pelvis and bucking hips—exuding sexuality—shocked middle-class adults. The more adults condemned rock-and-roll, the more teenagers loved it. Record sales tripled between 1954 and 1960, and Dick Clark's *American Bandstand* became the decade's biggest TV hit. As teens listened to 45-rpm records in their own rooms and to radios in their own cars, the music directed to them by such "outsiders" as Buddy Holly from West Texas, Richie Valens (Valenzuela) from East Los Angeles, and Frankie Lymon from Spanish Harlem nourished the roots of the coming youth revolt.

Portents of Change Teens cherished rock-and-roll for its frankness and exuberance. They elevated characters played by Marlon Brando in *The Wild One* (1954) and James Dean in *Rebel Without a Cause* (1955) to cult status for rejecting society's mores. They delighted in *Mad* magazine's ridiculing of the phony and pretentious in middle-class America. They customized their cars to reject Detroit's standards. All were signs of their variance from the adult world, of their distinct community.

Nonconformist writers known as the **Beats** expressed a more fundamental revolt against middle-class society. In Allen Ginsberg's *Howl* (1956) and Jack Kerouac's *On the Road* (1957), the Beats scorned conformity, religion, family values, and materialism as much as they did conventional punctuation. They scoffed at the "square" America described by Kerouac as "rows of well-to-do houses with lawns and television sets in each living room with everybody looking at the same thing and thinking the same thing at the same time." They romanticized society's outcasts—the mad ones, wrote Kerouac, "the ones who never yawn or say a commonplace thing, but burn, burn, burn like fabulous yellow roman candles exploding like spiders across the stars." Outraging respectability, they glorified uninhibited sexuality and spontaneity in the search for "It," the ultimate authentic experience, foreshadowing the counterculture to come.

The mass media scorned the Beats, as they did all dissenters. *Look* magazine derided them as Americans "turned inside out. The goals of the Beats are *not* watching TV, *not* wearing gray flannel, *not* owning a home in the suburbs, and especially—*not* working." But some college youth admired their rejection of conformity and celebration of sexual experimentation. They read poetry and listened to jazz, and some students even protested capital punishment and demonstrated against the continuing investigations of the House Un-American Activities Committee. Others decried the nuclear-arms race. In 1958 and 1959, thousands participated in Youth Marches for Integrated Schools in Washington. Together with the Beats and rock music, this vocal minority of the "silent generation" heralded a youth movement that would explode in the 1960s.

CONCLUSION

A far more complex era than that implied in the stereotype of the "nifty fifties," the decade encompassed contradictions. Although mightier than any nation in history and basking in prosperity, many Americans felt uneasiness as the Cold War continued and boom times brought unsettling changes. Most were pleased that continuity rather than change characterized the switch from a Democratic to a Republican administration. Differing from Truman's policies more in degree than in kind, Eisenhower pursued a centrist course in domestic affairs. While tilting to the right in favoring private corporations, the Eisenhower administration left New Deal reforms in place, expanded existing social-welfare benefits, employed Keynesian deficit spending to curtail economic recessions, made no effort to hamper labor unionization, and proposed construction of a vast interstate highway system—the largest domestic spending program in the nation's history. The size and scope of the federal government expanded.

So did its involvement throughout the world. The Eisenhower administration followed that of Truman's in its determination to contain communism while putting new emphasis on the need to avoid nuclear war and to fight communism in the Third World. Eisenhower and Dulles gained short-term victories in local conflicts by clandestine means, ignoring the nationalistic yearnings and socioeconomic deprivations of the local peoples, and increasingly allying the United States with reactionary, repressive regimes.

The postwar era was one of unparalleled material prosperity for most Americans. Building on the accumulated savings and pent-up demand for consumerism from the

Second World War, high levels of government spending and new technologies that increased productivity spurred an economic boom that further enriched the rich, transformed the working class into the middle class, and left the poor isolated on a remote island of deprivation and powerlessness.

Overall, the United States in the 1950s seemed the very model of a contented, complacent society. There was, indeed, much conservatism and conformity. But there were also cracks in the picture of a placid people. Unrest coexisted with consensus. Along with bland TV programs, Americans saw a renaissance of creativity in the arts and literature. Racism remained omnipresent in American society, yet the African-American struggle to end white supremacy quickened its pace. In the courts, the NAACP ceased requesting that separate facilities really be equal and instead insisted that true equality required desegregation. In the streets, Martin Luther King, Jr., and the Southern Christian Leadership Conference employed the techniques of nonviolent civil disobedience to mobilize the black masses to attack Jim Crow. The passage of the first civil-rights acts since Reconstruction and Supreme Court decisions that nullified the legal foundations of segregation brought some gains. More vitally, they stimulated the hopefulness that spurred further protest by blacks, as well as by Hispanics and Native Americans.

The Beats and many intellectuals criticized the hypocrisies of postwar America; and some young people, unwilling to accept their parents' embrace of the status quo, became alienated and rebellious. But most middle-class whites ignored the inequities in American society and the voices of discontent. Enjoying their private pleasures, they rejected radicalism, extolled religion, and idealized traditional gender roles, domesticity, and togetherness. Busy working and consuming, they left for a future decade the festering problems of poverty, urban decay, and racial injustice, and the explosive consequences of a younger generation rejecting their parents' conformity and conservatism.

28

The Liberal Era, 1960–1968

THE KENNEDY PRESIDENCY, 1961–1963

Projecting an image of youthful vigor, **John F. Kennedy** personified the self-confident liberal who believed that an activist state could improve life at home and confront the communist challenge abroad. His wealthy father, Joseph P. Kennedy, seethed with ambition and instilled in his sons a passion to excel and to rule. Despite a severe back injury, John Kennedy served in the navy in World War II, and the elder Kennedy persuaded a popular novelist to write articles lauding John's heroism in rescuing his crew after their PT boat had been sunk in the South Pacific.

Esteemed as a war hero, John Kennedy used his charm and his father's connections to win election to the House of Representatives in 1946 from a Boston district where he had never lived. Although Kennedy earned little distinction in Congress, Massachusetts voters sent him to the Senate in 1952 and overwhelmingly reelected him in 1958. By then he had a beautiful wife, Jacqueline, and a Pulitzer Prize for *Profiles in Courage* (1956), written largely by a staff member.

Despite the obstacle of his Roman Catholic faith, the popular Kennedy won a first-ballot victory at the 1960 Democratic convention. Just forty-three years old, he sounded the theme of a "New Frontier" to "get America moving again."

A New Beginning   "All at once you had something exciting," recalled a University of Nebraska student. "You had a guy who had little kids and who liked to play football on his front lawn. Kennedy was talking about pumping new life into the nation and steering it in new directions." But most voters, middle aged and middle class, wanted the stability and security of Eisenhower's "middle way" promised by the Republican candidate, Vice President Richard M. Nixon. Although scorned by

CHRONOLOGY ,1960–1968

1960 • Sit-ins to protest segregation begin.

1961 • John F. Kennedy elected president
Peace Corps and Alliance for Progress created.
Bay of Pigs invasion.
Freedom rides.
Berlin Wall erected.

1962 • Cuban missile crisis.

1963 • Civil-rights demonstrations in Birmingham.
March on Washington.
Test-Ban Treaty between the Soviet Union and the United States.
Kennedy assassinated; Lyndon B. Johnson becomes president.
Betty Friedan, *The Feminine Mystique.*

1964 • Freedom Summer in Mississippi.
California becomes most populous state.
Civil Rights Act.
Gulf of Tonkin incident and resolution.
Economic Opportunity Act initiates War on Poverty.
Johnson elected president.

1965 • Bombing of North Vietnam and Americanization of the war begin.
Assassination of Malcolm X.
Civil-rights march from Selma to Montgomery.
César Chávez's United Farm Workers strike in California.
Teach-ins to question U.S. involvement in war in Vietnam begin.
Voting Rights Act.
Watts riot in Los Angeles.

1966 • Stokely Carmichael calls for Black Power.
Black Panthers formed.
National Organization for Women (NOW) founded.

1967 • Massive antiwar demonstrations.
Race riots in Newark, Detroit, and other cities.

liberals for his McCarthyism, Nixon was better known and more experienced than Kennedy, identified with the still-popular Ike, and a Protestant.

Nixon fumbled his opportunity, agreeing to meet his challenger in televised debates. More than 70 million tuned in to the first televised debate between presidential candidates, a broadcast that secured the dominance of television in American politics. Nixon, sweating visibly, appeared haggard and insecure; in striking contrast, the tanned, telegenic Kennedy radiated confidence. Radio listeners judged the debate a draw, but the

The Sit-Ins *The sit-ins of 1960 initiated the student phase of the civil-rights movement. Across the South, young black activists challenged segregation by staging nonviolent demonstrations to demand access to public facilities. Their courage and commitment reinvigorated the movement, leading to still greater grass-roots activism.*

far more numerous television viewers declared Kennedy the victor. He shot up in the polls, and Nixon never regained the lead.

Kennedy also benefited from an economic recession in 1960, and from his choice of a southern Protestant, Senate Majority Leader Lyndon B. Johnson, as his running mate. Still, the election was the closest since 1884. Only 120,000 votes separated the two candidates. Kennedy's religion cost him millions of popular votes, but his capture of 80 percent of the Catholic vote in the closely contested midwestern and northeastern states delivered crucial Electoral College votes, enabling him to squeak to victory.

Kennedy's inauguration set the tone of a new era: "the torch has been passed to a new generation of Americans." In sharp contrast to Eisenhower's reliance on businessmen (see Chapter 27), Kennedy surrounded himself with liberal intellectuals. For attorney general, he selected his younger brother Robert Kennedy, joking "I see nothing wrong with giving Robert some legal experience before he goes out to practice law."

"America's leading man," novelist Norman Mailer called him. Kennedy seemed more a celebrity than a politician, and his dash played well on TV. Aided by his wife, he adorned his presidency with the trappings of culture and excellence, inviting distinguished artists to perform at the White House and studding his speeches with quotations from Emerson. Awed by his grace and taste, as well as by his wit and wealth, the media extolled him as a vibrant leader and adoring husband. The public knew nothing of his fragile health, frequent use of mood-altering drugs to alleviate pain, and extra-marital affairs.

Kennedy's
Domestic Record

Media images obscured Kennedy's lackluster domestic record. The conservative coalition of Republicans and southern Democrats that had stifled Truman's Fair Deal also doomed the New Frontier. Lacking the votes, JFK rarely pressed Congress for social legislation, maintaining that "there is no sense in raising hell, and then not being successful."

JFK made stimulating economic growth his domestic priority. To that end he combined higher defense expenditures with investment incentives for private enterprise. In 1961 he persuaded Congress to boost the defense budget by 20 percent. He vastly increased America's nuclear stockpile, strengthened the military's conventional forces, and established the Special Forces ("Green Berets") to engage in guerrilla warfare. By 1963 the defense budget reached its highest level as a percentage of total federal expenditures in the entire Cold War era. Kennedy also persuaded Congress to finance a "race to the moon," which Americans would win in 1969 at a cost of more than $25 billion. Most importantly, Kennedy took his liberal advisers' Keynesian advice to call for a huge cut in corporate taxes, which would greatly increase the deficit but would presumably provide capital for business to invest. This would stimulate the economy, increase tax revenues, and thus create a better life for all Americans. When the Kennedy presidency ended in November 1963, the proposed tax cut was bottled up in Congress. Military spending, continued technological innovation, heightened productivity, and low-cost energy, however, had already doubled the 1960 rate of economic growth, decreased unemployment, and held increases in inflation to 1.3 percent a year. The United States was in the midst of its longest uninterrupted economic expansion.

The boom would both cause further ecological damage and provide the affluence that enabled Americans to care about the environment. It would build on an older conservation movement, emphasizing the efficient use of resources, a preservation movement (focusing on preserving "wilderness"), and the fallout scare of the 1950s, which raised questions about the biological well-being of the planet. The publication in 1962 of Rachel Carson's *Silent Spring* (see Chapter 27), documenting the hazards of pesticides, intensified concern. Additionally, postwar prosperity made many Americans less concerned with increased production and more concerned with the quality of life. In response, Kennedy appointed an advisory committee that warned against widespread pesticide use. In 1963, Congress passed a Clean Air Act, regulating automotive and industrial emissions. After decades of heedless pollution, Washington hesitatingly began to address environmental problems.

Cold War Activism

In his inaugural address Kennedy proclaimed, "we shall pay any price, bear any burden, meet any hardship, support any friend, oppose any foe to assure the survival and success of liberty." He launched a major military buildup and surrounded himself with Cold Warriors who shared his belief that American security depended on superior force and the willingness to use it. At the same time, he gained congressional backing for economic assistance to Third World countries to counter the appeal of communism. The Peace Corps, created in 1961, exemplified the New Frontier's liberal anticommunism. By 1963, five thousand Peace Corps volunteers were serving two-year stints as teachers, sanitation engineers, crop specialists, and health workers in more than forty Third World nations. They were, according to liberal historian and Kennedy aide Arthur Schlesinger, Jr., "reform-minded missionaries of democracy."

In early 1961 a crisis flared in Laos, a tiny, landlocked nation created by the Geneva agreement in 1954. There a civil war between American-supported forces and Pathet Lao rebels seemed headed toward a communist triumph. In July 1962 Kennedy agreed to a face-saving compromise that restored a neutralist government but left communist forces dominant in the countryside. The accord stiffened Kennedy's resolve not to allow further communist gains in Asia, which resulted in his deepening of the American commitment to support a noncommunist South Vietnam.

Spring 1961 brought Kennedy's first major foreign-policy crisis. To eliminate a communist outpost on America's doorstep, he approved a CIA plan, drawn up in the Eisenhower administration, to invade Cuba. In April, fifteen hundred anti-Castro exiles, "La Brigada," stormed Cuba's Bay of Pigs, expecting their arrival to trigger a general uprising to overthrow Fidel Castro. It was a fiasco. Deprived of air cover by Kennedy's desire to conceal U.S. involvement, the invaders had no chance against Castro's superior forces. Although Kennedy accepted blame for the failure, he neither apologized nor ceased attempting to topple Castro.

In July 1961, Kennedy met Soviet premier Nikita Khrushchev in Vienna to try to resolve a peace treaty with Germany (see Chapter 26). Comparing American troops in the divided city of Berlin to "a bone stuck in the throat," Khrushchev threatened war unless the West retreated. A shaken Kennedy returned to the United States and declared the defense of West Berlin essential to the Free World. He doubled draft calls, mobilized 150,000 reservists, and called for increased defense spending. The threat of nuclear war escalated until mid-August, when the Soviets constructed a wall to seal off East Berlin and end the exodus of brains and talent to the West. The Berlin Wall became a concrete symbol of communism's denial of personal freedom until it fell in 1989.

To the Brink of Nuclear War

In mid-October 1962, aerial photographs revealed that the Soviet Union had built bases for intermediate-range ballistic missiles (IRBMs) in Cuba, capable of striking U.S. soil. Smarting from the Bay of Pigs disaster, fearing unchecked Soviet interference in the Western Hemisphere, and believing that his credibility was at stake, Kennedy responded forcefully. In a somber televised address, he denounced the "provocative threat to world peace" and announced that the United States would "quarantine" Cuba—impose a naval blockade—to prevent delivery of more missiles and would dismantle by force the missiles already in Cuba if the Soviets did not do so.

The world held its breath during the **Cuban missile crisis.** The two superpowers appeared on a collision course toward nuclear war. Soviet technicians worked feverishly to complete missile launch pads, and Soviet missile-carrying ships steamed toward the blockade. American B-52s armed with nuclear bombs took to the air, and nearly a quarter-million troops assembled in Florida to invade Cuba. Secretary of State Dean Rusk gulped, "We're eyeball to eyeball."

"I think the other fellow just blinked," a relieved Rusk announced on October 25. Kennedy received a message from Khrushchev promising to remove the missiles if the U.S. pledged never to invade Cuba. As Kennedy prepared to respond positively, a second, more belligerent message arrived from Khrushchev insisting that American missiles be withdrawn from Turkey as part of the deal. Hours later an American U-2 reconnaissance plane was shot down over Cuba. It was "the blackest hour of the crisis," recalled a Kennedy aide. Some advisers urged an immediate invasion, but the president, heeding Robert Kennedy's advice, decided to accept the first message and ignore the second one. The next morning Khrushchev pledged to remove the missiles in return for Kennedy's noninvasion promise. Less publicly, Kennedy subsequently removed U.S. missiles from Turkey.

The full extent of the crisis became known only after the end of the Cold War, when the Russians disclosed that Soviet forces in Cuba had possessed thirty-six nuclear warheads as well as nine tactical nuclear weapons for battlefield use. Soviet field commanders had independent authority to use these weapons. Worst of all, Kennedy had not known that the Soviets already had the capability to launch a nuclear strike from Cuba. Speaking in 1992, former secretary of defense Robert McNamara recalled the pressure on Kennedy to invade and the likely consequence: "No one should believe that U.S. troops could have been attacked by tactical nuclear warheads without the U.S.'s responding with nuclear warheads. . . . And where would it have ended? In utter disaster."

Chastened by coming to the brink of nuclear war, Kennedy and Khrushchev installed a telephone "hot line" so that the two sides could communicate instantly in future crises, and then agreed to a treaty outlawing atmospheric and undersea nuclear testing. These efforts signaled a new phase of the Cold War, later called détente, in which the superpowers moved from confrontation to negotiation. Concurrently, the Cuban missile crisis escalated the arms race by convincing both sides of the need for nuclear superiority.

The Thousand-Day Presidency

On November 22, 1963, during a trip to Texas to shore up his reelection chances, John and Jackie Kennedy rode in an open car along Dallas streets lined with cheering crowds. Shots rang out. The president slumped, dying, his skull and throat shattered. Soon after, aboard Air Force One, Lyndon B. Johnson was sworn in as president.

Grief and disbelief numbed the nation. Millions of Americans spent the next four days in front of their TV sets staring at replays of the murder of accused assassin Lee Harvey Oswald in the Dallas city jail by a nightclub owner; at the somber state funeral, with the small boy saluting his father's casket; at the grieving family lighting an eternal flame at Arlington National Cemetery. Few who watched would forget. Kennedy had helped make television central to American politics; now, in death, it made him the fallen hero-king of Camelot.

The assassination made a martyr of JFK. More admired in death than in life, the public ranked him as one of the very few "great" presidents, associating him with a spirit of energy and innovation. While Kennedy loyalists continued to stress his intelligence and his ability to change and grow, most historians pointed to his lack of achievements and the discrepancy between his public image and his private philandering. Some also deplored his aggressive Cold War tactics, his raising unrealistic expectations, and his vast expansion of presidential powers.

Kennedy's rhetoric expressed the new liberalism, but he rarely translated ideals into deeds. He frequently compromised with conservatives and segregationists in Congress; economic expansion came from spending on missiles and the space race, not on social welfare and human needs. Partly because his own personal behavior made him beholden to FBI director J. Edgar Hoover, JFK allowed the agency to infringe on civil liberties, even as the CIA plotted with the Mafia to assassinate Fidel Castro. (Scholars are still trying to untangle the plots and policies that enmeshed the Kennedy brothers, Hoover, organized crime, and the national security agencies.)

Internationally, Kennedy left a mixed record. He signed the world's first nuclear-test-ban treaty, yet initiated a massive arms buildup. He compromised on Laos but deepened U.S. involvement in Vietnam. He came to question the need for confronting the Soviet Union yet insisted on U.S. global superiority and aggressively prosecuted the Cold War. He did so, moreover, by increasing the powers of the White House staff. As never before, a small group of aides, personally loyal to the president, secretly dominated policy making.

Yet, JFK inspired Americans to expect greatness, aroused the poor and the powerless, and stimulated the young to activism. Dying during the calm before the storm, he left his successor soaring expectations at home and a deteriorating entanglement in Vietnam. His legacy and assassination would shatter illusions and optimism, leading millions of Americans to doubt their government and their future.

The Struggle for Black Equality, 1961–1968

Following the lunch-counter sit-ins, civil-rights activists tried to convince Kennedy to act on their behalf. He would not do so, fearing it would split the Democratic Party, immobilize Congress in filibusters, and jeopardize his reelection. He viewed civil rights as a thorny thicket to avoid, not a moral issue. He balanced his appointment of a record number of African-Americans to federal jobs with the nomination of white segregationists to judgeships. He stalled for two years on his promise to outlaw discrimination in federally funded housing by executive order, and then issued a weak order that barely made a dent in segregation. Only action by civil-rights groups that secured public favor held out the possibility of forcing Kennedy's hand.

Nonviolence and Violence

In spring 1961, the Congress of Racial Equality (CORE) organized a "freedom ride" through the Deep South to dramatize the flouting of a 1960 Supreme Court edict banning segregation in interstate transportation facilities. It aroused white wrath. Mobs beat the freedom riders in Anniston, Alabama, burned a bus, and mauled the protestors in Birmingham, making the freedom rides front-page news. Yet only after further assaults on the freedom riders in Montgomery did Kennedy, fearful that the violence would undermine American prestige abroad, deploy federal marshals to restore peace. And only after scores more freedom rides and the arrests of hundreds of protesters did the president prod the Interstate Commerce Commission to enforce the law. Only crisis, not moral suasion, forced Kennedy to act.

Many of the freedom riders were members of the **Student Nonviolent Coordinating Committee (SNCC)**, formed in April 1960 by participants in the sit-ins. SNCC stressed both the nonviolent civil disobedience strategy of Martin Luther King, Jr., and the need to stimulate local, grass-roots activism and leadership. In fall 1961, it chose Albany, Georgia, as the site of a campaign to desegregate public facilities. Despite King's involvement, wily local authorities avoided the overt violence that had won the freedom riders national sympathy. Without the national indignation that brought a White

House response, the Albany movement collapsed. But the lesson had been learned by civil-rights leaders.

It had not been learned by southern whites. An angry mob rioted in fall 1962 when a federal court ordered the University of Mississippi to enroll James Meredith, a black air force veteran. Rallying behind Confederate flags, troublemakers laid siege to the campus, attacking the federal marshals who escorted Meredith to "Ole Miss." The clash left two dead and scores injured before thousands of troops quelled the violence and protected Meredith's right to attend the university of his home state.

The African-American Revolution

As television coverage of the struggle for racial equality brought mounting numbers of African-Americans into the movement, civil-rights leaders applied increasing pressure on Kennedy to intervene. They realized that it would take decades to dismantle segregation piecemeal; the only practical remedy would be comprehensive national legislation, backed by the power of the federal government, guaranteeing full citizenship for African-Americans. To get such legislation from the Kennedy administration, they would need to induce an outrage by segregationists that would cause millions of Americans to demand that the president act.

Determined to expose the violent extremism of southern racism, **Martin Luther King, Jr.,** launched nonviolent marches, sit-ins, and pray-ins in Birmingham, Alabama. The most rigidly segregated big city in America, Birmingham's officials had even removed a book from the library that featured white and black rabbits. Past violence by whites against civil-rights protestors had earned the city the nickname "Bombingham," and the black neighborhood, "Dynamite Hill." Few doubted Police Commissioner Eugene "Bull" Connor's pledge that "blood would run in the streets of Birmingham before it would be integrated."

When jailed for instigating a march that a local court had prohibited, King penned the "Letter from Birmingham Jail." It detailed the humiliations of racial discrimination and segregation. It vindicated the nonviolent struggle against Jim Crow. And it justified civil disobedience to protest unjust laws, such as segregation statutes.

> We know through painful experience that freedom is never voluntarily given by the oppressor; it must be demanded by the oppressed. Frankly, I have yet to engage in a direct-action campaign that was "well-timed" in the view of those who have not suffered unduly from the disease of segregation. For years now I have heard the word "Wait!" It rings in the ear of every Negro with piercing familiarity. This "Wait" has almost always meant "Never." We must come to see, with one of our distinguished jurists, that "justice too long delayed is justice denied."

In May, thousands of schoolchildren, some only six years old, joined King's crusade. The bigoted Connor lost his temper. He unleashed his men—armed with electric cattle prods, high-pressure water hoses, and snarling attack dogs—on the nonviolent demonstrators. The ferocity of Connor's attacks, caught on camera and television, horrified the world.

"The civil-rights movement should thank God for Bull Connor," JFK remarked. "He's helped it as much as Abraham Lincoln." Indeed, Connor's vicious tactics seared the nation's conscience and pushed Kennedy to help negotiate a settlement that ended the demonstrations in return for an agreement by the city's department stores to desegregate their facilities and to hire black workers. By mid-1963, the rallying cry "Freedom

Now!" reverberated through the land as all the civil-rights groups became more militant, competing with each other in assisting ad hoc, local protests. The number of protests soared. Most were spontaneous initiatives led by black women who put their bodies on the line to compel changes at the community level. Concerned about America's image abroad as well as the "fires of frustration and discord" raging at home, Kennedy could no longer temporize. The government must propose changes in race relations, he reasoned; otherwise blacks would turn to violent leaders and methods. When Governor George Wallace refused to allow two black students to enter the University of Alabama in June 1963, Kennedy forced Wallace—who had pledged "Segregation now! Segregation tomorrow! Segregation forever!"—to capitulate to a court desegregation order.

On June 11, the president went on television to define civil rights as "a moral issue" and to declare that "race has no place in American life or law." A week later, Kennedy proposed a bill outlawing segregation in public facilities and authorizing the federal government to withhold funds from programs that discriminated. As the bill bogged down in Congress, civil-rights adherents planned to march on Washington to muster support for the legislation.

The March on Washington, 1963   The idea for a March on Washington had originally been proposed by A. Philip Randolph in 1941 to protest discrimination against blacks in the defense mobilization (see Chapter 25). Twenty-two years later, Randolph revived the idea and convinced the major civil-rights leaders to support a March on Washington for Jobs and Freedom.

A quarter of a million people, including some fifty thousand whites, converged on Washington, D.C., on August 28, 1963. It was the largest political assembly to date. After a long, sweltering day of speeches and songs, Martin Luther King, Jr., took the podium to remind Americans that the hopes generated by the Emancipation Proclamation had still not been fulfilled.

Summoning images of shackled, hobbled black slaves, he maintained, "The life of the Negro is still sadly crippled by the manacles of segregation and the chains of discrimination. . . . One hundred years later, the Negro is still not free." He described the promises of the Declaration of Independence as "a sacred obligation," which has proved to be, for African-Americans, a bad check. But, he roared, we have come to collect on the promise, to cash the check "that will give us upon demand the riches of freedom and the security of justice." Blacks would not brook delay or gradualism: "This sweltering summer of the Negro's legitimate discontent will not pass until there is an invigorating autumn of freedom and equality." He warned: "There will be neither rest nor tranquility in America until the Negro is granted his citizenship rights. The whirlwinds of revolt will continue to shake the foundations of our nation until the bright day of justice emerges." As the multitude cheered, King concluded by reiterating his dream of true brotherhood in America.

King's eloquence did not speed passage of the civil-rights bill. It did not end racism or erase poverty and despair. It did not quell the rage of white racists. In September, the Ku Klux Klan bombing of a black church in Birmingham killed four girls attending Sunday school. (Not until 2002 was the last of the four main suspects brought to justice.) It did not prevent the ghetto riots that lay ahead, or the white backlash that would ultimately smother the civil-rights movement. Yet King had turned a political rally into a historic event, recalling America to the ideals of justice and equality, to the fundamental notion that the color of one's skin ought never be a burden in American life.

The Civil Rights and Voting Rights Acts

Kennedy's assassination brought to the White House a southerner, Lyndon Johnson, who knew he had to prove himself on the race issue or the liberals "would get me. They'd throw up my background against me. . . . I had to produce a civil rights bill," he later wrote, "that was even stronger than the one they'd have gotten if Kennedy had lived." Johnson succeeded in doing just that, employing his vast skills to toughen the bill and break a southern filibuster in the Senate.

The **Civil Rights Act** of 1964, the most significant civil-rights law in U.S. history, banned racial discrimination and segregation in public accommodations. It outlawed bias in federally funded programs; granted the federal government new powers to fight school segregation; and created the Equal Employment Opportunity Commission (EEOC) to enforce the ban on job discrimination.

The Civil Rights Act did not address the right to vote. So CORE and SNCC activists, believing that the ballot held the key to power for southern blacks, mounted a major campaign to register black voters. They organized the Mississippi Freedom Summer Project of 1964 to focus on the state most hostile to black rights. Although 42 percent of Mississippi's population, blacks were only 5 percent of the registered voters. A thousand students, from nearly two hundred colleges and universities, volunteered to help register black voters and to teach the practices of democracy and black history in "Freedom Schools" that emphasized African-American self-worth. Harassed by Mississippi law-enforcement officials and Ku Klux Klansmen, the activists endured the firebombing of black churches and civil-rights headquarters, as well as arrests and even murders.

Although they registered only twelve hundred blacks to vote, the civil-rights workers enrolled nearly sixty thousand disfranchised blacks in the Mississippi Freedom Democratic Party (MFDP). In August 1964, they took their case to the national Democratic convention. "I was beaten till I was exhausted," Fannie Lou Hamer, the twentieth child of poor sharecroppers, told the convention. "All of this on account we wanted to register, to become first class citizens. If the Freedom Democratic party is not seated now, I question America." The MFDP was not seated. To stop a threatened walkout by southern white delegates, Johnson forged a compromise that offered two at-large seats to the MFDP and barred delegations from states that disfranchised blacks from all future conventions. The compromise pleased no one. The MFDP rejected it as a "token" gesture and left the convention in a huff. Within SNCC, the failure of the Democrats to support seating the MFDP delegates proved to be a turning point in their disillusionment with liberalism.

In 1964, most blacks still shared the optimism of Martin Luther King, Jr., and over 90 percent of African-American voters cast their ballots for the Democrats, leaving Johnson and the liberals in firm control. King now set his sights on opening the voting booths to blacks. Determined to win a strong voting-rights law, the SCLC organized mass protests in Selma, Alabama, in March 1965. Blacks were half the population of Dallas County, where Selma was located, but only 1 percent were registered to vote.

King knew he again had to create a crisis to pressure Congress to act. He masterfully provoked Selma's county sheriff, Jim Clark, every bit as violence-prone as Birmingham's "Bull" Connor, to reveal his brutality, arresting and beating thousands. When civil-rights activists sought to march from Selma to Montgomery, to petition Governor George Wallace, they were clubbed, shocked with cattle prods, and tear-gassed by lawmen. Showcased on TV, the spectacle provoked national outrage. Johnson grasped the mood of the country and delivered a televised address urging Congress to pass a

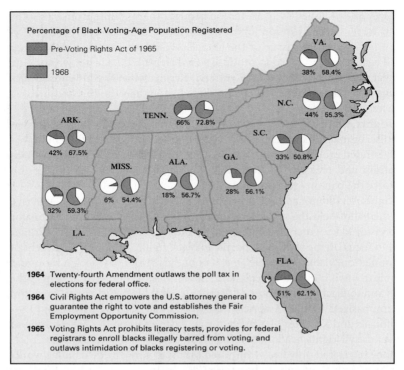

MAP 28.1 Voter Registration of African-Americans in the South, 1960–1968

As blacks overwhelmingly registered to vote as Democrats, some former segregationist politicians, among them George Wallace, started to court the black vote, and many southern whites began to cast their ballots for Republicans, inaugurating an era of real two-party competition in the South.

voting-rights bill, beseeching all Americans, "Their cause must be our cause, too." Because "it's not just Negroes, really, it's all of us who must overcome the crippling legacy of bigotry and injustice. And," invoking the movement's anthem, "we *shall* overcome."

Signed by the president in August 1965, the **Voting Rights Act** invalidated the use of any test or device to deny the vote and authorized federal examiners to register voters in states that had disfranchised blacks. The law dramatically expanded black suffrage, boosting the number of registered black voters in the South from 1 million in 1964 to 3.1 million in 1968, and transformed southern politics.

The number of blacks holding office in the South swelled from fewer than two dozen in 1964 to nearly twelve hundred in 1972, including half the seats on Selma's city council and the first two African-Americans elected to Congress from the former Confederacy since the nineteenth century. Electoral success brought jobs for African-Americans, contracts for black businesses, and improvements in facilities and services in black neighborhoods. Most importantly, as Fannie Lou Hamer recalled, when African-Americans could not vote, "white folks would drive past your house in a pickup truck with guns hanging up on the back and give you hate stares. . . . Those same people now call me Mrs. Hamer."

Fire in the Streets   The civil-rights movement changed, but did not revolutionize, race relations. It ended legal segregation, broke the monopoly on political power in the South held by whites, and galvanized a new black sense of self-esteem. The movement raised hopes for the possibility of greater change and legitimated protest. But its inability to transform equality of opportunity into equality of results underscored the limitations of liberal change, especially in the urban ghetto. The movement did not bring African-Americans economic equality or material well-being, and the anger bubbling below the surface soon boiled over.

On August 11, 1965, five days after the signing of the Voting Rights Act, a scuffle between white police and blacks in Watts, the largest African-American district in Los Angeles, ignited the most destructive race riot in decades. For six days thousands of blacks looted shops, firebombed white-owned businesses, and sniped at police officers and firefighters. When the riot ended, thirty-four people were dead, nine hundred injured, and four thousand arrested. Blacks in Chicago and Springfield, Massachusetts, then took to the streets, looting, burning, and battling police.

The violence in 1965 proved to be just a prelude to a succession of "long hot summers." In the summer of 1966, more than a score of ghetto outbreaks erupted in northern cities. Blacks rioted to force whites to pay heed to the squalor of the slums and to the brutal behavior of police in the ghetto—problems that the southern civil-rights movement had ignored. Extensive poverty and the unequal distribution of income and wealth in the nation, moreover, had exacerbated all the racial problems of the inner cities. Frustrated by the allure of America's wealth portrayed on TV and by what seemed the empty promise of civil-rights laws, black mobs stoned passing motorists, ransacked stores, torched white-owned buildings, and hurled bricks at the troops sent to quell the disorder.

The following summer, black rage at oppressive conditions and impatience with liberal change erupted in 150 racial skirmishes and 40 riots—the most intense and destructive period of racial violence in U.S. history. In Newark, New Jersey, twenty-seven people died and more than eleven hundred were injured. The following week, Detroit went up in smoke in the decade's worst riot. As the fires spread, so did the looting. Children joined adults in racing from store to store to fill their arms with liquor and jewelry; cars pulled up to businesses so they could be stocked with appliances. By the time the Michigan National Guard and U.S. army paratroopers quelled the riot, forty-three people had died, two thousand were injured, and seven thousand had been arrested. Then in 1968, following the assassination of Martin Luther King, Jr. (see Chapter 29), black uprisings flared in the ghettos of a hundred cities. The 1964–1968 riot toll would include some two hundred dead, seven thousand injured, forty thousand arrested, and at least $500 million in property destroyed—mostly white-owned stores and tenements that exemplified exploitation in the ghetto.

A frightened, bewildered nation asked why such rioting occurred just when blacks achieved many of their goals. Militant blacks saw the uprisings as revolutionary violence to overthrow a racist, reactionary society; poet Imamu Amiri Baraka (formerly LeRoi Jones) termed them spontaneous rebellions against authority. The Far Right saw them as evidence of a communist plot. Many conservatives described them as senseless outbursts by troublemakers. The administration's National Advisory Commission on

Bobby Seale and Huey Newton *Founded by Bobby Seale and Huey Newton in Oakland, California, in response to police brutality against African-Americans, the Black Panther Party was organized along semimilitary lines and advocated fighting for black justice, in Newton's words, "through the barrel of a gun."*

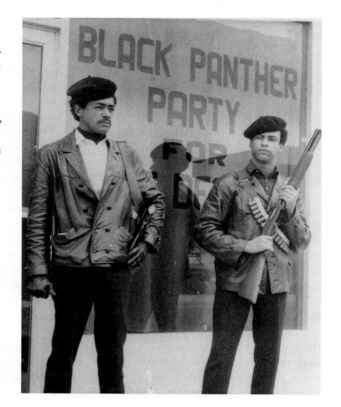

Civil Disorders (known as the Kerner Commission) blamed them on an "explosive mixture" of poverty, slum housing, poor education, and police brutality caused by "white racism." Warning that "our nation is moving toward two societies, one black, one white—separate and unequal," the commission recommended increased federal spending to create new jobs for urban blacks, construct additional public housing, and end de facto school segregation in the North. Johnson and Congress, aware of the backlash against the War on Poverty as well as the cost of the war in Vietnam, ignored the warning. "Each war feeds on the other," observed Senator William Fulbright, "and, although the President assures us that we have the resources to win both wars, in fact we are not winning either of them."

"Black Power"   For many young African-Americans, liberalism's response to racial inequality proved "too little, too late." The demand for **Black Power** sounded in 1966 paralleled the fury of the urban riots; it expressed the eagerness of militant activists for militant self-defense and rapid social change. The slogan encapsulated both their bitterness toward a white society that blocked their aspirations and their rejection of King's commitment to nonviolence, racial integration, and alliances with white liberals.

Derived from a long tradition of black nationalism, Black Power owed much to the militant rhetoric and vision of Malcolm X. Born in Omaha, Nebraska, in 1925, the son of a preacher active in the Marcus Garvey movement, Malcolm Little pimped and sold drugs before being jailed in 1946. In prison, he converted to the Nation of Islam (NOI), the Black Muslim group founded by Wallace Fard and led by Elijah Muhammad (Elijah Poole). Released in 1952 and renamed Malcolm X, as a symbolic repudiation of his "slavemaster" name, he quickly became the Black Muslims' most dynamic street orator and charismatic leader, bringing black nationalism to public attention.

Building on separatist and nationalist impulses with deep roots in the black community—racial solidarity and uplift, self-sufficiency, and self-help—Malcolm X called on blacks to "wake up, clean up, and stand up" to achieve true independence. "I don't see any American dream," he declared. "I see an American nightmare." He urged blacks "to recapture our heritage and identity." He wanted them to see themselves with their "own eyes not the white man's," and to separate themselves from the "white devil." Ridiculing civil-rights leaders like King—"just a twentieth-century Uncle Tom"—for emphasizing desegregation instead of the social and economic problems that beset most African-Americans, he insisted that blacks seize their freedom "by any means necessary." "If ballots won't work, bullets will," he said. "If someone puts a hand on you, send him to the cemetery." In February 1965, after he broke with the Nation of Islam to find a more effective approach to solving the problems of blacks, Malcolm X was murdered by three Black Muslim gunmen. He was not silenced. He became a martyr, and his account of his life and beliefs, *The Autobiography of Malcolm X* (1965), became the main text of the rising Black Power movement and its celebration of a new black consciousness.

Two days after winning the world heavyweight championship in 1964, boxer Cassius Clay shocked the sports world by announcing his conversion to the Nation of Islam and his new name, Muhammad Ali. Refusing induction into the armed services on religious grounds, Ali was found guilty of draft evasion, stripped of his title, and exiled from boxing for three and a half years during his athletic prime. Inspired by the examples of Ali and Malcolm X, and bitter at the failure of the established civil-rights organizations to achieve a fundamental distribution of wealth and power, young, urban African-Americans abandoned civil disobedience and reformist strategies. They embraced the word *black* and a new agenda based on racial identity. In 1966 CORE and SNCC changed from interracial organizations committed to achieving integration nonviolently to all-black groups advocating racial separatism and Black Power "by any means necessary." To SNCC chairman Stokely Carmichael, racial integration was "a subterfuge for the maintenance of white supremacy" that implied the superiority of white institutions and values.

The boldest champion of self-determination for African-American communities was the Black Panther Party for Self-Defense. Founded in Oakland, California, in 1966 by Huey P. Newton and Bobby Seale, it urged black men to become "panthers— smiling, cunning, scientific, striking by night and sparing no one." Although the Panthers also sponsored community centers and school breakfast programs, they attained national notoriety from their fearsome paramilitary style and shootouts with the police. Expressing contempt for the nonviolent, church-based civil-rights movement, Newton claimed that the "heirs of Malcolm X have picked up the gun." Violent confrontations with police and the FBI left many of its members dead or in prison, effectively destroying the organization and, together with the riots, splintering the black-white civil-rights alliance and contributing to the rightward turn in politics.

Although the concept remained imprecise, ranging from notions of black capitalism to local control of schools to revolutionary schemes to overthrow the American system, Black Power exerted a significant influence. Its origins lay in the racial pride and spirit of resistance bred by generations of white oppression; and most African-Americans took it to mean gaining the power to make the decisions that governed their day-to-day lives and destinies, to define their own goals, and to lead their own organizations. Empowerment was the key to its meaning. Scores of new community self-help groups and self-reliant black institutions exemplified it, as did the establishment of black studies programs at colleges, the mobilization of black voters to elect black candidates, and the encouragement of racial pride and self-esteem—"black is beautiful." The "Godfather of Soul," James Brown sang, "Say it loud—I'm black and I'm proud," and as never before African-Americans rejected skin bleaches and hair straighteners, gave their children Islamic names and Kwanzaa gifts instead of Christmas presents, and gloried in soul music. Artists and writers produced work rooted in the black experience that resonated with a black audience. "I may have lost hope," SCLC leader Jesse Jackson had students repeating with him, "but I am . . . somebody. . . . I am . . . black . . . beautiful . . . proud. . . . I must be respected." This message reverberated with other marginalized groups as well, and helped shape their protest movements.

Liberalism Ascendant, 1963–1968

Although a firm New Dealer in the 1930s, **Lyndon Baines Johnson** came to be distrusted by liberals as "a Machiavelli in a Stetson" and regarded as a usurper by Kennedy partisans. He had achieved his highest ambition as a result of the assassination of a

The LBJ Treatment *Not content unless he could wholly dominate friend as well as foe, Lyndon Johnson used his body as well as his voice to bend others to his will and gain his objectives.*

popular president in Johnson's home state of Texas. Though just nine years older than JFK, he seemed a relic of the past, a back-room wheeler-dealer, as crude as Kennedy was smooth, as insecure as his predecessor was self-confident.

Yet Johnson had substantial political assets. He had served in Washington almost continuously since 1932, accruing enormous experience and a close association with the Capitol Hill power brokers who controlled the legislative process. He excelled at wooing allies, neutralizing opponents, building coalitions, and achieving results. He loved the political maneuvering and legislative detail that Kennedy loathed.

Johnson's first three years as president demonstrated his determination to prove himself to liberals. He deftly handled the transition of power, won a landslide victory in 1964, and guided through Congress the greatest array of liberal legislation in U.S. history, surpassing the New Deal agenda. But LBJ's swollen yet fragile ego could not abide the sniping of Kennedy loyalists, and he frequently complained that the media did not give him "a fair shake." Wondering aloud, "Why don't people like me?" Johnson labored to ensure that everyone shared in the promise of the American Dream, and to vanquish all foes at home and abroad. Ironically, in seeking consensus and adoration, Johnson would divide the nation and leave office repudiated.

Johnson Takes Over

Calling for quick passage of the tax-cut and civil-rights bills as a memorial to JFK, Johnson used his skills to win passage of the Civil Rights Act of 1964 (see pp. 895) and a $10 billion tax-reduction bill, which produced a surge in capital investment and personal consumption that spurred economic growth and shrank the budget deficit. More boldly, Johnson declared "unconditional war on poverty in America."

Largely invisible in an affluent America, according to Michael Harrington's *The Other America* (1962), some 40 million people dwelled in substandard housing and subsisted on inadequate diets. Living with little hope in a "culture of poverty," they lacked the education, medical care, and employment opportunities that most Americans took for granted. To be poor, Harrington asserted, "is to be an internal alien, to grow up in a culture that is radically different from the one that dominates the society."

LBJ championed a campaign to bring these "internal exiles" into the mainstream. Designed to promote greater opportunity, to offer a "hand up, not a handout," the Economic Opportunity Act (1964) established the Office of Economic Opportunity to wage "unconditional **war on poverty.**" Its programs included a Job Corps to train young people in marketable skills; VISTA (Volunteers in Service to America), a domestic peace corps; Project Head Start, to provide free compensatory education for preschoolers from disadvantaged families; a Community Action Program to encourage the "maximum feasible participation" of the poor in decisions that affected them; and public-works and training programs.

Summing up his goals in 1964, Johnson offered his vision of the **Great Society.** First must come "an end to poverty and racial injustice." In addition, the Great Society would be a place where all children could enrich their minds and enlarge their talents, where people could renew their contact with nature, and where all would be "more concerned with the quality of their goals than the quantity of their goods."

The 1964 Election

Johnson's Great Society horrified the "new conservatives," such as William F. Buckley and the college students who belonged to the Young Americans for Freedom (YAF). The most persuasive criticism came from Arizona senator **Barry Goldwater,** who had voted against the Civil Rights Act. A product of the twentieth-century West, Goldwater was an outsider fighting the power of Washington, a fervent anticommunist, a proponent of individual freedom. He railed against liberalism's reliance on deficit spending and on a powerful federal government to cure social ills. He advocated as little federal governmental intervention in the economy as possible, and opposed government efforts to expand and protect civil rights and liberties. And he proposed that the U.S. roll back communism in the world rather than just contain it.

Johnson's advocacy of civil rights frightened southern segregationists and blue-collar workers in northern cities who dreaded the integration of their neighborhoods, schools, and workplaces. Their support of Alabama's segregationist governor George Wallace in the spring 1964 presidential primaries heralded a "white backlash" against the civil-rights movement.

Buoyed by this backlash, conservatives took control of the GOP in 1964. They nominated Barry Goldwater for the presidency and adopted a platform totally opposed to liberalism. Determined to offer the nation "a choice not an echo," Goldwater lauded his opposition to civil-rights legislation and his vote against the censure of McCarthy. In Appalachia, he denounced the War on Poverty, in Tennessee he called for the sale of the TVA to private interests, in the Midwest he opposed high price supports for farmers, and in the retirement community of St. Petersburg, Florida, he advocated scrapping social security. "We have gotten where we are," he declared, "not because of government, but in spite of government." Goldwater also accused the Democrats of a "no-win" strategy in the Cold War, hinting that he might use nuclear weapons against Cuba and North Vietnam. His candidacy appealed most to those angered by the Cold War stalemate, by the erosion of traditional moral values, and by the increasing militancy of African-Americans. His campaign slogan, "In your heart you know he's right," allowed his liberal opponents to quip, "In your guts you know he's nuts."

LBJ and his running mate, Senator Hubert Humphrey of Minnesota, depicted Goldwater as an extremist not to be trusted with the nuclear trigger. When the Arizonan charged that the Democrats had not pursued total victory in Vietnam, Johnson appeared the apostle of restraint: "We are not going to send American boys nine or ten thousand miles from home to do what Asian boys ought to be doing for themselves."

LBJ won a landslide victory, 43 million votes to Goldwater's 27 million. Goldwater carried only Arizona and five southern states. The GOP lost thirty-eight seats in the House of Representatives, two in the Senate, and five hundred in state legislatures. Many proclaimed the death of conservatism. Rather, it heralded a grass-roots revival of antigovernment westerners, economic and religious conservatives, and anti-integrationist whites that presaged the Right's future triumph. It transformed the Republicans from a moderate, eastern-dominated party to one decidedly conservative, southern, and western. It built a national base of financial support for conservative candidates; catalyzed the creation of new conservative publications and think-tanks; energized volunteers like Phyllis Schlafly to campaign for Goldwater and stay involved in politics; mobilized future leaders of the party, like Ronald Reagan; and led to Richard Nixon's "southern strategy" (see Chapter 29). But in the short run, the liberals controlled all three branches of government.

Triumphant
Liberalism

"Hurry, boys, hurry," LBJ urged his aides. "Get that legislation up to the hill and out. Eighteen months from now ol' Landslide Lyndon will be Lame-Duck Lyndon." Johnson flooded Congress with liberal proposals—sixty-three of them in 1965 alone. He got most of what he requested.

The Eighty-ninth Congress—"the Congress of Fulfillment" to LBJ, and Johnson's "hip-pocket Congress" to his opponents—enlarged the War on Poverty and passed a milestone voting-rights act. It enacted **Medicare** to provide health insurance for the aged under social security, and a **Medicaid** health plan for the poor. By 1975 the two programs would be serving 47 million people, and account for a quarter of the nation's total health-care expenditures. The legislators appropriated funds for public education and housing, for aid to Appalachia, and for revitalizing inner-city neighborhoods. They also created new cabinet departments of transportation and of housing and urban development (the latter headed by Robert Weaver, the first African-American cabinet member), and the National Endowments for the Arts and the Humanities.

Of enormous future significance, Congress enacted the **Immigration Act of 1965,** abolishing the national-origins quotas of the 1920s and transforming America's racial and ethnic kaleidoscope. Annual legal immigration would increase from about 250,000 to well over a million, and the vast majority of new immigrants would come from Asia and Latin America. Less than 1 percent of the U.S. population in 1960, Asian-Americans would be more than 4 percent in 2000; and the Hispanic population would increase from 4.5 percent in 1970 to nearly 12 percent in 2000. This increasing population diversity vastly expanded the nation's culinary, linguistic, musical, and religious spectrum.

The Great Society also battled what LBJ described as the problem "of vanishing beauty, of increasing ugliness, of shrinking open space, and of an overall environment that is diminished daily by pollution and noise and blight." In 1964 Congress passed the National Wilderness Preservation Act, setting aside 9.1 million acres of wilderness. It established Redwood National Park and defeated efforts to dam the Colorado River and flood the lower Grand Canyon; strengthened the Clean Water and Clean Air Acts; protected endangered species; preserved scenic rivers; and lessened the number of junkyards and billboards. Responding to the uproar caused by Ralph Nader's revelations about unsafe cars, Congress set the first federal safety standards for automobiles and required states to establish highway safety programs.

The Great Society increased opportunity and improved the lives of millions. The proportion of the poor in the population dropped from 22 percent in 1960 to 13 percent in 1969; infant mortality declined by a third; Head Start reached more than 2 million poor children; and African-American family income rose from 54 percent to 61 percent of white family income. The percentage of blacks living below the poverty line plummeted from 40 percent to 20 percent. But in part because Johnson oversold the Great Society and Congress underfunded it, liberal aspirations outdistanced results.

Despite its many successes, the Great Society remained more a dream than a reality for some. The war against poverty, Martin Luther King, Jr., asserted, was "shot down on the battlefields of Vietnam." In 1966, Johnson spent twenty times more to wage war in Vietnam than to fight poverty in the United States. Yet the perceived liberality of federal spending and the "ungratefulness" of rioting blacks alienated many middle- and working-class whites. Others resented liberal regulation of business and the growing intrusiveness of government. The Democrats' loss of forty-seven House seats in 1966 ended the dominance of liberalism in Congress.

The Warren Court in the Sixties   The Supreme Court, led by Chief Justice Earl Warren, did much to promote the liberal agenda. Kennedy's appointment of two liberals to the Court, and Johnson of two more, including Thurgood Marshall, the Court's first black justice, resulted in a solid liberal majority that expanded individual rights to a greater extent than ever before in American history.

In a series of landmark cases, the Court prohibited Bible reading and prayer in public schools, limited local power to censor books and films, and overturned state bans on contraceptives. It ordered states to apportion legislatures on the principle of "one person, one vote," increasing the representation of urban minorities.

The Court's upholding of the rights of the accused in criminal cases, at a time of soaring crime rates, particularly incensed many Americans.

Criticism of the Supreme Court reached a climax in 1966 when it ruled in **Miranda v. Arizona** that police must advise suspects of their right to remain silent and to have counsel during questioning. In 1968, both Richard Nixon and George Wallace would win favor by promising to appoint judges who emphasized "law and order" over individual liberties.

VOICES OF PROTEST

The aura of liberalism in the 1960s markedly affected Native Americans Hispanic-Americans, Asian-Americans, and women. They, too, were inspired by Kennedy's rhetoric, by Johnson's actions, and by the assertive outlook of Black Power. Each followed the black lead in challenging the status quo, demanding full and equal citizenship rights, emphasizing group identity and pride, and seeing its younger members push for ever more radical action.

Native American Activism   In 1961 representatives of sixty-seven tribes drew up a Declaration of Purposes criticizing the termination policy of the 1950s as a subterfuge for neglect (see Chapter 27). In 1964 hundreds of Indians lobbied in Washington for the inclusion of Native Americans in the War on Poverty. Indians suffered the worst poverty, the most inadequate housing, the highest disease and death rates, and the least access to education of any group in the United States. Native American life expectancy, just 44 years, was a third less than that of other Americans. President Johnson responded by establishing the National Council on Indian Opportunity in 1965. It funneled more federal funds onto reservations than any previous program. Johnson also appointed the first Native American to head the Bureau of Indian Affairs (BIA) since 1870, and promised to erase "old attitudes of paternalism." Advocating Indian self-determination, Johnson insisted in a special message to Congress in 1968 on "the right of the First Americans to remain Indians while exercising their rights as Americans."

Militant Native Americans, meanwhile, began to organize. The National Indian Youth Council, organized in 1961, sponsored demonstrations and marches, and Native Americans in the San Francisco Bay Area established the Indian Historical Society in 1964 to present history from the Indian point of view. By 1968 younger Indian activists, calling themselves "Native Americans," demanded "Red Power." They voiced dissatisfaction with the accommodationist approach of their elders, the lack of protection for Indian land and water rights, the desecration of Indian graves and sacred sites, and legal prohibitions against certain Indian religious practices. They mocked Columbus Day and staged sit-ins against museums that housed Indian bones. They established reservation cultural programs to reawaken spiritual beliefs and teach Native languages. The Wampanoag in Massachusetts named Thanksgiving a National Day of Mourning. The Navajo and Hopi protested strip-mining in the Southwest, and the Taos Pueblo organized to reclaim the Blue Lake sacred site in northern New Mexico. The Puyallup held "fish-ins" to assert old treaty rights to fish in the Columbia River and Puget Sound, and in 1968 the Supreme Court declared that states could not invalidate fishing and hunting rights that Native Americans had acquired in treaties.

The most militant group, the **American Indian Movement** (AIM), was founded in 1968 by Chippewas, Sioux, and Ojibwa living in and around Minneapolis. Its goals were to promote the traditional ways of Native Americans, prevent police brutality and harassment of Indians in urban "red ghettos," and establish "survival schools" to teach Indian history and values. It established a "powwow circuit" to publicize Indian protest activities across the country, and in November 1969 AIM occupied Alcatraz Island in San Francisco Bay. Citing a Sioux Indian treaty that unused federal lands would revert to Indian control, an armed AIM contingent held the island for nineteen months before being dispersed. They made Alcatraz a symbol of the conditions on reservations: "It has no running water; it has inadequate sanitation facilities; there is no industry, and so unemployment is very great; there are no health care facilities; the soil is rocky and unproductive." The occupation helped foster a new sense of identity among American Indians. As one participant glowed, "we got back our worth, our pride, our dignity, our humanity."

AIM's militancy aroused other Native-Americans to be proud of their heritage. Their members "had a new look about them, not that hangdog reservation look I was used to," Mary Crow Dog remembered, and they "loosened a sort of earthquake inside me." Many of the eight hundred thousand who identified themselves as Indians in the 1970 census did so for the first time.

Hispanic-Americans Organize | The fastest-growing minority, Latinos, or Hispanic-Americans, also grew impatient with their establishment organizations. The Mexican American Political Association and other organizations had been able to do little to ameliorate the dismal existence of most of the 5 million Hispanic-Americans. With a median annual wage half the poverty level, with 40 percent of Mexican-American adults functionally illiterate, and with de facto segregation common throughout the Southwest, Latinos like **César Estrada Chávez** turned to the more militant tactics and strategies of the civil-rights movement.

Born on an Arizona farm first cultivated in the 1880s by his grandfather, Chávez grew up a migrant farm worker, joined the U.S. navy in World War II, and then devoted himself to gaining union recognition and improved working conditions for the mostly Mexican-American farm laborers in California—suffering from extremely high rates of illiteracy, unemployment, and poverty. A charismatic leader who, like Martin Luther King, Jr., blended religion with nonviolent resistance to fight for social change, Chávez led his followers in the Delano vineyards of the San Joaquin valley to strike in 1965. Similar efforts had been smashed in the past. But Chávez and United Farm Worker (UFW) cofounder Dolores Huerta organized consumer boycotts of table grapes to dramatize the farm workers' struggle. They made La Causa, as the farm workers' movement became known, part of the common struggle of the entire Mexican-American community and part of the larger national movement for civil rights and social justice. For the first time, farm workers gained the right to unionize to secure better wages; and by mid-1970, two-thirds of California grapes were grown under UFW contracts. Just as the UFW flag featured an Aztec eagle and the Virgin of Guadalupe, Chávez combined religion, labor militancy, and Mexican heritage to stimulate ethnic pride and politicization.

Also in the mid-1960s young Hispanic activists began using the formerly pejorative terms *Chicano* and *Chicana* to express a militant sense of collective identity and solidarity for all those of Mexican descent. They saw themselves as a people whose heritage had been rejected and whose culture had been taken from them. They insisted on their self-selected name to highlight pride in Mexico's culture and revolutionary tradition, and their insistence on self-determination: "Our main goal is to orient the Chicano to *think* Chicano so as to achieve equal status with other groups, not to emulate the Anglo."

Rejecting assimilation, Chicano student organizations came together in *El Movimiento Estudiantil Chicano de Aztlan* (MEChA) in 1967. They led Chicano high-school students in Los Angeles, Denver, and San Antonio in boycotts of classes (called "blowouts") in 1968 to protest poor educational conditions in their schools and to demand bilingual education. Congress responded by enacting legislation that encouraged school districts to adopt bilingual education programs to instruct non-English speakers in both English and their native language. Chicanos demonstrated at colleges to obtain courses that emphasized the history, art, language, and literature of Mexican-Americans. At the inaugural Chicano Youth Liberation Conference in 1969, they adopted *El Plan Espiritual de Aztlan,* a manifesto of cultural and political nationalism, and, on September 16, Mexican Independence Day, they led high-school students carrying placards emblazoned with "Viva la Raza!" in the First National Chicano Boycott of schools throughout the Southwest.

Similar zeal led poet Rodolfo "Corky" Gonzales to found the Crusade for Justice in Colorado in 1965 to fight police brutality, foster Chicano culture, and improve job opportunities for Mexican-Americans. It led Reies Lopez Tijerina to form the *Alianza Federal de Mercedes* in New Mexico to reclaim land usurped by whites in the 1848 Treaty of Guadalupe Hidalgo. It also led Jose Angel Gutierrez and others in Texas to create an alternative political party in 1967, *La Raza Unida,* to elect Latinos and instill cultural pride. Four Mexican-Americans would win seats in Congress in the 1960s, including Senator Joseph Montoya of New Mexico. Chicano activism also led to the expansion of the one person, one vote concept in much of the Southwest. It pushed many more Hispanics to go to college and to get involved in local politics; it helped create the first major English-speaking-and-writing intellectual community in the history of Latinos in the United States; and it ushered in a "brown is beautiful" vogue and the paramilitary Brown Berets.

Puerto Ricans in New York City founded the Young Lords, which they too modeled on the Black Panthers. They published *Palante* ("forward in the struggle"), which, like the newspapers *La Raza* in Los Angeles and *El Papel* in Albuquerque, popularized movement strategies and aims. The Young Lords started drug treatment programs, and hijacked ambulances and occupied a hospital to demand better medical services in the South Bronx. They also blockaded the streets of East Harlem with trash to force the city to provide improved sanitation services for the six hundred thousand Puerto Ricans living there.

Asian-American Activism

Like their counterparts, young activists with roots in East Asia rejected the term *Oriental* in favor of *Asian-American,* to signify their new ethnic consciousness. Formed at the University of California in 1968, the **Asian American Political Alliance** brought together Chinese-, Filipino-, and Japanese-American students. It encouraged Asian-Americans to claim their own cultural identity and, in racial solidarity with their "Asian brothers and sisters," to protest against the U.S. war in Vietnam. Many Asian-American students condemned the war as a racist attack upon the peoples of Southeast Asia and as a violation of the sovereignty of a small Asian nation.

As did other ethnic groups, Asian-American students marched, sat in, and went on strike to promote causes emphasizing their unique identity. Mainly in California, Hawaii, and New York, they campaigned for courses on Asian-American studies, and some universities, like the City College of New York, set up interdisciplinary departments. Students from the Philippines and South Korea organized protests against the repressive dictatorships in their homeland, while those from Samoa denounced the damage caused by nuclear testing in the Pacific islands.

Many Asian-American activists focused on improving the lives of their compatriots in need. In 1968, they organized demonstrations and marches in San Francisco to protest the poor housing and medical facilities in Chinatown, and led a struggle to save a low-income residential facility for Chinese and Filipino men. Others worked with trade union organizers to upgrade the pay and working conditions of Asians in garment manufacturing and in hotel and restaurant jobs. The Redress and Reparations Movement, initiated by third-generation Japanese Americans, agitated to force the government to make restitution for the wartime internment.

None of these movements for ethnic pride and power could sustain the fervent activism and media attention that they attracted in the late sixties. But by elevating the consciousness and nurturing the confidence of the younger generation, each contributed to the cultural pride of its respective group, and to the politics of identity that would continue to grow in importance.

A Second Feminist Wave

The rising tempo of activism in the 1960s also stirred a new spirit of self-awareness and dissatisfaction among educated women. A revived feminist movement emerged, profoundly altering women's view of themselves and their role in American life.

Several events fanned the embers of discontent into flames. The 1963 report of John Kennedy's Presidential Commission on the Status of Women documented occupational inequities that were similar to those endured by minorities. Women received less pay than men for comparable work; and they made up only 7 percent of the nation's doctors and less than 4 percent of its lawyers. The women who served on the presidential commission successfully urged that the Civil Rights Act of 1964 prohibit gender-based as well as racial discrimination in employment.

Dismayed by the Equal Employment Opportunity Commission's reluctance to enforce the ban on sex discrimination in employment, these women formed the **National Organization for Women (NOW)** in 1966. A civil-rights group for women, NOW labored "to bring women into full participation in the mainstream of American society." It lobbied for equal opportunity, filed lawsuits against gender discrimination, and mobilized public opinion against sexism.

NOW's prominence owed much to the publication of Betty Friedan's critique of domesticity, *The Feminine Mystique* (1963). Friedan's account of unfulfilled housewives deplored the notion that women should seek fulfillment solely as wives and mothers. Suburban domesticity—the "velvet ghetto"—left many women with feelings of emptiness, silently wondering, "Is this all?" Friedan urged women to return to school and to pursue careers that would establish their own, independent identity. What she called "the problem that has no name"—the deep but unexpressed feeling that home-making was not enough—resonated with many educated middle-class women. It informed them that they were not alone, and gave them a vocabulary with which to express their dissatisfaction.

Still another catalyst for feminism came from the involvement of younger women in the civil-rights and anti–Vietnam War movements. These activists had gained confidence in their own potential, an ideology to understand oppression, and experience in the strategy and tactics of organized protest. They also became conscious of their own second-class status, as they were sexually exploited and relegated to menial jobs by male activists. In the words of two women deeply involved in the civil-rights movement:

> Assumptions of male superiority are as widespread and deep-rooted and every much as crippling to the woman as the assumptions of white supremacy are to the Negro. . . . [We need to] stop the discrimination and start the slow process of changing values and ideas so that all of us gradually come to understand that this is no more a man's world than it is a white world.

The young women who shared such thoughts would soon create a women's liberation movement more critical of sexual inequality than NOW.

Women's Liberation

In 1968 militant feminists adopted "consciousness-raising" as a recruitment device and a means of transforming women's perceptions of themselves and society. Tens of thousands of women assembled in small groups to share experiences and air grievances. They learned that others felt dissatisfaction similar to their own. "When I saw that what I always felt were my own personal hangups was as true for every other woman in that room as it was for me! Well, that's when my consciousness was raised," a participant recalled. Women came to understand that their personal, individual problems were in fact shared problems with social causes and collective solutions—"the personal is political." They saw the power dynamics in marriage, the family, and the workplace. Consciousness-raising opened eyes and minds, and begot a sense that "sisterhood is powerful."

Women's liberation groups employed a variety of publicity-generating and confrontational tactics. In 1968 radical feminists crowned a sheep Miss America to dramatize their belief that such contests degraded women, and set up "freedom trash cans" in which women could discard high-heeled shoes, girdles, and other symbols of subjugation. They demanded inclusion in the Boston Marathon, no longer accepting the excuse that "it is unhealthy for women to run long distances." Overcoming male condescension and ridicule, they established health collectives and shelters for abused women, created day-care centers and rape crisis centers, founded abortion-counseling services and women's studies programs. They demanded equality in education and the workplace, and protested the negative portrayals of women in the media and advertising. Terms like *male chauvinist pig* entered the vocabulary and those like *chicks* exited. Some feminists claimed patriarchy, the power of men, to be the main cause of all oppressions and exploitations. Most rejected the notion that women were naturally passive and emotional, or that they suffered from "penis envy."

Despite a gulf between female radicals and liberals, they set aside their differences in August 1970 to join in the largest women's rights demonstration ever. Commemorating the fiftieth anniversary of woman suffrage, the Women's Strike for Equality brought out tens of thousands of women to parade for the right to equal employment and safe, legal abortions. By then the women's movement had already pressured many financial institutions to issue credit to single women and to married women in their own names. It had filed suit against numerous colleges and universities to secure salary raises for women faculty members victimized by discrimination, and ended newspapers' practice of listing employment opportunities under separate "Male" and "Female" headings. Guidelines that required corporations receiving federal funds to adopt nondiscriminatory hiring practices and equal pay scales had been established; and by 1970 more than 40 percent of all women held full-time jobs outside the home.

The right to control their own sexuality and decisions whether to have children also became a feminist rallying cry. In 1960 "the Pill" came on the market, giving women greater freedom to be sexually active without the risk of pregnancy (see Technology and Culture: The Pill). Many women, aware of the dangers of illegal abortions, pushed for their legalization. Some challenged demeaning obstetrical practices. Others explored alternatives to hospital births and popularized alternatives to radical mastectomy for breast cancer. Although antifeminism persisted, many women had become aware, in historian Gerda Lerner's words,

> that they belong to a subordinate group; that they have suffered wrongs as a group;
> that their condition of subordination is not natural, but societally determined; that
> they must join with other women to remedy these wrongs; and finally, that they
> must and can provide an alternative vision of societal organization in which
> women as well as men will enjoy autonomy and self-determination.

THE LIBERAL CRUSADE IN VIETNAM, 1961–1968

The activist liberals who boldly tried to uplift the downtrodden also went to war to contain communism and export democracy. Kennedy escalated Eisenhower's efforts in Vietnam in order to hold "the cornerstone of the Free World in Southeast Asia, the keystone in the arch, the finger in the dike." Johnson resolved, "I am not going to lose Vietnam, I am not going to be the president who saw Southeast Asia go the way China went." They would make a stand. The war in Vietnam pursued by liberals ended the era of liberalism. The nation's longest, most controversial, and only losing war ended the liberal consensus and divided the United States as had nothing since the Civil War.

Kennedy and Vietnam

Following the compromise settlement in Laos, President Kennedy resolved, as had President Eisenhower, not to give further ground in Southeast Asia. He feared the likely success of the nationalist guerrilla movement led by Ho Chi Minh, which sought to overthrow the American puppet government in Saigon and unify the country under communist rule, unless the United States acted. Accordingly, JFK ordered massive shipments of weaponry to South Vietnam, stepped up clandestine operations against the North, and increased the number of American forces stationed in Vietnam from less than seven hundred in 1960 to more than sixteen thousand by the end of 1963. Although he never instituted the massive troop buildup advocated by some in the Pentagon, JFK refused

The Pill

The pill to prevent conception had many fathers and at least two mothers. Most of them were initially concerned with world overpopulation, not women's sexual freedom. In Margaret Sanger (see Chapter 21) and Katharine McCormick, heir to the International Harvester Company fortune, the goals of the movements for birth control and for population control meshed. The two women wanted a safe, inexpensive contraceptive that would be easy to use in the poverty-stricken slums of the world. In the postwar climate that favored technological solutions to social problems, they recruited Gregory Pincus, a pharmaceutical scientist working in a small Massachusetts laboratory grandly called the Worcester Foundation for Experimental Biology. Pincus desperately needed money to keep his lab afloat. Assured of McCormick's support to the tune of $2 million, he went to work in 1950 on Sanger's request for an oral contraceptive that would be as simple to use and as plentiful as aspirin.

Like most scientists, Pincus drew heavily on the earlier work of others. Chemists in the 1930s had synthesized estrogen, the female hormone that prevents ovulation (stopping the female body from forming and releasing an egg). Others had worked on progestin, the hormone in the ovaries that keeps sperm from fertilizing an egg. Pincus utilized their experiments with rabbits, as well as Carl Djerassi's synthesis of steroids and the work of gynecologist Dr. John Rock. None of these scientists had birth control on their minds. Indeed, Rock, a Catholic, was seeking an effective hormonal pill to help women get pregnant.

After years of experimenting with hundreds of combinations of substances, Pincus and his collaborator, Dr. M. C. Chiang, synthesized a mixture of estrogen and progestin that they believed safe and effective in suppressing ovulation in most women. In dubiously ethical practices, Pincus set up field trials with psychiatric patients and male prisoners (thinking it might work on men). Puerto Rico was the site for his first large-scale clinical trial of the oral contraceptive—because he could "attempt in Puerto Rico certain experiments which would be very difficult in this country." He followed that with tests in Haiti. Called Enovid, and produced by the G. D. Searle drug company, the pills were approved by the Food and Drug Administration (FDA) in 1957, but for gynecological disorders—not as a contraceptive.

At the time, thirty states still had laws banning or restricting contraceptive use, and most drug companies feared the controversy such a pill would arouse. The other drug companies left it to G. D. Searle to ask the FDA to approve the drug as a contraceptive. In May 1960 the FDA approved Enovid for contraceptive use. It did so, in large part, because of widespread concern about overpopulation and the threat of communism. Many feared that a teeming nonwhite underclass was tailor-made for a communist takeover, and thought the likelihood of that threat could be minimized by controlling population and thus reducing hunger, poverty, and disease in the world.

Many American women embraced the new technology with enthusiasm, and Enovid unexpectedly helped to foster a sexual revolution in the United States. By

1965, despite being condemned as immoral by the Catholic Church and denounced as a technology of genocide by African-American militants, "the Pill" (as it was commonly called) had become the most popular form of birth control in the United States, used by 6.5 million married women (unmarried women were not counted in official reports). In 1968 Americans spent as much on the Pill as on all other contraceptive methods combined. By 1970 more than 10 million American women were "on the Pill."

Pincus was deluged with fan letters. A grateful user in St. Paul kissed his picture in the newspaper, "for this is the first year in her eight years of marriage that she has not been pregnant." And in a song named "The Pill," Loretta Lynn sang, "All these years I've stayed at home while you had all your fun/ And ev'ry year that's gone by another baby's come/ There's gonna be some changes made right here on Nurs'ry Hill/ You've set this chicken your last time, 'cause now I've got the Pill."

Although widespread use of the Pill and the sexual revolution occurred together, the former did not cause the latter. Primarily married women consumed the Pill in the 1960s. It would take larger social changes in the United States before doctors would readily prescribe it for unmarried women, before the young would claim sexual pleasure as a right, and before a woman's liberation movement would be strong enough to insist on a woman's right to control her own sexuality. Permissiveness resulted more from affluence and mobility, from changed attitudes and laws, than from the Pill. Still, the Pill disconnected fears of pregnancy from the pursuit of sexual pleasure, and breaking reproductive shackles made sexual freedom more likely. The greater degree of autonomy and choice in women's sexual-reproductive lives changed the experience and meaning of sex, in and out of marriage.

The Pill has not been a universal panacea. One woman's medical miracle became another's social concern and a third woman's health problem. High amounts of estrogen in the early pills caused blood clots and strokes, disabling many women. Because the Pill was available only with a doctor's prescription, the oral contraceptive increased doctors' control over the sexual lives of women. While conservatives sought to stem the tide of promiscuity and pornography they blamed on the Pill, feminists charged that women bore the costs of contraception because men controlled the medical profession and pharmaceutical industry. At the same time, liberalized sexual behavior proved less emancipating and more exploitative than feminists first expected, and the disagreement about such issues as birth control, abortion, premarital sex, and obscenity hastened the demise of the liberal consensus.

To date, the Pill has neither significantly limited population growth in the Third World nor ended the scourge of unwanted pregnancies in the United States. It has changed the dynamics of women's health care and altered gender relations. The first medicine produced for a social, rather than therapeutic, purpose, it remains the pharmaceutical swallowed as a daily routine by more humans than any other prescribed medication in the world.

Questions for Analysis

- To what extent is the Pill the cause of the sexual revolution?

- What have been the chief negative and positive consequences of the development of the Pill?

to accept a unified, communist Vietnam. He feared it would lead to a Republican-led, anticommunist backlash, damaging him politically. Like Eisenhower, he believed that letting "aggression" go unchecked would lead to wider wars (the Munich analogy), and that the communist takeover of one nation would lead to others going communist (the domino theory). Kennedy viewed international communism as a monolithic force, a global enemy controlled by Moscow and Beijing. Seeing Third World conflicts as tests of America's, and his own, will, he determined to show the world that the United States was not the "paper tiger" that Mao Zedong (Mao Tse-tung) mocked.

To counter Vietcong, or National Liberation Front (NLF), gains in the countryside, the United States dropped both chemical defoliants to destroy vegetation and deprive the Vietcong of natural cover, and napalm bombs—whose petroleum jelly burned at 1,000 degrees and clung to whatever it touched, including human flesh. It also forcibly uprooted Vietnamese peasants and moved them into fortified villages, or "strategic hamlets," to prevent infiltration by the Vietcong. But South Vietnamese president Diem rejected American pressure to gain popular support through reform measures, instead crushing demonstrations by students and Buddhists. By mid-1963, Buddhist monks were setting themselves on fire to protest Diem's repression, and Diem's own generals were plotting a coup.

Frustrated American policy makers concluded that only a new government could prevent a Vietcong victory and secretly encouraged a coup by Vietnamese army officers to overthrow Diem. On November 1, the military leaders struck, captured Diem and his brother, and shot them. Although the United States promptly recognized the new government (the first of nine South Vietnamese regimes in the next five years), it too made little headway against the Vietcong. JFK now faced two unpalatable alternatives: increase the combat involvement of American forces or withdraw and seek a negotiated settlement.

What Kennedy would have done remains unknown. Less than a month after Diem's death, John Kennedy himself fell to an assassin's bullet. His admirers contend that by late 1963 he favored the withdrawal of American forces after the 1964 election. "It is their war," he said publicly; ". . . it is their people and their government who have to win or lose the struggle." Yet the president followed this comment with a ringing restatement of his belief in the domino theory and a promise that America would not withdraw from the conflict. He had already transformed Eisenhower's "limited-risk gamble" into a major American military commitment, and he and his advisers continued to hold that an American victory in Vietnam was essential to check communism in Asia. National Security Adviser McGeorge Bundy, Secretary of Defense Robert McNamara, and Secretary of State Dean Rusk would counsel Kennedy's successor accordingly.

Escalation of the War
Now it was Johnson who had to choose between intervening decisively or withdrawing from an inherited conflict that three previous presidents had insisted the communists must not win. Privately describing Vietnam as "a raggedy-ass fourth-rate country" undeserving of American blood and dollars, LBJ feared that an all-out American military effort might lead to World War III. He foresaw that full-scale engagement in "that bitch of a war" would destroy "the woman I really loved—the Great Society." Yet Johnson also accepted the domino theory and Munich analogy, and thought that only American resolve would prevent a wider war. He, too, feared being thought "a coward, an unmanly man," and worried that a pullout would leave him vulnerable to conservative

MAP 28.2 The Vietnam War, to 1968

Wishing to guarantee an independent, noncommunist government in South Vietnam, Lyndon Johnson remarked in 1965, "We fight because we must fight if we are to live in a world where every country can shape its own destiny. To withdraw from one battlefield means only to prepare for the next."

accusations that he was "soft" on communism and to the destruction of his liberal programs.

Trapped between unacceptable alternatives, Johnson expanded the war, hoping that U.S. firepower would force Ho Chi Minh to the bargaining table. But the North Vietnamese and NLF calculated that they could gain more by outlasting the United States than by negotiating. So the war ground on.

In 1964 Johnson took bold steps to impress North Vietnam with American resolve and to block his opponent, Barry Goldwater, from capitalizing on Vietnam in the presidential campaign. In February he ordered the Pentagon to prepare for air strikes against North Vietnam. In May his advisers drafted a congressional resolution authorizing an escalation of American military action, and in July LBJ appointed General Maxwell Taylor, an advocate of escalation, as ambassador to Saigon.

In early August, North Vietnamese patrol boats allegedly clashed with two U.S. destroyers in the Gulf of Tonkin. Evidence of the attack was unclear, yet Johnson announced that Americans had been victims of Hanoi's "open aggression on the high seas." Johnson condemned the attacks as unprovoked, never admitting that the U.S. ships took part in covert raids against North Vietnam. He ordered air strikes on North Vietnamese naval bases and asked Congress to pass the previously prepared resolution giving him the authority to "take all necessary measures to repel any armed attack against the forces of the United States and to prevent further aggression." Assured by the president that this meant no "extension of the present conflict," the Senate passed the **Gulf of Tonkin Resolution** 88 to 2, and the House 416 to 0.

Privately, LBJ called the resolution "grandma's nightshirt—it covered everything." He considered it a mandate to commit U.S. forces as he saw fit. The blank check to determine the level of force made massive intervention more likely; and having once used force against North Vietnam made it easier to do so again. But the resolution would eventually allow opponents of the war to charge that Johnson had misled Congress and lied to the American people, as he would do again when he assured the public during the 1964 campaign that he would neither deploy American troops to fight in Vietnam nor extend the war by bombing North Vietnam.

The Endless War

Early in 1965, Johnson ordered "Operation Rolling Thunder," the sustained bombing of North Vietnam. It aimed to "break the will of North Vietnam" and force Hanoi to negotiate, to boost the morale of the Saigon government, and to stop the flow of soldiers and supplies coming from North Vietnam via the so-called Ho Chi Minh Trail. But despite the dropping of eight hundred tons of bombs a day on North Vietnam between 1965 and 1968, three times the tonnage dropped by all the combatants in World War II, it failed to achieve its objectives.

Unable to turn the tide by bombing, Johnson committed U.S. combat troops. Adopting a "meat-grinder" or attrition strategy, Johnson sought to inflict unacceptable casualties on the communists to force them to the peace table. Johnson sent 485,000 troops (a greater military force than the U.S. had deployed in Korea) to Vietnam by the end of 1967. But superiority in numbers and weaponry did not defeat an enemy that could choose when and where to attack and then melt back into the jungle. Determined to battle until the United States lost the will to fight, Hanoi matched each American troop increase with its own. No end was in sight.

Doves Versus Hawks

First among pacifists and socialists, then on college campuses, and lastly in the wider society, a growing number of Americans opposed the war. In March 1965, students and faculty at the University of Michigan staged the first teach-in to raise questions about U.S. intervention. All-night discussions of the war followed at universities from Maine to Oregon. Some twenty-five thousand people, mainly students, rallied in Washington that spring to protest the escalation, giving the antiwar movement crucial television coverage. In 1966, large-scale campus antiwar protests erupted. Students demonstrated against the draft and university research for the Pentagon. They proved to be only a prelude to 1967's massive Spring Mobilization to End the War in Vietnam protests in

LBJ's Vietnam Nightmare   *The Vietnam War spelled Johnson's undoing. Young peace demonstrators made known their feelings about the president's role in the war during a massive antiwar protest at the Pentagon in October 1967.*

New York and San Francisco, which drew half a million participants, and the October demonstrations at the Pentagon by another hundred thousand.

Intellectuals penning essays against the war, clergy holding peace vigils, and women lobbying Congress for "a peaceful solution" joined the chorus of opposition to the war. Some decried the massive bombing of an underdeveloped nation; some doubted that the United States could win at any reasonable cost; some feared the demise of the Great Society and liberalism. In 1967, prominent critics of the war, including Democratic senators William Fulbright, Robert Kennedy, and George McGovern, pediatrician Dr. Benjamin Spock, and Martin Luther King, Jr., spurred hundreds of thousands to participate in antiwar protests.

Critics also noted that the war's toll fell most heavily on the poor. Owing to college deferments, the use of influence, and a military-assignment system that shunted the better-educated to desk jobs, lower-class youths were twice as likely to be drafted and, when drafted, twice as likely to see combat duty as middle-class youths. About 80 percent of the enlisted men who fought in Vietnam came from poor and working-class families.

TV coverage of the war further eroded support. Scenes of children maimed by U.S. bombs and of dying Americans, replayed nightly, laid bare the horror of war and undercut the optimistic reports of government officials. Americans shuddered as they watched U.S. troops, supposedly winning the hearts and minds of the Vietnamese, burn villages and desecrate burial grounds.

Yet for every protestor shouting "Hell No, We Won't Go!" many more war supporters affixed bumper stickers reading "America, Love It or Leave It!" Until 1968, most Americans either supported the war or remained undecided. "I want to get out, but I don't want to give up" expressed a widespread view. They were not prepared to accept a communist victory over the United States.

Equally disturbing was how polarized the nation had grown. **"Hawks"** would accept little short of total victory, whereas **"doves"** insisted on negotiating, not fighting. Civility vanished. As Johnson lashed out at his critics as "nervous Nellies" and refused to de-escalate the conflict, demonstrators paraded past the White House chanting, "Hey, hey, LBJ, how many kids did you kill today?" By 1968, the president had become a virtual prisoner in the White House, unable to speak in public without being shouted down. So ended an era of hope and liberalism. Few Americans now believed in Kennedy's assurance that the nation could "pay any price, bear any burden, meet any hardship, support any friend, oppose any foe."

CONCLUSION

The Kennedy style of "can-do" vigor and liberal rhetoric captivated the media and obscured a so-so domestic record. Stymied by the conservative coalition in Congress, Kennedy did more to stimulate hope than to achieve change. Others would force changes from the bottom up, and the next president, Lyndon Johnson, would persuade Congress to make a reality of the liberal ideal of an activist government promoting a fairer life for all Americans. Fed up with the more legalistic, cautious strategy of the civil-rights movement in the past, young African-Americans initiated a new direct action phase in black America's struggle for equal rights. Their activism, bubbling up from the local level, led to the landmark Civil Rights and Voting Rights Acts, which ended the legality of racial discrimination and black disfranchisement, provided greater equality of opportunity for African-Americans, and nurtured the self-esteem of blacks. However, the laws left untouched the maladies of the urban black ghetto. There, unfulfilled expectations and frustrated hopes exploded into rioting, which, in turn, triggered a white backlash that undermined support for the liberal agenda.

That agenda had prompted Johnson to secure the Civil Rights Act and a tax cut in 1964. Then came the Great Society legislation promoting health, education, voting rights, urban renewal, immigration reform, federal support for the arts and humanities, protection of the environment, and a war against poverty—the most sweeping liberal measures since the New Deal, and a significant enlargement in the role of the federal government in the lives of most Americans.

This outpouring of liberal measures, along with the model of the African-American struggle for justice, inspired other minorities and women to fight for equality and dignity. Native Americans, Hispanic-Americans, Asian-Americans, and women took to the streets to demand their fair due. Subsequently, their younger, more militant activists, like their black counterparts, also parted ways with liberals over means and ends.

Most of all, the Vietnam War destroyed the liberal consensus. To prevent South Vietnam from being taken over by the communists, Kennedy significantly increased the number and fighting role of American advisers in Vietnam and gave the green light for a coup to overthrow Diem, the unpopular head of the government in Saigon. Inheriting a deteriorating limited war from Kennedy, LBJ also chose to escalate America's involvement, hoping to force North Vietnam to negotiate a compromise. Three years later, a half-million American troops were stationed in Vietnam, and the United States was dropping more bombs on Vietnam than had been dropped in World War II. Still, the United States was no closer to achieving its objective; and the nation was now polarized. While the administration claimed to see the light at the end of the tunnel, critics saw the light as a speeding train about to crash into American society.

29

A Time of Upheaval, 1968–1974

THE YOUTH MOVEMENT

In the 1950s, the number of American students pursuing higher education rose from 1 million to 4 million, and the number doubled to 8 million in the 1960s. By then, more than half the U.S. population was under thirty years of age. Breaking with its forty-year tradition, *Time* magazine in 1967 selected the entire baby-boom generation as its "Man of the Year." Their sheer numbers gave the young a collective identity and guaranteed that their actions would have impact. And not just in the United States. Major student demonstrations shook the governments of Japan, Korea, Turkey, and Venezuela in 1960 alone.

Most baby boomers followed conventional paths. They sought a secure place in the system, not its overthrow. They preferred beer to drugs, and football to political demonstrations. They joined fraternities and sororities and majored in subjects that would equip them for the job market. Whether or not they went to college—and fewer than half did—the vast majority had their eyes fixed on a good salary, a new car, and a traditional family. Many disdained long-haired protesters and displayed "My Country— Right or Wrong" bumper stickers.

Some politically engaged young people mobilized on the right, joining organizations like Young Americans for Freedom (YAF), which by 1970 boasted fifty thousand members—far more than any other student group. These youths idolized Barry Goldwater, not John Kennedy. They demanded a rollback of big government at home and called for victory in Vietnam. While many adhered to traditional values, other young conservatives embraced libertarian notions. Although a part of a conservative movement that would grow increasingly more powerful in the future, YAF was overshadowed in the 1960s by young activists in the New Left.

Toward a New Left Although a tiny minority of youth, an insurgent band of liberal arts majors and graduate students got the lion's share of attention. This liberal-minded minority welcomed the idealism of the civil-rights movement and the rousing call of President Kennedy for service to the nation. They admired the mavericks and outsiders of the fifties: iconoclastic comedian Mort Sahl; Beat poet Allen Ginsberg; and pop-culture rebel James Dean.

In June 1962, some sixty students adopted the Port Huron Statement. Determined not to be a "silent generation," they issued a broad critique of American society and a call for more genuine human relationships. Proclaiming themselves "a new left," they gave birth to the **Students for a Democratic Society (SDS).** Inspired by the sit-ins and freedom rides, SDS envisioned a nonviolent youth movement transforming the United States into a "participatory democracy" in which individuals would participate in making the decisions that affected their lives. SDS assumed that people who controlled their own lives would value love and creativity, and would end materialism, militarism, and racism.

The generation of activists who found their agenda in the Port Huron Statement had their eyes opened by the police dogs and fire hoses in Birmingham, the assassination of President Kennedy, and the destruction of Vietnam brought so graphically into their homes by television. Most never joined SDS, instead associating with what they vaguely called "the Movement" or "the New Left." Unlike the Leftists of the 1930s, they rejected Marxist ideology and emulated SNCC's rhetoric and style. Many became radicalized by the rigidity of campus administrators and mainstream liberalism's inability to achieve fundamental change. Only a radical rejection of compromise and consensus, they presumed, could restructure society along humane and democratic lines.

From Protest to Resistance Returning from the Mississippi Freedom Summer to the Berkeley campus of the University of California in fall 1964, Mario Savio and other student activists ventured to solicit funds and recruit volunteers near the campus gate, a spot traditionally open to political activities. Prodded by local conservatives, the university suddenly banned such practices. That led Savio to found the **Berkeley Free Speech Movement (FSM),** a coalition of student groups insisting on the right to campus political activity. Likening the university to a giant machine, and its students to interchangeable machine parts, Savio insisted, "There is a time when the operation of the machine becomes so odious, makes you so sick to heart, that you've got to put your bodies upon the gears and upon the wheels . . . and you've got to make it stop." More than a thousand students joined Savio in a sit-in on the administrative "gears." Their arrests led to more demonstrations and a strike by nearly 70 percent of the student body.

By 1965 Mario Savio's call for students to throw their bodies upon "the machine" until it ground to a halt had reverberated on campuses nationwide. The FSM catalyzed a wave of campus protests. Students sat in to halt compulsory ROTC (Reserve Officers' Training Corps) programs, rallied to protest dress codes and parietal rules, and marched to demand changes in the grading system. They demanded fewer required courses, smaller classes, and teaching-oriented rather than research-oriented professors. They threatened to close down universities unless they admitted more minority students and stopped doing research for the military-industrial complex.

The escalation of the war in Vietnam, and the abolition of automatic student deferments from the draft in January 1966, turned the Movement into a *mass* movement.

CHRONOLOGY, 1964–1974

1964 • Berkeley Free Speech Movement (FSM).
The Beatles arrive in the United States.

1965 • Ken Kesey and Merry Pranksters stage first "acid test."

1966 • Abolition of automatic student deferments from the draft.

1967 • March on the Pentagon.
Israeli-Arab Six-Day War.

1968 • Tet offensive.
Martin Luther King, Jr., assassinated; race riots sweep nation.
Students take over buildings at Columbia University.
Robert F. Kennedy assassinated.
Violence mars Democratic convention in Chicago.
Vietnam peace talks open in Paris.
Richard Nixon elected president.

1969 • Apollo 11 lands first Americans on the moon.
Nixon begins withdrawal of U.S. troops from Vietnam.
Woodstock festival.

1970 • United States invades Cambodia.
Students killed at Kent State and Jackson State Universities.
Beatles disband.
Earth Day first celebrated.

1971 • United States invades Laos.
Swann v. *Charlotte-Mecklenburg Board of Education.*
New York Times publishes Pentagon Papers.
Nixon institutes wage-and-price freeze.
South Vietnam invades Laos with the help of U.S. air support.

1972 • Nixon visits China and the Soviet Union.
SALT I agreement approved.
Break-in at Democratic National Committee headquarters in
Watergate complex.
Nixon reelected president.

1973 • Vietnam cease-fire agreement signed.
Senate establishes special committee to investigate Watergate.
President Salvador Allende ousted and murdered in Chile.
Vice President Spiro Agnew resigns; Gerald Ford appointed vice president.
Roe v. *Wade.*
Yom Kippur War; OPEC begins embargo of oil to the West.
Saturday Night Massacre.

1974 • House Judiciary Committee votes to impeach Nixon.
Nixon resigns; Ford becomes president.

Popularizing the slogan "Make Love—Not War," SDS organized teach-ins, sponsored antiwar marches and rallies, and harassed campus recruiters for the military and the Dow Chemical Company, the chief producer of flesh-burning napalm and Agent Orange, the chemical used to defoliate Vietnam forests. In 1967 SDS leaders encouraged even more provocative protests. With the rallying cry "From Protest to Resistance," they supported draft resistance and civil disobedience in selective service centers, and clashed with federal marshals during the "siege of the Pentagon" in October's "Stop the Draft Week." At the Spring Mobilization to End the War in Vietnam, which attracted a half-million antiwar protesters, SDS members led the chants of "Burn cards, not people" and "Hell, no, we won't go!" By 1968 SDS claimed one hundred thousand members on three hundred campus chapters.

Spring 1968 saw at least forty thousand students on a hundred campuses demonstrate against war and racism. Most, but not all, stayed peaceful. In April militant Columbia University students shouting "Gym Crow must go" took over the administration building and held a dean captive to denounce the university's proposed expansion into Harlem to construct a gymnasium. The protest then expanded into a demonstration against the war and university military research. A thousand students barricaded themselves inside campus buildings, declaring them "revolutionary communes." Outraged by the harshness of the police who retook the buildings by storm and sent more than a hundred demonstrators to the hospital, the moderate majority of Columbia students joined a boycott of classes that shut down the university. Elsewhere, students in France, Germany, Ireland, Italy, Japan, and Mexico rose up to demand reform that year. In Prague, Czechoslovakian students singing Beatles songs battled Soviet tanks.

1969 saw the high point of the Movement with the New Mobilization, a series of huge antiwar demonstrations culminating in mid-November with a March Against Death. Three hundred thousand protestors came to Washington, D.C., to march through a cold rain carrying candles and signs with the names of soldiers killed or villages destroyed in Vietnam. By then, antiwar sentiment pervaded national institutions, and by 1972 it would be dominant. In sharp contrast to the apolitical students of the 1950s, youth in the 1960s proved themselves able to influence what affected their own lives.

Kent State and Jackson State

A storm of violence in spring of 1970 marked the effective end of the student movement as a political force. On April 30, 1970, Richard M. Nixon, LBJ's successor, jolted a war-weary nation by announcing that he had ordered U.S. troops to invade Cambodia, a neutral Indochinese nation that had become a staging area for North Vietnamese forces. Nixon had decided to extricate the United States from Vietnam by "Vietnamizing" the ground fighting (that is, using South Vietnamese troops instead of Americans) and intensifying bombing. Students, lulled by periodic announcements of troop withdrawals from Vietnam, now felt betrayed.

At Kent State University in Ohio, as elsewhere, student frustrations unleashed new turmoil. Radicals broke windows and torched the ROTC building. Nixon branded the protesters "bums," his vice president compared them to Nazi storm troopers, and the Ohio governor slapped martial law on the university. Three thousand National Guardsmen in full battle gear rolled onto the campus in armored personnel carriers.

"My God, They're Killing Us"   *Following President Nixon's announcement of the military incursion into Cambodia, a formally neutral nation, many colleges exploded in anger. To quell the protests at Kent State University, where more than a thousand students clashed with local police, Ohio National Guardsmen fired on students, killing four. News of the shootings outraged many students nationwide, touching off yet another round of campus protests, which led hundreds of colleges to cancel final exams and shut down for the semester.*

The day after the guard's arrival, six hundred Kent State students demonstrated against the Cambodian invasion. Suddenly a campus policeman boomed through a bullhorn, "This assembly is unlawful! This is an order—disperse immediately!" Students shouted back, "Pigs off campus!" Some threw stones. With bayonets fixed, the guardsmen moved toward the rally and laid down a blanket of tear gas. Hundreds of demonstrators and onlookers, choking and weeping, ran from the advancing troops. Guardsmen in Troop G, poorly trained in crowd control, raked the retreating students with M-1 rifle fire. When the shooting stopped, four students lay dead and eleven wounded. None was a campus radical.

Ten days later, Mississippi state patrolmen responding to a campus protest fired into a women's dormitory at historically black **Jackson State College,** killing two students and wounding a dozen others. Nationwide, students exploded in protest against the violence, the war, and the president. Student strikes closed down four hundred colleges, many of which had seen no previous unrest. The war had come home.

The nation was polarized. Although many students blamed Nixon for widening the war and applauded the demonstrators' goals, most Americans blamed the victims for the violence and criticized students for undermining U.S. foreign policy. They had enough of sit-ins at local draft boards, antiwar demonstrations, and draft-card burnings. Patriotism, class resentment of privileged college students, and a fear of social chaos animated America's condemnation of protesters. Many Kent townspeople shared the view of a local merchant who asserted that the guard had "made only one mistake—they should have fired sooner and longer." A local ditty promised, "The score is four, and next time more."

Legacy of Student Frenzy
The campus disorders after the invasion of Cambodia were the final spasm of a tumultuous movement. When a bomb planted by three antiwar radicals destroyed a science building at the University of Wisconsin in summer 1970, killing a graduate student, most young people condemned the tactic. With the resumption of classes in the fall, the fad of "streaking"—racing across campus in the nude—more reminiscent of the 1920s than the 1960s, signaled a change in the student mood. By then, Nixon had significantly reduced the number of young men being drafted, and the entire conscription system was soon to be ended, decreasing student opposition to the war. In addition, antiwar activists turned to other causes, or to communes, careers, and parenthood. A handful of radicals went underground, committing terrorist acts that justified the government's repression of the remnants of the antiwar movement. The New Left fell victim to government harassment, to its own internal contradictions, and to Nixon's winding down the Vietnam War.

The consequences of campus upheavals outlived the New Left. Student radicalism spurred the resentment of millions of Americans, helping shatter the liberal consensus. It gave religious evangelicals, southern segregationists, and blue-collar workers yet another reason to vote conservative, and propelled Republicans like Ronald Reagan to prominence. In 1966 he won California's governorship by denouncing Berkeley demonstrators and Watts rioters. The actor-turned-politician then won a resounding reelection victory by condemning young radicals. "If it takes a bloodbath, let's get it over with," he declared. "No more appeasement!" Nationwide, Republicans gained office with similar promises, heralding a vital change in American politics from liberalism to conservatism.

The New Left had, however, helped mobilize public opposition to the Vietnam War. It energized campuses into a force that the government could not ignore, and it made continued U.S. involvement in Vietnam difficult. The Movement also liberalized many facets of campus life and made university governance less authoritarian. Dress codes and curfews virtually vanished; ROTC disappeared entirely from some campuses, and went from a requirement to an elective at others; minority recruitment increased, and Black Studies programs proliferated; and students gained a larger role in decision making on campus.

Some New Left veterans remained active in 1970s causes, especially environmentalism, consumer advocacy, and the antinuclear movement. Female students in the Movement formed the backbone of a women's liberation movement. These involvements, however, fell short of the New Left vision of remaking the social and political order. While masses of students could be mobilized in the short run for a particular cause, only a few made long-term commitments to Movement activism. The generation that the New Left had hoped would be the vanguard of radical change preferred pot to politics, and rock to revolution.

THE COUNTERCULTURE

The alienation and hunger for change that drew some youths into radical politics led others to cultural rebellion, to focusing on personal rather than political change, to discarding middle-class values, attitudes, and practices. Rejecting the repressed authority of the established order, hardcore **hippies** disdained employment and consumerism, preferring to make what they needed, share it with others, and not want what they did not have. Love, cooperation, community, and immediate gratification became their mantra. In the second half of the 1960s they joined communes and tribes that glorified liberation from monogamy and private property. In urban areas such as San Francisco's Haight-Ashbury district and Atlanta's Fourteenth Street—"places where you could take a trip without a ticket"—they experimented with drugs, mysticism, and uninhibited sexuality. Some embarked on an almost religious quest for "authenticity" and "personal fulfillment." Historian Theodore Roszack called them "a **'counter culture'** . . . a culture so radically disaffiliated from the mainstream assumptions of our society that it scarcely looks to many as a culture at all, but takes on the alarming appearance of a barbarian intrusion."

Hippies and Drugs Illustrative of the gap between the two cultures, one saw marijuana as a "killer weed," a menace to health and life, and the other thought it a harmless social relaxant. In the absence of scientific evidence proving the drug dangerous, at least half the college students in the late sixties tried marijuana. A minority used hallucinogenic or mind-altering drugs, particularly LSD. The high priest of LSD was Timothy Leary, a former Harvard psychologist fired in 1963 for encouraging students to experiment with drugs—to "tune in, turn on, drop out." On the West Coast, writer Ken Kesey and his followers, the Merry Pranksters, conducted "acid tests" (distributing free tablets of LSD in orange juice), and created the "psychedelic" craze of Day-Glo-painted bodies gyrating to electrified rock music under flashing strobe lights.

The counterculture sought a world in which magic and mysticism replaced science and reason, and where competitive individuals became caring and loving. Some youths distanced themselves from middle-class respectability, flaunted outrageous personal styles ("do your own thing"), and expressed contempt for consumerism by wearing surplus military clothing, torn jeans, and tie-dyed T-shirts. Especially galling to adults, many young men sported shaggy beards and long hair. Typical of the generation that had been schooled in the deprivation and duty of the 1930s and 1940s, Governor Ronald Reagan of California defined a hippie as one "who looked like Tarzan, walked like Jane, and smelled like Cheetah."

Musical Revolution Popular music both echoed and developed a separate generational identity, a distinct youth culture. In the early 1960s folk songs protesting war and racism mirrored the early decade's optimistic idealism. Bob Dylan sang hopefully of changes "blowin' in the wind" and indignantly of changes that would "shake your windows and rattle your walls."

"Beatlemania" swept the country in 1964. They would soon be joined by the Rolling Stones, the Motown rhythm-and-blues black performers, and eardrum-shattering acid rockers—each extolling "sex, drugs, and rock-and-roll" for a generation at war.

In August 1969, four hundred thousand young people gathered for the **Woodstock festival** in New York's Catskill Mountains to celebrate their vision of freedom and harmony. For three days and nights, they reveled in rock music and openly shared drugs, sexual partners, and contempt for the Establishment. The counterculture heralded Woodstock as the dawning of an era of love, peace, and sharing—the Age of Aquarius.

In fact, the counterculture's luster had already dimmed. Prominent rock performers died of drug overdoses. The pilgrimage of "flower children" to the Haight-Ashbury district of San Francisco and to New York's East Village in 1967 brought a train of rapists and dope peddlers. In December 1969, hippie Charles Manson and his "family" of runaways ritually murdered a pregnant movie actress and four of her friends, and the Rolling Stones hired the Hell's Angels motorcycle gang to guard them at the rock concert at the Altamont Raceway near San Francisco. While the Stones performed, the Hell's Angels terrorized spectators and stabbed and stomped a young black man to death. In 1970, the Beatles disbanded. On his own, John Lennon sang, "The dream is over. What can I say?"

Advertisers awoke to the economic potential of the youth culture, using "rebellion" and "revolution" to sell cars and jeans. Most youths found conventional jobs and adopted traditional lifestyles. Although cynics concluded that counterculture values were not deeply held, its rosy view of human nature and skeptical attitude toward authority continued to influence American education and society long after the 1960s. Self-fulfillment remained a popular goal, and the repressive sexual standards of the 1950s did not return.

The Sexual Revolution

The counterculture's "if it feels good, do it" approach to sex fit the hedonistic and permissive ethic of the 1960s. This shift in attitude and behavior accelerated the sexual revolution. Although the AIDS epidemic and the graying of the baby boomers in the late 1980s chilled the ardor of heedless promiscuity, liberalized sexual mores were more publicly accepted than ever before, making full gender equality a realizable goal.

Many commentators linked the increase in sexual permissiveness to waning fears of unwanted pregnancy. In 1960 oral contraceptives reached the market, and by 1970 ten million women were taking the Pill. Still other women used the intrauterine device (IUD, later banned as unsafe) or the diaphragm. Some states legalized abortion. In New York in 1970 one fetus was legally aborted for every two babies born. The Supreme Court's **Roe v. Wade** (1973) struck down all remaining state laws infringing on a woman's right to abortion during the first trimester (three months) of pregnancy. Further fueling the sexual revolution, many universities ended their rules on dormitory visits and living off campus, and the counterculture emphasized casual sex, public nudity, and a four-letter word as a revolutionary challenge to bourgeois "uptight Amerika."

By the end of the 1960s, the Supreme Court had ruled unconstitutional any laws restricting "sexually explicit" art with "redeeming social importance." Mass culture exploited the new permissiveness. *Playboy* featured ever-more-explicit erotica, and women's periodicals encouraged their readers to enjoy recreational sex. The commercial success of films given "R" or "X" ratings led Broadway producers to present plays featuring full-frontal nudity and mock orgies. Even television began to allow sexual jokes and frank discussions of once forbidden subjects. Identifying pornography and obscenity as "a matter of national concern," Congress established a special commission to suggest a plan of attack. Instead, the commission in 1970 recommended the repeal of all obscenity and pornography laws. By then, most barriers to expressions of sexuality had fallen in literature, Broadway plays, and Hollywood films.

Attitudinal changes brought behavioral changes, and vice versa. Cohabitation—living together without marriage—became thinkable to average middle-class Americans. Some marital counselors even touted "open marriage" (in which spouses are free to have sex with other partners) and "swinging" (sexual sharing with other couples) as cures for stale relationships. The use of contraceptives (and to some extent, even of abortion) spread to women of all religious backgrounds—including Roman Catholics, despite the Catholic Church's stand against "artificial" birth control.

Gay Liberation   Stimulated by the other protest movements in the sixties, **gay liberation** emerged publicly in late June 1969. During a routine raid by New York City police, the homosexual patrons of the Stonewall Inn, a gay bar in Greenwich Village, unexpectedly fought back. The furor triggered a surge of "gay pride," a new sense of identity and self-acceptance, and widespread activism. The gay liberation movement that emerged built on the reform-minded Mattachine Society and the Daughters of Bilitis, as well as other "homophile" groups that focused on equal rights and assimilation. But the new liberation movement went far beyond the "rights-based" organizations in brazenly asserting its sexual orientation, "We are going to be who we are."

Supporters of the Gay Liberation Front came primarily from the gay subcultures found in the largest cities. By 1973 some eight hundred openly gay groups were fighting for equal rights for homosexuals, for incorporating lesbianism into the women's movement, and for removing the stigma of immorality and depravity attached to being gay. That year, they succeeded in getting the American Psychiatric Association to rescind its official view of homosexuality as a mental disorder, and to reclassify it as a normal sexual orientation.

Simultaneously, several cities and states began to broaden their civil-rights statutes to include "sexual orientation" as a protected status, and in 1975 the U.S. Civil Service Commission officially ended its ban on the employment of homosexuals. Millions of gays had "come out," demanding public acceptance of their sexual identity.

The baby boomers transformed sexual relations as much as gender and racial relations. The institutions of marriage and family were fundamentally altered. Women could have access to birth control, abortion, and an active sex life with or without a male partner. But what some hailed as liberation others bemoaned as moral decay. Offended by openly gay men and lesbians, and by "topless" bars, X-rated theaters, and "adult" bookstores, many Americans applauded politicians who promised a war on immorality. The public association of the counterculture, the sexual revolution, and gay liberation with student radicalism and ghetto riots swelled the tide of conservatism as the decade ended.

1968: The Politics of Upheaval

The social and cultural upheavals of the late sixties unfolded against a backdrop of frustration with the war in Vietnam and disillusionment with liberalism. The stormy events of 1968 would culminate in a tempest of a political campaign and a turbulent realignment in American politics, the first since the New Deal.

The Tet Offensive in Vietnam   In January 1968 liberal Democratic senator **Eugene McCarthy** of Minnesota, a Vietnam War critic, announced that he would challenge LBJ for the presidential nomination. Experts scoffed that McCarthy had no chance of unseating Johnson, who had won the presidency in 1964 by the largest margin in U.S. history. The last time such an insurgency had been attempted, in 1912, even the wildly popular Teddy Roosevelt had failed. Yet McCarthy persisted, determined that at least one Democrat enter the primaries on an antiwar platform.

Suddenly, on January 31—the first day of Tet, the Vietnamese New Year—America's hopes for victory in Vietnam exploded, and with them LBJ's political fortunes. National Liberation Front (NLF) and North Vietnamese forces mounted a huge **Tet offensive,** attacking more than a hundred South Vietnamese cities and towns, and even the U.S. embassy in Saigon for a few hours. U.S. and South Vietnamese troops eventually repulsed the offensive, inflicting a major military defeat on the communists, who failed to unleash a general uprising against the government in Saigon or to hold any South Vietnamese city.

Victory, however, came at an enormous psychological cost. The dramatic initial reports of the media, highlighting the number of American casualties and the grand scope of the Tet offensive, undercut Johnson's and General Westmoreland's claims of imminent victory, of "light at the end of the tunnel." However much supporters of the war blamed the media for ignoring the heavy losses to the NLF and the North Vietnamese, thereby turning "victory" into "defeat," the Tet offensive deepened the growing mood of gloom about the war and intensified doubts that the United States could win at an acceptable cost. Public approval of the president's conduct of the war fell to just 26 percent in the immediate aftermath of Tet.

After Tet, McCarthy's criticism of the war won many new sympathizers. *Time, Newsweek,* and influential newspapers published editorials urging a negotiated settlement. NBC's news anchorman concluded that "the grand objective—the building of a free nation—is not nearer, but further, from realization." The nation's premier newscaster, Walter Cronkite of CBS, observed, "It seems more certain than ever that the bloody experience of Vietnam is to end in a stalemate." "If I've lost Walter," LBJ sighed, "then it's over. I've lost Mr. Average Citizen." The number of Americans who described themselves as prowar "hawks" slipped from 62 percent in January to 41 percent in March, while the antiwar "doves" jumped from 22 percent to 42 percent.

A Shaken President   Beleaguered, Johnson pondered a change in American policy. When the Joint Chiefs of Staff sought 206,000 more men for Vietnam, he turned to old friends for advice. Former secretary of state and venerable Cold Warrior Dean Acheson told him, "the Joint Chiefs of Staff don't know what they're talking about." Clark Clifford, once a hawk and now secretary of defense, concluded "that the military course we were pursuing was not only endless but hopeless."

Meanwhile, nearly five thousand college students had swarmed to New Hampshire to stuff envelopes and ring doorbells for Eugene McCarthy in the nation's first primary contest. "Clean for Gene," they cut their long hair and dressed conservatively so as not to alienate potential supporters. McCarthy astonished the experts by winning nearly half the popular vote in a state usually regarded as conservative.

After this upset, twice as many students converged on Wisconsin to canvass its more liberal voters. Expecting Johnson to lose, Senator **Robert Kennedy,** also promising to end the war, entered the Democratic contest. Projecting the familiar Kennedy glamour and magnetism, Robert Kennedy was the one candidate whom Johnson feared could deny him renomination. Indeed, millions viewed Kennedy as the rightful heir to the White House. Appealing to minorities, the poor, and working-class ethnic whites, Kennedy became, according to a columnist, "our first politician for the pariahs, our great national outsider."

On March 31, exactly three years after the marines had splashed ashore at Danang, Johnson surprised a television audience by announcing a halt to the bombing in North Vietnam. Adding that he wanted to devote all his efforts to the search for peace, LBJ startlingly announced, "I shall not seek, and I will not accept, the nomination of my party for another term as your president." Embittered by the personal abuse he had endured and reluctant to polarize the nation further, LBJ called it quits. "I tried to make it possible for every child of every color to grow up in a nice house, eat a solid breakfast, to attend a decent school and to get a good and lasting job," he grumbled privately. "But look at what I got instead. Riots in 175 cities. Looting. Burning. Shooting. . . . Young people by the thousands leaving the university, marching in the streets." Both physically and emotionally spent, LBJ lamented, "The only difference between the [John F.] Kennedy assassination and mine is that I am alive and it has been more torturous." Two days later, pounding the final nail into Johnson's political coffin, McCarthy trounced the president in the Wisconsin primary.

Ignored and often forgotten in retirement, Johnson died of a heart attack in January 1973—ironically, on the same day that the Paris Peace Accords ended America's direct combat role in Vietnam. In many ways a tragic figure, he had carried out Vietnam policies shaped by his predecessors and received little acclaim for his enduring domestic achievements, especially in civil rights and reducing poverty. Although he often displayed high idealism and generosity of spirit, the enduring image of LBJ remained that of a crude, overbearing politician with an outsized ego that masked deep insecurities.

Assassinations and Turmoil

Three days after the Wisconsin primary, a high-powered bullet from a sniper's rifle killed Martin Luther King, Jr., as he stood on a motel balcony in Memphis, Tennessee. Because of his increasing concern about poverty in America, and his plans for an upcoming Poor People's Campaign, King had gone there to support striking black sanitation workers. The assassin, James Earl Ray, an escaped convict and white racist, would confess, be found guilty, and then recant, leaving aspects of the killing unclear. As in the assassination of John Kennedy, it seemed too insignificant that one misfit was alone responsible. What was clear in 1968 was that the national symbol of nonviolent protest and progressive social change had been murdered. As the news spread, black ghettos in 125 cities burst into violence. Twenty blocks of Chicago's West Side went up in flames, and Mayor Richard Daley ordered police to shoot to kill arsonists. In Washington, D.C., under night skies illuminated by seven hundred fires, army units in combat gear set up machine-gun nests outside the Capitol and White House. The rioting left 46 dead, 3,000 injured, and nearly 27,000 in jail.

Entering the race as the favorite of the party bosses and labor chieftains, LBJ's vice president, **Hubert Humphrey,** turned the contest for the nomination into a three-cornered scramble. McCarthy remained the candidate of the "new politics"—a moral crusade against war and injustice directed to affluent, educated liberals. Kennedy campaigned as the tribune of the less privileged, the sole candidate who appealed to both the white ethnic working class and the minority poor. In early June, after his victory in the California primary, the brother of the murdered president was himself assassinated by a deranged Palestinian refugee, Sirhan Sirhan, who loathed Kennedy's pro-Israeli views.

The deaths of King and Kennedy further estranged young activists, convinced others of the futility of nonviolence, and devastated the already beleaguered forces of liberalism. The dream of peace and justice turned to despair. "I won't vote," a youth said. "Every good man we get they kill." "We shall not overcome," concluded a Kennedy speechwriter. "From this time forward things would get worse, not better. Our best political leaders were part of memory now, not hope."

While Kennedy's death cleared the way for Humphrey's nomination, increasing numbers of Democrats turned to third-party candidate George Wallace's thinly veiled appeal for white supremacy or to the GOP nominee Richard M. Nixon. The Republican appealed to those disgusted with inner-city riots and antiwar demonstrations. He claimed to have a "secret plan" to end the war, lambasted the liberal decisions of the Warren Court, and derided hippies and protestors. Nixon also said he would heed "the voice of the great majority of Americans, the forgotten Americans, the non-shouters, the non-demonstrators, those who do not break the law, people who pay their taxes and go to work, who send their children to school, who go to their churches, . . . who love this country." Tapping the same wellsprings of anger and frustration, but without Nixon's restraint, Wallace pitched a fiery message to southern segregationists and working-class northerners, denouncing welfare mothers, antiwar demonstrators, and black militants. If elected, Wallace vowed to throw "over-educated, ivory-tower" federal bureaucrats "into the Potomac," and to crack down on "long-hair, pot-smoking, draft-card-burning youth."

In August 1968, violence outside the Democratic National Convention in Chicago reinforced the appeal of both Wallace and Nixon. Thousands descended on the city to protest peacefully against the war. Some radicals, however, wanted to provoke a confrontation to discredit the Democrats, and a handful of anarchistic **"Yippies"** (the Youth International Party, led by counterculture guru Abbie Hoffman) sought to ridicule the political system by threatening to dump LSD in Chicago's water system and to release greased pigs in the city's crowded Loop area.

Determined to avoid the rioting that had wracked Chicago after King's assassination, Mayor Richard Daley denied demonstrators permits to march or engage in meaningful protest, and gave police a green light to attack "the hippies, the Yippies, and the flippies." The savagery of the Chicago police fulfilled the radicals' desire for mass disorder. On August 28, as a huge national television audience looked on and protesters chanted "The whole world is watching," Daley's bluecoats took off their badges and clubbed demonstrators, tossed tear gas at bystanders, and bloodied reporters and photographers. The brutality on the streets overshadowed Humphrey's nomination, tore the Democrats farther apart, and created an enduring image of them as the party of dissent and disorder. Although an investigative panel later described the melee as a "police riot," 70 percent of Americans supported the police violence against the protestors. The real victor in Chicago was conservatism.

Conservative Resurgence

Nixon capitalized on the televised turmoil to attract the support of voters desperate for "law and order." His TV campaign commercials flashed images of campus and ghetto upheavals. He portrayed himself as the candidate of the Silent Majority, "the working Americans who have become forgotten Americans." He criticized the Supreme Court for safeguarding criminals and radicals, vowed to get people off welfare rolls and on payrolls, and asserted that "our schools are for education—not integration."

Also appealing to the reaction against liberalism, George Wallace stoked the fury of the working class against "bearded anarchists, smart-aleck editorial writers, and pointy-headed professors looking down their noses at us." Promising to keep peace in the streets, he vowed that "if any demonstrator ever lays down in front of my car, it'll be the last car he'll ever lie down in front of." In September Wallace climbed to 21 percent in voter-preference polls. Although many shared his views, few believed he had any chance of winning, and either did not vote or switched to his opponents. Still, 14 percent of the electorate—primarily young, lower-middle-class, small-town workers—cast their votes for Wallace.

MAP 29.1 The Election of 1968

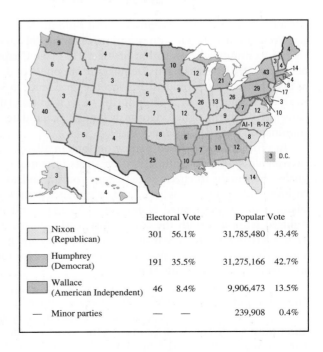

	Electoral Vote		Popular Vote	
Nixon (Republican)	301	56.1%	31,785,480	43.4%
Humphrey (Democrat)	191	35.5%	31,275,166	42.7%
Wallace (American Independent)	46	8.4%	9,906,473	13.5%
— Minor parties	—	—	239,908	0.4%

Nixon and Humphrey split the rest of the vote almost evenly. Nixon's 301 votes in the Electoral College was the narrowest triumph since Woodrow Wilson's in 1916. But, with Humphrey receiving just 38 percent of the white vote and not even close to half the labor vote, the long-dominant New Deal coalition was shattered and the liberal era ended.

The 57 percent of the electorate who chose Nixon or Wallace would dominate American politics for the rest of the century. While the Democratic Party fractured into a welter of contending groups, the Republicans attracted a new majority, many of whom lived in the Sunbelt—the metropolitan South, the sun country of Florida, the desert Southwest and Texas, and populous southern California. Kevin Phillips, whose advice to Nixon to focus on Sunbelt voters was published in 1969 as *The Emerging Republican Majority,* described its residents as "the pleasure-seekers, the bored, the ambitious, the space-age technicians and the retired—a super-slice of the rootless, socially mobile group known as the American middle class." Phillips also recognized the attraction of Sunbelt attitudes—on government spending, defense, race, and taxes—to residents in the suburbs and ethnic working-class neighborhoods of the North. So did the authors of *The Real Majority,* who deeply impressed Nixon with their assertion that the new key to a winning coalition was the "47 year old Catholic housewife in Dayton, Ohio whose husband is a machinist." Although she and her blue-collar husband had always voted Democratic, they would defect to the Republicans because of the couple's conservative views on black rioters, antiwar protesters, pornography, and drugs. Wooing these voters—who he named the Silent Majority in a 1969 speech—became the centerpiece of Nixon's political strategy.

NIXON AND WORLD POLITICS

A Californian of Quaker origins, Richard Milhous Nixon was elected to Congress as a navy veteran in 1946. He won prominence for his role in the House Un-American Activities Committee investigation of Alger Hiss (see Chapter 26) and advanced to the Senate in 1950 by accusing his Democratic opponent of disloyalty. He served two terms as Eisenhower's vice president, but lost the presidency to Kennedy in 1960 and the California governorship in 1962. Ignoring those who proclaimed the end of his political career, Nixon campaigned vigorously for GOP candidates in 1966, and won his party's nomination and the presidency in 1968.

In office, Nixon focused mainly on foreign affairs. Considering himself a master of *realpolitik*—a pragmatic approach stressing national interest rather than ethical goals—he sought to check Soviet expansionism and to reduce superpower conflict, to limit the nuclear-arms race, and to enhance America's economic well-being. He planned to get the United States out of Vietnam and into a new era of détente—reduced tensions—with the communist world. To manage diplomacy, Nixon chose **Henry Kissinger,** a refugee from Hitler's Germany and professor of international relations, who shared Nixon's penchant for secrecy and for the concentration of decision-making power in the White House.

Vietnamization | Nixon's grand design hinged on ending the Vietnam War. It was sapping American military strength, worsening inflation, and thwarting détente with China and the Soviet Union. Announcing the Nixon Doctrine in August 1969, he redefined America's role in the Third World as that of a help-

The My Lai Massacre *Under the command of First Lieutenant William Calley, the men of Charlie Company entered the small village of My Lai in March 1968 to attack the Vietcong believed to be there. Instead, they found unarmed civilians, mostly women and children, and massacred them. The military kept the incident secret for a year, but when news of the incident surfaced late in 1969 it became symbolic of the war's brutality and the futility of the U.S. effort in the Vietnam War.*

ful partner rather than a military protector. Nations facing communist subversion could count on U.S. support, but they would have to defend themselves.

The Nixon Doctrine reflected the president's recognition of war weariness by both the electorate and troops in Vietnam. Johnson's decision to negotiate rather than escalate had left American troops with the sense that little mattered except survival. Morale plummeted. Discipline collapsed. Army desertions rocketed from twenty-seven thousand in 1967 to seventy-six thousand in 1970, and absent-without-leave (AWOL) rates rose even higher. Racial conflict became commonplace. Drug use soared; the Pentagon estimated that two out of three soldiers in Vietnam smoked marijuana and that one in three tried heroin. The army reported hundreds of cases of "fragging"—enlisted men killing officers and noncommissioned officers.

The toll of atrocities against the Vietnamese also mounted. Increasing instances of Americans' dismembering enemy bodies, torturing captives, and murdering civilians came to light. In March 1968 an army unit led by Lieutenant William Calley massacred several hundred South Vietnamese in the hamlet of **My Lai.** The soldiers gang-raped girls, lined up women and children in ditches and shot them, and then burned the village. Revelations of such incidents, and the increasing number of returned soldiers who joined Vietnam Veterans Against the War, undercut the already-diminished support for the war.

Despite pressure to end the war, Nixon would not sacrifice U.S. prestige. Seeking "peace with honor," he acted on three fronts. First was "Vietnamization," replacing American troops with South Vietnamese. It was hardly a new idea; the French had tried *jaunissement* or "yellowing" in 1951, and it had not worked. By 1972, the U.S. forces had dropped from half a million to thirty thousand. Second, bypassing South Vietnamese leaders, Nixon sent Kissinger to negotiate secretly with North Vietnam's foreign minister, Le Duc Tho. Third, to force the communists to compromise despite the U.S. troop withdrawal, Nixon escalated the bombing of North Vietnam and secretly ordered air strikes on Cambodia and Laos. He told an aide,

> I want the North Vietnamese to believe I've reached the point where I might do anything to stop the war. We'll just slip the word to them that "for God's sake, you know Nixon is obsessed about communism. We can't restrain him when he's angry—and he has his hand on the nuclear button"—and Ho Chi Minh himself will be in Paris in two days begging for peace.

LBJ's War Becomes Nixon's War The secret B-52 raids against Cambodia neither made Hanoi beg for peace nor disrupted communist supply bases. They did, however, undermine the stability of that tiny republic. In early 1970, North Vietnam increased its infiltration of troops into Cambodia both to aid the Khmer Rouge (Cambodian communists) and to escalate its war in South Vietnam. Nixon ordered a joint U.S.–South Vietnamese incursion into Cambodia at the end of April 1970. They seized large caches of arms and bought time for Vietnamization. But the costs were high. The invasion ended Cambodia's neutrality, widened the war throughout Indochina, and provoked massive American protests against the war, culminating in the student deaths at Kent State University and Jackson State College.

In February 1971, Nixon had South Vietnamese troops invade Laos to destroy communist bases there and to restrict the flow of supplies southward from North Vietnam. The South Vietnamese were routed. Emboldened, North Vietnam mounted a major campaign in April 1972—the Easter Offensive—their largest since 1968. Nixon retaliated by mining North Vietnam's harbors and unleashing B-52s on its major cities. He vowed: "The bastards have never been bombed like they are going to be bombed this time."

America's Longest War Ends The 1972 bombing helped break the impasse in the Paris peace talks, stalemated since 1968. In late October, just days before the 1972 presidential election, Kissinger announced that "peace is at hand." The cease-fire agreement he had secretly negotiated with Le Duc Tho required the withdrawal of all U.S. troops, provided for the return of American prisoners of war, and allowed North Vietnamese troops to remain in South Vietnam.

Kissinger's negotiation sealed Nixon's reelection, but South Vietnam's President Thieu refused to sign a cease-fire permitting North Vietnamese troops to remain in the South. An angry Le Duc Tho then pressed Kissinger for additional concessions. Nixon again resorted to massive B-52 raids. The 1972 Christmas bombing of Hanoi and Haiphong, the most destructive of the war, roused fierce opposition domestically and globally but broke the deadlock. Nixon's secret reassurance to Thieu that the United States would "respond with full force should the settlement be violated by North Vietnam" ended Saigon's recalcitrance.

The Paris Accords, signed in late January 1973, essentially restated the terms of the October truce. The agreement ended hostilities between the United States and North Vietnam, but left unresolved the differences between North and South Vietnam, guaranteeing that Vietnam's future would yet be settled on the battlefield.

The war in Vietnam would continue despite fifty-eight thousand American dead, three hundred thousand wounded, and an expenditure of at least $150 billion. Twenty percent of the Americans who served in Vietnam, nearly five hundred thousand, received less-than-honorable discharges—a measure of the desertion rate, drug usage, antiwar sentiment in the military, and immaturity of the troops (the average U.S. soldier in Vietnam was just nineteen years old, seven years younger than the average GI in World War II).

Virtually all who survived, wrote one marine, returned "as immigrants to a new world. For the culture we had known dissolved while we were in Vietnam, and the culture of combat we lived in so intensely . . . made us aliens when we returned." Beyond media attention on the psychological difficulties of readjusting to civilian life, which principally fostered an image of them as disturbed and dangerous, the nation paid little heed to its Vietnam veterans—reminders of a war that Americans wished to forget.

Relieved that the long nightmare had ended, most Americans wanted "to put Vietnam behind us." The bitterness of many veterans, and of hawks and doves, moderated with time. Few gave much thought to the 2 million Vietnamese casualties, or to the suffering in Laos, or the price paid by Cambodia. In 1975, the fanatical Khmer Rouge (Cambodian communists), led by Pol Pot, took power and turned Cambodia into a genocidal "killing field," murdering some 2 million, an estimated third of the population.

"We've adjusted too well," complained Tim O'Brien, a veteran and novelist of the war. "Too many of us have lost touch with the horror of war. . . . It would seem that the memories of soldiers should serve, at least in a modest way, as a restraint on national bellicosity. But time and distance erode memory. We adjust, we lose the intensity. I fear that we are back where we started. I wish we were more troubled."

Détente

Disengagement from Vietnam helped Nixon achieve **détente** with the communist superpowers. These developments, the most significant shift in U.S. foreign policy since the start of the Cold War, created a new relationship among the United States, the Soviet Union, and China.

Presidents from Truman to Johnson had refused to recognize the People's Republic of China, to allow its admission to the United Nations, and to permit American allies to trade with it. But by 1969 a widening Sino-Soviet split made the prospect of improved relations attractive to both Mao Zedong and Nixon. China wanted to end its isolation; the United States wanted to play one communist power off against the other; and both wanted to thwart USSR expansionism in Asia.

In June 1971, Kissinger began secret negotiations with Beijing, laying the groundwork for Nixon's historic February 1972 trip to China "to seek the normalization of relations." The first visit ever by a sitting American president to the largest nation in the world, it ended more than twenty years of Chinese-American hostility. Full diplomatic recognition followed in 1979.

Equally significant, Nixon went to Moscow in May 1972 to sign agreements with the Soviets on trade, technological cooperation, and the limitation of nuclear weapons. Fear of a Sino-American alliance and a desire to slow the incredibly expensive arms race made the Soviet Union eager for better relations with the U.S. The Strategic Arms Limitation Treaty (SALT I) froze each side's offensive nuclear missiles for five years, and committed both countries to strategic equality rather than nuclear superiority; and the Anti-Ballistic Missile (ABM) Treaty restricted the deployment by both sides of nation-wide missile-defense systems. Although they did not end the arms race, the treaties symbolized a first step toward that goal, reduced Soviet-American tensions and, in an election year, enhanced Nixon's stature.

Shuttle Diplomacy   Not even better relations with China and the Soviet Union ensured global stability. In the Middle East, Israel, fearing an imminent Arab attack, launched a preemptive strike on its neighbors in 1967, routing them in six days, and seizing Sinai and the Gaza Strip from Egypt, the West Bank and East Jerusalem from Jordan, and Syria's Golan Heights. Israel promised to give up the occupied lands in exchange for a negotiated peace, but the Arab states refused to negotiate with Israel or to recognize its right to exist. Palestinians, many of them refugees since the creation of Israel in 1948, turned to the Palestine Liberation Organization (PLO), which demanded Israel's destruction.

War exploded again in 1973 when Egypt and Syria attacked Israel on the Jewish high holy day of Yom Kippur. Only massive shipments of military supplies from the United States enabled a reeling Israel to stop the assault. In retaliation, the Arab states embargoed shipments of crude oil to the United States and its allies. The five-month embargo dramatized U.S. dependence on foreign energy sources, and then the spike in the price of crude oil from three dollars to more than twelve dollars a barrel sharply intensified inflation and spurred the use of nuclear power.

The dual shocks of the energy crisis at home and rising Soviet influence in the Arab world spurred Kissinger to engage in "shuttle diplomacy." Flying from one Middle East capital to another for two years, he negotiated a cease-fire, pressed Israel to cede some captured territory, and persuaded the Arabs to end the oil embargo. Although Kissinger's diplomacy left the Palestinian issue festering, it successfully excluded the Soviets from a major role in Middle Eastern affairs.

To counter Soviet influence, the Nixon administration also supplied arms and assistance to the shah of Iran, the white supremacist regime of South Africa, and President Ferdinand Marcos in the Philippines. Nixon-Kissinger *realpolitik* based American aid on a nation's willingness to oppose the Soviet Union, not on the nature of its government. The administration gave aid to antidemocratic regimes in Argentina, Brazil, and South Korea, as well as to Portuguese colonial authorities in Angola.

When Chileans elected a Marxist, Salvador Allende, president in 1970, Nixon secretly funded the CIA to support opponents of the leftist regime. The United States also cut off economic aid to Chile and blocked banks from granting it loans. In 1973 a military junta overthrew the Chilean government and killed Allende. Nixon quickly recognized the dictatorship, and economic aid and investment again flowed to Chile.

Although committed to containing communist influence, Nixon understood the limits of U.S. power and the changed realities of world affairs. Discarding the model of a bipolar conflict that had shaped American foreign policy since 1945, Nixon took advantage of the Sino-Soviet rift to improve relations with both nations. His administration also improved the U.S. position in the Middle East and ended American involvement in Vietnam. The politician who had built his reputation as a staunch Cold Warrior had initiated a new era of détente.

DOMESTIC PROBLEMS AND DIVISIONS

Richard Nixon yearned to be remembered as an international statesman, but domestic affairs kept intruding. He tried to reform the welfare system and solve complex economic problems. But the underside of Nixon's personality appealed to the darker recesses of the nation and intensified the fears and divisions among Americans.

The Nixon Presidency

Close observers of Nixon noted the multiple levels of his character. Beneath the calculated public persona hid a shadowy man who rarely revealed himself. Largely hidden was the insecure Nixon, suspicious and filled with anger. Seething with resentments, he believed enemies lurked everywhere, waiting to destroy him. Accordingly, he sought to annihilate his partisan enemies, particularly the "eastern liberal establishment."

The classic outsider, reared in pinched surroundings, physically awkward, unable to relate easily to others, Nixon remained fearful, even at the height of national power, that he would never be accepted. At the beginning of his administration, however, his strengths stood out. He spoke of national reconciliation, took bold initiatives internationally, and dealt with domestic problems responsibly.

Symbolic of his positive start, the nation celebrated the first successful manned mission to the moon. On July 21, 1969, the Apollo 11 lunar module, named *Eagle*, descended to the Sea of Tranquility. As millions watched on television, astronaut **Neil Armstrong** walked on the moon's surface and proclaimed, "That's one small step for man, one giant leap for mankind." Five more lunar expeditions followed, and in 1975 the space race essentially ended with the United States and the Soviet Union engaging in cooperative efforts to explore the rest of the universe.

The first newly elected president since 1849 whose party controlled neither house of Congress, Nixon cooperated with the Democrats to increase social-security benefits, build subsidized housing, expand the Job Corps, and grant the vote to eighteen-year-olds. Responding to the growing environmental awareness and energized environmental movement, which brought out 20 million Americans for the first Earth Day in 1970, the president approved new laws limiting pesticide use, protecting endangered species and marine mammals, safeguarding coastal lands, and controlling strip-mining. Nixon also signed bills creating the Occupational Safety and Health Administration (OSHA), to enforce health and safety standards in the workplace, and the Environmental Protection Agency (EPA), requiring federal agencies to prepare an environmental-impact analysis of all proposed projects.

Conservatives grumbled as government grew larger and more intrusive and as race-conscious employment policies, including quotas, were mandated for all federal contractors. Conservatives grew still angrier when Nixon unveiled the Family Assistance Plan (FAP) in 1969. A bold effort to overhaul the welfare system, FAP proposed a guaranteed minimum annual income for all Americans. Caught between liberals who thought the income inadequate and conservatives who disliked it on principle, FAP died in the Senate.

A Troubled Economy

Nixon inherited the fiscal consequences of President Johnson's effort to wage the Vietnam War and finance the Great Society by deficit financing—to have both "guns and butter." Facing a "whopping" budget deficit of $25 billion in 1969 and an inflation rate of 5 percent, Nixon cut government spending and encouraged the Federal Reserve Board to

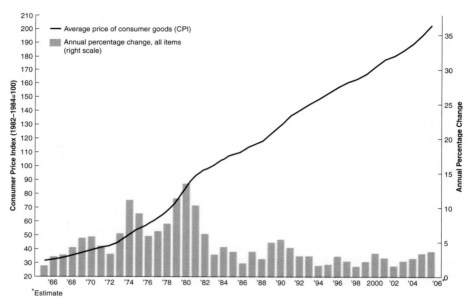

FIGURE 29.1 Inflation, 1965–2006

Inflation, which had been moderate during the two decades following the Second World War, began to soar with the escalation of the war in Vietnam in the mid-1960s. In 1979 and 1980 the nation experienced double-digit inflation in two consecutive years for the first time since World War I.

raise interest rates. The result was a combination of inflation and recession that economists called "stagflation" and Democrats termed "Nixonomics."

Accelerating inflation lowered the standard of living of many families and sparked a wave of strikes as workers sought wage hikes to keep up with the cost of living. It encouraged the wealthy to invest in art and real estate rather than technology and factories. Hence, more plants shut down, industrial jobs dwindled, and many displaced workers lost their savings, their health and pension benefits, and their homes.

Throughout 1971 Nixon lurched from policy to policy. Declaring "I am now a Keynesian," he increased deficit spending to stimulate the private sector. It resulted in the largest budget deficit since World War II. Then Nixon devalued the dollar to correct the balance-of-payment deficit. Finally, he imposed a freeze on wages, prices, and rents, a short-term fix that gave the economy a shot in the arm until after the 1972 election. Then Nixon again reversed course, replacing controls with voluntary—and ineffective—guidelines. Inflation zoomed as the Organization of Petroleum Exporting Countries (OPEC) boycott raised the price of crude oil, and sluggish growth dogged the economy throughout the decade.

Law and Order   Despite his public appeals for unity, Nixon hoped to divide the American people in ways that would bring about a realignment in politics and create a new Republican majority coalition. His "southern strategy" sought to attract Dixie's white Democrats into the GOP fold, while his stands on crime, drugs, antiwar protestors, and black militants wooed blue-collar laborers and suburbanites—voters whom political strategist Kevin Phillips described as "in motion between a Democratic past and a Republican future." To outflank George Wallace, Nixon opposed court-ordered busing and took a tough stand against campus unrest and black radicalism.

To combat the militants he despised, Nixon had the IRS audit their tax returns; the Small Business Administration deny them loans; and the National Security Agency illegally wiretap them. The FBI worked with local law officials to disrupt and immobilize the Black Panthers, the CIA illegally investigated and compiled dossiers on thousands of American citizens, and the Justice Department prosecuted antiwar activists and black radicals in highly publicized trials. Nixon himself drew up an "enemies list" of adversaries to be harassed by the government.

In 1970, Nixon widened his offensive against the antiwar movement. The Huston Plan called for extensive wiretapping and infiltrating of radical organizations, as well as break-ins to gather or plant evidence. But FBI chief J. Edgar Hoover opposed the plan as a threat to the bureau's power. Blocked, Nixon secretly created his own White House unit to discredit his opposition and ensure executive secrecy. Nicknamed **"the plumbers"** because of their assignment to plug government leaks, the team was headed by former FBI agent G. Gordon Liddy and former CIA operative E. Howard Hunt.

The plumbers first targeted Daniel Ellsberg, a former Defense Department analyst who had given the press the **Pentagon Papers,** a secret documentary history of U.S. involvement in Vietnam. On June 13 the *New York Times* began publishing the Pentagon Papers, revealing a long history of White House lies to Congress, foreign leaders, and the American people. Although the papers contained nothing about his administration, Nixon, fearing that they would undermine trust in government and establish a precedent for publishing classified material, sought to bar their publication. The Supreme Court, however, ruled that their publication was protected by the First Amendment. Livid, Nixon directed the Justice Department to indict Ellsberg for theft and ordered the plumbers to break into the office of Ellsberg's psychiatrist in search of information to discredit the man who had become a hero to the antiwar movement.

The Southern Strategy

Nixon especially courted whites upset by the drive for racial equality. The administration opposed extension of the Voting Rights Act of 1965, sought to cripple enforcement of the Fair Housing Act of 1968, pleaded for the postponement of desegregation in Mississippi's schools, and filed suits to prohibit the busing of children to desegregate public schools. In 1971, when the Supreme Court upheld busing as a constitutional and necessary tactic in *Swann* v. *Charlotte-Mecklenburg Board of Education,* Nixon condemned the ruling and asked Congress to enact a moratorium on busing. The strategy of wooing white southerners also dictated Nixon's Supreme Court nominations. To reverse the Warren court's liberalism, he sought strict constructionists, judges who would not "meddle" in social issues or be "soft" on criminals. In 1969 he appointed Warren Burger as chief justice. Although the Senate then twice rejected southern conservatives nominated by Nixon, the president succeeded in appointing Harry Blackmun of Minnesota, Lewis Powell of Virginia, and William Rehnquist of Arizona. Along with Burger, they steered the Court in a centrist direction, ruling liberally in cases involving abortion, desegregation, and the death penalty, while shifting to the right on civil liberties, community censorship, and police power.

As the 1970 congressional elections neared, Nixon encouraged his vice president, Spiro T. Agnew, to step up attacks on "hooligans, hippies, and radical liberals." Agnew assailed the Democrats as "sniveling hand-wringers," intellectuals as "an effete corps of impudent snobs," and the news media as "nattering nabobs of negativism." Liberals deplored Agnew's alarming alliterative allegations, but many others found them on target. The 1970 elections were a draw, with the GOP losing nine House seats and winning two Senate seats.

The Crisis of the Presidency

In his second inaugural, Nixon pledged "to make the next four years the best four years in America's history." Ironically, they would rank among its sorriest. His vice president would resign in disgrace; his closest aides would go to jail; and he would serve barely a year and a half of his second term before resigning to avoid impeachment.

The Election of 1972

Nixon's reelection appeared certain. He faced a deeply divided Democratic Party and counted on his diplomatic successes and the winding down of the Vietnam War to win over moderate voters. He expected his southern strategy and law-and-order posture to attract Wallace voters. Nixon's only possible worry, another third-party candidacy by Wallace, vanished on May 15, 1972, when Wallace was shot during a campaign stop and paralyzed from the waist down. He withdrew from the race, leaving Nixon a monopoly on the white backlash.

The Senate's most outspoken dove, **George McGovern** of South Dakota, capitalizing on antiwar sentiment, blitzed the Democratic primaries. He gained additional support from new party rules requiring state delegations to include minority, female, and youthful delegates in approximate proportion to their numbers. Actress Shirley MacLaine approvingly described California's delegation as "looking like a couple of high schools, a grape boycott, a Black Panther rally, and four or five politicians who walked in the wrong door." McGovern won the nomination on the first ballot.

Perceptions of McGovern as inept and radical drove away all but the most committed supporters. After pledging to stand behind his vice-presidential running mate Thomas Eagleton "1,000 percent" when it became known that Eagleton had received electric-shock therapy for depression, McGovern dumped him and suffered the embarrassment of having several prominent Democrats publicly decline to run with him. McGovern's endorsement of decriminalization of marijuana, immediate withdrawal from Vietnam, and pardons for those who had fled the United States to avoid the draft exposed him to GOP ridicule as the candidate of the radical fringe.

Remembering his narrow loss to Kennedy in 1960 and too-slim victory in 1968, Nixon left no stone unturned. To do whatever was necessary to win, he appointed his attorney general, John Mitchell, to head the Committee to Re-Elect the President (CREEP). Millions of dollars in campaign contributions financed "dirty tricks" to create dissension in Democratic ranks and paid for an espionage unit to spy on the opposition. Led by Liddy and Hunt, the "White House plumbers" had been created to plug the leaks concerning the secret bombing of Cambodia, which Nixon feared would increase congressional and public opposition to the war. In 1972 it received Mitchell's approval to wiretap telephones at the Democratic National Committee headquarters in the Watergate apartment and office complex in Washington. Early one morning in June 1972, a security guard foiled the break-in to install bugs. Arrested were James McCord, the security coordinator of CREEP, and several other Liddy and Hunt associates.

Earth Day, May 4, 1970 *Designed to alert people about the threats to the air, land, and water, the first Earth Day signaled the emergence of the modern environmental movement. It would put pressure on the federal government to take major steps in cleaning up the nation's environment and educate a generation of Americans to understand the ecology of the planet as a delicate, interconnected series of elements, in which damage to any single element damages many others.*

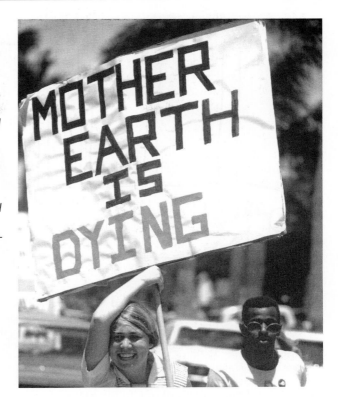

A White House cover-up began immediately. Nixon announced that "no one in the White House staff, no one in this administration, presently employed, was involved in this bizarre incident." He then ordered staff members to expunge Hunt's name from the White House telephone directory, to buy the silence of those arrested with $400,000 in hush money and hints of a presidential pardon, and to direct the CIA to halt the FBI's investigation of the Watergate break-in on the pretext that the investigation would damage national security.

With the McGovern campaign a shambles and Watergate seemingly contained, Nixon amassed nearly 61 percent of the popular vote and an overwhelming 520 electoral votes. Supported primarily by minorities and low-income voters, McGovern carried only Massachusetts and the District of Columbia. The election solidified the 1968 realignment. Nevertheless, the GOP gained only twelve seats in the House and lost two in the Senate, demonstrating the growing difficulty of unseating incumbents, the rise in ticket-splitting, and the decline of both party loyalty and voter turnout. Only 55.7 percent of eligible voters went to the polls (down from 63.8 percent in 1960).

The Watergate Upheaval
The scheme to conceal links between the White House and the accused Watergate burglars had succeeded during the 1972 campaign. But after the election, federal judge "Maximum John" Sirica, known for his tough treatment of criminals, refused to accept the defendants' claim that they had acted on their own. Threatening severe prison sentences,

Driving Southward and Backward *To outflank George Wallace and win the votes of both southern whites and urban blue-collar workers in the North, Nixon's "southern strategy" included delaying school desegregation plans and strong opposition to busing children to achieve racial balance in the schools.*

Sirica coerced James McCord of CREEP into confessing that White House aides had known in advance of the break-in and that the defendants had committed perjury during the trial. Two *Washington Post* reporters, Carl Bernstein and Bob Woodward, wrote a succession of front-page stories tying the break-in to illegal contributions and "dirty tricks" by CREEP. They had followed clues furnished by a secret informant named **"Deep Throat."** (Only in 2005 did W. Mark Felt, the former No. 2 man in the FBI, step forward at age 91 to unmask himself as the mysterious source.)

In February 1973 the Senate established the Special Committee on Presidential Campaign Activities to investigate. As the trail of revelations led closer to the Oval Office, Nixon fired his special counsel, John Dean, who refused to be a scapegoat, and announced the resignations of his principal aides, H. R. Haldeman and John Ehrlichman. Pledging to get to the bottom of the scandal, he appointed Secretary of Defense Elliot Richardson, a Boston patrician of unassailable integrity, as his new attorney general, and instructed him to appoint a special Watergate prosecutor with broad powers of investigation and subpoena. Richardson selected Archibald Cox, a Harvard law professor and a Democrat.

In May the special Senate committee began a televised investigation. Chaired by Sam Ervin of North Carolina, the hearings revealed the existence of a White House "enemies list," the president's use of government agencies to harass opponents, and administration favoritism in return for illegal campaign donations. Most damaging to Nixon, the hearings exposed the White House's active involvement in the Watergate cover-up. But the Senate still lacked concrete evidence of the president's criminality, the "smoking gun" that would prove Nixon's guilt. Because it was his word against that of John Dean, who testified that the president directed the cover-up, Nixon expected to survive the crisis.

Then another presidential aide dropped a bombshell by revealing that Nixon had installed a secret taping system that recorded all conversations in the Oval Office. The Ervin committee and Cox insisted on access to the tapes, but Nixon refused, claiming executive privilege. In October 1973, when Cox sought a court order to obtain the tapes, Nixon ordered Richardson to fire him. Richardson instead resigned in protest, as did the deputy attorney general, leaving it to the third-ranking official in the Department of Justice, Solicitor General Robert Bork, to dump Cox. The furor stirred by this "Saturday Night Massacre" sent Nixon's public-approval rating rapidly downward. Even as Nixon named a new special prosecutor, Leon Jaworski, the House Judiciary Committee began impeachment proceedings.

A President
Disgraced

Adding to Nixon's woes that October, Vice President Agnew, charged with income-tax evasion and accepting bribes, pleaded no contest—"the full equivalent to a plea of guilty," according to the trial judge. Dishonored, Agnew left office with a three-year suspended sentence and a $10,000 fine. House Minority Leader Gerald R. Ford of Michigan replaced Agnew.

In March 1974, Jaworski and the House Judiciary Committee subpoenaed the president for the tape recordings of Oval Office conversations after the Watergate break-in. Nixon released edited transcripts of the tapes, filled with gaps and the phrase "expletive deleted." Despite the excisions, the president sounded petty and vindictive.

Nixon's sanitized version of the tapes satisfied neither Jaworski nor the House Judiciary Committee. Both pressed for unedited tapes. In late July the Supreme Court rebuffed the president's claim to executive privilege. Citing the president's obligation to provide evidence necessary for the due process of law, Chief Justice Burger ordered Nixon to release the unexpurgated tapes.

In late July, the House Judiciary Committee adopted three articles of impeachment, accusing President Nixon of obstruction of justice for impeding the Watergate investigation, abuse of power for his partisan use of the FBI and IRS, and contempt of Congress for refusing to obey a congressional subpoena for the tapes. Checkmated, Nixon conceded in a televised address on August 5 that he had withheld relevant evidence. He then surrendered the subpoenaed tapes, which contained the "smoking gun" proving that the president had ordered the cover-up, obstructed justice, subverted one government agency to prevent another from investigating a crime, and lied about his role for more than two years. Certain that the Senate would vote to convict him if impeached, Richard Nixon, on August 9, 1974, became the first president to resign, and Gerald Ford took office as the nation's first chief executive who had not been elected either president or vice president.

CONCLUSION

Baby boomers took material comfort and their own importance for granted. Longing for meaning in their lives, as well as personal liberty, they sought a more humane democracy, a less racist and materialist society, and an end to the war in Vietnam. Failing to force a quick end to the war, the New Left became increasingly radical and violent. Most of the young, however, were more interested in "sex, drugs, and rock-and-roll." Ultimately, the student movement and counterculture helped prod the United States into becoming a more tolerant, diverse, and permissive society. They helped pave the way for the environmental movement and other causes in the 1970s, and spurred an end to America's longest war—which had cost the nation dearly in lives and dollars, in turning Americans against one another, and in diverting society from pressing needs.

The youth rebellion, racial rioting, and the Tet offensive in Vietnam brought politics to a boil in 1968. The year of assassinations and turmoil cost Democrats the White House, made Richard Nixon president, and triggered a conservative resurgence and major political realignment. Pursuing the national interest by *realpolitik,* Nixon and Kissinger adopted a strategy of "Vietnamization" while extending the American air war to Cambodia and Laos, and simultaneously holding secret negotiations with North Vietnam to end hostilities. At the same time, they opened the way for reduced tensions with China and the Soviet Union, enhancing the world outlook for peace, while also giving economic and military assistance to anticommunist dictatorships.

Equally vital to his political success, Nixon wooed whites upset by civil strife and the counterculture, and emphasized law and order to attract the silent majority concerned with the upsurge of criminality and breakdown of traditional values. Following a "southern strategy," he nominated conservatives for the Supreme Court, opposed extension of the Voting Rights Act and school busing for racial integration, and cracked down on peace advocates, militant blacks, and young radicals.

In 1972 the secret schemes Nixon had put in place to spy upon and destroy those who opposed his Vietnam policies began to unravel. His obsession for secrecy and his paranoia about those who opposed him brought his downfall. The arrest of the Watergate burglars and the subsequent attempted cover-up of White House involvement led to revelations of a host of "dirty tricks" and criminal acts, the indictment of nearly fifty Nixon administration officials and the jailing of a score of his associates, and a House Judiciary Committee vote to impeach the president. To avoid certain conviction, a disgraced Nixon resigned.

When his successor, Gerald Ford, took the oath of office, many Americans took pride in the smooth continuity of the political system and in its ability to curb excesses and abuses. Others worried that so many Americans had for so long just shrugged off Watergate as politics as usual, and that the Nixon scandals might never have come to light if not for coercion by a federal judge and the president's desire to tape and preserve his conversations. The deepening public disenchantment with politicians and disillusionment with government would last into the next century.

30

Conservative Resurgence, Economic Woes, Foreign Challenges, 1974–1989

CULTURAL TRENDS

As personal pursuits and leisure diversions shaped 1970s' American culture, women in large numbers entered the work force. The sexual revolution continued, but the shadow of AIDS introduced a sobering note. While antiwar and black-power protests faded, some activist causes rooted in the 1960s gained momentum, notably environmentalism, the women's movement, and gay rights. A conservative turn; a revival of evangelical religion; and sharp divisions over abortion, homosexuality, and other issues also shaped 1970s' culture.

Personal Pursuits and Diversions   The Vietnam War shattered the early-1960s' liberal consensus, and the radical New Left movement soon fragmented as well, creating political turmoil on the Left. The Watergate crisis, in turn, temporarily disoriented conservatives. With politics in disarray, personal preoccupations beckoned.

Some young people practiced Transcendental Meditation or joined the Reverend Sun Myung Moon's Unification Church. Others embraced the International Society for Krishna Consciousness, whose shaved-head, saffron-robed followers added an exotic note in airports, city streets, and college campuses. Several thousand rural communes arose as some counterculture veterans sought to escape the urban-corporate world, practice organic farming, revive old technologies, and live in harmony with nature. Most of these ventures proved short-lived.

By the early 1980s, journalists discovered the "Yuppie" (young urban professional), preoccupied with physical fitness and consumer goods. The stereotype had some basis in fact. Physical well-being became a middle-class obsession. Yuppies jogged and exercised, ate pesticide-free natural foods, and stopped smoking when medical evidence linked cigarettes to lung cancer and heart disease. The actress Jane Fonda, earlier an antiwar and antinuclear-power activist, promoted a series of exercise videos beginning in 1982. In a process known as gentrification, yuppies purchased and restored run-down inner-city apartments, often displacing poor and elderly residents in the process.

Self-improvement could easily turn selfish. Novelist Tom Wolfe satirized the "Me Generation." *Newsweek* magazine, proclaiming "the Year of the Yuppie" in 1984, commented, "[T]hey're making lots of money, spending it conspicuously, and switching political candidates like they test cuisines."

In the cultural arena, the politically engaged songs of the 1960s gave way to disco, suitable for dancing but carrying little cultural weight. Blockbuster movies like *Jaws* (1975), *Rocky* (1976), *Star Wars* (1977), and *E.T.* (1982) offered escapist fare. *Happy Days*, the top TV show of 1976–1977, evoked nostalgia for the 1950s. The TV series *Dallas*, chronicling the steamy affairs of a Texas oil family, captivated millions in the early 1980s. Walt Disney World, the Disney Corporation's sprawling Florida theme park, opened in 1971 and proved enormously popular. Football's Super Bowl and other sports extravaganzas attracted vast TV audiences.

Cable TV, introduced in the early 1970s, broadened viewers' options. By 1988, over half of U.S. homes had cable. Innovations in consumer electronics also shaped the era. By the early 1990s, 70 percent of U.S. households had VCRs (videocassette recorders), enabling users to tape TV shows for later viewing and to rent movies on cassette. In the music field, the compact disc (CD), introduced in 1983, offered high-quality sound. In a development of great future significance, the late 1970s also saw the advent of the personal computer.

American culture in these years was not all escapism and technological novelties, however. Bruce Springsteen's songs such as "Darkness at the Edge of Town" (1978) evoked the stresses of working-class life and bleakly described widening class divisions in America. Springsteen's "Born in the USA" (1984) told of a young man "sent . . . to a foreign land to go and kill the yellow man" who now finds himself "in the shadow of the penitentiary" with "[n]owhere to run . . . , nowhere to go." Bob Dylan's "Blood on the Tracks" (1974) expressed distrust of authority while celebrating defiant outsiders.

The 1970s also saw the rise of punk rock, an aggressively anti-establishment genre promoted by such groups as the Sex Pistols, the Ramones, and the Clash; of Tejano (Spanish for "Texan") music, which spread from Texas to win national popularity thanks to performers such as Selena Quintanilla, before her murder by a deranged fan in 1995; and of rap or hip-hop, with roots in Jamaican reggae music and West African storytelling traditions. Rap, beginning in the 1970s in poor black New York City neighborhoods, and involving free-form improvised recitations, gained a broad following in the 1980s and beyond.

Along with escapist movie fare, directors also produced brilliant films exploring the darker side of American life. Robert Altman's *Nashville* (1975) offered a disturbing vision of cynical mass-culture producers, manipulative politicians, and alienated drifters. Roman Polanski's *Chinatown* (1974) probed the corruption beneath the sunny surface of southern California life. *Network* (1976) explored the mass media's potentially

CHRONOLOGY, 1974–1989

1974 • Richard Nixon resigns presidency; Gerald Ford sworn in.
Indian Self-Determination Act.

1975 • South Vietnamese government falls.
Mayagüez incident.

1976 • Jimmy Carter elected president.

1977 • Panama Canal treaties ratified.
Introduction of Apple II computer.
Gay Pride parades in New York and San Francisco.

1978 • Carter authorizes federal funds to relocate Love Canal residents.

1979 • Menachem Begin and Anwar el-Sadat sign peace treaty at White House.
Second round of OPEC price increases.
Accident at Three Mile Island nuclear plant.
Carter restores full diplomatic relations with the People's Republic
of China.

1980 • Alaska Lands Act.
Soviet invasion of Afghanistan.
Iran hostage crisis.
Ronald Reagan elected president.

1981 • Major cuts in taxes and domestic spending, coupled with large increases
in military budget.
AIDS first diagnosed.

1982 • Equal Rights Amendment dies.
CIA funds contra war against Nicaragua's Sandinistas.
Central Park rally for nuclear-weapons freeze.

1983 • 239 U.S. marines die in Beirut terrorist attack.
U.S. deploys Pershing II and cruise missiles in Europe.
Reagan proposes Strategic Defense Initiative (Star Wars).
U.S. invasion of Grenada.

1984 • Reagan defeats Walter Mondale to win second term.

1984–1986 • Congress bars military aid to contras.

1985 • Rash of airline hijackings and other terrorist acts.

1986 • Congress passes South African sanctions.
Immigration Reform and Control Act.

1987 • Congressional hearings on Iran-contra scandal.
Stock-market crash.

1988 • Reagan trip to Moscow.

Breaking the Gender Barrier   *Martha Fransson, the sole female member of the Class of 1970 at the Tuck School of Business at Dartmouth College, poses with her classmates.*

destructive power. *The Deer Hunter* (1978) dramatized the Vietnam War's psychological aftermath. Such work, too, is part of the cultural legacy of the decade.

Changing Gender Roles and Sexual Behavior   Many women's lives changed dramatically in these years. Spurred by a resurgent women's movement as well as by inflation pressures (see below), the number of women working outside the home leaped from under 20 million in 1960 to nearly 60 million by 1990.

Women's wages still lagged behind those of men, however, and the workplace remained gender-segregated. Women were concentrated in such fields as nursing, teaching, retail sales, and secretarial work, while men dominated management positions and the professions. But even this changed as women entered the ranks of management. (Top management remained a male preserve, however, a phenomenon known as the "glass ceiling.") By the early 1990s the legal and medical professions were nearly 20 percent female, while growing numbers of women in professional schools of all kinds promised more changes ahead.

As women pursued higher education or careers, their median age at first marriage rose from twenty in 1960 to twenty-four in 1990. The birthrate fell as well, and by 1980 the statistically average U.S. family had 1.6 children, far below earlier levels. In the wake of the landmark *Roe* v. *Wade* decision of 1973 (see Chapter 29), the number of abortions rose from about 750,000 in 1973 to more than 1.5 million in 1980 and then leveled off.

The challenge to prevailing sexual codes and taboos posed by the 1960s' counterculture had long-lasting effects. In 1960 about 30 percent of unwed nineteen-year-old U.S. women reported having had sexual experience. By 1980 more than half did, and the figure rose higher by 2000. The number of unmarried couples living together jumped from 523,000 in 1970 to 3.5 million by 1993.

FIGURE 30.1 **Women in the Work Force, 1950–2005**

After 1960 the numbers of American women who were wage earners surged upward. Both the women's movement and economic pressures encouraged this trend. *Source:* U.S. Department of Labor, Bureau of Labor Statistics (www.bls.gov).

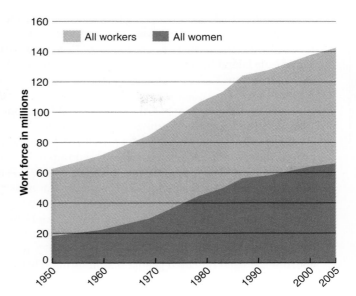

The freer attitude toward sex received a setback with the spread of the deadly viral infection **AIDS** (acquired immune deficiency syndrome), first diagnosed in 1981. AIDS spread mainly among sexually active homosexuals and bisexuals, intravenous drug users sharing needles, and persons having sexual intercourse with these high-risk individuals. (Early in the epidemic some persons, including tennis star Arthur Ashe, contracted AIDS through blood transfusions.) Though the worst lay ahead, more than thirty-one thousand Americans had died of AIDS by the end of the 1980s.

Medical authorities warned against unprotected sex. The message was driven home when film star Rock Hudson died of AIDS in 1985, and basketball superstar Earvin ("Magic") Johnson and Olympic diver Greg Louganis announced that they carried the HIV virus, a precursor of AIDS. While the epidemic emboldened some Americans to express their hatred of homosexuality (see below), it also stimulated medical research and an outpouring of concern. A large AIDS quilt honoring victims toured the nation. Under the shadow of AIDS, many Americans grew more cautious in their sexual behavior. The exuberant 1960s slogan "Make Love, Not War" gave way to a more somber message: "Safer Sex."

The Persistence of Social Activism

The environmental-protection movement, a legacy of the 1960s, grew stronger in the 1970s. Older organizations such as the Sierra Club and the Wilderness Society, as well as new ones such as Greenpeace, won fresh recruits. Greenpeace was founded in 1971 when Canadian activists protested a planned U.S. nuclear test on an island in the Bering Sea. The U.S. branch, established soon after, worked to preserve old-growth forests and protect the world's oceans. By 2000, Greenpeace had 250,000 U.S. members. The Save the Whales campaign, launched by the Animal Welfare Institute in 1971, opposed the slaughter of the world's largest mammals by fleets of floating processing factories to provide dog-and-cat food.

Environmentalists also targeted the nuclear-power industry. Adopting techniques from the civil-rights and antiwar campaigns, activists protested at planned nuclear-power plants. The movement crested in 1979 when a partial meltdown crippled the **Three Mile Island** nuclear-power plant in Pennsylvania. A Jane Fonda movie released at the same time, *China Syndrome,* portrayed a fictitious but plausible nuclear-power disaster caused by a California earthquake. The Three Mile Island accident, coupled with a far more serious one at the Chernobyl nuclear-power plant in the Ukraine in 1986, deepened public concerns about nuclear power.

Of the 1960s' many legacies, the revitalized women's movement (see Chapter 28) proved most enduring. The National Organization for Women (NOW), founded in 1966, boasted nearly fifty thousand members by 1975. Feminist support groups and Gloria Steinem's *Ms.* magazine (1972) spread the message. While NOW remained mainly white and middle class, African-American, Latina, and Asian women organized as well. Women workers agitated for better wages and working conditions (see below).

With the movement's growth came political clout. The National Women's Political Caucus (1971) promoted a feminist agenda. By 1972, many states had liberalized their abortion laws and outlawed gender bias in hiring. That same year Congress passed an

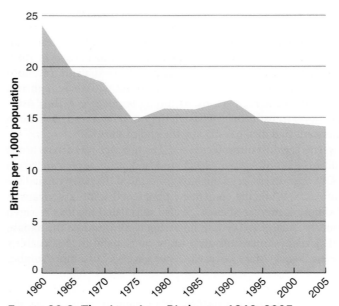

FIGURE **30.2 The American Birthrate, 1960–2005**

Families of five or six children or more were once common in the United States, and the birthrate remained high in the baby-boom years of the later 1940s and the 1950s. (The nearly 80 million children of the baby boomers, born between 1982 and 1995, were dubbed "echo boomers.") The U.S. birthrate fell dramatically from 1960 to the mid-1970s, rose slightly, and then resumed its downward trend after 1990. *Source:* National Center for Health Statistics, U.S. Dept. of Health and Human Services.

equal rights amendment (ERA) to the Constitution barring discrimination on the basis of sex. Twenty-eight states quickly ratified it, and ultimate adoption seemed likely. Other feminist organizations defended women's reproductive rights in the face of a conservative backlash against *Roe* v. *Wade* (see below).

The women's movement splintered in the late 1970s, as Betty Friedan and other moderates opposed the lesbians who were becoming more assertive (see below). The moderates also deplored the strident rhetoric of some radical feminists and criticized their downgrading of motherhood and homemaking. In *The Second Stage* (1981), Friedan added family-protection issues to the feminist agenda.

Conservatives worried that women's changing roles would weaken the family. Women themselves conceded the stresses of balancing career and family, but few pined for the era when child care, housework, and volunteerism had defined "women's sphere." As the 1980s ended, many American women enjoyed unprecedented opportunities, but barriers persisted and complex issues remained.

As we saw in Chapter 29, many gay men and lesbians "came out of the closet" in the 1970s, openly avowing their sexual preference and protesting job discrimination and harassment. In 1977, "Gay Pride" parades drew seventy-five thousand marchers in New York City and three hundred thousand in San Francisco, a center of gay activism. Two years later, a national gay and lesbian civil-rights parade attracted one hundred thousand marchers to Washington, D.C. More taboos fell as Elaine Noble, an avowed lesbian, won a seat in the Massachusetts legislature in 1974 and Harvey Milk, an openly gay candidate, was elected to the San Francisco board of supervisors in 1977. In 1987 Massachusetts congressman Barney Frank acknowledged his homosexuality.

Organizations like the National Gay Task Force, founded in 1973 (and later renamed the National Gay and Lesbian Task Force), and a militant New York group called ACT-UP (1987) demanded the repeal of anti-gay laws and passage of legislation protecting homosexuals' civil rights. Responding to the pressure, many states and cities repealed laws against same-sex relations between consenting adults and barring job discrimination on the basis of sexual orientation.

Grass-Roots Conservatism
But a backlash was building, rooted in the 1960s and earlier. The sixties was a polarizing decade. While the counterculture and antiwar protests drew media attention, many Americans deplored what they viewed as the decade's radical excesses. As blue-collar and white ethnic Democrats reacted against what they saw as the party's takeover by hippies and radical leftists, their traditional party loyalty eroded. As we saw in Chapter 29, Richard Nixon exploited this disaffection to win the White House in 1968.

The conservative resurgence had even deeper roots. **William F. Buckley** had launched the conservative *National Review* magazine in 1955; founded Young Americans for Freedom in 1960; and started a conservative TV talk show, *Firing Line*, in 1966. Barry Goldwater's 1964 presidential campaign alerted conservatives both to their potential power within the Republican Party and to the importance of broadening their appeal beyond the hard-core conservative loyalists who had rallied to the far-right John Birch Society, founded in 1958.

The career of Phyllis Schlafly, devout Roman Catholic, law-school graduate, mother of six, and tireless activist, illustrates the movement's post-1960 evolution. Schlafly's *A Choice Not an Echo* (1964) championed Goldwater and denounced the Republican

Party's liberal, East Coast wing. Her *Phyllis Schlafly Report,* begun in 1967, attacked the New Left and the counterculture. In the 1970s, Schlafly and her organization, The Eagle Forum, focused on hot-button cultural issues such as abortion; gay rights; and the Equal Rights Amendment, which she fiercely opposed.

In local communities, especially in the fast-growing South and West, conservatives found each other, shared their concerns, and mobilized politically. This process was especially evident in southern California's Orange County, a region recently transformed from ranches and citrus groves to suburban developments. Orange County conservatives—mostly upwardly mobile white evangelical Protestants, often newcomers from the East—were intensely anticommunist, dismayed by 1960s' radicals, and suspicious of the "liberal intellectuals" dominating the media and national politics. Political scientist Lisa McGirr describes their political mobilization:

> At living room bridge clubs, at backyard barbecues, and at kitchen coffee klatches, the middle-class men and women of Orange County "awakened" to what they perceived as the threats of communism and liberalism. Sensing an urgent need for action, they forged study groups, multiplied chapters of national right-wing organizations, and worked within the Republican party to make their voices heard. In so doing, they became the cutting edge of the conservative movement in the 1960s.

Foreshadowing changes ahead nationally, Orange County helped elect **Ronald Reagan** governor of California in 1966 and in 1978 helped pass Proposition 13, a state referendum calling for deep cuts in property taxes. Conservative think tanks like the Heritage Foundation, founded by the Colorado beer baron Joseph Coors in 1973, instructed local conservatives as they solidified their ideology.

As Schlafly's campaigns illustrate, 1970s' conservatives mobilized around specific issues, especially abortion. In the wake of *Roe* v. *Wade,* a "Right to Life" movement led by Roman Catholic and conservative Protestant activists pressed for a constitutional amendment outlawing abortion. The "murder of the unborn," they charged, eroded respect for human life. "Pro-life" advocates rallied, signed petitions, and picketed abortion clinics and pregnancy-counseling centers.

Responding to the pressure, Congress in 1976 ended Medicaid funding for most abortions, in effect denying this procedure to the poor. Most feminists, by contrast, adopted a "pro-choice" stance, arguing that women and their physicians, not the government, should make reproductive decisions. Opinion polls reflected deep divisions, although a majority favored the "pro-choice" position. Handing conservatives another victory, President Nixon in 1972 had vetoed a bill setting up a national network of daycare centers, criticizing its "communal approach to child-rearing." The Equal Rights Amendment, denounced by Schlafly and other conservatives, died in 1982, three states short of the three-fourths required for ratification.

Gay and lesbian activism particularly inflamed conservatives, who saw it as evidence of society's moral collapse. TV evangelist Jerry Falwell thundered, "God . . . destroyed the cities of Sodom and Gomorrah because of this terrible sin." In 1977, singer Anita Bryant led a campaign against a Miami ordinance protecting homosexuals' civil rights. "God created Adam and Eve, not Adam and Bruce," she pointed out. Thanks in part to Bryant's efforts, voters repealed the ordinance. Soon after, readers of *Good Housekeeping* magazine voted Bryant "the most admired woman in America." Other cities, too, reversed earlier measures favoring gay rights.

In 1978, as the backlash intensified, a member of the San Francisco board of supervisors fatally shot gay board-member Harvey Milk and Milk's ally, Mayor George Moscone. "[T]he city weeps" headlined the *San Francisco Examiner*. When the killer received a light sentence (after claiming that eating sugary junk foods had impaired his judgment), riots erupted in the city. In 1980 disco singer Donna Summer, popular in the gay community, announced her religious conversion and speculated that God had sent AIDS "to punish homosexuals."

Evangelical
Protestants
Mobilize

The conservative movement also found expression in the rapid growth of evangelical Protestantism, with its emphasis on strict morality, biblical inerrancy, and a personal "born again" conversion experience. Evangelical denominations such as the Assemblies of God and the Southern Baptist Convention grew explosively in the 1970s and 1980s, as did independent suburban megachurches such as Chuck Smith's Calvary Chapel in Orange County, typically conservative theologically and culturally. Meanwhile, liberal denominations such as the Methodists, Congregationalists, and Unitarians, whose ministers had rallied behind the civil-rights and antiwar movements, lost members.

Many evangelicals plunged into politics. As one observed in 1985, "I always thought that churches should stay out of politics. Now it seems almost a sin not to get involved." Evangelicals had pursued social reform before the Civil War, including the abolition of slavery, and their modern-day successors also preached reform, but of a conservative variety. Jerry Falwall's Moral Majority, founded in 1979 as a "pro-life, pro-family, pro-moral, and pro-America" crusade, actively supported conservative candidates.

Pat Robertson, head of the Christian Broadcasting Network and host of its popular *700 Club*, mounted an unsuccessful presidential bid in 1988. Another leading evangelical, the Reverend Tim LaHaye of San Diego, was active in Christian Voice, a group that encouraged grassroots organizing to promote conservative causes. In 1981 LaHaye founded the Council for National Policy, a secretive conservative lobbying organization.

While battling abortion, homosexuality, and pornography, often in alliance with conservative Catholics, evangelicals also attacked the Supreme Court's 1962 *Engel v. Vitale* decision banning organized prayer in public schools as a violation of the First Amendment. While pushing to reverse this ruling, evangelicals also advocated home schooling and private Christian schools, to shield children from what they saw as the secularist (nonreligious) values and lax morals pervading the public schools. Most evangelicals also embraced militant anticommunism.

Not all evangelicals were political conservatives. Most African-American evangelicals, in particular, remained loyal to the Democratic Party. In general, however, resurgent evangelicalism went hand in hand with the larger conservative movement of the 1970s.

For many evangelicals, Bible prophecy reinforced their political mobilization. Hal Lindsey's *The Late Great Planet Earth* (1970), a popularization of one system of prophetic interpretation, was *the* nonfiction best seller of the 1970s. Lindsey found the Soviet Union, communist China, the Arab-Israeli conflict, the United Nations, the European Union, and growing domestic wickedness all foretold in the Bible. He urged true believers to rally on the side of righteousness as the End approached.

Christian bookstores, radio stations, and TV evangelists fueled the revival. Along with Falwell's *Old Time Gospel Hour* and Robertson's *700 Club*, popular broadcasts included Jim and Tammy Bakker's *PTL* (Praise the Lord) program and Jimmy Swaggart's telecasts from Louisiana. The so-called electronic church suffered after 1987 amid sexual and financial scandals, but the evangelical resurgence continued. In a world of change, evangelicals found certitude, reassurance, and a sense of community in their shared faith. In the process, they profoundly influenced late-twentieth-century American life.

ECONOMIC AND SOCIAL CHANGES IN POST-1960s AMERICA

Inflation, industrial decline, and other economic problems offered a troubling counterpoint to the cultural and political developments of these years. Many white-collar professionals and people involved with the emerging information-based economy prospered. Others, however, including displaced factory workers, did not. Although many African-Americans enjoyed upward mobility as the civil-rights revolution expanded opportunities, others remained in poverty. While Native Americans faced adversities, the 1970s also brought brighter prospects and a new assertiveness in pursuing treaty rights. Shifting patterns of immigration, meanwhile, changed the nation's ethnic and demographic profile, with major implications for the future.

A Changing Economy

Disturbing economic developments influenced U.S. politics and shadowed the lives of millions of Americans in the 1970s. Largely owing to surging oil prices (see below), the inflation rate spiked to around 11 percent in 1973, dipped a bit, and then soared to almost 14 percent by 1980. Overall, consumer prices more than doubled from 1970 to 1980. This grinding rate of inflation battered American families, drove many wives into the work force out of necessity, and turned hard-pressed taxpayers against the welfare programs adopted during past Democratic administrations.

The ranks of family farmers, once revered as the backbone of America, thinned in these years. In 1960 about 6 percent of the U.S. labor force worked on farms; by 1994 the figure was 2.5 percent. As farm youth migrated to the cities, the dwindling ranks of small-farm operators often took second jobs to make ends meet. Overall farm production increased, however. As big operators bought and consolidated failing farms, average farm size grew from 375 to 430 acres between 1970 and 1990, and farms of several thousand acres were not unusual. Large-scale wheat, corn, and soybean production involved major capital investment and heavy-duty equipment, and factory farms dominated poultry and hog production. Federal subsidy programs encouraged the rise of giant agribusinesses. As Secretary of Agriculture Earl Butz put it: "Adapt or die." In the 1985 film *The Trip to Bountiful,* an aging Texas woman, movingly played by Geraldine Page in an Oscar-winning role, pays a nostalgic visit to her girlhood farm home, only to find it falling to ruin.

Industrial stagnation, or **deindustrialization,** worsened the era's economic woes. In a process that would intensify in the future (see Chapter 32), the steel and automobile industries were especially hard hit. As soaring gasoline prices boosted sales of more fuel-efficient foreign imports, U.S. car makers suffered. U.S. purchases of foreign cars, mainly from Japan, grew from 2 million in 1970 to 4 million in 1989. Facing severe production cutbacks, GM, Ford, and Chrysler laid off more than 225,000 workers.

Longer-term sources of industrial decline included aging machinery, inefficient production methods, and fierce competition from foreign companies using state-of-the-art equipment, paying lower wages, and unburdened by the pension plans and other benefits enjoyed by U.S. workers. As auto plants, steel mills, and other midwestern industries laid off workers, the unemployment rate reached 8.5 percent in 1975. In one five-year period, 1979–1983, 11.5 million U.S. workers lost jobs because of plant closings and production cutbacks. Statistics cannot convey the anxiety and disruption experienced by workers, their families, and entire communities as once-secure jobs vanished. Service-sector employment grew by 55 percent in the 1970s, partially counterbalancing the losses, but for laid-off factory workers, this was cold comfort.

As imports increased, the United States in 1971, for the first time in the twentieth century, ran a trade deficit. (That is, the total value of imports exceeded the total value of exports.) Trade deficits became the rule from 1976 on, and, as we shall see, their size mushroomed in the 1980s and beyond. As U.S. dollars flowed abroad to cover this trade imbalance, the domestic economy suffered.

As industrial workers lost jobs, the union movement weakened. In 1960, 31 percent of U.S. workers belonged to unions; in 1985, the figure stood at 18 percent, with further declines ahead. Some workers did join unions in these years, mainly teachers, public employees, flight attendants, and service workers, many of whom were female. The Coalition of Labor Union Women, founded in Chicago in 1974, encouraged unionization by women workers. Declared one delegate: "You can . . . tell [George Meany, head of the ALF-CIO] there are three thousand women in Chicago, and they didn't come to swap recipes." Female-dominated labor unions focused not only on wages but also on such issues as maternity leaves. While important in labor history and women's history, however, service-sector unionization only slowed, but did not reverse, the overall decline of union membership.

The Two Worlds of Black America Millions of blacks experienced significant upward mobility in these years, thanks to the civil-rights movement. In 1965, black students accounted for under 5 percent of total college enrollment; by 1990 the figure had risen to 12 percent, close to their proportion in the general population. By 1990 some 46 percent of black workers held white-collar jobs. TV's *Cosby Show,* a late-1980s comedy in which Bill Cosby played a doctor married to a lawyer, portrayed this upwardly mobile world.

Outside this world lay the inner-city slums, inhabited by perhaps a third of the black population. Here, up to half the young people never finished high school, and the jobless rate soared as high as 60 percent. As jobs disappeared owing to suburbanization, deindustrialization, and urban decline, inner-city black communities were hard hit. In 1980, the poverty rate among African-Americans stood at 32 percent, three times the rate for non-Hispanic whites.

Cocaine and other drugs pervaded the inner cities. Some black children recruited as lookouts for drug dealers eventually became dealers themselves. With drugs also came violence. In the 1980s, a young black male was six times as likely to be murdered as a young white male. In Los Angeles, two rival gangs, the Bloods and the Crips, accounted for more than four hundred killings in 1987. Warned the psychologist Jewelle Taylor Gibbs: "Young black males in America's inner cities are an endangered species . . . , [the] rejects of our affluent society."

In truth, despite the tough **Comprehensive Drug Abuse Act** of 1970, drug abuse affected all social levels, including yuppies, show-business celebrities, and young corporate executives. It was even glorified in movies, songs, and rock concerts. But drug use and drug trafficking particularly devastated the inner cities.

Unmarried women—mostly young and poor—accounted for nearly 60 percent of all black births in 1980. Scarcely beyond childhood themselves, these single mothers often survived on welfare payments. Buffeted by complex social and economic forces, and at risk of becoming a permanent underclass, the mainly nonwhite inner-city populations posed a major social challenge. Both significant upward mobility and educational advances by African-Americans, and serious social problems among those left behind in the inner cities, would continue into the twenty-first century (see Chapter 32).

To compensate for past racial discrimination, some cities set aside a percentage of building contracts for minority businesses. Some educational institutions reserved slots for minority applicants. These so-called **affirmative-action** programs faced court challenges, however. In *Bakke* v. *United States* (1978), a pivotal case brought by a rejected white medical-school applicant, the Supreme Court overthrew the quota system by which a California medical school had tried to increase its minority enrollment. In 1989, the Supreme Court invalidated a Richmond, Virginia requirement that 30 percent of building contracts go to minority businesses. The courts, did, however, uphold programs to encourage minority businesses or minority-student enrollment in higher education, so long as they did not involve specific quotas.

Brightening
Prospects for
Native Americans

Building on their occupation of Alcatraz Island in San Francisco Bay (see Chapter 28), members of the militant American Indian Movement briefly occupied the Bureau of Indian Affairs in Washington in 1972, and in 1973 took over a trading post at Wounded Knee, South Dakota, site of an 1890 Indian massacre by the U.S. army (see Chapter 17). In response to spreading protests, the **Indian Self-Determination Act** of 1974 granted tribes control of federal aid programs on the reservations and oversight of their own schools.

The 1990 census recorded more than 1.7 million persons as American Indians, in contrast to some eight hundred thousand in 1970. This upsurge reflected not only natural increase and ethnic pride, but also economic advantages associated with tribal membership. Under a 1961 law permitting them to buy or develop land for commercial and industrial projects, tribes launched business ventures ranging from resorts to mining and logging operations. They licensed food-processing plants, electronics firms, manufacturing enterprises, and gambling casinos on tribal lands, providing jobs and income.

Indian tribes also reasserted long-ignored treaty rights through the Indian Claims Commission, a federal agency set up in 1946. In 1971, the Native peoples of Alaska won 40 million acres and nearly $1 billion in settlement of treaty claims. In 1980, the Sioux were awarded $107 million for South Dakota lands taken from them illegally. The Penobscot Indians in Maine won claims based on a 1790 federal law. In 1988, after years of protests, the Puyallup tribe of Washington State received $162 million in settlement of their claim that the city of Tacoma occupied land granted them in the 1850s. Among other projects, the Puyallups laid plans to restore salmon runs on the Puyallup River.

Sid Gutierrez, Astronaut
Hispanics entered all arenas of American life in the late twentieth century. Gutierrez, a native of Albuquerque, New Mexico, piloted space shuttle Columbia *on a 1991 NASA mission.*

High rates of joblessness, alcoholism, and disease persisted among Indians. But renewed pride, economic ventures, and progress in asserting treaty rights offered hope. In the popular culture, movies such as *Little Big Man* (1970) and *Dances with Wolves* (1990), while idealizing Indians, represented an improvement over the negative stereotypes of earlier films.

New Patterns of Immigration

These years saw a steady influx of immigrants, both legal and illegal. Whereas most immigrants once arrived from Europe, some 45 percent now came from the Western Hemisphere and 30 percent from Asia. As in the past, economic need drew these newcomers. In oil-rich Mexico, for example, falling oil prices in the 1980s worsened the nation's chronic poverty, spurring many to seek jobs in the north. But life in the United States was often harsh. In 1980, some 26 percent of persons of Hispanic origin in the United States lived in poverty, twice the national rate. Despite adversity, Hispanic newcomers preserved their language and traditions, influencing U.S. culture in the process. Many neighborhoods of Los Angeles, Miami, and other major cities were wholly Hispanic.

Millions of Hispanic immigrants lacked official documentation. Working long hours with few legal protections, these migrants, mostly Mexicans and Haitians (as well as Puerto Ricans, who are U.S. citizens), sweated in the garment trades, cleaned houses, held low-paying service-sector jobs, and labored in agricultural fields. The **Immigration Reform and Control Act** of 1986, an update of the 1965 Immigration Act (see Chapter 28), outlawed the hiring of undocumented immigrants, but offered legal status to aliens who had lived in the United States for five years. Debates over immigration policy persisted, however, as did efforts to tighten U.S. border controls (see Chapter 32).

Immigration from Asia climbed as newcomers arrived from South Korea, Vietnam, and the Philippines. The motive, again, was primarily economic, though many Hmong (pronounced "mong"), the indigenous people of Indochina who had supported the United States in the Vietnam War, came for political reasons. Valuing education, many Asian immigrants advanced academically and economically. The younger generation, torn between new and old, sought to balance family and group loyalties with the appeal of the larger society beyond.

YEARS OF MALAISE: POST-WATERGATE POLITICS AND DIPLOMACY, 1974–1981

In the aftermath of the Vietnam failure and Richard Nixon's disgrace, Presidents **Gerald Ford** and Jimmy Carter grappled with domestic and foreign problems. Amid inflation, recession, and industrial stagnation, unease gripped the nation. Globally, the later 1970s brought mostly humiliations, from the final Vietnam withdrawal to a maddening hostage crisis. The familiar polarities of the Cold War blurred as problems in the Middle East and elsewhere highlighted issues the United States would face in the future.

The confident 1950s and early 1960s, when prosperous America had savored its role as the Free World's leader, equal to any challenge, now seemed remote. A nation long convinced that it was immune to the historical forces that constrained other societies seemed prey to forces beyond its control. But while the Vietnam experience encouraged isolationist tendencies, events made clear that America could not evade global involvement.

The Caretaker Presidency of Gerald Ford, 1974–1977

Gerald Ford took the presidential oath on August 9, 1974, following Richard Nixon's forced resignation. A Michigan congressman who had been House minority leader before becoming vice president, Ford conveyed a likable decency as he urged Americans to move beyond the "long national nightmare" of Watergate. The honeymoon soon ended, however, when Ford pardoned Richard Nixon for "any and all crimes" committed while in office. Ford said he wanted to help heal the body politic, but many Americans reacted with outrage.

On domestic issues, Ford proved more conservative than Nixon, vetoing a series of environmental, social-welfare, and public-interest measures, among them a 1974 freedom of information bill granting citizens greater access to government records. The Democratic Congress overrode most of these vetoes.

Economic problems dogged Ford's presidency. In 1973, oil prices had shot up as a result of an Arab oil embargo and price hikes by the **Organization of Petroleum Exporting Countries** (OPEC), a marketing consortium formed in 1960. The United States, heavily dependent on imported oil, felt the shock as surging prices of gasoline, heating oil, and other petroleum-based products worsened the inflationary spiral and produced long lines of angry drivers at gas stations. In October 1974, Ford unveiled a program of voluntary price restraint dubbed "Whip Inflation Now" (WIN), but prices continued to zoom. When the Federal Reserve Board tried to cool the economy by raising interest rates, a severe recession resulted. Unemployment approached 11 percent by 1975. As oil and gas prices soared, Americans for the first time since World War II struggled to curb energy consumption. Congress set fuel-efficiency standards for automobiles in 1975 and imposed a national speed limit of fifty-five miles per hour.

National morale sank further in April 1975 when the South Vietnamese government fell, ending two decades of U.S. effort in Vietnam. The TV networks chronicled desperate helicopter evacuations from the U.S. embassy in Saigon (soon renamed Ho Chi Minh City) as North Vietnamese troops closed in. A few weeks later, Cambodia seized a U.S. merchant ship, the *Mayagüez*. A military rescue ordered by Ford freed the thirty-nine *Mayagüez* crew members but cost the lives of forty-one U.S. servicemen. As the nation entered the election year 1976—also the bicentennial of the Declaration of Independence—Americans found little reason for optimism.

The Outsider as Insider: President Jimmy Carter, 1977–1981

Gerald Ford won the 1976 Republican nomination despite a challenge from former California governor Ronald Reagan. **Jimmy Carter,** a Georgia peanut grower and former governor, swept the Democratic primaries by stressing themes that appealed to post-Watergate America: his honesty, his status as a Washington outsider, his evangelical Christian faith. As his running mate, Carter chose a northern liberal, Minnesota senator Walter Mondale.

Carter's early lead eroded as voters sensed vagueness in his program, but he won by a narrow margin. The vote broke along class lines: the well-to-do went for Ford; the poor, overwhelmingly for Carter. The Georgian swept the South and received 90 percent of the black vote. Despite the rising conservative tide, popular revulsion against Nixon and Watergate temporarily interrupted the Republican advance, and Carter won.

Underscoring his outsider image, Carter rejected the trappings of what some had called Nixon's "imperial presidency." On inauguration day, with his wife and daughter, he walked from the Capitol to the White House. In an echo of Franklin Roosevelt's radio chats, he delivered some TV speeches wearing a sweater and seated by a fireplace. To broad public approval, he appointed a number of women and members of minority groups to federal judgeships.

Despite the populist symbolism and gestures of inclusiveness, Carter never framed a clear political philosophy. Liberals and conservatives both claimed him. Relying on young staff members from Georgia, he avoided socializing with politicians. A graduate of the U.S. Naval Academy and former nuclear-submarine engineer, Carter did best when focused on specific problems. He and Congress fought the recession with a tax cut and a modest public-works program, and the jobless rate fell to around 5 percent by late 1978. But with public opinion turning against "big government," he offered few proposals to deal with inner-city poverty, industrial decline, the trade imbalance, and other major problems.

Environmental issues loomed large for Carter, however, as they did for many Americans. In 1980, in a major victory for the administration, Congress passed the **Alaska Lands Act,** which set aside more than 100 million acres of public land in Alaska for parks, wildlife refuges, and national forests, and added twenty-six rivers to the nation's Wild and Scenic River System. Energy companies hoping to tap Alaska's oil fields protested, and laid plans to carry on the battle.

Carter confronted an environmental crisis in Niagara Falls, New York, where for years the Hooker Chemical and Plastics Corporation had dumped tons of waste in a district known as the Love Canal. In 1953, Hooker had covered the landfill with earth and sold it to the city. Schools, homes, and apartments soon sprang up, but residents complained of odors and strange substances oozing from the soil. In the later 1970s, tests confirmed that toxic chemicals, including deadly dioxin, were seeping into basements, polluting the air, and discharging into the Niagara River. Medical researchers found elevated levels of cancer, miscarriages, and birth defects among Love Canal residents. The Love Canal Homeowners' Association, founded by Lois Marie Gibbs, demanded action.

In 1978 President Carter authorized federal funds to relocate Love Canal families. In 1980, he declared the Love Canal situation a national emergency, freeing more federal money for relocation and clean-up. In late 1980, as his term ended, Carter signed legislation creating a federal "Superfund" to clean up the nation's most polluted industrial sites. The Alaska Lands Act, involving long-term wilderness preservation, and the Love Canal crisis, involving hazardous poisons, underscored the diversity of the environmental challenges facing the nation.

Overall, Carter's domestic record proved thin. Congress ignored his proposals for administrative reforms in the civil service and in the executive branch of government. His calls for a national health-insurance program, overhaul of the welfare system, and reform of the income-tax laws fell flat. "Carter couldn't get the Pledge of Allegiance through Congress," groused one legislator. His problems arose from his own ineptness, but also from the sharp conservative turn in the political climate.

Carter's foreign-policy record proved similarly mixed. As a candidate he had urged more emphasis on protecting human rights worldwide, in contrast to Henry Kissinger's single-minded focus on U.S. national interests. His secretary of state, Cyrus Vance, worked to combat abuses in Chile, Argentina, South Africa, and elsewhere. (Abuses by U.S. allies such as South Korea and the Philippines received less attention.)

In Latin America, Carter sought improved relations with Panama. Since 1964, when anti-American riots had rocked Panama, U.S. diplomats had been working on a new Panama Canal treaty that would address Panama's grievances. The Carter administration completed negotiations on treaties transferring the Canal Zone to Panama by 1999. Although these agreements protected U.S. security interests, conservatives attacked them as proof of America's post-Vietnam loss of nerve, and recalled Teddy Roosevelt's boldness in bringing the canal into existence. But in a rare success for Carter, the Senate ratified the treaties.

In dealing with America's Cold War adversaries China and the Soviet Union, Carter pursued the Nixon-Kissinger strategy of seeking better relations. After China's long-time leader Mao Zedong died in 1976, his successor, Deng Xiaoping, expressed interest in closer ties. Carter responded by restoring full diplomatic relations with Beijing in 1979, thus opening the door to scientific, cultural, and commercial exchanges. Relations remained rocky because of China's human-rights abuses, but the era of total hostility and diplomatic isolation had ended.

Toward the Soviet Union, Carter first showed conciliation, but toughness ultimately won out. In 1979, Carter and the Soviet leader Leonid Brezhnev signed the

SALT II treaty, limiting each side's nuclear arsenals. Senate ratification stalled, however, when advocates of a strong military attacked the treaty for allegedly favoring the Soviets. Support dissolved entirely in January 1980 when Russia invaded Afghanistan. The reasons were complex, but many Americans saw the invasion as proof of Moscow's expansionist designs. As U.S.-Soviet relations soured, Carter withdrew SALT II from the Senate and adopted a series of anti-Soviet measures. These included a boycott of the 1980 Summer Olympics in Moscow, which frustrated U.S. athletes, and an embargo on grain shipments to Russia, which angered midwestern farmers. This hard-line policy reflected the growing influence of Carter's national security adviser, Polish-born Zbigniew Brzezinski, who advocated a tough stance toward Moscow.

The Middle East: Peace Accords and Hostages

Carter's best and worst moments came in the Middle East. Despite Henry Kissinger's efforts, Israel and Egypt remained in a state of war. When Egyptian leader Anwar el-Sadat unexpectedly flew to Israel in 1977 to negotiate with Israeli prime minister Menachem Begin, Carter saw an opening. In September 1978, he hosted Sadat and Begin at Camp David, the presidential retreat in Maryland. The resulting **Camp David Accords** set a timetable for giving more autonomy to the Palestinians in the West Bank and Gaza, occupied by Israel since the 1967 war. In March 1979, the two leaders signed a formal peace treaty at the White House.

Carter's efforts for a broader Middle Eastern peace failed, however. Israel continued to build Jewish settlements in the occupied territories, and the other Arab states rejected the Camp David Accords. Islamic fundamentalists assassinated Sadat in 1981, and peace remained as elusive as ever.

A new Middle Eastern crisis erupted in 1979. For years, Iran had been ruled by Shah Mohammed Reza Pahlavi, who had come to power in 1953 with CIA help (see Chapter 27) and imposed a harshly repressive but pro-U.S. regime. For Washington, Iran under the shah represented a bulwark against Soviet expansion. Iran's Shiite Muslims, however, inspired by their exiled spiritual head, Ayatollah Ruhollah Khomeini, hated the shah and his ties to the West. In January 1979, amid rising Shiite unrest, the shah fled Iran. Khomeini returned in triumph, imposed strict Islamic rule, and denounced America.

In November, after Carter admitted the shah to the United States for cancer treatment, Khomeini supporters stormed the U.S. embassy in Tehran and seized more than fifty American hostages. Thus began a 444-day ordeal that nearly paralyzed the Carter administration. TV images of blindfolded hostages, anti-American mobs, and U.S. flags being used as garbage bags rubbed American nerves raw. A botched rescue attempt in April 1980 left eight GIs dead. Secretary of State Vance, who had opposed the rescue effort, resigned. Not until January 20, 1981, the day Carter left office, did the Iranian authorities release the hostages.

Troubles and Frustration as Carter's Term Ends

The decade's second oil crisis hit in 1979. When OPEC again boosted oil prices, U.S. gasoline prices edged toward the then-unheard-of level of $1 a gallon. The national mood soured as inflation surged and as lines of fuming motorists again surrounded gas stations. As the Federal Reserve Board battled inflation by raising interest rates, mortgages and business loans became prohibitively expensive. Economic activity stalled, worsening so-called **stagflation,** the combination of business stagnation and price inflation that characterized the U.S. economy through much of the 1970s.

For Carter, the lesson of the crisis was clear: the cheap, unlimited energy that for decades had fueled U.S. economic growth could no longer be counted on, and energy conservation demanded high priority. As early as 1977 Carter had created a new Department of Energy and proposed higher oil and gasoline taxes, tax credits for conservation measures, and research on alternative energy sources. Congress had passed a watered-down version of this energy bill in 1978, but Carter now decided that tougher measures were needed. However, he failed to resolve either the hostage crisis abroad or the energy crisis at home.

As with Herbert Hoover in the early 1930s, Americans turned against the remote figure in the White House. When Carter's approval rating sagged to 26 percent in mid-1979 (lower than Nixon's at the depths of Watergate), he retreated to Camp David and emerged to deliver a TV address that seemed to blame the American people for their collective "malaise" and "crisis of confidence." A cabinet reshuffle followed, but suspicions deepened that Carter himself was the problem. The 1980 Democratic convention glumly renominated Carter, but defeat in November loomed.

Carter's sudden emergence in 1976 illustrated how, in the TV era, a relative unknown could bypass party power brokers and win a national following. Voters longing to see integrity restored to the presidency had embraced him. Keenly analytical, Carter identified many emerging issues, including environmental protection; energy conservation; and reform of the nation's tax, welfare, and health-care systems. But in contrast to Franklin Roosevelt and Lyndon Johnson, he lacked the political skills to build a consensus around his proposed solutions. A post-presidential career of public service restored Carter's reputation, and brought him the Nobel Peace Prize in 2002. But when he left office in January 1981, few expressed regrets.

THE REAGAN REVOLUTION, 1981–1984

In 1980, with Carter's popularity abysmally low, Ronald Reagan, a Republican who promised a break with the past, won the presidency. The Reagan era saw mixed economic developments. It began with a recession, and ended with a stock-market crash. In between, however, inflation eased, business activity picked up, and the stock market surged. Nevertheless, continued industrial decline and inner-city problems created stubborn unemployment and pockets of real suffering. While Reagan's program of tax cuts, military spending, and business deregulation provided some economic stimulus, these policies also gave rise to mounting federal deficits and other problems.

An avid Cold Warrior, Reagan in his first term blasted the Soviets rhetorically, pursued a costly military build-up, and financed guerrillas seeking to overthrow leftist regimes in Latin America. Like other presidents before and since, he also grappled with crises in the Middle East.

Roots of the
Reagan Revolution

Ronald Reagan grew up in Dixon, Illinois, the son of an alcoholic father and a churchgoing evangelical mother. In 1937, after college and a stint as a radio sports announcer in Des Moines, he went to Hollywood for a screen test. His fifty-four films proved forgettable, but he gained political experience as president of the Screen Actors' Guild. A New

Dealer in the 1930s, Reagan had moved to the right in the 1950s, and in 1954 had become the General Electric Company's corporate spokesperson. In a 1964 TV speech for Barry Goldwater, he lauded American individualism and the free-enterprise system. As governor of California (1967–1975), he popularized conservative ideas and denounced campus demonstrators, but also proved open to compromise.

In the 1980 Republican primaries, Reagan easily bested his principal opponent, George H. W. Bush (father of the later President George W. Bush), whom he then chose as his running mate. Belying his sixty-nine years, he campaigned with youthful vigor. Posing the question "Are you better off now than you were four years ago?" Reagan garnered 51 percent of the vote in the general election to 41 percent for the Carter-Mondale Democratic ticket. (An independent candidate, liberal Republican John Anderson, collected most of the balance.)

Republicans gained eleven Senate seats, giving them a majority for the first time since 1955, and trimmed thirty-five seats from the Democrats' majority in the House of Representatives. The Republican successes revealed the power of conservative political action committees (PACs), which used computerized mass mailings focusing on emotional issues like abortion and gun control. (Liberal PACs used the same techniques, of course.)

Benefiting from the erosion of Democratic strength in the South fostered by George Wallace and by Richard Nixon's southern strategy, Reagan carried every southern state except Carter's own Georgia. He also swept every state west of the Mississippi except Minnesota and Hawaii. Over half of white blue-collar workers, once solidly Democratic, voted Republican. Of FDR's New Deal coalition, only black voters remained firmly Democratic.

Jerry Falwell and other politicized evangelicals helped Reagan's cause. Falwell's pro-Reagan Moral Majority registered an estimated 2 million new voters in 1980 and 1984. The organization disbanded after 1984, but Pat Robertson's Christian Coalition took its place, mobilizing conservative Christians to elect candidates to town councils and school boards as a prelude to expanded national influence.

Population changes also contributed to Reagan's success. While New York City, Chicago, Detroit, and other Democratic strongholds in the Northeast and Midwest had lost population in the 1970s, Texas, California, Florida, and other more conservative Sunbelt states had grown rapidly.

What underlay Reagan's appeal? First, voters frightened by stagflation welcomed his seemingly painless panacea: a big tax cut that would stimulate the economy. Moreover, Reagan's praise of self-help and private initiative struck many voters as preferable to the liberal ideology of "government handouts." His antigovernment rhetoric and dismissal of social-welfare programs like Lyndon Johnson's War on Poverty resonated with white middle-class and blue-collar Americans. Like his one-time political hero Franklin Roosevelt, Reagan promised voters a new deal. But unlike FDR, Reagan's new deal meant individualism, smaller government, lower taxes, and untrammeled free enterprise.

Reagan also embraced the cultural values of the emerging conservative movement. Many Americans at all socioeconomic levels found deeply disturbing the New Left politics, social turmoil, and sexual revolution of the 1960s, as well as legalized abortion, radical feminism, the gay-rights movement, sex and violence in the media, godless school textbooks, and the ban on school prayer. They longed for a return to a partially imagined time when life was simpler and traditional values prevailed.

Reagan, a seasoned actor and public speaker, wove these essentially negative themes into an appealing positive message of moral affirmation and support for "traditional values." At a time of national malaise, he seemed confident and assured. His unabashed patriotism, calls for military strength, and praise of America's greatness soothed the battered psyche of a nation traumatized by Vietnam, Watergate, and the multiple problems of the Ford and Carter years. Some thought Reagan glib and superficial, and his ideology fundamentally mean-spirited. But in 1980, a majority of voters found his hopeful and upbeat message persuasive and even inspiring.

Reaganomics

Reagan's economic program, called Reaganomics by the media, boiled down to the belief that U.S. capitalism, if freed from heavy taxes and government regulation, would achieve wonders of productivity. Reagan's first budget message proposed a 30 percent cut in federal income taxes over three years. Trimming this proposal slightly, Congress voted a 25 percent cut: 5 percent in 1981, 10 percent in 1982 and 1983.

To counterbalance the lost revenues, Reagan proposed cuts in such programs as school lunches, student loans, job training, and urban mass transit. Congress cut less than Reagan wanted, but it did slash more than $40 billion from domestic spending. Conservative southern Democrats joined Republicans in voting for these reductions. Not since FDR's Hundred Days of 1933 had government shifted gears so dramatically. Economists warned that the tax cut would produce huge federal deficits, but Reagan insisted that lower tax rates would stimulate business growth, pushing up tax revenues. In the Republican primary campaign, George Bush had ridiculed Reagan's rosy predictions as "voodoo economics," but once in the administration he tactfully remained silent.

Reaganomics also involved less government regulation of business. Deregulation had begun under Carter, but Reagan extended it into new areas such as banking, the savings-and-loan industry, transportation, and communications. The Federal Communications Commission cut federal rules governing the broadcast industry. The secretary of transportation cut regulations aimed at reducing air pollution and improving vehicle efficiency and safety.

The Rev. Pat Robertson *Head of the Christian Broadcasting Network (CBN) and founder of the Christian Coalition, Robertson helped mobilize evangelical Christians politically in the 1980s and beyond.*

Secretary of the Interior James Watt of Wyoming opened federal wilderness areas, forest lands, and coastal waters to oil, gas, and timber companies, and cut back on environmental-protection and endangered-species laws. Before coming to Washington, Watt had headed the Mountain States Legal Foundation, which spearheaded the so-called Sagebrush Rebellion, a movement of ranchers, farmers, and mineowners aimed at shifting federal lands in the West to state and county control. The Sierra Club and other environmental organizations protested Watt's privatizing approach, and petitions demanding his ouster garnered more than a million signatures. After a series of public-relations gaffes, Watt resigned in 1983.

Strongly pro-business, Reagan took a tough line against organized labor. In 1981, when the Professional Air Traffic Controllers Organization (PATCO) went on strike, Reagan invoked the 1948 Taft-Hartley law against strikes by federal employees, and ordered them back to work. When more than 11,000 PATCO members defied the order, Reagan fired them and barred them permanently from federal employment. (President Bill Clinton would reverse this order in 1993.) Reagan acted within the law, but other federal workers had struck in the past without such dire punishment.

Although Reagan's campaign against "big government" affected tax policy, corporate regulation, the environment, and other areas, it had little overall impact. The century-long growth of the federal budget and bureaucracy continued in the 1980s.

While implementing Reaganomics, the administration also faced the immediate problem of inflation. The Federal Reserve Board led the charge, pushing interest rates ever higher. This harsh medicine, coupled with a drop in oil prices, did its job. Inflation fell to around 4 percent in 1983 and held steady thereafter.

The Fed's high interest rates soon brought on a recession, however. By late 1982, unemployment stood at 10 percent. Reagan's cuts in social programs worsened the plight of the poor, including inner-city blacks and Hispanics. The Fed's policy also hurt U.S. exports. As foreign investors bought dollars to earn high U.S. interest rates, the dollar rose in value vis-à-vis foreign currencies, making U.S. goods more expensive abroad. With exports declining and U.S. consumers buying cars, TVs, and stereo systems made in Japan and elsewhere, the U.S. annual trade deficit shot up, reaching a whopping $111 billion in 1984.

Soaring federal deficits added to the economic muddle. Reagan's tax cuts reduced federal revenues without immediately producing the predicted business boom, while increased military appropriations far exceeded domestic spending cuts. With the budget and trade deficits mounting, the industrial sector struggling, and critics denouncing him as callous toward the poor, Reagan in 1982–1983 accepted a reduced rate of military spending, less drastic cuts in social programs, emergency job programs, and various tax increases disguised as "revenue-enhancement measures."

The economy remained worrisome through 1982. Like other recent presidents, Reagan appeared headed for failure. In the 1982 midterm elections, the Democrats regained twenty-six House seats. But 1983 brought an economic rebound. Encouraged by tax cuts, falling interest rates, better job statistics, and evidence that inflation had been tamed at last, consumers went on a buying binge and a booming stock market evoked memories of the 1920s. The five-year bull market actually began in August 1982. Money managers like Ivan Boesky, an apparent genius at stock transactions, became celebrities. E. F. Hutton and other brokerage firms advertised heavily to lure new investors. Corporate mergers proliferated. Chevron bought Gulf for $13 billion; GE acquired RCA (and its NBC subsidiary) for $6.3 billion. Banks and savings-and-loan companies, newly deregulated and flush with the deposits of eager investors, ladled out billions to developers planning shopping malls, luxury apartments, condominiums, and retirement villages. Through it all, the stock market roared on.

The Wall Street frenzy had an unsavory underside. In 1985, E. F. Hutton officials pled guilty to illegal fund manipulation. Ivan Boesky went to prison after a 1986 conviction for insider trading (profiting through advance knowledge of corporate actions). On October 19, 1987, the stock market crashed, reducing the paper value of the nation's stocks by 20 percent overnight. Thanks to prompt government action to ease credit, the market soon recovered, but the collapse had a sobering effect on giddy investors.

Even during the great bull market, economic problems persisted. The trade gap widened; the deficit passed $200 billion in 1986; and many farmers, inner-city poor, recent immigrants, and displaced industrial workers suffered through the boom times. But by 1988—just in time for another election campaign—the overall economic picture looked brighter than it had in years.

The "Evil Empire" and Crises in the Middle East

The anti-Soviet rhetoric of the late 1970s intensified during Reagan's first term. Addressing a convention of Protestant evangelicals, the president demonized the Soviet Union as "the focus of evil in the modern world." Anti-Soviet fury exploded in September 1983 when the Russians shot down a Korean passenger plane that had strayed into their airspace, killing all 269 aboard.

The administration's anti-Soviet obsession influenced its policy toward El Salvador and Nicaragua, two impoverished Central American nations caught up in revolutionary turmoil. The Reagan White House backed the Salvadoran military junta in its brutal suppression of a leftist insurgency supported by Fidel Castro's Cuba. A U.S.-backed moderate won El Salvador's 1984 presidential election, but the killing of the regime's opponents went on.

In Nicaragua, the Carter administration had initially granted aid to the Sandinista revolutionaries who overthrew dictator Anastasio Somoza in 1979. Reagan reversed this policy, claiming that the Sandinistas were turning Nicaragua into a procommunist state like Cuba. In 1982, the CIA organized and financed an anti-Sandinista guerrilla army, called the contras, based in neighboring Honduras and Costa Rica. The contras, with links to the hated Somoza regime, conducted raids, planted mines, and carried out sabotage inside Nicaragua that took a heavy toll of civilian lives.

For Reagan, the campaign to overthrow the Sandinistas and to control events in Latin America became an obsession. "The national security of all the Americas is at stake," he somberly told a joint session of Congress in May 1983. "[I]f we cannot defend ourselves there . . . the safety of our homeland would be put at jeopardy."

Fearing another Vietnam, Americans grew alarmed as details of this U.S.-run war leaked out. Congress voted a yearlong halt in U.S. military aid to the contras in December 1982 and imposed a two-year ban in 1984. Despite these prohibitions, the White House continued to funnel money contributed by foreign governments and right-wing groups in the United States to the contras. Reagan grudgingly backed a 1988 truce between the Sandinistas and the contras arranged by Central American leaders, but he still hoped for a contra victory.

UNITED STATES

ATLANTIC OCEAN

GULF OF MEXICO

MEXICO

NAFTA links U.S., Canada, Mexico in free-trade zone, 1994; U.S. intervenes to save Mexican peso, 1995.

Ongoing guerrilla activity and widespread poverty.

BELIZE

GUATEMALA

EL SALVADOR

Right-wing government and opposition leaders sign peace treaty, 1992.

HONDURAS

NICARAGUA

Staging area for anti-Sandinista rebel army (contras), organized and financed by U.S.

U.S. finances guerrilla army fighting leftist Sandinista government, 1982–1988. Anti-Sandinista coalition wins 1990 election.

COSTA RICA

PANAMA

Panama Canal

Panama Canal Treaties, 1978; U.S. invades Panama to capture Gen. Manuel Noriega, Dec. 1989.

PACIFIC OCEAN

BAHAMAS

CUBA

Migration of thousands of Cubans to U.S., 1980; withdrawal of Soviet aid, 1991.

Guantánamo

U.S. opens prison for "enemy combatants" from Afghanistan, 2003.

HAITI

Military coup, 1991; U.S. invasion restores President Aristide, 1994; Aristide overthrown, 2004; U.S., U.N. peacekeeping forces intervene.

JAMAICA

DOMINICAN REPUBLIC

PUERTO RICO (U.S.)

ST. KITTS AND NEVIS

ANTIGUA AND BARBUDA

DOMINICA

ST. LUCIA

BARBADOS

ST. VINCENT AND THE GRENADINES

TRINIDAD AND TOBAGO

GRENADA

Radical leftist government overthrown by U.S. intervention, Oct. 1983.

CARIBBEAN SEA

COLOMBIA

Flow of drugs to U.S. poses chronic problems.

VENEZUELA

Populist Hugo Chávez elected president, 1998; survives coup, 2002; urges resistance to U.S. "imperialism."

GUYANA

BRAZIL

Major economic expansion, 1980s, 1990s; civilian rule restored 1985; reformer Luiz da Silva elected president, 2002.

MAP 30.1 The United States in Central America and the Caribbean, 1978–2006

Plagued by poverty, population pressures, repressive regimes, and drug trafficking, this region has experienced turmoil and conflict—but also some hopeful developments—in recent decades.

Reagan's one unqualified success in Latin America involved the tiny West Indian island of Grenada, where a 1983 coup had installed a radical pro-Castro government. In October 1983, two thousand U.S. troops invaded Grenada and set up a pro-U.S. government. Democrats grumbled, but most Grenadians, as well as other West Indian governments, approved.

The Middle East, so frustrating to earlier administrations, also bedeviled President Reagan. Late in 1980, Iraq under strongman Saddam Hussein invaded its neighbor Iran. The incoming Reagan administration, hoping to slow the spread of Islamic fundamentalism as represented by Iran's anti-American Ayatollah Khomeini, backed Iraq in this bloody eight-year war. (Two decades later, under very different circumstances, the United States would invade Iraq to overthrow Saddam Hussein [see Chapter 32].)

Meanwhile, the conflict among Israel, the Palestinians, and Israel's Arab foes dragged on. Many Americans, remembering the Holocaust and admiring Israel's vibrant democracy, felt a strong bond with Israel, and the United States gave Israel large annual grants in military aid and other assistance. Many Bible-prophecy believers saw Israel's fate as connected to God's end-time plan. At the same time, the United States also gave extensive aid to Egypt and relied heavily on oil from Saudi Arabia and other Arab states that were strongly anti-Israel. Whipsawed by conflicting pressures, Reagan enjoyed no more success than other U.S. presidents in achieving peace in the region.

In 1981 Israel and the Palestine Liberation Organization (PLO) concluded a cease-fire. But the PLO continued building up forces at its base in southern Lebanon. In June 1982, when PLO extremists shot and critically wounded Israel's ambassador to Great Britain, Israeli troops under General Ariel Sharon, Israel's defense minister, invaded Lebanon, defeated the PLO, and forced its leaders, including chairman Yasir Arafat, to evacuate Lebanon.

This invasion deepened tensions among Lebanon's various Christian and Muslim factions. With Sharon's approval, a Lebanese Christian militia force entered two Palestinian refugee camps near Beirut to root out armed gunmen. Instead, in revenge for the earlier assassination of Lebanon's Christian president, they massacred hundreds of camp residents, including women and children. An Israeli inquiry judged Sharon negligent for permitting the militiamen to enter the camp, but found no evidence that he knew of the planned massacre beforehand. Sharon resigned as defense minister, but remained in the government.

After these events, Reagan ordered two thousand marines to Lebanon as part of a multinational peacekeeping force. The Muslims accused the Americans of favoring Israel and the Christian side, and in October 1983 a Shiite Muslim on a suicide mission crashed an explosive-laden truck into a poorly guarded U.S. barracks, killing 239 marines. Reagan had never clearly explained how the deployment served U.S. interests, and the disaster further discredited his policy. In early 1984 he withdrew the surviving marines. Reagan's efforts to promote a wider Middle East peace settlement proved equally ineffective. In September 1982, he tried to restart Arab-Israeli peace talks based on the 1978 Camp David Accords, but the effort failed.

Military Buildup and Antinuclear Protest

Insisting that post-Vietnam America had grown dangerously weak, Reagan launched a massive military expansion. The Pentagon's budget nearly doubled, reaching more than $300 billion by 1985. The buildup included nuclear weapons. Secretary of State Alexander Haig spoke of using "nuclear warning shots" in a conventional war, and other administration officials mused about the "winnability" of nuclear war. Despite popular protests across Europe, the administration deployed 572 nuclear-armed missiles in Western Europe in 1983, fulfilling a NATO decision to match Soviet missiles in Eastern Europe. The Federal Emergency Management Agency issued a nuclear-war defense plan whereby city-dwellers would flee to nearby small towns. A Defense Department official proposed backyard shelters as adequate protection in a nuclear war. "With enough shovels," he asserted, "everybody's going to make it."

Such talk, coupled with the military buildup and Reagan's anti-Soviet rhetoric, alarmed many Americans. A campaign for a verifiable multinational freeze on the manufacture and deployment of nuclear weapons won strong support. Antinuclear protesters packed New York's Central Park in June 1982. That November, voters in nine states, including California and Wisconsin, approved nuclear-freeze resolutions.

To counter the freeze campaign, Reagan in March 1983 proposed the **Strategic Defense Initiative** (SDI), a computerized anti-missile system involving space-based lasers and other high-tech components. Critics quickly dubbed the scheme "Star Wars," and experts warned of its monumental technical hurdles and the danger that it would further escalate the nuclear-arms race. Nevertheless, Reagan prevailed, and a costly SDI research program began.

Reagan Reelected   The 1984 Republican convention enthusiastically renominated Reagan and Bush. The convention, staged for TV, accented themes of patriotism, prosperity, and Reagan's personal charm. To his admirers, the president had fulfilled his promise to revitalize the free-enterprise system, rebuild U.S. military might, and make America again "stand tall" in the world. They applauded his tax cuts, his attacks on big government, and his tough stance toward the Soviets. The booming economy further strengthened his popularity.

Reagan's 1981 selection of Sandra Day O'Connor as the first woman justice on the U.S. Supreme Court had won widespread praise. So had his jaunty response in March 1981 when a ricocheting bullet fired by a deranged young man struck him in the chest. Rushed to the hospital, Reagan had insisted on walking in. "Please tell me you're all Republicans," he had quipped to physicians. (The attack disabled Reagan's press secretary, James Brady, who with his wife Sarah later joined the campaign for stricter gun control.)

The field of Democratic hopefuls included **Jesse Jackson,** an African-American civil-rights leader and former aide to Martin Luther King, Jr., who proposed a "rainbow coalition" of African-Americans, Hispanics, displaced workers, and other outsiders. In a surprisingly strong showing in the Democratic primaries, Jackson garnered 3.5 million votes and won in five southern states. But former vice president Walter Mondale came in first overall, and won the nomination with backing from labor unions, party leaders, and various interest groups. His vice-presidential choice, New York congresswoman Geraldine Ferraro, became the first woman to run on a major-party presidential ticket. Democratic campaigners criticized Reagan for runaway military spending, Cold War belligerence, massive budget deficits, cuts in social programs, and assaults on the government's regulatory powers.

Reagan and Bush won 59 percent of the popular vote and carried every state but Mondale's Minnesota plus the District of Columbia. Many white working-class voters again defected to Reagan. Despite Ferraro's presence on the Democratic ticket, a higher percentage of women voted Republican in 1984 than in 1980. Reagan's ideological appeal and his mastery of TV, combined with prosperity, had carried the day. The

Democrats still controlled the House of Representatives and many state and local offices, but the Republicans' post-1968 dominance of the White House—interrupted only by Jimmy Carter's single term—continued.

Some frustrated Democrats sought to reverse their image as a "big government" and "tax-and-spend" party dominated by special interests. In 1985 Arkansas governor Bill Clinton, Senator Al Gore of Tennessee, and other moderates formed the **Democratic Leadership Council** (DLC) to stake out a more centrist party position. In the early 1990s Clinton would use the DLC as a springboard for a presidential bid.

REAGAN'S SECOND TERM, 1985–1989

Economic problems persisted in Reagan's second term, and the president made two Supreme Court appointments. But events abroad—and a major scandal related to the administration's foreign policy—dominated these years. A dramatic and unexpected easing of Cold War tensions signaled the approaching end of that long conflict. Continued tensions in the Middle East and a wave of terrorist attacks made clear, however, that even a post–Cold War world would remain dangerous.

Supreme Court Appointments, Budget Deficits, the Iran-Contra Scandal

Reagan's second term brought some legislative achievements, including the Immigration Reform and Control Act, discussed earlier, and a tax-reform law that made the system fairer and spared some 6 million low-income Americans from paying any income taxes. Reagan reshaped the Supreme Court in 1986 by elevating William Rehnquist, a Nixon appointee, to the chief justiceship upon the retirement of Warren Burger, and appointing Antonin Scalia to replace him. Scalia would prove one of the Court's most outspokenly conservative members and a champion of the view that the "original intent" of the authors of the Constitution must prevail over later interpretations.

When another vacancy opened in 1987, Reagan nominated Robert Bork, a judge and legal scholar whose abrasive personality and inflexible views led the Senate to reject him. Reagan's next nominee withdrew after admitting that he had smoked marijuana as an adult. Reagan's third choice, Anthony Kennedy, a conservative California jurist, won quick confirmation.

Federal budget deficits—a byproduct of Reagan's tax cuts and military spending increases—surpassed $200 billion in 1985 and 1986, and hovered at about $150 billion for the next two years. This, coupled with the yawning trade gap and a savings-and-loan industry scandal related to deregulation (see Chapter 31), were Reagan's principal economic legacies.

The worst crisis of Reagan's presidency, the so-called **Iran-contra scandal,** began obscurely late in 1986 when a Beirut newspaper reported that in 1985 the United States had shipped, via Israel, 508 antitank missiles to Iran, America's avowed enemy. Admitting the sale, Reagan claimed that the goal had been to encourage "moderate elements" in Tehran and to gain the release of U.S. hostages held in Lebanon by pro-Iranian groups. In February 1987 a presidentially appointed investigative panel blamed Reagan's chief of staff, Donald Regan, who resigned.

More details soon emerged, including the revelation that Lieutenant Colonel Oliver North, a National Security Council aide in the White House, had secretly diverted prof-

President Reagan at the Berlin Wall, June 1987 *Celebrating the city's 750th anniversary, Reagan speaks before the Brandenburg Gate, with a part of the wall visible behind him. Erected in 1961, the Berlin Wall came to symbolize Europe's Cold War division. With his flair for the dramatic, Reagan directly challenged the leader of the Soviet Union: "Mr. Gorbachev, tear down this wall."*

its from the Iran arms sales to the Nicaraguan contras at a time when Congress had forbidden such aid. To hide this crime, North and his secretary had altered and deleted sensitive computer files and destroyed incriminating documents. North implicated CIA director William Casey in illegalities, but Casey's death thwarted this line of investigation.

In May 1987 a joint House-Senate investigative committee opened hearings on the scandal. The nation watched in fascination as North, resplendent in his marine uniform, boasted of his patriotism, and as National Security Adviser John Poindexter testified that he had deliberately concealed the fund-diversion scheme from Reagan. The committee found no positive proof of Reagan's knowledge of illegalities, but roundly criticized the lax management style and contempt for the law that had pervaded the Reagan White House. In 1989, North was convicted of obstructing a congressional inquiry and destroying and falsifying official documents. (The conviction was later reversed on the technicality that some testimony used against North had been given under a promise of immunity.) Although ultimately less damaging to the presidency than the Watergate scandal, the Iran-contra affair dogged the Reagan administration's final years as a serious abuse of executive power.

Other scandals plagued Reagan's second term, including allegations of bribery in military-procurement contracts. Attorney General Edwin Meese resigned in 1988 amid charges that he had used his influence to promote ventures in which he had a financial interest. In 1989 came revelations that former interior secretary James Watt and other prominent Republicans had been paid hundreds of thousands of dollars for using their influence on behalf of housing developers seeking federal subsidies.

Reagan's popularity seemed unaffected by all this dirty linen. The veteran actor possessed an uncanny ability to convey warmth and sincerity and to shrug off damaging revelations with a disarming joke. Some dubbed him the Teflon president—nothing seemed to stick to him. Moreover, a surprising turn of events in Russia would end his presidency on a high note.

Reagan's Mission to Moscow   A dramatic warming in Soviet-American relations began early in Reagan's second term. At meetings in Europe in 1985 and 1986, Reagan and the new Soviet leader, Mikhail Gorbachev, revived the stalled arms-control process. Beset by profound economic and political problems in Russia and by spreading unrest in Poland, East Germany, and elsewhere in the Soviet sphere, Gorbachev worked to reduce superpower tensions to gain breathing space as he struggled with mounting crises at home. His ambitious program involved nothing less than restructuring and democratizing the Russian government and economy, ending the Communist Party's absolute power, and loosening Moscow's grip on the sprawling Soviet Union and the satellite nations of Eastern Europe.

In June 1987, speaking near the Berlin Wall, President Reagan dramatically declared: "Mr. Gorbachev, tear down this wall!" That December, in Washington, the two leaders signed the **Intermediate-range Nuclear Forces (INF) Treaty,** eliminating 2,500 U.S. and Soviet missiles from Europe. This treaty, in turn, led to Reagan's historic visit to Moscow in May 1988, where the two leaders strolled and chatted in Red Square.

Some Reaganites protested as their hero, having earlier denounced the Soviet Union as an "evil empire," cozied up to the world's top communist. One conservative paper called Reagan's trip "a sad week for the free world." Reagan himself, with his usual confidence, pointed to Gorbachev's reforms and argued that "the evil empire" was becoming more benign. Most Americans welcomed improved relations with the Cold War enemy.

The INF treaty and Reagan's trip to Moscow marked the beginning of the end of the Cold War. Historians still debate the relative importance of Reagan's military buildup versus the Soviet Union's own internal weaknesses in bringing about this outcome. Whatever history's judgment on that point, the fact that one of America's most dedicated Cold Warriors presided over the early stages of its demise remains one of the ironies of recent American history.

The Middle East: Tensions and Terrorism   As relations with Moscow improved, conditions in the Middle East worsened. In 1987, Palestinians in Gaza and the West Bank rose up against Israeli occupation. In response, Secretary of State George Shultz (who had replaced Alexander Haig in 1982) proposed talks among Israel, the Palestinians, and Jordan on a plan for Palestinian autonomy. Israel refused to negotiate until the uprising ended, and the Palestinians rejected Shultz's proposals as not going far enough toward creating a Palestinian state. Over U.S. objections, Israel continued to build settlements in the disputed West Bank.

A deadly byproduct of the Middle East conflict was a series of bombings, assassinations, hijackings, and hostage-takings by anti-Israel and anti-American terrorists. At the 1972 Summer Olympics in Munich, Palestinian gunmen killed two Israeli athletes and took nine more hostage. In the ensuing gun battle with German police, all nine hostages died, along with five of the terrorists and a policeman.

In 1985, terrorists set off bombs in the Vienna and Rome airports and hijacked a TWA flight en route from Athens to Rome, holding the crew and 145 passengers hostage for seventeen days and killing one passenger, a U.S. sailor. That same year, four heavily armed men demanding the release of Palestinians held by Israel hijacked an Italian cruise ship, the *Achille Lauro,* dumping a wheelchair-bound Jewish-American tourist into the sea.

In 1986, the bombing of a Berlin disco club popular with U.S. troops killed two GIs and injured others. Accusing Libyan strongman Muammar al-Qadaffi of masterminding this and other attacks, Reagan ordered the bombing of Libyan military sites. But the terrorist attacks intensified in frequency. In December 1988, a concealed bomb detonated aboard Pan Am flight 103, en route from London to New York. It crashed near Lockerbie, Scotland, killing all 259 aboard, including many Americans. In 1991, the United States and Great Britain formally charged two Libyan officials in the attack. In 2001, after years of stalling by Qaddafi, a special Scottish court sitting in the Netherlands acquitted one of the men but convicted the other of murder and imposed a life sentence.

This cycle of terrorism reflected profound religious and political divisions in the Middle East. Hatred of Israel, and even denial of the Jewish state's right to exist, gripped parts of the Arab world, particularly among a growing Islamic fundamentalist movement. This movement appealed especially to poor, ill-educated young Muslims attracted by clerical calls for *jihad* (holy war in defense of Islam) against a secular West that seemed increasingly dominant militarily, economically, and culturally. The Palestinian leader Yasir Arafat bore responsibility as well, for leadership failures and missed opportunities. The stationing of U.S. troops in Saudi Arabia, as well as expanding Jewish settlements in the Palestinian territories, also fed the anger that fueled terrorist attacks.

Assessing the Reagan Years   After Nixon's disgrace, Ford's caretaker presidency, and Carter's rocky tenure, Ronald Reagan's two terms restored a sense of stability and continuity to U.S. politics. Domestically, Reagan compiled a mixed record. Inflation eased, and the economy improved after 1982. But the federal deficit soared, and the administration largely ignored festering social issues, environmental concerns, and long-term economic problems.

Reaganism offered little to the poor beyond the hope that free-enterprise capitalism, stimulated by tax cuts and deregulation, would generate enough jobs that everyone could improve their lot. Building on Richard Nixon's strategy (see Chapter 29), Reagan exploited the anxieties and resentments of middle-class white voters. He criticized affirmative-action programs and ridiculed the welfare system by passing along mythic stories about Cadillac-driving black "welfare queens" and poor people who used food stamps to buy lemons for their gin-and-tonics.

Reagan's critics dismissed his presidency as a time when self-interest trumped the public good, or, at best, as an interlude marked by nostalgia and drift rather than positive achievement. They noted how readily Reagan's celebration of individual freedom could morph into self-centered materialism. Apart from anticommunism and flag-waving patriotism, they contended, Reagan offered few goals around which all Americans could rally.

In 1988, former chief of staff Donald Regan, still smarting over his forced resignation, published a memoir that portrayed Reagan as little more than an automaton: "Every moment of every public appearance was scheduled, every word was scripted, every place where Reagan was expected to stand was chalked with toe marks." He also reported the central White House role of Nancy Reagan, and her reliance on a San Francisco astrologer in planning her husband's schedule. Others noted that Reagan's benign public image masked less appealing traits. One former aide called him "the most warmly ruthless man I've ever seen."

To his admirers, such criticism was itself mean-spirited, and beside the point. They credited Reagan for reasserting traditional values of self-reliance and free enterprise; criticizing governmental excesses; and restoring national pride with his infectious optimism and patriotism.

Reagan's militant anticommunism spawned the Iran-contra scandal, but also, his admirers believed, contributed mightily to America's victory in the Cold War—a victory whose full dimensions would become apparent after he left office.

Alzheimer's disease darkened Reagan's post-presidential years. He died in 2004, at ninety-three. But ideas underlying "the Reagan revolution" lived on, and still influence American politics.

Conclusion

After the turbulent 1960s, an escapist tone dominated popular culture in the 1970s, and many young people pursued personal and careerist goals. Activist energies survived, however, in a revitalized women's movement, a gay-rights campaign, and support for environmental causes. A grass-roots conservative movement gained momentum as well, however, reinforced by an evangelical religious revival. Opposing abortion, gay rights, costly social-welfare programs, and secular cultural trends, conservatives mobilized politically, laying the groundwork for Ronald Reagan's electoral victories.

Industrial decline, oil-price hikes, and runaway inflation caused serious economic problems through most of the 1970s. The 1980s, though bracketed by a recession and a stock-market crash, saw a five-year boom that brought prosperity to many. However, a persistent trade gap, massive federal deficits linked to President Reagan's tax cuts, and a continued erosion of factory jobs posed warning flags for the future.

Displaced industrial workers and inner-city minorities struggled in a high-tech economy that increasingly demanded advanced education and specialized skills. Many African-Americans enjoyed upward mobility, but others remained in poverty. Native Americans faced continuing deprivation but also new economic opportunities and benefits from long-ignored treaty rights. Immigration from Latin America and Asia, meanwhile, reshaped the nation's ethnic profile.

During his brief presidency, Gerald Ford proposed voluntarist strategies for battling inflation. President Jimmy Carter crafted strategies to address the energy crisis, environmental hazards, and other emerging issues. But as Americans reacted to successive oil shocks and setbacks abroad, neither president seemed up to the challenges confronting the nation. Carter brokered a peace settlement between Egypt and Israel, but the Iranian hostage crisis bedeviled his final fourteen months in office.

Ronald Reagan entered the White House in 1981 as a champion of conservative cultural values that many Americans saw as threatened, and a proponent of a political ideology stressing free enterprise, lower taxes, and a smaller government bureaucracy, coupled with military might and aggressive anticommunism. After a series of failed and frustrating presidencies, millions of Americans welcomed Reagan's optimism, uncomplicated patriotism, and firmly held political beliefs.

The so-called Iran-contra scandal, arising from the Reagan administration's secret military aid to Iran and from its determined effort to overthrow Nicaragua's leftist regime, preoccupied the nation in 1987. Reagan's reputation survived largely unscathed, however. U.S.-Soviet relations, after deteriorating in the late 1970s and early 1980s, improved dramatically in Reagan's second term. Mikhail Gorbachev, contending with grave economic and political problems in Russia and throughout the Soviet sphere, intensified by the need to match Reagan's defense buildup, took conciliatory steps that signaled the Cold War's end.

As the Cold War faded, however, worsening conditions in the Middle East and an upsurge of terrorism, which announced itself with assassinations, exploding bombs, and crashing airplanes, signaled the onset of an era no less hazardous in its way than the darkest days of the Cold War.

31

<hr>

Beyond the Cold War: Charting a New Course, 1988–2000

THE BUSH YEARS: GLOBAL RESOLVE, DOMESTIC DRIFT, 1988–1993

Ronald Reagan's vice president, **George Bush,** elected president in 1988, was a patrician in politics. Son of a Connecticut senator, Yale graduate, and World War II veteran, he had entered the Texas oil business, served in Congress, lost a Senate race, and been U.N. ambassador and CIA director before becoming Reagan's running mate in 1980.

As president, Bush compiled an uneven record. Internationally, he reacted decisively when Iraq invaded Kuwait, and he worked to ease Israeli-Palestinian tensions. His domestic record was thin, however, as he typically substituted platitudes for policy.

The Election of 1988   Vice President Bush easily won the 1988 Republican presidential nomination. In his acceptance speech, he called for a "kinder, gentler America" and pledged, "Read my lips: no new taxes." As his running mate he selected Senator Dan Quayle of Indiana, son of a newspaper publisher.

The field of Democratic contenders eventually narrowed to the black leader Jesse Jackson and Massachusetts governor Michael Dukakis. Jackson, urging concern for the poor and a war on drugs, ran well in the primaries. But Dukakis's primary victories in

1988 • George Bush elected president.

1989 • Massive Alaskan oil spill by *Exxon Valdez*.
Supreme Court, in several 5-to-4 decisions, restricts civil-rights laws.
U.S. invasion of Panama; Manuel Noriega overthrown.
China's rulers crush prodemocracy movement.
Berlin Wall is opened.

1990 • Federal Clean Air Act strengthened.
Americans with Disabilities Act passed.
Iraq invades Kuwait.
Recession (1990–1993).
Germany reunified; Soviet troops start withdrawal from Eastern Europe.

1991 • Persian Gulf War (Operation Desert Storm).
Hearings on Clarence Thomas's Supreme Court nomination.
Collapse of Soviet Union.

1992 • Supreme Court in *Planned Parenthood* v. *Casey* approves abortion restrictions but upholds *Roe* v. *Wade*.
President Bush commits U.S. troops in Somalia.
Bill Clinton elected president.

1993 • Congress approves NAFTA treaty.
Economy expands, stock market surges (1993–2000).
Clinton health-care reform plan fails (1993–1994).
Some eighty Branch Davidians die in fire as federal agents raid compound in Waco, Texas.
World Trade Center bombing kills six.

1994 • Christian Coalition gains control of Republican Party in several states.
Yasir Arafat and Yitzhak Rabin sign Oslo Accords at White House.
Clinton withdraws U.S. forces from Somalia.
United States joins the World Trade Organization (WTO).
Republicans proclaim "Contract with America"; win control of House and Senate; Newt Gingrich becomes Speaker.

1995 • Oklahoma City federal building bombed.
Dayton Accords achieve cease-fire in Bosnia; Clinton commits U.S. troops to enforce agreement.

1996 • Welfare Reform Act.
Clinton defeats Bob Dole to win second term.

1997 • Congressional battle over tobacco-industry regulation.

1998 • Clinton impeached by House of Representatives in sex scandal.

1999 • Senate dismisses impeachment charges.
Columbine High School shootings.
U.S. and NATO forces intervene in Kosovo.

2000 • George W. Bush wins presidency when Supreme Court ends Florida election dispute.

New York and California proved decisive. As his running mate, Dukakis chose Texas senator Lloyd Bentsen.

In the campaign Bush stressed Reagan's achievements while distancing himself from the Iran-contra scandal. Emphasizing peace and prosperity, he pointed to better Soviet relations, low inflation, and the 14 million new jobs created during the 1980s. A TV commercial aired by Bush supporters, playing on racist stereotypes, featured a black convict who committed rape and murder after his release under a Massachusetts prisoner-furlough program.

Dukakis emphasized his managerial skills. "This election is not about ideology, it's about competence," he insisted. He hammered at the failures of the "Swiss-cheese" Reagan economy (that is, full of holes) and urged "Reagan Democrats" to return to the fold. But Dukakis seemed wooden, and his dismissal of ideology made it difficult for him to define his political vision. Both candidates relied on TV-oriented "photo opportunities," vague slogans, and sound bites. Bush visited flag factories and military plants. Dukakis proved his toughness on defense by posing in a tank. Editorial writers deplored the "junk-food" campaign.

Bush won, carrying forty states and garnering 54 percent of the vote. Dukakis prevailed in only ten states plus the District of Columbia. The Democrats, however, retained control of Congress and most state legislatures.

The Cold War Ends As the Bush administration took power in Washington, the Soviet collapse symbolized by the opening of the Berlin Wall proceeded with breathtaking rapidity. Germany was reunited for the first time since 1945. Estonia, Latvia, and Lithuania, the Baltic republics annexed by Moscow in 1940, declared independence. The other Soviet republics moved toward autonomy as well.

In August 1991 President Bush and Mikhail Gorbachev signed a treaty in Moscow reducing their strategic nuclear arsenals by 25 percent. Secretary of Defense Dick Cheney proposed a 25 percent reduction in U.S. military forces over five years. NATO announced major troop reductions.

As the Russian Communist Party's centralized control collapsed and the economy sank into crisis, reformers called for a Western-style market economy. In August 1991, hard-line communists tried to overthrow Gorbachev. But thousands of Muscovites, rallied by Boris Yeltsin, president of the Russian Republic, protectively surrounded Moscow's parliament building, and the coup failed.

Exuberant crowds toppled statues of Lenin and Stalin. Leningrad resumed its pre-Soviet name, St. Petersburg. Late in 1991 most of the Soviet republics proclaimed the end of the USSR. Gorbachev, overwhelmed by forces he himself had unleashed, resigned. In Moscow, Boris Yeltsin filled the power vacuum.

Secretary of State James Baker, a longtime Bush ally, proceeded cautiously as these events unfolded. U.S. influence was limited, in any event, as long-suppressed forces of nationalism and ethnicity burst forth in Eastern Europe and in the former Soviet Union. Baker did work to ensure the security of the twenty-seven thousand nuclear weapons based in Russia and in newly independent Ukraine, Belarus, and Kazakhstan, and to prevent rogue states or terrorist groups from acquiring nuclear materials or know-how from these countries. As negotiations with Yeltsin and other leaders went forward, Bush announced further reductions in the U.S. nuclear arsenal.

For decades, the superpowers had backed their client states and rebel insurgencies in the Third World. As the Cold War faded, prospects brightened for resolving some local disputes. In Nicaragua, for example, Bush abandoned the U.S.-funded contra war against the leftist Sandinista government. Instead, Bush and Congress crafted a program aimed at reintegrating the contras into Nicaraguan life and politics. A multiparty anti-Sandinista coalition won the 1990 Nicaraguan elections.

Poverty and economic exploitation still plagued Latin America, however, and the flow of cocaine and heroin to U.S. cities from the region continued. In 1989, Bush ordered a U.S. invasion of Panama to capture the nation's ruler, General Manuel Noriega. Formerly on the CIA payroll, Noriega had accepted bribes to permit drugs to pass through Panama on their way north. Convicted of drug trafficking, he received a life prison term.

U.S. relations with the Philippines, a former colony and longtime ally, shifted as well. In 1991 the Philippines legislature ended an agreement permitting two U.S. naval bases in the islands. With the Cold War over, the Bush administration closed the bases.

Meanwhile, South Africa's policy of racial segregation, called apartheid, provoked growing protests by U.S. black leaders and campus activists. In 1986, over a Reagan veto, Congress had imposed economic sanctions against white-ruled South Africa, including a ban on U.S. corporate investment. Economic pressure by America and other nations strengthened a powerful anti-apartheid campaign in South Africa itself, led by Anglican bishop Desmond Tutu. The South African government in 1990 released black leader Nelson Mandela after years in prison and opened negotiations with Mandela's African National Congress. When South Africa scrapped its apartheid policy in 1991, President Bush lifted the sanctions. In 1994, underscoring the new political order in South Africa, Mandela was elected president.

In 1989, Chinese troops brutally crushed a pro-democracy demonstration in Beijing's Tiananmen Square, killing several hundred unarmed students and workers. A wave of arrests and public executions followed. The Bush administration curtailed diplomatic contacts and urged banks to postpone loans to China. But Bush, committed to U.S. trade expansion, did not break diplomatic relations or cancel trade agreements with Beijing.

As the Cold War faded, trade issues loomed large. America's trade deficit with Japan stirred special concern. Early in 1992, facing a recession and rising unemployment in an election year, President Bush turned an Asian trip into a trade mission. Joined by U.S. business leaders, he urged the Japanese to buy more U.S. products. The trade gap continued, however.

The Persian Gulf War, 1991 One foreign crisis brought a forceful response. On August 2, 1990, Iraq invaded its neighbor Kuwait. Iraq's dictator, Saddam Hussein, viewed Kuwait's ruling sheiks as Western puppets and asserted Iraq's historic claims to Kuwait's vast oil fields.

Under Saddam, Iraq had pursued chemical- and nuclear-weapons programs and threatened not only Kuwait but also other Arab nations and Israel. During the Iran-Iraq War, however, the United States had favored Iraq, and even assisted Saddam's military buildup (see Chapter 30). Now, however, confronted by Iraq's invasion of Kuwait, Washington protested vigorously.

Avoiding Lyndon Johnson's mistakes in Vietnam, Bush built a consensus in Congress, at the United Nations, and among the American people for a clear objective: Iraq's withdrawal from Kuwait. Deploying more than 500,000 U.S. troops to achieve that goal, Bush also built a coalition of thirty-four nations, including five in the Persian Gulf, which contributed an additional 160,000 troops.

MAP 31.1 The Mideast Crisis, 1980–2000

With terrorist attacks, the Iran-Iraq War, the Persian Gulf War, and the ongoing struggle between Israel and the Palestinians, the Middle East was the site of almost unending violence, conflict, and tension in these years.

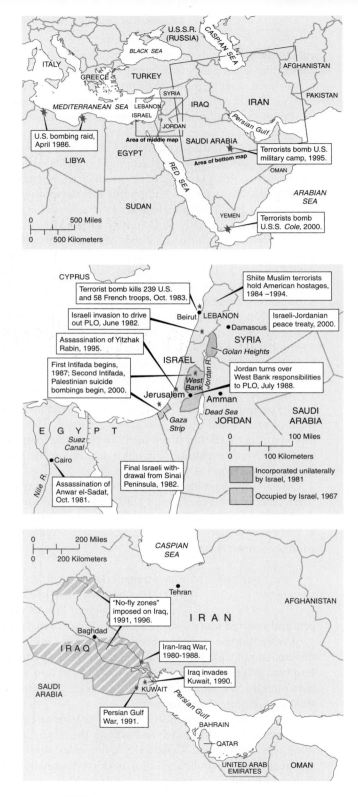

U.S. bombing raid, April 1986.

Terrorists bomb U.S. military camp, 1995.

Terrorists bomb U.S.S. *Cole*, 2000.

Area of middle map

Area of bottom map

Terrorist bomb kills 239 U.S. and 58 French troops, Oct. 1983.

Shiite Muslim terrorists hold American hostages, 1984–1994.

Israeli invasion to drive out PLO, June 1982.

Israeli-Jordanian peace treaty, 2000.

Assassination of Yitzhak Rabin, 1995.

First Intifada begins, 1987; Second Intifada, Palestinian suicide bombings begin, 2000.

Jordan turns over West Bank responsibilities to PLO, July 1988.

Final Israeli withdrawal from Sinai Peninsula, 1982.

Assassination of Anwar el-Sadat, Oct. 1981.

Incorporated unilaterally by Israel, 1981

Occupied by Israel, 1967

"No-fly zones" imposed on Iraq, 1991, 1996.

Iran-Iraq War, 1980-1988.

Iraq invades Kuwait, 1990.

Persian Gulf War, 1991.

Kuwait, 1991 *Burning oil fields, set ablaze by retreating Iraqis, provide an eerie backdrop to motorized U.S. troops participating in Operation Desert Storm, the high point of the Bush presidency.*

The UN imposed economic sanctions against Iraq and insisted that Saddam withdraw by January 15, 1991. On January 12, the Senate and the House endorsed military action. Most Democrats voted against war, favoring continued economic sanctions. The shadow of Vietnam hovered in the background as Americans debated another war.

The air war began on January 16. For six weeks B-52 and F-16 bombers pounded Iraqi troops, supply depots, and command centers in Iraq's capital, Baghdad. The air forces of other nations participated as well. In retaliation, Saddam fired Soviet-made Scud missiles against Tel Aviv and other Israeli cities, as well as against the Saudi capital, Riyadh. As TV news programs showed distant targets through aircraft bombsights and U.S. Patriot missiles intercepting incoming Scuds, the war resembled a glorified video game.

On February 23 two hundred thousand U.S. troops under General H. Norman Schwarzkopf moved across the desert toward Kuwait. Although rain turned the sand to soup, the army pushed on. Iraqi soldiers fled or surrendered en masse. U.S. forces destroyed thirty-seven hundred Iraqi tanks while losing only three. With Iraqi resistance crushed, President Bush declared a cease-fire, and Kuwait's ruling family returned to power. U.S. casualties numbered 148 dead—including 35 killed inadvertently by U.S. firepower—and 467 wounded. Iraqi military casualties, estimated at 25,000 to 65,000, included as many as 12,000 killed in the bombing campaign. The Iraqi government claimed that U.S. bombs also killed 2,300 civilians.

For President Bush, the **Persian Gulf War** proved that Americans were again ready to use military might to pursue national interests. "By God, we've kicked the Vietnam syndrome once and for all," he declared.

Some had urged President Bush to invade Iraq and overthrow Saddam Hussein. Bush and National Security Adviser Brent Scowcroft rejected this course, however. Invading Iraq, they feared, could involve an extended occupation and unleash sectarian conflict. Somewhat chastened, Saddam granted UN inspectors access to his weapons-production facilities. The UN also imposed "no-fly zones" on Iraqi aircraft, but Saddam's army brutally suppressed uprisings by Shiite Muslims in the south and ethnic Kurds in the north.

Home-Front
Problems and
Domestic Policies

In the early 1990s the impact of Reagan-era tax cuts and deregulation began to hit home. First came the collapse of the savings-and-loan (S&L) industry, provider of home loans and a modest but secure return to depositors. As interest rates had risen in the late 1970s because of inflation, the S&Ls had offered higher interest to attract deposits, even though their assets were mostly in fixed-rate mortgages. Money freed up by the Reagan tax cuts flowed into S&Ls with their high rates of return. Meanwhile, in the deregulation fervor, Congress eased the rules governing S&Ls, enabling them to make loans on risky real-estate ventures. As recession hit, many of these investments went bad. In 1988–1990, nearly six hundred S&Ls failed, especially in the Southwest, wiping out many depositors' savings.

Because the government insures S&L deposits, the Bush administration in 1989 set up a program to repay depositors and sell hundreds of foreclosed office towers and apartment buildings in a depressed real-estate market. Estimates of the bailout's cost topped $400 billion. "'Savings and loan,'" wrote a journalist, "has become synonymous with 'bottomless pit.'"

The federal deficit, a byproduct of Reagan's tax cuts and military spending, continued to mount. In 1990, Congress and Bush agreed on a deficit-reduction plan involving spending cuts and tax increases. Bush's retreat from his 1988 "no new taxes" pledge angered many voters. Despite the agreement, the deficit reached $290 billion in 1992. The Gulf War, the S&L bailout, and soaring welfare and Medicare/Medicaid payments sank the budget-balancing effort.

Making matters worse, recession struck in 1990. Retail sales slumped; housing starts fell. The auto industry, battered by Japanese imports, fared disastrously. GM cut its work force by more than seventy thousand. By 1992 the jobless rate exceeded 7 percent and the number of Americans living in poverty had risen by 2.1 million, to about 34 million. If 1984 was "morning in America," wrote a columnist, quoting a Reagan campaign slogan, this was "the morning after."

The recession worsened inner-city joblessness and despair. In April 1992, an outbreak of arson and looting erupted in a poor black district of Los Angeles. The immediate cause was black outrage (shared by many others) over a jury's acquittal of four white police officers whose beating of a black motorist had been captured on videotape. The riots left some forty persons dead and millions in property damage, underscoring the desperate conditions in the inner cities. When Bush came to Atlanta in 1992 to observe Martin Luther King Day, Dr. King's daughter, a minister, declared, "How dare we celebrate in . . . a recession, when nobody is sure whether their jobs are secure?"

Proclaiming himself the "education president," Bush called for national testing of schoolchildren and supported a voucher system to enable children to attend private schools at public expense. In the view of many educators, such proposals bore little relationship to the plight of many crowded and underfunded public schools.

The **Americans with Disabilities Act** of 1990, supported by Bush, barred discrimination against disabled persons in hiring or education. In an echo of the earlier African-American civil-rights campaign, Congress passed this law following demonstrations and lobbying by the disabled and organizations representing them. Thanks to this law, job opportunities for handicapped persons increased and the number of physically or cognitively impaired children attending public schools rose significantly.

Environmental concerns surged in 1989 when a giant oil tanker, the *Exxon Valdez,* ran aground in Alaska's Prince William Sound, spilling more than 10 million gallons of oil. The accident fouled coastal habitats, killed thousands of sea otters and shore birds, and jeopardized Alaska's herring and salmon industries. That summer, air pollution in more than one hundred U.S. cities exceeded federal standards. A 1991 Environmental Protection Agency study found that pollutants were seriously depleting the atmosphere's ozone layer, which reduces cancer-causing solar radiation.

Squeezed between public worries and corporate resistance to regulation, Bush compiled a mixed environmental record. In a bipartisan effort, the White House and the Democratic Congress agreed on a toughened Clean Air Act in 1990. (California and other states adopted even tighter auto-emission standards.) The government also began the costly task of disposing of radioactive wastes and cleaning up the contamination around nuclear facilities. On the other hand, the administration scuttled treaties on global warming, backed oil exploration in Alaskan wilderness preserves, and proposed to open protected wetlands to developers. Bush's self-serving speech to a UN environmental conference in Rio de Janeiro in 1992 further alienated environmentalists.

President Bush made two Supreme Court nominations. David Souter, a New Hampshire judge of moderate views, won easy confirmation in 1990. With **Clarence Thomas,** however, Bush continued Reagan's effort to shift the court sharply to the right. Bush nominated Thomas in 1991 to replace Thurgood Marshall, a black who had fought segregation as an NAACP lawyer. Thomas, also an African-American, supported right-wing causes and opposed affirmative-action programs. Having risen from poverty to attend Yale Law School and to head the Equal Employment Opportunity Commission (EEOC) under Reagan, Thomas viewed individual effort, not government programs, as the avenue of upward mobility for the disadvantaged. Noting his weak qualifications, critics charged Bush with playing racial politics.

In the Senate Judiciary Committee hearings, a former Thomas associate at EEOC, **Anita Hill,** accused him of sexual harassment. Thomas narrowly won confirmation, but Republican efforts to discredit Hill's testimony alienated many women. When women candidates did very well in the 1992 elections (see below), many observers concluded that resentment over the Thomas hearings had played a role.

On the Court, Thomas allied with Justice Antonin Scalia in upholding executive power, interpreting the Constitution narrowly, and championing conservative social issues. Overall, the Reagan/Bush appointments blunted the Supreme Court's liberal thrust that began in the 1930s and continued under Chief Justice Earl Warren and others. In 1990–1991, the Court narrowed the rights of arrested persons and upheld regulations barring physicians in federally funded clinics from discussing abortion with their patients. In *Planned Parenthood* v. *Casey,* a five-to-four decision in 1992, the Court affirmed *Roe* v. *Wade* but upheld a Pennsylvania law restricting abortion rights by imposing a twenty-four-hour waiting period and other requirements. Conservative activism was replacing liberal activism on the high court.

1992: Clinton Versus Bush, and a Third-Party Challenge

George Bush's approval ratings soared after the Persian Gulf War, only to fall below 50 percent as the recession hit. A 1991 *New York Times* editorial commented: "[Bush is] shrewd and energetic in foreign policy . . . , clumsy and irresolute at home. . . . The domestic Bush flops like a fish, leaving the impression that he doesn't know what he thinks or doesn't much care, apart from the political gains to be extracted from an issue."

Intimidated by Bush's post–Gulf War popularity, top Democrats stayed out of the 1992 presidential race. But Governor Bill Clinton of Arkansas took the plunge. Fending off reports of marital infidelity, Clinton defeated other hopefuls in the primaries and won the nomination. As his running mate, he chose Senator **Albert Gore, Jr.,** of Tennessee. In his acceptance speech, Clinton pledged action on environmental, health-care, and economic issues.

President Bush quashed a primary challenge by conservative columnist Pat Buchanan, but at the Republican Party convention Buchanan and evangelist Pat Robertson gave divisive speeches staking out deeply conservative positions on contested cultural issues. Delegates from Robertson's Christian Coalition cheered, but moderate Republicans deplored the party's rightward turn.

Political outsider **H. Ross Perot,** founder of a Texas data-processing firm, also entered the race. The nation's economic problems were simple, Perot insisted on TV talk shows; only party politics stood in the way of solving them. He proposed electronic "town meetings" by which the public would govern directly. At his peak of popularity, nearly 40 percent of the voters supported Perot. His eccentricities and thin-skinned response to critics cost him support, but he remained a wild card in the election.

Bush attacked Clinton's character and charged that he had evaded the Vietnam-era draft. As for the recession, Bush promised to put James A. Baker in charge of domestic affairs in a second term. Clinton, meanwhile, focused on the economy and the problems of the middle class. He pledged to work for a national health-care system, welfare reform, and programs to promote economic growth and new technologies.

Clinton won 43 percent of the vote to Bush's 38 percent. Perot amassed 19 percent—the best showing for a third-party candidate since Teddy Roosevelt in 1912. Clinton carried such key states as California, Ohio, and New Jersey; lured back many blue-collar and suburban "Reagan Democrats"; and did well in the South. Clinton's move to the center (see below), coupled with Bush's indecisiveness and the divisive Perot campaign, had brought him victory.

In the congressional races, thirty-eight African-Americans and seventeen Hispanics won seats. A California congressional district sent the first Korean-American to Washington. California also became the first state to elect two women senators, Barbara Boxer and Dianne Feinstein. Illinois elected the first African-American woman senator, Carol Moseley Braun. Overall, the new Congress included fifty-three women: six in the Senate and forty-seven in the House. Magazines hailed "The Year of the Woman." With Democrats in control of Congress and the executive branch, an end to the much-deplored Washington "gridlock" seemed possible.

THE CLINTON ERA BEGINS: DEBATING DOMESTIC POLICY, 1993–1996

In contrast to George Bush, a member of the World War II generation, **William Jefferson (Bill) Clinton** was the first president from the baby-boom generation that came of age in the era of JFK, Vietnam, and the Beatles. Born in Arkansas in 1946, he admired Elvis Presley, played the saxophone, and once considered becoming a pop musician. His early interest in politics led him to attend Georgetown University in Washington, D.C., Oxford University (as a Rhodes scholar), and Yale Law School, where he met his future wife, Hillary Rodham. He returned to Arkansas after graduation, ran unsuccessfully for Congress, but won the governorship in 1979, at age thirty-two.

Clinton's presidency soon encountered setbacks, and the 1994 midterm election produced a Republican landslide. The newly energized congressional Republicans pursued their conservative agenda, including—with Clinton's cooperation—sweeping welfare reform.

Shaping a Domestic Agenda In contrast to Republican predecessors like Nixon and Bush, Clinton preferred domestic issues to foreign policy. Of course, like all presidents, Clinton confronted serious diplomatic challenges. (See "Clinton's Foreign Policy: Defining America's Role in a Post–Cold War World" below.) For the most part, however, domestic policy dominated his attention.

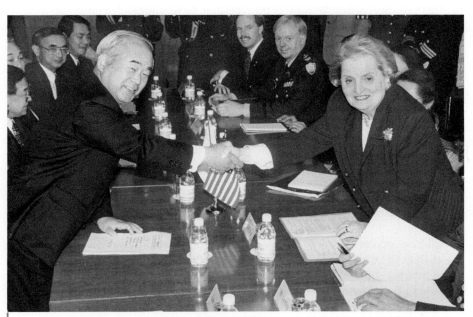

Secretary of State Madeleine Albright Meets with Japanese Defense Minister Fumio Kyuka, February 1997 *Appointed secretary of state by President Bill Clinton in 1996, the first woman to hold that post, Albright grappled with the complexities of a post–Cold War world.*

Clinton and Vice President Al Gore were leaders of the New Democratic Coalition, a group of moderates unhappy with the party's ultra-liberal, "tax and spend" reputation. To win back middle-class and blue-collar voters, Clinton's campaign stressed Middle America's concerns: jobs, health care, soaring welfare costs. As he steered the party toward the middle and muted its concern with the poor, traditional liberals and black leaders expressed uneasiness. Seeking middle ground on abortion, he said it should be "safe, legal, and rare." Clinton firmly endorsed environmental protection, a popular cause with voters. Indeed, Al Gore in 1992 had published an environmental manifesto, *Earth in the Balance*.

Lending symbolic support to the women's movement, Clinton named women to head the Departments of Justice, Energy, and Health and Human Services; the Council of Economic Advisers; the Environmental Protection Agency; the United Nations delegation; and the Bureau of the Budget. To fill a Supreme Court vacancy in 1993, he nominated Judge Ruth Bader Ginsberg. (When a second vacancy arose in 1994, Clinton chose moderate liberal Stephen G. Breyer, a federal judge in Boston.) In 1997 he named **Madeleine K. Albright** as secretary of state—the highest U.S. government office ever held by a woman.

Clinton's early effort to fulfill a campaign pledge to end homosexuals' exclusion from military service proved extremely contentious. A study commission eventually crafted a compromise summed up in the phrase "Don't ask, don't tell." According to this policy, so long as homosexual or bisexual soldiers do not openly reveal their sexual orientation, commanders may not investigate it.

On the economic front, Clinton proposed military-spending cuts and tax increases to ease the budget deficit. To combat the recession, he recommended programs to stimulate job creation and economic growth. In August 1993, Congress adopted Clinton's spending cuts and tax increases. But with the economy improving, the economic-stimulus package fell by the wayside.

Clinton also urged ratification of the **North American Free Trade Agreement** (NAFTA) negotiated by the Bush administration. This pact admitted Mexico to the free-trade zone that the United States and Canada had created earlier. While critics warned that U.S. jobs would flee to Mexico, NAFTA backers, including most economists, predicted a net gain in jobs as Mexican markets opened to U.S. products. Congress approved NAFTA in 1993, handing Clinton a welcome victory.

With Medicare and Medicaid costs exploding, health-care reform stood high on Clinton's "to do" list. From 1980 to 1992, government payments for these programs ballooned from 8 percent to 14 percent of the federal budget. Liberal critics also noted the uneven distribution of health care and the millions of citizens who lacked health insurance.

Clinton appointed his wife Hillary to head a health-care task force. This body, working mainly in secret, devised a sweeping plan for universal health insurance, with employers paying 80 percent of workers' costs. To cover start-up expenses, the plan proposed new tobacco taxes. The task force's cost-containment plan included health-care purchasing cooperatives, a national board to monitor costs, and caps on health-insurance premiums and on Medicare/Medicaid payments.

Lobbyists for doctors, the insurance industry, tobacco companies, and other groups ganged up to oppose the plan. Critics attacked the secretive way it had been formulated. By fall 1994, health-care reform was stalled. Clinton had misread public complaints about medical costs and bureaucratic red tape as support for radical change. But soaring costs, gaps in coverage, and other health-care problems guaranteed that this issue would remain on the political agenda.

Crime and welfare reform also ranked high among voter concerns. In 1994, Clinton proposed an anticrime bill including a ban on assault weapons and funds for more prisons and police officers. After much partisan maneuvering, Congress enacted a crime bill similar to Clinton's proposal.

In 1994, Clinton offered a welfare-reform bill. It required able-bodied recipients of payments from the government's major welfare program, Aid to Families with Dependent Children (AFDC), to go to work after two years, in a public-service job if necessary. The bill included job training and child-care provisions, as well as measures to force absent fathers ("deadbeat dads") to support their offspring. It also permitted states to deny additional payments to welfare mothers who had more children. Congress delayed welfare reform until 1995, however, when Republican majorities in both houses shaped their own bill.

By 1994, Clinton's popularity was sagging. Exploiting the "character issue," critics publicized the Clintons' earlier involvement in a shady Arkansas real-estate speculation, the Whitewater Development Company. The 1993 suicide of assistant White House counsel Vincent Foster, the Clintons' close friend, attracted conspiracy theorists. In 1994, Paula Jones, an Arkansas state employee, filed a lawsuit claiming that Clinton when governor had solicited sexual favors.

Favorable economic news helped Clinton weather the setbacks. By 1994, the unemployment rate had fallen to the lowest level in four years, and inflation remained well under control. The federal deficit dropped each year from 1993 to 1997. Nevertheless, by mid-1994 Clinton's approval ratings had sunk to 42 percent.

Sensing Clinton's vulnerability, the opposition grew bolder. Radio commentator Rush Limbaugh won fans for his jeering attacks on liberals. By 1994, Pat Robertson's **Christian Coalition,** with some nine hundred chapters nationwide, controlled several state Republican parties. With its passion and organizational energy, the religious Right represented an increasingly potent political force.

A Sharp Right Turn: Bill Clinton had run in 1992 as a "new Democrat," but by
1994–1996 1994 many voters saw him as an old Democrat of the big-government, "tax-and-spend" variety, beholden to gays, feminists, and other "special interests." To critics, Clinton's failed health-care plan embodied all the flaws of the New Deal/Great Society style of top-down reform.

Meanwhile, a network of organizations, from the Christian Coalition to the National Rifle Association, built on the conservative movement dating to the 1970s (see Chapter 30, "Grass–Roots Conservatism") to orchestrate a sharp rightward swing in the body politic. Heavily endowed conservative think tanks such as the Heritage Foundation and the American Enterprise Institute issued books and position papers promoting movements to downsize government, reduce welfare, slash taxes, deregulate business, and shift power from Washington to the states. A torrent of mass mailings and an endless drumbeat of conservative radio commentary denounced the "liberal elite" and inflamed differences over such hot-button issues as obscenity, abortion, gun control, gay rights, school prayer, "radical feminism," sex education, and an alleged erosion of "family values."

Normally, prosperity helps the party in power, but the recovery did little for ordinary Americans (see "An Uneven Prosperity"). In October 1994, an ominous 58 percent of Americans told pollsters that they felt no better off despite the economic upturn.

Republican congressman **Newt Gingrich** of Georgia mobilized the discontent. In a September 1994 ceremony on the Capitol steps, some three hundred Republican congressional candidates signed Gingrich's "Contract with America" pledging to propose tax cuts, congressional term limits, tougher crime laws, antipornography measures, a balanced-budget amendment, and other reforms. The Contract nationalized the midterm election, normally fought on local issues.

In November, voters gave the GOP control of both houses of Congress for the first time since 1954; increased the number of Republican governors; and cut down such Democratic giants as New York governor Mario Cuomo and Texas governor Ann Richards. Although only 38 percent of eligible voters went to the polls, the outcome signaled a significant rightward shift. Evangelical Christians, energized by politicized preachers like Falwell and Robertson, turned out in large numbers, mostly to vote Republican.

Republicans hailed the election as a further step in a conservative resurgence launched by Barry Goldwater in 1964. In the Senate, the reactionary Jesse Helms of North Carolina became chairman of the Foreign Relations Committee, and ninety-two-year-old Strom Thurmond of South Carolina, presidential candidate of the States' Rights (Dixiecrat) Party in 1948, headed the Armed Services Committee.

In the House of Representatives, a jubilant horde of 230 Republicans, 73 of them newly elected, chose Newt Gingrich as Speaker, made Rush Limbaugh an "honorary member," and set about enacting the Contract with America. A constitutional amendment requiring a balanced federal budget passed the House but narrowly failed in the Senate. House Republicans also targeted the Public Broadcasting System, accused of liberal bias, and the National Endowment for the Arts for funding projects some found offensive. Fulfilling pledges to combat pornography, Congress passed a Communications Decency Act strengthening the government's censorship powers. (In 1997, the Supreme Court ruled the law unconstitutional.)

The torrent of bills, hearings, and press releases recalled the heady days of the early New Deal and Lyndon Johnson's Great Society. Now, however, the activist energy came from the conservative side of the political spectrum.

The architect of this revolution, Newt Gingrich, stumbled in 1995 when he first accepted, and then turned down, a $4.5 million advance from a publishing house owned by Rupert Murdoch, a media tycoon with interests in federal legislation. Journalists also focused on Gingrich's network of political action groups, dubbed "Newt, Inc.," funded by corporate money and conservative foundations. The 1994 election also signaled a go-it-alone view of America's world role. The Contract with America largely ignored foreign policy, and key Republican legislators pushed isolationist views. Jesse Helms denounced the United Nations, criticized environmental treaties, and belittled UN peacekeeping efforts and America's foreign-aid program. Congressional Republicans refused to pay $1 billion in past UN dues. Bending to the shifting political winds (and to Pentagon objections), the Clinton administration rejected a multinational treaty banning land mines.

Savoring their electoral triumph, conservatives renewed the battle for welfare reform. They offered two arguments. The first was economic. AFDC, with 14.2 million women and children on its rolls, cost about $125 billion in 1994, including direct payments, food stamps, and Medicaid benefits, a sharp jump since 1989. Though dwarfed by the benefits enjoyed by the middle class through social security, Medicare, farm subsidies, and various tax loopholes, this was still a heavy budgetary drain. The second argument was ideological: the belief that welfare had become a "lifelong entitlement" that encouraged indolence and irresponsible behavior and trapped recipients in a multigenerational cycle of dependence. Many observers linked the soaring rate of out-of-wedlock births to AFDC policies that paid mothers higher benefits for each child. Though partially based on stereotypes rather than empirical data, such views were widely held.

As a broad consensus gradually emerged that the existing welfare system had serious flaws, the debate focused not on whether to change it, but how. While Clinton favored federally funded child care and job-training programs to ease the transition from welfare to work, Republicans argued that businesses, the states, and private agencies could best provide these services. Clinton vetoed two welfare bills that lacked the safeguards he thought essential.

At last, in August, as another presidential campaign unfolded, Clinton signed the landmark **Welfare Reform Act of 1996.** Reversing sixty years of welfare policy, the law ended the largest federal program, AFDC. Instead, states would now receive block grants to develop their own programs within strict funding limits and guidelines limiting most recipients to two years of continuous coverage, with a five-year lifetime total.

Supporters argued that ending welfare as a lifetime entitlement would encourage personal responsibility. Critics warned of the effects on inner-city welfare mothers lacking education or job skills. Traditional Democratic liberals such as Massachusetts senator Edward Kennedy, as well as advocates for children, the poor, and minority groups, argued that Clinton had not fought strongly enough to protect welfare recipients in negotiating with congressional Republicans.

The direst predictions did not materialize. From 1996 to 2005 the number of families on welfare fell by 57 percent, and the birthrate among unmarried women leveled off. The percentage of unmarried mothers in the work force rose from around 48 percent in 1996 to around 65 percent in 2000, although many held low-paying, unskilled jobs, and changed jobs frequently. On balance, however, most observers rated welfare reform at least a qualified success.

THE ECONOMIC BOOM OF THE 1990S

The 1990s saw one of the longest periods of sustained economic growth in U.S. history. Productivity increased, unemployment fell, and inflation remained low. Prosperity helped cut crime rates and reduce welfare rolls. Federal deficits dropped as tax revenues increased. In 1998, for the first time since 1969, the federal budget actually showed a surplus.

For some, the surging stock market stimulated the urge to get rich quick, acquire more possessions, and enjoy the good times. But real wages lagged behind the stock market, and workers who lacked the skills required by the emerging knowledge-based economy faced difficulties. America's participation in an increasingly global economy fueled economic growth, but when foreign economies faltered, the U.S. economy stumbled as well.

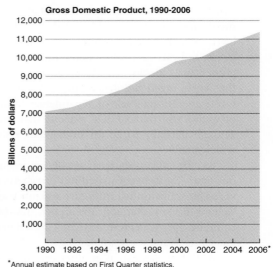

FIGURE 31.1 The U.S. Economy, 1990-2006

The unemployment rate fell, and the gross domestic product rose during the boom years of the 1990s. As recession hit in 2001, however, the jobless rate increased and the GDP flattened (see Chapter 32). *Source:* Unemployment Rate Chart: Bureau of Labor Statistics, U.S. Department of Labor; GDP: U.S. Department of Commerce. http://www.bea.gov/bea/dn/gdplev.xls

An Uneven Prosperity

The economic boom of the 1990s had various sources, but the new products, efficiencies, and business opportunities associated with the personal computer and the information revolution were certainly crucial (see Chapter 32). Rising international trade, a low inflation rate, and the Federal Reserve Board's low interest rates all helped sustain the boom. Unemployment, which stood at 7.5 percent in 1992, fell to 4 percent by 2000. Corporate earnings soared. The gross domestic product, a key economic indicator, rose nearly 80 percent in the decade.

Wall Street boomed as stock prices far outran many companies' actual value or earnings prospects. From under 3,000 in 1991, the Dow Jones Industrial Average edged toward 12,000 by early 2001. New investors flocked into the market. By 1998, nearly 50 percent of U.S. families owned stock directly or through their pension plans. The rising stock market stimulated a quest for luxury goods and leisure pursuits (see below). In 2000, Americans spent $105 billion on new cars; $107 billion on video, audio, and computer equipment; and $81 billion on foreign travel. As in 1929, a few economists warned that the market's inevitable downturn could have severe consequences. As early as 1996 Federal Reserve Board chairman Alan Greenspan warned of "irrational exuberance" in the stock market, but with little effect.

Information-technology (IT) stocks proved especially popular. The NASDAQ composite index, loaded with technology stocks, soared from under 500 in 1991 to over 5,000 by early 2000. Some stock offerings by IT start-up companies hit fantastic levels, turning young entrepreneurs into paper millionaires. Brokers who managed these offerings (and profited as the stock prices rose) hyped them with glowing assessments of new companies' prospects.

Corporate mergers multiplied as companies sought to improve their profitability. In 2000, the communications giant Viacom swallowed CBS for $41 billion, and the pharmaceutical company Pfizer acquired rival Warner-Lambert for $90 billion. In the biggest merger of all, the Internet company America Online (AOL) acquired Time-Warner (itself the product of earlier mergers) for $182 billion.

The prosperity was very unevenly distributed, however. From 1979 to 1996 the portion of total income going to the wealthiest 20 percent of Americans increased by 13 percent, while the share going to the poorest 20 percent *dropped* by 22 percent. Commented economist Richard Freeman in 1998, "The U.S. has the most unequal distribution of income among advanced countries—and the degree of inequality has increased more here than in any comparable country." Adjusted for inflation, the buying power of the average worker's paycheck fell or remained flat through much of the period from 1986 to 2000. As corporations maintained profits by "downsizing" and cost cutting, job worries gnawed at many Americans. The growing service sector included not only high-income white-collar positions and IT work, but also low-paying jobs in fast-food outlets, custodial work, car washes, telemarketing, and so forth.

While many service workers, teachers, and other white-collar groups belonged to unions, only 13.5 percent of the total labor force was unionized in 2000, weakening this means by which workers had historically bettered their wages and job conditions. Unions' political clout diminished as well. Congress ratified the 1993 NAFTA treaty, for example, despite protests from organized labor.

Job-market success increasingly required special training and skills, posing problems for high-school graduates, displaced industrial workers, and welfare recipients entering the labor force. Overall employment statistics also obscured racial and ethnic variables. In 2000, the jobless rate for blacks and Hispanics, despite having dropped, remained significantly higher than the rate for whites. In short, while the economic boom benefited many, a wide gap separated those who prospered and those who experienced minimal gains or none at all.

America and the Global Economy
As the NAFTA agreement made plain, foreign trade ranked high on Clinton's agenda. When the U.S. trade deficit hit $133 billion in 1993, including a $59 billion trade gap with Japan, Clinton, like his predecessor, pressured the Japanese to buy more U.S. goods.

Clinton also preserved trading ties with China despite Beijing's human-rights abuses and one-party rule. Clinton welcomed Chinese president Jiang Zemin for a state visit in 1997 and visited China in 1998. This reflected economic realities. China had become America's fourth largest trading partner, after Canada, Mexico, and Japan. In 2000, when U.S. imports from China surpassed $100 billion, Congress granted China the same status as America's other trading partners, rather than making trade with China dependent on year-by-year agreements.

Economic **globalization** increasingly shaped U.S. policy. When the Mexican peso collapsed in 1995, jeopardizing U.S.-Mexican trade and threatening to increase illegal migration northward, Clinton quickly granted Mexico $40 billion in loan guarantees.

In 1997–1998, when political corruption and other factors weakened the economies of Thailand, South Korea, Indonesia, and other Asian nations, the Clinton administration worked to promote stability in the region. Chaos especially threatened Indonesia, the world's fourth most populous nation, ruled until 1998 by an aging autocrat. Working through the International Monetary Fund, the administration sought to reduce the regime's corruption and strengthen Indonesia's faltering economy.

As the Asian economic crisis spread, Japan's banks faltered, the Tokyo stock market fell, and the yen lost value. This, in turn, unsettled the U.S. stock market and jeopardized U.S. exports and investments in Asia. Recognizing the threat, the administration pressed Japan to undertake needed economic reforms. As Brazil and Argentina also sank into recession, analysts questioned how long the U.S. boom could continue. All these developments underscored how deeply the United States had become enmeshed in a complex global economy (see Beyond America—Global Interactions: The Challenge of Globalization).

CLINTON'S FOREIGN POLICY: DEFINING AMERICA'S ROLE IN A POST–COLD WAR WORLD

Bill Clinton preferred domestic issues to foreign policy. Yet America could not withdraw from the world. When Clinton's attention turned abroad, he faced four key challenges: protecting U.S. trade and investment interests (see "America and the Global Economy"); using American power wisely as Russia, Eastern Europe, and the Balkans emerged from the Soviet era; promoting peace between Israel and the Palestinians; and responding to security threats, including nuclear proliferation and terrorism by Muslim extremists.

The Balkans, Russia, and Eastern Europe in the Post-Soviet Era
The aftershocks of the Soviet collapse unsettled the region of southeastern Europe known as the Balkans. In Yugoslavia, an unstable nation comprised of Serbia, Bosnia, Croatia, and other enclaves and administrative divisions, the ruling communist party gave up power in 1990. In 1991–1992, as Yugoslavia broke apart, Serbian forces launched a campaign of "ethnic cleansing" in neighboring Bosnia. This meant supporting Bosnia's ethnic Serbs while killing or driving out Muslims and Croats. Incited by Serbia's president Slobodan Milosevic, Serbian troops overran UN-designated "safe havens" and slaughtered Muslims. When a UN peacekeeping force failed to stop the killing, a joint U.S. and NATO operation launched air strikes against Bosnian Serb targets in August 1995.

Later in 1995, the Clinton administration flew the leaders of Bosnia's warring factions to Dayton, Ohio, for talks. The resulting Dayton Accords imposed a cease-fire and created a framework for governing the region. Clinton committed twenty thousand U.S. troops to a NATO force in Bosnia to enforce the cease-fire.

In 1998, Serbian forces attacked Muslims in Serbia's southern province, **Kosovo.** Early in 1999, as the bloodshed continued, NATO, under U.S. leadership, bombed Serbian facilities in Kosovo and in Serbia itself, including Belgrade, the capital. This reliance on air power, with minimal risk of U.S. casualties, became Clinton's preferred form of military engagement. Haunted by Vietnam, American public opinion wavered as well, appalled by the suffering and refugee crisis in the Balkans as well as in Rwanda (see below), but wary of expanding U.S. involvement. In June 1999, however, U.S. troops joined a NATO occupying force in Kosovo. With the Serbian army restrained, the refugees trickled back. Slobodan Milosevic was overthrown in 2001, and the new

Serbian government, eager for Western aid, delivered him to a war-crimes tribunal at the Hague. The trial ended inconclusively with Milosevic's death in 2006.

Although Russia generally backed Serbia, a traditional ally, Russian forces joined in NATO's occupation of Kosovo. Facing unrest among its own Muslim population, Russia in 1995–1996 invaded the breakaway Islamic republic of Chechnya. Some called this unpopular conflict Russia's Vietnam. Amid these troubles, Russia's hasty conversion to a free-market economy triggered an economic crisis and massive corruption that threatened the survival of President Boris Yeltsin. Having given Russia billions in loans, the Clinton administration watched anxiously as chaos threatened.

U.S. diplomacy also continued to focus on the safe disposal of nuclear weapons in the former Soviet Union. In the 1993 **Strategic Arms Reduction Treaty** (START II), the United States and Russia agreed to cut their long-range nuclear arsenals by half. This left many deactivated nuclear weapons in Russia, Ukraine, Kazakhstan, and Belarus. Both the Bush and Clinton administrations used diplomacy, economic aid, and technical assistance to assure the secure destruction of these weapons.

Despite U.S. disapproval of the Chechnya war and concern over Boris Yeltsin's alcoholism and increasingly erratic behavior, Clinton continued to support the Russian president. In 1999, the administration backed Russia's admission to the Group of Seven (G-7), the world's leading industrial nations. In the same year, however, over Russia's protests, NATO with U.S. support admitted three new members from the former Soviet bloc—Hungary, Poland, and the Czech Republic. With Yeltsin's resignation in December 1999, Prime Minister Vladimir Putin, a former agent of the KGB, the Soviet secret police, succeeded him as president.

The Middle East: Seeking an Elusive Peace, Combating a Wily Foe

After hopeful beginnings, Clinton's pursuit of peace in the Middle East failed. The 1987 Palestinian uprising, or Intifada, against Israel's military occupation of the West Bank and Gaza (see Chapter 30) continued into the 1990s. Prospects for peace brightened in 1993, after Israeli and Palestinian negotiators meeting in Norway agreed on a six-year timetable for peace. The so-called Oslo Accords provided for a Palestinian state, the return of most Israeli-held land in the West Bank and Gaza to the Palestinians, and further talks on the claims of Palestinian refugees and the final status of Jerusalem. In 1994, President Clinton presided as Israeli prime minister Yitzhak Rabin and Yasir Arafat, head of the Palestine Liberation Organization, signed the agreement at the White House.

The bloodshed continued, however, and in 1995 a young Israeli opposed to the Oslo Accords assassinated Rabin. Israel's next election brought Benjamin Netanyahu of the hard-line Likud Party to power. Suicide bombings by Palestinian extremists in 1996–1997 killed some eighty Israelis, triggering retaliatory attacks. Under U.S. pressure, Netanyahu in 1998 agreed to withdraw Israeli forces from some West Bank areas in return for security guarantees. But as attacks continued, Netanyahu halted the withdrawal. Jewish settlements, with accompanying highways, checkpoints, and infrastructure, spread across Palestinian territory. By 2000, the West Bank and Gaza had an estimated two hundred thousand Israeli settlers. Secretary of State Madeleine K. Albright struggled to persuade the two sides to resume negotiations.

Ehud Barak of Israel's more moderate Labour Party became prime minister in 1999. In July 2000, Clinton invited Barak and Arafat to Camp David. In these talks, Barak made major concessions, reportedly including Israel's withdrawal from 95

The Challenge of Globalization

A Chicago advertising copywriter, dressed casually in a top sewn in Bangladesh, jeans made in India, and shoes manufactured in South Korea, finishes a day spent working on the Toyota account. Coming home, she goes jogging (wearing her Nikes made in Brazil), orders Vietnamese take-out, and turns on her television (imported from Japan) to watch a CNN report, relayed live via satellite, of a deadly earthquake in Java. At her computer (assembled in Mexico), she clicks the website of a London-based humanitarian organization and makes a credit-card contribution to aid the victims. After checking the Nikkei stock index in Tokyo, she settles down to enjoy a book of Italian Renaissance art, printed in Hong Kong.

This is globalization. By a convergence of economic, technological, and cultural trends, humanity is becoming increasingly interconnected and interdependent.

A surge in world trade is globalization's most obvious manifestation (see "America and the Global Economy"). Total world exports of goods and services in 2004 neared $11 trillion. American consumer products—from computers, TVs, microwaves, and cell phones to sneakers, clothing, and toys—mostly come from abroad. So does information. Americans seeking help with computer problems typically talk to technicians in Dublin, Manila, New Delhi, or Bangalore.

The first effort to regulate world trade, in 1947, was the General Agreement on Tariffs and Trade, or GATT (see Chapter 26), which in 1995 became the World Trade Organization (WTO).

With 149 member nations, the WTO works to reduce trade barriers and resolve trade disputes. The European Union (EU) and the North American Free Trade Association (NAFTA) set trading policies and arbitrate trade disputes within their regions.

Despite such agencies, international trade remains contentious. U.S. and European aircraft builders battle for market share. American media companies protest China's failure to prosecute black marketeers who pirate their CDs and DVDs. Exporters of agricultural commodities to America denounce Washington's farm subsidies as a hidden tariff. When Canadian cattle ranchers and timber companies secured a WTO ruling against discriminatory U.S. trading practices, the United States simply ignored the ruling.

Economic globalization can be painful as well as turbulent. As Japanese and other foreign automakers increased their U.S. market share, American automakers fired thousands of workers (see Chapter 32). In response, Toyota and other foreign automakers point to the U.S. jobs created by their manufacturing, marketing, and advertising.

Globalization pervades the corporate world. The world's largest corporations, whatever their home base, are global in scope. GM, Ford, Caterpillar, and other U.S. businesses operate worldwide. Seattle-based Starbucks sells coffee in thirty-seven countries.

European and Asian conglomerates are major players in the United States. In 2005, foreign investment in U.S. companies totaled $1.5 trillion. The U.S. holdings of the German-based Bertelsmann Group include the book publishers Doubleday, Random House, and Knopf; the magazines *Family Circle, Parents,* and *McCall's;* and the Arista and RCA record labels.

Economic globalization stirs opposition, often with good reason. American labor leaders and activists charge that multinational corporations, working through local contractors, operate factories where the workers, often young women, live in prison-like barracks away from their families, laboring long hours at repetitive tasks for a pittance in wages with no benefits. Environmentalists deplore these factories' dismal environmental record. Activists pressure Wal-Mart and other mass marketers to monitor their foreign suppliers' labor policies more strictly. The annual WTO meetings, from Seattle in 1999 to Hong Kong in 2005, regularly attract protesters who charge the United States and other rich nations with contributing to environmental degradation through their trading policies and exploiting workers in poor countries.

Most economists argue that, on balance, globalization benefits America. U.S. popular-culture products and some information-technology innovations, for example, are highly sought after abroad. But globalization has also meant major disruptions for U.S. workers and raised troubling ethical and public-policy issues.

Some fear that globalization compromises national sovereignty. A political firestorm erupted in 2006 when a company based in Dubai, an Arab emirate in the Persian Gulf, acquired a British firm that manages America's East Coast ports. Politicians angrily complained that even port security was being outsourced (that is, shifted abroad). The Dubai company backed off, seeking a U.S. buyer for this portion of its operations.

Globalization is more than trade, jobs, and finance. In today's world, issues of life and death transcend national borders. Environmental hazards such as global warming require a global response (see Chapter 32, "Technology and Culture: Developing New Tools for Measuring Global Warming"). Public-health dangers—from malaria, tuberculosis, and AIDS to impure water and a threatened avian flu pandemic—preoccupy international health organizations.

As the Beatles and the Rolling Stones first demonstrated in the 1960s, globalization is also a cultural phenomenon. Celebrity musicians and orchestra conductors jet around the world. U.S. movies, TV series, and popular music attract a global following. For millions, Coca Cola and McDonald's symbolize American culture. American televangelists spread their beliefs globally via communications satellites. Americans, in turn, listen to West African popular music; savor Thai, Ethiopian, and Cuban food; practice Yoga and T'ai Chi; buy CDs by Scandinavian rock groups; play Japanese video games; and enjoy British comedy or Puerto Rican jazz festivals on public television.

Satellite TV and the Internet have created a global communication grid. In December 2004, when a tsunami triggered by an Indian Ocean earthquake killed thousands of people in Indonesia and other countries, magazines, TV, and Internet websites carried heart-rending images of the devastation, producing a world-wide outpouring of contributions, volunteer relief efforts, and fundraising concerts.

But cultural globalization also stirs protests, with the United States a frequent target. Cultural nationalists in France and other countries try to erect barriers against the inroads of American movies, TV, and fast food. Islamist fundamentalists denounce the popular culture of the West, with its global saturation, as a threat to Islamic values and practices.

More than forty years ago, in *Understanding Media* (1964), the Canadian scholar Marshall McLuhan foresaw an emerging "global village." Wrote McLuhan: "[A]fter more than a century of electronic technology, we have extended our central nervous system itself in a global embrace, abolishing both space and time." The intervening decades amply confirmed McLuhan's insight. For better or worse, globalization—and the reactions against it—have become driving forces in our comtemporary world.

Questions for Analysis

- What economic, technological, and cultural developments underlie globalization?

- In what specific ways does globalization affect your everyday life?

percent of the West Bank and all of Gaza; the creation of a Palestinian state; Palestinian control of East Jerusalem; and the transfer of Jerusalem's Temple Mount, sacred to both Muslims and Jews, to a vaguely defined "religious authority." In return, the PLO would end hostilities and give up further claims on Israel.

Arafat rejected Barak's offer, however, and the summit failed. In September, the Likud leader Ariel Sharon—with nearly one thousand Israeli soldiers and police—made a provocative foray onto Temple Mount, symbolically asserting Israel's control of the site. Soon after, Palestinians launched a new Intifada against Israel. In 2001, Israelis elected Sharon prime minister. As Clinton left office, the Israeli-Palestinian conflict raged on (see Chapter 32).

Iraq also demanded Clinton's attention. After the Persian Gulf War, the United Nations had imposed strict sanctions on Iraqi oil exports and set up an inspection system to prevent Iraq from building chemical or nuclear weapons. In 1997, when Saddam Hussein barred UN inspectors from certain sites, Clinton dispatched ships, bombers, and thirty thousand troops to the Persian Gulf. He sought to rally support for a military strike, as George Bush had done in 1991, but France, Russia, and various Arab states resisted. Clinton drew back after the UN secretary general, Kofi Annan, secured Saddam's agreement to open inspections. Saddam soon reneged, however, and the crisis continued (see Chapter 32).

Nuclear
Proliferation,
Terrorism, and
Peacekeeping
Challenges

Nations that signed the 1968 Nuclear Nonproliferation Treaty pledged not to develop nuclear weapons. India and Pakistan, long at odds over Kashmir, did not sign, however, and in 1988 India tested a nuclear bomb. Despite urgent pleas from the United States and other powers, Pakistan followed suit. Both the Bush and Clinton administrations imposed sanctions on the two countries, but the spread of nuclear weapons in this region deepened proliferation fears.

Communist North Korea also roused concern. Despite having signed the Nonproliferation Treaty, North Korea began a program of nuclear-weapons development and missile testing. In 1994, facing UN economic sanctions and the loss of $9 billion in international assistance, North Korea pledged to halt its nuclear-weapons program. In 1999, confronting famine and economic crisis, North Korea suspended long-range missile testing in return for an easing of U.S. trade and travel restrictions. The country's nuclear intentions remained worrisome.

Attacks by anti-American Islamic extremists continued. In February 1993, a powerful bomb exploded in a parking garage beneath one of the towers of New York's World Trade Center. Six persons died in the blast and hundreds were injured as fifty thousand workers hastily evacuated. Five Islamic militants, including a blind Egyptian sheik, Omar Abdel Rhaman, the alleged mastermind, were arrested. Three, including Sheik Omar, were convicted of murder and given life sentences.

In 1992, President Bush had committed some twenty-six thousand U.S. troops to a UN humanitarian mission to Somalia, an East African nation afflicted by civil war and famine. As the warring factions battled, forty-four Americans were killed, including eighteen murdered in Mogadishu, Somalia's capital. President Clinton withdrew the U.S. force in 1994, and the UN mission ended a year later. Later evidence implicated anti-American Islamic extremists loyal to **Osama bin Laden** in the Mogadishu killings. A wealthy Saudi Arabian and Islamic fundamentalist militant, bin Laden had been expelled from Saudi Arabia in 1991 and taken refuge in Sudan, where he financed large-scale construction and agricultural projects but also planned anti-Western terrorist activities.

Two bombings at U.S. military installations in Saudi Arabia in 1995–1996 killed twenty-four Americans. On August 7, 1998, simultaneous bomb blasts at the U.S. embassies in Nairobi, Kenya, and Dar-es-Salaam, Tanzania, killed 220, including Americans and many local people. U.S. intelligence again pinpointed Osama bin Laden as the mastermind of the attacks. Expelled from Sudan in 1996, bin Laden had shifted his base of operations to Afghanistan, where he organized terrorist training camps. Clinton ordered cruise missile strikes on one of bin Laden's Afghan camps as well as on a suspected chemical-weapons factory in Sudan allegedly financed by bin Laden. A U.S. grand jury indicted bin Laden on charges of planning the embassy attacks and also of inciting the earlier killing of GIs in Somalia.

In 1999, Clinton called for redoubled efforts against rogue states and terrorist groups in danger of acquiring nuclear, chemical, or biological weapons. "[W]e are involved here in a long-term struggle . . . ," declared Secretary of State Albright. "This is, unfortunately, the war of the future." Underscoring Albright's grim assessment, on October 12, 2000, a bomb aboard a small boat in the harbor of Aden, Yemen, ripped a gaping hole in the U.S. destroyer *Cole,* killing seventeen sailors.

Closer home, in Haiti, a Caribbean island-nation wracked by poverty and disease, a military junta overthrew President Jean-Bertrand Aristide in September 1991 and terrorized his supporters. In 1991–1993, thousands of Haitians set out for Florida in leaky boats, only to be intercepted by the U.S. Coast Guard and returned to an uncertain fate in Haiti. Pressured by Haitian-Americans and U.S. black leaders, the Clinton administration supported a 1994 UN resolution authorizing military action against the junta. With a U.S.-led invasion flotilla anchored offshore, the junta's leaders went into exile, and Aristide, backed by a U.S. occupation force, resumed the presidency. (Ten years later, facing another uprising, Aristide again went into exile, and a UN peacekeeping force arrived to maintain order.)

A New World Order Painfully Emerges The peaceful post–Cold War era that many had anticipated seemed an ever-receding mirage as Americans of the 1990s confronted international issues of maddening complexity.

The USS *Cole* After a Suicide Bombing During a Refueling Stop in the Port of Aden, October 2000 *The bomb, concealed in a small boat that came alongside the Cole, killed seventeen U.S. sailors and injured many more. These years saw a rising level of terrorist attacks by anti-American militants based in the Middle East and in North Africa.*

The Soviet adversary had collapsed, and the threat of global thermonuclear war receded, but crises still flared around the world. Like firefighters battling many small blazes rather than a single conflagration, policy makers now wrestled with a baffling tangle of issues. Somalia, Bosnia, Iraq, Kosovo, North Korea, Pakistan, Afghanistan, Israel, the Palestinians, shadowy terrorist cells—all demanded attention.

Confronting such complexities, some citizens simply gave up. In a 1997 poll, only 20 percent of Americans said that they followed foreign news, down sharply from the 1980s, with the biggest drop among young people. TV coverage of events abroad fell by more than 50 percent from 1989 to 1995. Seeking to clarify the confusing world situation, analysts noted at least four large-scale trends in the post–Cold War era:

- First, economic considerations played an ever-greater role in international affairs. Multinational networks of trade, communications, and finance increasingly shaped America's foreign-policy interests. (See Beyond America—Global Interactions: The Challenge of Globalization.)

- Second, a growing chasm divided the prosperous, comparatively stable industrialized world from societies marked by poverty, disease, illiteracy, and explosive population growth. This vast gulf helped spawn resentment, hatred, and even terrorism.

- Third, despite and partially because of a globalizing economy and mass culture, ethnic divisions and religious fundamentalisms intensified. The lethal ethno-religious conflict in the former Yugoslavia was far from unique. Similar clashes erupted in many other regions. In the tiny Central African Republic of Rwanda, as many as a million people perished in genocidal violence in 1994, as militias of the ruling Hutu ethnic group systematically massacred members of the once-dominant Tutsi group. Thousands more fled in panic, creating a massive refugee crisis. (The 2004 film *Hotel Rwanda*, about a courageous Rwandan hotel manager who sheltered over a thousand Tutsi refugees, conveys the horror of the genocide.) Traumatized by the Somalia fiasco, President Clinton failed to intervene.

  As Muslim fundamentalists denounced Western liberalism and secularism, a small but lethal minority embraced violence as a religious duty. Some Israeli Jews (supported by U.S. Christian fundamentalists) claimed a God-given right to Palestinian lands. In India, violence erupted in 1992 when Hindu militants destroyed an ancient Muslim mosque they claimed had been built on an even more ancient Hindu shrine. Tensions increased when a fundamentalist Hindu party gained power in India in 1998.

- Finally, the United Nations worked to define its role in the new era. With the Cold War's end, many Americans pulled back from engaging with the world community. Some even demanded U.S. withdrawal from the United Nations. Others, however, found reason to hope that the United Nations, long a pawn of the superpowers' conflict, might at last function as its supporters had hoped in 1945. Indeed, by 2000 more than forty thousand UN peacekeeping forces and civilian personnel were serving in fifteen world trouble spots. UN agencies addressed global environmental, nutritional, public-health, and human-rights issues. UN-sponsored judicial bodies brought to justice perpetrators of terrible deeds in Bosnia, Rwanda, and elsewhere.

Despite the countertrends, opinion polls indicated that most Americans supported internationalist approaches to world problems and viewed the UN favorably, despite its flaws and shortcomings. While attention to foreign affairs sometimes flagged, Americans could become engaged when they understood an issue in human terms. With the Cold War over, America's position as simply one player—albeit a major player—in a truly global order became inescapably clear.

THE CLINTON ERA ENDS: DOMESTIC POLITICS, IMPEACHMENT, DISPUTED ELECTION, 1996–2000

Straddling the political center, Bill Clinton won reelection in 1996. His second term saw a battle over tobacco-industry regulation, a commitment of U.S. forces in Kosovo, and a final effort to resolve the Israeli-Palestinian dispute. It is mainly remembered, however, for a sex scandal that led to Clinton's impeachment—a crisis that further poisoned a contentious political climate. A disputed presidential election in 2000 did little to heal the nation's divisions.

Campaign 1996 and After: Battling Big Tobacco; Balancing the Budget

Bill Clinton had won the nickname "the Comeback Kid" after a long-shot victory in the 1992 New Hampshire primary, and after the 1994 Republican landslide he again hit the comeback trail. The Republicans suffered a black eye in 1995 when House Speaker Newt Gingrich, battling Clinton over the budget, twice allowed a partial government shutdown.

Clinton got another lucky break: a weak Republican opponent. When General Colin Powell, the popular former chairman of the Joint Chiefs of Staff, declined to run, Kansas senator Bob Dole, a partially disabled World War II hero, won the nomination. The seventy-three-year-old Dole ran a lackluster campaign, and Clinton won with 49 percent of the vote, to Dole's 41 percent. (The Texas maverick H. Ross Perot garnered 8 percent.) The Republicans held control of Congress, though GOP legislators proved less combative than after their 1994 triumph.

Fundraising scandals marked the 1996 contest as TV advertising continued to drive up campaign expenses. A Democratic fundraiser with links to Indonesian and possibly Chinese businesses raised $3.4 million. After an event at a Los Angeles Buddhist temple attended by Vice President Al Gore, priests and nuns sworn to poverty contributed over a hundred thousand dollars to the Democratic cause. The money apparently came from Asian businessmen seeking favor with the administration.

Tobacco regulation, a major public-health issue, loomed large in Clinton's second term. In 1997, facing lawsuits by former smokers and by states saddled with medical costs linked to smoking-related diseases, the tobacco industry agreed to pay some $368 billion in settlement. The agreement limited tobacco advertising, especially when directed at young people.

Since the agreement required government approval, the debate now shifted to Washington. Southern legislators close to the tobacco companies defended the industry, but the Clinton administration backed a bill imposing tougher penalties, higher cigarette taxes, and stronger antismoking measures. Supporters of this bill documented the industry's manipulation of nicotine levels and targeting of children. The industry struck back with a $40 million lobbying campaign and heavy contributions to key legislators, killing the bill. The Republican Party, commented John McCain, Arizona's maverick Republican senator, appeared to be "in the pocket of the tobacco companies."

In 1998, the tobacco industry reached a new settlement, scaled back to $206 billion, with forty-six states. In 1999, Clinton ordered the Justice Department to sue the tobacco industry for $280 billion to cover Medicare costs for treating smoking-related illnesses. (In 2005 a federal judge threw out this lawsuit, and the Supreme Court rejected the government's appeal.)

Following his strategy of offering modest proposals that appealed to progressives without alienating moderates, Clinton in his January 1998 State of the Union address offered some initiatives to help the poor, such as enrolling the nation's 3 million uninsured children in Medicaid. But he also introduced proposals attractive to the middle class (college-tuition tax credits; extending Medicare to early retirees) and to fiscal conservatives (reducing the national debt; shoring up social security). Some liberals dismissed the speech as "Progressivism Lite," but it had political appeal, and under normal conditions would have certified Clinton's political comeback.

Scandal Grips the White House

But conditions were not normal. Even as Clinton spoke, scandal swirled around the White House. Adultery charges had long clung to Clinton, and now he faced the Paula Jones sexual-harassment suit, dating from his days as Arkansas governor. The Supreme Court had helped Jones's case by permitting lawsuits against sitting presidents.

Seeking to show a pattern of sexual harassment, Jones's lawyers subpoenaed Clinton and quizzed him about reports linking him to a young White House intern, **Monica Lewinsky.** The president denied everything, as did Lewinsky. As the rumors became public (via an Internet website devoted to political gossip), Clinton denounced them as false. Hillary Clinton blamed "a vast right-wing conspiracy." In fact, political conservatives *were* digging for damaging information on Clinton, and he helpfully provided them with ample material. Clinton settled Paula Jones's suit by paying her $850,000, but more problems awaited. In telephone conversations illegally taped by her "friend" Linda Tripp, Monica Lewinsky had described an affair with Clinton from 1995, when she was twenty-one, through early 1997. In January 1998, Tripp passed the tapes to Kenneth Starr, an independent counsel appointed to investigate the Clintons' murky real-estate dealings in Arkansas. At Starr's request, FBI agents fitted Tripp with a recording device and secured further Lewinsky evidence.

Starr's investigation now shifted to whether Clinton had committed perjury in his Paula Jones testimony and if he had persuaded Lewinsky to lie. In August, after jail threats and a promise of immunity, Lewinsky admitted the affair before Starr's grand jury. Soon after, in videotaped testimony, Clinton admitted "conduct that was wrong" with Lewinsky but denied a "sexual relationship" under his narrow definition of the term. In a brief TV address, Clinton conceded "inappropriate" behavior with Lewinsky, but called his testimony in the Jones lawsuit "legally accurate" and attacked Starr as politically motivated.

Other presidents had pursued extramarital affairs, but by the 1990s changing standards, sexual-harassment laws, and the glare of media publicity had made such behavior more objectionable and harder to conceal. Unsurprisingly, the scandal unfolded in tabloid headlines, late-night television jokes, Internet humor, and conservative radio talk shows.

In a September 1998 report to the House Judiciary Committee, Kenneth Starr narrated the Clinton-Lewinsky affair in lurid detail. He recommended impeachment on the grounds that Clinton had committed perjury, influenced others to do so, and obstructed justice by retrieving gifts he had given Lewinsky and coaching his secretary on his version of events.

The Judiciary Committee, on a party-line vote, forwarded four articles of impeachment to the House of Representatives. In a similarly partisan vote, the House approved and sent to the Senate two articles of impeachment: perjury and obstruction of justice. Clinton thus became the first president since Andrew Johnson to be impeached (though Nixon came close).

Opinion polls sent the Republicans an ominous message: most Americans opposed impeachment. In the 1998 midterm elections, as the impeachment process unfolded, the Democrats gained five House seats.

Since removing a president requires a two-thirds Senate vote and the Republicans held only fifty-five Senate seats, the impeachment process seemed foredoomed. Nevertheless, in January 1999 the trial began. As Chief Justice William Rehnquist presided, House Republicans presented their case. White House lawyers challenged what one called a "witches' brew of speculation."

Through it all, Clinton's approval ratings soared. While people deplored his behavior, few believed that it met the Constitution's "high crimes and misdemeanors" standard for removal from office. With the economy booming and Clinton's political positions generally popular, the public appeared willing to tolerate his personal flaws. Further, many saw him as the target of Republican zealots.

On February 12, the Senate rejected the impeachment charges and ended the trial. While some Republicans spoke darkly of a double standard of justice, most Americans simply felt relief. In January 2001, as he left office, Clinton admitted to perjury, paid a $25,000 fine, and lost his law license for five years.

While escaping the worst, Clinton had suffered grievous damage, mostly self-inflicted. He remained active in his final two years in office, committing U.S. forces to Kosovo and working to resolve the Israeli-Palestinian dispute, for example, but the scandal unquestionably eroded his leadership and tarnished his presidency.

The Republican Party suffered as well, as some of its most partisan members took center stage, rubbing raw the divisions roiling the nation. In 1999 Newt Gingrich, closely identified with the impeachment effort, and embroiled in ethical controversies and issues involving his marital life, resigned as Speaker and left Congress.

Election 2000: Bush Versus Gore

As the 2000 campaign got under way, the Democrats, bouncing back from the impeachment crisis, confidently nominated Vice President Al Gore for the top job. As his running mate, Gore chose Connecticut senator Joseph Lieberman, making him the first Jewish-American candidate on a major party ticket. (Barry Goldwater, the Republican presidential candidate in 1964, was of Jewish ancestry, but his father had converted to the Episcopal faith.) The fact that Lieberman had denounced the Lewinsky affair and Clinton's attempted cover-up helped insulate Gore from the "sleaze factor" in the Clinton legacy.

The Republican contest narrowed to Arizona senator John McCain, a former prisoner of war in Vietnam, and Texas governor **George W. Bush,** son of the former president. McCain, a champion of campaign-finance reform and a critic of corporate influences in his party, made a strong bid. Bush, however, with powerful backers and a folksy manner, won the nomination. His running mate Dick Cheney, defense secretary in the first Bush administration, had more recently headed the Halliburton Corporation, a Texas energy company. The Green Party nominated consumer advocate Ralph Nader.

Both Gore and Bush courted the center while trying to hold their bases. For Bush, this meant corporate interests, religious conservatives, and the so-called Reagan Democrats in the middle and working classes. Gore's base included liberals, academics and professionals, union members, African-Americans, and many Hispanics.

Gore pointed to the nation's prosperity (downplaying signs of weakness) and pledged to extend health-care coverage and protect social security. In televised debates Gore was far more articulate and displayed greater mastery of detail than Bush. But the vice president, tainted by fund-raising scandals in the 1996 campaign, had image problems. Many voters found him pompous. The factual mastery he displayed in the debates struck some as arrogant. Eager to prove his political independence, Gore distanced himself from Clinton, despite the president's popularity.

Bush, with an easygoing manner but little national or foreign-policy experience, was widely seen as a lightweight wholly dependent on family influence. As one Texas Democrat quipped, "George was born on third base and thought he had hit a home run." Calling himself a "compassionate conservative," Bush subtly reminded voters of Clinton's misdeeds by promising to restore dignity to the White House. Polls showed that most voters agreed with Gore on the issues, approved the Democrats' economic policies, and conceded Gore's intellectual edge. Ominously for Gore, however, they preferred Bush as a person. The election seemed a toss-up.

The resulting disputed election worsened the partisan rancor of these years, so evident in the impeachment crisis. Gore won the popular vote by more than 500,000, but the Electoral College remained up for grabs. The struggle narrowed to Florida, whose twenty-five electoral votes would determine the outcome.

Flaws in Florida's electoral process quickly became apparent. In Palm Beach County, a poorly designed ballot led several thousand Gore supporters to vote for Pat Buchanan, running on Ross Perot's Reform Party ticket. In other counties with many poor and African-American voters, antiquated voting machines rejected thousands of ballots in which the paper tabs, called "chads," were not fully punched out. When Gore supporters demanded a hand count of these rejected ballots, Bush's lawyers sued to stop the recounts. Florida's secretary of state, Katherine Harris (the co-chair of Bush's Florida campaign and an ally of Florida governor Jeb Bush, the candidate's brother), refused to extend the deadline for certifying the vote, making a recount more difficult.

On November 21 the Florida Supreme Court, with a preponderance of Democrats, unanimously ruled that a hand recount should constitute the official result. Bush's lawyers appealed to the U.S. Supreme Court. Despite a well-established precedent of letting state courts decide electoral disputes, the justices accepted the case. Overturning the Florida ruling, the Supreme Court on December 4 sent the case back to Tallahassee for clarification.

Meanwhile, on November 26, Katherine Harris had certified the Florida vote, awarding Bush the state. But on December 8, ten days before the scheduled Electoral College vote, the Florida Supreme Court ordered an immediate recount of all suspect ballots. "At this rate," mused a radio commentator, "the Inaugural Ball will be a surprise party."

The U.S. Supreme Court again heard an appeal, and on December 12, by a 5-to-4 vote, halted the recount. Gore conceded the next day. Five Supreme Court justices (all Republican appointees) had made George W. Bush president. Ralph Nader also helped Bush's cause. Had the 97,488 Floridians who voted for Nader not had that option, Gore would probably have won the state and the presidency.

The election produced an evenly divided Senate. Each party had fifty senators, giving Vice President Cheney the deciding vote. (The Republicans narrowly held the House of Representatives.) **Hillary Rodham Clinton** won election as senator from New York, becoming the first presidential wife to pursue an independent political career. Overall, the new Senate included thirteen women, a record number.

As he left office, Bill Clinton issued presidential pardons to 167 people, including his half-brother, in trouble on drug charges; persons caught up in Clinton-related scandals; and white-collar offenders who had White House influence or were big Democratic contributors, including a commodities trader holed up in Switzerland to avoid trial for tax evasion and other crimes. Despite Clinton's political skills and good intentions, few expressed regret as he left Washington.

Would George W. Bush heal the nation's divisions and pursue a wise foreign-policy course? Americans waited hopefully.

CULTURAL TRENDS AT CENTURY'S END

American life in the 1990s reflected both the decade's prosperity and its cultural conflicts. While the newly rich flaunted their wealth and Americans pursued leisure diversions, undercurrents of violence also marked the decade. As cultural disagreements deepened, the values of openness and tolerance for diversity seemed under threat.

Affluence and a Search for Heroes The economic boom of the 1990s produced instant fortunes for some and an orgy of consumption that set the decade's tone. Wall Street and Silicon Valley spawned thousands of youthful millionaires. In 1997, surveying the lifestyles of the newly rich, *Vanity Fair* magazine described New York as "the champagne city, making the brash consumption of the 1980s look like the depression." Elegant restaurants offered absurdly expensive cigars and rare wines, and exclusive shops sold $13,000 handbags. In 1999, the nation's top one hundred advertisers spent $43 billion promoting their goods.

The boom also encouraged a hard-edged "winner take all" mentality like that of the Gilded Age, when the rich had turned their backs on the larger society. In *Bowling Alone: The Collapse and Revival of American Community* (2000), political scientist Robert Putnam found diminished civic engagement and weakened interest in public issues, as evidenced by declines in voting, political activism, and civic participation. He even claimed to find less informal socializing, from dinners with friends to card parties and bowling leagues. While some saw the Internet as a new form of community, Putnam viewed it as further evidence of a diminished public sphere.

Anecdotal evidence supported Putnam's conclusions. A 1997 survey of college students found that 77 percent expected to become millionaires. *The Prayer of Jabez* (2000), a best-selling motivational book, cited a shepherd's prayer recorded in the Bible ("Bless me indeed, and enlarge my territory") as a key to success. "If Jabez had worked on Wall Street," wrote the author, "he might have prayed 'Lord, increase the value of my investment portfolio.'"

With the stock market surging, the Cold War over, and new threats only coming into focus, many Americans set out to enjoy themselves. Attendance at the Disney theme parks in Florida and California neared 30 million in 2000. The sales of bulky sport-utility vehicles (SUVs) soared. When a White House press secretary was asked in 2001 if people should reduce consumption to conserve energy, he replied, "[I]t should be the goal of policy makers to protect the American way of life—the American way of life is a blessèd one."

As in the 1980s, the mass culture offered escapist fare. Popular movies included historical extravaganzas like *Braveheart* (1995) and *Gladiator* (2000). The 1997 blockbuster *Titanic,* with spectacular special effects, grossed $600 million. The top-rated TV show of 1999–2000, *Who Wants to Be a Millionaire?*, celebrated raw greed. So-called reality shows like *Survivor* offered viewers a risk-free taste of the hazards that American life itself (at least for the privileged) conspicuously lacked.

Millions avidly followed TV coverage of the 1995 trial of O. J. Simpson, a former football star accused of killing his former wife and her friend. The 1996 murder of a six-year-old Colorado girl whose parents had pushed her into child beauty pageants similarly mesmerized the public. The Clinton sex scandals often seemed little more than another media diversion in a sensation-hungry decade.

However, as in the 1980s, popular-culture evidence can also suggest a more complex picture. For example, some critics interpreted *Titanic,* which sided with its working-class hero in steerage against the rich snobs in first class, as a comment on America's widening class differences. One even called the movie "an exercise in class hatred." The 1992 Clint Eastwood western *Unforgiven,* winner of the Academy Award for best picture, expressed nostalgia for an era when life presented rugged challenges and hard moral choices. The same longings, some suggested, underlay the tide of admiring biographies of past heroes, such as Stephen Ambrose's *Eisenhower* (1991) and David McCullough's *Truman* (1993).

Americans of the 1990s also relived the heroic era of World War II in TV specials, books such as Tom Brokaw's *The Greatest Generation* (1998), and movies like *Saving Private Ryan* (1998) and *Pearl Harbor* (2001). The *New York Times* columnist Frank Rich saw *Pearl Harbor* as "more about the present than the past," reflecting longing "for what is missing in our national life: some cause larger than ourselves." Concluded Rich: "Even those Americans who are . . . foggy about World War II . . . know intuitively that it was fought over something more blessed than the right to guzzle gas."

Outbursts of Violence Stir Concern

A popular 1999 film, *American Beauty,* and TV's *The Sopranos,* an HBO series about a mobster and his family, which debuted in 1999, explored dark impulses and violent undercurrents in American life. The violence was not limited to pop-culture fantasy. True, the overall crime rate fell nearly 20 percent between 1992 and 2000—a decline experts attributed to prosperity, stricter gun-control laws, a drop in the young male population, the waning crack-cocaine epidemic, and tougher sentencing rules. (The U.S. prison population approached 2 million by 2000.)

But bursts of violence punctuated the decade. The annual toll of gun deaths exceeded twenty-eight thousand in 2000. Multiple shootings drew special attention. In 1999 an Atlanta man distraught by investment losses shot and killed nine employees at a financial firm. Also in 1999, two students at Columbine High School near Denver fatally shot twelve students and a teacher before committing suicide. These episodes produced anxious discussions of America's obsession with firearms, the alleged breakdown of parental authority, and the influence of mass-media violence. After the Columbine massacre President Clinton again called for stricter gun-control laws, but the firearms lobby, led by the National Rifle Association, fought such efforts.

The violence sometimes reflected the intensity of the nation's culture wars. In 1998, two youths tortured and murdered a gay student at the University of Wyoming, Matthew Shepard, because of his sexual orientation. As the abortion controversy raged, some "pro-life" advocates turned violent. In 1995 an anti-abortion activist fatally shot a physician and his bodyguard outside a Florida abortion clinic, and an unstable youth murdered two people and wounded five others at a clinic near Boston. In 1997 bombers struck abortion clinics in Tulsa and Atlanta. The following year, a Buffalo physician who performed abortions was shot dead.

Criticizing the NRA *Amid a wave of school shootings, a political cartoonist offered a sardonic comment on the National Rifle Association's enthusiastic defense of the right to gun ownership.*

On April 19, 1995, in the decade's most horrifying burst of mass violence, five thousand pounds of explosives concealed in a rental truck demolished the nine-story Murrah Federal Building in Oklahoma City, Oklahoma. The blast killed 168 people, including 19 children in the building's day-care center. Police soon arrested Timothy McVeigh, a Gulf War veteran with vague links to secretive antigovernment militia groups obsessed with conspiracy theories. McVeigh, convicted of murder, was executed in 2001. A coconspirator, Terry Nichols, received a life sentence.

The **Oklahoma City bombing** came precisely two years after a government raid on the Waco, Texas, compound of the Branch Davidians, an apocalyptic religious sect led by David Koresh, charged with firearms violations. An earlier raid in February 1993 had left four government agents and six Davidians dead. The April raid ended tragically when fires probably set by Koresh and others erupted inside the compound as federal tanks moved in, leaving some eighty Branch Davidians dead. Timothy McVeigh claimed that his Oklahoma City attack was in retaliation for the deaths at Waco.

Culture Wars: A Broader View Fortunately, the decade's culture wars typically involved words and symbolic gestures, not bullets and bombs. For example, the Smithsonian Institution canceled a 1995 exhibit marking the fiftieth anniversary of the atomic bombing of Japan when politicians and veterans' organizations attacked it for documenting the bombs' human toll and for presenting differing views of President Truman's decision.

But if the culture wars, whose origins lay in the 1960s, did not often descend into violence, they did involve fierce contests that some viewed as nothing less than a struggle for the nation's soul. The Christian Coalition's attempted takeover of the Republican Party was part of a larger campaign to reverse what conservatives saw as America's moral decay. In the nineteenth century, cultural conflicts had pitted native-born Protestants against Catholic and Jewish immigrants. During the Cold War, the ideological menace had been external: atheistic communism, centered in Moscow. Now many Americans applied the same black-and-white world view to the home front, and searched for the enemy within.

The struggle unfolded on many fronts, from televangelists' programs, bookstore shelves, and radio talk shows to school-board protests, shouting matches at family-planning clinics, and boycotts of TV shows deemed immoral. Religious conservatives proposed a constitutional amendment permitting prayer in classrooms and called for a renewal of traditional morality and "family values." Other groups criticized history textbooks for being insufficiently patriotic or excessively multicultural.

As gays and lesbians grew more vocal politically (and more visible in the media), conservative politicians at the state and local level continued to mobilize against their demands for equality. The Southern Baptist Convention, America's largest Protestant denomination, urged a boycott of Disney World because it had unofficially sponsored "Gay Pride" days.

The fast-growing evangelical and charismatic churches, including suburban mega-churches with thousands of members, denounced society's wickedness and the government's complicity in the moral decline. In 1997 some seven hundred thousand men representing a conservative Protestant movement called Promise Keepers rallied in Washington, D.C., for a day of prayer, hymn singing, and pledges to reclaim moral leadership of their households. President Clinton's sexual misdeeds underscored for conservatives the moral rot they saw eating away at America.

Pat Robertson's *The New World Order* (1991) saw much of world history as a vast conspiracy that will soon end in the rule of the Antichrist. The best-selling *Left Behind* series of novels (1995–2004), coauthored by the conservative activist Tim LaHaye (see Chapter 30) and loosely based on certain biblical prophecies, described an End Time apocalypse in which Jesus Christ and an army of true believers will destroy the sinister forces of evil increasingly dominating the modern world.

The culture warriors experienced frustration as well as successes. The Christian Coalition and other religious conservative groups complained bitterly about Republican politicians who courted their votes but ignored their agenda once in power.

In *One Nation After All* (1998), sociologist Alan Wolfe reported on his interviews with middle-class Americans, whom he found accepting of diversity and suspicious of extremist positions. The virtues of tolerance and live-and-let-live, Wolfe suggested, still prevailed in Middle America. As one of Wolfe's interviewees reflected, "[W]e can't just stand back and whine about the ways things are. . . . We've got to move forward and trust that we can . . . get to a solution eventually." In its optimism and moderate tone, such a perspective captured a deep-seated pragmatic approach to cultural differences, and struck a cautiously encouraging note amid the clash of contending viewpoints as the twentieth century ended.

CONCLUSION

As the Soviet Union's collapse transformed the international order, President Reagan's successor, George Bush, confronted new challenges. Bush successfully handled the major foreign crisis he faced, rallying home-front support and mobilizing a multinational coalition to repel Iraq's invasion of Kuwait. Domestically, however, Bush faltered in dealing with a recession, racial violence, and environmental hazards, and in 1992 he lost to the Democrat Bill Clinton.

The failure of Clinton's sweeping health-care reform plan, coupled with other missteps, laid the groundwork for a Republican landslide in the 1994 midterm elections. Adapting to a more conservative political climate, Clinton signed a welfare-reform bill sponsored by Republicans. A rebounding economy that stimulated a stock-market boom helped Clinton's political standing. While the good times benefited some, including white-collar service workers and those involved with computer-based information technologies, most inner-city residents and displaced industrial workers did not share in the general prosperity.

Internationally, the Clinton administration worked to combat nuclear proliferation and joined in multinational efforts to halt ethnic violence in the Balkans. Clinton stood aside as genocidal slaughter overwhelmed Rwanda, however, and despite his determined peacemaking efforts, the Israeli-Palestinian conflict raged on.

The political and cultural conflicts of the later 1990s were intensified by the political mobilization of conservative Christian evangelicals; by differences over such emotion-laden issues as abortion and homosexuality; and by Clinton's own indiscretions. Caught in lies as he tried to conceal an embarrassing sex scandal, Clinton was impeached by a highly partisan House of Representatives. Though he escaped removal from office, his reputation suffered. In the disputed 2000 presidential election, finally resolved by the Supreme Court, George W. Bush, son of the former president Bush, defeated Vice President Al Gore.

Newly affluent Americans flaunting their wealth helped set the cultural tone of the 1990s. However, outbursts of violence, from school shootings to a catastrophic bombing in Oklahoma City, coupled with profound cultural divisions and a poisonous political climate, left many citizens feeling deeply apprehensive as the nation entered a new century.

32

Global Dangers, Global Challenges, 2001 to the Present

AMERICA UNDER ATTACK: SEPTEMBER 11, 2001, AND ITS AFTERMATH

Although George W. Bush had campaigned as a centrist, his early appointments and proposals suggested a hard-line conservative approach. On September 11, 2001, a horrific attack by airplane hijackers on U.S. buildings and citizens riveted the nation's attention. Targeting the mastermind of the attack, Bush mobilized a multinational coalition to invade Osama bin Laden's stronghold in Afghanistan. He also secured new laws and reorganized federal agencies to tighten homeland security. Insisting that Iraq's dictator Saddam Hussein had conspired in the 9/11 attacks and possessed weapons of mass destruction, Bush launched an invasion of Iraq as well.

The Bush Administration Begins

George W. Bush, who turned fifty-five in 2001, was a president's son and a senator's grandson. After graduating from Yale, serving in the Texas Air National Guard during the Vietnam War, and earning an MBA at Harvard, Bush entered the oil business in Texas. He was known for partying and drinking, but a religious conversion and marriage to Laura Welch stabilized his life. Bush's business ventures failed, but in 1989 he joined a group that bought the Texas Rangers baseball team. This visibility, plus family connections, helped him win the Texas governorship in 1994 and the Republican presidential nomination in 2000. **Richard (Dick) Cheney** became his running mate (see Chapter 31).

Bush named **Colin Powell,** former head of the Joint Chiefs of Staff, as secretary of state, making him the highest-ranking African-American to serve in a presidential administration. **Condoleezza Rice** of Stanford University, also African-American, became national security adviser even though her academic specialization, Soviet affairs, had become less relevant with the end of the Cold War.

Other Bush appointees were, like Vice President Cheney, veterans of earlier Republican administrations with corporate ties. Secretary of Defense **Donald Rumsfeld** had held the same post under President Ford and later headed a pharmaceutical company. Treasury Secretary Paul O'Neill had been CEO of Alcoa Corporation. Army Secretary Thomas E. White came from Houston's Enron Corporation. The Republican right wing welcomed ultra-conservative John Ashcroft as attorney general.

As we shall see, on issues from taxes and energy to education and medical research, Bush proposed measures that reflected the interests of the wealthy; corporate America; and the religious right, whose alienation had helped defeat his father in 1992. Bush's conservative appointments and domestic policies troubled many moderate Republicans, including Vermont senator James Jeffords, who in May 2001 left the Republican Party to become an independent. (With Jeffords's vote Senate Democrats briefly regained the majority, only to lose it in the 2002 elections.) By the summer of 2001, Bush's approval rating had fallen to about 50 percent. But all this faded as the administration and the nation faced an awesome crisis.

Day of Horror: September 11, 2001

On the morning of **September 11, 2001,** three commercial airplanes hijacked by terrorists slammed into the Pentagon outside Washington, D.C., and the twin towers of New York's World Trade Center. As Americans watched in horror, the blazing towers collapsed, carrying more than 2,800 men and women to their deaths. The Pentagon attack left 245 dead on the ground. A fourth plane crashed in Pennsylvania when heroic passengers prevented terrorists from hitting another target, possibly the White House. At the World Trade Center, nearly 350 firefighters and 23 police officers perished. Along with the dead on the ground, 246 passengers and crew, plus 19 hijackers, died in the four planes.

The hijackers deliberately targeted symbols of U.S. economic and military power. The destruction of the World Trade Center that terrorists had attempted in 1993 (see Chapter 31) had now tragically been achieved. The government soon identified the hijackers, all Muslims from the Middle East, and traced their movements before September 11, including enrollment in flight-training schools in Florida, Oklahoma, and Minnesota.

Terrorism—whether assassinations or the bombing of buildings, buses, ships, and planes—was familiar elsewhere, and had taken many American lives, civilian and military, in the 1980s and 1990s. But not since the War of 1812 had foreign enemies attacked major cities on the U.S. mainland. As the nation mourned, political divisions faded. Flags appeared everywhere. The World War II anthem "God Bless America" enjoyed renewed popularity. Editorial writers evoked memories of the 1941 Japanese surprise attack at Pearl Harbor. "United We Stand" proclaimed banners, billboards, and bumper stickers. President Bush urged Americans to distinguish between a few Islamic terrorists and the world's 1.2 billion Muslims, including some 6 million in America. Nevertheless, U.S. Muslims faced hostility and even violence.

CHRONOLOGY, 2001–2006

2001 • Bush administration repudiates Kyoto protocol on emission standards.
Congress passes $1.35 trillion tax cut bill.
Stockmarket falls; Enron Corporation collapses; wave of corporate bankruptcies and scandals.
Congress passes No Child Left Behind Act.
U.S. withdraws from ABM (Anti-Ballistic Missile) Treaty and begins missile defense system.
Terrorist attacks on World Trade Center, Pentagon (September 11).
U.S. and allied forces defeat Taliban regime in Afghanistan.
Captured Taliban fighters and others imprisoned at Guantánamo Bay, Cuba.
USA-Patriot Act passed.

2002 • Bipartisan Campaign Reform Act (McCain-Feingold law).
Department of Homeland Security created.
Sarbanes-Oxley Act tightens business accounting regulations.
Bush secretly authorizes National Security Administration to spy without warrants.
Republicans gain in midterm elections.

2003 • U.S. and coalition forces invade Iraq (March 21).
North Korea withdraws from Nuclear Non-Proliferation Treaty.
Prescription-drug benefits added to Medicare.

2004 • Revelation of abuses at Baghdad's Abu Ghraib prison.
George W. Bush wins second term, defeating John Kerry.

2005 • Congress passes Energy Act.
Bush signs bill barring "cruel, inhuman, and degrading" treatment of prisoners.
Trade deficit and budget deficit hit record levels.
Bush names John Roberts and Samuel Alito to Supreme Court.
Hurricane Katrina devastates New Orleans.
Lobbyist Jack Abramoff indicted on multiple criminal charges.

2006 • Tom Delay resigns House seat.
Congressional report documents government failures in Hurricane Katrina response.
Radical Hamas organization wins Palestinian elections.
Iran resumes nuclear enrichment program.
U.S. sells India nuclear fuel and reactor parts.
GM and Ford announce major layoffs.
Congress debates immigration-law changes; Hispanic immigrants march in major cities.
Democrats gain control of both houses in midterm elections
Resignation of Defense Secretary Donald Rumsfeld.

When the damaged New York Stock Exchange reopened after six days, stock prices plunged. They soon recovered, but consumer confidence remained fragile. The airline and travel industries reeled as jittery travelers canceled trips. "Vacant Rooms, Empty Tables, and Scared Tourists," headlined a New York newspaper.

In October, an editor at the *National Enquirer,* a tabloid that had attacked Osama bin Laden, died of anthrax, a rare bacterial disease, contracted from spores mailed in a letter. Letters containing anthrax spores next appeared in the offices of NBC news and two senators. Police closed the Senate Office Building for decontamination. Four other persons, including two postal workers, died from anthrax-tainted mail. As panic spread, scientists traced the spores to a U.S. research laboratory, and investigators focused on finding a domestic perpetrator rather than a foreign terrorist.

Confronting the Enemy in Afghanistan

President Bush on September 12 declared the attacks an "act of war." On September 14, the Senate unanimously authorized Bush to use "all necessary and appropriate force" to retaliate and to prevent future acts of terrorism. On September 20, addressing a joint session of Congress, a somber Bush blamed the attack on a terrorist network called **al Qaeda** ("the base") headed by Osama bin Laden in Afghanistan. Bin Laden, the renegade son of a wealthy Saudi Arabian contractor, was already under indictment for the 1998 attack on U.S. embassies in Africa (see Chapter 31). He had long denounced America for supporting Israel and for stationing "infidel" troops on Saudi soil. (Ironically, the United States had backed bin Laden in the 1980s, when he was

America Under Attack *Rescuers remove a flag-draped body from the ruins of the World Trade Center.*

fighting Russian forces in Afghanistan.) A videotape in which bin Laden boasted of the attack and laughed about the massive damage, discovered by U.S. forces in Afghanistan, confirmed his responsibility. Though bin Laden claimed to be defending Islam, most Islamic leaders repudiated him. Among the poor in some Arab cities and Palestinian refugee camps, however, the attacks produced celebratory demonstrations.

Bush announced his determination to uproot al Qaeda. He also targeted al Qaeda's protectors, the Taliban, a Pakistan-based movement of strict and militant Muslims, which had controlled Afghanistan since 1996. This phase of America's antiterrorist effort enjoyed broad international backing. Despite the pro-Taliban sympaties of Muslim fundamentalists in Pakistan, that country's military government endorsed Bush's campaign. British prime minister Tony Blair offered strong support. On October 7, U.S., British, Canadian, Pakistani, and other forces launched the attack. For the first time, NATO forces fought in defense of a member nation. Anti-Taliban groups within Afghanistan, gathered in a loose coalition called the Northern Alliance, assisted in the campaign as well.

The Taliban soon surrendered Kabul, the Afghan capital, and other strongholds. By mid-December, despite sporadic resistance, the United States and its allies claimed victory. Hundreds of captured al Qaeda fighters were sent to the U.S. base in **Guantánamo Bay,** Cuba. In June 2002, with U.S. support, Afghan tribal leaders established a new government and named an interim prime minister, Hamid Karzai. Afghanistan's eighty-nine-year-old former king, back in Kabul after years in exile, endorsed the effort. Osama bin Laden remained at large, however, and many al Qaeda loyalists retreated to mountainous eastern Afghanistan and prepared to fight on. The top Taliban leader, Mullah Omar, went into hiding as well.

Tightening Home-Front Security

Bush's September 20 speech also signaled a broader response to the attacks. America would target not only al Qaeda, he said, but "every terrorist group of global reach," and employ not only military strikes but "covert operations, secret even in success." Americans would experience "the delays and inconveniences that may accompany tighter security," he warned, and they must "give law enforcement the additional tools it needs to track down terror here at home."

In one step to shore up domestic security, Congress late in 2001 required that the nation's 28,000 airport security personnel be U.S. citizens and meet performance standards set by a newly created Transportation Security Administration. But other aspects of the open-ended antiterrorism campaign hinted at by Bush proved more controversial. The Justice Department detained hundreds of Middle Easterners living in the United States, some for minor visa violations, and held them without filing charges or even revealing their names. Some local police officials, troubled by civil-liberties issues, resisted this wholesale roundup of persons simply on the basis of their ethnicity or national origin.

The **USA-Patriot Act,** the administration's sweeping antiterrorist bill passed by Congress in October 2001, extended the government's powers to monitor telephone and e-mail communications and library patrons' Internet searches. Civil-liberties organizations protested. Even some conservatives, traditionally suspicious of big government, questioned this expansion of federal power. (Despite growing reservations, Congress renewed the Patriot Act in 2005, though with some modifications.) In November 2001, Bush signed an executive order empowering the government to try

Map 32.1 Afghanistan and Pakistan

After the attacks of September 11, 2001, U.S. and NATO forces at-
tacked the terrorist organization al Qaeda, based in Afghanistan.
Afghanistan's radical Islamist Taliban regime was overthrown, but many
fighters retreated to the mountains along the Afghan-Pakistan border.
As of late 2006, Afghanistan remained violent and unsettled, and al
Qaeda leader Osama bin Laden was still at large.

noncitizens accused of fomenting terrorism in secret military tribunals rather than in
civil courts. While precedent existed for such tribunals in wartime, this order, issued
without consulting Congress, roused widespread criticism. In 2002, news media reported disturbing evidence of missed clues before the 9/11 attack. In August 2001, for
example, a Minnesota flight school had warned the FBI that a suspicious person named
Zacarias Moussaoui had tried to enroll. Moussaoui had been arrested on immigration
charges, but the Justice Department had denied an FBI request for permission to check

his computer. (After September 11 Moussaoui's link to bin Laden was documented, and in 2006 he was tried in Virginia and sentenced to life in prison.) Administration officials also acknowledged that through the summer of 2001, President Bush's daily security briefings had included warnings of an al Qaeda plot to hijack a U.S. airliner.

To coordinate antiterrorism efforts, Congress created a new cabinet-level **Department of Homeland Security** in November 2002. The new department absorbed the Coast Guard, the Customs Service, the Federal Emergency Management Agency (FEMA), the Immigration and Naturalization Service, and other agencies. The FBI and the CIA remained independent. The department's first head, former Pennsylvania governor Tom Ridge, announced a color-coded system to alert citizens to the level of national-security danger. Skeptics doubted whether such warnings, and a reshuffling of existing agencies, actually increased security.

In 2003 Bush named a blue-ribbon commission, headed by Republican Thomas Kean, a former New Jersey governor, and Democrat Lee Hamilton, a former congressman, to examine pre-9/11 intelligence failures. The commission's 2004 report pinpointed a lack of communication between the FBI, the CIA, and other agencies, and called for a restructuring of U.S. intelligence operations. In 2005 Bush named John Negroponte, a career diplomat, as Director of National Intelligence, to coordinate fifteen civilian and military intelligence agencies, including the CIA. Nevertheless, when Thomas Kean was asked about homeland security in 2006, he replied: "It's not a priority for the government right now. . . . [A] lot of the things we need to do . . . to prevent another 9/11 just simply aren't being done." Critics noted that most incoming shipping containers went unchecked, and U.S. chemical plants remained vulnerable.

The Campaign in Iraq, 2003–2004

Although Afghanistan remained unstable and Osama bin Laden uncaptured, the administration's attention shifted elsewhere. In his January 2002 State of the Union address, President Bush identified Iran, Iraq, and North Korea as an "axis of evil." Of the three, Iraq loomed largest. Iraq's ruler, Saddam Hussein, had been a thorn in America's flesh since the Persian Gulf War, which had left him weakened but still in power. In a barrage of speeches, Bush, Vice President Cheney, Defense Secretary Rumsfeld, and National Security Adviser Rice accused Saddam of complicity in the 9/11 attacks and of stockpiling or developing nuclear, chemical, and biological weapons.

This shift of focus to Iraq was orchestrated by a close-knit group of Republican **neoconservatives.** (The term, meaning "new conservatives," originally applied to one-time Democrats who favored a militant anti-Soviet foreign policy in the Cold War and who turned to the Republican Party when the Democratic Party shifted leftward in the 1960s.)

This group advocated an aggressive foreign policy dedicated to spreading democracy in the Arab world and beyond. Skeptical of multilateral approaches, neoconservatives believed that the United States, as the world's superpower, should act alone to pursue its goals. Such a policy, they believed, would advance freedom and create a safer environment for Israel, America's ally in the Middle East. Prominent neoconservatives included Paul Wolfowitz, Douglas Feith, and Richard Perle, who all held positions in Rumsfeld's Pentagon; Gary Adelman, a former Reagan administration official; and William Kristol, editor of *The Weekly Standard,* a political journal. For neoconservatives, democratizing Iraq was a first step in their ambitious agenda.

The call for invading Iraq proved controversial from the start. Critics challenged the administration to prove its claims. A preemptive war would not only violate U.S.

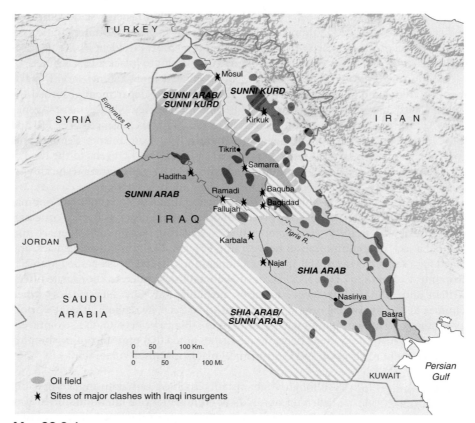

MAP 32.2 Iraq

With Saddam Hussein's overthrow by U.S.-led forces in 2003, violence erupted among Iraq's ethnic and religious groups, including the majority Shia Muslims concentrated in the southeast and the minority Sunni Muslims, who had ruled the country under Saddam and earlier.

principles, they charged, but could also drag on for years, unleash anger across the Arab world, and undermine the larger antiterrorist campaign. Great Britain's Tony Blair backed the administration, but other NATO allies, as well as Russia and most Arab leaders, objected. To counter the rush to war, they called for a UN resolution demanding that Iraq readmit UN weapons inspectors, who had departed in 1998 when Iraq blocked their access to some sites.

In October 2002, Congress passed a resolution sponsored by the administration authorizing President Bush to "defend the national security of the United States against the continuing threat posed by Iraq." While Republicans overwhelmingly supported the resolution, Democrats were divided, fearful of opposing Bush on an issue he called vital to American security. As Lyndon Johnson had cited the Gulf of Tonkin Resolution to justify escalating the Vietnam War (see Chapter 28), President Bush would later use this resolution as the legal basis for invading Iraq. Bush also presented the case against Saddam in a UN address.

As the November 2002 midterm elections approached, President Bush, enjoying post-9/11 approval ratings close to 70 percent, campaigned tirelessly, stressing his leadership in the war on terror. Democrats hammered at the recession, corporate scandals, and Bush's environmental record. With 9/11 memories still raw, Bush's talk of terrorism hit home. As a Colorado voter commented: "[W]e need protection and I don't want to see President Bush get stalemated . . . [in] protecting our country." The outcome strengthened Bush's hand, as Republicans regained control of the Senate and increased their House majority. In the wake of the defeat, the House minority leader, Missouri's Richard Gephardt, resigned. Nancy Pelosi of California replaced him, the first woman of either party to hold this position.

Bolstered by the election, the administration pushed its Iraq invasion plans. In November 2002 the UN Security Council imposed tough new weapons-inspection requirements on Iraq. Baghdad agreed, and UN inspectors returned. They soon withdrew, however, as U.S. and British forces assembled in the Persian Gulf. In a February 2003 UN speech, Secretary of State Colin Powell, relying on evidence supplied by the CIA, insisted that Saddam Hussein was developing weapons of mass destruction (WMDs).

The war began on March 19, 2003, as U.S. cruise missiles rained down on Baghdad. The land invasion commenced on March 21. U.S. and British troops moved first into southern Iraq, populated by Shiite Muslims who had been brutally oppressed by Saddam. Securing the oil fields around Basra, the invaders moved north. Field commanders, encountering unexpected guerrilla resistance, raised caution flags, but the top commander, General Tommy Franks, dismissed their warnings. In early April, U.S. troops occupied Baghdad and toppled a large statue of Saddam. As the regime fell and Saddam fled, basic services in the city collapsed and widespread looting erupted.

On May 1, after a navy jet had brought him to the aircraft carrier *Abraham Lincoln* off San Diego, President Bush declared major combat operations over. A banner behind him proclaimed "Mission Accomplished." Bush named L. Paul Bremer, a career Foreign Service officer, to administer civil affairs in Iraq. Two of Saddam's sons died resisting arrest in July. Saddam himself was captured in December, and later put on trial.

Iraq's Sunni Muslims, though a minority, had long dominated Iraqi politics. Resisting their loss of power, they mobilized to expel the invaders. Bremer's decision to disband the Iraqi army and dismiss all government officials who had served under Saddam created a power vacuum, encouraging sectarian violence. Radical Muslim fighters from outside Iraq, led by a Jordanian, Abu Musab al-Zarqawi, added to the unrest. So did a fiery young Shiite cleric, Moqtada al-Sadr, popular among Baghdad's poor. Anti-American and anti-Sunni, al-Sadr also feuded with senior Shiite religious leaders.

Conditions worsened through 2004 as bombings, kidnappings, and deadly highway blasts caused by improvised explosive devices (IEDs) occurred daily. In March, insurgents ambushed and killed four U.S. employees of a security company, and burned their bodies. In June, Paul Bremer transferred power to a provisional Iraqi government headed by Iyad Allawi. A physician who had led a London-based anti-Saddam movement, Allawi had close ties to Western intelligence agencies. But little changed. In September, the toll of U.S. dead in Iraq passed 1,000. As the year ended, the war that the Bush team had launched so confidently seemed mired in bloodshed and violence. Vice President Cheney had predicted that the Iraqis would welcome the Americans as liberators. The head of the CIA had assured Bush that victory would be a "slam dunk." Now reality blasted such wishful thinking.

POLITICS AND THE ECONOMY IN BUSH'S FIRST TERM, 2001–2005

Although the 9/11 attacks and their aftermath dominated Bush's first term, the administration also proposed a series of economic and social initiatives. Debate over these measures unfolded amid a sharp recession and a cascade of corporate bankruptcies and scandals.

Economic Reverses and Corporate Scandals The prosperity and stock-market boom of the 1990s (see Chapter 31) barely outlasted the decade. As Asian and Latin American economies faltered, the U.S. economy suffered as well. In March 2001, the stock market recorded its worst week since 1989, falling by 6 percent. The high-flying Silicon Valley information-technology companies, which had led the boom of the later 1990s, were especially hard hit. An estimated 250 such businesses collapsed in a few months' time. As the market value of the surviving companies plummeted, instant millionaires watched their portfolios shrivel.

Few shed tears when luxury boutiques and pricey restaurants suffered reverses. But the recession that began in Silicon Valley and Wall Street soon spread. Industrial production dropped, and every state lost jobs. Service-sector employment fell faster in the last quarter of 2001 than in any comparable period since the 1940s. Unskilled workers and former welfare recipients seeking entry-level jobs struggled. By June 2003, with the unemployment rate at 6.4 percent, 2.6 million workers had lost their jobs.

The longest economic boom in American history had ended with a thud. The Bush administration, having inherited a budget surplus, now projected years of deficits. To stimulate the economy, the Federal Reserve Board cut interest rates eleven times in 2001, to a forty-year low. A wave of corporate bankruptcies and scandals, particularly in the energy and telecommunications fields, further eroded investor confidence. Business deregulation, a culture of greed, and the emergence of new information-based enterprises and complex corporate structures that investors did not understand well had created a situation that invited fraudulent corporate practices.

Houston's Enron Corporation, with close ties to the administration, was an early casualty. A marketer of electric power, Enron flourished in the 1990s and moved into utilities and telecommunications. In 2000, claiming revenues of $101 billion, Enron ranked seventh in *Fortune* magazine's list of America's top corporations. The end came abruptly. Late in 2001 Enron filed for bankruptcy and admitted to falsifying profit reports. More than five thousand Enron workers lost both their jobs and their retirement funds, which consisted mostly of Enron stock. Shortly before the collapse, Enron founder Kenneth Lay and other top officials had sold their Enron stock, profiting handsomely. The Chicago accounting firm that had certified Enron's financial reports collapsed as well. Enron's chief financial officer pled guilty to criminal charges and cooperated with the prosecution. In 2006, a Houston jury convicted Lay and former Enron CEO Jeffry Skilling on multiple counts of fraud and conspiracy. The company's logo, a crooked "E," seemed all too appropriate. Lay died of a heart attack in July 2006.

The overextended fiber-optics industry, having laid 100 million miles of optical fiber worldwide in 1999–2001, stumbled badly as recession hit. Lucent Technologies, a telecommunications giant, cut nearly one hundred thousand jobs in 2001. In 2002 WorldCom, America's second-largest telecommunications company, admitting that it had overstated profits by billions, filed for bankruptcy and fired seventeen thousand employees. CEO Bernard Ebbers, convicted of securities fraud in 2005, received a twenty-five-year prison sentence.

The parade continued. John T. Rigas, head of Adelphia Corporation, the nation's sixth-largest cable company, was arrested in July 2002 with his two sons for a fraud that cost stockholders $2.5 billion. He received a fifteen-year prison term. In September, Dennis Kozlowski, the CEO of Tyco, an industrial products and service company, was indicted along with Tyco's chief financial officer for looting the company of $600 million. Kozlowski's trial included testimony about a $6,000 shower curtain for his New York apartment and a $2 million Mediterranean birthday party for his wife. Kozlowski received a long prison sentence, was fined $70 million, and was ordered to repay Tyco $134 million.

Top mutual-fund managers faced charges of increasing their bonuses by advising investors to buy stocks at inflated prices while privately disparaging the same stocks. "Let's put lipstick on this pig," one analyst joked to another, discussing a stock he was pushing. Under investigation by New York attorney general Eliot Spitzer, the Wall Street investment firm Merrill Lynch paid $200 million in fines.

Despite some positive economic news, the stock market fell through much of 2002 and early 2003, as traumatized investors remained wary. Executives who had been celebrities in the 1990s now faced public hostility if not criminal investigation. The University of Maryland business school took students on field trips to penitentiaries where white-collar inmates warned them to be honest. Declared the chairman of Goldman Sachs, a Wall Street investment bank, "I cannot think of a time when business . . . has been held in less repute."

Politicians responded to mounting public anger. President Bush delivered a stern speech upholding business morality. In July 2002 Congress passed the Sarbanes-Oxley Act, named for its sponsors, which imposed stricter accounting and financial reporting rules and toughened criminal penalties for business fraud.

Stimulated by low interest rates, the U.S. economy grew by 4.2 percent in 2004 and 3.5 percent in 2005. But this growth was unevenly distributed geographically, being heavily concentrated west of the Mississippi. Also, while the real income of the nation's richest 1 percent increased by more than 12 percent in 2004, the average real income of the remaining 99 percent grew by only 1.5 percent. Job growth remained weak. Discussing these data, the economist Paul Krugman wrote: "[I]t's a great economy if you're a high-level corporate executive or someone who owns a lot of stock. For most other Americans, economic growth is a spectator sport." By mid-2006, even this uneven recovery faltered. As oil prices soared, world conditions deteriorated, and the Federal Reserve Board raised interest rates to combat inflation, job growth slowed, and the jittery stock market again sank.

The Republican Domestic Agenda In February 2001, fulfilling a campaign promise, President Bush proposed a $1.6 trillion cut in income taxes over a ten-year period. Though the measure reduced all rates, wealthy taxpayers received the highest percentage reduction. As the recession began, Bush argued that the cuts would stimulate investment and speed recovery. Democrats attacked the bill for favoring the rich, and warned that slashing taxes, as President Reagan had in 1981, would produce huge federal deficits.

In May Congress passed a $1.35 trillion tax cut—lower than Bush's proposal and somewhat less slanted toward the rich. Mounting budget deficits predictably followed, erasing the surplus Clinton had achieved. Economists, estimating lost federal revenue over a twenty-year period at $4 trillion, warned of a mountainous national debt. Nevertheless, the Republican-led Congress added another $320 billion in tax cuts in 2003 and $95 billion in 2005.

The administration's 2001 energy bill emerged from secret meetings of oil and gas executives with Vice President Cheney, himself a former head of Halliburton, an energy company. Kenneth Lay, a major GOP contributor, played a key role before Enron's collapse. The bill proposed more nuclear power plants; eased environmental regulations on energy companies; and included incentives to expand coal, oil, and natural-gas production, including drilling in Alaska's **Arctic National Wildlife Refuge** (ANWR). President Bush defended the bill as a way to reduce U.S. dependence on foreign oil.

The 9/11 attacks and all that followed intervened, but in August 2005 Congress passed an energy bill. It granted $14.5 billion in tax breaks to oil, natural gas, coal, and nuclear-power companies; exempted them from some environmental laws; and eased the process of securing permits to drill or mine on public lands. The law offered a one-year tax credit for purchasers of hybrid vehicles and energy-efficient appliances and included incentives for research on renewable and cleaner energy sources, including ethanol, made from corn, which won supporters in the corn belt. The law did not approve drilling in ANWR, but Alaska's powerful senator, Ted Stevens, vowed to continue that fight. Despite lobbying by environmental groups, it did not tighten vehicle fuel-efficiency requirements, even on gas-guzzling trucks and SUVs. Overall, said one critic, the measure was "Christmas in August" for the energy companies.

On education, Bush pushed a program he labeled **"No Child Left Behind."** As governor of Texas, Bush had addressed education issues, and the subject interested his wife Laura, a former school librarian. Embracing education reform also enhanced his image as a "compassionate conservative." Bush's plan called for standardized national tests in grades four and eight to measure reading and math skills, with penalties for schools that fell short. In 2001, Congress mandated annual testing. Fourth-grade reading scores improved somewhat by 2003, but eighth-grade reading and math scores showed little change. Some schools, focusing on raising test scores, cut back art, music, history, and other subjects. Poorly performing schools, often in disadvantaged neighborhoods, protested the threatened penalties. The massive federal intrusion in public education, historically a local matter, troubled some conservatives.

Christian conservatives ranked among Bush's strongest supporters in 2000. Moving quickly to reward them, Bush in 2001 created an Office of Faith-Based and Community Initiatives to funnel federal grants to churches for social programs. Under this initiative, grants went to anti-abortion groups, organizations promoting teenage sexual abstinence, and prison ministries run by evangelicals. Operation Blessing, a charity operated by televangelist Pat Robertson, received $22 million in direct grants and food surpluses. A black church in Milwaukee led by a prominent Republican received $1.4 million.

Bush's education plan also included a voucher system by which children could attend private or religious schools at taxpayers' expense. Congress rejected this proposal, but some states introduced their own voucher plans. By 2006 some 4,000 private and church-sponsored schools were partially supported by student vouchers. Some did well; others showed no better results than the public schools; and some 400 had closed for various reasons.

President Bush also sought favor with Christian conservatives, who overwhelmingly oppose abortion, by restricting stem-cell research. Stem cells are produced during an early stage of human embryo development, and fertility clinics often have "surplus" fertilized embryos. Since stem cells can develop into more specialized human cells, they are valuable for medical research. Some anti-abortion groups oppose research using fertilized embryos, however. In a 2001 presidential directive, Bush permitted federal funding of research on a handful of existing stem-cell lines, but barred funding for research on stem cells harvested from human embryos in the future. Medical researchers warned that this restriction could inhibit their work.

Campaign Finance Reform and the Election of 2004
As political campaign costs soared, reformers worked to curb the endless fundraising the system required. They especially targeted so-called soft money contributions to political parties that then flowed on to specific candidates. Big soft-money contributors ranged from (mostly Republican) business lobbies, anti-abortion groups, and the National Rifle Association to (mostly Democratic) labor unions, trial lawyers, and teachers. In the 2000 election, soft-money contributions reached $400 million.

In 2002 President Bush signed a reform bill co-sponsored by Arizona Republican John McCain and Wisconsin Democrat Russell Feingold. It banned soft-money contributions; barred fake TV "issue ads" designed to influence elections; and included other provisions to reduce the power of money in politics. As lobbying organizations sought loopholes and challenged the law on free-speech grounds, its ultimate impact remained unclear.

As the 2004 election approached, Howard Dean, a physician and former Vermont governor, emerged as the early frontrunner for the Democratic presidential nomination. Dean criticized the Iraq War and Democrats who had supported it. Like Jimmy Carter in 1976, he bypassed party leaders and appealed directly to voters. He built a following via the Internet, especially on college campuses. But while Dean's candor energized the Democratic base, it also alienated many voters. In the Iowa primary kicking off the campaign, he finished a weak third behind Senators **John Kerry** of Massachusetts and John Edwards of North Carolina. When he again lost to Kerry in the New Hampshire primary a week later, his campaign faded. Nevertheless, Dean had bluntly criticized the Iraq War while other leading Democrats hung back. He also demonstrated the Internet's potential for fundraising and rallying support.

John Kerry won the nomination. Democratic strategists hoped that his military record as a decorated Vietnam War veteran would neutralize charges that Democrats were weak on defense. He named Senator Edwards, a successful trial lawyer, as his running mate. George W. Bush and Dick Cheney again headed the Republican ticket. Bush began the campaign with a massive war chest of some $150 million from corporate sources and wealthy donors called "Pioneers." Bypassing the McCain-Feingold restrictions on organizational contributions, the Pioneers raised money from friends and colleagues. Of 246 "Pioneers," 104 later received appointments in the Bush administration.

In the campaign, Kerry criticized the administration's response to 9/11. Although he had voted for the Patriot Act and supported a Senate resolution approving the use of force in Iraq as a last resort, Kerry now accused Bush of misleading the nation about Saddam Hussein, and criticized parts of the Patriot Act as threats to civil liberties. President Bush defended both the Iraq conflict and the Patriot Act as crucial to the war on terrorism. Citing Kerry's changing positions, Republicans accused him of "flip-flopping" indecisiveness.

Attacking Bush's environmental record, Kerry called for vigorous enforcement of environmental laws, tougher fuel-efficiency standards, and more support for renewable energy. Highlighting Bush's less than distinguished military record, Kerry played up his tour in Vietnam. At the Democratic convention he opened his acceptance speech with a salute and the line: "I'm John Kerry, and I'm reporting for duty." (Anti-Kerry TV commercials questioned his Vietnam record and emphasized his 1971 antiwar testimony before the Senate Foreign Relations Committee on behalf of Vietnam Veterans Against the War.) Kerry, a Catholic, sought to counter Bush's edge with evangelical Christians. "I don't wear my religion on my sleeve," he said in his acceptance speech. "But faith has given me values and hope to live by, from Vietnam to this day."

The candidates' positions on cultural issues reflected national divisions. Kerry opposed the death penalty; Bush supported it. Kerry supported *Roe* v. *Wade;* Bush favored a ban on all abortions except in rare circumstances. Kerry backed stricter gun control; Bush opposed it.

The divisive issue of same-sex marriage loomed large during the campaign. In 2004, San Francisco's mayor challenged California law by allowing same-sex couples to marry, and the Massachusetts Supreme Court ruled that banning same-sex marriage violated the state constitution's equal-rights guarantee. As gay and lesbian couples in San Francisco and Massachusetts applied for marriage licenses, opinion polls found 63 percent of Americans opposed to same-sex marriage. (By 2006 that figure had dropped to 51 percent.) While Kerry favored leaving this issue to the states, Bush endorsed a constitutional amendment banning gay marriage. As eleven states added referenda banning same-sex marriage to the fall ballot, the issue energized religious conservatives. The referenda passed by lopsided margins in all eleven states, and Bush won in nine of the eleven, including closely contested Ohio.

On election day, Bush garnered 51 percent of the popular vote to Kerry's 48 percent. Kerry won New England, New York, and Pennsylvania. In the Upper Midwest he carried Michigan, Illinois, Wisconsin, and Minnesota. California, Oregon, and Washington also fell his way. In the rest of the nation, the majority went for Bush. Bush narrowly won the Electoral College vote, with Ohio the pivotal state. Republicans gained a net of four Senate seats and four House seats. In South Dakota, a Republican defeated Tom Daschle, the Senate Democratic leader. Voters most worried about terrorism, as well as evangelical Christians and other cultural conservatives, overwhelmingly voted Republican.

Kerry had won the two largest states, California and New York, and 55 percent of voters under thirty—an age group that increased its strength at the polls by 9 percent between 2000 and 2004—voted Democratic. In Illinois, a charismatic young Democrat, Barak Obama, won election to the Senate. Overall, however, a tax-cutting president seen as a leader in the "war on terror" and a defender of embattled conservative cultural values had eked out a narrow victory.

The election highlighted the political role of new technologies. MoveOn.org and democracyforamerica.com, two Internet-based Democratic initiatives that emerged from the campaign, continued to raise funds and to generate e-mail and telephone campaigns in support of liberal candidates and causes. Hundreds of bloggers (independent website operators) sustained a freewheeling flow of political commentary. While conservative organizations had long mobilized their supporters via magazines, direct mail, radio, and TV, liberals appeared to have the edge in the new arena of Internet-based activism, especially among young people.

Indeed, the popular culture offered many challenges to conservative ideology. Michael Moore's 2004 documentary *Fahrenheit 9/11* mounted a sharp and witty critique of the administration's response to 9/11. *Democracy Now,* a left-oriented news program, was available on radio, the Internet, and some public TV stations. Singers Bruce Springsteen and Neil Young and the Dixie Chicks country trio stirred controversy for their outspoken criticism of Bush. Even on talk radio, a conservative bastion, individuals such as Bill Maher and Al Franken voiced opposing views.

The 2004 election again underscored the political role of organized groups. Conservative organizations and those on the religious right, some dating to the 1970s (see Chapters 30 and 31), remained active. Highlighting such volatile issues as gay marriage and school prayer, Pat Robertson's Christian Coalition, Donald E. Wildmon's American Family Association, James Dobson's Focus on the Family, and other groups mobilized Bush's base of religious and cultural conservatives. These groups, too, used the Internet to promote their cause.

But organizations opposed to the conservative agenda were active as well. People for the American Way, the American Civil Liberties Union, Planned Parenthood, the Sierra Club, Amnesty International, the Union of Concerned Scientists, Emily's List (which supported women candidates who endorsed liberal and feminist goals), and many other groups advocated for liberal candidates or rallied opposition to administration policies they opposed. Even among evangelical Christians, support for Bush was not unanimous. Jim Wallis, founder of the evangelical Sojourners movement based in Washington, D.C., sharply criticized the religious right in his *Sojourners* magazine and his book *God's Politics: Why the Right Gets It Wrong and the Left Doesn't Get It* (2005). Ronald Sider, founder of Evangelicals for Social Action, called on evangelicals to embrace such issues as peacemaking, concern for the poor, and environmental protection. In full-page newspaper ads in 2006, leading evangelicals challenged the administration's environmental and energy policies.

FOREIGN POLICY IN A THREATENING ERA

By 2005, two years into the Iraq War, insurgent violence and sectarian conflict raged unabated. Home-front support eroded amid accusations of prisoner abuse, illegal spying in the name of security, and deceptions in the administration's case for invading Iraq. The continuing Israeli-Palestinian struggle, threats of nuclear proliferation, and rising international concern about environmental hazards further challenged U.S. policy makers.

The Continuing Struggle in Iraq; Sagging Home-Front Support

In his second inaugural address in January 2005, Bush described the Iraq War as part of a global campaign to spread democracy, "with the ultimate goal of ending tyranny in our world." The speech echoed Woodrow Wilson's 1917 war message proclaiming America's mission to make the world "safe for democracy" (see Chapter 22). But Secretary of State Colin Powell, who had privately opposed the war, had resigned in November 2004; Bush named National Security Adviser Condoleezza Rice to replace him.

Chaos in Iraq: Aftermath of the Destruction of the Imam Ali Mosque in Najaf, August 29, 2003 *As Shiite Muslims crowded into the mosque for Friday prayers, a massive car bomb killed at least 125 people, including a top Shiite religious leader, and destroyed the mosque, one of Shia Islam's holiest shrines. The bombing was part of a pattern of worsening sectarian violence in Iraq following the U.S.-led invasion.*

In Iraq the conflict dragged on, with daily news of roadside IEDs, suicide bombings, kidnappings, and assassinations. A Sunni-led insurgency centered in Baghdad and a region north of the city called the "Sunni triangle." Determined to prevent a government of Shiites allied with the Kurds of northern Iraq, Sunnis organized a campaign of disruption, targeting police, soldiers, and government officials. A February 2005 bombing at a police recruiting station near Baghdad killed 127 and wounded many more. U.S. troops periodically raided Sunni strongholds. A November 2004 operation in Fallujah, involving more than 10,000 U.S. and Iraqi forces, left 38 Americans dead and 275 wounded. Typically, however, the insurgents returned once the troops withdrew. Suicide attacks by outside fighters, including al Qaeda loyalists, added to the unrest.

Amid the turmoil, U.S. attempts to train an Iraqi army faltered, as did the reconstruction effort. In Baghdad and other cities, electricity and other basic services remained unpredictable. A subsidiary of the Halliburton Company, once headed by Vice President Cheney, with $3.6 billion in reconstruction contracts awarded with no bidding competition, faced accusations of fraud and overcharging. Company officials denied wrongdoing and noted the difficulty of working in a war zone. Oil exports, Iraq's major income source, remained below prewar levels. Amid widespread corruption, some funds from oil sales were diverted through shadowy channels to the insurgents.

Bringing democracy to Iraq proved equally difficult. Sunnis boycotted a January 2005 election to choose a National Assembly. Dominated by Shiites, the Assembly chose as prime minister Ibrahim al-Jaafari, a Shiite religious party leader with links to the radical cleric Moqtada al-Sadr, whose private militias attacked Sunnis, U.S. soldiers, journalists, and foreign contractors. Sectarian hatred worsened when U.S. troops found a secret prison and torture center run by the Interior Ministry of the Shiite-dominated government. Sunnis accused Shiite militias and even rogue Interior Ministry "death squads" of targeting Sunni leaders for kidnapping and killing and detonating car bombs in Sunni neighborhoods and commercial districts.

Sunnis participated in a second round of parliamentary voting in December 2005, but the vote followed sectarian lines, and the violence continued. In one day in January 2006, suicide bombers killed more than sixty Shiite pilgrims in Karbala and more than fifty applicants for police jobs in Ramadi. In February, suicide bombers destroyed a revered Shiite shrine, the golden-domed Al-Askariya Mosque in Samarrah, triggering anti-Sunni reprisal attacks. (The Kurds in northern Iraq, hoping for an eventual independent Kurdish state, mostly remained aloof from the carnage.)

Nearly four thousand Iraqi security forces and civilians died in sectarian violence in the first four months of 2006. Thousands of fearful refugees found shelter in makeshift camps. As the estimated Iraqi death toll since March 2003 topped 50,000, former prime minister Allawi observed: "If this is not civil war, then God knows what civil war is." In April 2006, another Shiite politician, Nouri al-Maliki, replaced al-Jaafari as prime minister. Maliki announced plans for tightened security and a program of "national reconciliation," but the sectarian and insurgent killings, kidnappings, and bombings only intensified.

Historically a patchwork of ethnic and religious groups ruled by successive Persian, Greek, and Arab invaders, Iraq was governed by British colonial administrators after World War I and became an independent nation only in 1932. Whether it could avoid fragmenting into separate Sunni, Shiite, and Kurdish enclaves amid the chaos that followed Saddam's overthrow remained deeply problematic.

The 133,000 U.S. troops fought few open battles, but casualties continued. By October 2006 more than 2,700 GIs had been killed in Iraq and more than 20,000 wounded, nearly half of them severely. Casualties among journalists, contractors, and other U.S. civilians in Iraq pushed the grim total still higher. Combined with operations in Afghanistan, the war's cost stood at around $440 billion, with billions more in prospect. As other nations in the coalition withdrew their forces, the burden fell more heavily on the United States.

In November 2005, Pennsylvania congressman Jack Murtha urged immediate withdrawal from Iraq. A decorated Vietnam veteran with a hawkish record on military matters, Murtha had initially supported the war but now labeled it "a flawed policy, wrapped in an illusion." Similar calls came from across the political spectrum. "[T]he American objective in Iraq has failed," the conservative leader William Buckley bluntly declared. Observed the liberal *New York Times:* "Iraq is becoming a country that America should be ashamed to support, let alone occupy." Amid spreading sectarian violence, journalist Tom Friedman reflected: "The fate of the entire U.S. enterprise now hangs in the balance . . . ; once this kind of venom gets unleashed, it poisons everything." By May 2006, according to the Harris poll, Bush's approval ratings had fallen below 30 percent.

As the war lost support, criticism of the administration's decision for war intensified. In *Against All Enemies: Inside America's War on Terrorism* (2004), President Bush's former counterterrorism coordinator, Richard Clarke, reported that the day after 9/11, Bush had repeatedly pressured him to focus on Saddam Hussein. Under scrutiny, the key arguments in the administration's case for invading Iraq, Saddam's alleged WMD program and his connections to 9/11, both crumbled. After the invasion, CIA investigators found no WMDs in Iraq. President Bush's claim in his 2003 State of the Union address that Iraq had imported uranium from Africa proved false, and no credible evidence linked Saddam to the 9/11 attacks.

Were these distortions deliberate? The Senate Intelligence Committee and a presidential commission looking into prewar intelligence failures concluded that the CIA had supplied faulty or incomplete information on Iraq's alleged WMD program. But the Senate inquiry also found "significant pressure" by administration officials on the CIA to link Saddam to al Qaeda. Much evidence suggested that Cheney and other officials "cherry picked" intelligence that strengthened the case against Iraq, and downplayed contradictory data.

Critics also questioned Secretary of Defense Rumsfeld's prewar assurances that a small U.S. ground force equipped with high-tech weaponry could achieve victory, and that Iraq's army would switch sides once Saddam fell. When army chief of staff General Eric Shineski told Congress in March 2003 that success in Iraq would require several hundred thousand troops, Rumsfeld had derided this estimate as "far from the mark."

The Pentagon's lack of planning for post-invasion pacification and reconstruction faced intense criticism. In *Cobra II: The Inside Story of the Invasion and Occupation of Iraq* (2006), retired general Bernard Trainor and a co-author identified these lapses as crucial errors that underlay Iraq's descent into sectarian violence. In April 2006 Bush rejected a call by six retired generals for Rumsfeld's dismissal. "I am the decider," he declared, "and I decide what is best. And what's best is for Don Rumsfeld to remain as secretary of defense."

Evidence of prisoner mistreatment deepened home-front uneasiness. In April 2004, revolting photographs surfaced showing the abuse and sexual humiliation of Iraqis held by U.S. forces at Baghdad's Abu Ghraib prison. The army transferred Lieutenant General Ricardo Sanchez, commander of ground forces in Iraq, to Germany; demoted the general in command of the Abu Ghraib prison; and court-martialed some participants. One ringleader received a ten-year prison sentence and a dishonorable discharge. However, despite evidence that the army's interrogation guidelines encouraged abuses, the repercussions initially went no higher.

Further allegations soon surfaced charging prisoner abuse in Afghanistan, in Iraq, and at Guantánamo Bay, where more than 500 men seized in Afghanistan were held. In a secret 2002 memo, Justice Department lawyer John Yoo argued that the Geneva Conventions protecting prisoners of war did not apply to persons the president designated as "enemy combatants." The only interrogations that constituted torture, Yoo wrote, were those causing "death, organ failure, or serious impairment of bodily functions." All else was permissible. Yoo's "torture memo," approved by White House counsel (and future attorney general) Alberto Gonzales, became public in 2004, unleashing more controversy.

In 2004, the International Committee of the Red Cross described interrogation methods at Guantánamo as "tantamount to torture." A 2005 report by Amnesty International, a prisoner-rights organization, similarly alleged human-rights violations at

U.S. military prisons. One technique singled out for criticism was "water boarding," in which the victim is nearly drowned.

The Bush administration claimed the right to hold these prisoners without trial as "enemy combatants" as long as the "war on terrorism" continued. The army asserted that its interrogation techniques were "safe, secure, and humane." As of early 2006, only ten of the detainees had been formally charged. Evidence also surfaced that the CIA had secretly transported detainees to an uncertain fate in Egyptian and Eastern European prisons. UN agencies and officials in Great Britain, Spain, and other countries called upon the United States to close the Guantánamo facility.

In 2005, defying the White House, Congress passed an amendment proposed by Senator John McCain to a military appropriations bill. McCain's amendment outlawed "cruel, inhuman, and degrading" treatment of prisoners. McCain, who had been tortured as a POW in Vietnam, argued that information secured through torture is unreliable. For the United States to condone torture, he cautioned, placed captured American soldiers in greater jeopardy. Bush signed the bill, but in an increasingly common practice he issued a "signing statement" asserting, in effect, that he was not bound to obey the McCain amendment.

Deepening civil-liberties concerns, Americans learned in 2005 that President Bush in 2002 had secretly authorized the National Security Agency (NSA) to tap U.S. citizens' overseas phone calls and e-mails without securing a warrant from a special court created in 1978 to review requests for such clandestine surveillance. (The NSA, so secret that it has been jokingly called "No Such Agency," was created by President Truman in 1952.) John Yoo, author of the so-called "torture memo," also crafted the Justice Department memo justifying this action.

Defending this spying as vital to catching terrorists, Bush and Attorney General Gonzales argued that the September 2001 congressional resolution authorizing the president to use "all necessary and appropriate force" to prevent future attacks covered the NSA's monitoring of U.S. citizens' phone records without a warrant. Evidence that the NSA had electronically monitored domestic as well as foreign phone calls and e-mails, and that the FBI had targeted peace groups and journalists for surveillance, deepened the sense of uneasiness.

Bush's "signing statement" asserting his right to ignore the McCain antitorture amendment was one of many such pronouncements by which the president "interpreted" bills he was signing. Such "signing statements" have no constitutional standing. The Constitution empowers presidents to veto bills and grants Congress the power to override vetoes by a two-thirds vote. Bush's actions bypassed this constitutional procedure. The *New York Times,* criticizing Bush's "out-of-control sense of his powers in combating terrorism," editorialized in May 2006: "This president seems determined not to play by any rules other than the ones of his own making."

Early in 2006 Wisconsin senator Russell Feingold proposed a resolution censuring Bush for unconstitutional actions. A CBS News opinion poll found that most Americans thought that Bush had exceeded his authority in approving warrantless NSA spying on U.S. citizens. Even many Republicans, traditionally suspicious of governmental excesses, found Bush's actions disturbing. Congress took no action on Feingold's proposal, however.

In June 2006, the U.S. Supreme Court rejected the administration's claims that it could set up special military tribunals, not bound by the usual rules of courtroom procedure, to try the Guantánamo prisoners. Such tribunals, the Court held, violated both federal law and the Geneva Conventions governing the treatment of prisoners of war. In a broader sense, the Court rejected the Bush administration's claim that it could pursue the war on terrorism with little regard for Congress, the Constitution, or international law.

Adding to the accumulation of disturbing developments, *Time* magazine in March 2006 reported that in November 2005, U.S. marines had killed twenty-four unarmed Iraqi men, women, and children in the town of Haditha in Iraq's Anbar Province after a roadside IED had killed a member of their unit. In July 2006, four GIs and one recently discharged GI were charged with raping and murdering a fifteen-year-old Iraqi girl and killing three members of her family in a village near Baghdad. As military criminal-justice teams investigated these alleged incidents, and subsequent cover-ups, memories of the Vietnam era massacre at My Lai stirred uneasily.

Central to America's relationships with the Muslim world was U.S. support for Israel and for a "two state" solution recognizing Palestinian interests. On this front, prospects seemed bleak. When Palestinian leader Yasir Arafat rejected the Camp David peace plan and a second Palestinian Intifada began in 2000 (see Chapter 31), violence in the region escalated. Ariel Sharon of the hard-line Likud Party, elected Israel's prime minister in February 2001, demanded an end to violence before talks could resume. In response, Arafat insisted that protests would continue so long as Israel fostered Jewish settlements in Palestinian territory. In June 2002, Israel began building a security barrier, partially extending into the West Bank, to control access and prevent suicide attacks.

A U.S.-sponsored "road map to peace," proposed in 2003, called on the Palestinians to renounce violence and on Israel to withdraw from the West Bank and support a Palestinian state. Peace prospects briefly brightened in November 2004 when Arafat died and Mahmoud Abbas, a moderate, replaced him. In August 2005 Israel withdrew all Jewish settlements from Gaza.

But in this conflict, one step forward always seems to be followed by two steps back. In January 2006, Palestinian elections gave victory to the radical Hamas organization, which had perpetrated many attacks on Israeli civilians and even denied Israel's right to exist. The United States, the European Union, Russia, and the UN, collectively called the Quartet, called on Hamas to renounce violence and recognize Israel. When Hamas refused, the Quartet halted its regular grants to the Palestinian Authority.

After Sharon suffered a stroke in January 2006, his deputy Ehud Olmert succeeded him. While pursuing plans to withdraw from parts of the West Bank, Olmert announced that three large Jewish settlements would remain. He also asserted Israel's unilateral right to set its borders with the West Bank; extend the intrusive security barrier; and determine the future of Jerusalem, a highly sensitive issue. All Palestinian groups rejected any settlement that left West Bank territory under Israeli control; denied full sovereignty to a Palestinian state; and left Jerusalem's future status up to Israel.

Violence exploded in June 2006 as Palestinian militants in Gaza killed two Israeli soldiers on the border and kidnapped a third. Israel retaliated with heavy bombing in Gaza. Tensions escalated as Hezbollah, a militant organization supported by Iran and Syria and based in southern Lebanon, killed three Israeli soldiers, kidnapped two more, and lobbed scores of rockets into northern Israel, including the major city of Haifa. Denouncing this "act of war," Israel bombed not only Hezbollah bases but also the Beirut airport and bridges and highways throughout Lebanon, resulting in heavy property damage and loss of life. As in Iraq, America's influence in mediating this deepening conflict seemed steadily to diminish.

Nuclear Proliferation Threats

Although the end of the Cold War had reduced fears of the ultimate nightmare, global thermonuclear war, nuclear-related issues remained. President Reagan's antimissile "Star Wars" initiative (see Chapter 30), downgraded by President Clinton, was revived by George W. Bush. A modest, ground-based missile-defense system was technically feasible, supporters argued, and could protect America against a missile attack from North Korea or other "rogue states." Bush's proposed system violated the 1972 Anti-Ballistic Missile (ABM) Treaty between the United States and Russia. But Russian president Vladimir Putin, eager for U.S. investment and NATO membership, agreed to abandon the ABM Treaty if both sides further reduced their nuclear arsenals. The Bush administration agreed, and in 2002 the ABM Treaty officially lapsed. Soon after, Bush and Putin signed a treaty pledging to reduce their nuclear weapons by two-thirds within ten years, and NATO granted Russia a consultative relationship, though not full membership. In 2002 work began at Fort Greely, Alaska, on a ground-based missile-defense system. Despite test failures, eight interceptor missiles were in place by 2006.

Meanwhile, the administration joined with other nations to address the specter of nuclear proliferation, especially in North Korea and Iran. Isolated and impoverished North Korea, ruled by an eccentric dictator, Kim Jong Il, displayed an almost paranoid suspicion of outsiders. (The presence of more than 30,000 U.S. troops in South Korea, combined with President Bush's inclusion of North Korea in the "axis of evil" in his 2002 State of the Union address, doubtless contributed to North Korea's edginess.)

Claiming to fear a U.S. attack, North Korea boasted of its nuclear-weapons program (see Chapter 31), and in 2003 withdrew from the Nuclear Non-Proliferation Treaty. Six-nation negotiations led by China got nowhere, as North Korea demanded economic aid, one-on-one talks with the United States, a U.S. pledge not to attack, and assistance with its nuclear-power program. A North Korean long-range missile test in July 2006, although unsuccessful, deepened tensions. North Korea appeared to be using nuclear bluster to achieve other goals, but the proliferation risk could not be ignored.

Dissidents in Iran, meanwhile, revealed in 2002 the existence of uranium-enrichment laboratories needed for nuclear-power development, but also essential for building nuclear weapons. Many suspected that Iran had secured vital information from Abdul Khan, a Pakistani nuclear scientist who had confessed to passing nuclear know-how to other nations. Iran suspended its nuclear program in 2004 but resumed it early in 2006 after Mahmoud Ahmadinejad's election as president. A fiery nationalist, and Islamic fundamentalist, Ahmadinejad taunted America, called the Holocaust a myth, and said Israel "should be wiped off the map." He denied that Iran sought nuclear weapons, but insisted on its sovereign right to develop nuclear power.

In February 2006, the International Atomic Energy Agency (IAEA), backed by the United States, the European Union, and Russia, reported Iran to the UN Security Council for violating IAEA inspection guidelines. Amid talk of possible U.S. military action, Secretary of State Rice pursued the diplomatic path, working with European allies to offer Iran incentives to comply with UN guidelines.

On another front, in March 2006 President Bush agreed to sell India fuel and parts for its nuclear-power reactors even though India had secretly developed nuclear weapons and refused to sign the 1970 Nuclear Non-Proliferation Treaty. Bush said the agreement would help a democratic ally meet its energy needs and reduce fossil-fuel emissions. Critics said the agreement weakened the nonproliferation cause and undermined efforts to prevent North Korea and Iran from going nuclear.

A Widening Trade Gap and China's Growing Power   As the pace of globalization increased (see "Beyond America— Global Interactions: The Challenge of Globalization," Chapter 31), the most immediate impact for the United States was a surging trade deficit, which hit a record $726 billion in 2005. This massive imbalance mainly reflected rising prices on imported oil; surging foreign car sales, particularly from Japan (see below); and a yawning trade gap with China. With China's admission to the **World Trade Organization** in 2001, its exports boomed. Low-paid Chinese workers now produced many of the export goods formerly made in South Korea, Taiwan, and other Asian nations. In 2005, as American consumers snapped up Chinese-made clothing, sneakers, housewares, toys, electronics, and appliances, the U.S. trade deficit with China neared $202 billion. In 2006, even the U.S. State Department purchased 15,000 computers from a Chinese-owned company.

As imports grew, so did protectionist pressures. In 2002, Bush slapped tariffs on steel imports from China, the EU, and other nations, even though this violated WTO rules. He lifted the tariffs in 2003 as the EU threatened to retaliate against Florida citrus and other U.S. exports.

U.S. manufacturers complained that China artificially manipulated its currency, the yuan, to make Chinese exports cheaper. In 2005, as Congress threatened tariffs on Chinese imports, China partially eased controls on the yuan and promised eventually to let market forces determine its value. This would raise the price of Chinese imports, benefiting U.S. manufacturers.

The situation was complex, however. Cheap Chinese imports helped U.S. retailers keep their prices low. When U.S. textile manufacturers pressured Bush to impose quotas on clothing imported from China, Wal-Mart and other discount chains fought the effort. Also, many Chinese imports were produced for U.S. companies that reaped the profits when these goods were sold. As one economist noted: "While China gets the wage benefits of globalization, it does not get . . . the profits of globalization." Finally, many products labeled "Made in China" were manufactured elsewhere, with only the final assembly in China.

With a GDP approaching $2 trillion in 2004, China was the world's fourth-largest economy, behind the United States, Japan, and Germany. Some economists predicted it would be first in twenty years. On a 2005 visit to Beijing, President Bush acknowledged China's centrality in the global marketplace and in the U.S. economy while criticizing the regime's repressiveness and its restraints on religious freedom. Others attacked China's poor environmental record, including massive greenhouse-gas emissions. A U.S. visit by Chinese leader Hu Jintao in 2006 revealed a similar combination of wariness and recognition of the two nations' interdependence. With 40 percent of its 1.3 billion people living at the subsistence level, China urgently needs continued economic development, and for this, the U.S. market is crucial. As a Chinese diplomat wrote in *Foreign Affairs* in 2005: "[China] must maintain a close relationship with the United States if its modernization efforts are to succeed. . . . [A] cooperative partnership with Washington is of primary importance to Beijing."

Environmental
Hazards Become
a Global Concern

Three Mile Island, Love Canal, and the *Exxon Valdez* disaster (see Chapters 30 and 31) all underscored modern technology's environmental risks. A 1986 nuclear-power plant explosion at Chernobyl in the Ukraine and a 1984 disaster in Bhopal, India, in which deadly gases from a U.S.-owned chemical plant killed seventeen hundred people, highlighted the global scope of these risks. Environmental issues remained central in the early twenty-first century.

With the Cold War over, the United States helped Russia, Ukraine, and Kazakhstan dispose of their nuclear-weapons materials (see Chapter 31). America also faced the task of disposing of its own radioactive waste from nuclear-weapons facilities, uranium and plutonium from dismantled nuclear weapons, and spent fuel rods from aging nuclear-power plants. Since these materials will remain deadly for thousands of years, the issue proved highly contentious. In 2002, over protests by local politicians, President Bush designated Yucca Mountain in the Nevada desert as the nation's nuclear-waste disposal site. Scientists warned of seismic activity and corrosive water seepage in the area, but planning proceeded, with the facility scheduled to open by 2010.

Other environmental hazards threatened as well. Acid rain carrying sulfur dioxide and other pollutants from U.S. factories and vehicle exhaust damaged Appalachian forests and Canadian lakes. As fluorocarbons from aerosol cans, refrigeration equipment, and other sources depleted the atmosphere's ozone layer, more solar radiation reached the earth's surface, increasing skin-cancer risks. Air and water pollution posed global health hazards, from respiratory ailments to deadly intestinal diseases. Above all, **global warming** posed a long-range hazard. (See Technology and Culture: Developing New Tools for Measuring Global Warming).

The United States, with other industrialized and developing nations, was deeply implicated in these global environmental trends. With under 5 percent of the world's population, America accounts for 25 percent of global energy consumption. And this energy comes heavily from the fossil fuels that figure prominently in global-warming discussions. To be sure, environmental laws had some effect. With stricter emission standards, U.S. vehicles and factories produced one-third less carbon monoxide from 1970 to 2003. Air quality in some cities, notably Los Angeles, improved. But other key indicators of environmental pollution worsened. A 2005 EPA study found that U.S. motor vehicles were, on average, significantly less fuel efficient than they had been in the late 1980s.

The Bush administration's environmental record was mixed at best. On taking office, Bush halted the EPA's implementation of measures to reduce carbon dioxide emissions from power plants. Government scientists who questioned administration policies were marginalized. In 2002, when the EPA cited scientific data confirming global warming, Bush dismissed it as "a report put out by the bureaucracy." The administration's energy program (see above) downplayed the environmental impact of fossil-fuel consumption. Conservation might be a "sign of personal virtue," said Vice President Cheney, but had no place in energy-policy discussions. Rejecting calls for stricter emission laws and fuel-efficiency standards, the administration instead touted distant and uncertain alternative energy sources, such as hydrogen-powered fuel cells.

A UN-sponsored conference on global warming, held in Kyoto, Japan, in 1997, drafted a protocol setting strict emission targets for industrialized nations. President Clinton had signed it but did not submit it for Senate ratification, fearing defeat. President Bush repudiated the protocol entirely, charging that it would jeopardize

America's standard of living. He criticized the document for exempting developing nations such as China and India, which are, indeed, major polluters.

At a follow-up conference in Bonn, Germany, in 2001, delegates from 178 nations crafted a new plan for cutting fossil-fuel emissions designed to meet U.S. objections. Again, the administration rejected it. The Bonn treaty was "not in [America's] interests," declared National Security Adviser Condoleezza Rice. The revised **Kyoto Accords** went into effect in 2005, with only the United States, Australia, India, and China refusing to cooperate. Reviewing this record, the head of the EPA under President Richard Nixon commented: "[T]his administration is not a conservative administration. . . . [I]t's a radical administration. It represents a radical rollback of environmental policy going back . . . many, many years."

SOCIAL AND CULTURAL TRENDS IN CONTEMPORARY AMERICA

In the late twentieth and early twenty-first centuries the long-term migration from the Northeast, Midwest, and Plains states to the South and West continued, as did the flow of immigrants from Asia and Latin America. Fundamental economic changes affected millions of Americans, benefiting some but creating difficulties for others, including displaced industrial workers and inner-city residents.

An Increasingly Diverse People

The rapid growth, geographic mobility, and ethnic diversity long characteristic of U.S. society continued in these years, as did the historic shift to the South and West, reflecting both internal migration and immigration patterns. The West added 10.4 million residents in the 1990s, with California alone increasing by more than 4 million. Maricopa County, Arizona (which includes Phoenix), grew by nearly 1 million. The South expanded by nearly 15 million in the decade.

Household arrangements continue to evolve. The proportion of "traditional" families headed by a married heterosexual couple fell from 74 percent in 1960 to 50 percent in 2004. People living alone made up 26 percent of households in 2004, while 4.2 percent of households were maintained by unmarried partners. Commenting on these statistics, the *New York Times* observed, "[T]he nuclear family is not the only kind of family or even the only healthy kind of family. In modern America no type of family can really be recognized to the exclusion of all others."

The graying of the baby-boom generation (those born between 1946 and 1964) pushed the median age from around 33 in 1990 to 36 in 2004, the highest in American history. On the public-health front, average life expectancy at birth rose from seventy-four to seventy-seven between 1980 and 2002. (Life expectancy differs by gender, race, and other variables, however.) The decline in cigarette smoking by Americans continues, falling to under 25 percent of the population in 2004. Ominously, however, nearly 40 percent of 18- to 25-year-olds are smokers.

America is becoming increasingly diverse and multicultural. Growing immigration from Asia and Latin America in recent decades reversed a long decline in the proportion of foreign-born persons in the population. From a low of about 5 percent in 1970, this figure reached nearly 12 percent in 2004.

The population of 299 million (as of mid-2006) is about 13 percent Hispanic, 12 percent black, 4 percent Asian, and 1 percent American Indian. The Asian category includes persons who trace their ancestry to India, China, the Philippines, Vietnam, Laos, India, Korea, and elsewhere. The number of persons with ancestral roots in Haiti (where the languages are Creole and French) reached 385,000 by 2000. Some 6 million Muslims, mainly from the Middle East and North Africa, add to the ethno-religious mix.

The nation's Hispanics (who may be of any race but share a common language, Spanish) are nearly 60 percent of Mexican origin, with Puerto Ricans, Cubans, and Salvadorans comprising most of the balance. With their high birthrate, Hispanics are predicted to comprise 25 percent of the population by 2050. (The name most frequently given male babies in California and Texas in 1999 was José.) Many Mexicans working in the United States bypassed immigration checkpoints, making dangerous treks across the desert led by guides called "coyotes." As border controls tightened, they took more perilous routes, and in 2003–2005 over 800 died making the attempt. (See "Debating Immigration" below.)

Upward Mobility and Social Problems in a Multiethnic Society
While these groups faced problems, opportunity beckoned. For African-Americans, median family income in 2003 approached $30,000. While well below the median for non-Hispanic white families ($47,777), this was 14 percent higher, in constant dollars, than the 1990 figure. College-educated blacks enjoyed significantly higher earnings, while the number of black-owned businesses reached 1.2 million in 2002. Of black high-school graduates in 2005, 57 percent went on to college. Reversing a long trend, many blacks moved from the North to the South after 1990, strengthening the thriving black middle-class and professional communities in Atlanta and other cities. The substantial black middle and professional classes, in short, are growing and thriving.

But blacks in the inner cities, where the unskilled have few job prospects, school dropout rates soar, and drug trafficking is pervasive, face a different reality. The black unemployment rate of 11 percent in 2005 (already twice the national rate) zoomed to 50 percent among men aged 22–30 lacking a college education, and 72 percent among high-school dropouts. By age thirty-five, nearly a third of black males lacking a college education have served prison time.

Inner-city black women face risks as well, particularly drug use, HIV/AIDS infection, and out-of-wedlock pregnancy. In 1970, unmarried women accounted for 37 percent of black births; in 2002, the figure stood at 68 percent. Many of these births were to teenage girls, reducing their prospects for education and employment. (Out-of-wedlock births to white women rose as well, but at a far lower rate.)

But the inner cities present hopeful trends as well, as church leaders, dedicated community activists, and private agencies such as Baltimore's Center for Fathers, Families, and Workforce Development work to provide opportunities and break the cycle of self-destructive behavior. Battling urban violence, several cities sued gun manufacturers for injuries or deaths caused by unregistered firearms. The manufacturers deliberately overproduced guns, the suits alleged, knowing that many would be sold illegally. In April 2006 the mayors of New York, Boston, Milwaukee, and other cities held a summit conference to address the plague of illegal guns.

Developing New Tools for Measuring Global Warming

Since the time of the Industrial Revolution, technology has brought great benefits to humanity, but at a cost. The technologies we rely on for light, heat, transportation, and countless other benefits consume enormous amounts of energy. The resulting emissions are having major environmental effects, including, most scientists argue, an impact on global warming, with profound future implications.

The fact of global warming is beyond dispute. The Earth's average temperature rose by one degree Fahrenheit in the twentieth century, and the rate of increase shot up after 1970. The century's ten hottest years came after 1985, and 2005 was the hottest year ever recorded. Global warming is real, reported the National Science Foundation in 2001, and likely to intensify.

Nearly all scientists also agree that carbon dioxide, methane, and other gases from fossil-fuel combustion in factories, homes, and motor vehicles contribute significantly to global warming. Just as the glass of a greenhouse traps the sun's heat, so the carbon dioxide, methane, and other "greenhouse gases" blanketing the Earth prevent solar heat from escaping. In 2005, a report issued by the leading scientific bodies of the United States, Canada, France, Italy, Germany, Great Britain, Japan, China, India, Russia, and Brazil concluded that "most of the warming in recent decades can be attributed to human activities."

From 1980 to 2003, U.S. carbon dioxide emissions from fossil fuels grew from 4.7 to 5.8 million metric tons. The output from India and China increased enormously in these same years.

Naturally occurring greenhouse gases are essential. Without their warming effect, the Earth would be a frozen waste. But in recent decades, these gases have increased to dangerous levels. Throughout Earth's known history, carbon dioxide levels remained within a range of 180 to 300 parts per million. However, beginning around 1950 the level crept up. In 2005 it reached 380 parts per million, trapping more solar heat and driving up temperatures. As polar ice melted, sea levels rose 6 to 8 inches.

Projecting current trends, scientists predict a 40 percent increase in carbon dioxide emissions by 2020, with a corresponding surge in global warming. If this happens, scientists foresee not only hotter temperatures, but also still higher sea levels from melting polar ice, disrupted climatic conditions affecting crops and plant and animal habitats, and ferocious tropical storms caused by the rise in ocean temperatures.

The impact of global warming can already be seen. Storm surges are destroying homes in Shishmaref, an Inupiat village on an island in northwestern Alaska, as a protective ice barrier melts. In 2002, the residents voted to move farther inland to preserve their community. As one said: "[P]eople here in Alaska are like everyone else. We want to keep our culture alive."

The mountain pine beetle, a pest that arrived with rising temperatures, has devastated millions of acres of spruce forest in Alaska and western Canada. As the permafrost melts, Alaskan highways are buckling, houses in Fairbanks are developing cracks, and the stability of Alaska's oil pipeline from Prudhoe Bay to Valdez is threatened.

Technology not only contributes to global warming, but also enables scientists to document the phenomenon. Hundreds of weather stations track temperature changes worldwide. Botanists and entomologists record shifts in plant and insect distribution as temperatures rise. In 2005, amphibian-disease experts reported a massive decline in rare Latin American frog species because of a spreading fungus they attributed to global warming. Australian researchers report dying coral reefs as ocean temperatures rise.

Two satellites, nicknamed Tom and Jerry, launched from a former Russian ICBM site in 2002, are measuring the polar icecaps. Using these data, scientists reported in 2006 that Antarctica's icecap is melting at a rate of thirty-six cubic miles per year—180 times the annual water consumption of Los Angeles. Satellite data show a similar melt-off in the Greenland and Arctic Ocean icecaps.

Using ice-core sampling, scientists are tracing carbon dioxide levels over vast periods of time. In the 1990s, a team of U.S., Russian, and French scientists extracted a two-mile-long ice core in Antarctica and examined trapped air bubbles to measure carbon dioxide levels over a 440,000-year span. In 2005, European researchers reported on ice cores extending back 650,000 years. Both teams concluded that current carbon dioxide levels far exceed any levels found in that incredibly long time span. As one scientist observed: "There's no natural condition that we know about in a really long time where the greenhouse

gas levels were anywhere near what they are now."

Using computer simulations, climatologists predict greater temperature increases by 2100. The resulting polar melting could increase sea levels up to five feet, endangering coastal cities from Boston to San Francisco. In low-lying Bangladesh, flooding could displace 6 million people.

Mass-culture technologies heighten public awareness. Hundreds of Internet websites discuss global warming. In 2006 alone, the PBS science program *Nova* aired a global-warming episode; Al Gore's film *An Inconvenient Truth* documented the dangers; and an HBO special, *Too Hot Not to Handle,* urged grass-roots action to reduce greenhouse gases.

Hollywood has used lurid plots and awesome special effects to dramatize global warming. In *Waterworld* (1995), melting polar ice inundates the whole world. Isolated floating communities shelter the only survivors except for Kevin Costner, a mutant who has developed gills. In *Day After Tomorrow* (2004), freaky weather triggered by global warming floods Manhattan, pounds Tokyo with giant hailstones, and finishes off Los Angeles with killer tornadoes. In the 2006 animated film *Ice Age: The Meltdown,* lovable creatures including Manny the Mammoth and Syd the Sloth flee to safety as melting ice threatens their habitat.

Fanciful as they are, such mass-culture productions translate sober scientific warnings into mass-culture fare. As a reviewer of *Day After Tomorrow* noted: "It's . . . a depressing comment on our crippled political culture . . . that it takes [a movie] to do what environmental groups have been trying to do for decades: get the message out about global warming."

The technologies underlying our fossil-fuel-based economy now threaten human well-being. But other technologies enable us to document the danger; alert the public; and research solar, wind, thermal, and other power alternatives. The Kyoto Accords represent a major multinational commitment to reducing greenhouse gases. The U.S. government has set emissions standards for factories and some vehicles, but California and other states have enacted even stricter standards. Research on hybrid vehicles that are far more fuel efficient is going forward.

How each society responds to the crisis is a matter not only of science or technology, but of political will. Whether that response will match the magnitude of the challenge remains an urgent question as the global community, including the United States, confronts its future.

Questions for Analysis

- What technologies help scientists document global warming?

- What strategies are being used to reduce greenhouse gases?

Among Native Americans, renewed tribal pride and activism continued. Citing Article VI of the Constitution, which describes all U.S. treaties as "the supreme law of the land," tribes sued to enforce the 331 Indian treaties ratified between 1778 and 1871. Indian gambling casinos, approved by Congress in 1988, proliferated. Connecticut's giant Foxwoods Casino, run by the Mashantucket Pequots, earned $6 billion annually. As they competed for casino licenses, Indian tribes became major political contributors (see below). Many citizens deplored the spread of gambling, and some Indians lamented the tribal conflicts and social disruption the casinos brought in their wake. But casino income did enable tribes to support schools, museums, community centers, job training, and substance-abuse programs.

The Hispanic population, too, resisted sweeping generalizations. While Mexican-Americans concentrated in the Southwest and West Coast, many lived in other regions as well. Cubans, Puerto Ricans, and other Hispanic groups, as well as Haitians, resided mainly in Florida, New York, New Jersey, and Illinois. Many Hispanics were well educated, prosperous, and upwardly mobile. Hispanic households' median income rose to $33,000 by 2003, and unemployment among Hispanics dropped from 9 percent in 1995 to 5.5 percent in early 2006. The 1.6 million Hispanic-owned businesses in 2002 represented a 31 percent increase in five years.

In 2004, 22 percent of Hispanics were living in poverty, many in inner-city neighborhoods plagued by gangs, alcohol and drug addiction, teen pregnancy, and erratic school attendance. Religion and family loom large in Hispanic culture, but stressful social conditions took their toll. Many unskilled Hispanic newcomers took poorly paid jobs as gardeners, maids, day laborers, and migrant farm workers. As the British journal *The Economist* wrote in 1998, "Wherever the booming [U.S.] economy cries out for workers . . . the ever-arriving and ever-progressing Latinos will move in. Nothing daunts them."

Americanization, Twenty-first-Century Style *Recent immigrants from Afghanistan join a fitness class in Fremont, California, in 2001.*

Hispanics, like other immigrant groups, mobilized to promote their interests. In 2005, more than five thousand Hispanics held elective public office, including Los Angeles mayor Antonio Villaraigosa, the city's first Hispanic mayor since 1872. Though Hispanics have tended to vote at lower rates than non-Hispanic whites, 7.6 million cast ballots in 2004, making them an increasingly important constituency.

Of the nation's 13 million Asian-Americans in 2004, 75 percent had arrived since 1980. This group, too, presents a variegated picture, though with certain commonalities. Prizing education and supported by family networks, many followed a trajectory of academic achievement and upward mobility. In 2004 nearly 50 percent of adult Asian-Americans held college degrees. Among Asian-American high-school graduates in 2005, the college-enrollment rate neared 90 percent.

After passage of the Immigration Reform Act of 1965, many Indian doctors, engineers, and academics emigrated to America, often joined later by parents and other family members. In Fremont, California, the Asian population grew from 19 percent in 1990 to 40 percent in 2000, with many of the newcomers working in nearby Silicon Valley. The Hmong comprise was yet another distinct Asian immigrant group contributing a new strand to American life.

By 2050, demographers calculate, no single ethno-racial group will be a majority in America. Non-Hispanic whites, in other words, while still a plurality, will simply be another minority. Many Americans of mixed origins, like the golfer Tiger Woods, of Thai, Chinese, African-American, and American Indian ancestry, resist being pigeonholed. From 1960 to 2000, the number of interracial married couples in the United States rose

FIGURE 32.1 U.S. Population by Race and Hispanic Origin, 2000 and 2050 (Projected)

By 2050, the Census Bureau projects, with some 40 million Asian-Americans, 90 million Hispanics, and 60 million African-Americans, non-Hispanic whites will constitute less than half the total U.S. population. *Source:* U.S. Census Bureau, 2000.

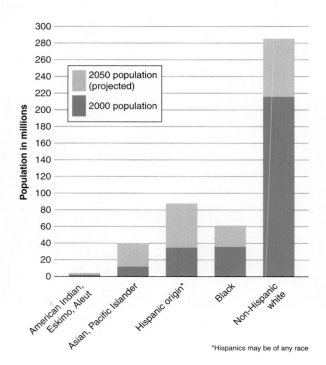

*Hispanics may be of any race

from 149,000 to 1.5 million. Recognizing these realities, in 2000 the Census Bureau permitted citizens to check more than one racial category, or none at all.

Not everyone welcomed the new diversity, and the phenomenon of "white flight" continued. Between 1990 and 1995 both Los Angeles and New York lost more than 1 million native-born inhabitants, approximately equal to the new arrivals from Asia and Latin America. Language became a major battleground. While some campaigned to make English America's "official language," others called for school instruction in children's native tongue, or at least bilingual classes. Interestingly, a 1998 study found that immigrant children themselves overwhelmingly wished to learn and speak English in school.

In an increasingly diverse nation, some observers foresaw a society divided psychologically if not physically along lines of race, ethnicity, religion, or national origin. In a 2005 Los Angeles poll, 70 percent of blacks and 64 percent of Hispanics rated race relations as "poor" or "not so good." The 2005 movie *Crash*, winner of the Academy Award for best picture, portrayed a society seething with racial and ethnic hostility. Whether through a shared awareness of prejudice or economic inequity, or in reaction to the anonymity of mass society, many people clearly seek the reassurance of a clear-cut group identity. Others retreat into enclaves defined by wealth, profession, or social status. The persistence of the culture wars and abusive political rhetoric (see Chapter 31) deepens the divisions.

In such a situation, what does it mean to be "American"? In his 1908 play *The Melting Pot*, Israel Zangwill, a Jewish immigrant from England, foresaw the blending of immigrants into a common national identity. A century later, Zangwill's metaphor has faded, in part because its advocates usually assumed that entering the "melting pot" meant abandoning one's ethnic roots and cultural traditions and conforming to an Anglo or northwestern European model. If the "melting pot" model doesn't work, what will unite this diverse society? Americans share a common identity as consumers of goods and mass-culture entertainment. Is this enough? Can the nation's civic culture match its commercial and leisure culture? The answer remains unclear.

The "New Economy" and the Old Economy   In *The Coming of Post-Industrial Society: A Venture in Social Forecasting* (1973), sociologist Daniel Bell offered a remarkably accurate prediction of changes in the U.S. economy. In the late nineteenth and early twentieth centuries, America's mainly farm economy gave way to one driven by industrial production. As the twentieth century ended, an equally profound transformation occurred: the decline of industry and the rise of a professional and service-based economy. Farming and manufacturing continued, of course, but not as major sources of employment.

A snapshot of the U.S. labor force in 2004 tells the story. In a work force of 140 million, 62 percent held white-collar jobs, ranging from business and financial management and professions such as medicine, the law, teaching, engineering, telecommunications, and computer programming to sales, office work, and careers in the entertainment and leisure fields. Lower-paid service-sector workers in health care, personal services, custodial work, and food-related occupations comprised another 16 percent. A mere 23 percent worked in fields that as recently as 1960 had dominated the labor market: manufacturing, farming, construction, and transportation. Daniel Bell's "post-industrial society" has become a reality.

The rewards of the new economy were unevenly distributed. Some young people with the necessary education, skills, and contacts found exciting challenges and good salaries in the new electronics, programming, and telecommunications fields. For less-privileged youths, supermarkets, car washes, fast-food outlets, and discount superstores provided entry-level jobs, but few long-term career prospects. For displaced industrial workers, the impact could be devastating.

Globalization contributed to the transformation of the U.S. economy. The availability of cheap imported products hastened the decline of U.S. manufacturing, from toys and textiles to steel and automobiles. As VW, Toyota, Honda, Subaru, and other foreign automakers grabbed more U.S. sales, America's automakers, in trouble since the 1970s (see Chapter 30), faced a crisis. Ford's market share fell from 25 percent in 2000 to 17 percent in 2005. Early in 2006, Ford announced plans to eliminate up to 30,000 jobs and close 14 factories. Chrysler (now Daimler-Chrysler through merger with a German firm) faced problems as well. As gas prices hit $3 a gallon in 2006, sales of SUVs and light trucks, moneymakers for U.S. automakers in the 1990s, plummeted, worsening the crisis.

General Motors, another icon of America's industrial might, having lost $10.6 billion in 2005 and watched its stock price tumble by 50 percent, announced plans to lay off 30,000 of its 113,000 factory workers and thousands of white-collar employees, and close or scale back a dozen plants. Workers willing to quit were offered buyouts of up to $140,000. Said one GM engineer: "This once was the premier company . . . to work for. You were at the top of the heap, the major leagues. . . . Today, you know this company is crumbling around you." Delphi, GM's parts supplier, went bankrupt in 2006 and prepared to close most of its twenty-nine U.S. plants. GM's pension and medical costs for 1.1 million retirees and their families, written into union contracts in better times, added to the crushing burden. One wit described GM as a health-care company that also makes cars. In other countries with national health-insurance plans paid for by taxes, governments rather than individual companies cover these costs.

Altogether, in 2000–2006 the big three automakers announced plans to cut some 140,000 jobs. In these circumstances, the long decline in union membership continued, sinking to only 12 percent of the work force in 2004. As unions grew weaker, workers had less bargaining power to resist wage cuts and other concessions demanded by management. As if to rub salt in the wound, Toyota, poised to overtake GM as the world's largest carmaker, set an all-time monthly U.S. sales record of 220,000 vehicles in March 2006. The big foreign automakers took pains to emphasize that they are also major U.S. employers. Toyota boasts of supporting 386,000 U.S. jobs through its nine manufacturing plants in seven states plus its dealerships, parts suppliers, R&D centers, and advertising agencies. Toyota's Camry plant in Georgetown, Kentucky, alone employs 7,000 workers. In auto making, as throughout the U.S. economy, globalization's effects are complicated. One thing is clear, however: the economic order familiar to the parents and grandparents of today's youth is gone forever.

DOMESTIC POLICY SINCE 2004

President Bush called for social-security reform and expanded prescription-drug benefits for seniors, but his domestic policies did little to lift his approval ratings. The administration's slow response to the devastation of Hurricane Katrina in 2005 brought new charges of incompetence. Bush sought to preserve his conservative legacy through two Supreme Court appointments, but a mushrooming federal deficit, lobbying scandals, blatant congressional spending on pet projects, and soaring gasoline prices as oil companies reported record profits further soured the public mood as the 2006 midterm elections approached.

Funding Social Security and Health Care as the Federal Deficit Soars Since social-security was introduced in 1935, conservative Republicans have argued for its abolition or privatization. Launching his second term, Bush called for a partial privatization of social-security, enabling workers to shift some of their social-security funds to private investment accounts. Bush pushed this proposal heavily, but the public remained cool. Most citizens preferred a government-run program to the uncertainties of the market. Democrats dismissed the idea as simply another expression of the administration's ideological commitment to privatization and to reducing the government's role in the economy.

In 2003, the Republican Congress expanded the 1965 Medicare program (see Chapter 28) to cover part of seniors' prescription-drug expenses beginning in 2006. Drug costs worried older Americans, but the plan proved extremely complicated, and many seniors felt more aggravation than gratitude as they battled the red tape. "I have a Ph.D., and it's too complicated to suit me," said one. Democrats criticized the plan as designed to benefit drug firms and insurance companies more than retirees. Since retirees vote in large numbers, their frustration worried GOP strategists.

The prescription-drug benefit further burdened an already costly program. In 2004, Medicare and Medicaid, the government's health-insurance systems for the elderly and the poor, cost $600 billion, more than double the 1990 figure. These costs, along with social-security benefits, will soar even higher as baby boomers retire. These entitlement programs, plus Iraq War costs and interest payments on the $9 trillion national debt, produced explosive federal deficits. The deficit, $319 billion in 2005 was projected to surpass $420 billion in 2006.

Despite such numbers, Bush insisted that his tax cuts be made permanent. This action, budget experts predicted, would drive the deficit over $500 billion by 2015. As Washington issued bonds to cover the growing debt, China and other foreign governments awash in dollars because of the U.S. trade deficit snapped them up. But economists warned that this method of funding the debt would eventually dry up, leaving future generations of Americans to pay off the massive debt racked up during the Bush years.

Worsening the deficit crisis, Congress members continued the long-standing practice of quietly inserting into spending bills special provisions known as "earmarks" that benefited their districts. A 2005 highway bill included 6,000 earmarks promoting pet projects, including two "bridges to nowhere" proposed by Alaska senator Ted Stevens. In a 2006 spending bill covering Iraq War and Hurricane Katrina costs, legislators added $14 billion for unrelated pet projects.

Hurricane Katrina Tests the Bush Administration   In August 2005, **Hurricane Katrina** struck the Gulf Coast, taking as many as 1,400 lives. Coastal areas of Alabama, Mississippi, and Louisiana suffered massive damage. Disrupted shipping on the Mississippi River hurt corn and soybean growers far to the north. Katrina and a subsequent hurricane smashed oil refineries and offshore oil rigs.

The most catastrophic damage hit New Orleans, the legendary "Big Easy" at the mouth of the Mississippi. Much of the city lies below sea level, protected by levees from the Gulf of Mexico and Lake Pontchartrain. Over the years, developers had drained thousands of acres around New Orleans. This had not only done severe ecological damage but also increased the flood hazard by eliminating the sponge-like marshlands that could absorb the water when Lake Pontchartrain overflowed. Inadequate levees and poor levee maintenance, revealed in post-storm investigations, had heightened the danger.

As levees burst under Katrina's storm surge, rampaging water flooded New Orleans's lower sections, populated mainly by poor blacks. Many residents drowned or died awaiting rescue. Others escaped with their lives as houses and possessions disappeared. Thousands poured into New Orleans's Superdome, which soon became a squalid disaster zone. Buses transported others to cities as far away as Houston. Some died of heat prostration as they waited along highways for rescue. The toll among the elderly and residents of nursing homes and hospitals was especially high. The longer-term impact was equally devastating, as public schools, churches, and hospitals closed their doors. Tulane University and the city's other institutions of higher education experienced major disruptions. In May 2006, New Orleans's population was only about 40 percent of its pre-storm level.

As New Orleans endured the worst natural disaster in recent U.S. history, the government response at all levels was appallingly inadequate. While many New Orleans police officers performed well, others disappeared, either caring for their own families or overwhelmed by the crisis. State and federal officials did little better. FEMA head Michael Brown, a political appointee with no disaster experience, proved hopelessly ineffectual. Though initially praised by Bush ("Heck of a job, Brownie"), he soon resigned. President Bush made token visits and delivered a TV speech in the city's historic district, but the administration's performance did not match the president's rhetoric.

A 2006 congressional report documented the scope of the failure. A FEMA official who observed a major levee break on Monday, August 29, had urgently notified Michael Brown, who immediately alerted the Department of Homeland Security and the White House. Yet the next day Homeland Security director Michael Chertoff flew to a meeting in Atlanta unrelated to Katrina, and President Bush, vacationing in Texas, expressed pleasure that New Orleans had "dodged the bullet." The distribution of emergency relief funds involved massive fraud. FEMA spent $900 million on 26,000 mobile homes, many of which sat empty and unused. Despite the post-9/11 reorganization of the security bureaucracy, Hurricane Katrina revealed the same pattern of slow response and failed communication among responsible officials.

By summer 2006 no coherent plan had emerged for reconstructing New Orleans's destroyed districts or bringing back the city's scattered residents. The levees were hastily repaired, yet no one knew how they would withstand future hurricanes. Recovery in the hardest-hit parts of the city remained stalled. As streets stood silent and empty, with no electricity and rows of shattered and abandoned houses, sections of New Orleans resembled a ghost town.

Extending Republican Influence: From the Supreme Court to K Street

When Supreme Court justice Sandra Day O'Connor, a Reagan appointee who had emerged as a key swing vote in many 5–4 decisions, announced her retirement in July 2005, Bush nominated as her replacement federal appeals-court judge John G. Roberts, Jr., who had held posts in the Reagan Justice Department and White House. When Chief Justice William Rehnquist died in September, Bush nominated Roberts as chief justice. He won easy Senate confirmation while revealing little about his judicial philosophy.

To fill the second vacancy, Bush chose White House counsel Harriet Miers, a longtime Texas friend and adviser. While conservatives criticized Miers on ideological grounds, others questioned her qualifications. When Miers withdrew, Bush nominated Samuel Alito, Jr., a federal appeals-court judge enthusiastically supported by conservatives. As a Justice Department lawyer in the Reagan administration, and later as a judge, Alito had espoused a very broad view of the powers of the executive branch—a view embraced by the Bush administration to justify its actions at home and abroad after 9/11.

At his confirmation hearings Alito recalled his humble Italian-American origins, but proved equally unwilling to discuss his judicial philosophy. This frustrated Democrats who feared that he might vote to overturn *Roe* v. *Wade* and join Antonin Scalia and Clarence Thomas (President Bush's two favorite justices) in upholding White House claims to vast powers. Critics also worried that he would interpret the Constitution so narrowly as to restrict the court's engagement with social-justice and civil-rights issues. Alito, too, won confirmation, though on a much closer vote than Roberts.

The Court now had five Roman Catholic justices, something unthinkable in earlier eras of anti-Catholic prejudice.

In a challenge to *Roe* v. *Wade,* the South Dakota legislature in 2006 passed an extreme abortion ban with no exceptions even for rape or the mother's health. This law was sure to face legal challenge, perhaps reaching the Supreme Court. Public opinion on abortion remained remarkably consistent, with most leading polls showing about 55 percent of Americans supporting legal abortions with certain restrictions, 24 percent favoring no restrictions at all, and 20 percent believing that all abortion should be banned.

As Supreme Court politics drew the nation's attention, so did the growing influence of Washington lobbyists. Lobbying has been a part of American politics from the beginning. (The term comes from the fact that individuals seeking to influence legislation gathered in the lobbies of the Capitol or state legislatures to buttonhole politicians, because they were barred from the actual legislative chambers.) Today, many Washington lobbyists, often ex-legislators or legislative aides, have offices on K Street, near the White House.

Lobbyists' influence grew enormously during the ascendancy of Congressman Tom DeLay of Texas, nicknamed "the Hammer," the Republican majority whip (1995–2003) and majority leader (2003–2005). The ranks of registered lobbyists expanded from around 15,000 in 2000 to nearly 33,000 in 2005, with many more unregistered ones. Implementing a plan dubbed "the K Street project," DeLay pressured lobbying organizations to hire Republicans, and he extracted campaign contributions from lobbyists seeking to influence legislation. In 2003 DeLay engineered a Texas congressional redistricting under which Republicans gained five seats, a step toward the larger goal of creating a permanent Republican majority.

A series of high-visibility cases in 2005 focused attention on lobbyists and the role of money in politics. In September, DeLay resigned as majority leader after his indictment by a Texas grand jury for violating state election laws. In November, a San Diego Republican congressman admitted accepting more than $2 million in bribes and unreported campaign contributions from defense contractors. In December, a federal grand jury indicted Jack Abramoff, a high-flying Washington lobbyist with close ties to DeLay, who soon resigned from Congress. The indictments of Abramoff and a top aide alleged that they had obtained millions of dollars from corporations interested in influencing legislation, including $82 million from Indian tribes promoting their casino interests. Laundered though dummy organizations such as the "Capital Athletic Foundation," much of this money went as bribes or campaign donations to Congress members—mostly Republicans but also some prominent Democrats—while Abramoff himself allegedly siphoned off millions. Pleading guilty at his hearing early in 2006, Abramoff admitted "a multitude of mistakes." Both DeLay and Abramoff had close connections with President Bush, but the White House denied any wrongdoing.

DeLay and Abramoff emerged as symbols of a corrupt system by which lobbyists influenced legislation through contributions, gifts, lavish dinners, expensive golf junkets, and hiring politicians' relatives. Republican congressman Bob Ney of Ohio, chair of the powerful Committee on House Administration, came under Justice Department scrutiny for a golf vacation in Scotland funded by Abramoff and for involvement in a 2002 Abramoff scheme by which a Texas Indian tribe seeking a casino permit gave Ney's campaign committee $32,000. As public disgust mounted, politicians scrambled to return Abramoff's contributions, distance themselves from lobbyists, and regulate lobbyists' behavior more strictly. Said Democratic senator Christopher Dodd of Connecticut: "There's a sign that's now up in front of the Capitol. It says 'Not for Sale.'" Whether the flurry of reform would reduce the power of money in government in the long run remained unclear.

Debating Immigration

The thorny issue of immigration reform surged to prominence in 2006. Attention focused on the estimated 11 million illegal immigrants, 78 percent of them from Mexico or elsewhere in Latin America, up from 3.9 million in 1992. Many worked for low wages in a "shadow economy" as migrant agricultural laborers, motel cleaners, janitors, gardeners, fast-food employees, and nursing-home attendants, or in food-processing plants such as Cargill, or Tyson, the poultry company.

In 2001, President Bush had proposed a "guest worker" program by which short-term immigrants would receive temporary work visas requiring them to return to their own country when the permit expired. The 9/11 attacks and the Iraq War temporarily eclipsed the issue, but when the administration introduced an immigration-reform bill late in 2005, it again seized public attention.

The debate was complex, and emotions ran high. Some invoked America's tradition of welcoming newcomers, symbolized by the Statue of Liberty, and argued that the

Antonio Villaraigosa, Mayor-Elect of Los Angeles, May 2005 *The first Hispanic mayor of Los Angeles since the 1870s, Villaraigosa speaks on the phone beneath a photo of John and Robert Kennedy, his political heroes. His election symbolized the growing political power of the nation's rapidly expanding Hispanic population.*

undocumented immigrants did the hard but necessary work that few others would do. Others argued that if undocumented immigrants working for low wages were excluded, the law of supply-and-demand would push up the wages for these jobs and U.S. citizens would take them, increasing opportunities for the unemployed.

As the debate went on, private citizens in the Southwest organized the Minuteman Project in 2005 to monitor the U.S.-Mexican border and report illegal entries to the Border Patrol. Late in 2005, the House of Representatives passed a tough immigration bill introduced by Wisconsin's James Sensenbrenner. This bill criminalized illegal aliens and required their deportation. It also called for the construction of a 700-mile barrier along the U.S.-Mexican border and made it a felony for anyone, including ministers, priests, and health-care providers, to help undocumented immigrants.

Reaction to the Sensenbrenner bill was swift. Catholic bishops denounced the criminalizing of aid to illegal immigrants, and advised priests to disobey such a law. In March and April 2006, immigrant advocates organized protest demonstrations in Los Angeles, Phoenix, Chicago, and other cities. Over half a million marched in Los Angeles; 100,000 in Chicago. Said Jessica Aranda, an organizer of the Chicago rally: "Our community is coming into our own, and realizing our own power." Spanish-language radio stations and TV channels—an increasingly important segment of the mass media—supported the demonstrations.

A backlash quickly erupted. "My first thought is anger, folks," declared right-wing radio pundit Rush Limbaugh. When Hispanic stations broadcast "Nuestro Himno," a Spanish version of "The Star-Spangled Banner," some citizens angrily protested.

In the Senate, meanwhile, a bipartisan bill provided for beefed-up border control, but also established procedures by which undocumented immigrants could eventually secure citizenship. Opponents denounced this as a covert form of "amnesty" for illegal immigrants.

With the Hispanic vote up for grabs (some called it "the sleeping giant of American politics"), and with many native-born citizens angry about illegal immigration, both parties proceeded cautiously. The final legislative outcome remained uncertain.

The Election of 2006

Mid-term elections often focus on local issues. In 2006, however, the voters rendered a stinging judgment on the Iraq War, the Republican Congress, and the Bush administration. Even President Bush admitted that his party had taken a "thumping." In the House of Representatives, the Democrats won at least 29 seats, to regain the majority. They also won control of the Senate, by the barest of margins, 51-49. The number of women in the Senate inched upward, from 14 to 16, a record high. Also, for the first time since 1994, a majority of governorships—28—fell into Democratic hands. In Massachusetts, Deval Patrick became only the second African American elected governor since Reconstruction.

The results made clear voters' discontent over the nation's direction, and especially over the Iraq War, from the deceptions with which it was launched to the disastrous way it was conducted. Facing this reality, President Bush the day after the election announced the resignation of Defense Secretary Donald Rumsfeld, the chief architect of the war.

Other issues influencing the outcome were massive federal budget deficits and a constant stream of corruption and personal scandals that dominated the news in the months before the election. Facing all these negatives, the Republicans could not capitalize on favorable economic news, such as a rising stock market, lower gas prices, and falling unemployment.

New technologies loomed large in the campaign, including computerized phone banks, video cameras and blogs that publicized candidates' embarrassing gaffes, and even the personal websites on YouTube. Millions of voters used sophisticated (but sometimes problem-prone) touch screen and optical scanner machinery for the first time.

The Democratic victories meant new Congressional leadership in 2007: Harry Reid of Nevada as Senate Majority Leader, and Nancy Pelosi of San Francisco as Speaker of the House of Representatives, the first woman to hold that post. At a victory party in Washington, D.C., Pelosi told her fellow Democrats: "Today we have made history. Now let us make progress." Despite the euphoria of victory for the Democrats and the sting of defeat for Republicans, politicians in both parties recognized that America faced grave problems at home and abroad, and that leaders of all political persuasions, backed by an informed and engaged citizenry, would have to work together to put the nation back on course.

CONCLUSION

George W. Bush's presidency had scarcely begun when the attacks of September 11, 2001, shocked the nation. Americans supported Bush as he mobilized an attack on al Qaeda terrorists in Afghanistan, and Congress overwhelmingly passed the administration's antiterrorism legislation, the USA-Patriot Act. The invasion of Iraq, promoted as an antiterrorism measure, won broad initial support.

As the stock market fell sharply and scandal rocked corporate America, Bush called for tax cuts that favored the wealthy and measures to increase domestic fossil-fuel production. Bush's education program involved universal testing in reading and math, plus public funding of private charter schools.

Domestic support for the war eroded amid worsening sectarian violence in Iraq, revelations of abuses by the U.S. military and domestic spying in the name of security, and skepticism about the administration's case for invading Iraq. Other troubling world developments included worsening Israeli-Palestinian relations; nuclear programs in North Korea and Iran; and China's growing economic and military power. As global warming and other environmental hazards roused concern, the Bush administration downplayed the threat, advocated voluntarist responses, and rejected international efforts to address the crisis.

Major social trends in these years included continuing migration to the South and West, chronic inner-city problems, and increasing ethnic diversity as the Hispanic and Asian populations grew. On the economic front, the long-term shift from industrial production to an information-based and service economy proceeded, and a massive tide of foreign imports stirred uneasiness, especially in the troubled domestic auto industry.

Several developments heightened public frustration after 2004, as Bush's second term began, including a growing federal deficit and pressures on Medicare and social security as the baby boomers retired. Washington's flawed response to the devastation of Hurricane Katrina; influence-peddling scandals; and legislators' lavish spending on pet projects deepened many citizens' skepticism about the integrity and competence of government. As job worries focused attention on illegal immigrants, various strategies emerged for dealing with the problem.

In 2001, accepting the Nobel Peace Prize a few weeks after 9/11, UN Secretary General Kofi Annan said: "We have entered the third millennium through a gate of fire." But Annan went on to evoke the vision that had inspired the UN's founders in 1945. Despite the hatred and inequalities dividing nations and peoples, he insisted, the fate of all Earth's inhabitants is interconnected. The task of the twenty-first century, he said, is to achieve "a new, more profound awareness of the sanctity and dignity of every human life, regardless of race or religion. . . . Humanity is indivisible."

As we conclude this history of America and its people, what is the "enduring vision" of our title? There is, of course, no single vision, but many. That is part of America's meaning. Nor is this a vision of a foreordained national destiny unfolding effortlessly, but rather of successive generations' laborious, often frustrating struggle to define what their common life as a people should be. For all the failures, setbacks, and wrong turns, the shared visions, at their best, are rooted in hope, not fear. In 1980, Jesse de la Cruz, a Mexican-American woman who fought for years to improve conditions for California's migrant workers, summed up the philosophy that kept her going: "Is America progressing toward the better? . . . We're the ones that are gonna do it. We have to keep on struggling. . . . With us, there's a saying: *La esperanza muere al ultimo*. Hope dies last. You can't lose hope. If you lose hope, that's losing everything."

Credits

Photo Credits

CHAPTER 16 *p. 482:* Courtesy of Special Collections, LSU Libraries, Louisiana State University. *p. 492:* Schlesinger Library, Radcliffe Institute / Harvard University. *p. 494:* The Museum of the Confederacy, Richmond, Virginia. *p. 502:* Collection of The New-York Historical Society, image 50819.

CHAPTER 17 *p. 523:* (left) National Anthropological Archives / Smithsonian Institution, Washington, D.C. *p. 523:* (right) National Anthropological Archives, neg. 07-0222 / Smithsonian Institution, Washington, D.C. *p. 527:* Kansas Collection, University of Kansas Libraries. *p. 520:* Alaska and Polar Regions Archives, Elmer E. Rasmunson Library, University of Alaska.

CHAPTER 18 *p. 551:* Frank and Marie-Therese Wood Print Collections, Alexandria, Virginia. *p. 564: Harper's Weekly*, March 26, 1877. *p. 568:* Library of Congress. *p. 573:* Museum of American Political Life, University of Hartford, West Hartford, Connecticut.

CHAPTER 19 *p. 582:* Lewis W. Hine photo, 1909, Courtesy George Eastman House. *p. 594:* from the Sophia Smith Collection, Smith College. *p. 603:* from the Collection of The Henry Ford Museum and Greenfield Village. *p. 612:* © Bettmann / Corbis.

CHAPTER 20 *p. 621:* The Granger Collection, New York. *p. 628:* Library of Congress. *p. 637:* Collection of David J. and Janice L. Frent. *p. 644:* National Archives.

CHAPTER 21 *p. 650:* Brown Brothers. *p. 660:* Courtesy Philadelphia City Archives. *p. 670:* Library of Congress. *p. 678:* © Bettmann / Corbis.

CHAPTER 22 *p. 690:* The Granger Collection, New York. *p. 701:* U.S. Military History Institute. *p. 715:* Collection of David J. and Janice L. Frent.

CHAPTER 23 *p. 723:* Walter P. Reuther Library / Wayne State University. *p. 731:* Courtesy of the Arizona Historical Society, Tucson, AHS #62669. *p. 738:* Frank Driggs Collection / Getty Images. *p. 742:* Library of Congress.

CHAPTER 24 *p. 755:* © Bettmann / Corbis. *p. 767:* Library of Congress. *p. 770:* Library of Congress. *p. 777:* Library of Congress.

CHAPTER 25 *p. 784:* Thomas McAvoy / TIMEPIX / Getty Images. *p. 795:* Myron H. Davis. *p. 804:* National Archives. *p. 818:* U.S. Army / Franklin D. Roosevelt Library, Hyde Park, New York.

CHAPTER 26 *p. 826:* Courtesy Indiana University Archives. *p. 832:* National Archives. *p. 838:* © Bettmann / Corbis. *p. 843:* Hy Peskin / TIMEPIX / Getty Images.

CHAPTER 27 *p. 859:* © Bettmann / Corbis. *p. 862:* AP Images. *p. 876:* Courtesy of Motorola Museum © 1955 Motorola, Inc. / Picture Research Consultants and Archives. *p. 882:* © Bettmann / Corbis.

CHAPTER 28 *p. 888:* © Bettmann-Corbis. *p. 898:* AP Images. *p. 900:* Lyndon B. Johnson Presidential Library, Austin, Texas. *p. 915:* © Bettmann / Corbis.

CHAPTER 29 *p. 921:* John Filo / Getty Images. *p. 931:* Ron Haeberle / TIMEPIX / Getty Images. *p. 939:* Flip Schulkel / Black Star / Stock Photo. *p. 940:* Cartoon News International.

CHAPTER 30 *p. 946:* Courtesy Tuck School of Business Archives, Dartmouth College, Hanover, New Hampshire. *p. 955:* NASA / Johnson Space Center. *p. 962:* © Wally McNamee / Bettmann / Corbis. *p. 969:* AP Images.

CHAPTER 31 *p. 979:* Bruno Barbey / Magnum Photos. *p. 983:* Yoshikazu Tsuno / Getty Images. *p. 996:* AP Images. *p. 998:* Cartoon Stock, Ltd.

CHAPTER 32 *p. 1010:* Dan Tellock / Gamma / Zuma Press. *p. 1022:* AP Images. *p. 1035:* Monica Almeida / The New York Times. *p. 1042:* David Hume Kennerly / Getty Images.

Text Credits

CHAPTER 26 *p. 837:* From *American Promise*, Vol. 2, 4th ed., by James A. Henretta et al. Reprinted with permission of Bedford/St. Martin's.

Index

Warren, Earl, 904; as chief justice, 857–858

Warren Court, 857–858; Nixon and, 928, 938; in 1960s, 904

Wars and warfare: in Africa, 995; in Balkans, 990–991; guerrilla war in Philippines, 644–645; outlawing of, 726. *See also* Trench warfare; *and entries for specific wars and battles*

Warsaw Pact, 835

Washburn, Henry D., 544

Washington, Booker T., 630, 666–667

Washington, D.C.: beautification of, 659; bonus marchers in, 754; Ku Klux Klan in, 742 (illus.); race riots in, 928; Randolph, A. Philip, and, 813; Youth Marches for Integrated Schools in, 884. *See also* March on Washington

Washington Naval Arms Conference, 726

Washington Post, 703, 940

Washington (state): railroads and, 527; statehood for, 530

Watchdog agencies, 680. *See also entries for specific agencies*

Water: running, 589; use of, 590; waste of, 590; in West, 544, 675–676. *See also* Irrigation

"Water boarding," 1025

Water cannons, 536

Water systems, 660

Watergate scandal, 939–941, 943, 956

Waters, Ethel, 737

Waterworld, 1033

Watson, Tom, 626–627, 629, 636

Watt, James, 963, 970

Watterson, Henry, 562

Watts (Los Angeles), riot in (1965), 897–898

"Waving the bloody shirt," 510, 618, 622

WCTU, *see* Woman's Christian Temperance Union (WCTU)

WEAF (New York), 732

Wealth: of corporate executives, 1016–1017; in industrial America, 571–572; Veblen on, 651. *See also* Elites

Wealth gap, 608

Wealth of Nations, The (Smith), 578

Wealth Tax Act, 764

Wealthy: in cities, 588; in suburbs, 588, 590; tax cut for, 1008; World War II and, 800

Weapons: after World War I, 726; chemical and biological, 995; nuclear, 831; in World War II, 797–798, 801–802. *See also* Nuclear weapons; *and entries for specific weapons*

Weapons of mass destruction: enemy civilians in World War II and, 822; Iraq and, 1013–1015, 1024

Weapons of mass destruction (WMD), 1024

Weary Blues, The (Hughes), 737

Weaver, James B., 620, 627, 632

Weaver, Robert, 903

Wedding Present, The (1936), 780

Weekly Standard, The, 1013

Wehrmacht (German army), 804

Welch, Joseph, 854

Welfare capitalism, 724, 747. *See also* Social welfare

Welfare programs, 952

"Welfare queens," 971

Welfare reform, 985–987, 988 (illus.)

Welfare Reform Act (1996), 987

Welfare system: overhaul of, 936; Roosevelt, Franklin D., and, 760

Welles, Orson, 783

Wellesley, 594, 721

Wells, H. G., 783

Wells-Barnett, Ida, 667, 669

Welsh immigrants, 583

Welty, Eudora, 874

West: bonanza farms in, 538–539; cattle ranching in, 536–538, 636 (map); conservation movement in, 645–646; dams in, 867; defense spending in, 865; Farmers' Alliance movement in, 625; farming in, 530; in Great Depression, 768; Homestead Act and, 528–529; Indians in, 516, 518–526, 520 (map); Japanese-American detention camps in, 816–817; legends of, 542–544; markets in, 530; mining in, 534–536, 636 (map); myth of, 542–544; Okies in, 777; Oklahoma

land rush in, 539, 542; planning for, 768; railroads and, 526–528; settlement of, 526–532, 531 (map); society in, 530–532; strikes in, 576–577; trans-Mississippi, 516, 518–526; Turner's frontier thesis and, 542; water in, 675–676; woman suffrage in, 531, 618; during World War II, 798. *See also* Southwest; *and entries for specific territories and states*

West, Mae, 661, 780

West Bank, 991–992, 1016–1017, 1026

West Berlin, Kennedy, John F., and, 890

West Germany, 834, 840–841

West Indies, Danish, 737

West Virginia, coal mines, 655

Western Europe, Marshall Plan for, 833–834

Western Front, in World War I, 700 (illus.)

Western Hemisphere: immigration from, 739–740. *See also entries for specific regions*

Westinghouse, George, 556–557

Westinghouse Company, 556–557, 649, 660, 732

Westmoreland, William, 926

Wetback, 880

"Wets," in Prohibition, 745

Weyler, Valeriano, 641

Wharton, Edith, 702

What Social Classes Owe to Each Other (Sumner), 578

Wheat, 626; boom in, 538–539

Wheeler, Candace, 607

Wheeler, Edward L., 640

Wheeler and Wilson (manufacturer), 506

"Where Is the Difference?" (political cartoon), 621 (illus.)

"Whip Inflation Now" (WIN), 957

"Whiskey ring" scandal, 504

White, Andrew D., 593–595

White, Dan, 950

White, Thomas E., 1008

White, William Allen, 653, 761

White Caps (Las Gorras Blancas), 533

White Citizens Councils, 857

White flight, 877, 1036

White League, 511